"A fascinating history and account of what suicide is and how suicide prevention is actually practiced. It is the best, easy-to-read, comprehensive book written by a layperson for the lay reader with which to enter the world of 'suicidology.'"

—Edwin S. Shneidman, professor of thanatology emeritus, University of California, and author of *The Suicidal Mind*

# November of the Soul

The Enigma of Suicide

## George Howe Colt

SCRIBNER

New York London Toronto Sydney

SCRIBNER
1230 Avenue of the Americas
New York, NY 10020

Library of Congress Cataloging-in-Publication Data
Colt, George Howe.
November of the soul: the enigma of suicide / George Howe Colt.
p. cm.
Originally published: New York: Summit Books, c1991.
Includes bibliographical references and index.
1. Suicide. I. Title.
HV6545.C598 2006
362.28—dc22                           2005056327

ISBN-13:  978-0-671-50996-5
ISBN-10:  0-671-50996-9
ISBN-13:  978-0-7432-6447-1 (Pbk)
ISBN-10:  0-7432-6447-9 (Pbk)

For information regarding special discounts for bulk purchases,
please contact Simon & Schuster Special Sales
at 1-800-456-6798  or  business@simonandschuster.com

Originally published in hardcover as *The Enigma of Suicide*

*Grateful acknowledgment is made for the following permissions:*

Extract from *The Poems of Stanley Kunitz, 1928–1978,* by Stanley Kunitz, copyright © 1971 by Stanley Kunitz. By permission of Little, Brown and Company. Extract from *The Children of Night* by Edwin Arlington Robinson (New York: Charles Scribner's Sons, 1897), courtesy of Macmillan Publishing Company, A Division of Macmillan, Inc. Extract from *Suicide Solution,* words and music by Joan Osbourne, Robert Daisley and Randy Rhoads, copyright © 1981 Essex Music International, Venice, CA. Used by permission. Extract from *The Savage God* by A. Alvarez. Published by George Weidenfeld and Nicholson, Ltd. Extract from *The Vital Balance* by Karl Menninger, copyright © 1963 by Karl Menninger, M.D. Reprinted by permission of Viking Penguin, a Division of Penguin Books USA, Inc. Extract from *The Collected Poems of A. E. Housman,* copyright © 1936 by Barclays Bank Ltd. Copyright © 1964 by Robert E. Symons. Copyright © 1965 by Holt Rinehart and Winston, Inc. Reprinted by permission of Henry Holt and Company, Inc. Extract from *Wanting to Die* by Anne Sexton, copyright © 1966 by Anne Sexton. Reprinted by permission of Houghton Mifflin Co. Extract from "Perhaps Love," lyrics by John Denver, copyright © 1980 Cherry Lane Music Publishing Co., Inc. International Copyright Secured. All Rights Reserved. Used by permission.

*For Anne*
*Then, now, always*

# CONTENTS

# INTRODUCTION

DURING THE MONTHS that followed September 11, 2001, I could not help noticing what pains the op-ed pages of America's newspapers took to make clear that the terrorists who steered jets into the World Trade Center towers and the Pentagon were not *real* suicides. The implication was that these men had nothing in common with the troubled souls we think of—and feel compassion toward—when we hear the profoundly unsettling word *suicide.*

It is understandable that we would be reluctant to find any commonality between unhappy people who deserve our sympathy and mass murderers—and, to be sure, there are great differences. And yet the terrorists *were* suicides, albeit of a particular but hardly unique strand in the history of self-destructive behavior. Indeed, the post-9/11 editorialists seemed unaware that for much of recorded history, suicide has been seen primarily not as a private act of desperation but as a public statement with a larger social meaning. Suicides have often been depicted not as miserable, helpless victims but as rational masters of their own fates, sacrificing themselves in the name of protest, idealism, or subversion by committing what the French sociologist Émile Durkheim called altruistic suicide (a difficult label to apply to the events of 9/11, but, from its executors' skewed perspective, an accurate one). These terrorists were nothing new—except, perhaps, in the magnitude of their destruction.

To find an analogue, one need look back only fifty years to the kamikaze, the Japanese pilots who flew their fighter planes into American aircraft carriers in the South Pacific during the waning months of World War II. One could, of course, look much further back, to the early Christian martyrs, who believed that by killing themselves they would receive posthumous glory and enter the kingdom of heaven in a state of blissful sinlessness. (Indeed, so many Christians killed themselves in the first few centuries AD that the church was forced to redefine suicide as a mortal sin.) By contrast, the contemporary terrorist earns cultural veneration for killing others, and his suicide is merely a lethal side effect. By the standards of antiquity, the September 11 hijackers could well have seen themselves as modern versions of Samson, who knew that when he pulled down the Philistine temple, he, too, would die.

At the same time, they—along with the Palestinian, Iraqi, and Tamil suicide bombers who populate our front pages—may not be as different as we might think from the despondent, often psychiatrically distressed people we consider to be "typical" suicides (as if there were such a thing). As time has passed, a more complex picture has emerged in which such terrorists appear to be neither selfless martyrs nor (as the 9/11 editorialists would have it) vindictive cowards but troubled young men and, occasionally, women who, finding little meaning in their lives, are psychologically and culturally primed to be swept away by a cause, especially one whose apparent largeness of purpose might lend them dignity. They are less akin, perhaps, to clear-eyed Cato and the other so-called rational suicides of antiquity than to those cultists who swallowed poisoned Kool-Aid and followed Jim Jones to their deaths in the Guyana jungle, or to the harried zealots in Waco, Texas, who, at the behest of a charismatic leader named David Koresh, fired on federal agents until they were themselves killed. In their confusion, rage, and feelings of powerlessness, they had something in common with the boys who turned their guns on their schoolmates at Columbine High School before turning them on themselves. In some ways, in fact, they may not be that far removed from any despairing person who looks, often in the wrong places, for something that will lend his life meaning and ends up finding death.

Though their motivations may differ, people who kill themselves, whether they are suicide bombers or depressed teenagers, believe—mistakenly—that there are no alternative paths. Indeed, in the months after 9/11, my mind kept returning to those men and women on the upper floors of the World Trade Center who, with fire behind them, jumped to their deaths. This seemed to me the literal expression of the psychological experience faced by most suicidal people: they feel they have no choice.

---

I raise these points as a way of suggesting that when it comes to suicide, there is very little new under the sun. Suicide has likely been with us as long as life and death have been with us. In the fifteen years since the original version of this book was published, the essentials haven't changed. People are killing themselves at about the same frequency, in about the same ways, and for about the same reasons as in 1991. At the same time, there have been a number of developments in the intervening years that make updating and revising this book not only worthwhile but necessary.

In 1991, Americans were horrified by the soaring rate of adolescent suicide, and by the way these suicides seemed to come in bunches. Schools were rushing to get suicide prevention programs into place; the question of how these programs worked—or whether they worked at all—was just beginning to be asked. Since then, the adolescent rate has plateaued and fallen, there has been a wealth of new research into the causes of youth suicide, and the debate about how to prevent it has been heated. These developments will be discussed in part one. Nevertheless, the adolescent rate remains far higher than it was in the 1950s, and communities continue to be devastated by clusters of teenage suicides.

When this book was first published, suicide was understood to be caused by a variety of psychological, sociological, biological, and spiritual factors. Fifteen years later, the conceptual framework hasn't changed, but the relative emphases on these factors have shifted. The past decade has seen an expanded understanding of the biological ingredients of depression and suicide. Part two brings the history of suicide up-to-date by describing the work of neurobiologists who track down chemical changes in the brain that tell us why some people may be more prone to taking their own life. Part three, which discusses the range, patterns, and motivations of suicidal behavior, has been updated to reflect current trends: for instance, that suicide rates are growing in rural areas; that gay suicide is a subject of increasing controversy; and that rates in many of the former states of the Soviet Union have become the highest in the world.

When I originally wrote this book, Prozac, the initial entry in a class of antidepressants known as selective serotonin reuptake inhibitors (SSRIs), had recently been introduced. These new medications have undoubtedly saved many lives; some credit them with the drop in the adolescent suicide rate. But they have not come without controversy. Several studies have suggested that though the SSRIs are more effective than their less sophisticated predecessors in reducing depression, they may actually be responsible for triggering suicidal behavior in some young people. The advent of the SSRIs has encouraged a related development. Fifteen years ago, the treatment of depressed and suicidal people, to be discussed in part four, usually involved a combination of psychotherapy and psychopharmacology, working in a more or less equal (if at times uneasy) partnership; since then, the biological approach has become ever more dominant. The result of the trend toward medication, reinforced by the ascendancy of HMOs, which emphasize treating mental health in primary-care settings, is that a suicidal person today is far more likely to be treated by an internist or a family physician than by a psychiatrist, psychologist, or social worker.

When this book was first published, it had been only a few weeks since the Hemlock Society, a group advocating the legalization of physician-assisted suicide and euthanasia, had published *Final Exit,* a manual for the terminally ill that offered detailed instructions on how to take one's own life. It had been only ten months since Jack Kevorkian had used his suicide machine to carry out the first of his more than 130 so-called medicides. Yet only the most optimistic right-to-die advocate—or her most pessimistic opponent—could have foreseen that within three years, Oregon voters would make it legal for doctors in their state to prescribe lethal doses of medication for terminally ill patients. Perhaps nowhere in the field of suicide has there been a more dramatic evolution than in what has been called the right to die. Although the ethical issues have changed little in fifteen years—or in fifteen centuries—the legal and practical developments have come at an astonishing rate. Not surprisingly, the right to die, which will be discussed in part five, remains a raw and contentious subject, as evidenced in the collective national hysteria occasioned by the case of Terri Schiavo in the spring of 2005. Indeed, as this book went to press, the Supreme Court was due to hear an appeal by the federal government that would, if approved, essentially void the Oregon Death with Dignity Act.

In 1991, the devastated friends and family members left behind after a suicide were just beginning to speak out. Since then, survivors of suicide, as they are known, have become a powerful voice in suicide prevention: advocating for research, bringing attention to depression and suicide as public health issues, and chipping away at the stigma that has encrusted the subject of suicide over the last two millennia. Their story is told in part six.

---

When I began the reporting for this book, my personal experience with suicide was minimal. In the years following its publication, this seemed to surprise and, occasionally, even to disappoint people. Just a few months ago, a man I met at a dinner party, who had himself suffered suicidal depression decades earlier, challenged my right to write about a subject with which I had no intimate experience. I explained that my book was not a memoir but a work of journalism, in which I had sought out and learned from those people who *had* had intimate experiences with suicide. I also explained (as I wrote in the preface to the first edition) that I believe all of us, to varying degrees, have been touched in some way by suicide—whether someone we know has considered, attempted, or completed suicide; whether we have considered or attempted it ourselves; or whether we've acted in self-destructive ways that fall short of the actual act.

Since the book was published, however, I have, unfortunately, had closer contact with the subject. One of the people I love most in the world made what researchers call a "nearly lethal" suicide attempt. (He survived and, with the help of psychotherapy and antidepressant medication, put a life back together that is now full and happy.) Several years later, my beloved mother-in-law, a member of the Hemlock Society, took her own life while suffering from terminal breast cancer and Parkinson's disease. In the former instance, I experienced a kind of sorrow that made my previous experiences of sorrow seem unworthy of the word; in the latter, my sadness was leavened by the knowledge that my mother-in-law had ended her life with the determination and independence with which she had lived it. These experiences made me return to this project both with a greater admiration for those who have struggled with self-destructive impulses and with a more profound empathy for those whose lives have been bruised by suicide, including—and especially—those people I interviewed for these pages. Although I did not say this to my dinner companion, if I had had that loss and that near loss before I had started work on this book, I suspect I would never have been able to write it.

---

This book was originally published as *The Enigma of Suicide,* a title selected by its publisher. I would like to be able to say that I changed it for this edition because it was no longer true. Alas, despite the strides we have made over the last fifteen years, suicide remains an enigma. The first time around, I had hoped the book could be called *November of the Soul,* a phrase that for many years had struck me as an uncannily accurate description of the feeling that lies at the heart of that enigma. This time my publisher agreed.

On the first page of *Moby-Dick,* Ishmael describes the onset of a morbid depression that makes him pause before coffin warehouses and bring up the rear of every funeral procession he meets. He calls it a "damp, drizzly November in my soul." Whenever that feeling comes over him, Ishmael knows what he must do. "Cato throws himself upon his sword," he tells us; "I quietly take to the ship." Would that all suicidal people knew they had a choice other than death.

# PREFACE TO THE FIRST EDITION

NOT LONG AFTER I started the research for this book, I attended a conference in Boston on "Suicide: Assessment and Management." My notebooks soon filled with information about warning signs, risk factors, mother-infant bonding, and countertransference hate. "Empathy with despairing people requires the therapist to give up the psychological distance between himself and the patients he might ordinarily like to maintain," said one psychiatrist, a dapper fellow in a bow tie. "We must meet the patients in the howling desert where the unfinished business of early childhood has left them." On my right a middle-aged psychologist in a pin-striped suit copied the statement verbatim into his leatherbound notebook. There seemed to me to be something slightly absurd about hundreds of psychiatrists, psychologists, and social workers in a thickly carpeted hotel ballroom under ten-foot crystal chandeliers being exhorted to meet the patient in the howling desert. As the conference ended and we walked out, I wondered how many of us were prepared to do so.

It was a Friday night in January, and the Boston streets, still shiny with the afternoon's rain, were crowded with honking cars. Everyone was in a hurry to get home and begin the weekend. In the subway station a thin young man with a saxophone played "Summertime." But the evening was chilly, the trains were running late, and as the platform filled, the waiting commuters grew irritated. "Get us home!" shouted a bearded old man.

After the subway finally arrived, it traveled only one stop when a voice over the loudspeaker informed us that the electricity had been shut off between this station and the end of the line. Buses would deliver us to our destinations. Grumpy and impatient, the crowd spilled back into the streets. "What is it?" called out passersby. "Is it a fight? Did somebody die?"

I found a seat on the bus near the back. Behind me two young men complained loudly about having been forced off the subway. Suddenly they stopped talking and turned to look out the window. The flickering blue lights of police cars mingled with spotlights at the far end of a side street. Word filtered through the bus that the subway line had been closed down because the tracks, after coming aboveground, passed a cathedral from whose steeple a young man was threatening to jump.

"They got the whole street blocked off," said the older of the two boys behind me. "Fire trucks, police, and everything."

"Shit, man, if he really wanted to do it, he'd just run up there and jump," said the younger boy disdainfully. He snickered, "Hell, I say go ahead and jump, but not on *my* time."

The older boy, his voice quieter, said, "Why does he want to do that? Why does he want to die?"

"He don't want to die," said the younger boy. "He just wants to get his face on TV."

They laughed, but the older boy fell silent again. "Ever think of doing something like that? I don't understand it."

"I'd *never* do it," said the younger boy. "I mean, I like the hell out of living."

"Maybe he got no reason for living," said the older boy.

"Then go ahead and jump," said the younger boy, recovering some of his bravado. "Or do it alone—go home, turn on the water, and slit your wrists. Get it done and let the rest of us go home. We got places to go."

"People to see," said the older.

"Drugs to do," said the younger. He giggled, the other boy joined in, and they began to talk about their plans for the evening. At the next stop they got off the bus, jostling each other, laughing as they disappeared into the night.

When the bus reached the end of the line, I persuaded my brother, who had been waiting there for me in the car, to drive back to Boston. I wanted to find out what had happened to the man on the steeple. By the time we returned to the cathedral, however, the crowds were gone. A lone police car was parked in front. The officer told me that a drunken twenty-year-old man who had broken up with his girlfriend had climbed the scaffolding surrounding the steeple and stayed there, 150 feet up, seventy minutes before policemen, firefighters, and two priests managed to talk him down. He had been taken to the hospital for psychiatric observation. Now, saying he had to file his report, the sergeant excused himself and drove off.

The cathedral was in a rough-looking neighborhood whose streets were dark and deserted. The night was quiet except for the sporadic clatter of the subway, which, back in operation, swept by overhead. I looked up at the steeple and tried to imagine where the jumper might have stood.

Then I noticed a man about fifty feet from me, staring at the cathedral, his arms resting on the iron fence that surrounded the churchyard. I walked over and asked him whether he'd seen what had happened. No, he said, but he had heard about it. His voice was soft and listless. He wore old jeans, a flannel shirt, and a blue parka that was shiny with dirt. Shocks of gray hair stuck out from under his black wool cap. His face was thin and his beard was flecked with white. I guessed he was in his late thirties.

I shook my head. "Thank God he didn't jump," I said.

"Yeah," said the man. He asked me if I was a reporter. I said no, but I was writing a book on suicide.

"Oh." He nodded. "I'm a prime candidate."

"Why?" I asked.

"Because . . . things get you down," he said. I must have looked confused because he added, "There is an entire group of people in this country that gets put down, kept down, and ignored."

"By whom?"

"By everyone. By the federal government, by the laws, by big business." He saw that I wasn't convinced. "I'll tell you what happened to me. I used to be a *person,* with an office and a degree and an apartment and a car and a life. I had a girlfriend, but she was a married woman and when her husband found out, he came to my house and punched me out and . . ."

As we stood side by side gazing up at the church, he told me of the breakup with his girlfriend, of financial troubles, of legal difficulties, of friends pulling away, of life in his cramped apartment, of his deep depression. As the story unraveled I had the sinking feeling that this could be a long evening, and I was cold because I had left my jacket in the car, where my brother waited with the engine running. "And I was committed to a mental hospital," he was saying. "Once you've been in there, our society says you're no good." He paused. "I have no money. I have no job. My life is ruined. But don't worry, I'm not going to run up there and jump now." He shook his head. "But I think about killing myself every day."

"What do you do when you feel like killing yourself?"

"I call a prevention center."

"Do they help?"

"Sometimes, yeah."

I shivered. "You're freezing," he said. He reached over and touched me lightly on the back. I shivered again but not from the cold. He took an almost empty pack of Marlboros from his jacket pocket and offered me one. I shook my head, and he lit one for himself. He took a puff and began to talk more about his broken life in the same leaden voice.

---

In the years since then, I have thought often of that evening. My encounters with the psychiatrists, the boys on the bus, and the lonely man at the cathedral gate raised many of the questions that this book attempts to explore. Between 1 and 2 percent of all Americans die by suicide, and some 4 or 5 percent make a suicide attempt at some point in their lives. Very few of us have not known someone, however distantly, who has taken his or her own life. In the course of writing this book, I talked with several hundred people who had intimate experience with suicide—people who had made attempts, family and friends of people who had killed themselves, psychiatrists, social workers, members of the clergy, biologists, hot line volunteers. But perhaps more surprising and, in some cases, more illuminating were the hundreds of other people I met in the course of my daily life who ended up telling me their stories. These included a middle-aged Scandinavian woman sitting next to me on a train who told me she'd been so depressed she had tried to hang herself with a belt earlier that year; a young minister I met at a restaurant who was about to take over a small Virginia parish in which there had recently been several teenage suicides; a woman at a bus stop whose mother, a cancer patient, was considering taking a fatal overdose; a man I met at a party who believed that anyone who *hadn't* considered suicide must not have explored the true meaning of life; a psychiatrist haunted by thoughts of a patient who had killed herself eight years earlier; a young artist who told me that one evening shortly after she had moved to New York City she was eating dinner when the body of an upstairs neighbor fell past her window.

When I began the research that led to this book, I was surprised by the sheer volume of writing on the subject. As I turned from a seventeenth-century clergyman's sermon on the sin of suicide to a neurobiologist's paper on serotonin imbalance to a philosopher's defense of the right to suicide to a novelist's description of a character's suicidal depression, I was struck by how fragmented and lacking in context the suicide literature seemed. Each book or paper approached the subject from a different perspective, and reflected little knowledge of—or interest in—any insights from outside its own narrow focus. This parochialism was true, too, of the majority of mental health professionals and researchers I interviewed, many of whom were unaware of related developments even within their own fields. As our knowledge of suicide has deepened we have come to realize that the subject involves many different disciplines. Yet it seems to me that even a preliminary understanding of suicide is incomplete without some familiarity with all avenues of exploration.

This book is an attempt to bring some of those different vantage points together. It endeavors to put current thinking about suicide into a historical perspective by tracing the way people have thought and felt about the subject during the last four thousand years. It explores the various motives and meanings that suicide may have had to the people who killed themselves and the explanations offered by so-called experts. It discusses who commits suicide and why certain people and certain groups are more vulnerable than others. It explores the range of self-destructive behaviors, including those that do not immediately end in death: alcoholism, Russian roulette, and so on. It looks at the methods of suicide and the psychological significance those methods may have. And it describes the problems faced by those left behind after a suicide and how they deal with them.

Most people feel that suicide is a tragedy that should be prevented. But how can we prevent it when our understanding of its causes is still imperfect? This book attempts to describe the state of the art of suicide prevention, in crisis centers, therapists' offices, hospitals, and the halls of government. It also raises the question of whether there are some suicides—those of terminally ill people, for example—in which intervention is inappropriate.

The book opens with a discussion of adolescent suicide. In 1983, as I started my research, a rash of teenage suicides in Plano, Texas, drew the national media's attention. Indeed, the rate of adolescent suicide had nearly tripled since 1950. Suddenly, magazines, newspapers, and television shows trumpeted the "national epidemic" of suicide that seemed to plague upper-middle-class suburbs. Although I was aware that even at its highest the rate of adolescent suicide remained lower than for older Americans, I was intrigued by the issues this "epidemic" raised—and by how many of them were the same issues that had been raised for centuries in many different countries. And so when eight adolescents in the tricounty area north of New York City killed themselves during a four-month period in 1984, I decided to investigate the so-called Westchester cluster. Although every suicide is unique and suicide has different meanings and motives for different groups, according to age, race, religion, and so on, a detailed examination of this particular rash of suicides serves as an introduction and exploration of some issues inherent in all suicides. By beginning with a look at how suicide affected one age group in one area in one year, I hope to offer a window into the larger subject of self-destruction.

While I was researching this book, I was frequently asked whether I had a suicide in my family. People were, I think, surprised when I told them the answer was no. I, in turn, was surprised at their assumption that my interest in the topic must have been compelled by intimate personal experience. After all, what other subject touches so intensely on so many aspects—ethical, psychological, biological, cultural—of human life? Who could not be interested in such a subject? As I worked on the book, I also recalled the times that suicide had touched my life in various ways and with varying degrees of seriousness—my early fascination with Hart Crane, Sylvia Plath, Anne Sexton, and other suicidal writers; the vow I made with my best friend, when we were both caught up in the romantic angst of being sixteen, to swim out to sea and drown if we were still alive at twenty-five; the alcoholism that has frequently blighted my family tree; the pain and confusion I felt in college when I learned that a classmate had jumped to his death from a dormitory window. And although I have never thought seriously of taking my own life, I remember the occasional urge to find out what would happen if I swerved my car into the opposite lane; the desire to find a way to stop living—without dying—when a relationship of many years broke up; the drinking binges in college and graduate school that I realized only later were an expression less of collegial bonhomie than of fear and loneliness.

Certainly, these were relatively tame encounters with self-destruction, no more and probably no less than most people I know have experienced. I describe them to show not that I am closer to the subject than other people, but that the subject has touched all of us in some way—and to suggest that even the most extreme suicidal depression is but an extension of feelings most of us have had at some point in our lives. By the end of my research I had also come to believe that any of us, if sufficiently pushed by genes, bad luck, ill health, or a combination of these factors, might be drawn to the precipice. Part of my purpose in writing this book is therefore to chip away at some of the barriers our culture erects between "normal" people and "suicidal" people—barriers that I believe we erect from the fear that the difference is so slight.

———————

As the man at the cathedral went on, part of me wanted to stay, to find a place to talk with him over cups of hot coffee, not because I thought he was going to climb the steeple and jump, not because I believed I could get him his former life back, but because he was lonely and depressed and had asked for help. But I saw the evening stretch out before me, filled with the sadness of his life and the dullness of his voice. I thought of my brother waiting in the car, of the drive out to the well-lighted house in the suburbs where dinner was waiting. I thought of how callous the young men on the bus had sounded, and my guilt prodded me to stay. But already my brain was furnishing my heart with excuses: this man was probably crazy; this man *wasn't* crazy, and he didn't need my help; I was exhausted after a long day at the conference.

He may have sensed my thoughts, for when I shivered once more, he said kindly, "You're cold. You should go home." He said good-bye and began to walk away. "Take care," I said. Then, because that sounded lame, I added, ". . . of yourself." I took a step toward the car. "Take care of yourself," I called once more. I opened the door and slid into the warm car. Then I turned and watched him stuff his hands into his pockets and disappear into a dark side street.

# 1

# ADOLESCENT SUICIDE

---

# I

# JUSTIN

JUSTIN CHRISTOPHER SPOONHOUR
OCTOBER 10, 1969
10:20 A.M.
7 LB 20 IN

THE GOLD LETTERING stands out against the cover of the white photograph album, now beige with age, coffee-spattered, and held together by tape. Inside, 114 snapshots, with captions written by the proud mother, lovingly document Justin Spoonhour's first few years. *Justin was less than three hours old:* a picture of "Boy Spoonhour" in his hospital bassinet, a white blanket covering all but a puckered face with a pale shadow of hair. *First day home:* his mother, Anne, breast-feeding. *At a month, he was easy to shop with—but where do you put the packages:* Justin asleep in a supermarket shopping cart. *About four and a half months—getting very fat and sassy:* Justin snug in a comfy chair, a grinning, diapered Buddha.

Slowly, in the album's pages, the prunish infant becomes an energetic, red-cheeked child moving happily through a succession of milestones: Justin's first Christmas; Justin sitting up; Justin learning to crawl; Justin's first tooth; Justin standing; Justin beaming (*Working on teeth five and six*); Justin's first birthday; Justin's first step; Justin's second Christmas; Justin standing on a chair (*Pausing for a souvenir photo atop Mt. Everest—I did it all myself*).

From the beginning, Justin Spoonhour was treated like a little adult. "We never talked baby talk to him," says his father, Giles. "We always talked English." Justin responded in kind: his first word was "McGovern" (his parents had volunteered for the senator's 1972 presidential campaign), and his first sentence was "MerrillLynchBullishAmerica." He was raised on a diet of *Sesame Street.* Even after he learned how to change channels, he spurned cartoons and stayed tuned to the educational television station. The Spoonhours' house in Putnam Valley, New York, was crammed with books, and Justin was reading before he entered kindergarten.

At elementary school, Justin's precociousness was not the only thing that set him apart from his classmates—there was also his appearance. Justin seemed to have a permanent rumple. His blond hair often hung down to his shoulders, uncombed; his shirts were untucked, his clothes unironed, his sneakers untied, and his fly frequently unzipped. He suffered from a bedwetting problem until the age of eleven. Doctors prescribed an antidiuretic, but it helped only temporarily. His parents set an alarm clock in his bedroom so he could go to the bathroom in the middle of the night, but by then it was often too late. The problem embarrassed Justin, and Anne and Giles didn't want to make him more self-conscious by questioning him. So each morning Anne would check his sheets and remind Justin to take a bath. Occasionally he forgot. At school he became a target for teasing: "Justin, you greaseball, did you ever hear of soap?" To his classmates the issue wasn't that Justin was messy so much as that he was peculiar. One morning he walked into class wearing a three-piece suit for no apparent reason. At lunch the other children giggled and discussed how "stupid" it was. And even though he had worn a suit, they noticed, his hair was still uncombed.

Justin dismissed the teasing with a cutting remark or a simple "Shut up." He never got into fights; he just walked away. At recess, while his classmates played, he usually sat alone, and when the class split into groups for an activity, Justin was always left out until the teacher chose a group for him. He was rarely invited to his classmates' houses, and although his parents encouraged it, he seldom brought anyone home from school. Justin's few friends tended, like him, to be on the fringes of grade school society: a foster child with a wild temper; a chubby boy with glasses and an attaché case; a shy boy who stuttered. On the rare occasions that Justin did bring home a friend, they inevitably quarreled and ended up playing by themselves. While his grades were good, Justin's marks for "cooperation" were low. "It wasn't so much 'Justin doesn't get along,'" says Anne, "as 'Justin doesn't even relate.'"

Anne and Giles weren't as concerned as some parents might be that their son was "different." They were "different" themselves. Their three-bedroom home in Lookout Manor, a small, isolated neighborhood, had a somewhat anarchic air. Four or five cats had the run of the house, dishes often went unwashed, and tilted pictures were likely to remain that way. "Housekeeping," admits Anne, "was not a high priority." Giles and Anne had no rules about clothing or hair. They dressed casually themselves and paid little attention to what was in or out of style. "Giles and Anne were nonconformists from the word go," says a townsperson. "And they chose to live in a community where conformity is the watchword."

Putnam Valley, fifty miles north of New York City, had been settled by farmers in the eighteenth century. By the early twentieth century it was principally a summer resort. After World War II, when newly built highways made commuting to Manhattan possible, people moved into the summer houses and lived there year-round. By the time Justin was born, Putnam Valley was a conservative, largely middle-class bedroom community of about ten thousand people (the population doubled in summer), many of whom worked in Manhattan. Although Putnam Valley was growing, its residents were spread over a wide area, and the community still had a rural feel. The commuter train didn't stop there, and the closest thing to a town center was Oregon Corners, a group of shops clustered around a four-way intersection. "This is a very small town," the librarian told me. "There's a great deal of interaction among citizens and a great deal of knowledge about one another." As the local newsweekly, *The Community Current,* observed, "There are no secrets in Putnam Valley."

Anne grew up in Putnam Valley. Her parents were what some townspeople called "senior hippies." Her father, who managed a millionaire's estate, wore his hair in a ponytail, and their house was a haven for hitchhikers and runaways. Local schoolteachers still remembered Anne as an exceptionally gifted student. They also remembered how willful and independent she was. At various times she wanted to be a veterinarian, a rodeo rider, a Formula One race car driver, a police officer. After two years as a drama student at Ithaca College, she returned home to live with her parents and work at a nearby department store. Every Monday night she drove to the Friars of the Atonement Seminary in Garrison to play the flute in their folk masses. There she met Giles Spoonhour, a tall priest with a surprisingly soft voice, blue eyes, and a sudden, booming laugh. "He was very different from most men I knew—better read, better spoken," says Anne. "He was more tolerant and compassionate. And he wanted to make changes in the world." She and Giles talked earnestly about religion, politics, and Vietnam and found they agreed on most counts. They even shared a passion for science fiction.

Giles was the eldest of three brothers raised in a conservative Catholic family in Chicago. Like Justin, Giles was a precocious, somewhat withdrawn child. He planned on becoming a mechanical engineer, but halfway through the Illinois Institute of Technology he met an elderly woman who ran a Catholic retreat outside the city. Their long philosophical talks convinced Giles there was more to the world than engineering, and despite opposition from his parents, he entered the priesthood. However, after thirteen years as a theology student, parochial-school teacher, and parish priest, Giles became disillusioned with the orthodoxy of the Church. He wanted to marry and have children. By the time he met Anne he had decided to give up the priesthood. Several months later Giles left the seminary, and he and Anne were married.

Settling down in Putnam Valley, the Spoonhours put their political convictions into practice. As a social worker in nearby Peekskill, Giles counseled troubled families. Anne became a reporter for Putnam Valley's weekly newspaper, writing spirited articles and editorials. They were active in the Democratic Club and belonged to a discussion group that explored new directions in Christianity. Although Giles was no longer a priest, he continued to perform weddings and baptisms as a member of the Federation of Christian Ministries, which stirred up gossip and occasional criticism in the strongly Catholic town. While Anne was admired for her energy and conviction, she had too much substance for those who concentrated on style. "Anne uses long words and doesn't do small talk," says a friend. "At eleven in the morning people want to talk about their shopping, their mothers-in-law, and their children. Anne wants to talk about the plight of the American Indian." After reading an article in *Newsweek* about ethnic and handicapped adoptees, Giles and Anne decided to adopt at least one "hard to place" child. Three years after Justin was born, they adopted Leah, an eighteen-month-old black, albino girl from Louisiana. She and Justin soon developed a fierce sibling rivalry.

If their classmates were encouraged by their parents to achieve in grades and sports, Justin and Leah were encouraged to become independent, morally responsible individuals. "We assumed they would go to college, but they were going to be whatever they bloody well wanted to be," says Anne. "We encouraged them not to just go with the herd. We wanted to bring them up as reasonably pacifist and humane people." She pauses. "Do you encourage a kid to be a conformist for the sake of his own happiness, or do you cross your fingers and hope he has enough strength of character to tolerate the kind of singling out he's going to get if he's different—and maybe survive it to be happy later on?"

When Justin was eight, he told his parents that he wanted to join the Cub Scouts. They bought him a blue uniform and drove him back and forth to den meetings. But Justin didn't like it. "He really wasn't into making like a little Indian and doing crafty stuff and being a Cub and a Bear and a Wolf and a Webelos and all that junior fraternity stuff," says Anne. "I don't know how much of that attitude he may have absorbed from me, because I was not an organization person. Boy Scouts are great for kids who are going to be backslappers and chummy and rah-rah all their lives. But for somebody who is being raised as an individual, somebody who really wants to do things of significance or do nothing, that's not where it's at." After half a dozen meetings, Justin stopped going.

Justin seemed more interested in creating his own world than in fitting into any preexisting social structure. Far more fascinating to him than the nature hikes and knot-tying of the Cub Scouts were the cosmic realms of Middle

Earth or outer space. In his reading, Justin was drawn to fantasy and science fiction. He devoured Madeleine L'Engle's *A Wrinkle in Time,* and when his fourth-grade class was assigned the first volume of C. S. Lewis's *Chronicles of Narnia,* he quickly went on to finish the rest of the series. Then he read and reread Tolkien's *The Lord of the Rings.* He spent his allowance on comic books—*Superman, Superboy,* and *Legion of Super-Heroes.* He saw the film *Star Wars* several times and decorated his room with posters of Luke Skywalker and Darth Vader, and with models of intergalactic spacecraft.

Although Justin had few friends his own age, he got along well with the younger children in his neighborhood, and they often played war in the woods across the street from the Spoonhour home. Unlike school, this was a society in which Justin was the leader. He made himself the general, and his "soldiers" admired the elaborate worlds he created, complete with secret salutes, codes of conduct, and courts-martial. When Justin chose to do something, he threw himself into it, planning it down to the last detail, and when others didn't fit in the way he'd imagined—if a neighborhood soldier didn't carry out orders according to military protocol—he could get exasperated and angry. He had a clear sense of how he felt the world ought to operate. Anne remembers taking him for a riding lesson and seeing him get thrown from the horse. "He grabbed the reins and started to get back on, but first he looked the horse in the eye and very reasonably explained, 'Now listen, horse, you're not supposed to do that because I'm supposed to be the boss and I'm on top!'"

Justin spent most of his time alone in his room at the rear of the house, reading or listening to the radio. From his mother he inherited a taste for folk and classical music, which developed into a passion for Bach, Mozart, and, above all, Beethoven. His favorite piece of music was the Ninth Symphony. Justin's room, cluttered with flea-market bric-a-brac, was usually a mess, his bed rarely made, his clothes on the floor, his baseball gloves and archery bows in a corner. Justin had built his own bookshelves where he kept his *Narnia* set, Tolkien books, *Peanuts* comic books, *Mad* magazine anthologies, Plato's *Meno, 2500 Insults,* Asterix comics, *The Encyclopedia of American History,* and the *World Book Encyclopedia* his parents had bought when he was five. His library overran the shelves into boxes on the floor; whenever his parents couldn't find one of their own books, they knew where to look. On one wall was a huge Confederate flag an uncle had given him. On another wall was an old map of Putnam County. Justin covered a third wall with aluminum foil, partly to brighten up and partly to warm the poorly insulated room. On his door Justin posted a sign:

DO NOT DISTURB
DO NOT ENTER
TRESPASSERS WILL BE SHOT
5 CENTS TO ENTER

Justin's affinity for spending time alone was encouraged by the demands of the Spoonhour household. When Justin was three, Giles took a new job as a drug counselor in New York City, a two-hour commute each way. By the time the children were stirring at 7 a.m., he was usually gone. Anne worked odd hours at the newspaper, was trying her hand at writing novels, and served as a volunteer for the town's ambulance corps. Giles's and Anne's community activities kept their schedules erratic, and one or both of them were often busy in the evenings. "There was a certain amount of running in and out and coming and going," says Anne, "but we tried to make it a point to schedule a couple of meals a week together." If she and Giles weren't going to be home for dinner, Anne left a casserole for the children to heat up. If that wasn't possible, Justin and Leah were capable of fixing themselves something to eat. Justin had been cooking since he was seven and enjoyed it. Sometimes, however, it was as if four self-reliant grown-ups were sharing the house at Lookout Manor.

---

Justin and Leah were treated as adults partly from the necessity of their parents' schedules and partly because that was the way their parents had been raised. "I was not spanked, I was reasoned with," remembers Anne, "and I tried to do the same with Justin." Anne proudly recalls being complimented by a woman who'd seen her in school with Justin and Leah. "She was very impressed because I was explaining things to the kids as though they were adults." Giles also tried to reason with his children, but occasionally his temper would explode. "When I was in a disciplining state of mind, I had a tendency to get very loud," he says, "and I know that this was scary for Justin and Leah." A sports fan who got so excited he would shout himself hoarse at games, Giles coached some of the town's recreational teams. In Justin's sixth-grade year, Giles coached him in midget basketball. Justin, who was not naturally athletic, played second string. "I tried not to single him out for special consideration or special criticism," says Giles. "I tried to treat him like all the other boys." Yet several parents remarked at how much more exacting he was of Justin. One woman got quite upset at baseball games because Giles yelled at Justin if he struck out.

Yet there were many moments of family happiness. At unexpected times Justin would sneak up behind Anne and give her a hug. "You're a good little mommy," he'd say. Giles and Justin occasionally threw a football, played chess, or went swimming in nearby Lake Oscawana. His mother often invited him along when she drove into Oregon Corners on errands, and they talked earnestly about politics and the environment. On weekends the Spoonhours picked apples and strawberries together, browsed flea markets, went to church, and ate out, sometimes at a restaurant, sometimes at McDonald's or Burger King. And though Justin usually went to his room after dinner, from time to time the family watched *M*A*S*H,* with Giles's laughter booming over the rest, or went to a movie. Or they would be out driving in Anne's beat-up old Chevy Nova, with the sound track to *Peter Pan* on the tape deck, and she and Leah and Justin would belt out "I Won't Grow Up."

At school Justin was a step ahead of most of his classmates—at least in the subjects that interested him. The consensus on his report cards was "Brilliant but doesn't try." Some things came easily to him, and he invested little effort in those that didn't. When his grades slipped, he could usually buckle down in time to get his accustomed B average by semester's end. Unlike his classmates he didn't agonize over his report card. In sixth grade, because of his high IQ, he was placed in an accelerated track for gifted children. While others in the project lorded their status over their classmates, Justin didn't seem to care; he skipped assignments, floundered through the program, and was not asked to return the following year. When it appeared that he might be held back a class because his grades were so poor, Giles and Anne took him to a psychologist. Justin was placed in a group with other youngsters who lacked what the school tactfully called "socialization skills." They met once a week to play games, talk, and eat pizza.

Though Justin had few friends his own age, he got along well with adults. At school he sought out the company of teachers, with whom he had vigorous philosophical discussions about ecology, nuclear disarmament, and the state of the world. What his classmates saw as "different," many adults saw as "special." Lora Porter, the Putnam Valley librarian, never thought of Justin as peculiar, perhaps because she, too, as she says, is considered "a bit of a kook." Justin, who felt at home at the library from an early age, delighted Porter by asking her to recommend books for him. The summer after Justin's seventh-grade year, Anne would drop him and Leah off at the library on her way to the newspaper office. They spent the day there, reading and helping out at the children's story hour. "I always sort of knew they hadn't had breakfast," says Porter, "so I'd send Justin to the store down the road for some rolls and oranges."

Like many others, Porter treated Justin as an adult. "There was no other way to treat him." When she became embroiled in a controversy over whether a fundamentalist group should be allowed to use the library for meetings, she talked about it with Justin. "His mother had written some strong articles in the paper supporting my civil liberties position. Justin had read them, and he brought up the subject when he came to the library. Though he was very young, he discussed the issue with the understanding of a mature mind. I remember him saying, 'I guess you really have to take a stand.'"

Justin and Leah became the official library puppeteers, putting on shows for children during vacations. Starting with theatrical kits, Justin designed and embellished sets for a series of fairy tales. For *Rumpelstiltskin* he found some straw and sprayed it with gilt to resemble the gold the dwarf spun. He and Porter had lengthy deliberations about lighting techniques and sound effects. "We discussed the shows as if we were Mike Nichols and his producer," she remembers. Using the library's elaborate puppet theater, Justin, Leah, and two of Leah's friends performed *Puss in Boots, The Three Little Pigs,* and *Hansel and Gretel* for flocks of small children who sat on the floor in openmouthed awe. Justin, working several puppets at once, expertly adapted his voice to each character. When the play was over, Lora Porter asked the puppeteers to step out from behind the red velvet curtain. When Justin heard the applause, his face always broke into a huge smile.

---

As Justin entered adolescence, the contrast between him and his peers grew still sharper. At Putnam Valley Junior High, Justin's class gradually sifted into cliques. "There were three groups," explains one of his classmates. "There was the cool group, the burnouts. They were the kids who were the first to start smoking, drank a lot, used drugs, talked back to teachers, and spent a lot of time in detention. Then there was the sort of easygoing group—not trying to be tough, not real burnouts, a little bit academic. Then there were the losers—kids who couldn't do sports, who were ugly, or who didn't really care much about anything. Maybe they liked one another, but nobody liked them. And then there was Justin. He was a group in himself."

Justin obviously wasn't cool, and he was too intense to be in the easygoing group. He didn't qualify for the losers' group either. He wasn't ugly—a girl in his class grudgingly admits that, combed and washed, "he would have looked just as good as anybody else." Although he didn't excel in sports, he wasn't hopeless. And though he cared about many things, the things he cared about were, to his classmates, the wrong things. He preferred chess to checkers, cats to dogs, archery to soccer. He preferred reading to hanging out at the Jefferson Valley Mall. After school, when most seventh-grade boys were playing ball, Justin was one of three males to sing in the school chorus. While his classmates' Walkmans were tuned to rock, the radio in Justin's room was tuned to classical. In music class, when the students were asked to present reports, virtually everyone chose rock bands and snickered as they stood in front of their peers playing tapes by Prince, Black Sabbath, or The Cars. Justin chose Beethoven. He brought in an armful of articles and books, played a recording of a piano concerto, and clenched his fists with passion as he described Beethoven's work.

In junior high "cool" boys wore concert jerseys with pictures of rock groups, designer jeans, and expensive new basketball sneakers. Justin wore flannel shirts, generic jeans that were usually too short, and black dress shoes or dirty white high-top sneakers. Once, when his mother bought him a pair of designer jeans, Justin made sure to cut off the label before wearing them. In gym class, while the athletes preened in shorts and T-shirts no matter how cold the weather, Justin wore a stained oversize sweat suit. Whatever he wore was unironed, untucked, often unwashed, and sometimes backward. His classmates hurled insults: "Wash your hair." "Is that the only shirt you own?" "You smell." "Why do you listen to that classical crap?" "Get a life." Justin would shrug off their taunts, which made his tormentors all the madder. Justin wasn't like them, but he didn't seem to *want* to be like them. Says one classmate, "He brought most of this stuff on himself by not trying to fit in."

But when Justin tried to fit in, he was not allowed. In seventh grade he persuaded the track coach to let him be team manager. He traveled with the squad to their meets, cheered for his classmates, and kept careful records of their times. Justin was proud of his position, and he had letters put on the back of his sweatshirt that spelled out TRACK MANAGER. But while the team admitted Justin did a thorough job, he remained an outcast. "Theoretically, he was part of the team, but nobody really liked him," says a team member. "On bus trips he sat up front with the coaches or by himself because he knew nobody else would sit with him, or if he sat with somebody, they'd just give him heck all the way there or hold their nose or something like that." Justin managed the team for two years. Eventually, the letters on his sweatshirt started to fall off, and it read CK    AG R.

There were occasional moments of acceptance: when Justin made a difficult move in a basketball game; when he had a solo in the school chorus. In seventh grade, after he had a minor hip operation, his classmates clamored to borrow his crutches, and suddenly Justin was the center of attention. But after two weeks the crutches were gone and so was the attention.

Mike LoPuzzo was the closest thing to a friend Justin had. Although he was considered part of the easygoing group, Mike himself was a little different—for his music report in seventh grade, Mike had chosen to explicate the genius of Frank Sinatra. He dressed neatly, wore his hair short and carefully parted, and carried a briefcase to school. He was earnest, tolerant, and precocious, qualities not highly prized by his peers. But because he was a big, strong fellow, he wasn't teased much. He had watched the kids badger Justin since fifth grade when his family had moved to Putnam Valley from the Bronx, and although he had occasionally chimed in, he felt sorry for Justin and admired the way he handled the situation. In seventh and eighth grades, when the class divided up for projects, Mike didn't groan like the others when the teacher put Justin in his group, and they occasionally talked about school, movies, and books. Sometimes Justin brought in collections of *Doonesbury* cartoons to show him—Justin was partial to Zonker, a long-haired, leftover-sixties type. Mike found Justin interesting to talk to and liked his dry sense of humor. But, says Mike, they never ate lunch together, talked on the phone, or saw each other outside school. "Justin never said a word about his parents or his home life," says Mike. "He never talked about girls or about problems. He never talked about his personal life, and he never asked me about mine."

Nor did Justin talk about being teased. "It never seemed to bother him—he was always a happy-go-lucky kind of person," says Mike. "He would just put his head down and say, 'Aaargh.' No matter how all the students were down on him, he always seemed to bounce back." Mike once asked Justin why he didn't wash his hair. "If you washed and combed it, then people wouldn't bother you," he said. Justin shrugged, and Mike didn't press it. "To me it seemed like such a simple solution, but to him maybe it was symbolic," says Mike. "Maybe he was trying to send the world a message: 'Does physical appearance matter that much? What's important is inside.' Besides, Justin had more important things to worry about, like Beethoven and Shakespeare."

But even Mike admits that he may have drawn back a little from Justin: "Sometimes I was afraid that other people would treat me the way they treated him." When the eighth grade took its annual four-day trip to Washington, D.C., Justin ended up rooming with Mike. "We chose roommates before we went down," says Mike, "four to a room. Me and two friends were together in one room. Naturally, nobody wanted Justin. I think he was just hoping for someone to ask him, so I said, 'Yeah, come on with us.'" When they arrived at their hotel after the four-hour bus ride, everyone was excited and rambunctious. "We started messing up Justin's bed," says Mike. "He'd make it up, and then we'd pull it apart again. We got a little carried away. Justin was on the verge of tears. I'd never seen him that upset before. We kept apologizing, but he wouldn't talk to us. Later I went over to him and said, 'Jeez, I'm sorry, Justin, we were only kidding around. We didn't mean to hurt your feelings.' He said it was all right, and we shook hands." It was the only time Mike ever saw the teasing get to Justin.

Giles and Anne were aware that Justin was teased. "It had come up a couple of times in conferences," says Anne, "but I had not bothered to go to them for a couple of years. I got tired of hearing the same thing that my mother heard about me and what I'm sure Giles's parents heard about him, and what every parent under the sun hears in conferences: 'Your little bastard isn't working up to his full potential.' Well, I say if he isn't disruptive in class, let's let it go. If he stares out the window, well, so did Edison. For that matter, they thought Einstein was retarded." At his son's basketball games, Giles overheard jokes about Justin's bed-wetting and his sloppy clothes. He once saw one of Justin's teammates throw a basketball at him on the sidelines. At home Giles would ask him about the teasing, but Justin dismissed it, saying, "Ah, they're just idiots."

Justin's eccentricities exasperated even his teachers. He was often late to class, rarely raised his hand unless the topic interested him, and turned in careless work. "I think some of the teachers had almost the same attitude that we kids did," says one of his classmates. "They wanted to avoid him. They wouldn't go out of their way to call on him or make him comfortable. When Justin didn't turn in his homework in English class, the teacher would get mad at him. There was another kid who didn't do his assignments, either, but the teacher laughed at him because he was really lovable. But Justin wasn't, so she'd get annoyed. In homeroom my friend and I came in late almost every day. The teacher would smile and shake his head. But when Justin was late, he'd get pretty perturbed." And while some teachers welcomed Justin's extracurricular attention, others were less receptive. "Justin always tried to hang around with the teachers, maybe because he had no friends," says a classmate. "Some of them would sort of ignore him, or they'd wave him off—like 'not this kid again.' They didn't treat him badly, but they treated him like an outsider just as much as the kids did."

And yet Justin seemed to relish being different. As treasurer of the Grace United Methodist Church Youth Group, he concocted elaborate fund-raising schemes such as breakfasts and bake sales while the other five children planned football games, video parties, and trips to the beach. When one of his ideas was rejected, Justin immediately tried to devise another project that would meet with their approval. The group expected Justin to hatch grand ideas; it was a running joke that Justin always wanted to be president of something. Justin often seemed to delight in dissenting just for the sake of testing his peers. When everyone else voted for *Superman* for a pizza and video party, Justin fought for *Star Wars* although they'd all seen it before. One time when the group was planning the music for a party, Justin said he wouldn't attend because he liked only classical music. After all the arguing, however, Justin usually went along with the majority.

"He had his clashes with his peers, but on the whole I think he related rather well," says Marion Cox, pastor at Grace United Methodist and leader of its Youth Group. "I don't think he had an enemy in our group. There were times when he would take the opposite tack from everyone else and just push and push and push, and the kids would get down on him. But it was never unfriendly. They'd just say, 'Oh, that's Justin.'" Cox had moved to Putnam Valley a few years before and was still getting settled in the community. "He and Justin got along famously," says Anne Spoonhour. "Justin was aware that Reverend Cox was something of an outsider." Justin appreciated Cox's corny jokes, and he liked to tease him that his sermons were too long and "dry as dust." Cox, who was married but had no children, took something of a paternal interest in Justin. "He was a very lively boy with an impish sense of humor," says Cox. "He liked to test you. But just as you were about to get exasperated, he'd have a twinkle in his eye as if to say, 'Now really, don't take it all *that* seriously.'"

During the summer after eighth grade, Justin spent a week at a Methodist youth camp. It was his first time away from home. The dozen campers slept in lean-tos and cooked their own meals. Justin loved it, but he came on a bit strong at first, giving orders the way he did as "general" of his neighborhood army. The night before the campers returned home, the pastor who led the camp held a small Communion service. As part of the service he told the group, "Before you take the sacraments, if you feel there's something you need to say to someone because you haven't understood him rightly or perhaps you mistreated him in some way, now is the time to apologize." There was a pause, and then all eleven campers lined up in front of Justin.

---

The next fall Justin entered ninth grade at Putnam Valley Junior High. In the previous year he had grown rapidly. "Every time I looked up, he seemed to have grown another inch and put on another ten pounds," says Giles. At five-eleven and 140 pounds, Justin was gangly but broad-shouldered. The features on his round face had grown larger and sharper. When Lora Porter saw him at Christmastime, she noticed how much he looked like his father. Anne bought him a new sports jacket, brown corduroy with elbow patches, size 20 collegiate.

That same fall Leah entered seventh grade. Although her appearance—a tall, skinny body topped by a pale face and a shock of frizzy white hair—made her a more obvious target for teasing than her brother, Leah possessed a certain sheer nerve that drew people to her. She quickly found herself at the center of a tight circle of friends; whatever the "norm" was that Justin wasn't part of, Leah was at its core. While Justin ate alone at lunch in his last year at the school, his sister, in her first year, was surrounded by giggling friends. Unlike Justin, Leah was often asked home by her classmates, and they frequently visited the Spoonhour house for afternoons and sleepovers. Justin would arrive home to find his sister and her cronies gossiping to a background of heavy metal music. He would groan and yell at them to keep quiet. "You're weird," the girls would answer. "Why don't you go read a book," Justin replied scornfully. "Don't you do anything with your head except wear hair on it?"

Justin and Leah's rivalry had always been strong, though no worse than that of other siblings their age, Anne and Giles thought. They were intensely competitive playing board games, and at Youth Group meetings they occasionally argued. Justin needled Leah about her marathon telephone calls, her cooking, and her taste in books, while she teased him about his taste in TV. Their musical preferences were a particular problem; their parents finally decreed that they must alternate afternoons in control of the stereo. Genuine love lay beneath the teasing, Anne believes.

Justin seemed to be making modest social progress of his own. That summer his psychologist had agreed that Justin didn't need the socialization group anymore. And while Justin had no real friends, he had a small circle of what Anne calls "associates" with whom he played Dungeons & Dragons. Given the basic instruction manual for his thirteenth birthday, he quickly became an avid player. He spent long hours alone in his room filling stacks of notebook paper with maps, sketches of new characters, and equations calculating the characters' chances for survival. He occasionally played the game with a few people at recess or lunch. Although Justin rarely used the telephone, since discovering "D and D" he might call a classmate to discuss a character he had just created or to make plans for a D and D session. In October, for his fourteenth birthday, he asked his parents for a D and D party. A half dozen boys arrived at noon and stayed through the evening, poring over battle plans at the dining room table, filling up on pizza and popcorn, and taking occasional breaks to throw a football in the yard.

Justin had another way to step out of his own world into one over which he had more control. He had grown up listening to his parents' recordings of *West Side Story* and *The Fantasticks* and had attended several Broadway shows on school trips or with his parents. After seeing *Can-Can* on the eighth-grade trip to Washington, Justin said, "When I grow up, I want to be rich enough to be a Broadway producer so I can revive all the good old musicals." He also talked about an acting career. In eighth grade he played the title role in the school production of *Whatever Happened to Ebenezer Scrooge?*, a contemporary sequel to Dickens's *A Christmas Carol.* He threw himself into the part of the crotchety old miser, wearing his nonprescription spectacles offstage, nattering on in his "Scrooge" voice. "When he got a role, he took it very seriously," remembers Anne. "He would truly identify with the character." Although Drama Club was hardly the cool thing for Putnam Valley boys, his classmates had to admit that Justin was talented.

In ninth grade he was cast as a curmudgeonly senator in *Outrageous Fortune.* Playing opposite him was Diana Wolf, a classmate who had also been in *Scrooge.* "At first it was like I didn't want to shake his hand, but the drama teacher took me aside and said, 'He's different—just give him a chance.' " Diana and Justin got along fairly well. In *Outrageous Fortune,* Justin had some trouble with his lengthy role, particularly with one long speech. "He knew his lines, but he was so nervous he'd start stuttering and garbling the words," says Diana. "He'd get frustrated and ask to start again." She and Justin devised a remedy. "At one point he was supposed to be showing me something in his briefcase, so we taped some of his lines in there." Opening night did not go well for Justin. Before the curtain he wanted to make his hair neat for the show. He went from cast member to cast member asking to borrow a comb. Each of them said sorry, he didn't have one. Onstage, recalls Diana, "he messed up so badly we all had to cover for him." When his mother saw the production, however, she was impressed. "Most of the kids acted the way eighth and ninth graders act—flat line readings with a lot of hesitation and missed cues. But Justin *was* that senator."

Onstage Justin seemed to be able to express things more freely than he could in real life. In *Scrooge,* Justin's character had legions of elves working for him. "Justin really liked the role because he got to be in charge," says a cast member. "Usually people picked on him and didn't listen to him. But in the show he was the boss, and he could yell at people." Similarly, in *Outrageous Fortune,* Justin played another adult who got to tell off the other characters.

Offstage Justin was less and less able to attract attention. "After a while I think people got used to him, and they just ignored him, which probably drove him even more crazy," says a classmate. "I guess it's more or less like a wart on your foot. First it bothers you, then you think it's gross, and then after a while you just don't notice it anymore."

At home Justin kept his problems hidden. Anne had taken a job as a dispatcher for the Putnam Valley Police Department and worked many evenings; Giles commuted to his job in Manhattan. Although their schedule of volunteer activities was busier than ever, they believe they spent as much time as they could with their children, as much as most parents. If Justin needed more, he didn't show it. "Very rarely would he approach us to talk about things or ask for help," says Giles. "Very rarely would he take the initiative." Adds Anne, "But it's not as if he was taking his problems to anyone else as far as we know. He just didn't express his problems, period." It was difficult to tell when Justin was upset. He rarely raised his voice and never threw tantrums; when angry, he grew quiet and disappeared into his room. Occasionally, however, Justin left a curious clue to his mood. Several times Giles came home to find a pile of wood shavings on the living room floor. When he asked Justin about it, he learned that Justin, exasperated over the failure of some scheme, had taken a knife and a stick and begun whittling.

As Justin grew older, Giles felt frustrated at not being closer to his son. "I would have liked to have more conversations with him about what was going on in his life," he says. "I remember going through a lot of turmoil in my own adolescence and not having anyone I could sit down and talk to. I never had heart-to-heart talks with my father, and I was looking forward to having them with my son. I was hoping that as he became interested in girls, we could talk about that. I had ideas that I wanted to share with him about what to say and what to do and what not to say and what not to do."

But Justin rarely talked about girls. "In a lot of ways he didn't know what he was yet," says Anne. "Sex almost hadn't entered the picture. He was still in the 'girls are to throw rocks at' stage." Justin spoke admiringly of a young actress on *Buck Rogers,* and once, chatting with his mother, he mentioned a girl he had known in seventh grade who was, he allowed, "pretty okay." But as far as Anne knows, Justin never mentioned his feelings to the girl. "He was very male-oriented," says Giles. "He did not seem to have much of an interest in girls. I was a little concerned about that." Girls were even less interested in Justin. When asked what his female classmates thought of him, one girl responds matter-of-factly, "Nothing." She explains, "No girl would go out with him because it would be so damaging to her reputation. I mean unless she were incredibly ugly or drugged out, she wouldn't be seen with him unless he totally changed."

Giles attempted to get closer to his son: "I tried to do it as naturally as possible. I didn't want to make a point of 'Okay, now we're going to sit down and talk.' There were times that we would talk about things, and I was hoping that from general worldwide problems we could get down to specifics in his own life. But I was not very successful in getting him to open up." Though the issue of sex came up, it tended to come up as another dinner-table topic, like hunger in third-world countries. "I can't remember having a 'man to man' talk with him or anything like that," says Giles. "It was always in a family context with his mother and me and sometimes even his sister there. We would talk about it in general, about young people getting involved sexually."

In November, Giles and Justin watched *The Day After,* a made-for-TV movie depicting the aftermath of a nuclear holocaust. Justin, who tended to take the world's problems to heart, had often fretted over the disarmament issue. When the program was over, Giles could tell that Justin was upset. "I knew it had a strong impact on him because ordinarily he talked about these things, but this time he didn't. He seemed dispirited." Giles tried to draw him out but was unsuccessful. "It was as if he were in a state of shock and couldn't talk about it. He seemed to get the feeling that nuclear destruction was almost inevitable." That night Justin lay awake and wept, thinking about the movie and what could happen. The next day he wrote a letter to the president saying that he had been so concerned about the threat of nuclear holocaust that he hadn't slept. Couldn't we find a better way of solving our problems? Justin never mailed the letter.

As the New Year began, Justin was brimming with plans. He intended to perform puppet shows at the library during February recess. He had started writing science fiction stories. He had arranged John Denver's song "Perhaps Love" as a solo with chorus backup and planned to audition with it for the spring musical. He was excited about returning to camp—this time he wanted to stay for two weeks. He was trying to persuade his parents to let him attend a summer Dungeons & Dragons convention in Minnesota. He was already talking about what kind of party he wanted for his fifteenth birthday the following October, and he was campaigning for a new archery bow as a junior high school graduation present. "It's only $169, Mom," he'd plead as he danced around her. "I really need it if I'm going to be an Olympic archer."

In February his Honors English class read *Julius Caesar* aloud. Justin, who adored Shakespeare, lugged his massive two-volume edition of the complete plays into class each day, but the teacher, exasperated, told him he had to use the same paperback as the other students. Justin won the role of Caesar, which he read with great feeling and flourish. Though he tended to show off a bit, the class was impressed.

On Sunday evening, February 12, there was a Youth Group meeting. Justin had pushed for the session, at which he unveiled an elaborate scheme to raise funds for scholarships to camp. He proposed a flea market and barbecue modeled on the church's annual barn sale. Reverend Cox didn't want to quash Justin's enthusiasm, but he said it didn't seem practical. He suggested a car wash or a bake sale. He promised to discuss Justin's plan at the next board meeting. The other boys and girls in the group agreed that Justin's project was too complicated. Although Justin quickly changed the subject and proposed that next week his parents talk to the group about their work in emergency services, Cox could tell that Justin felt deflated. That evening when Giles picked up his son, he asked him how the meeting had gone. "Well," said Justin, "they shot me down again." They talked about it a little on the way home, and Giles knew Justin was disappointed because he was so quiet.

Tuesday, February 14, was Valentine's Day. Justin was up in time to have a quick breakfast with his father before Giles left for work. Then he and Leah caught the bus for school. That morning Justin got a French test back. He had done well and showed his paper to Mike LoPuzzo, to his guidance counselor, and to anyone else who would look. "This is the best I ever did," he exulted. After lunch Reverend Cox happened to be at the school discussing plans for the annual career day with the principal when Justin walked into the office. Cox, remembering Justin's defeat at Youth Group, asked him how he was doing. Justin said he was fine and told Cox about his success on the French test. In English class that afternoon Justin performed the role of Caesar with his customary panache.

At the end of class the teacher handed out Valentine's Day carnations. Each year the Student Council took orders for flowers at one dollar apiece, and just before school let out on February 14 they were distributed. Coaches bought them for members of their teams; friends bought them for friends; and some bought them for classmates they had crushes on. While popular students received several—one pretty ninth grader received eight—some people didn't get any. Justin, of course, was one of them. "I don't think it bothered him," says a classmate. "I'm sure he didn't send one, so I'm sure he didn't expect to receive any." Justin told Mike he would bring him another book of *Doonesbury* cartoons tomorrow.

When Anne returned from shopping at three, Justin and Leah were already back from school. She had bought Justin some jelly beans and a valentine but decided to save them until Giles got home so that he could sign the card, too. Justin was out playing with a friend. Anne called him in and kissed him good-bye, then left for her four-to-midnight shift as police dispatcher. When Giles arrived home around six-thirty, it was already cold and dark. Leah was inside playing with a friend. Giles asked her where her brother was. Leah said she had gone out for a while and, when she returned, Justin was gone. Giles thought this was a little odd. On the living room floor there was a pile of wood shavings.

Giles went outside and called for Justin. When he chooses to use it, Giles has a booming voice that carries quite a distance; often when Justin was out playing or even when he was indoors at a friend's house, Giles would call to him and Justin would hear and come home. This time there was no answer.

Giles grew concerned. He telephoned a few of the neighbors and the parents of some of Justin's classmates. No one had seen him. Between calls Giles went to the door and shouted his son's name into the night.

Giles worried that Justin had fallen and hurt himself or that he might have made wisecracks to some older teenagers and they had ganged up and beaten him. Once before when Justin had disappeared, that is what Giles had feared. Justin, eleven at the time, had been with friends at Lake Oscawana, about a half mile from home. At dusk Giles and Anne had called his friends, who said Justin had walked home alone hours before them. Giles recruited some neighbors, and they had fanned out and searched the area between the Spoonhours' house and the lake, calling his name. They didn't find him. They phoned the police, who hurried over. While Giles and Anne were in the living room telling the police what they knew, in walked Justin, rubbing his eyes, wondering what all the fuss was about. He had been asleep for hours in the storage room and had just awakened.

Giles hoped that this time around something similar would happen, but by ten-thirty, after trying everyone he could think of, he called Anne, who thought of some more people to call. At eleven-fifteen, Giles called Anne again and said he was really worried and wanted her to come home. Anne arranged for someone to finish her shift. A friend at the station offered to help, and grabbing a couple of battery-powered searchlights, they drove quickly to Lookout Manor. When they got home, the three of them began searching the neighborhood, calling Justin's name. Giles looked around the rocks where Justin and his band liked to play war; Anne searched the yard. Then she and her friend crossed the road and walked into the woods, their flashlights cutting tunnels of light in the dark. About a hundred yards from the house Anne heard her friend cry out, "Oh my God." She started toward the sound of his voice, but he came crashing forward, shouting at her to stay put. He ran toward the house, yelling for Giles. Anne turned on her light and saw her son, his eyes dilated, his tongue swollen and protruding, hanging from a tree.

––––––––––

The following morning one of Justin's teachers was driving to school when news of his death was broadcast on the radio. She was so shocked she nearly drove off the road. News travels fast in Putnam Valley, and by the time students arrived at school, many of them had heard. Students and teachers clustered in the halls crying, and as new arrivals were told, some of them burst into tears. The first reaction of a few students was "Good—he's gone," but when the truth sank in, they were stunned into silence. Diana Wolf hadn't listened to the radio that morning, and when she arrived at school, she heard a girl spreading the news. "I went up to her and said, 'What are you talking about?' She said, 'Justin hung himself. My mother heard it on the radio.' I said, 'I don't believe you.' I went to my homeroom teacher and asked him if it was true. He had yelled at Justin for being late just the day before. He looked down and said, 'Yes.' In my first class everybody was talking about it. One kid said, 'Well, it's the only thing Justin ever did right. He finally did something right.'"

At his locker that morning Mike LoPuzzo heard the talk about Justin and prayed that it wasn't true. "I thought, 'Jeez, I hope nothing happened to him, because these people don't give a damn about him, they're gonna love it.'" First period he was alone in a classroom, minding computers for a teacher, when he looked out the window and saw several policemen talking to Justin's father. "I knew then that something had really happened." Mike thought of the *Doonesbury* book Justin had promised to bring him that day. "In a strange way I felt that he let me down," he says. He felt even more let down by the thought that his classmates had finally gotten to Justin. "I was mad at him. 'Why did you let them get to you?' I said to myself. 'That's just what they wanted. How could you let those idiots push you over the edge?'" Later that day a school counselor approached Mike. "I hear you were friends with Justin," he said. "Well, I really wasn't his friend, but I was friendly to him," Mike replied. After he said it he felt guilty and wondered why he had been defensive.

Early that morning, Richard Brodow, the superintendent of Putnam Valley schools, was having his car fixed at a garage when he got a call from the school telling him what had happened. Brodow, who had known Justin enough to say hello to him by name, was stunned. The biggest problems he had faced as superintendent of the small, eleven-hundred-student district had been budget fights—just the day before he had steered a lengthy but productive budget meeting. The idea of a suicide seemed unbelievable. "As an administrator you may be trained in curriculum, you may be trained in personnel, you may be trained in supervision," he says, "but this is something that you're never trained for."

There had been suicides in Putnam Valley before, including those of teenagers, but they had been met with hushed silence, almost as if people had agreed to pretend they hadn't occurred. However, even if Brodow had wanted to bury the news, which he didn't, the notion of business as usual was absurd. When he arrived at the school during the first period, students were still gathered in the halls, sobbing. His teachers were doing their best to cope, but many of them were as bewildered as the students. It was obvious that no lessons could be conducted—the entire school was essentially in shock. Brodow telephoned Peekskill High School and asked them to send over two counselors, who, in addition to Putnam Valley's psychologist and guidance counselor, would visit each classroom to discuss Justin's suicide and answer questions. Students were told that counselors were also available in the guidance office to talk privately. The staff drew up a list of students who seemed particularly distressed, and a counselor met with each of them. Their parents were called and told that their children should be watched closely over the next several days. After-school activities were canceled; the flag was lowered to half-mast.

For many students Justin's suicide was their first experience with death. That the death was of someone their own age was frightening; that it was intentional was incomprehensible. Students who had teased Justin were terrified that they had driven him to suicide. "Why did I pick on him?" they said. "Why did I tell him he smelled?" Others felt guilty for tolerating the teasing or for ignoring Justin. "I think he was just too good for us," one child told a counselor. Teachers wrestled with their own feelings of guilt. They worried that they had not treated Justin as well as they might have, that they had missed signs, that somehow they could have prevented his death.

The last class of the day was Honors English, in which Justin had played Julius Caesar with such intensity twenty-four hours earlier. Today, the guidance counselor spoke to the class about Justin's death. He had met with Justin the day before to discuss his schedule for his first year at high school. Justin had seemed cheerful and confident, said the counselor, but perhaps he had already made his decision to kill himself, and that had made him seem happy. Diana Wolf, who had kept control over herself all day, began to weep. At the end of the day when Brodow, over the public address system, asked the school to stand for a moment of silence in Justin's memory, Diana couldn't stop sobbing. When she got home, she went to her room, took out her journal, drew a fat black X instead of the day of the week, and wrote: "One of my classmates, Justin Spoonhour, hung himself last night. He's dead. Our class of 115 is now a class of 114. I'll never see him again. . . . Nothing like this has ever happened to me before. I can't handle it. Right now I'm crying uncontrollably. This is awful. I don't know what to do. I don't want to take a shower. I don't want to go for a walk or go to sleep. I haven't eaten all day, and I don't intend to because I might throw it up. I'm going to watch 'The Guiding Light' now. I better blow my nose first. Justin, underneath, we did love you. Why did you do it?"

Over the next few days the entire town struggled to answer that question. Certainly, many people were aware that Justin Spoonhour had been "a square peg in a round hole," as they said, and that he had been ostracized for it. But he had never complained or indicated that he was unhappy or depressed, and he had never spoken of death. He had endured the teasing for years—why had he killed himself now? Some were convinced it had been an accident, that Justin had been playing around and had gone too far. A few people murmured that Justin had become so involved in Dungeons & Dragons that he had been unable to distinguish fantasy from reality and had committed suicide as part of the game. Others felt that on Valentine's Day, when the whole world was supposed to be in love, the years of isolation had finally gotten to him. Still others suggested that Justin may have gotten the idea of killing himself from the newspaper. Ten days earlier, thirteen-year-old Robbie DeLaValliere had been found hanging from a tree in the town park in Peekskill, ten miles south of Putnam Valley. His suicide had made headlines in the local papers. Justin had not known DeLaValliere, and no one had heard him mention the boy's death, but people wondered if he had read about it and decided that he had found a solution to his problems.

But there were no convincing answers. Justin himself had left no note, and although everyone kept expecting someone—a friend to whom he might have confided his plans, perhaps—to come forward with an explanation, no one did. There were rumors, of course. Some said that Justin had fought with his English teacher that afternoon; others claimed that he had been given a flower as a Valentine's Day joke. One student said that on the school bus a few weeks before his death, Justin had showed him a noose he had fashioned from a piece of string. "See?" Justin had said. "This is a strong knot." But that was all he had said. It was just another stray clue that seemed significant only in retrospect, like the pile of wood shavings Giles had found on the living room floor. But while the clues were inconclusive, it seemed that Justin, in the end, had been resolute. The coroner determined that he had hanged himself about six o'clock, three hours after getting home from school, with a rope from the cellar.

Most of Justin's classmates came to the wake, including many of those who had harassed him. One boy with whom Justin had had a shoving match at a basketball game a few months earlier came several times, each time with different friends. Many of the children wept, and a few became hysterical as they approached the open casket where Justin lay in his size 20 collegiate jacket, his chorus sweater, and a burnt-orange turtleneck, borrowed from a friend of Anne's, to cover the rash where the rope had bitten into his neck. Justin looked handsome and neat, but not too neat. Before the wake Anne's best friend had leaned over the casket and mussed his hair.

Friday at noon, several hundred people packed Grace United Methodist Church for Justin's funeral. More than half his class attended with their parents. Reverend Cox, who had stayed up until 2 a.m. writing the eulogy, spoke of his shock at Justin's death. He wondered why Justin hadn't come to him, why he hadn't recognized any signs of unhappiness, and he concluded that perhaps he had attributed an adult maturity to Justin that he did not have so early in his life. As for reasons, said Cox, we can speculate, but only God can know. Giles, one hand on Justin's coffin, spoke of the terrible irony of a father burying his son. "I had been looking forward to sharing so many things with him—school and college and career choices and helping him struggle with adolescent problems and dating and getting serious and choosing someone and raising a family. . . . I will miss him, and I'm convinced I will see him again." Giles nearly broke down several times. "I shaved this morning with the razor I was going to give to Justin," he said. "My God, my son wasn't even old enough to shave yet." When Anne sang a hymn to her son, the church was pierced with sobs. "There are no answers for what happened," she told Justin's classmates. "But if you want to honor my son, you will try to love and be more aware of each other." The organist played the "Ode to Joy" from Beethoven's

Ninth Symphony, and Justin's drama teacher sang "Perhaps Love," the song
Justin had hoped to sing in the spring concert:

> Perhaps love is like a resting place
> A shelter from the storm.
> It exists to give you comfort
> It is there to keep you warm.
> And in those times of trouble
> When you are most alone,
> The memory of love will bring you home.

On a gray, drizzly day Justin was buried a quarter mile from the church at
Rose Hills Memorial Park. Giles and Anne had placed several things in the
casket with their son: the sheet music to "Perhaps Love," some Beethoven
tapes including a recording of the Ninth Symphony, and the jelly beans and
valentine that Justin had never received.

# II

# THE SLOT MACHINE

ON THURSDAY EVENING, two days after Justin Spoonhour's death, a public meeting was held at Putnam Valley Junior High. The topic of the meeting, which had been called by school superintendent Richard Brodow, was "Adolescents in Crisis," but everyone knew it was really about suicide. Although 250 chairs had been set up in the auditorium, by the time the meeting started, people were standing in back. The audience consisted mostly of parents and teachers but included some teenagers. Diana Wolf and Mike LoPuzzo were there.

Kenneth Schonberg, a pediatrician from nearby Chappaqua whom Brodow had asked to speak, could feel the tension in the room. He had conducted meetings like this before. Nine months earlier in the town of North Salem, fifteen miles east of Putnam Valley, a high school girl had hanged herself in the restroom of a drive-in movie after a quarrel with her boyfriend. A month later the boy hanged himself in his family's home. Schonberg had spoken to the town's anxious parents. He sensed that tonight's crowd was even more tense because the suicide had occurred so recently. Although he knew he could give them no real answers, he wanted to ease their fears, to put Justin's death in some perspective. He gave a brief overview of adolescent suicide and talked about the complexities of parent-child relationships. He said that feelings of anger, guilt, fear, and sadness were natural responses to the tragedy. "What you must understand and let your children know is that they are not to blame for what happened."

Although Justin was on everyone's mind, his name was rarely mentioned. Parents worried that what had happened to Justin could happen to their own children. A couple whose son had known Justin was concerned because he didn't want to talk about Justin's death. A mother who had been taking notes asked, "What if a youngster denies feeling suicidal but he walks the floor all night?" Another mother wondered, "How do you make your child talk about it if he doesn't want to?" Schonberg suggested that parents not force the issue but ask gently whether something was on their child's mind and be ready to listen. "Ninety-nine percent of this is not to prevent another suicide," he said, "but to make your kids feel comfortable talking about it." One woman voiced the fear shared by most parents at the meeting: "What happens if we go through all this, we talk about it, and we have another one?" Said Schonberg, "It's the same chance as lightning hitting twice in the same place. There's no reason for anyone to think that this is a contagion. Just because it happened to one child doesn't mean it will happen again."

Near the end of the meeting a gray-haired man stood and said, "I've been a resident of this community for a long time, and I can remember previous incidents of this kind. What disturbs me is that it takes an event like this to bring us together. Kids want to talk, but parents don't. We as parents should discuss these things." He sat down to applause.

By the end of the meeting there was a feeling of catharsis and a sense that the community was pulling together. As they drifted out, people greeted their friends and neighbors. Many of them stopped to thank Schonberg and to pick up a directory of crisis services available in the area and a list of "the warning signs of suicide." As couples drove home on the winding roads of Putnam Valley that night, they talked about their families. Some looked in on their sleeping children when they got home. One woman phoned each of her children around the country. "I want you to know I love you," she told them. "I want you to know you can talk to me."

That night, not long after the meeting ended, twenty-five miles south of Putnam Valley in a town called North Tarrytown, an eighteen-year-old boy named Jimmy Pellechi shot himself in the head.

---

Much of what Kenneth Schonberg told Putnam Valley parents about suicide that evening was new to them. Because they tend to avoid the subject until it hits close to home, most people are shocked when they find out how many people choose to end their own lives. In 2002, the most recent year for which statistics are available, 31,655 Americans completed suicide. On an average day eighty-seven Americans kill themselves, twelve of them under twenty-five years of age, five, like Justin, under twenty. In a country with one of the highest murder rates in the world, more than half again as many people kill themselves as are killed by others.

Still, the government-certified statistics are believed to be lower than the actual numbers, because families may cover up evidence, rearrange a death scene, or hide a suicide note in order to qualify for insurance benefits or to avoid stigma. Some coroners and medical examiners have been known to classify a death as suicide only when the circumstances are unequivocal—when a note has been left (about 15 to 20 percent of all cases) or the victim is found hanging. They may overlook shooting, jumping, overdosing, drowning, and other methods that can be interpreted as accidents. Studies in the 1980s concluded that suicide rates were underreported by as much as 50 percent; more recent research places the figure at closer to 10.

For many years suicide was associated with older white males. Four times as many males as females complete suicide, and the rate rises with age. Over the last five decades, however, a dramatic change has taken place. While the overall suicide rate has remained fairly stable, the rate for adolescents (aged fifteen to twenty-four, as defined by federal statisticians) tripled, from 4.5 suicides per 100,000 in 1950 to 13.8 per 100,000 in 1994. (Underreporting may be particularly prevalent for adolescents, for whom accidents are the leading cause of death, accounting for 40 percent of all fatalities.) During those years advances in medicine lowered the mortality rate for every age group in America except fifteen-to-twenty-four-year-olds, whose rate rose, largely because of the increase in suicides. Most of those suicides were male; five times as many males as females in this age group kill themselves, compared with the four-to-one ratio in the population at large. "The real importance of this is that it shows a real, fundamental change in the phenomenon of suicide in this country," Mark Rosenberg, an epidemiologist at the Centers for Disease Control and Prevention (CDC), told reporters. "Whereas a few years ago it might have been your grandfather . . . now it's your son."

Hearteningly, over the last decade, the adolescent suicide rate has stabilized and slightly decreased, to 9.9 in 2002. Yet suicide remains the third leading cause of death among fifteen-to-nineteen-year-olds, behind accidents and homicides, and the second leading cause of death for twenty-to-twenty-four-year-olds, behind accidents. (While most of the attention has focused on teenagers, a more media-genic demographic, the rate of suicide in the college-age group is 50 percent higher than among high school students.) To illustrate the magnitude of the loss, psychiatrist Kay Jamison compared the number of suicide deaths among males under age thirty-five with those from two more highly publicized causes of death among men in the last four decades. She found that during the Vietnam War, there were almost twice as many suicides (101,732) as war deaths (54,708), and during the height of the HIV/AIDS epidemic, nearly 15,000 more young men died from suicide than from AIDS.

Suicide deaths, however, represent only one extreme of adolescent suicidal behavior. Official statistics on attempted suicide are not kept, but for every adult suicide there may be as many as twenty-five attempts; for every adolescent suicide, there may be one hundred or more. Psychologist Kim Smith of the Menninger Foundation, assembling data from several studies, has suggested that 2 percent of all high schoolers have made at least one suicide attempt, which would mean that 2 million high schoolers, at some point in their lives, have attempted suicide. Most of them are female. While five times as many adolescent males kill themselves, three times as many females make attempts. And a great many more adolescents *think* about killing themselves: In 2002, a CDC survey reported that during the previous year, 19 percent of high school students had "seriously considered" suicide, 15 percent had formulated a plan, 9 percent had made an attempt, and nearly 3 percent had made an attempt that required medical attention. In another survey, high school and college students were asked, "Do you think suicide among young people is ever justified?" Forty-nine percent said yes.

Although clinicians had long been aware of the rising rate of adolescent suicide, national attention turned to the problem only in the mideighties, spurred by the growing recognition that adolescent suicides tend to come in bunches. In 1983, when eight teenagers in fourteen months killed themselves in the wealthy Dallas suburb of Plano, youthful suicide became a big story. Suddenly, suicide seemed to be snatching, according to the media, "the best and the brightest," who had "everything to live for"—the football captain and the cheerleader as well as the loner and the delinquent. Across the country the questions poured out: Why was the adolescent rate increasing so rapidly? Why these bunches of young suicides? Why are young people so unhappy? Why are they killing themselves?

---

No one knows exactly why people kill themselves. Trying to find the answer is like trying to pinpoint what causes us to fall in love or what causes war. There is no single answer. Suicide is not a disease, like cancer or polio. It is a symptom. "People commit suicide for many reasons," says psychologist Pamela Cantor. "Some people who are depressed will commit suicide, and some people who are schizophrenic will commit suicide, and some people who are fine but impulsive will commit suicide. We can't lump them all together." And just as there is no one explanation for the four thousand adolescent suicides each year, there is no one explanation for any particular suicide. While it is often said that suicide may be committed by twelve different people for twelve different reasons, it may be just as true to say that one person may choose death for twelve different reasons or one hundred different reasons— psychological, sociological, and biological factors that finally tighten around one place and time like a knot.

Although some adolescent suicides are said to come "out of the blue," the vast majority of young people who kill themselves can be found, on closer inspection, to have had clearly discernible and often long-standing difficulties. Certainly, although Justin Spoonhour's suicide was unexpected, there were many possible contributing factors that might be emphasized by different experts according to their professional orientations. After his death some Putnam Valley townspeople said, "He killed himself because he wasn't given a flower on Valentine's Day." Although this was a risibly simplistic response, a psychiatrist might point out that Justin's rejection on Valentine's Day mirrored rejections he had experienced throughout his life by his classmates. Others observed, "He killed himself because he was different—he liked Beethoven and everyone else listened to Michael Jackson." Although listening to Beethoven is not commonly known to cause suicide, it was one example of Justin's isolation and how that isolation led to ostracism. Even his few attempts to belong to the "mainstream"—joining the Cub Scouts, becoming the track manager—were met with scorn. Another psychiatrist might point to the high standards Justin set for himself, standards that were difficult for the rest of the world to live up to. His being "different" was encouraged by parents who were themselves somewhat different. A third psychiatrist might point to the lack of a stable family life. Although the child of an intact marriage, Justin was often alone at home, both because of his lack of friends and because his parents' activities kept them away. Justin seemed, in fact, to be most at home in the fantasy world he created. A fourth psychiatrist might point to Justin's eccentricities, conclude that he had suffered from an undiagnosed "adjustment disorder," and suggest that he should have tried a course of antidepressants.

Other experts would highlight other influences. A sociologist might point out the effect of changing social mores and the difficulties faced by a child of sixties parents growing up in the conservative eighties. Although much of Justin's isolation seemed to be self-imposed, another sociologist might stress that in rural towns like Putnam Valley, making and keeping friends is especially difficult when they are all a car ride away. A philosopher might point to Justin's extreme sensitivity to the problems of the world, especially his apparent anxiety over the nuclear threat. A physician or a developmental psychologist would certainly observe that all of these influences were heightened by the traditional chaos of puberty, a time when biological changes were shaking up Justin's universe and he was beginning to grapple with questions of sexuality. A neurobiologist might wish to have analyzed Justin's cerebrospinal fluid in an attempt to learn whether his decision might have been linked to abnormally low levels of a brain chemical called serotonin.

All of these responses might be correct, but separately, no one of them would be the truth. Like the blind men who grab different parts of the elephant and misidentify the beast, suicide experts, exploring suicide from their own perspectives, end up supplying only part of the whole. "Suicide is a biological, sociocultural, interpersonal, dyadic, existential malaise," says Edwin Shneidman, a psychologist who has devoted his life to the study of suicide. Shneidman's definition is cumbersome, but it may be the most accurate we have.

What are some of these "biological, sociocultural, interpersonal, dyadic, existential" variables? Over the last twenty-five years, there has been increasing evidence that some of the most important variables may be biological. Studies of completed suicides have suggested that more than 90 percent occur in individuals with a diagnosable psychiatric disorder—a catchall that covers everything from schizophrenia to alcohol abuse to less easily defined categories such as "conduct disorder." Over those same years, researchers have found genetic underpinnings for many of those afflictions, including depression, schizophrenia, alcoholism, and substance abuse. Although there is evidence that younger adolescent suicide victims may have lower rates of psychopathology than do adults, it is clear that in a great many adolescents, suicide and suicidal behavior are associated with a diagnosable, and treatable, psychiatric disorder. Yet mental illness doesn't by itself lead to suicide; while an estimated 90 percent of completed suicides of all ages have a psychiatric disorder, more than 95 percent of people with psychiatric disorders do not kill themselves.

Of the some three hundred mental illnesses listed in the *Diagnostic and Statistical Manual of Mental Disorders,* a few are particularly associated with suicide. Although schizophrenia, alcohol and drug abuse, and borderline personality disorder, among others, all carry increased risk, the disorder with which suicide has most closely been identified is depression. Indeed, for many years suicide was linked almost exclusively to depression, as if there were a threshold—different for every person—that one could not bear to sink below. Suicide was seen as depression's last stop. Although clinicians have since recognized that many people who are not depressed kill themselves, experts nevertheless estimate that six of every ten people who die by suicide suffer from major depression, in either its bipolar form (also known as manic depression) or its unipolar form (often called major depression). If alcoholics who are depressed are included, the figure jumps to nearly eight in ten. According to the National Institute of Mental Health (NIMH), people who suffer from clinical depression have a rate of suicide twenty-five times that of the general population. About 15 percent of Americans will suffer from clinical depression at some point in their lifetime. Thirty percent of all severely depressed patients will attempt suicide; 15 percent will ultimately complete. If mild depression is included, the rate of completed suicide drops to about 3 percent. Of the two main forms of depression, bipolar disorder is the more strongly linked to self-destruction; while an estimated one in five people with major depression will attempt suicide, nearly one-half with bipolar disorder will try to kill themselves.

Until three decades ago, however, psychiatric wisdom held that children and adolescents did not experience depression. This belief was based primarily on Freud, who said that depression was anger turned inward by the superego. Children and adolescents, it was believed, did not have fully developed superegos and thus could not get depressed. They could be moody and sad, but such feelings were attributed to the vicissitudes of growing up. The reluctance to recognize depression in younger people no doubt contributed to the belief that adolescent suicide was rare and was another reason why so many young suicides were cataloged as accidents.

These days, it is accepted that children and adolescents can suffer from depression, although they may manifest different symptoms from those of adults. Children and younger adolescents tend to camouflage depression with overt behavior, acting out their feelings through restlessness and temper tantrums—what psychiatrists used to call masked depression. Older adolescents may show signs of masked depression, such as promiscuity and excessive risk-taking, but they also display classic adult symptoms—insomnia, loss of appetite, inability to concentrate. They may also show irritability, restlessness, aggression, and, particularly in those suffering from bipolar disorder, outbursts of rage. Symptoms are often difficult to recognize because the angst of normal adolescence so often resembles depression. One in twenty teenagers suffers from clinical depression; if mild depression is included, the number jumps to one in five. In a study of the health problems of fifty-six hundred adolescents, depression was second only to colds in frequency. "I think that depression, in a funny way, is an inevitable part of adolescence," Paul Walters, former director of health services at Stanford University, told me. "In fact, if you *don't* get depressed, I think there's something wrong."

Although major depression has consistently been found to be the most prevalent disorder among adolescent suicide victims, situational depression, caused by a reaction to an event—a poor grade, the loss of a relationship—can also be lethal. Such depressive episodes, however intense, may be brief and, coming as they do at a stage of life in which an individual is groping for autonomy and identity, are developmentally normal. Feeling blue after not getting into one's first-choice college is as appropriate as feeling happy after scoring a winning touchdown. But many adolescents who experience situational depression don't realize that it won't last forever. They tend to keep their sadness to themselves. They may believe that depression is a sign of weakness. They may worry that they are going crazy.

"One kind of person most likely to kill himself is someone experiencing a depressive reaction for the first time," says psychologist Douglas Powell, who worked at Harvard University Health Services for many years. "Young people who are depressed often think that one thing, one event, will make it all better—a good grade, a boyfriend. It's important to help them realize that it's perfectly possible to have a date that isn't earth-shattering, and that even if it's not such a great time, you're still the same person afterward and it's not the end of the world." Depressed adolescents are apt to blame themselves for feeling bad and to punish themselves for imagined failures. "Kids who have never experienced failure go into a tailspin when they get a twenty-three on a biochemistry test," says Chicago psychiatrist Derek Miller. "One of the most important things we can do for our children is build some failure into their lives so they learn that it is possible to fail without being a failure." San Francisco psychiatrist Jerome Motto drew applause at a conference on adolescent suicide when he suggested, "Early on, we should give children puzzles they can't solve—and then give them love when they fail."

While depression and suicide are closely related, depression is not the only answer; for every teenage suicide there are hundreds of depressed teenagers. And depression is twice as common in females as males, yet suicide is four times more common in males. Clinicians have struggled to isolate the factors that separate suicidal depression from depression, but they tend to come up with abstractions such as "loneliness," "isolation," "low self-esteem," and "a profound sense of worthlessness." Psychiatrist Aaron Beck, the founder of cognitive therapy, cites "hopelessness" as the key factor, and in a series of studies has shown it to be a strong predictor of suicide in depressed patients. (Psychiatrist Calvin Frederick goes two *h*'s further: "helplessness, hopelessness, and haplessness.") Comparing twenty-six depressed patients who had completed suicide with twenty-six depressed patients who had not, a group of clinicians found that while hopelessness, rage, self-hatred, and anxiety were more prevalent among those who had completed suicide, "the acute affective state most associated with a suicide crisis was desperation." Still other clinicians have found a significant relationship between hopelessness and what psychiatrists call "locus of control." People who believe that the outcomes of events are due to forces outside themselves, and whose sense of self-esteem is based on what others think of them, tend to feel more hopeless than those who feel that events are contingent on their own actions. Adolescents who depend on others for a sense of self-worth may find a reason to live in someone or something else. They put all their eggs in one basket—a sport, a grade, a person—which then becomes all-important. Often that reason may be a boyfriend or girlfriend. "If the adolescent has no other sources of self-esteem, the relationship becomes tremendously overvalued," says Samuel Klagsbrun, a psychiatrist in Westchester County. "It becomes the foundation of the person's life. 'If the other person loves me, I'm okay.' But if that goes, it's as if everything goes—because there's nothing left to bank on."

As early as 1938, psychiatrist Gregory Zilboorg noted the greater frequency of parental death in the history of suicidal people and suggested that the loss of a family member when the child was at the height of the Oedipus complex or in the transition to puberty led to a morbid identification with the dead person and rendered the child especially susceptible to suicide. "This is probably the most primordial cause of suicide in the human breast," he concluded. Since then, many studies of suicide have found a high incidence of parental loss. Examining fifty suicidal patients of all ages, psychiatrists Leonard Moss and Donald Hamilton identified what they called a "death trend"—95 percent of the patients had suffered the loss of a close relation. In 75 percent of the cases, the deaths had occurred before the end of adolescence. A University of Washington study of 114 completed and 121 attempted suicides found that the death of a parent had occurred significantly more often in the childhood of the actual suicides than in that of the attempted suicides. They concluded that an inability to come to terms with a parent's death in childhood leads to an inability to cope with loss in later life. "Loss in all of its manifestations is the touchstone of depression—in the progress of the disease and, most likely, in its origin," wrote the novelist William Styron in *Darkness Visible,* a harrowing account of his descent into suicidal depression. Although Styron traces his illness to genetic vulnerability—like him, his father had been hospitalized for severe depression—he ascribes an even more important role to the death of his mother when he was thirteen.

If that early parental loss is by suicide, it may be even more debilitating; people who have had suicide in their family are eight times more likely to complete suicide themselves. Whether that heightened risk is due to the disruption caused by parental psychiatric illness, to inherited vulnerability to depression (or another psychiatric illness associated with suicide), to what psychologists call modeling—the fact that once certain behaviors are introduced into a family, they may become more acceptable, in the same way that the offspring of dentists are more likely to become dentists themselves—or to a combination of these, or to some other factor, is a subject of controversy. It will be discussed further in part two.

Death is not the only way in which adolescents may lose someone close to them. Not surprisingly, suicidal young people are apt to come from families where there have been problems. Comparing 505 children and adolescents who had attempted suicide with a control group, psychiatrist Barry Garfinkel found that the attempters came from families that showed more "disintegration." Families of attempters had higher rates of medical problems, psychiatric illness, substance abuse, paternal unemployment, and completed or attempted suicide. Both parents were present in fewer than half the families. (Numerous studies of completed suicide have found high rates of parental psychopathology—particularly depression and substance abuse.) In a study of 120 young suicide victims in the New York metropolitan area, Columbia University epidemiologist Madelyn Gould found that certain psychosocial factors increased suicide risk among adolescents even beyond the risk attributable to psychiatric illness. The most notable ingredients: problems at school or at work, a family history of suicidal behavior, poor parent-child communication, stressful life events, nonintact family of origin, a mother with a history of depression, a father with a history of trouble with the police. Child psychiatrist Cynthia Pfeffer of Cornell University Medical College found that parents of suicidal children were subject to intense mood shifts, lacked the ability to delay gratification, and were extremely dependent and incapable of communicating with or guiding their children. In short, they were like children themselves.

Given these findings, it is hardly surprising to learn that family cohesion is a protective factor; one study found that students who described their family life as one of mutual involvement, shared interests, and emotional support were five times less likely to be suicidal than were adolescents who had the same levels of depression or life stress but were raised in less tightly knit families.

One of the strongest risk factors for suicide is childhood trauma, which can not only trigger a range of immediate effects, from low self-esteem to substance abuse to delinquent behavior to difficulty forming attachments—all of which are associated with suicide risk—but can also increase the chances of developing depression, substance abuse, and other psychiatric disorders associated with suicide. (Nearly half of all abuse victims develop at least two disorders by age twenty-one.) Over the last decade, neurobiologists have found that childhood trauma can derail the developing brain, causing potentially lifelong alterations in cognitive development and disrupting its stress response system, rendering children more vulnerable to later stressful events as well as to the development of psychopathology. Of the many types of childhood trauma, sexual abuse is the strongest risk factor, implicated in an estimated 9 to 20 percent of adult suicide attempts. A review of twenty studies concluded that adults with a history of physical or sexual abuse in childhood are up to twenty-five times more likely to attempt suicide. The greater the trauma—duration, use of force, relationship of perpetrator to victim, whether or not penetration occurred—the greater the risk of suicide. "Violence is a learned response to frustration and anger," says Harvard epidemiologist Eva Deykin, whose study of 159 adolescents who had attempted suicide found a frequent incidence of physical or sexual abuse. "An individual who is exposed to child abuse might incorporate that response, turning aggression inward, as a means of coping with outside infringements."

In much of this research, science merely confirms common sense. A child who grows up in a dysfunctional household is more apt to have problems later on. But these "problems" may erupt in a variety of ways; no one has yet pinpointed which are more likely to lead to suicide and which to drug abuse, alcoholism, or other symptoms of unhappiness. Every risk factor mentioned thus far—depression, parental loss, abuse—causes stress and pain that may be expressed in a variety of self-destructive behaviors, all of which are connected to suicide like stars in a constellation. Studies have found high rates of attempted suicide among juvenile offenders, among homeless and runaway youths, among drug and alcohol users, among teenage mothers, among cigarette smokers. While these studies have led some nonclinicians to the simplistic conclusion that drugs, crime, and teenage pregnancy can cause suicide, they indicate that unhappy adolescents are turning to a variety of self-destructive and risk-taking behaviors to cope with their pain. They are all forms of communication; suicide is merely the most radical. And adolescents who use these other methods are more apt to turn to suicide if their communication goes unanswered. Says counselor John Tiebout, "Today teenagers have to go to more and more extremes to get what they want. And maybe suicide fits into that dynamic. Being depressed or getting high is not a strong enough way to communicate to the world how miserable and fucked-up you are."

If these problems are accompanied by substance abuse, they are especially likely to end in suicide. Autopsies tell us that one-third to one-half of teenage suicides are under the influence of alcohol or drugs shortly before they kill themselves, while nearly one-third of teenage attempters are drunk or high shortly before they attempt. The Department of Health and Human Services has estimated that three in ten adolescents have drinking problems. While drugs and alcohol don't cause suicide—after all, millions of teenagers drink or use drugs and do not kill themselves—under their influence, underlying rage is more readily translated into aggression. Alcohol is a depressant, which can make an already depressed person more depressed, and as "liquid courage" it can lower inhibitions and release suicidal impulses. (Those impulses are far more likely to be acted on if guns are available; teenagers who use firearms are five times more likely to have been drinking than those who use other methods.) A Houston study of 153 adolescents who had made "nearly lethal" suicide attempts—attempts that would have ended in death if someone hadn't intervened—found that drinking within three hours of the attempt was the most important alcohol-related risk factor, more important even than alcoholism or binge drinking. Drugs and alcohol themselves offer a withdrawal, a step away from reality and a step toward suicide. Alcohol abuse is one of many self-destructive behaviors that have been called slow suicide. Sometimes, however, it is not so slow, as in the case of a fifteen-year-old Colorado boy who went to a party and drank nine cans of beer, a quart of bourbon, and half a bottle of whiskey. He died that night.

No matter how self-destructive urges are manifested, the sources of an adolescent's need to harm himself, directly or indirectly, are often difficult to trace. While many suicides come from broken, disturbed homes, a great many more children from troubled homes turn out fine. And more than a few suicides grow up in intact, loving families. What makes one child grow up liking himself and another child grow up hating himself?

Some psychiatrists believe that the seeds of self-esteem and the ability to cope with stress are planted in mother-infant bonding, the connective tissue of looks, touches, and words that forms between mother and child within the first year of the child's life. When a crying baby gets a gentle, loving response, he develops what psychoanalyst Erik Erikson calls "basic trust." He is more apt to grow up feeling loved and lovable, to develop a sense of self-worth and a belief that he is not powerless in the world. The English psychoanalyst John Bowlby, a pioneer in the study of bonding, demonstrated that young children are upset by even brief separations from their mother. If the child's cries or tantrums are ignored, the child, he says, may adopt a permanent pose of detachment that may render him unable to form meaningful relationships for fear of being abandoned, as he felt he once was by his mother. "A baby repeatedly left to cry alone ultimately learns to give up and tune out the world," says psychologist Lee Salk. "This is learned helplessness and possibly the beginning of adult depression."

Orthodox Freudians trace the roots of adolescent suicide back to mother-infant bonding. "Nearly every suicidal child we've seen has suffered a break, a problem, in the mother-infant bond," write the authors of *A Cry for Help,* a book about adolescent suicide. ". . . We must realize that the suicidal impulse can be engrained within the first few months of life." But to blame suicide on bonding failure, one would be obliged to trace that failure back to how *that* mother bonded with *her* mother, and so on. The seeds of trust planted in infancy merely provide the base on which a sense of self-esteem is built. That sense is constantly reinforced or undermined by subsequent life experiences. In adolescence, however—an especially vulnerable stage in which a young person is beginning the process of breaking away from his parents and searching for his own identity—conflicts over separation and dependence are at their most intense. "The child who feels unloved in infancy or in early life, whether perceived or true, is more likely to grow up feeling unloved and unwanted, and unable to love and be loved," says psychologist Pamela Cantor. "This may cause difficulty in forming meaningful relationships and lead to frustration, anger, and depression."

For years, researchers have tried to find a genetic marker for suicide. They haven't found it, but they have found evidence of a specific biological link to suicidal behavior. By analyzing the cerebrospinal fluid of those who have attempted suicide and studying the brains of those who have died by suicide, neurobiologists have discovered that some suicidal people, regardless of psychiatric diagnosis, have lower than average levels of a brain chemical called serotonin. They have found these abnormalities in suicidal people as well as in impulsive, aggressive individuals, often in association with depression. Researchers have suggested that serotonin dysregulation is a biological trait that predisposes to suicide; a depressed person with low serotonin function is more likely to respond to a stressful experience by acting impulsively or aggressively or both—and that action may include a decision to attempt suicide.

Although the serotonin research, which will be discussed in part two, is extraordinarily promising, much remains to be learned. Only a fraction of suicides are linked to serotonin dysfunction—how large a fraction is not yet known—and serotonin depletion is also found in people who aren't suicidal, just frustrated or depressed. Furthermore, the research has yet to be replicated in adolescents. Yet these findings may help explain why a large proportion of young male suicides—the highest risk category among adolescents—has been found to have a combination of depression and antisocial or aggressive behaviors, often complicated by drug or alcohol use. Many of them have a history of disciplinary problems at school or with the law. Psychiatrists at the Los Angeles Suicide Prevention Center found that over 40 percent of the suicidal youngsters they studied had had physical fights with family members. In a recent survey of high school students, the CDC found that those who had attempted suicide during the preceding twelve months were nearly four times more likely to have reported fighting than those who hadn't attempted suicide. Studying suicides age nineteen and under in the New York metropolitan area, psychiatrist David Shaffer found that a minority of suicides—mostly girls—showed a picture of uncomplicated depression, while the largest diagnostic group, about 25 percent—mostly boys—was composed of adolescents with both aggressive and antisocial symptoms and depression.

Such a description certainly fit Jimmy Pellechi, the eighteen-year-old who shot himself in North Tarrytown two days after Justin Spoonhour's death. A big, awkward adolescent, Jimmy dropped out of high school during senior year, drank heavily, never backed down from a fight, spent evenings racing with friends on his motorcycle, and had what his best friend described as an "I don't give a fuck" attitude and what older townspeople called "a death wish." One night, after drinking heavily, Jimmy telephoned the girl he had been seeing and told her that he had a gun and if she didn't promise to stop going out with other boys, he would kill himself. She refused. Jimmy put his father's shotgun to his head and pulled the trigger.

For the depressed and suicidal teenager, the breakup of a relationship may be what clinicians call the "precipitating" or "triggering" event. In Madelyn Gould's study of adolescent suicide, nearly half of the 120 victims had experienced a recent disciplinary crisis or interpersonal loss—a suspension from school, an appearance in court, a breakup with a girlfriend or boyfriend. After such an incident an adolescent may feel he has failed and that his failure is unacceptable to his parents, his peers, or himself. Teenagers arrested for the first time on charges of drunken driving and jailed overnight, for instance, are often overwhelmed by shame. Feeling they cannot face the outside world, they may take their own lives, often during the first few hours of confinement. (One young man, jailed on a minor charge, hanged himself while his parents were in the next room posting his bail.) Adolescents confused about their sexuality may commit suicide rather than admit to themselves or their parents that they might be gay. "In all the teenage suicides we see," says Judy Pollatsek, a counselor in Washington, D.C., "the kids always have some secret and are terrified that someone is going to find out." A few hours after learning she was pregnant, a fourteen-year-old girl, fearing her parents' reaction, killed herself by kneeling in front of a train. Suicide is often an impulsive act; among adolescents, especially so. In the Houston study of nearly lethal suicide attempts, almost 25 percent of the adolescents reported that fewer than five minutes passed between their decision to kill themselves and their actual attempt.

The triggering event need not be momentous. One often reads newspaper accounts of teenagers who kill themselves for seemingly trivial reasons: the fourteen-year-old boy who, according to his parents, shot himself because he was upset about getting braces for his teeth that afternoon; the girl who killed herself moments after her father refused to let her watch *Camelot* on television. For Justin Spoonhour, not receiving a flower on Valentine's Day or having his plans rejected by his church's Youth Group may have been the triggering event. Such incidents are often misinterpreted by the media or even by family and friends as the "reason" for a suicide, but they are usually the culmination of a long series of difficulties. "Interpersonal loss, perceived, actual, or anticipated, oftentimes is the last blow," says psychologist Alan Berman. "A relationship, a breakup, or a fight with one's parents may open wounds of deeper pain." The triggering event may seem to verify the lack of self-worth the teenager may have felt all along. "They are like a trivial border incident which triggers off a major war," wrote A. Alvarez in *The Savage God*.

The triggering event may seem inconsequential to adults, but it may be a matter of life and death to the teenager. "If youth is the season of hope, it is often so only in the sense that our elders are hopeful about us; for no age is so apt as youth to think its emotions, partings, and resolves are the last of their kind," wrote George Eliot in *Middlemarch*. "Each crisis seems final, simply because it is new." Says psychiatrist Samuel Klagsbrun, "For adolescents, the moment is everything. They think, 'I've got pain, and the pain is lasting for more than two minutes—that means the pain will last forever.'"

To an adolescent in pain, suicide can seem like an instant cure. This is "like treating a cold with a nuclear bomb," as one therapist puts it. "When young people are suicidal, they're not necessarily thinking about death being preferable, they're thinking about life being intolerable," says Sally Casper, former director of a suicide prevention agency in Lawrence, Massachusetts. "They're not thinking of where they're going, they're thinking of what they're escaping from." Casper recalls a fifteen-year-old girl who came to her agency one day. "In one pocket she had a bottle of sleeping pills, and in the other she had a bottle of ipecac, a liquid that makes you want to vomit. She said, 'I want to kill myself, but I don't want to be dead. I mean, I want to be dead, but I don't want to be dead forever, I only want to be dead until my eighteenth birthday.'"

This girl was indulging in what clinicians call magical thinking. Like Wordsworth, who observed, "Nothing was more difficult for me in childhood than to admit the notion of death as a state applicable to my own being," suicidal adolescents may not fully understand the permanence of death. They may describe it as a sanctuary, a womb, a long sleep, or a tranquil vacation. They may feel, in the words of the theme song from *M\*A\*S\*H*, that "suicide is painless" and what comes afterward is pleasant. They might agree with

Peter Pan: "To die will be an awfully big adventure." But at some level they may not realize that it is an adventure from which they cannot return. "I thought death would be the happiest place to be," a seventeen-year-old Texas girl who had attempted suicide three times after breaking up with her boyfriend told *Newsweek*. "I thought it would be like freedom, instantly. You'd be flying around happy and you wouldn't be tied down to earth."

"Suicidal teenagers may be grieving over some sort of loss in their lives, whether it be that of their self-esteem, a relationship, or a family problem," says Los Angeles child psychiatrist Michael Peck. "But if you could say to them, 'Don't commit suicide because I can get you away from the pain without dying,' they'd likely be ready to do it." A study by psychologists Roni Cohen-Sandler and Alan Berman found that suicidal children have a black-and-white perspective. In solving problems they give up looking for alternative solutions and become frustrated and depressed. And the pain may become so great that death is seen as the only option. As one fourteen-year-old girl told Berman, "If I died, I wouldn't hurt as much as I do now."

"Suicidal adolescents suffer from tunnel vision," says psychologist Pamela Cantor. "They are looking down a long tunnel, and all they see is darkness. They don't know where they are in the tunnel; they think it goes on forever. They don't know that there is light at the other end." Perhaps more accurately, at a certain point the suicidal adolescent believes that there *is* light at the end of the tunnel and that light is suicide. This was expressed by a depressed four-teen-year-old girl who made repeated suicide attempts, one of which was fatal. About a year before she died, she wrote this poem:

> *I wandered the streets,*
> *I was lonely; I was cold.*
> *Weird music filled the air.*
> *It grew louder and louder.*
> *There was no other sound—*
> *Only weird, terrible music.*
> *I began to run as though I was being chased.*
> *Too terrified to look back,*
> *I ran on into the darkness,*
> *A light was shining very brightly, far away.*
> *I must get to it.*
> *When I reached the light,*
> *I saw myself,*
> *I was lying, on the ground.*
> *My skin was very white.*
> *I was dead.*

Serotonin dysfunction, locus of control, and impulsiveness may help us understand some of the factors that might lead a young person to suicide, but they do little to explain the 300 percent jump in the adolescent suicide rate from the midsixties to the midnineties—or to explain its recent, modest decline. To account for the three-decade jump, a host of explanations have been proposed: the unraveling of America's moral fiber, the breakdown of the nuclear family, school pressure, peer pressure, parental pressure, parental lassitude, child abuse, drugs, alcohol, low blood sugar, TV, MTV, popular music (rock, punk, heavy metal, or rap, depending on the decade), video games, promiscuity, lagging church attendance, increased violence, racism, the Vietnam War, the threat of nuclear war, the decrease in the average age of puberty, the media, rootlessness, increased affluence, unemployment, capitalism, excessive freedom, boredom, narcissism, Watergate, disillusionment with government, lack of heroes, movies about suicide, too much discussion of suicide, too little discussion of suicide. While none of these factors have been proved to have more than an incidental correlation with the rising rate of suicide, all of them represent very real reasons why, as one psychiatrist says, "it may be more difficult to be a kid today than at any other time in history."

According to psychiatrist Calvin Frederick, "The primary underlying cause of the rising suicide rate among American youth seems to be a breakdown in the nuclear family unit." While the disintegration of the nuclear family is an easy target—it has been blamed for everything from asthma to schizophrenia—there is evidence that at a developmental stage when they are most in need of it, adolescents have been receiving less support. In the same years that the adolescent suicide rate tripled, so, too, did the divorce rate. A causal relationship to suicide cannot be proved, of course—indeed, a few studies have suggested that divorce as a factor in adolescent suicide may be attributable to underlying psychiatric problems in the adolescent and/or his parents. Yet a correlation exists: while more than 50 percent of American couples eventually divorce, an estimated 70 percent of adolescents who attempt suicide come from divorced families. Even where there are two parents in the house, they are not likely to be home. Along with 91 percent of America's fathers, half the mothers of preschoolers and two-thirds of all mothers with children over six now work outside the home. Parents increasingly subcontract child-raising duties to day care, babysitters, and, most of all, to children themselves. Cross-cultural studies show that parents in the United States spend less time with their children than parents in any other nation in the world.

An adolescent's diminishing support extends beyond the nuclear family. The pioneer spirit that once sent American families west in search of opportunity now sends them crisscrossing the country in pursuit of upward mobility, leaving behind the traditional backing of friends and extended family. Over a five-year period, one-quarter of the population moves. Both the executive blueprint for success and the blue-collar struggle to stay employed demand more movement than ever and result in less chance for a child to make a place for himself. There are new schools to attend, new cliques to break into, new identities to establish. The Houston study of nearly lethal suicide attempts found that among the factors increasing the likelihood of an attempt were frequency of moving, distance moved, difficulty staying in touch, and recentness of move—especially if that move took place within the previous twelve months. When their sixteen-year-old son killed himself a year after the family moved for the fifth time, one Texas couple decided to have the body cremated. "Where would we bury him? Where is home?" said his mother. A sixteen-year-old whose family had moved from New Rochelle to Shaker Heights to Houston hanged himself from an oak tree in the backyard of their rented house, leaving a note: "This is the only thing around here that has any roots."

Over the last several decades there has also been a fundamental change in child-rearing philosophy: parents have been encouraged to give their children "space." But with too much space, teenagers may feel as if they're growing up in a vacuum. "Once childhood is over, there is a tendency for parents to stop parenting," says psychiatrist Michael Peck. "They just say, 'If that's the way you feel, do your own thing.' And so all the things that kids used to do at age seventeen or eighteen, they're being given the freedom to do at twelve and thirteen. Many parents are afraid to teach their children, afraid to set rules and enforce them. But a feeling that they can do anything they want is terrifying to kids." Peck says many of the suicidal young people he sees in his practice get little clear-cut guidance, lack goals, and feel "a sense of floating along in time without direction." Left to their own devices, adolescents are turning to sex, drugs, and alcohol earlier than ever. By age fifteen an estimated one-third have had intercourse. By sixth grade one-third have tried beer or wine and one-tenth have tasted hard liquor. A *Weekly Reader* survey found 30 percent of fourth graders felt peer pressure to drink. Young people who begin drinking before they turn fifteen are four times more likely to become alcohol-dependent than those who start between the ages of fifteen and twenty-one.

Parents who struggled hard to get where they are can't fathom why their children are so distressed. "I know two or three other people whose children have been suicidal, and the kids always blame the parents," a St. Louis woman, whose seventeen-year-old daughter had recently taken a nonfatal overdose, told me. "I don't think it's all mom and dad's fault. I don't think these kids learn how to be responsible for themselves. They can't handle the slightest rejection, not only by parents but by boyfriends, and in school. My husband and I grew up in what is now the ghetto. When we went to school, you were lucky if your dad had a job. The stress you had was whether your father came home with a paycheck, whether you had enough for bus fare to school, whether there was food on the table. For kids today the stress is 'Do I have an Izod shirt? What boy am I going with?' I've talked to more people who say, 'My son won't go to school today unless he has Nike sneakers.' I have a friend whose son has been going with a girl. When she tried to break off the relationship, he attempted suicide. So his mother bought him a car, thinking it would help.

"I think they've had it easy. We overindulge them. We've given them material things, but we haven't made them responsible people. As long as you say yes, they're fine. The minute you say no, they're off the deep end. To this day, my daughter never says, 'I attempted suicide,' she says, 'My parents *drove* me to it.' But you can't blame everything in the world on parents; you have to learn how to cope with these things. If it's the parents' fault, why didn't *I* turn out this way? I had a mom who never knew I was there and a father who beat me. But I never blamed them. I just figured that's the way it was. When we were young, we were so busy trying to survive, we didn't have *time* to think about committing suicide."

With parents acting like peers, where do adolescents learn to cope in a crisis? "I've had more kids tell me, 'I don't know how people solve problems—I've never seen anybody do it in my life,'" says Dallas pediatrician John Edlin. "Adults of the current generation have great difficulty dealing with the pain in their lives. What do you do if you have a fight? You get a lawyer and get separated. What do you do if something goes wrong at work? You get a lawyer to see if you can sue the boss. There's no feeling that things can be worked at. Kids pick that up. Why work it out? I won't be going to this school tomorrow. My parents divorce each other. What are my role models for how to handle pain?"

While parents spend an average of two minutes a day communicating with their child, the television set spends an average of three and a half hours a day with their child. The average American will watch more TV by the time he is six than he will spend talking to his father for the rest of his life. (A study of 156 preschoolers found almost half preferred watching TV to being with their fathers.) By the time he graduates from high school, he will have logged twenty thousand hours in front of the TV, compared with eleven thousand in the classroom. Parted from this third parent, children may experience severe separation anxiety. Television doesn't cause suicide, of course, but adolescents often watch it to reduce loneliness and may thus become less likely to develop real relationships. A thirteen-year-old boy whose family had recently moved to northern California was reluctant to go to his new school because he was overweight. He stayed in his room and watched the television he had been given as a reward for earning good grades at his previous school. His father removed the TV from his room, telling him he would get it back when he returned to school. Hours later the boy shot himself, leaving a note that said, "I can't stand another day of school and especially another minute without television."

Real life may pale next to television. "TV bombards kids with the glamorous and the thrilling, and then they have to go out and live their lives, and their lives are not glamorous and thrilling," says a high school counselor. "TV doesn't help kids understand that life on a day-to-day level can be boring and mundane and upsetting. Being held up to that image when you have to face the realities of your life can be discouraging, if not depressing." And on TV no problem is so great that it can't be solved in an hour.

Often the solution is achieved by violence. By the time he is graduated from high school, the average child will have witnessed two hundred thousand acts of violence, forty thousand murders, and at least eight hundred suicides on television. One study computed that murder is one hundred times more prevalent on television than it is in reality, and that television crime is twelve times more violent than crime in real life. "Television has brought about the virtual immersion in violence into which our children are born," George Gerbner, dean of the Annenberg School of Communications at the University of Pennsylvania, told a House subcommittee during hearings on "The Social/Behavioral Effects of Violence on Television" in 1981. Since then, more than a thousand studies have concluded that children saturated in television violence—or in video game violence—are more apt to solve their own problems that way. At a Congressional Public Health Summit in 2000, six prominent medical groups warned that children exposed to media violence tend to exhibit increased anti-social and aggressive behavior; to be less sensitive to violence and victims of violence; to view the world as violent and mean; to see violence as an acceptable way to settle conflicts; and to want to see *more* violence—on TV, in video games, and in real life.

Violence on television—or in movies, video games, and books—reflects violence in the outside world, and the chicken-or-the-egg question of precedence will continue to be debated. Whatever the cause, violence as a solution is increasingly used inside and outside the family. And a teenager ready to explode is more likely than ever to have the means at hand. As the adolescent suicide rate tripled from the 1950s to the 1990s, the rate of gun ownership in the United States soared, as did the rate of youth suicide by firearms. "The increase in the use of guns accounts for almost all of the increase noted in youthful suicide," psychologist Alan Berman observed.

Personal struggles can appear even more hopeless when the outside world seems no better off—when on any given day a teenager can pick up a newspaper or turn on a television and learn about starvation in Africa, terrorism in the Middle East—or in the United States—and an abundance of murders, muggings, accidents, and natural disasters. At the breakfast table children pour milk from a carton that bears the faces of children their age who are missing and perhaps kidnapped; in coloring books they fill in a picture of a boy running from a stranger who has offered him a ride; at the mall they are fingerprinted so they will more easily be traced if they disappear. Teenagers live in a paradoxical world in which the 350,000 commercials they see by the time they graduate high school tell them to be the fastest, the strongest, the brightest, the best-looking, the wealthiest, and the winningest, while forty thousand TV murders, the morning paper, and the evening news tell them they might not be alive tomorrow. Adolescents are caught between these extremes, and the gap between who they are and who they are told they should be grows larger. And the powerlessness of the outside world to solve its problems may match the powerlessness a teenager feels inside. Faced with an increasing sense of impotence, an adolescent may believe that the one thing he still owns is his life, and suicide is the only way he can exercise control over his universe. *If I can't control my life, I can control my death.* And to that growing number of voices chanting "USA! USA! USA!" and "We're number one! We're number one!" which beats like a tom-tom on a teenager's brain, there is a flip side, expressed in the lone answering voice of the seventeen-year-old senior who, at his high school graduation in Massachusetts, stepped to the podium and announced, "This is the American way," pulled a gun from beneath his robe, and shot himself, although not fatally.

---

None of this explains a single suicide, of course, but it describes the background against which young people choose to live or die. "What we're doing is looking at a rising suicide rate and trying to determine what is different now from twenty-five years ago," psychologist Pamela Cantor told me at the height of the adolescent suicide "epidemic." "You can point to the rising divorce rate. You can point to increased mobility. You can point to two-career families. And therefore that's what gets blamed. I think they are responsible, but maybe they're not. It may just be correlation because you can also point to the fact that the weather has gotten colder." She smiled wryly. "I'm not being facetious. We just don't know what the answers are."

In 1971, teaching a psychology course at Boston University, Cantor asked her class how many had seriously considered suicide. All but two students raised their hands. Cantor had been studying suicide ever since. Her private practice consisted primarily of young women, many of whom had attempted or threatened suicide. Cantor had traveled the country speaking to students, teachers, and clinicians about adolescent suicide. She had been president of the American Association of Suicidology and chair of the National Committee for Youth Suicide Prevention. Over the years she had been asked hundreds of times why the rate was rising, and in a voice filled with concern and urgency, she had tried to answer that question.

When I spoke with her, Cantor expressed her concern not only as a psychologist but as the working mother in a high-achieving, two-career family in a wealthy Boston suburb. She fretted about her own parenting; as a therapist she had vast knowledge of its hazards and, as a parent, of its rewards. She was keenly aware of how different her children's world was from the world she knew growing up on Long Island in the fifties, with Debbie Reynolds and June

Allyson for role models. "There's no safe place anymore," she told me. "When I was young, our safe place used to be larger than just our home. I could gain mastery over my world by going to the village to get a loaf of bread, by going out for a tuna fish sandwich, by walking to and from school. I could take the train into New York City and stroll up and down Fifth Avenue. I had a great sense of freedom and autonomy without any real threat of danger. Today, when we get out of the car, we lock it; when we get in the car, we look in the backseat. We look under the car before we get in. One Sunday I left the kitchen window open. My husband and children were home. I went to see a friend, and when I came home, I found that a man had climbed through the window and wandered through the house and nobody ever saw him. We keep the window locked now. It's ridiculous. And sad. And this is not only part of my life but part of my children's. Surely it affects their attitude and their well-being. Does it lead to suicide? I don't know.

"The suicide literature is very frustrating. I feel that frustration when I speak to parents because I will go through the list of things that have been pointed to as factors, and I always come up feeling empty because when you're all through, it really doesn't help you determine what to do and what not to do. Yet people want the answer, and I don't blame them—I want it, too. That is why this subject is so frightening for parents, because you can't say, 'If you do a, b, and c, you will protect your children from suicide, and if you do d, e, and f, you will lead them down the path of self-destruction.' The bottom line seems to me that if a person likes himself, he won't kill himself. But how do you get children to like themselves? What do you do? And even if you do everything you think you're supposed to do and you give them love and a sense of security and a feeling that you care, some kids still don't like themselves. And some kids who *do* like themselves go through periods when they *don't*. One evening my daughter told me she didn't like being herself because she wasn't popular. But she has *lots* of friends. How seriously do you take it? When do you listen? When don't you listen? When do you do something? You have to follow your instincts, and I guess all I'm saying is that the best you can do is give children two parents who genuinely love them." She sat back in her chair and shrugged.

---

In the years since I spoke with Pam Cantor, the adolescent suicide rate has dropped—from a high of 13.8 in 1994 to 9.9 in 2002. If the reasons for the three-decade rise are murky, the reasons for the recent decline are hardly less so. One of the most frequently cited reasons for the increase was the greater exposure of adolescents to drugs and alcohol, yet there has been no clear decline in drug or alcohol use by young people over the last decade. Others have pointed to the falling rate of firearm use among high school students following the 1994 Brady Bill, which required federally licensed firearms dealers to run a background check and receive authorization from a national database before making a sale. Yet the proportion of suicides by firearm remained unchanged between 1988 and 1999, and a comparison of states that did and did not pass the Brady Bill statutes showed no effect on the proportion of firearm suicides, except in elderly men. Many therapists attribute the decrease in adolescent suicide to the extraordinary increase in antidepressants prescribed for adolescents; between 1987 and 1996, the annual rate of antidepressant use more than tripled among those age six to nineteen in the United States. Indeed, studies have shown that adolescent suicide rates have dropped in those countries where the use of antidepressants has increased. Yet clinical trials have found that antidepressants have had little effect on reducing depression in adolescents and may, in fact, *cause* suicidal behavior in a tiny minority of pediatric patients, a phenomenon to be discussed in part four. The declining rate in the 1990s may have been due, in part, to increased public awareness of depression and of the warning signs of suicide. Or it may have been due to the booming economy during that decade; over the century, one of the few steadfast correlates has been that the suicide rate rises as the economy falls. A few researchers just throw up their hands and remind us that the suicide rate has always been subject to inexplicable cycles, dips, and blips.

The recent decline in the adolescent suicide rate, however, serves as a reminder that while even one adolescent suicide is too many, the vast majority of American teenagers maneuver through adolescence without killing themselves. In 2002, for instance, 40,496,000 of 40,500,000 adolescents chose not to commit suicide. Although suicide is the third leading cause of death among adolescents, young people have the lowest suicide rate of any age group. While most people wonder why so many adolescents kill themselves, some clinicians suggest that we have the question backward. Why don't more adolescents kill themselves? And why do so many consider it and then back away? Psychiatrist Robert Litman, who has studied suicide for nearly half a century, talks about something he calls "the suicide zone." He believes that suicide-vulnerable individuals move in and out of periods of suicidal risk—sometimes for brief periods, sometimes for moderate or long periods—as their life circumstances fluctuate. But of all those people who enter that zone, few actually kill themselves. "For every hundred people at high risk," he says, "only three or four will actually commit suicide over the next couple of years."

For that to happen, says Litman, a multitude of things must occur. "It's like a slot machine," he says. "You can win a million dollars on a slot machine in Las Vegas, but to do that, six sevens have to line up on your machine. In a sense it's the same with suicide." Those spinning sevens represent all the biological, psychological, and sociological variables that are associated with suicide—depression, broken family, serotonin dysfunction, triggering event, and so on. "In order to commit suicide, a lot of things have to fall together at once, and a lot of other things have to *not* happen at once," says Litman. "There's a certain random element determining the specific time of any suicide and, often, whether it happens or not."

In Litman's slot machine metaphor, suicide is conceptualized as an exceedingly rare event that requires everything to be in alignment for it to take place—a sort of perverse, malevolent music of the spheres. "It's as if you need to have six strikes against you," Litman says. "And we're all walking around with one or two or three strikes. Then you get into a big crisis and you have four strikes. But to get to all six takes some really bad luck."

# III

# BRIAN

---

BRIAN HART WAS the kind of young man who would have been prized by the classmates who scorned Justin Spoonhour. Handsome, athletic, and outgoing, Brian was as much in the thick of things as Justin was isolated and alone. Brian grew up in a large, loving family in Bedford Hills, an upper-middle-class community halfway between Putnam Valley and New York City. As hard as Justin tried to be different, Brian tried hard to be one of the guys, but he could never succeed to his satisfaction. He grew up with one large strike against him, one that ultimately set him apart every bit as much as Justin Spoonhour.

---

Family photographs seem to cover every surface of Patrick and Mary Hart's modest home: grade school portraits, graduation pictures, baptisms, first communions, birthdays, weddings, Thanksgivings, Christmases, and St. Patrick's Days. "The Rogues' Gallery," Pat and Mary call it. When they come downstairs in the morning or go up to bed at night, they are surrounded by the smiling faces of their children. Home and family are important to the Harts. Pat grew up less than a mile from this house, on the estate where his father was superintendent. When Pat was sixteen, his father died, and Pat had to go to work to support his mother and two younger siblings. Mary grew up on Long Island, but the family was broken up during the Depression when her father lost his job. After living with various aunts for two years, Mary was reunited with her family in Mount Kisco. Pat and Mary met in the eighth grade but didn't date until junior year. Pat played basketball and baseball; Mary was prom queen. In their graduation portraits, which hang side by side at the top of the stairs, they look serene, Mary ravishingly beautiful, Pat confident and strong. Their heads are cocked, gazing up and off to the right, looking, as the photographer no doubt intended, toward the future.

Four years after graduating, Pat and Mary were married. During the next four years they had five children, the last two, twins. Pat got up long before dawn for his job as a milkman, then went to night school for his college degree. After working as an officer for the local Teamsters union, he became a federal labor mediator. Mary raised the family and did volunteer work. Seven years after the twins were born, agreeing that they had never had time to truly savor raising a child because they were always busy caring for the next, Pat and Mary decided to have one more child—"the last hurrah," as Mary says. "The gang" was thrilled with the news. When the Harts drove up to church on Easter Sunday in their nine-seater Pontiac, they leaned out of every window. "Guess what!" they yelled. "We're going to have another baby!"

As an infant, Brian was like an only child with seven doting parents. Each morning when Mary woke, she never knew in whose room Brian would be: the first child to wake would lift Brian from his crib, take him to his or her own bed, and feed him his bottle. As soon as the children got home from school, they would drop their books and run through the house looking for their baby brother. Brian was the little prince of the family. If he wanted anything, he was given it; if he was hurt in any way, there was hysteria; if there was an activity, he was included. But gradually his brothers and sisters went off to college or to jobs, and by the time he was twelve, Brian was the only child left at home.

One Saturday morning in October of his seventh-grade year, Brian was playing with friends in the next-door neighbor's backyard. Though Brian had never been allowed to play with toy guns, they were using the friend's BB rifle. By accident one of the boys fired a shot that hit another in the eye. Brian was close enough to hear the splat. Pat, hearing screams, went to the door in time to see the other children, terrified, fleeing the scene, followed by Brian, one arm around the injured boy, whose eye was streaming blood. When Brian returned from walking the boy home, he went into the backyard where the boy had been shot and gathered up the bloodstained leaves from the ground. At the brook behind his house he knelt and carefully washed the blood from each leaf.

Though Brian didn't talk about the incident, his parents could tell it bothered him. He began to have problems concentrating in school. His teachers said that while most of the time Brian was bright, eager, and responsive, at times he was withdrawn, almost "out of it." (In the elections at the end of the year, his classmates would vote Brian Most Popular and also Most Moody.) They suggested he get professional help. Although reluctant—Brian's therapy would be a family first—the Harts found a respected young psychiatrist named Eugene Kornhaber, who began seeing Brian once a week. Brian was initially resentful, but he grew reconciled to being in therapy and would joke to his family and friends about his "shrink."

Brian seemed to be getting along well until the following year when the Harts' beagle, Kelly, died. Kelly was kept tied to the clothesline on a running leash, and the Hart children had been told never to let her loose because the commuter railroad tracks ran behind the house. But Brian occasionally took Kelly across the tracks to play on the hill. One day while Kelly was crossing the tracks, a train approached. Brian called her, but Kelly panicked and ran in front of the train. The train hit her, and Brian saw Kelly tossed between the cars. After the train passed, Brian heard a weak bark and ran to Kelly just as another train approached from the opposite direction. He darted in front of the engine, grabbed Kelly from the tracks, and jumped off the embankment. Brian rushed her to the house—he could hear her bones grind as she moved—but she died within the hour. Brian buried her in the backyard. That night Brian couldn't stop crying. He was sure that he had led Kelly to her death.

Though he rarely talked about them, these two incidents would haunt Brian throughout his life. Years later doctors would point to them as crucial traumas in his development. Because the injured boy, who had to get a glass eye, was on the Harts' property when he was hit by the BB, the Harts were involved in a lawsuit that wasn't settled until Brian was seventeen. In eleventh grade, Brian wrote an essay in which he described the guilt he felt over Kelly's death. Sometimes when he walked into the backyard, he could still hear her howling in pain.

After Kelly's death, Brian's ups and downs became more pronounced. When Brian was up, his determination, exuberance, and sense of humor were infectious. He was extraordinarily handsome, with sandy hair, blue-green eyes, and a wide grin. Girls developed instant crushes on him, teachers were reminded of why they had gone into teaching, and friends' parents wondered why their sons couldn't be as charming as Brian Hart. "With Brian, nothing was halfway," says his mother. "He didn't do anything gradually, he'd jump right in, feetfirst." When Brian took up jogging, he immediately started running five miles a day—and won two medals for ten-kilometer races. When he became interested in cooking, he tested recipes on his parents and made plans to write a cookbook. When he became interested in girls in eighth grade, he fell in love at least once a week. When Brian was up, he believed anything was possible. Watching a TV show in which a New York Giants football player discussed the upcoming season with pessimism, Brian composed a four-page letter to the Giants' administration, telling them a player with that attitude shouldn't be on the team—a person should never give up.

At times, however, Brian was remote and morose. "Sometimes he was afraid to be alone. He'd walk out with me—not with me but behind me, like a puppy, afraid to let me out of his sight," says Mary, who had been elected town clerk. "Sometimes he would call the office and ask me to come home and talk to him. I'd drop everything and rush home, and then he wouldn't talk." When his parents asked him what was wrong, he would say, "I'm just low." At night when he went upstairs and his parents, sitting in the living room, looked up, Brian demanded, "What are you staring at?" After an eighth-grade basketball game, Brian's father kidded him about a play in which the player he was guarding had cut around him to score a basket. Brian was silent for a moment, then said quietly, "Dad, you shouldn't criticize me." Pat was taken aback but realized that Brian just wasn't the type to be teased. When Brian asked his mother not to come to his games, she was saddened that he might be embarrassed by her presence—the Harts had always attended their children's activities—but she agreed. "If this was the only way he could function, without our being too close, that was all right," she says.

Finding a balance between showing their love for Brian and not putting pressure on him was frustrating. Pat and Mary fretted about Brian's grades, which fluctuated with his moods. They suspected that he smoked marijuana, and they knew he drank with his friends in the neighborhood. Liquor occasionally disappeared from their cabinet, and for a while they kept it locked in the basement. The Harts were especially concerned about alcohol because Pat had had a drinking problem years earlier. There were occasional arguments and fights, and once when Brian was in the eighth grade, his mother marched him down to the local Alcoholics Anonymous office, where a counselor gave Brian a talking-to. More often the Harts tried to give their son space. "At that point we were beginning to walk on eggs," says Mary. "We were hoping that everything was working and that the psychiatrist was able to help." Dr. Kornhaber told the Harts that their son's case was difficult to diagnose, and he was having a hard time pinpointing what should be done. But though he wasn't sure what was wrong, everyone agreed that things were not quite right.

The summer before tenth grade, the Harts sent Brian to a camp in Maine. Brian's letters home described the swimming, boating, and hiking in exuberant detail. He seemed to be involved in everything. Although Brian had failed math that spring and would have to pass a special examination before returning to school, he solved the problem in typical Brian style: he found a pretty girl at the camp who also needed instruction, and they canoed daily across the river to the house of a math tutor. When the Harts picked him up at summer's end, Brian was euphoric. "We felt we had a different Brian back," says Mary. "He was happy and confident, he knew he was going to pass the test, and he was on top of the world." The day of the test Pat returned from a meeting to find a phone message from Brian: "Your stupid son managed to get an eighty-six in math and just wanted to let you know!"

Two months later, in mid-October, Brian took the Preliminary Scholastic Aptitude Test. When Mary picked him up at school that afternoon, she found him surrounded by five of his friends. "I don't know what's the matter with Brian," one of them said, "but he's just not with it." When Brian got in the car,

Mary knew immediately that something was seriously wrong. Brian's face was expressionless, and he could barely speak. "I couldn't do anything" was all he could say. "I couldn't do anything." Later, the Harts were told that Brian had checked off the same answer for almost every question on the test.

The next day, after examining Brian, Dr. Kornhaber told the Harts that Brian was having a psychotic episode and would have to be hospitalized. (The Harts would later learn that Brian had tried to kill himself that morning by pulling a plastic bag over his head and wrapping an extension cord around his neck.) Although they hardly understood what was happening themselves, Pat and Mary explained to Brian that something in him had snapped and needed to be fixed, and that he would have to go to the hospital. Brian seemed almost to welcome the news, and he packed an overnight bag with two pairs of pants and a sweater, enough clothes for a few days.

Brian would be in the hospital for nine months.

The Harts had been warned by Dr. Kornhaber that when someone enters a psychiatric hospital for the first time, his psychosis may initially increase, both because the doctors are likely to experiment with various medications, which can take weeks or even months to evaluate, and because of the change of environment. Still the Harts were unprepared for their first visit with Brian, two days after they had driven him to Stony Lodge, a private hospital in Ossining. The Harts were escorted through two locked doors and into a stark common room in which several men gazed numbly at a television. Brian stood in the doorway on the far side of the room. He was neatly dressed in a white T-shirt and corduroy pants, but he looked pale and terrified. He didn't move. The Harts went to him and put their arms around him, and the three of them hugged and wept. In a tiny voice Brian said over and over, "I'm scared. I'm scared. I'm scared."

Brian thought his parents had abandoned him. "Why am I here?" he kept saying. His parents tried to reassure him that it was for the best, but they were unnerved. Heavily medicated with Thorazine, an antipsychotic drug commonly used to sedate patients, Brian had difficulty speaking and couldn't articulate his fears. He just squeezed their hands so hard he left marks. Driving home that afternoon, Pat and Mary were deeply shaken. "We wondered if we were doing the right thing," says Mary. "But people that know say you're doing the right thing. You're putting your whole life in the hands of strangers." Says Pat, "We wondered if we'd ever have him back. We wondered if we'd ever have him right." Wild ideas flashed through Mary's mind. She thought of fleeing with her son into the woods and taking care of him there.

The next months were agonizing. The BB gun lawsuit had recently gone to court, and Brian was terrified that his family would lose their house and all their possessions because of the incident. At the same time, he insisted he wasn't as sick as the other patients, that he would be back in school soon. After a month or so he seemed to improve. He began to make friends with other young patients. He refinished chairs and tables in the woodworking shop, made pottery and paintings for family Christmas presents, and kept up his schoolwork with a tutor. Brian was anxious to go home, and his parents, telling him to try to take things day by day, continued to pay the tuition at his private school each month in the hope that he would soon be well enough to return. They visited him as often as they could; after Brian started improving, Mrs. Hart drove over almost every night. "I used to watch TV when a commercial would come on and say, 'Did you hug your child today?' And, oh . . . I'd feel so awful. And I'd get in the car and take off to Ossining to see Brian."

Eventually, Brian was allowed home for weekends, during which he did all the things he used to do—football games and skiing with his family, movies and pizza with his friends. But he didn't seem to be getting truly better, just having up days and down days. At times he would be what his parents came to think of as "good Brian"—bubbling over with energy. Other times he was depressed. Brian and his father usually went to the Giants game on Sunday afternoons. Afterward, Brian would go home for dinner; sometimes, though, he would ask to be driven straight back to the hospital, and the Harts knew he was feeling down. At one game in December, Patrick sensed that Brian was not really conscious of what was happening on the field, and he asked him if he wanted to leave. Brian said yes, and Pat drove him straight back to Stony Lodge. The following day Mary got a call from the psychiatrist in charge, who told her that Brian had disappeared.

With images of dragnets combing the roads and radio bulletins warning the public about "an escapee from the mental hospital," a frantic Mary Hart called the Bedford chief of police, whom she knew in her job as town clerk. They drove the streets between Ossining and Bedford Hills but saw no sign of Brian. Shortly after they got back to her house, Brian walked in the door. "I'm home," he said. He had left the hospital after breakfast and walked seven miles through the woods. Mary was overjoyed that her son was safe, but as she hugged him, she knew she had to tell him he had to go back. While Brian changed his clothes, she made him a chicken sandwich, then she drove him to the hospital. Brian was quiet. "To this day," says Mary, "I'll never forget the look he gave me as I took him back: How could you do this to me? How could you do this to me?"

That spring the doctors, who still hadn't settled on a diagnosis, decided to try Brian on lithium, a drug used successfully to treat manic depression, an illness characterized by extreme mood swings and having strong genetic roots. For Brian (whose illness would indeed eventually be diagnosed as manic depression), lithium seemed to be a miracle drug. He was no longer subject to drastic mood swings. Says Mary, "He was himself again."

In July, as he approached the day of his release, Brian wrote in his journal about his feelings on leaving the hospital after nine months:

Today I hit a landmark. Today for the first time since late February I was and am depressed. Not really heavily depressed like I used to be, but a kind of melancholy, silent mood. . . . I figured out why I was depressed. I'm going to leave this land of make-believe where everyone is nice and so much like you. No matter how much I cursed and damned this place, no matter how long I prayed, hoped, dreamed, and begged to get out of here, it still was a heavy big part of my life I'll never forget. I've made friends here. I've grown accustomed to this life. Being babied and looked after. I'm used to it but at the same time sick to death about it. I want my independence back! Give me Liberty or give me Death! I'm happy to say I'm alive enough to say that. You see, if I didn't come here I surely would of found some way and enough guts to end my life. Kill myself. Now I'm ok, I want life. I want, need challenge, excitement and a girlfriend. Not necessarily in that order.

What I'm saying is that I want and deserve to be let out. The question is, will I want to come back to the false security like I described in the last passage? Only time will tell.

Brian had his heart set on returning to Kennedy High, but on the advice of his doctors and teachers the Harts decided he should go to a special school for a year, to phase him back gradually into the mainstream. That fall Brian entered the Anderson School in Staatsburg-on-Hudson, forty-five miles north of Bedford Hills, a small, coed, residential high school for students "whose behavior, emotional, and/or family problems are hindering their educational process." The school's fifty students took standard courses in math, English, and history but received extra attention and counseling from a staff of special education teachers, mental health workers, nurses, and physicians. In the first weeks after he arrived Brian held himself aloof, trying hard to show that he was much less troubled than his classmates. He succeeded so well that some of the staff wondered whether there had been some mistake—one counselor referred to Brian as "Jack Armstrong, all-American boy." But Brian's polish began to wear off. One night during a fire drill he stayed in his bed staring at the ceiling. When staff members came to get him, they were shocked when he refused to move and began cursing at them.

With only three ninety-minute classes a day, academics at Anderson were designed not to push the student, but Brian pushed himself. He arrived early to class, sat in the front row, always did his homework, and, given an option to rewrite a paper, usually took it. He loved to read—Tolkien, Dickens, and Stephen King were his favorites—and always seemed to have a stack of books under his arm. At a school where to be called "not a problem" was high praise, Brian was "an ideal student," according to Sandy Martin, his English teacher. "I remember one day when the kids had been giving me a rough time and I'd had it," she says. "After class Brian came up and said, 'I want you to that I really appreciate your putting up with their BS. I get angry when people fool around when you're trying to teach something.' That made my day. I remember I wanted to hug him, but he was not a kid you could hug. He wanted to be hugged, but if you touched Brian, he would tense up."

While he was well liked by his teachers and classmates, Brian had no close friends at Anderson. "The other kids thought he was great, but Brian couldn't believe it," says Sandy Martin. "Inside he didn't think he was worthy. He'd say, 'Why would anyone want me?'" His lack of confidence was especially apparent with girls. Although he desperately wanted a girlfriend, and with his good looks and charm, girls flocked around him, Brian couldn't seem to make the right connection. Because Anderson had a four-to-one ratio of boys to girls, few of his classmates had girlfriends. Yet Brian felt inadequate for not having one.

There was another reason why having a girlfriend was especially important to Brian. At about this time he began to talk to his mother about his fears that he might be gay. During eighth grade he had been propositioned by a man in the town park. Brian had fled. His psychiatrist suggested he tell the police, but Brian worried that the police would assume he was homosexual. Brian didn't mention the incident again, but he told his mother that when they had put him in the hospital, he had been terrified that it was a whorehouse for men. Mary listened to her son, but Brian was so popular with girls, she didn't believe his fears were justified. "What's the difference?" she would say. "Stop beating yourself over it—you are what you are." Brian's counselor at Anderson also felt his fears were groundless, stemming from common adolescent panic at being unable to connect with the opposite sex. But Brian remained troubled; talking with his mother, he would hold his hands up and shake his head sadly. "These hands," he would say. "They're such feminine hands."

Worries about his sexuality made Brian feel even further from the normalcy he strove for. Brian didn't want to be a "special case," but it bugged him that to be "normal" he had to take pills twice a day and have his blood level measured once a month. And so part of trying to be normal was skipping his lithium, which he called a "weakness." "I refuse to take it anymore," Brian would announce to a friend. "I'm going to try to do it on my own." When he was feeling good, Brian would persuade himself that he could manage without lithium, and he would stubbornly try to overcome his mood swings through sheer force of will. Other times he would get high and forget to take it. Without the lithium, however, he would sink into depression. At meals, where he was usually at the center of a laughing group of students, he would sit alone, staring into space like a robot. If someone asked him to go for a walk or play a game, he would reply in a monotone, without looking up, that he didn't feel like it. "He would phase out and you couldn't get through to him," says one teacher. "It was as if there were a plastic shield around him that you couldn't penetrate. You'd want to take him by the shoulders and shake life back into him." The difference between Brian's highs and lows was so great that at staff meetings it was common to hear teachers say, "Which Brian are we talking about?"

Brian's two moods are strikingly juxtaposed in his journal. Four months after arriving at Anderson he described his feelings about the school, concluding:

> It's kind of funny, but I'm due out of here in June, too. To go home, with Mom, Dad, and Vicky, good pup. That's kind of fun, no, sad. Because chances are I'll be due to leave there to college in a year after I get home, then on my own. It seems so unfair to me that two years of my life could have been taken away from me like that. I feel cheated, as surely my parents do too. The pain and guilt they must have felt signing their baby into a loony bin, to get him back for themselves two years later, only to send him away again. Oh Mom and Dad, I love you so much. Please forgive me.

Six weeks later Brian circled the entry and wrote below it in a scrawled, angry hand:

> I read that now and all that seems like total BULLSHIT! It's like a script to a soap opera. Reading that is like cutting your way out from the bottom of a giant bowl of spaghetti with clam sauce. No matter how fast or how much you chop, you fall, sink deeper and deeper, gasping for air, almost drowning from a roomful of smoke, then fog, then finally rain of liquid lead.

Underneath he drew a picture of a man disappearing beneath a massive weight. Only the man's hands are visible as he struggles to stay alive.

One Friday afternoon near the end of his first year at Anderson, Brian's friends became concerned about him. The students at Anderson were a tight-knit group, bound together by their troubles. If a student played hooky for an evening or was involved in drinking or drugs, his friends typically covered for him, but when someone was in a deep depression, they alerted the staff. Suicide attempts at Anderson were frequent—almost one per week, according to a teacher. Most were not life-threatening—cuts from flip-top cans, razors, knives, or glass, or minor overdoses of medication. When Brian seemed to be withdrawing that weekend, his friends spoke to his teachers. On Saturday morning when Brian discussed suicide with some of his friends at breakfast, again those teachers were alerted. But it was too late. Shortly after breakfast Brian disappeared.

The next week was a blur of telephone calls and search posses. The school believed Brian might head out West to see one of his sisters. The Harts hired a private investigator, who was convinced that Brian had not left the area. The students at Anderson were somber—almost all of them had considered or attempted suicide at some point, and they were fearful that they might come in one morning to learn that Brian had been found dead. "In all honesty people expected to find him hanging in the woods," says an Anderson teacher. The police searched the shores of the Hudson for Brian's corpse. The Harts never believed that Brian would kill himself but feared he might have a psychotic break, wander off someplace, and be hit by a train. As the days went by and the chances of Brian's being found alive grew slim, they were terrified that perhaps this time they had lost him forever. Friday morning at the breakfast table, six days after he had disappeared, they began to discuss where to bury Brian. That afternoon when Mary got home from work, she heard a soft, apprehensive voice on the answering machine: "Mom, I'm all right. Can you come get me? I'll call back."

Fifteen minutes later the phone rang. It was Brian. He was calling from a pay phone in a park twelve miles from school. Mary sped up Route 9, furious at every red light, terrified that Brian wouldn't be there when she arrived. Though it was seven o'clock when she pulled into the park, it was still light out. Families ate at picnic tables and children's voices pierced the warm summer night. Then she saw Brian walking across the field toward her, his jeans and sweatshirt coarse with grime, his hair tangled, his face shadowed by a week's growth of beard. People at the picnic tables eyed him nervously. Mary put her arms around him, but Brian, self-conscious, said, "Let's get in the car." Not long after they got on the road, Brian asked his mother for a hug. Mary stopped the car and clutched her son tightly.

Brian had no idea how long he had been gone. All he remembered of that week were a few images: lying in a gutter in the rain, hearing people call his name but being unable to respond; finding a deserted hunter's cabin in the woods where he had eaten a jar of moldy peanut butter; sneaking down to the park at night to scavenge watermelon rinds and other scraps from the garbage pails; wading into the Hudson River with the intention of drowning but then walking out. When he talked about that week with his counselor at Anderson, his eyes widened with fear. "Jesus, what a thing to do," Brian would say. "How could I go through that?" For almost a year, the terror of that week would return to Brian like a sudden chill.

After going AWOL, even Brian realized that returning to Kennedy was out of the question. But once he was back on lithium, his senior year at Anderson went smoothly. He earned an A in an expository writing course at a local community college. He was accepted at all four colleges he applied to and decided to attend the State University of New York at Brockport, a small liberal arts college near Rochester. When he came back to Anderson after a weekend at home and told people about his new girlfriend, he was so enthusiastic that one teacher thought he had invented her. Mary, a pretty, red-haired girl Brian had known at Kennedy, was devoted to Brian. She visited him as often as possible, drove him back on Sunday nights after weekends together, and wrote him long, encouraging letters almost every day. Brian's parents were so delighted that even when Mary's mother called to tell them that she and her husband had come home unexpectedly and found Brian and Mary in bed, they couldn't be too angry—Brian was so happy.

Brian felt closer to the mainstream than he had in years. In an essay for his class on "The Modern Age," he wrote:

Anderson is an escape. It is an escape from real life. It is more relaxed and less distressing. I am bored of this make-believe world, and I am anxious to graduate to the real world. I have become too comfortable in this safe, get-over world. But there have been times when I needed this escape like a man with a bullet wound cries for morphine. The realization of my departure is solidifying as my graduation day grows nearer each passing moment. But I jump for the chance of change! So I will take everything I have learned about myself and people, as well as everything else I have learned and move on. . . . I will move on, change, and weep later.

Brian graduated from Anderson first in his class of eighteen, winner of the prize for Best Attitude, and valedictorian, as voted by the teachers. In his address, he urged his classmates to make use of what they had learned at Anderson as they went on to face new challenges. He concluded:

On behalf of the graduating class I thank each teacher, dorm parent, social worker, cook, kitchen worker, maintenance man, housekeeper, administrator, secretary, as well as our parents and our families for their support and guidance whether or not they knew they gave it. We must leave to be born again, to start fresh, to take our second chance with an understanding of why we had it: We are loved and we are believed in. Thank you.

That summer Brian dove back into the mainstream with a vengeance, as if trying to make up for lost time. He worked as a clerk in a department store by day and as a busboy in a restaurant at night. Then he partied with his old Kennedy friends. His parents would hear him come home as late as two or three in the morning. He occasionally skipped his lithium, and his mother grew tired of asking him whether he had taken it. He was going to be alone at college, and he would have to learn. Brian saw less of his girlfriend, Mary. He wanted to "cool" the relationship before his freshman year at Brockport.

As late August approached, Brian started to get apprehensive. At a precollege orientation seminar at a nearby hotel, the other young men and women had acted so sure of themselves; they knew what they wanted to major in, and their careers seemed planned and focused. Brian's aspirations—forestry, social work, and the Peace Corps were among the possibilities he had mentioned—were as changeable as his moods. He fretted that although he had been a star at Anderson, an Anderson education was not as rigorous as that offered by public high schools. He worried that he might not be up to college. One night shortly before school started, when his parents were out to dinner, they got a call from Brian asking if he could come and talk to them. He arrived at the restaurant in a panic. He had been talking to another college-bound Anderson friend whose nervousness had kindled Brian's fears. His parents tried to calm him, telling him he didn't *have* to go, but Brian's response was "I'll go, I'll go." The night before they drove him to Brockport, Brian seemed dazed. He couldn't decide what to pack, although he had been planning all summer. On the ride up, as he talked about the courses he wanted to take, Brian was clearly anxious. At registration he thought he saw someone from Bedford Hills. He was upset—it seemed that even as a college freshman hundreds of miles from home, he couldn't start out with a fresh slate.

That fall Brian worked hard to be like everyone else. In early October, when Pat drove up for Parents Weekend, he was impressed at how Brian seemed to be a part of everything, at how many people knew him. They went to a football game, to a play, and to church. But though it had all the earmarks of a typical college weekend, Pat could tell Brian was on edge, straining hard to have him think that things were under control.

One night not long after that weekend, the Harts received a call from Brian, who was weeping and said he couldn't handle college. "Oh my God," Mary thought. "Why don't you come home," she said. "Everything will be okay." Brian told her he was calling from the phone booth in the school cafeteria, and he didn't want the other students to see him crying. Mary told him to stay there. She called Dr. Kornhaber, who called Brian. They had a long talk, and Brian managed to get through the night and remain in school.

Once again Brian was up and down. The Harts would receive a ten-page letter full of plans and projects, telling them he was going to stop fooling around and get down to work and that they shouldn't worry. Brian was taking his lithium, they could tell. Then there would be a phone call at two in the morning and a thin, lonely voice asking, "Are you okay? Is everything okay?" When Sandy Martin, his English teacher at Anderson, who had received many spirited, chatty letters from Brian, called him in November, Brian was stoned. "I'm losing it," he told her. "I'm partying too much." His grades were sinking, and he had skipped several midterm exams. He said that he was hanging out with the drug crowd and didn't have enough self-control to break away. Searching for a spark of the old Brian, Sandy encouraged him to make a list of things he needed to do to get his act together. Brian said he would do it, but he sounded drained and sad.

"At Thanksgiving vacation when I picked up Brian at the train station, he was wearing blue jeans and a white, cable-knit Irish sweater and he looked terrific," says Mary Hart. "He got in the car, but when I asked him if he wanted to drive, he said no. I knew something was off. He started talking about his girlfriend, Mary. 'She's been so good to me, and I've been so bad to her,' he kept saying. He cried and started pounding the seat with his fist. I had never seen him this disturbed, and I said, 'Brian, you're frightening me. I think we'd better go to the hospital.' He said, 'No, I'm all right. I am just really, really upset.' I held his hand, and he squeezed mine so tight I thought he might break it."

On Thanksgiving Day, at a family reunion at their cousins', Brian's sister told her mother that something seemed wrong with Brian. Mary Hart went downstairs where Brian and his cousins were watching a football game. She saw immediately that Brian was "not right." He was gripping the chair tightly, with a dazed expression on his face. "We'll go home now, Brian," said Mary. "Good," Brian said in a remote, clipped voice. "Good. Yeah. I want to go home." As they walked into their house, Brian turned to his mother and waved both hands at her, as if shooing her away. "It was the oddest thing," she recalls. "He was looking at me, but he was seeing something that he didn't want to see and he kept waving his hands, as if to say, 'Please go away.' I realized afterward that he was hallucinating."

The next day Pat took Brian to Dr. Kornhaber, who told them that Brian's blood levels were unbalanced and would have to be stabilized. Brian later admitted that he hadn't been taking his lithium at school and to compensate had gobbled a handful of tablets on the train home. Kornhaber recommended hospitalization. Brian said no. Kornhaber said if Brian refused, he could not take responsibility for him. Brian reluctantly gave in. That afternoon his parents drove him to Stony Lodge. As they pulled in the drive, Brian looked out the window. "I was in this place for my sixteenth birthday," he said quietly, "and it looks as if I'm going to be in it for my nineteenth birthday."

Once again Brian believed that he would be at the hospital for only a few days. But this time, instead of being edgy to get out, by the end of the month he stopped asking when he would be released. His parents grew concerned that he was becoming too comfortable there, that he might be giving up. Nevertheless, when the doctors decided Brian was ready to go home, provided he found a job, Mary realized she wasn't sure she was ready. "I didn't know if I could take it, if he was going to get into drugs again," she says, shaking her head. "We had tried just about everything. We had tried Brian at home. We had tried freedom at college. Now home and work. I didn't think he was well enough to come home. I just felt things were not quite right." Meanwhile, the insurance for Brian's hospitalization was running out. "Everything seemed to be going down the tubes, and Brian just didn't seem to be getting better," says Mary. Her frustration concerned the doctors, who suggested Pat and Mary begin family therapy with Brian. The Harts agreed. After seven weeks in the hospital, Brian was discharged.

Brian found a job almost immediately. Jim Candon, a supervisor at the Margaret Chapman School in Hawthorne, says he will never forget his interview with Brian: "I asked him what made him think he was right for the job. Brian said, 'Because I have a lot of love to give.' I interpreted that to mean he needed a lot of love." The Margaret Chapman School is a school for profoundly retarded children, many of whom cannot perform even simple tasks for themselves. As a teacher's aide Brian dressed the children, toilet trained them, brushed their teeth, washed their hands and faces, combed their hair, fed them, and assisted them in the classroom with their drawing and counting. Many new staff members are squeamish when asked to brush a child's teeth or wipe his bottom, but Brian showed no reluctance, even volunteering for tasks that others refused to do. The staff realized that Brian had a gift for working with these children. Playing basketball with kids who could barely move, he would guide them around, encouraging them, getting them involved in the game. In class he persuaded a little girl who had always drawn with only one crayon to use four other colors. "There was an immediate bonding between Brian and the kids," says Jim Candon. "He had a gentleness about him, a way of being able to reach the kids without the necessity of verbal expression. These children were real human beings to Brian. He always treated them as normal, not retarded. I think he found in the children a reflection of his own brokenness, and thus, more than any of us, could empathize. He could see the human being beneath the mask, the real person struggling, aching, and reaching out for understanding."

Once again Brian was full of plans. He talked about his work at Chapman with his parents, overflowing with ideas for programs, passionate about the need for funding to help retarded children. He talked about returning to school for a degree in special education so he could make a career of this work. Reconciled to living at home for the time being, he began buying plants and hanging posters of rock groups on his bedroom wall. With his first paycheck from Chapman he bought a stereo. He worked double shifts to help save for a car. He enrolled in a sculpture course at Westchester Community College and talked about clearing a space in the cellar for a studio. He constructed a collage from magazine photographs of his favorite things—skiing, travel, wildlife, and women—and hung it on his bedroom wall. He jotted down lists of things he planned to do.

But just as it had at Anderson and at Brockport, Brian's period of normalcy began to fray. Once again the Harts could tell he wasn't taking his lithium. He grew a scraggly beard and dressed less neatly; at his grandmother's birthday dinner he was the only man without a tie. He hadn't talked to his girlfriend, Mary, since before Thanksgiving, and he spent most of his free time with Melinda, a sixteen-year-old girl he had met at the hospital who had been a member of the fast crowd. He had started smoking pot again, going to parties, and coming home late. He began to skip his sculpture class; he stopped getting to work on time. Some days he didn't show up at all. Questioned by his parents, he would offer vague answers and half-truths. While the Harts were concerned, they agreed that they shouldn't hector Brian. Once again, they were walking the fine line between protecting and intruding.

One evening in January, Brian called his parents from a bar in the nearby town of Mahopac. He would hitchhike home, he said. It was a cold night, and several inches of snow lay on the ground. As the evening wore on and Brian hadn't returned, the Harts grew concerned. Pat drove to the bar. Brian wasn't there. Pat combed the roads between Mahopac and Bedford Hills, and finally saw Brian hitchhiking. When Brian got in, Pat could tell his son had been drinking heavily, and he questioned him about it. Suddenly Brian reached for the door handle and tried to jump from the moving car. His father grabbed his arm and tried to hold him as he slowed the car. When the car stopped, Brian jumped out. Pat got out of the car and chased him through the snow. Brian swore at his father. "Leave me alone!" he screamed. "Leave me alone!" Pat finally tackled his son and held him down. But as soon as he got up, Brian took off again. Pat caught up with him again, but Brian shook loose and rolled under a guardrail and down a ravine toward a two-lane parkway. Pat was terrified that Brian would be hit by a car, but he saw Brian get up and cross the road. Pat got back in his car and tried to follow. When he reached the exit ramp from the parkway, he saw Brian lying on the road. He stopped the car and pleaded with Brian to come home. "You don't want to miss work," he said. "Yeah, they love me, those kids," Brian kept saying. "I love those kids and they love me." But Brian broke loose again and ran off into the night. Pat finally drove home, feeling frightened and powerless.

Mary went out to look for Brian and found him downtown. She pulled up beside him, opened the door, and said, "Come on in, Brian." Brian lunged at the car and kicked one of the headlights. Mary drove farther down the road and parked where she thought he couldn't see her. She wanted to stay close to her son in case he fell or passed out in the snow. When Brian spotted the car, he walked up and spat at it. "Leave me alone," he shouted. "I'm not an alcoholic. Leave me alone." Then he stomped off. Mary went home.

Half an hour later, as Pat and Mary sat in the living room, they heard the back door open. Brian walked in. Nobody said a word as he went straight up to his room.

The following morning Brian showed up at his mother's office at the town hall and asked to borrow her car. He wouldn't say where he was going, he just insisted that it was important. Feeling uneasy but wanting to let him know she still trusted him, Mary gave him the keys. When he returned, he gave her a big hug and told her he had been to Alcoholics Anonymous. "This is the first of ninety meetings in ninety days," he said. But his enthusiasm for AA lasted only a few sessions. He continued to drink and to have his ups and downs, but now there were more downs than ups. Brian was verbally abusive to his parents, and they could tell he was doing drugs again. Brian's friends were away at college, and he had more or less pulled away from everybody except Melinda, with whom he now spent much of his free time. One day Mary called her and asked her to persuade Brian to go to work. That Tuesday night Mary arrived home to find Brian at the dining room table, sketching, and saying over and over again, "Fucking bitch. Fucking bitch. Fucking bitch." Mary, who had to prepare for a town board meeting that night, went to her room and closed the door. Brian stormed in, swearing at her. She lost her patience. "Get out of here," she shouted. "Just get out of this room." Brian stomped into his own room, which adjoined his parents', and banged on the wall.

On Thursday, boiling with anger at his parents, Brian announced to Dr. Kornhaber that he refused to attend any more family sessions. But by Friday morning he had changed his mind, and their therapy session was their best ever. Brian was more open and forthright than he had been in some time. He acknowledged that he'd been drinking and smoking pot and even gave them a rundown of the drugs he'd tried at college—cocaine, acid, and angel dust. He admitted that he had been lax in his attendance at work, and he vowed to apologize to his boss. He talked about saving money for a car and about returning to school part-time. Though Pat and Mary couldn't help thinking, "Here we go again, off on another roll," they were elated.

Brian got a haircut, shaved his beard, and even washed his clothes—every last shirt and sock. His apology was accepted at Chapman, and Brian worked Saturday and Sunday. Sunday afternoon he visited Melinda, but instead of staying out late as usual, he was home by suppertime. Mary cooked veal parmigiana, Brian's favorite dish.

After dinner Brian and his parents sat in the living room and talked. They didn't discuss anything in particular; it was just a pleasant, relaxed conversation—about college, the New York Giants, Melinda, how he'd appreciated his mother making veal parmigiana, how he'd started smoking pot in the sixth grade, the rock concert he planned to attend the following Saturday night. "It was nothing spectacular," says Mary. "It was just a mother and a father and a son talking." But after all the troubles and frustrations, during which Brian and his parents had become almost adversarial, the evening was so relaxed and normal that Mary was overwhelmed with relief. She believed that this might be the beginning of a new level of honesty between them. Now, looking back, she thinks that her son was saying good-bye.

The following evening, when Mary and Pat got home, there was a note on the kitchen blackboard: "Gone for a walk. Going to stop at library. Don't worry. Love, Brian." An hour and a half later, as they sat in the living room, they heard a thump in the attic. They rushed upstairs. Brian was walking down the attic steps. His mother asked him what he'd been doing in the attic, a rarely visited storage area. "Looking for books," he said. The Harts knew it was too dark to see much up there. Brian said he'd used matches. Pat, concerned about the fire hazard, started to get angry, but Mary gave him a look, and they didn't pursue the matter.

Later, Mary was sitting in her bedroom when Brian came in. He looked pale, and she noticed a red mark on his neck. Brian told her it was just a rash. She said it didn't look like a rash. Brian admitted that he had bought a rope that day and had been trying to hang himself in the attic. But his ears had started popping and the rope had slipped. Mary was unnerved, but because Brian had been in such good spirits the past few days, she did not really believe him, and she remembered a counselor telling them years before that if someone has to tell you about a suicide attempt, it's not serious. "Come on, Brian," she said. "Wasn't that stupid." She even teased him a little—there wasn't even room enough to stand up straight in the attic. When she and her husband talked about it later, they agreed that if Brian had *really* wanted to kill himself, he would have done it. In any case, Brian was scheduled to see Dr. Kornhaber at noon the following day.

In the morning Brian talked with his mother in the kitchen before she left for work. He seemed a little shaky but not unusually so. "I don't know what I'm going to do, Mom," he said. "I just don't know." "Just try and take it day by day, Brian," his mother said. "Day by day." They talked about the previous evening, and she kidded him lightly: "Why did you pick the attic? We wouldn't have found you for days." "Well, I wouldn't want to bother anybody," said Brian. She joked, "Sure, we would have smelled you in about three days." They talked briefly about Arnold Caputo, a nineteen-year-old college sophomore who had hanged himself three weeks earlier in his parents' home in Mount Vernon, fifteen miles south of Bedford Hills. Mary said what a shock it must have been for his family to find him.

Brian seemed okay. He told her his plans for the day. He was borrowing her car to do some errands—to fill a prescription for lithium and buy some toothpaste—before meeting Dr. Kornhaber at noon. When Brian left at eight-thirty, he gave his mother a big hug and a kiss. "Good-bye, Ma," he said. "Good-bye, Brian," she said. "Drive carefully."

At eleven Pat called Dr. Kornhaber from his office, as he usually did before Brian's sessions, to tell him how things had been going since the last meeting. He described how pleasant and relaxed the weekend had been, but when he told him about Brian and the rope in the attic, the psychiatrist was immediately concerned. He told Pat to try to reach Brian. Pat called home, but Brian wasn't there. Mary hadn't heard from Brian either. Brian missed his noon appointment. At two Dr. Kornhaber called Mary and urged her to go to the police department and report Brian as missing and suicidal. Mary thought he was overreacting—Brian had been gone only a few hours—but the psychiatrist insisted. She thought the police would find him immediately because the whole town knew the license plate with the Harts' initials—MFH–PJH. But as the afternoon wore on, she grew increasingly anxious. Yet even that night as she and her husband lay in bed unable to sleep, listening for Brian, they believed he would return. "I fully expected him to come in," says Mary, "because this wasn't the first time it had happened, and in the past he had always turned up."

Next morning at work, every time the phone rang Mary picked it up expecting it to be Brian saying, "I'm home." She couldn't concentrate. Shortly before noon she called her husband, who hadn't gone to work that day, and asked him to come and get her. When she got home, she made some phone calls to members of the family. While she was talking to her daughter in California about Brian's disappearance, she heard a knock on the front door. Mary hurried downstairs. The police lieutenant was telling her husband that the car had been found at the rear of Oakwood Cemetery in Mount Kisco, several miles from their house, the motor still running, vacuum hoses carrying exhaust from the tailpipes into the car. Brian might have been in the car as long as twenty-four hours. Pat and Mary Hart were amazed to find that mixed in with the shock and the sadness there was a feeling of relief. "It was over," says Pat. "He was in such a struggle within himself, and that struggle was finally over." Mary says, "Brian had found his peace at last."

---

The funeral was held on St. Patrick's Day. St. Matthias, a small Catholic church, was filled with more than two hundred people. Mary's brother, a monsignor who had baptized Brian, said the Mass. Brian's three brothers and three friends, two from Kennedy and one from Anderson, were pallbearers. At Mary's request the organist added some traditional Irish music to the recessional. "The funeral was quite impressive, actually," says Mary. "Brian would have been very uncomfortable about all the fuss, I'm sure. He didn't like to be fussed over."

In the following weeks Pat and Mary talked with their children, laughing and weeping as they shared memories of Brian's ups and downs. They talked with Dr. Kornhaber, who had been stunned by Brian's death. They looked everywhere for a note. They searched the house, scoured the car, checked the pockets of Brian's clothes, and even played through the tape on the tape recorder in case he had recorded a last message. Each day they checked the mail, thinking he might have written them a letter, but they found nothing. Although Mary recognized that even if they found one it could never fully explain Brian's death, she would have liked to find something.

They also read through Brian's journals and notebooks, hoping to gain some insight, some clues. They didn't find a single key that explained everything; they learned little that was new or surprising. But they realized his highs had been higher, his lows lower, and the change from one to the other more abrupt than they had known. His journal brimmed with bittersweet evidence of his determination: his hopes, schemes, pep talks, self-exhortations, and renewed vows to start afresh. Even in the last week of his life he had compiled lists of things he wanted to buy for his room—posters, plants, sketchbooks—as well as notes about goals for his art and ideas about where to market his work. The last thing Brian wrote was a note to himself on his clipboard Thursday night, four days before his death: "I'm going to stop the pot. I'm going to get it together. I'm going to clean up my act."

# IV

# SOMETHING IN THE AIR

———

A FEW HOURS AFTER Brian's body was found, the media began calling. In the days that followed, as the Harts struggled with their shock over Brian's death, they also struggled with the flood of journalists who clogged the telephone lines at Mary's office and patrolled Bedford Hills in search of interviews. One afternoon Pat came home to find a television reporter waiting in his driveway. Pat politely refused to answer her questions, but when he opened the front door, the reporter began to follow him in. After she was finally persuaded to leave, she drove into Bedford Hills and found a teenager on the street to interview. That night the Harts watched the evening news as a boy who had never met Brian was asked why teenagers kill themselves. "I guess these rich kids don't know what to do with their time," he replied.

Brian's death made the headlines in every newspaper the Harts saw: "Suicide Stuns W'chester," wrote the *New York Post,* and in the following edition: "Town Mourns Suicide Teen." The *New York Times* was more cautious: "Another Teen-Ager Is Believed a Suicide in Westchester Area." The *Gannett Westchester Reporter Dispatch* wondered, "Another Teen-age Suicide?"

Brian Hart's death brought the number of teenage suicides in the Putnam-Westchester area to five in less than six weeks. Ten days after the suicide of Robbie DeLaValliere on February 4, 1984, Justin Spoonhour had hanged himself. Two days later eighteen-year-old Jimmy Pellechi shot himself. Eight days later Arnold Caputo, nineteen, hanged himself in his parents' home in Mount Vernon. And now Brian. With each death the press coverage grew exponentially, and by now the "Westchester suicides," as they were called, were the top story on the nightly news, not only in New York but across the country. The suburbs north of New York City responded with a growing feeling of panic. At first many had believed that the series of suicides was a coincidence. None of the teenagers had known each other or attended the same school. But as the toll began to mount, the suspicion grew that these deaths were somehow connected. Had one suicide triggered another? Can reading about suicide in the newspaper or hearing about it on TV cause suicide? Is suicide contagious? When would it stop? *Would* it stop? Who was next?

Certainly the hysteria was contagious. Crisis hotlines, school officials, guidance counselors, and therapists were swamped by calls from anxious parents seeking reassurance. "My son's been withdrawn lately," they'd say. "I don't want him to end up like those other boys." News programs publicized the warning signs of teenage suicide, and parents checked their children for symptoms of depression. "You get paranoid," said the Westchester mother of a thirteen-year-old at a workshop on adolescent suicide. "You look for red eyes to see if he hasn't been sleeping. You look to see if he's sleeping too much."

Therapists struggled to explain the situation. Suicide, said one Westchester psychiatrist, is "a contagious illness. It's not something that spreads from one person to another, like a cold. It's something that's in the air, in the culture, in the environment." In an article on the "Westchester suicides," Susan Blumenthal, head of the Suicide Research Unit at the National Institute of Mental Health, speculated that suicide could become "sort of like punk rock—something that catches on." Even Westchester County mental health commissioner Eugene Aronowitz, who had from the start firmly insisted the suicides were unconnected, was ruffled. "They seem to be related to each other because one seems to be kicking off the other," he told Tom Brokaw on *NBC Nightly News,* "so to that extent, until we put a stop to it in some way, we've got an epidemic here."

On April 7, three weeks after Brian Hart's death, eighteen-year-old Kelly Keagan of Carmel, a small town in Putnam County, hanged herself in her dormitory room at Mount St. Mary College in Newburgh.

On Friday, May 25, seventeen-year-old Charles Castaldo Jr. shot himself in the head in a bedroom of his father's home in Greenburgh, near Scarsdale.

The following Monday nineteen-year-old Kevin Harlan was found hanging in a stairwell outside a church in the tiny middle-class community of Sparkill across the Hudson River in Rockland County. His death brought the number of teenage suicides in the tricounty area north of New York City to eight in four months.

---

As horrifying as the "Westchester suicides" were, they were hardly unique. Indeed, they merely added to the growing evidence that youth suicides tend to occur in bunches, evidence that, in the 1980s, focused America's attention on adolescent suicide as never before. Even as Justin Spoonhour and Brian Hart were taking their lives, in Arlington, Texas, a Dallas suburb, there were five youth suicides in the first four months of 1984. In Beverly Hills, California, there had been three between January and April. And before that, starting in February 1983, there had been eight in fourteen months in Plano, Texas. In Columbus, Ohio, there had been five in a single month, including three freshmen at the same high school in one weekend. In 1982, in Cheyenne, Wyoming, there had been three in seventeen days. In 1980, in Englewood, Colorado, three in five months at the same high school. In 1979, in West Milford, New Jersey, six in twenty months. Beginning in 1978, in the North Shore suburbs of Chicago, twenty-eight in seventeen months.

Was there something in one suicide that acted as a "triggering incident" for another? Did each successive suicide lower the threshold for the next, as a firecracker, once lit, detonates the rest of the string? Adding to the fear was the confusion of the experts who struggled to explain the phenomenon. Their bafflement was reflected in the variety of words they used to describe the various episodes: *epidemic, rash, copycat syndrome, serial suicides, ripple effect, cascade, clump, contagion, fever, outbreak, chain, follow the leader, domino effect.* Eventually, they would settle on the slightly more clinical-sounding *cluster.*

While these terms seem to suggest that self-destruction might be catching, in the fashion of measles or the flu, suicide doesn't pick its victims that randomly. Researchers have long suspected that when one suicide occurs, it may lower the threshold for vulnerable people in the same geographic vicinity. People with a previous suicide in the family, as we have learned, have an incidence of suicide eight times higher than the general population. Yale researchers Bruce Rounsaville and Myrna Weissman studied sixty-two patients who were seen in an emergency room following suicide attempts; four had made their attempt within four weeks after the suicide or suicide attempt of someone to whom they were close. In three of the four cases a similar method was used. They concluded that clustered suicidal behavior was not infrequent. In certain settings, often confined places in which there is a rigid social structure, one suicide seems to spur others. Clusters have occurred in prisons, boarding schools, colleges, army barracks, and mental hospitals. After a suicide most hospitals routinely place the rest of the patients under heightened security or "suicide watch."

Adolescents, at a developmental stage in which they are highly suggestible, may be especially prone to imitation in suicide. Various estimates suggest that clusters may account for 1 to 5 percent of teen suicides—suicides that wouldn't have occurred at that time if the victims hadn't been "exposed." "When a suicide happens, even people who don't know the person are affected," says former Harvard psychologist Douglas Powell, who has counseled students after campus suicides. "One always has the thought, 'This could happen to me. Is it *going* to happen to me? If it happened to *him* and *he* didn't seem troubled . . .' " One adolescent suicide will, in a sense, bring other suicidal adolescents to the surface, but experts agree that the suicide can influence only someone who is already vulnerable. "Reading about a suicide does not *make* someone suicidal," emphasized Judie Smith, the program director at the Suicide and Crisis Center in Dallas who worked with Plano students, parents, and teachers after the 1983 cluster. "But if that person is already at risk of suicide, the media reports may inadvertently convey the message that it's okay to kill yourself, that suicide is an acceptable solution to your problems." Westchester psychiatrist Samuel Klagsbrun says, "When one kid actually goes ahead and does the unthinkable, it's almost as if it gives permission to others to also do the unthinkable."

The more attention a suicide provokes, the more a "permission" is apt to seem like an invitation. "The way we handle this frightens me," says psychologist Pamela Cantor. "There is often so much adulation after a teenage suicide—they name a school building after him, they have a ceremony, they dismiss school for the day. A kid who has felt lonely and out of it can suddenly go from being a nonentity to being a hero." A letter to columnist Ann Landers described a thirteen-year-old Cincinnati girl who had been unable to make the cheerleading squad or to get admitted into any campus club. When she won a raffle at a pizza parlor entitling her to a pizza dinner for fifteen, she turned down the prize, saying she didn't have fourteen friends. A few weeks later she killed herself. At her funeral more than two hundred schoolmates signed the guest book, wept, and placed flowers on her casket.

After Arnold Caputo was buried, front-page articles described the posthumous outpouring of grief and affection for the young rock musician, noting that according to his wishes he was buried with his guitar. "Is it important for us to know that?" wonders a Westchester high school counselor. "A troubled kid who reads that may say, 'Hey, I'll go out with my basketball or my hockey stick.'" Like Tom Sawyer, who enjoyed fantasizing about the effect of his death on the Widow Douglas, a vulnerable teenager may imagine the effect of his suicide on those left behind. "I've talked to lots of people, like over a hamburger at lunch, about who would be at our funerals if we died," says a Texas teenager. "If you're feeling depressed one day and you feel you don't have any friends, you think, 'If I died, whoever came to my funeral would be my friends.'" A suicidal teenager may have a magical belief that he'll be able to savor the reaction to his death. But unlike Tom Sawyer, he won't be around to attend his own funeral. A lonely, overweight thirteen-year-old California boy who shot himself wrote in his suicide note, "Please tell my classmates what happened and watch if they are sad or if they laugh."

If the notion of imitation seems understandable, there is disagreement on what constitutes a cluster. In 1983, Plano, a well-to-do bedroom community twenty miles from Dallas, became embedded in the national consciousness as a prototype when eight adolescents—seven of them students at the same school—killed themselves within fourteen months. (There were, as well, at least sixteen attempts.) After the fourth suicide the national media descended on Plano and competed to describe its expensive homes, manicured lawns, and six-foot "privacy fences." It was, as one newspaper noted, a town in which adolescents seemed to have "everything to live for." The town resented the attention, and many people blamed the press for the subsequent suicides. The story was a natural: Plano fit a stereotype as the dark underside of the American dream. "Suicides in Paradise," headlined the *Los Angeles Herald Examiner.* "Teen-age Suicide in the Sun Belt—An Idyllic Dallas Suburb Is Discovering the Sorrows of Rootlessness and Isolation" was the headline in *Newsweek.* The *San Antonio Light:* "Plano: Where Suicide Is Preppy."

But tagging upwardly mobile boomtowns as incubators for adolescent suicide gave communities like Plano an undue share of notoriety. Over the past few decades, clusters have taken place in cities, suburbs, Inuit villages, farming communities, and on college campuses and Indian reservations. In some instances subsequent suicides knew a previous victim; in others they may have heard of other suicides through word of mouth or the media. Some clusters drew a great deal of publicity; others were hardly mentioned. In some the adolescents used similar methods; in others they used a variety.

When the media turned to the teenage suicides occurring north of New York City, it treated Westchester and Plano as if they were virtually interchangeable. *Ladies' Home Journal,* for instance, portrayed Westchester County as "a sprawling bedroom suburb that could be the definition of upward mobility." Television news reports ran footage of gracious homes, rolling hills, and young girls show-jumping horses. The word *affluent* was used so often that it made wealth sound like a terminal illness. "'Contagious' Teen Suicides Worry Town" was the headline for a story in the *Dallas Times Herald,* which like many other accounts dismissed the "affluent suburb" of New York as if the suicides had occurred in a single community, not in eight different towns in three different counties with a total population of more than a million. The eight teenagers, in fact, represented a variety of socioeconomic backgrounds and lived in towns ranging from the prosperous bedroom community of Mount Vernon, to rural Putnam County, to the racially mixed, largely blue-collar towns of Peekskill and North Tarrytown. The majority came from families whose circumstances could be described as modest. Most of the victims' families had lived in their communities for many years. None of the victims knew one another or attended the same school. None of the suicides was directly linked to a previous suicide, although the teenagers may have read or heard about them. It would have been difficult not to because almost every day there seemed to be another newspaper article or television spot about the "Westchester suicides."

The press was prone to make the cluster larger than it actually was. When Christopher Ruggiero, the seventeen-year-old son of the fire chief in Pelham, was found hanged by his bathrobe sash in his bedroom closet on February 21, five days after Jimmy Pellechi's death, most newspapers assumed he had become the fourth suicide in the Westchester cluster. Several days later the county medical examiner said that Ruggiero's death was not a suicide. People were perplexed. Then an article appeared in the *New York Times* on autoerotic asphyxiation (AEA). A practice familiar to medical examiners and coroners but little known to the public, AEA is a form of masturbation in which erotic sensation is enhanced by decreasing oxygen to the brain, usually by means of a noose around the neck. Although sexual pleasure, not death, is the goal, an estimated five hundred to one thousand practitioners a year—most of them young white males—go too far, become unconscious, and asphyxiate. Whether or not it results in death, the practice is clearly masochistic, risk-taking behavior. Yet deaths due to AEA are ruled accidents. Many, however, are mistakenly classified as suicides. In Christopher Ruggiero's case, although his death was lumped with the other suicides, swelling the Westchester cluster beyond its actual extent, the medical examiner ultimately ruled that the death was due to "undetermined circumstances."

What exactly is a cluster? Are some adolescents more vulnerable to suggestion than others? Are some towns more vulnerable than others? Do suicides cluster by method? In Plano, four were by carbon monoxide, four were by gunshot; in Westchester, five of eight were by hanging. What are the geographical boundaries of a cluster? If a teenager in New Jersey reads about a cluster in New York and kills himself, is he part of the New York cluster or the possible beginning of a New Jersey cluster? Do clusters spawn clusters? Did Plano beget Westchester? Do older people commit suicide in clusters? If there were a cluster in Harlem instead of an affluent suburb like Plano, would we hear about it? Have there always been clusters or is the media merely reporting them more fully? Does reporting contribute to clusters? Are certain kinds of coverage more lethal than others?

---

While the term *cluster* is new, the phenomenon it describes is probably as old as suicide itself. As Forbes Winslow, an English physician, observed in 1840, "The most singular feature connected with the subject of suicide is, that the disposition to sacrifice life has, at different periods, been known to prevail epidemically, from a perversion, as it has been supposed, of the natural instinct of imitation."

There are several ways in which "the natural instinct of imitation" can work. Throughout history, during times of religious persecution, political oppression, or social upheaval, there have been instances in which a city, a country, or a religious group has been swept by a collective impulse to suicide. Classical Greek and Roman history is filled with accounts of entire towns and armies that chose death over surrender. When Philip of Macedon besieged the city of Abydos, he triggered a frenzy of suicide among its inhabitants. Hoping to stanch the self-slaughter, he withdrew his army for three days. When he returned, there was no one left alive. In AD 73, Jewish zealots defending the fortress of Masada in Israel chose death over surrender to the besieging Roman legions. Nine hundred and sixty men, women, and children died. In 1190, in York, England, more than five hundred Jews under siege by idle ex-crusaders killed one another to avoid persecution and torture; at Verdun in 1320, another five hundred did the same. In 1944, after surrendering to Allied troops, much of the Japanese population of Saipan completed suicide. Soldiers blew themselves up with grenades; civilians walked off cliffs or drowned themselves in the Pacific.

Collective suicide has also been occasioned by plague. "In the year of Grace 665," wrote Roger of Wendover, a thirteenth-century monk and historian, "there was such an excessive mortality in England, that the people crowded to the seaside, and threw themselves from the cliffs into the sea, choosing rather to be cut off by a speedy death than to die by the lingering torments of the pestilence." Seven centuries later the Black Death of 1348–50 spurred an even greater toll of suicides, including many Jews who, falsely accused of causing the plague by poisoning the wells, burned themselves to escape the gentiles' fury. In *A Journal of the Plague Year,* his imaginative reconstruction of London's Great Plague of 1665, Daniel Defoe wrote, "Some threw themselves out at windows or shot themselves, or otherwise made themselves away, and I saw several dismal objects of that kind." An outbreak of smallpox among American Indians on the Central Plains during the 1830s set off an equally virulent outbreak of suicide. As one observer noted, "Very few of those who were attacked recovered their health; but when they saw all their relations buried, and the pestilence still raging with unabated fury among the remainder of their countrymen, life became a burden to them, and they put an end to their wretched existence, either with their knives and muskets, or by precipitating themselves from the summit of the rock near their settlement. The prairie all around is a vast field of death, covered with unburied corpses."

Collective suicide often occurs in the face of an enemy less tangible than a disease or an army but no less real to its victims. In the mid-seventeenth century, the Old Believers, a Russian Orthodox sect that insisted the Antichrist was to arrive in 1666, burned their villages around them. In less than a decade some twenty thousand had taken their own lives. In Tiraspol, Russia, in 1897, twenty-eight members of a religious sect buried themselves alive to escape the census, which they regarded as sinful. In May 1910, when it was widely believed that the earth was about to pass through the tail of Halley's comet, clusters of suicides were reported in Spain, France, and the United States. In 1978, under the spell of their charismatic leader, Jim Jones, who persuaded them that their way of life was threatened by a hostile outside world, 912 members of the People's Temple drank cyanide-laced grape Kool-Aid at Jonestown, Guyana. Collective suicide has even been occasioned by ecstasy. During the dancing manias of the fourteenth century, hundreds of frenzied Italians and Germans tarantellaed off the cliffs.

In these instances a collection of individual impulses seems to detonate simultaneously, often under the influence of a leader who acts as a sort of lethal pied piper. At other times, a single suicide seems to set off a chain reaction in which the act of suicide is passed like a baton from despairing person to despairing person, often using the same method. In ancient Greece, Plutarch described such an episode:

> A strange and terrible affliction once came upon the maidens of Miletos from some obscure cause—mostly it was conjectured that some poisonous and ecstatic temperament of the atmosphere produced in them a mental upset and frenzy. For there fell suddenly upon all of them a desire for death and a mad impulse towards hanging. Many hung themselves before they could be prevented. The words and tears of their parents and the persuasions of their friends had no effect. In spite of all the ingenuity and cleverness of those who watched them, they succeeded in making away with themselves.

The epidemic abated when city magistrates decreed that the corpses of suicides would henceforth be dragged naked through the marketplace, whereupon, as author A. Alvarez observed, "vanity, if not sanity, prevailed." Similar rashes of suicide among women are said to have occurred in Marseille and Lyons during the Renaissance. In 1792, after a soldier hanged himself from a beam at Les Invalides hospital in Paris, five other wounded soldiers hanged themselves from the same beam within a fortnight, and a total of fifteen took their lives before the corridor was closed. After the suicides of two of his grenadiers at Saint-Cloud, Napoleon issued an order asserting that "to abandon oneself to grief without resisting, and to kill oneself in order to escape from it, is like abandoning the field of battle before being conquered." (Napoleon himself had contemplated suicide as a melancholy teenager and is said to have attempted it by overdosing on opium after the death of his mistress, Josephine.) In 1928, in Budapest, after 150 drownings were recorded during the months of April and May, a "suicide flotilla" patrolled the Danube, saving nine of ten would-be suicides. Primitive tribes, recognizing the possibility of contagion, have devised more direct remedies. In *African Homicide and Suicide,* anthropologist Paul Bohannan writes, "The East African societies all destroy the tree on which or the hut in which the suicide occurred, burning it and the rope expressly so that an epidemic of suicides will not occur."

Adolescents may be especially susceptible to imitation. "A child is more open to suggestion than an adult, in suicide as in all other matters," observed David Oppenheim in 1910. "In fact, the power of suggestion shows itself with horrifying clarity in many youthful suicides." Oppenheim, a professor of classical languages in Vienna, was speaking in Sigmund Freud's living room at a meeting of the Vienna Psychoanalytic Society. The meeting, perhaps the first interdisciplinary symposium on suicide, had been called in response to a crisis that bore remarkable similarity to the situation in the United States in 1984. An epidemic of adolescent suicide seemed to be sweeping Europe, Russia, and the United States around the turn of the century. In Moscow, to cite just one example, seventy children in a single school district took their lives between May 1908 and October 1910. The epidemic was widely reported in the press, and writers, doctors, and clergymen rounded up a familiar list of suspects: illegitimacy, divorce, excessive ambition, lack of discipline in the schools and in the home, and a general weakening of the moral fiber. "To all this may be added the weakmindedness which springs from forced, hothouse education, begun too early and goaded on too fast . . . ," wrote one American critic. "Boys and girls to-day are often men and women in the experience of life and its excitements, and *ennuyés* or *blasés* at an age when their grandparents were flying kites and dressing dolls."

Those words could have been written today, and the discussion that took place in Freud's living room in 1910 was not unlike those heard at dozens of recent youth suicide symposiums. Freud's distinguished panel talked about the social conditions that made suicide more likely, while noting that the focus must be on psychological vulnerability to stress rather than on the stress itself. They criticized journalists who oversimplified or sensationalized the problem, and raised concerns about the role of imitation. "The sensational fashion in which so many newspapers present such news [of a suicide]," observed Karl Molitor, "and the aura of martyrdom they delight in placing around these unfortunates, can all too easily induce another victim to follow the fatal example." They called for better research and for suicide prevention education.

One issue raised in Freud's living room that is increasingly debated today is the effect of music and literature on imitation. Certain books, videos, movies, and music are accused of acting as spurs to suicide. An oft-cited name on the list of rock musicians whose lyrics have been said to inspire suicide is Ozzy Osbourne. "Suicide is the only way out / Don't you know what it's really all about," sang the heavy-metal star in "Suicide Solution," from his album *Speak of the Devil.* The song was a favorite of John McCollum's. A nineteen-year-old from Indio, California, one October night he went to his bedroom, put *Speak of the Devil* on the stereo, put on the headphones, and shot himself with his father's pistol. His father filed suit against Osbourne and his record company, claiming that Osbourne's "violent, morbid, and inflammatory music . . . encouraged John McCollum to take his own life."

Each generation has its Ozzy Osbourne. Two hundred years ago it was Johann Wolfgang von Goethe, whose novel *The Sorrows of Young Werther* (published in 1774, when the author was twenty-four) is perhaps the most famous prod to youthful suicide in history. The hero is an angst-ridden young man who shoots himself when his love for a married woman goes unrequited. The book touched a nerve. Like Werther, young men all over Europe dressed in blue tailcoats and yellow waistcoats. Like Werther, they talked and acted with exaggerated sensitivity. And, like Werther, some of them shot themselves. Romantic suicidal melancholy was dubbed Wertherism, and those whose suicides were linked to the book were said to have been suffering from Wertheritis. Goethe biographer Richard Friedenthal writes, "One 'new Werther' shot himself with particular *éclat:* having carefully shaved, plaited his pigtail, put on fresh clothes, opened *Werther* at page 218 and laid it on the table, he opened the door, revolver in hand, to attract an audience and, having looked round to make sure they were paying sufficient attention, raised the weapon to his right eye and pulled the trigger." The book was banned in Leipzig and Copenhagen; when an Italian translation appeared in Milan, the Catholic clergy bought up and destroyed the entire edition.

Goethe was not the only author whose works, according to some people, encouraged a preoccupation with death and suicide. In an 1805 sermon, "The Guilt, Folly, and Sources of Suicide," New York City minister Samuel Miller asserted that "the mischievous influence on popular opinions produced by many dramatic representations and by licentious novels, may probably be considered as leading to many cases of the crime before us." As the Romantic Age bloomed, Byron's *Manfred,* Chateaubriand's *René,* and Lamartine's *Raphael* were all accused of sparking suicides and were duly reviled by the clergy. Even Thomas Paine's 1796 treatise, *The Age of Reason,* was accused of sponsoring suicides by "weakening the moral principles."

In 1928, when thirteen boys and girls killed themselves in thirteen weeks in the town of Liesva in the Ural Mountains, investigators from Moscow found they had been members of a suicide club formed in honor of Sergei Esenin, a Russian poet who had hanged himself in 1925. The students held meetings at which they discussed Esenin's poetry and debated "Is life worth living?" and "Is suicide justified?" In 1936, in Budapest, the suicides of eighteen young people were linked to the popularity of a ballad called "Gloomy Sunday." The lyrics of "The Hungarian Suicide Song," as it came to be known, concluded with the words "My heart and I have decided to end it all." (Thirty-two years later, Reszo Seress, the song's composer, jumped to his death from his apartment window.) In the late forties, many adolescent suicides in the United States and Canada were attributed to the pernicious effects of horror comic books; in Montreal, policemen initiated a campaign to ban them from the newsstands. More recently, several films have been accused of romanticizing suicide and triggering the deaths of young people. *The Deer Hunter,* a film about the Vietnam War that contains a graphic depiction of Russian roulette, has been linked by researchers to at least forty-three Russian roulette deaths since its release in 1978. After the death by hanging of Robbie DeLaValliere, the first of the Westchester cluster, many people blamed the film *An Officer and a Gentleman,* in which a charismatic young naval cadet hangs himself. DeLaValliere had seen the film and had talked of it frequently before his death by hanging.

As Goethe himself noted, however, art reflects rather than creates the mood of a time. Robbie DeLaValliere was a troubled youngster long before he saw *An Officer and a Gentleman.* And John McCollum, the heavy-metal fan who killed himself while listening to "Suicide Solution," had other problems besides Ozzy Osbourne. According to news reports, he had dropped out of school in the ninth grade and had "had some trouble with the law," including an arrest for drunken driving. (His father's suit against Osbourne was dismissed by a judge, who commented, "Trash can be given First Amendment protection, too.") As one columnist observed, "We must grieve with Jack McCollum for the loss of his son. But there's no reason to blame the artist who may have been his son's only solace in a hostile and extremely unbearable world." At a conference on youth suicide, a young woman in the audience voiced a similar point of view: "Maybe we should look at rock music not as a cause of problems but as a symptom of our time. Instead of condemning our youth we should start listening to them. And instead of banning their music we should start listening to it."

Long before Plano and Westchester, media accounts of actual suicides were blamed for triggering further suicides. In 1828, English physician George Man Burrows wrote, "When the mind is beginning to aberrate, [it is] very essential to prevent persons affected by moral causes or inclined to suicide, from reading newspapers, lest the disposition and the mode be suggested by something similar." While Burrows recommended that vulnerable people be kept from newspapers, William Farr, director of vital statistics for the British Registrar-General's office, urged the press to control themselves. "No fact is better established in science than that suicide (and murder may perhaps be added) is often committed from imitation," he wrote in 1841. "A single paragraph may suggest suicide to twenty persons; some particular, chance, but apt expression, seizes the imagination, and the disposition to repeat the act, in a moment of morbid excitement, proves irresistible. Do the advantages of publicity counterbalance the evils attendant on one such death? Why should cases of suicide be recorded at length in the public papers, any more than cases of fever?"

The debate reached its climax at the turn of the century. After the *New York World* published the article "Is Suicide a Sin?" in 1894, the *New York Times* accused the *World* of provoking an unprecedented number of suicides. A rash of Cleveland, Ohio, suicides in 1910 was attributed to press coverage, and in 1911 the National Association of Retail Druggists protested newspaper reports publishing the dosages of poisons used in suicide attempts as "inducing morbid people and criminals to use these poisons." That same year, at the annual meeting of the American Academy of Medicine, statistician Edward Bunnell Phelps denounced "the pernicious influence of neurotic books and newspapers" as "an accomplice in crimes against the person." He singled out morbid literature and plays, newspaper accounts of suicides, and lurid tales in the Sunday supplements—a "literary chamber of horrors" from which he culled a few examples: "The City of the Suicide Germ," "Chain of Suicides Strangely Arise from Love Match," and "The Pathetic Mystery of Suicide on the Eve of Marriage—What Secret Hides Behind the Recurring Tragedies of Self-Destruction at the Brink of Nuptial Union, Even Where Every Known Promise Is for a Happy Future."

Did morbid literature and sensational newspaper accounts of suicide really increase the number of suicides? Or were the suicides that were blamed on the printed word the deaths of troubled people who would have killed themselves anyway? The sociologist Émile Durkheim believed the latter. In his landmark 1897 study, *Le Suicide,* he reviewed the research linking suicide and suggestion and concluded that the effect of imitation on the national level of suicides was minimal. Those few suicides that might be triggered by suggestion, he said, would eventually have occurred in any case; a book like *Werther* or a sensational newspaper report merely hastened the timing.

Seventy-seven years later, David Phillips, a thirty-year-old Princeton-trained sociologist, disputed this conclusion. Checking the vital statistics of the United States against the *New York Times* index for front-page stories on suicide since World War II, he found that suicides increase significantly in the month after a highly publicized suicide story. The greater the publicity, the greater the increase. For instance, the suicide of Marilyn Monroe in 1962 spurred a 12 percent jump (197 more suicides than would have been expected in the month following her death). Phillips also found that the increase occurs primarily in the geographic area in which the story is published. Finding that there was no matching "dip" in the rate after the publicity had died down, Phillips concluded that these deaths were "extra" suicides, not inevitable suicides that would otherwise have taken place a little later. Phillips called this phenomenon "the Werther effect."

While his work offers compelling evidence linking suggestion and suicide, Phillips is careful to emphasize that the media story does not itself cause suicide. "The factors that drive a person to suicide may build up over many years," he says. "I've been investigating only one aspect of it. I'm studying the trigger and not what loaded the gun." Phillips goes on to speculate on how that trigger might be squeezed: "A suicide story in the newspaper may be a sort of natural advertisement. Just as, suppose, watching television, I have this strange vague feeling inside me, but I can't put a label on it. Then I see an ad for McDonald's, and I say to myself, 'Come to think of it, I think that strange vague feeling I have is hunger. And there are various ways to assuage my hunger, but now I've seen this option suggested, I think I'll go to McDonald's.'

"Now it's possible that unhappy people out there, who may or may not realize they're unhappy, read the story about Marilyn Monroe's suicide and become aware that they *are* unhappy and maybe also become aware of an option to end their unhappiness. They may feel they have been given permission because they see another person has done it. Maybe they say, 'Gee, if even Marilyn Monroe is feeling bad enough to do this, shouldn't I do it, too?'"

Over the years, numerous other studies have found evidence for the Werther effect. Researchers agree that the magnitude of the effect is related to the amount, duration, and prominence of the coverage; it is especially strong if the story is placed on the front page, with large headlines. Not surprisingly, it is more pronounced in those whose demographic characteristics—age, gender, nationality, and so on—resemble those of the victim. In nearly every study, however, teenagers have been shown to be especially susceptible.

The likability of the victim also makes a difference. The 1978 mass suicide at Jonestown, for instance, did not trigger a spike in the suicide rate. Similarly, news accounts of murder followed by suicide have had no effect, perhaps, researchers suggest, because of the "nonattractiveness" of the victims. After the highly publicized 1999 tragedy at Columbine High School in Littleton, Colorado, in which two teenage boys shot and killed twelve students and one teacher before killing themselves, one might have expected an increase in adolescent suicidal ideation. But an ongoing, yearlong CDC survey of high school students from fifty states allowed researchers to compare those who filled out the survey *before* Columbine with those who filled it out afterward. The percentage of students considering suicide decreased significantly following the tragedy, a result attributed by the survey's authors to the nature of the media coverage. Although stories about the homicide victims focused on the outpouring of grief among their families and friends, stories about the suicide victims focused on the social problems they'd experienced at school.

While Phillips himself has provided evidence that the contagion effect extends to television news coverage of suicide, studies analyzing the effect of *fictional* television suicides have been less conclusive. But there is evidence to suspect that TV portrayals of self-destruction may lead to increased rates of suicide and suicide attempts, often using the same methods depicted in the shows. A 1999 English survey of patients presenting in forty-nine emergency rooms during the week following an episode of a popular TV series in which a teenager had overdosed on paracetamol found cases of self-poisoning up 17 percent. Twenty percent of the attempters said the broadcast had influenced their decision to take an overdose, while 17 percent said that the show had influenced their choice of drug. While the impact of film portrayals of suicide on the rate remains unproven, it is clear that the rate of cinematic suicide is rising. An examination of American films from 1917 to 1997 found that the portrayal of suicide in films has increased dramatically; nearly one in ten films now depicts a suicide or a suicide attempt. Whether this is a case of art imitating life or life imitating art is not yet apparent. (At least one study asks whether cyberspace—in the form of suicide-themed Web sites, where young people gather to discuss the subject and argue the merits of potential methods—may be fertile ground for the contagion effect.)

"If the mass media were to reduce the publicity of suicide stories, it's pretty clear that the number of suicides would go down," says Phillips, pointing out that several studies have documented a decrease in suicide deaths during newspaper strikes. Nevertheless, he opposes censorship. "I grew up in South Africa, where the press was controlled and individual freedom substantially limited. I think it would be extremely unfortunate if my studies were used as ammunition to pressure the media to change their coverage. If the media want to do this voluntarily, it's up to them." In 1987, following a highly publicized three-year rash of suicides by jumping in front of subway trains in Vienna, the Austrian Association for Suicide Prevention alerted journalists to the possible negative effects of excessive coverage and suggested alternative, less sensational strategies. When the amount of reporting on the deaths dropped, subway suicides and nonfatal attempts by that method fell more than 80 percent in the next six months, while the total number of Viennese suicides declined as well. In 1994, the CDC, acknowledging that "it is not news coverage of suicide per se, but certain types of news coverage, that promote contagion," issued recommendations for the media. They urged journalists to avoid referring to suicide in the headline, to minimalize morbid details, to avoid publishing photographs of the death site or the funeral, to omit technical information about the suicide method, to avoid glorifying the victim with descriptions of grieving relatives and classmates, to avoid simplistic explanations ("Boy, 10, Kills Himself Over Bad Grades"), and to acknowledge that suicide is never caused by a single factor but by a complex interaction of many factors, usually involving a history of psychosocial problems.

Was anybody listening? Four years later, the Annenberg Public Policy Center reviewed a year's worth of suicide coverage in nine of this country's highest-circulation newspapers, as well as three years' worth in the *New York Times*. Seven of the nine papers featured the word *suicide* in at least half their stories' headlines, often in sensationalized fashion ("Eighth-Grade Sweethearts in a Love Suicide" was one 1995 *New York Times* headline). In 60 percent of the *New York Times* articles, either the fact of suicide or the method was mentioned in the headline, yet only 8 percent cited depression as a possible factor. Many of the stories included explicit details about the method used. It was hardly surprising that the newspapers had ignored the CDC guidelines; interviewing sixty-one reporters and fifteen editors who had reported on acts of suicide, the Annenberg Center found that the journalists had never heard of the guidelines. Some were unaware that certain types of coverage could increase copycat suicide, and even those who were familiar with the phenomenon expressed doubts about its validity.

On at least one occasion in this country, voluntary media restraint has had encouraging results. In 1994, when charismatic grunge rock star Kurt Cobain shot himself, experts expected a wave of copycat suicides. Rather than portraying Cobain as a misunderstood latter-day Werther, however, most news stories highlighted Cobain's depression and substance abuse problems, while providing names and places to turn to if readers needed counseling. Cobain's widow publicly and rather vituperatively expressed not only her grief but her anger at the senselessness of his death and at his abandonment of their nineteen-month-old daughter. A study published two years later found Cobain's death had no effect on the adolescent suicide rate.

---

In 1984, however, the media could not restrain itself. Suicide and suicide clusters were a hot story. Ironically, the focus on clusters may allow us to overlook the extent of youth suicide generally. While spotlighting "affluent suburbs" such as Plano, for instance, the Dallas papers virtually ignored the fact that the teen suicide rate was far higher in their own city. And Westchester County alone would have a total of six teenage suicides in 1984, compared with an average of five over the previous eight years and fewer than the high of seven in 1979. In that case, the 1984 suicides barely qualified as an "epidemic," which is defined as "more than would normally be expected," leading some to suggest that the "Westchester cluster" was a statistical mirage.

On February 16, 1985, seventeen-year-old David Balogh of Tarrytown was found in a car parked at a landfill, dead from carbon monoxide poisoning. In the following three weeks there were three more adolescent suicides in Westchester County, the same number as in 1984 when the suicides had ignited media and public hysteria. "Last year at this time it was chaos," a high school counselor told me. "This year there hasn't been a peep. No calls from the media. Nobody mentions the word *cluster.*" Said a local psychologist, "I'd like to think it's because the media is more sensitive to the issue, but the more cynical side of me wonders if it isn't just old news."

With or without media attention, adolescent suicides continued in the tri-county area. But gradually the suicides became just a part of the overall rate of adolescent suicide in the United States. Some people say, in fact, that the attention showered on the Westchester suicides of 1984 was, in fact, ultimately beneficial because it focused attention on the problem of adolescent suicide after many years of silence. "I think the way the media dealt with that particular episode had some very positive results," Westchester pediatrician Kenneth Schonberg told me a few years later. "Despite the fact that, in all honesty, that was not a very exceptional year. Unfortunately, adolescents are dying at a rather constant rate from suicide, and it wasn't restricted to the late winter and early spring of 1984. Eighty-four or eighty-three . . . which was it? I forget already."

# V

# DANA

---

"I USED TO LIE in bed and imagine what my life could be like. I'd set up these great scenes in my mind. In my favorite I'd be driving down the road and there'd be a car accident, and I'd jump out and save the guy's life, and it would be in all the newspapers—'Hero Saves the Day.' Or I'd go to college, become a doctor, and every hospital in the country would want me because I'd pioneered some new operation. Or I'd win the Olympics in swimming—every distance, every stroke imaginable. Or I'd be out at a romantic dinner, the kind you see on TV, where the camera focuses on the couple staring into each other's eyes. The man would be tall, with a great body. Rugged good looks. Like Tom Selleck. And he couldn't live without me."

At seven on a Tuesday morning in March, Dana Evans heard her mother leave for work. She rolled over and went back to sleep. It was a school day, but she didn't feel like going. When she woke again, it was nine-thirty. She turned on the television set at the foot of her bed. Then she got up, shuffled downstairs to the living room, and poured herself a mug of vodka—straight, as always. She knew that if she added tonic, she wouldn't get drunk as fast. Then she climbed back into bed and stared at the TV. Dana paid little attention to the game show. She sipped her vodka and thought about how miserable her life was.

Although Dana, a high school senior, had often been told she was smart, she rarely did her homework, skipped school at least once a week, and was failing several classes. Although she was a promising swimmer, she had quit the team at the end of her junior year. Although she had a cute face and brown, curly hair, she was convinced she was ugly. She had never had a boyfriend and was certain she never would. She had no close friends. Her parents were divorced. Her father lived in Texas, and her mother, who worked two jobs, was rarely home. Her older sister was away at college. While her classmates were obsessed with boyfriends and college plans, Dana spent most of her time sleeping, watching television, drinking, or getting high.

Suddenly Dana slammed the mug of vodka down on her bedside table, pulled on some jeans and a T-shirt, and stomped angrily through the apartment, pausing occasionally to punch the wall. Her head rang with imagined insults:

> *Here you are again, hanging out, doing nothing.*
> *Well, that's cuz no one wants to be with you.*
> *That's cuz you're an asshole and you're ugly.*
> *Well, so, what do you expect?*
> *Well, you're stupid.*
> *Well, you're ugly.*
> *Well, you're a fucking asshole.*
> *Well, then fuck it.* Today's the day.

It was eleven-thirty. Dana realized that she would have to hurry. Tammy, a classmate who was staying with Dana and her mother, was due home at five-fifteen. Dana had always imagined that she'd leave a note telling her mother, her sister, and Tammy that she loved them. Now she decided against it—let them wonder, she told herself. She thought about where to do it. "I decided I'd better use the bathroom because from what I'd read, that's where everyone kills themselves," she says. "Plus if I got the bedroom rug dirty"—there is no trace of irony in her voice—"my mother would *kill* me."

At noon Dana went to her room and fished a razor blade from her purse. She walked into the bathroom and locked the door. "And then I just started," she says. "I cut my wrists. I watched the blood go into the sink, and because the sink was already wet, the blood spread out and I realized how neat it looked." She made vertical and horizontal slices on both wrists, lightly at first, and then, after taking a breath, deeply. "It hurt, but I didn't mind," she says. "It was almost as if I wanted it to hurt because I wanted to be tough." Every so often she paused. "Everything in the bathroom is white," she says. "White tile walls and white tile floors. I had to keep stopping and cleaning up because I didn't want to make a mess. I poured water in the sink so the blood would go down the drain. I'd rest my arms on my pants to soak up the blood so it wouldn't get on the floor." Dana felt herself grow weak, but she kept cutting. Then she stopped for a moment, looked at herself in the mirror, and said aloud, "Good-bye."

While attention to adolescent suicide has focused primarily on completed suicide, for every adolescent who dies, there are at least twenty—some say as many as one hundred—who make an attempt. Although no official statistics are compiled for suicide attempts, in 2002 an estimated 125,000 visits to emergency rooms in this country were made by adolescents who had attempted suicide. Many more made attempts that didn't require medical attention.

For years attempted and completed suicide were regarded as psychologically similar acts, differing only in their outcome. It is for this reason, in part, that until a few decades ago, people who attempted suicide and survived were called "unsuccessful" or "failed" suicides; those who died were called "successful." The suicide attempter was regarded as a double failure—not only at life but at death. Most suicide research, in fact, was based on attempters—who were available to be interviewed—and then generalized to include completers. Clinicians now maintain, however, that attempters and completers form two different though overlapping groups, each with its own goals and motivations.

Completers tend to be older than attempters; 50 percent of all attempters are under age thirty; attempts peak between sixteen and eighteen years of age. Completers tend to be male: four times as many men as women kill themselves. Attempters tend to be female: three times as many women as men attempt suicide. "Suicide is masculine, suicide attempts are feminine," summarizes Diane Ryerson, a social worker who runs suicide prevention programs in the schools. "Girls use it as a form of communication, guys use it to permanently punish." In *Night Falls Fast,* psychiatrist Kay Jamison suggests that part of the gender disparity is attributable to the fact that females are at least twice as likely as males to suffer from depression. "Although depression is more common in women, their depressive illnesses may be less impulsive and violent than those of men; this in turn may make women less likely to use violent methods and more likely to use relatively safer means such as self-poisoning," she writes. Seventy-five percent of completers shoot or hang themselves, while 70 to 90 percent of all attempters swallow pills and about 10 percent cut their wrists, methods that allow more time for rescue. Men, Jamison adds, are more likely than women to feel there is a stigma attached to a "failed" attempt; less likely than women to seek psychiatric help; and far more likely to abuse alcohol or drugs and to own guns—risk factors that make a suicide attempt more likely to end in death. Attempts are often made in settings that make survival not only possible but probable. Ninety percent of adolescent suicide attempts take place at home, 70 percent while parents are in the house.

Given these figures, it is tempting to assume that people who complete suicide truly want to die and people who attempt merely want attention. However, many people who complete suicide don't intend to die. Some lack knowledge of pharmacology and unintentionally overdose. Some mistakenly count on rescuers arriving in time to save them. On the other hand, some attempters who seem bent on dying end up living. People have survived six-story jumps or bullets in their heart. In *King Lear,* when blind Gloucester leaps from what he believes is a Dover cliff but is actually level ground, he is, in intent, making a serious suicide attempt. With adolescents, who are prone to risk-taking behavior, the line of intention is particularly difficult to draw. Suicide attempts range from swallowing a dozen aspirin in full view of one's mother to jumping off the Golden Gate Bridge. Clearly, one attempter has a greater determination to die than the other, but every suicide or suicide attempt has its own degree of ambivalence. "Most people who commit suicidal acts do not either want to die or to live," psychiatrist Erwin Stengel has written. "They want to do both at the same time, usually the one more, or much more, than the other."

While a suicide attempt is a move toward death, it may also be a way of moving toward other people. The person who threatens to jump from a building is an example. "The man up there is saying, 'Look at me. See how bad I feel,'" says psychologist Norman Farberow. "Sitting on the ledge of a building is a tremendous effort at communication." People use such an extreme form of expression—"a desperate version of holding their breath until turning blue," psychiatrist Mary Giffin has called it—because other forms have failed or because they have never learned more effective ways of asking for help. It may also be a last-ditch attempt to change a seemingly intolerable situation. In *A Cry for Help,* Giffin described a thirteen-year-old Illinois girl who, one week after her father moved out of the house, slashed her wrists in the bathtub shortly before she knew her mother would be bathing. "I didn't really want to die," she said later. "I just hoped and prayed that if Mom and Dad knew how upset and unhappy I was, Dad would move back in."

Clinicians have used a variety of expressions to describe such low-lethality attempts: manipulative behavior, histrionic suicide attempts, abortive suicides, fake suicides, psychological blackmail, suicidal gestures. Because death is clearly not the object, these attempts are often dismissed as not serious. But the line between serious and not serious is a fine one. *"Gesture?"* says Warren Wacker, former director of Harvard University Health Services. He smiles ironically. "If someone slashes her wrists lightly, it's a gesture. If she cuts deeper, it ain't." As Wacker suggests, making that distinction can be dangerous. "Clinicians use these terms pejoratively," says psychiatrist Douglas Jacobs, "but just because an attempt is minor does not mean a patient is not suicidal." A Michigan youth hospitalized after a suicide attempt was chided by the doctor, "This wasn't very serious, was it?" The young man says, "It's like if you're saved, it wasn't serious. If you succeed, they should have taken you seriously." Indeed, those who make a low-lethality attempt may be even more troubled than those who make a medically serious attempt; one study concludes that they are more likely to have chronic psychiatric problems, a higher number of previous attempts, and greater rates of physical or sexual abuse. Those who make repeated low-lethality attempts, often by wrist-cutting or overdosing, may be another psychologically distinct group: they generally use self-destructive behavior as a way of dealing with stress, tend to have more chronic symptomatology, poorer coping skills, and a higher rate of suicidal and substance abuse behaviors in their family histories.

Clinicians and parents, dismissing an attempt as attention-getting, may refuse to give that attention—or they may give the wrong kind. Some doctors show anger toward attempters: A woman who had made numerous cuts on her wrists was told by her emergency room physician, "If you really want to do a good job, why don't you just take a knife and make a real good, deep cut." A sixteen-year-old Texas girl who slashed her wrists says, "The doctor told me he'd sew me up so I could see the scar and for the rest of my life I would never forget what I'd done. And he did, too." Parents—anxious, terrified, angry—may minimalize or deny the attempt. One study found that only 38 percent of treatment referrals after an adolescent attempt were acted on. Another found that only 41 percent of families came for further therapy following the initial session. "It's often difficult to get parents to acknowledge the problem because they *are* the problem," says child psychiatrist Peter Saltzman. After making an attempt, one of Saltzman's patients was told by his father, "Next time, jump off the Bourne Bridge."

An adolescent whose suicide attempt is belittled or ignored may feel forced to take more drastic action. One young girl, after an argument with her parents, slashed her wrists lightly. For several mornings in a row she appeared at the breakfast table wearing short-sleeved shirts that clearly revealed her fresh scars. When this attempt at communication failed, she slashed an artery.

If dealt with improperly, a "failed" suicide may lead to a face-saving "success." Long-term follow-up studies show that 10 to 15 percent of those who attempt suicide will eventually kill themselves, 2 percent within a year. An estimated 25 to 40 percent of those who complete suicide have made a previous attempt. Among adolescents, those who have attempted suicide are at far greater risk for completing—one study puts the figure at three times greater for girls, thirty times greater for boys. In *A Cry for Help,* the authors describe a lonely sixteen-year-old Minneapolis boy who believed his father paid more attention to his Cadillac than to his son. One night after leaving a note on his bulletin board saying that he was an outcast at school, he stole the keys to the Cadillac and smashed into an oak tree in the front yard. After spending several months in the hospital recuperating from his injuries, he was pronounced "straightened out." But he came home to find little had changed. Eight months after his first attempt, his mother found him behind the wheel of his father's brand-new Cadillac, dead from carbon monoxide poisoning.

---

A bright, outgoing girl, Dana Evans received good grades in elementary school, played war with the neighborhood kids, and went home to a hot supper each evening in a split-level ranch house in a small town eighty miles north of Manhattan. "We had a dog, two kids, a two-car garage, and two cars," she says with a touch of sarcasm. "It was all so perfect." But all was not so perfect. At nine months she developed spinal meningitis, and not long afterward her mother noticed Dana had difficulty bending her right leg. Over the next eighteen years dozens of specialists would be unable to pinpoint the problem. As a child Dana did prescribed exercises daily, had a slight limp, and wore a shoe with a built-up sole to compensate for her shorter left leg. At school she was called names like "peg leg" and "the polio kid." Although Dana tried to ignore the taunts, she was self-conscious about her leg and never wore a dress except on Thanksgiving and Christmas.

Dana was also affected by the friction between her parents. She felt intimidated by her father, a quiet, remote engineer whom she desperately wanted to please. He often gave her the vague feeling that he would have preferred a son. When she was seven, he asked her if she wanted to be in a swim meet. She said yes. "When the gun went off, everybody dove in except me," Dana recalls. "I didn't know that was the signal. Eventually, I dove in. Halfway down the pool I started crying because everybody else had finished and I was still in the middle of the pool." But Dana was determined to please her father, and she doggedly went to swim practice. Swimming soon became an important part of her life.

When Dana was nine, her parents separated, and she and her mother and older sister moved into a massive apartment complex in a neighboring town. To support the family Mrs. Evans returned to work full-time as a secretary and also took a weekend job as a waitress. To relieve her loneliness she went to singles bars with friends several nights a week. "Before, my mother had always been there when I came home from school," says Dana. "Now I had to carry a key because I was the first one home. At first I thought, 'Hey, this is great—no one around to tell me what to do.'" Dana learned to smoke, and she and her sister smuggled boys into the house when their mother was out. "But after a while it wasn't so much 'Great, there's no mother around,'" says Dana, "as 'Where's my mother?'"

Even when Dana's mother was home, there was little communication. A pragmatic woman, Mrs. Evans had her hands full trying to support her family and move on after her divorce. She was reluctant to discipline her daughter because she felt Dana had suffered enough already from the leg problem. When Dana didn't do her chores, her mother overlooked it. When she caught Dana smoking, she let her off with a warning. When Dana got drunk for the first time, her mother said, "All kids try it—just don't make it a habit." Dana found herself wishing that she could get a stronger reaction from her mother. Dana never talked about her problems, and her mother rarely asked. "I don't think we ever sat and chatted about our feelings," says Mrs. Evans. "I think it's because parents in my generation did not. Adults were adults and children were children. There was no such thing as 'parent effectiveness training.' Today, if the kid comes home and kicks the cat, you're supposed to say, 'Did you have a rotten day at school?' Back then you'd scold them for kicking the cat! My father and mother didn't deal on a feeling level with each other, let alone with their children." She shrugs. "So my children and I did not get into personal, emotional subjects. But I perceived that as being the way all parents were with their children."

Dana's father, who lived with his second wife and her two daughters, was even less of an influence. Dana dreaded their weekends together. Although he rarely criticized her, she believed that nothing she did ever pleased him. Yet she longed for his approval. One day when Dana was thirteen, after picking up Dana and her sister for the weekend, her father told them that his company was transferring him to Texas. Dana felt wounded. "I think I knew rationally that he was not moving to get away from us, but I didn't understand why he wanted to move so far away when his children lived here," she says. "I remember feeling, 'Jesus Christ, if they transferred you to the *moon,* you'd go.'"

Dana also had difficulty getting noticed at school. Because of a series of operations on her knee, she missed fifty-three days of her seventh-grade year and found it hard to make a place for herself in the huge new junior high. "At school there were the jocks and the nerds and the heads," she says. "I swam, but for a club team, not for the school, so I wasn't a jock. And I had a deep aversion to the nerds. That's not a group you become a member of by choice; you're born into it. So I never really fit in anywhere." But late in her seventh-grade year, when Dana was twelve, she found a way of belonging. A classmate asked her if she wanted to buy a joint, and Dana said sure. "I took it home and hid it in the back of my desk, and one afternoon after school I sat on my bed and smoked it. It was great. I loved being high. It put me in such a different head than I had been in all my life. Everything looked so different. Everything looked okay."

Once Dana found an identity, she pursued it with a vengeance. Dana and the other druggies would meet at lunch in the woods in back of school and get high. She stopped wearing the corduroy slacks with color-coordinated blouses that her mother bought her and wore old jeans, T-shirts, and concert jerseys emblazoned with the names of favorite rock bands. She wore mirror sunglasses and a cloth cap pulled low over her eyes. A Walkman filled her ears with rock music. From her weight lifting and swimming she developed huge shoulders, arms, and biceps, which she liked to show off by rolling up her sleeves. She cultivated a swagger and a glare that kept people at a distance. She became friends with a tough girl named Stacey. "We'd meet in the girls' bathroom and get high next to the open window so no one could smell anything," says Dana. "If anyone was there when we went in, it was like 'This is our office, get out.' And they would."

Dana also began to drink heavily. She had first tasted alcohol as a child when, fetching beers for her father, she was rewarded with the first sip. At age eleven, at a family dinner in an Italian restaurant, she and her cousins managed to sneak a carafe of wine down to the children's end of the table. Dana drank most of it and blacked out. By thirteen she was stealing from the liquor cabinet and pouring water into the bottles so her mother wouldn't suspect. "She kept one bottle of everything, so I'd take a little of each and have a mug with vodka, gin, and bourbon." By the end of eighth grade, Dana was drinking or getting high almost every day.

As Dana began to get attention for the first time, her behavior became more and more extreme. "In trying to fit in somewhere and to get people to realize that I existed, I did some really weird things." In the hallways she was apt to push girls up against a wall and threaten them. In science class she stole her classmates' lab books, ripped out their homework if they were ahead of her, and poured hydrochloric acid on their experiments. She even intimidated some of the teachers. At the end of class when her science teacher asked the students to push in their chairs, Dana glared at her and kicked her chair out from behind her. "My general attitude toward the world was 'Don't mess with me or I'll kill you,'" says Dana. "I loved it when people were scared of me." Dana was proud of her new nickname: Tuffie. She liked the idea that she cared about nothing, and nothing could get to her.

For years swimming had been the one thing Dana truly cared about. She loved the feel of her body hitting the cold water and the grueling discipline of laps. During the day she might get high, mouth off to teachers, and wear sloppy clothes, but every weeknight she worked out with her club team. "I *occasionally* went to school," she says. "I *always* went to practice." But the more she partied, the more practices she skipped. Sometimes she'd show up high. She kept a pint of J&B Scotch in her gym bag, which she sipped on "trips to the bathroom." She quarreled with the coach, a gentle, earnest man who had gone out of his way for Dana ever since she had joined the team, picking her up for meets and staying late to help her develop a new racing start because her knee didn't bend enough for the standard position. After a race she would ignore his congratulations, leaving him standing there with his hand out. Sometimes she swore at him or gave him the finger. "I'd get kicked out of practice about once a week," she says. "Afterward I'd try to apologize, but it would come out all wrong. He'd say, 'You can't tell me to go fuck myself in front of the other kids,' and I'd *want* to say, 'I don't know why I swear at you because I really like you,' but I'd end up saying something stupid like 'Well, you deserved it.' And he'd say, 'Don't talk to me like that.' And I'd say, 'Well, fuck you.'" Dana shrugs. "I wanted to be friends with him, but I was holding back so much from everything. I was like a snake keeping people away from me."

In March of Dana's junior year she and her coach argued over whether she would be allowed to miss part of an important meet to attend the junior prom. The coach excused her from a few events. Dana says, "If you don't go to the prom, the word is out, like 'She's a loser, she'd have to *pay* somebody to take her.'" Nobody had asked Dana, so, as time was running out, she invited a boy in her chemistry class whom she hardly knew. "It was a disaster," she says. "We were assigned to a table with people we didn't know. We hardly talked the whole night. Afterward we went with another couple to an Italian restaurant where I got smashed. My date didn't drink a drop. He thought we were all pretty stupid. So the rest of us drank and drank and drank, and then we all drove down by the tracks to watch the sunrise. I passed out in the car."

Four hours later Dana stood on the starting block for the hundred-yard freestyle. She was still drunk. "When the gun went off, I dove into the water and my stomach turned. I swam to the other end, did a flip turn, swam back, and did another flip, and when I came up and took a breath, I got some water in my mouth, which happens occasionally. But this time I just stood up and got out of the pool. It was the first time I had ever not finished a race."

Dana stayed on the team for two more months. One day in June she threw her sweat suit at the coach. "I don't need your shit anymore," she said, walking out. "Swimming was my life," says Dana. "I spent ten years doing it, and in one day I just threw it all away."

Without swimming, Dana had little left but her identity as a druggie. "Senior year I just said, 'Screw it—I'm going the whole nine yards,'" she remembers. "I sort of said good-bye." She got high at school almost every day and began using hashish and mescaline as well as marijuana. She cut school at least once a week, forging excuses from her mother, and spent the day in bed sipping vodka and watching reruns of *Jeopardy!, I Love Lucy,* and *The Brady Bunch.* If she went to school, she would come home in the afternoon and drink and sleep until her mother arrived. Sometimes she would just put on a sad record and smoke pot. Without swim practice she spent nights in front of the TV, drinking. "I knew every single show from six o'clock until eleven," she says. "I was like a walking *TV Guide.*" At parties she got drunk or high as quickly as possible. "There was no such thing as stopping when I got a buzz on—it was 'Go for it.' My big worry was that other people would drink too much, because the more they drank, the less there was for me." At the beginning of a party she would hide a few bottles of beer to make sure there would be enough for her to get drunk. "At school on Monday morning, people would tell me what I'd done that weekend," she says. "Even good friends told me I drank too much. And I *knew* I drank too much. But I knew I had to. I had to take a break from life. I was depressed when I wasn't drinking, and I thought drinking would save me, I thought it was like my best friend. But the drunker I got, the less fun it was."

Although it seemed everyone around her had a boyfriend, Dana had never had one. Occasionally, a friend would include her in a double date, but Dana wasn't much interested. "I thought I must be a lesbian 'cause I didn't like guys. I didn't like girls either, though. I thought maybe I was asexual." She tried not to think about it. "I just hoped it would all go away, that I'd grow up and everything would be fine. But I figured that even if I ended up liking guys, there wasn't much hope since I wasn't pretty. Dating seemed like a big pain in the ass anyway. First you have to explain yourself to somebody and get to know him, and then you gotta get closer, and then you fight, and then you stop seeing each other, and you both get really hurt."

Dana talked to no one about her sexuality, her depression, her drinking, or about anything else personal, not even to Tammy, a classmate who came to live with the Evanses when her own parents moved from the area. Dana and Tammy would gossip for hours, but Tammy did most of the talking, primarily about boys she was interested in. Anyway, thought Dana, with her silky hair, perfect figure, and steady boyfriend, how could Tammy understand what Dana was feeling? "We were like two different grades of people—she was like large Grade A, and I was . . . day-old bread, twenty percent discount." Even if there had been someone to talk to, Dana wouldn't have talked. The last thing in the world she would admit was that she felt scared.

Dana knew she was depressed, but in the back of her mind she expected things to get better when she turned eighteen. "I thought that adults had it infinitely easier than kids and that the day I turned eighteen and became an adult, my whole life was going to magically fall into place." On the night of her eighteenth birthday Dana had a party at her house. About twenty people came, most of them druggies. To celebrate that Dana was of legal drinking age, Mrs. Evans bought the beer. Among her friends' presents were an enormous joint and a silver mug inscribed with Dana's nickname. Dana made full use of both gifts, and long before the party was over, she passed out. "The next day I woke up hung over. Nothing had changed. It was just . . . Sunday morning. I thought, 'Well, here I am, I'm eighteen, but I still don't know what I want to do with my life. If anything.'"

Dana had long been fascinated by the subject of suicide. "I used to read everything about it I could get my hands on," she says. "I wrote a paper in eleventh-grade English on suicide—the statistics, men versus women. I got a B-plus." Dana had never consciously considered it as an option, but about two months before her birthday she started carrying a razor blade in her wallet. She had found it in the family toolbox, where it was kept for scraping expired registration stickers off the car windshield. At first it was a kind of toy she was fond of playing with, carving patterns on desks, but gradually she began to think of it as a means of escape. "It was my security blanket: 'Well, if it gets too bad, I'll just bail out.'"

About a month after her eighteenth birthday Dana knew she was going to kill herself. "I didn't know what it would be like to be dead, but I knew it would be better than this," she says. "I wasn't setting a date, but I knew it would be soon. I was walking around thinking, 'Hey, it doesn't matter what happens 'cause I ain't going to be here!' I was just waiting for the right time." Even now Dana is not sure how she chose the day. Later she told people it was because she had an English test the following morning, but "that was just to give them an answer they'd understand." By the time she used the razor blade she felt so angry at herself and at the world that even after she slumped to the white tile floor of the bathroom, she continued to hack away insistently at her wrists, her arms, and her legs until she slipped into unconsciousness.

When Dana woke, a blur of policemen and paramedics hovered over her, asking her name, wrapping gauze on her wrists, reaching for the razor blade in her hand. Dana said nothing but squeezed her fist tighter, as if the blade were a jewel they were trying to steal. When they carried her downstairs, she fought and kicked, breaking the dining room window. They tied her down on a stretcher and loaded her into the ambulance. On the ride to the hospital a medical technician tried to soothe her. "Everything is going to be okay," he said softly. Dana thought, "How the fuck would *you* know?"

In the emergency room Dana received seven stitches on each wrist. Afterward, as she lay tied to a cot, she dimly recognized Tammy, who had come home early from school to find Dana in a pool of blood on the bathroom floor, and her mother, who had arrived home from work just after the ambulance had left. Dana kept moaning that she wanted to go home, but the doctors had signed ninety-day commitment forms. The doctors suggested the state hospital, but Mrs. Evans refused to consider it and chose a private psychiatric hospital in Westchester County. Dana was put in a straitjacket, loaded into an ambulance, and driven to the hospital, where a nurse made her strip, gave her a hospital gown, and told her to get in bed. "These are going into the garbage," said the nurse, holding up Dana's bloody jeans. "Don't fuck with my pants," snarled Dana, frightened but determined to be tough. Her mother came in to say goodbye. "When she leaned over to kiss me," says Dana, "one of her tears dropped on my face. I said, 'You're dripping on me.'"

For the first few days in the hospital Dana refused to talk. Even after she gave in, she stared at the floor as the doctors administered a battery of psychological tests. Three times a week she met with a psychologist. "Therapy was a joke," says Dana. "He'd ask me how I felt and I'd talk about how I hated hospital food, and he'd tell me stories from his college days." The psychologist prescribed Mellaril, an antipsychotic, but when Dana gained weight, she refused to take it. He recommended that she attend meetings of Alcoholics Anonymous in a nearby town. Escorted to her first session, Dana wore a Yukon Jack whiskey T-shirt—though when she realized the other people were serious about not drinking, she folded her arms across her chest so they couldn't read the logo. But she was skeptical. "I didn't think I had a drinking problem," she says. "I didn't think the problem was me—I thought that things *around* me had to get better. I thought if only my mother were happy, then I'd be happy. Or I'd think if I fell in love and got married, I'd be fine. Or if only I went to a good school. Or if only I found some friends." She shrugs. "I didn't think I belonged in the hospital because a hospital was for crazy people, and I wasn't crazy. I thought if someone would just fix my life, I could go home, and everything would be fine."

Dana came to like the hospital. She made friends with three girls her age, and they smuggled alcohol, drugs, and boys into the girls' ward. In many respects her life was no different from the way it had been at home except that she didn't have to go to school, cook meals, or clean up. "All in all, once I learned the system and how to get around it, I had a ball." She even found her first boyfriend, a young patient from Pennsylvania. One night when they got permission to watch TV together, they turned out the lights and made love on the ward floor—Dana's first time. The boy was discharged not long afterward, however, and after a few brief phone conversations, he stopped calling.

As time went by, however, Dana grew anxious to get out. She told the doctors what she thought they wanted to hear—that she was getting better, that she would stop drinking, that she didn't want to hurt herself anymore. In July, after four months at the hospital, Dana was discharged.

---

That fall, Dana enrolled as a freshman at a college on Long Island. "I was going to start all over again where no one knew me," she says. "I thought, 'This is it. I'm going to meet new people, maybe find a boyfriend, and live the good old college life. I'll just be somebody different this time.'" Her first night at school Dana unpacked, arranged her clothes in her bureau, and studied the school's catalog. The second night she went to a beer party down the hall, played a drinking game called Pass Out, went back to her room, threw up, and passed out.

Dana had drunk little during the month she had been at home, but once she had ruined her clean slate at the party, she figured, "Why not? I've already blown it." Soon she was drinking every day again. Her bottom desk drawer became her liquor cabinet. Of the $50 weekly food allowance her parents gave her, she spent all but $3 on liquor; with the rest she bought a packet of bouillon cubes and a can of powdered juice mix. She rarely went to class, and though she opened the books on her desk every night, she never got around to reading them. Her roommate moved out to live with friends down the hall, and the two girls with whom Dana shared a bathroom were seniors she rarely saw. While her classmates lived "the good old college life"—flinging Frisbees across the quad, shouting conversations from dorm to dorm, aiming their stereo speakers out the window and blasting music throughout the campus— Dana spent almost all of her time alone in her room, drinking and watching television.

One Friday night in early November, Dana was in the laundry room when she ran into a boy from down the hall with whom she occasionally talked about sports. They ended up in her room watching TV. Although the boy didn't drink, Dana did—"I don't mind drinking alone, I'm used to it," she assured him. Later that night she blacked out. When she woke up shortly before dawn, the boy was in bed next to her. "I assumed we'd had sex," she says. "I didn't ask. I didn't want to know." Promising that he would stop by and see her later that morning, he stumbled back to his room. Dana realized she didn't even know his last name.

Dana spent Saturday staring at her textbooks, hating herself, hating the boy, but wanting him to come back. Saturday night, as rock music from the dormitory dance floated through her window, Dana stayed in her room drinking, watching TV, falling asleep, waking, watching TV, drinking.

When Dana woke up Sunday, there was a half bottle of rum on her bureau and the television was on. She spent the afternoon finishing the bottle and growing more depressed. "I had no friends. I wasn't doing any work. I knew that even if I finished the semester, I would flunk everything anyway. I was thinking, 'Here we are again. Everything's just the same, and I managed to do it in two months.'" That evening she rummaged through the toolbox her mother had given her to help decorate her room and found a small knife with a two-inch blade. "This time I wanted to do it right," she says. "I knew I had all the time in the world because no one ever came to my room. I could sit in that apartment for days, and nobody would come looking for me." She sat down at her desk and began to slice into her wrists, just as she had done nine months before. After making repeated cuts she decided to try her jugular vein because she knew it would be quicker, but when she got up to use the bathroom mirror, drunk and weak from loss of blood, she fell back into her chair.

No one ever did come looking for her, but the dormitory's resident assistant, looking for Dana's roommate, knocked on the door, let himself in with his passkey, and found Dana instead. Five minutes later the police came into her bedroom. This time they were not gentle; they twisted her arm until she dropped the knife, tied her wrists and ankles tight, and strapped her to a stretcher. At the busy hospital, an orderly walked by and saw her cursing and struggling to free herself. "I wish you *had* died," he said.

---

The second time around at the hospital was no more effective than the first. Although her old buddies were gone, Dana found a new pack of friends to party with. But as the months passed and her friends were discharged, and new patients entered and were themselves discharged, Dana realized she didn't want to leave. "I wanted to live there," she says. "I didn't have to work, all my meals were made, and I had friends." She didn't tell anybody this—like the others, she bad-mouthed the hospital and submitted frequent requests for a discharge hearing, which she always ripped up before it was too late. When she was finally allowed to go, she ran through the ward shouting, "I'm getting out of this jail! I'm free!" But inside she was terrified.

Dana was released on the Fourth of July weekend. Her mother was away with her boyfriend in Vermont. Dana and her best friend from the hospital spent the weekend cruising Dutchess County. "I drove around with a beer in one hand and a joint in the other," Dana remembers. When her friend, out on a weekend pass, returned to the hospital on Sunday afternoon, Dana was restless and lonely. She decided to drive down to the hospital and see her friend. When she arrived, still drunk and high, the staff wouldn't let her leave. They didn't even bother readmitting her; they just tore up her discharge papers. She had been out only forty-eight hours.

When Dana called her mother that night and told her she was back at the hospital, she was surprised by her response. "Usually my mother came running down with clothes and cigarettes and money and sympathy." This time Mrs. Evans said that she and her boyfriend were going to California for a wedding, as planned, and they would see Dana when they got back in ten days. Dana was angry. The doctors were also less tolerant. They allowed Dana no visitors or phone calls, forbade her to talk to other patients, and plotted her daily schedule down to the minute. Although this infuriated her, Dana had time to think. "I began to realize I was getting tired of it all," she says. "I knew I couldn't stay at the hospital for the rest of my life, but I also knew I couldn't handle it outside."

Dana's mother and her boyfriend came to see her the night they got back from California. The three of them sat outside in the warm summer evening. Mrs. Evans asked Dana if she thought she had a problem. Dana surprised herself by saying, "Yeah. I do." "Is it alcohol or drugs?" her mother asked. "Well, sort of both." "Do you want to stop?" her mother asked. "No," said Dana. "I like it." Dana was surprised. After so many months of automatically saying she was getting better, that things were going to be different, for the first time she felt she was telling the truth.

Dana admitted to her mother that if she had any hope of improving, she couldn't stay at this hospital—it made life too easy for her. Dana was discharged one day in August, and the following day her mother drove her to Four Winds, a psychiatric hospital in nearby Katonah.

From the very first day Dana realized that Four Winds was going to be different. At the other hospital there had been a few hours of therapy a week; at Four Winds there were more than twenty. At the other hospital it had been simple to smuggle in drugs and alcohol; at Four Winds the no-drugs/no-alcohol rule was enforced with urine tests and frequent hall checks. Transgressors were immediately asked to leave. At the other hospital Dana had controlled her therapy sessions; at her first Four Winds session, when Dana kept her eyes on the floor, the therapist, a young social worker named Terry, suddenly stopped talking and literally pulled her head up. Dana was scared. That night she called her mother in tears. "These people are weird," she cried. "You've got to get me out of here."

At the old hospital Dana felt it had always been the patients versus the staff. Here, she realized, people worked at getting well. "At the other hospital, if you showed any sign of being interested in treatment, it was like 'What's wrong with you?'" she says. "At Four Winds, if you *weren't* into treatment, you were on the outside." In group therapy the staff leader would ask, "All right, who wants to work today?" The other patients raised their hands. Dana never did. She kept her arms crossed and her eyes on the floor. Sometimes she'd get dragged into the discussion, but she got out as soon as possible. "Dana, what do you think?" the leader would ask. "I don't think," she would say.

One day in therapy Terry criticized her for being cruel to the other patients. Dana felt herself begin to cry. She kept her head down until she was able to stop so that Terry couldn't see her tears. "I couldn't believe that he'd gotten to me," she says. "*No one* was supposed to get to me. I was so pissed off at myself." When the session was over, Dana ran back to her room and made light cuts all over her arm. "I was at the point where I knew that killing myself was not going to help, but I needed to release the pressure. Out in the world or even at the other hospital you could drink or get high or talk. At Four Winds I couldn't drink or get high, and I wasn't talking to anybody, aside from saying, 'Fuck you.' So I found another way." About once a week, after she had verbally abused someone or when someone had penetrated her wall for a moment, she would feel guilty. "Whenever I felt upset about something, I always thought it was my fault. And because it was my fault, I felt I deserved to be hurt." She would come back to her room and scratch her arms with a metal triangle she had cut from a soda can and hid in her drawer. They were superficial scrapes; the nurse would clean and bandage them, and Dana would roll her sleeves down as if nothing had happened.

One night, about three months after Dana had arrived at Four Winds, there was a meeting of the patients in her unit. Dana, as always, sat in sullen silence, arms folded across her chest. Suddenly everyone in the group turned on her. "We're sick and tired of you," they said. "You haven't done anything since you got here. If you didn't feel so damn sorry for yourself, maybe you could do something. But since you're not doing anything, why don't you leave?" Even her best friend, a patient named Lucy, joined the attack. Dana was stunned, but she kept her head down, saying nothing. After the meeting she spent the night shooting pool in a fury, sending balls flying off the table. "I felt betrayed," she says. Next morning her favorite nurse cornered her. "I hear they really gave it to you last night—it's about time," she said. "You know they're right." "No, I don't," said Dana. "Yes, you do," said the nurse. The following day in group therapy when the staff member asked, "Who wants to work today?" Dana raised her hand.

After so many years of carefully constructing defenses to keep the world at bay, opening up was slow, painful, and frightening. "How do I change what I think?" Dana would ask Terry. "Just change it," he would answer. "How?" "Just act as if you cared about yourself." "If it's fake, I'm not going to act it." "Just give yourself a break. Once in a while don't talk like that about yourself." "But that's acting." "It's a first step." They would end up shouting at each other, and Dana would stalk out of the room. Gradually, however, her armor began to chip away. Both staff and friends tried to support Dana's efforts. "I still had a sharp tongue, but now every time I swore, even the most timid person would say, 'I don't like that.' If someone said hello and I said, 'Hey, bitch,' they'd say, 'Don't call me bitch,' and I'd apologize."

After many arguments with Terry, Dana even put aside her jeans and T-shirts for corduroys and blouses. The first time she wore them, a young male patient called out, "Well, look at the young lady, don't she look pretty?" Dana ran to her room and climbed back into her jeans. She told Terry that if she was going to change, people couldn't tease her. "You can't program people," he said. "You have to risk it." Two days later she tried again. The same boy gave her a wolf whistle. Dana cringed but kept walking.

Dana had never let people get close to her. "I could be friends with someone, but there was always an unspoken agreement that *I* could get to know *them,* but *they* weren't allowed to get to know *me,*" she says. Before, when her friends saw that Dana was depressed and asked her what was wrong, she would say "Nothing." If they persisted, she would swear at them. Now when they asked her what was wrong, Dana would start to say "Nothing" but catch herself and say "I don't know." "It was a start," admits Dana. "After a while they'd say 'What's wrong?' and eventually I'd be able to tell them."

Dana soon had a true test of her progress when her father came to Four Winds. Although he had often been in New York on business, he had never visited Dana during any of her hospitalizations. They had never talked about her suicide attempts or her therapy. He had phoned her occasionally, but their conversations were so stilted she stopped accepting calls. In the weeks before his visit Dana worked in therapy on being open with her father. In psychodrama the instructor made her and another patient, who played her father, sit back-to-back—"because you two never face each other." "Dana, how are your grades?" her "father" would say. "Fine," said Dana. The instructor would stop her, and they would try again. "Dana, how are your grades?" "I'm not doing well." "Why not?" "'Cause I'm not studying much." Gradually, Dana was able to be more open about her treatment and her plans for the future. But as the day of her father's visit approached, she was terrified.

When her father and his wife arrived, Dana gave them a quick tour of Four Winds. "They'd already eaten dinner at the hotel, but they took me to a diner so I could have a hamburger," she says. "I was very nervous. I had never said a word to my father about my drinking, but I told him I was an alcoholic and

I was going to AA five times a week. I told him about my treatment. I told him I had problems getting close to people. I told him about all the things Terry and I were working on, and when I finished, he said, 'Well, that's good. I took you to dinner to tell you I'm moving to Japan.'" Dana was crushed, but she kept her composure while they had coffee. After they dropped her off at Four Winds, she rushed down to the smoking room and wept.

The following day she and her father met with Terry for a therapy session. Terry told her father some of the reasons Dana felt she couldn't relate to him. Her father nodded thoughtfully, and when Terry had finished, he admitted that it was difficult for him to talk about feelings because he hadn't been brought up to do so. "But you two need to talk to each other," said Terry. "Do you think you could try?" "Sure, we can try," said Mr. Evans.

As she walked her father to his car, Dana said, "There's something else you don't know." She rolled up her sleeves and showed him her arms, criss-crossed with scars. "I used to cut myself," she said. "Oh," he said. "Well, thank you for telling me." There was an awkward silence, and Dana said she had better get back to the group. They said good-bye, and Dana went inside.

"It could have been worse," Dana says now. "I was worried he'd just say 'I've had it with you.' And though he didn't say 'Please get well,' he never said 'I don't care about you.' For him that was something—that he said we'd try."

---

That spring Dana continued to open up. In therapy, as she and her mother began to talk about her mother's work, about her boyfriends, about Dana's leg, and about the divorce, they became more understanding of each other's struggles. At AA meetings Dana began to take an active role, making the coffee, setting up chairs, participating in discussions. "I was actually letting a few people get to know me a little bit," says Dana. "It was terrifying. I had never trusted anybody. I always thought if I told someone something, they'd print it in the local paper. Terry told me I had to risk it." Dana and Lucy became even closer. "I would tell her something that I thought would be embarrassing, and she would say, 'Oh, I did that, too.'" In April, Dana was scheduled to have major surgery to replace her kneecap. She was so afraid the operation would fail that she couldn't talk about it in group. But a few nights before the operation Dana went to Lucy and said, "I'm terrified." It was the first time she had ever admitted to anyone that she could be frightened. On the eve of the operation Lucy stayed up all night with her.

Dana spent three weeks in a hospital in Manhattan. She thought that while she was away, they would forget about her at Four Winds, but Terry called her every day. A staff social worker visited her three times a week. Every so often the unit nurse would call on the ward phone, and the patients would take turns talking to her. One day a friend from the ward walked into her room. "What are you doing here?" asked Dana. Then Nan, the head nurse, entered, followed by

Lucy. They wheeled Dana down to the solarium. "There were fifteen people out there!" says Dana. "Half the unit! I couldn't believe it. It was great! I figured I wouldn't see those people for three weeks. They didn't tell me they were coming down. They'd posted a sign-up sheet—'Sign up if you want to see Dana'— so no one *forced* them to go." She smiles. "More people wanted to go, but there wasn't enough room."

In May 1984, two months after Brian Hart's death, Dana was discharged from Four Winds.

# VI

# "Use the Enclosed Order Form to Act Immediately. You Could Save a Life"

---

ON A SPRING MORNING two years after Justin Spoonhour's death, George Cohen walked into a social studies classroom at White Plains High School carrying a slide projector and a tape recorder. Setting them on a desk, he pulled a white screen down from the row of furled maps above the blackboard. The bell rang. While Cohen set up his projector, a stream of tenth graders flooded the room. He observed them for a moment before asking for quiet. Cohen, a middle-aged man, was dressed in a brown tweed jacket and striped tie, but his mop of dark, curly hair, pudgy face, and ready grin gave him a rumpled, informal look. "I've asked your teacher to let me come in and talk to you today," he said. "I'm here for two reasons. The first reason is that the problem of teenage suicide has grown tremendously. Three times as many kids kill themselves today as when I was in high school. The second reason is that everyone in this room can do something about it."

Cohen began his program with a sixteen-minute slide show describing the extent of teenage suicide, the warning signs of depression, and how to help in a crisis. As the slides progressed, some of the students watched intently. One girl took notes as furiously as she chewed her gum. Others were less attentive— a girl whispered to a friend at the next desk, a boy studied his history book, a

111

girl fished a compact from her purse and began meticulously to apply eye shadow. Gradually, however, the whispering stopped; the boy looked up from his homework, the girl abandoned her makeup. Soon the only sound in the room was the voice of the narrator and the click of the slide projector.

The slide show offered some basic information about suicide and its prevention. Suicides rarely happen out of the blue; experts say four of five people who kill themselves leave clues to their plans. Some clues are behavioral—giving away prized possessions, for example. If someone gives his watch or music collection to a friend, he may be trying to say good-bye. Other clues are verbal. When someone says "You won't be seeing me around anymore" or "The world would be better off without me," he may be thinking of suicide.

Although there are few precise indications of when a depressed adolescent will turn to suicide, there are signs that suggest when an adolescent is experiencing depression severe enough to warrant concern: sudden changes in behavior (for instance, when someone who takes great pride in his appearance neglects himself); dramatic changes in appetite; sudden weight gain or loss; sleeping difficulties (insomnia or a desire to sleep all the time); poor performance in school; trouble concentrating; unexplained lethargy or fatigue; loss of interest in friends, hobbies, or social activities; increased drug or alcohol use; constant feelings of worthlessness or self-hatred; excessive risk-taking; a philosophical preoccupation with death, dying, or suicide.

When the slide show was over, Cohen paced in front of the class. "After seeing this, what feelings are you left with?" he asked. "Sad," said a girl sitting in the front row. Cohen nodded. "How many of you have known someone who has thought about or attempted suicide?" Eleven of twenty students raised their hands. "What was it like?" he asked. "It was scary," said another girl. "You'd worry about her every minute, wondering whether or not she would do it." Another girl added, "It was confusing because it seemed like she had everything she wanted. I couldn't understand why she would want to do that." Cohen turned to the girl who had been putting on makeup. "Did you know her?" he asked. "What was it like for you?" The girl looked up. "I didn't believe her," she said. "Why?" asked Cohen. "Because she came right out and said she was going to do it." Heads nodded agreement. "That's the toughest part—knowing whether they really mean it or not," said a boy in the back who had seemed to sleep through the film. "They may just be trying to get attention," someone murmured. Cohen looked up. "Sometimes people will joke about it—'Man, I'm gonna kill myself,'" he said. "But it's important to ask, 'Are you serious?'" Too often, he told them, out of uneasiness or fear, a friend may laugh off a plea or ignore a clue. And one of the biggest myths about suicide is that people who talk about it won't do it. "It's very important to take them seriously."

Cohen had an easygoing, cheerful manner, and he quickly established a rapport with the students. He always asked a student his name; the next time that student raised his hand, Cohen remembered it. "What do you say to someone who has told you he's thinking of killing himself?" Cohen asked the class. "I'd say, 'Let's go get help,'" suggested one boy. "I'd ask why," said a girl. "That's good," said Cohen. "Depressed people feel hopeless, and one of the things they need most is someone to listen." A girl with hoop earrings said, "I would tell her that I care about her." Cohen nodded. "Yes, it's important to let them know that you care," he said. "And there's something else I'd like you to tell them. I'd like you to tell them, 'Don't do it.' Sometimes people have made their decision, but they need to hear someone who cares say no.

"What if a friend makes you promise to keep a secret, and then he tells you he's going to kill himself? What do you do?" After a moment of silence a young man spoke up: "I'd tell somebody and get help anyway. If that person is a true friend, you'd care enough to want to keep him around." Another boy nodded. "It's someone's *life*," he said. "You keep a secret when it's about a boyfriend or a girlfriend, but not when it's someone's life." Some of the kids worried that breaking a promise might anger their friend, but they nodded agreement when Cohen said, "It's better to have a live angry friend than a dead one."

Cohen asked the students to whom they would turn for help, and the students named the school nurse, school counselor, and school social workers. Cohen mentioned the two school psychologists; not one of the students had heard of them or knew where their offices were. When Cohen suggested parents, the kids chuckled and shook their heads. "They'd just get hysterical," said one girl. "What would they say?" asked Cohen. A girl sitting in back affected a high, shrill voice: "Oh, *my* baby wouldn't do that." The class burst into laughter. "Yes, you may get a lot of denial," said Cohen, "but it's a good idea to talk to the parents because they have the responsibility." Cohen also suggested the local suicide hotline. He passed out a list of warning signs and resource numbers and asked if there were any more questions. "Thank you for letting me talk to you," said Cohen. "If anyone wants to talk more, let me or your teacher know." The bell rang, chairs scraped on linoleum, and the students rushed out to their next class.

Two or three times a week Cohen, a human relations specialist with the White Plains Public Schools, brought his projector to classrooms, auditoriums, church basements, and libraries throughout Westchester County to talk to teenagers, teachers, social workers, and parents about suicide. His thirty-nine-minute program, designed to fit into a high school period, was sponsored by the Westchester County Mental Health Association Interagency Task Force on Adolescent Depression and Suicide, of which Cohen was chairperson. The group's imposing name belied the modesty of its operation. It was formed in 1979 after two suicides and five attempts in five months at the same high school in Chappaqua left Westchester County health professionals realizing how little they knew about the subject. The Task Force, an unpaid volunteer group of teachers, counselors, and therapists, began meeting regularly. Although

Westchester had one of the largest mental health budgets per capita of any county in the nation, it had no specific suicide prevention program directed at adolescents. In the fall of 1982 the Task Force began offering this program, free of charge, to high schools in the county. While some schools welcomed the program, the Task Force met resistance from administrators who believed that talking about suicide would only encourage a youngster to commit it. Others felt that suicide prevention was not the school's responsibility; it was a family matter. Others feared that if students were exposed to the program, teachers and counselors would be overwhelmed with students wanting to talk about their troubles. Some said there was simply no need for the program; in *their* school, suicide was not a problem.

In 1984, as the "Westchester suicides" made headlines, demand for the program soared. Many of the schools that had been reluctant were suddenly eager. As far as Cohen knew, none of the students who had seen the program had completed suicide. "But even if a youngster went out and killed himself after seeing it," he told me, "I wouldn't back away from the program because I know a lot of youngsters are getting help because of it." After almost every program, while he was putting away the projector, a student would approach Cohen to tell him about a friend she was worried about or about her own suicidal thoughts. "One night at ten I got a call from a girl who had seen the program in class. She said, 'I have a friend in the next room who wrote a note that says she's going to kill herself.' I told her to keep her friend there, and I was able to get over and talk to the kid and get her into the hospital. Today, I see that kid walking around the streets of White Plains, and I feel terrific. Without the program I'm not sure her friend would have known what to do."

———

While Cohen's presentation may seem tame, it would have been unthinkable fifteen years earlier. At that time, although there were three hundred suicide prevention centers across the country, there were no programs aimed at younger people. Prevention was geared toward adults, whose rate was highest. In a 1969 article on reducing adolescent suicide, recommendations made by suicide "experts" ranged from the suggestion that students be "encouraged to participate in extracurricular activities" to increasing "the relevance of education to the modern world." No one broached the idea of actually educating teenagers about suicide—that, it was assumed, would be too dangerous. Many schools prohibited talking about suicide in any context; the only mention of it might occur in English class when the students read *Hamlet* or Hemingway. If a student completed suicide, teachers were expressly forbidden by school administrators to discuss it with students. It was simply not a school matter; these were "crazy kids"—they must be, or why would they kill themselves?

In 1974, a decade before the "Westchester suicides," eleven teenagers killed themselves in San Mateo County, a string of bedroom communities south of San Francisco. Today it would be called a cluster. At the time it wasn't called anything; as was the case elsewhere, schools generally hushed up the deaths. Charlotte Ross, director of the Suicide Prevention and Crisis Center of San Mateo County, found that all eleven teenagers had left clues recognizable to people with training in suicide prevention. Over several days, for example, a sixteen-year-old asked his teacher, "Do you have to be crazy to kill yourself?", wrote the word *death* across the back of his hand, and one morning told a friend he was "going to heaven very soon." That day in class the boy slipped a revolver from a brown paper bag and killed himself.

Later that year Ross attended a World Health Organization conference that asserted that suicide among youth had reached "epidemic" proportions. Ross returned from that meeting determined to try a new approach to preventing adolescent suicide. Adapting the program she used to train her hotline volunteers, she went into the schools and trained teachers to recognize and respond to signs of depression and suicide. She found that students were crying out for help but not getting it. Teachers were dealing with suicide threats and attempts more and more frequently but had never been told what to do. They were terrified of responding to veiled suicidal messages for fear of putting the idea into a student's head. "We had cases where an English teacher would receive an essay on suicide and return it to the student corrected for grammar," said Ross, who taught the teachers not to be afraid to ask specifically about suicide.

The program worked. Teachers reported increased confidence in dealing with the subject, and there were more calls to the prevention center from adolescents as well as from teachers and administrators asking for advice. But training teachers didn't reach the heart of the problem. In a survey of 120 high school students asking to whom they would turn in a suicidal crisis, 109 said they would turn first to a friend. Parents were perceived as part of the problem, "unable to understand, but able to interfere," observed Ross, while guidance counselors were for "getting you into college." Ross decided to go into the classrooms to teach students themselves about warning signs, depression, and how to help one another.

Spurred by anxiety over the adolescent suicide "epidemic," suicide prevention in the schools soon reached epidemic proportions. All across the United States, social workers and counselors went into health classes and assemblies to teach students, teachers, administrators, and parents about suicide. A slew of pamphlets, films, slide shows, seminars, and curricula on adolescent suicide were developed. Public service announcements on radio and television, featuring Bette Midler, Mariette Hartley, and Nancy Reagan, urged teenagers to choose life ("If you have suicide on your mind, wait a minute. I'm Mariette Hartley . . ."). Largely through Ross's efforts, in 1983, California became the first state to mandate suicide prevention programs in schools. Several other states quickly followed suit. By 1986 there were more than a hundred school-based programs in the United States, reaching an estimated 180,000 students. Mark Fisher, former director of the Suicide and Crisis Center in Dallas, could have been describing most of these programs when he said, "Our goal is to help youngsters, sometime during junior high or high school, learn the warning signs of suicide in the same way they would learn the warning signs of an impending heart attack, and come up with sort of an emotional CPR: that when you know someone who's suicidal or you recognize suicidal things in yourself, you know exactly what to do—the people to contact and the resources available."

The programs ranged from free, one-shot presentations like George Cohen's to the "comprehensive" curriculum offered by the South Bergen Mental Health Center in New Jersey, in which teachers and school personnel, then parents, and finally the students themselves were trained over several months. While most programs were aimed at high school students, a clinic in Plainville, Connecticut, trained high schoolers to teach and counsel students down to the fifth grade about suicide prevention. The Dayton, Ohio, Suicide Prevention Center performed puppet shows about death and dying for elementary school children. Although the shows did not deal specifically with suicide, the topic often came up in discussion. ("Children with a clearer understanding of the nature of death may be expected to choose suicide as a less attractive behavior during a time of depression or agitation in their lives," concluded two assistant professors at Wright State University in a monograph on the puppet show.) On Chicago's North Shore, where twenty-eight suicides in seventeen months beginning in 1978 brought it the title The Suicide Belt, young social workers were dispatched to school and community hangouts—smoking lounges, gymnasiums, hamburger joints—to meet with kids on their own turf. A prevention center in Ithaca, New York, sent its young counselors into local high schools, where they hung out in the gym, cafeteria, and carpentry shop and made themselves available to any students who wanted to talk. Several prevention centers sponsored telephone hotlines on which teenagers counseled teenagers, while others offered group therapy in which suicidal adolescents met weekly with a psychologist or social worker to discuss parents, schools, friends, drugs, sex, and suicide. In Westchester County several teenagers who had attempted suicide performed skits about suicide at area high schools, then led discussions. Another Westchester County prevention organization helped students act out key scenes from *Romeo and Juliet,* encouraging them to write alternative, nonsuicidal endings. A California group developed suicide-prevention-themed video games.

The array of options was bewildering. I recall attending a conference sponsored by the American Association of Suicidology at which a table near the registration desk was stacked with brochures hawking dozens of mail-order curricula appealing to a range of budgets. For $6.60, William Steele offered *Preventing Teenage Suicide* ("A must for every parent and those who work with teenagers"), a workbook that included "rating scales, assessment guides, guided discussions, actual situations, role-playing scripts, methods of communicating and helping, quizzes about suicidal issues, situations and the suicidal person." For $48.95, a Denver psychologist marketed *Youth in Crisis,* an "action manual" that "motivates the reader to become a community leader in youth suicide prevention" and was "presented in a durable, attractive three-ring binder allowing for reproduction of various forms and instruments provided." For $150, Southwest Associates, Inc. Management Resources/Nexus Plans, an affiliate of Netcare Corporation, advised me to "Order Your Copy Today" of its manual, which would help me develop and institute "a comprehensive school-based and community program for preventing the *Number Two Killer* of our Teenagers today—SUICIDE." (In its excitement, Southwest Associates, Inc., miscalculated; suicide was—and is—the *third* leading cause of death for teenagers.) For $395, LexCom Productions of Columbia, South Carolina, offered "a sensitive, insightful two-part video series" with "vivid slice-of-life vignettes." The company urged me to "use the enclosed order form to act immediately. You could save a life."

While no doubt well intentioned, the programs were unsettling. They held out the promise that a recipe existed for preventing suicide and that *they* knew the ingredients. As a culture, we had gone from a time when no one talked about suicide to a time when virtually any talk about it was considered good. Schools without programs were deemed "neolithic" and "resistant." Wrote Westchester psychiatrist Samuel Klagsbrun, "Any school administrator that stands in the way of an intelligent adolescent suicide program, which includes a healthy discussion with teenagers, has to be able to live with death on his or her hands." But what was an intelligent program? In the field of suicide prevention, mere good intentions were often taken as the litmus test of worth, though few of these programs had been evaluated and their effectiveness depended largely on who taught them. And while most programs revolved around teaching the warning signs, a few maverick educators took other approaches—one of which seemed to have more in common with the tactics used at Miletos in 500 BC than with those used in George Cohen's classroom.

Convinced that the rise in adolescent suicide was due in large part to a romanticized conception of death and self-destruction, Victor Victoroff, chief of psychiatry at Huron Road Hospital in Cleveland, decided to show teenagers what he called "the real face of suicide." In his presentations to high schools, Victoroff showed graphic color slides of young people who had come to emergency rooms following suicide attempts: a girl whose stomach was being pumped; a girl with slit wrists; a boy whose face had been blown away by a gunshot. He displayed the suture kits used to sew up wounds, the tracheotomy kits used to cut new air holes for breathing, the tubes used to pump stomachs. He handed out a "suicide packet" that contained a card bearing the phone number of the local suicide hotline and a cotton pad soaked in ipecac. "I ask them to smell the ipecac—it really stinks—and I tell them, 'This is what we pour down people's throats after an overdose,'" Victoroff told me. "I make it clear that being treated for a suicide attempt is likely to be one of the more unpleasant experiences a person may have to endure. I explain how many attempters end up half-blind or paralyzed. I want them to know that playing around with suicide is a dangerous game." At this point, after offering squeamish audience members a chance to leave—"few do," he said—Victoroff showed slides of completed suicides on the autopsy table: examples of suicide by strangulation, stabbing, poisoning, electrocution, asphyxiation, and gunshot. He concluded his presentation by asking everyone in the audience to "kill themselves." "I get out a clock and say, 'Now we're all going to commit suicide. I want you to hold your breath for thirty seconds.' As they hold their breath, I tell them that they are lying in bed. They have taken pills and the poison is beginning to work. Then I tell them they have four minutes left before they lose consciousness and die." Victoroff paused. "The point is that I'll use any means I can to cut through the romantic haze that sometimes surrounds suicide. I want the students to know that suicide is not romantic at all. It's hard and dirty, and it involves a lot of heartache and agony." By the time I spoke with him, Victoroff estimated that he had made his presentation to ten or fifteen thousand adolescents. "And until somebody tells me what I'm doing is wrong," he told me, "I'm going to continue."

Who could say whether Victoroff's scare tactics or Cohen's touchy-feely approach worked better—or whether any of these programs worked at all? Although there was anecdotal evidence of their efficacy—Victoroff, for instance, told me that over the years he had received a stack of letters from would-be suicides thanking him for dissuading them from their plans—there were few objective evaluations. And although a rising tide of opinion suggested that talking about suicide was the best prevention, some people worried that programs promoting openness about suicide might in fact encourage it by making the act seem less forbidden. They pointed to the drug education programs of the early seventies, which did not markedly affect the drug abuse problem. In one of the first rigorous evaluations of suicide prevention efforts, Columbia University psychiatrist David Shaffer studied the effects of three different programs in New Jersey high schools. While there was no evidence that the programs caused wide distress, neither was there widespread attitude change, though a few students who were already suicidal became even *more* upset after being exposed to the program. Calculating that the number of students who might be saved by such programs was minuscule, Shaffer concluded that their possible benefits were outweighed by their possible harm. "I believe there should be a moratorium on suicide awareness programs directed at students," he told a stunned audience at the 1988 annual meeting of the American Association of Suicidology.

Distorted and magnified by the media ("Do-Gooders to Rescue Again, but Are They Killing Your Kids?" was the headline in the *Palm Beach Post*), Shaffer's broadside had a dramatic effect. "The negative publicity set us back ten years," says Diane Ryerson, founder of the South Bergen program and former director of the AAS Prevention Division, who has trained more than two hundred schools and mental health agencies in suicide prevention. "People were suddenly afraid to implement programs, schools didn't want to get involved, and we couldn't get money to evaluate the programs that already existed. People began to question whether we *should* be talking about suicide in the schools at all." Despite efforts by prevention movement veterans to "de-Shafferize" schools, as one of them puts it, many smaller, less established programs folded, including George Cohen's Westchester Interagency Task Force, whose sponsors suddenly began to worry that the program might inspire copycat suicides.

Emboldened by Shaffer's outspokenness, other critics surfaced. Some claimed that school programs often used inaccurate or exaggerated data. Others faulted them for being unable to reach certain high-risk populations: runaways, dropouts, the incarcerated. Others fretted that programs placed an unreasonable burden on young people and suggested they train community "gatekeepers"—police, clergy, coaches, physicians—instead. A study of 115 school-based programs found that most consisted of a brief, onetime lecture on the warning signs, in which suicide was portrayed as a response to extreme stress that, given sufficient pressure, could happen to anyone. Only 4 percent of the programs mentioned that suicide is usually linked to a psychiatric disorder. "By deemphasizing or denying that most adolescents who commit suicide are mentally ill, these programs misrepresent the facts," warned a blistering 1993 report in *American Psychologist*. "In their attempt to destigmatize suicide in this way they may be, in fact, normalizing the behavior and reducing potentially protective taboos." A 1994 CDC summary of programs recommended forging closer links between prevention programs and existing community mental health resources, increasing attention on young adults (a group at far higher risk than teenagers), encouraging parents to restrict their children's access to lethal means, and integrating suicide material into broad-based adolescent health curricula rather than running suicide-specific programs. While admitting that there was no evidence that prevention programs actually *contributed* to suicidal behavior, a 1998 survey found "no justification" for them.

It is likely that school suicide prevention programs are neither so harmful as their detractors claim nor as beneficial as their most passionate advocates suggest. In the past few years, however, several studies of comprehensive, carefully considered, second-generation programs have found that they influenced attitudes toward suicide, made troubled students and their friends more likely to seek help, and even contributed to a reduction of suicidal behavior. A 2004 study of twenty-one hundred students in Connecticut and Georgia who had taken the SOS High School Suicide Prevention Program, which combines screening for depression with education about suicide and mental illness, found that those who had gone through the program were 40 percent less likely to have attempted suicide over the following three months than a control group. "Shaffer has perpetrated a myth that programs are harmful—and there's no basis for that," says John Kalafat, a psychologist at Rutgers University who studied countywide programs in New Jersey and Florida and found significant reductions in youth suicide rates following the programs that did not occur either nationally or elsewhere in those states. Encouraged by these findings, programs are beginning to return to the classroom. Several states—Colorado, Washington, Maine, and Florida—are developing comprehensive prevention curricula. Shaffer himself, suggesting that programs emphasize "case finding," has developed TeenScreen, in which high schoolers fill out a brief questionnaire asking them about suicide risk factors; if the responses indicate that he or she may be at risk, the student then fills out a "comprehensive" computerized mental health evaluation. The results are reviewed by a clinician who interviews the student and decides whether he or she should be referred for treatment. TeenScreen is now used by schools and clinics in thirty-four states. Critics of the program point out that the vast majority of students in distress— 78 percent according to one study—turn first to peers and are reluctant to confide in an adult, albeit an adult disguised as a questionnaire. They also suspect that, given the notorious mood swings of adolescence, a onetime test might allow many troubled teens to slip through the cracks. "Teens may be suicidal tomorrow but not today," as Ryerson puts it.

Whatever the approach, the tragic nature of adolescent suicide makes it likely that there will always be programs for its prevention. Following the suicide of their seventeen-year-old son, Mike, in 1994, a Colorado couple, Dale and Dar Emme, acknowledging that Mike had been in trouble but hadn't known how to ask for help, printed up cards with the message *It's OK to Ask4Help!* on one side and information on where to find help on the other. Thus began the Yellow Ribbon Suicide Prevention Program, in which the Emmes and other "trainers" talk to schools and communities about depression and suicide, hand out Yellow Ribbon cards, urge parents and kids to wear the yellow ribbon, and (for $10) sell Link, a nine-inch stuffed toy bear sporting a yellow ribbon on his chest and an "Ask-for-Help" card in his backpack, "to let you know you are NEVER alone." The Emmes estimate that they have trained over two hundred thousand people, and Yellow Ribbon now has chapters in all fifty states and forty-eight other countries. "More than **2,500** LIVES HAVE BEEN SAVED!" proclaims its Web site. "5 MILLION Yellow Ribbon Cards have been distributed. 42,000 letters asking for help & telling of lives saved have been received. . . . Why do prevention programs in schools and communities? *Because they work!*"

# VII

# BEGINNING TO CLOSE
# THE DOOR

---

TWO YEARS AFTER being discharged from Four Winds, Dana Evans was
on the dean's list at a local community college. She hadn't taken a drink or
used drugs during that time. She attended three AA meetings a week and had
started a chapter at school. She had told several friends that she was an alcoholic, one or two friends that she was in a psychiatric hospital, and no one
about her suicide attempts. She was living at home. She and her mother were
getting along better. "We're not best friends or anything, but it's okay. We talk
about work and school. Sometimes we even share makeup."

When I met Dana, she looked like a different person from the one she was
in her drinking days. She was slim, pretty, and neatly dressed. Although she
was witty and sharp, able to make others laugh easily, her own laughter came
self-consciously, and her defensiveness and anger occasionally flared. Her
biggest problem, she told me, was loneliness. She had few friends at college,
and though she remained close to some of her Four Winds friends, she spent
much of her time by herself. "I've still got a long way to go. It takes a long time
to break an eighteen-year habit. At Four Winds, when Terry and I started working on how to relate to people, I was at ground zero. And in two and a half
years you don't exactly become proficient at making bosom buddies. But it's
only going to get better as my confidence grows and I get more used to
doing things and not caring so much about what people think." Dana laughed.
"'Cause I still care what Joe Schmo thinks, and who the hell is he? I don't even
know him!"

In the first few months after Brian's death, Mary Hart visited her son's grave several times a day. It helped her to stand there and talk to him. "I could say things to him, and he couldn't talk back." Sometimes she would shout at him, "Why did you do this, you dumb kid? Why?" For a long time she and her husband believed that if Brian had taken his medication regularly, he would still be alive. While her husband kept his feelings more to himself, Mary felt an endless, restless need to talk about Brian's death. The weight of his suicide threatened to crush her. "One day I found myself in the garage thinking all I have to do is to trip this button and close the garage door, and I'd be asleep, too."

Mary and Pat began seeing a therapist, and gradually Mary's rage and frustration dissipated. "I had been looking for Brian around every corner. It was hard for me to say, 'This is the end,' but after awhile I realized that this was his choosing and there was nothing more. The therapist helped me begin to close the door."

Nevertheless, there were unexpected reminders: going down to the cellar to fetch something and coming across Brian's skis; looking through her recipe file and finding a note in Brian's handwriting on the back of one: "Ma, I've gone to the mall to look for some Christmas gifts"; waking at four in the morning and feeling the need to pore over the roster of people at Brian's wake. She continued to visit Brian's grave several times a week, but when she spoke to him, she was more gentle. "I talk about the things we'll never know—what he would have looked like, what his children would have been like, what he might have done. And about the pain he must have gone through . . . and how much I wish we could have understood that pain more."

Two years after their son's death, Sandy Martin, Brian's English teacher at Anderson, sent the Harts some snapshots she had taken of Brian. As they looked at them, the Harts realized that these were probably the last new photographs they would ever see of their son. Pat hung one of them in the Rogues' Gallery, a picture of Brian in a bright red polo shirt, flashing a broad smile.

---

"Whatever caused Justin Spoonhour's death, we all had a part in it," Lora Porter, the Putnam Valley librarian, told me. "We failed him by not raising our children to be kinder to one another. Do you remember that line from *South Pacific*? 'You've got to be carefully taught to hate.' Well, the same thing applies to love. You've got to be taught to love and respect, and I don't think we do that enough."

With money donated by members of the library board, Porter ordered some special animal puppets and sewed labels on them that said JUSTIN'S PUP-

PETS. Having worked with hundreds of children over the years, Porter was surprised at the hold Justin's memory had on her. In her heart of hearts she still thought of his death as an accident, although her head told her it wasn't. If Justin could only have survived adolescence, Porter believed, he would have blossomed. "He was just marking his time through childhood. In another few years he would have graduated high school and been out on his own. I think he would have come into his own when he became an adult. And I would like so much to have known him when he grew up. I would have liked to have him as a friend. The world needs people like Justin. There are too many pedestrians. Justin could fly."

On the day after Justin's suicide his English class was due to read aloud the scene in which Julius Caesar is killed. As they began, the irony stunned the class for a moment, but no one said anything. The teacher took over the role of Caesar, and they finished the play as quickly as they could. In the first few days two dozen junior high school students saw guidance counselors; the second week, only a few sought help, and by the third week, recalled one administrator, things were "back to normal." "Nobody talked about it," said a student. "He was just crossed off the attendance list, everyone was careful not to mention his name, and it was like that was that."

There were a few official observances. At the spring concert the chorus director played Beethoven's "Ode to Joy" in Justin's memory. His class dedicated its yearbook, *Tiger '84,* to him: under the lyrics of "Perhaps Love" there were four photographs of Justin, including curmudgeonly poses from *Scrooge* and *Outrageous Fortune,* as well as his formal graduation portrait. The caption read, "Putnam Valley Junior High deeply regrets the loss of Justin Spoonhour." At graduation Justin's name was not mentioned. On the first anniversary of his death teachers were reminded to be particularly alert in case students remembered the date and were upset. But no one mentioned it or came to the counselors for help. And yet a visitor to the cemetery that day found that some children had left notes and flowers on Justin's grave.

"I'm not sure a school ever gets over something like this," Superintendent Richard Brodow says. "It's something you always remember, and you *should* always remember because it lets us know how vulnerable we are." Brodow's forthright handling of the tragedy was praised by parents and teachers, and over the following year, when other schools in the area experienced suicides, they turned to him for advice. Brodow wrote about Justin's suicide in a short essay, which begins with a quote from Jean Giraudoux: "Out of the heart of darkness comes the light." Brodow firmly believed that the school learned something from the tragedy. "Certainly there is more awareness and sensitivity on everyone's part for youngsters who have difficulty." But the next year, after Justin's classmates had moved on to high school, the new ninth graders found another outcast to pick on—teasing him, calling him names, urinating in his locker.

Mike LoPuzzo saved all the newspaper clippings about his friend's death. He attended all the town meetings on suicide, sitting near the front, listening attentively. Although at first he thought that Justin had killed himself because of the teasing, Mike realized that couldn't be the entire answer—Justin had endured it all his life. "He didn't leave us a note. He didn't want to make it easy for us. He wanted to leave us with questions. He wanted us to think about it. Maybe he was saying, 'Take a look at yourselves.'"

Two years after Justin's death Diana Wolf was surprised to find herself thinking of her former classmate once more. "I wear contact lenses, and sometimes I have problems with them and have to use glasses. And when I wear them, I don't like the way I look at all. One day at school I was wearing glasses and I was feeling bad. I didn't like the way my hair had come out, I wasn't wearing flattering clothes, and I was feeling fat and ugly. In English class some kids were being snotty to me, and in social studies my regular work partner wasn't there. Usually I'm pretty popular, but this time I couldn't find anyone to be my partner, and I felt terrible.

"After school I was walking home alone from the bus. It was a damp, drizzly day. I felt lonely and pretty miserable because I just hadn't fit in. It was the worst feeling, that not fitting in. I was really depressed. But I went home and took off those glasses. I showered, put on some different clothes, and managed to get my lenses back in. I felt so much better just because I accepted myself again. And then I suddenly thought, 'What I felt like for one day is what Justin must have felt like all the time.'"

Anne and Giles Spoonhour quickly tried to put their son's death behind them. Two days after the funeral they kept their appointment to speak at Justin's Youth Group about their emergency services work. They talked for almost two hours to the children about how to handle a crisis, what resources were available, and so on—without once breaking down. Early on, Anne made a conscious decision not to look back. "My thinking was, 'It can't be undone, no matter who did it or why. Now what are you going to do? Let's get on with it.'" She threw herself into her work as police dispatcher, became a member of the volunteer fire department, worked as steward chairman of the church, and wrote long letters to the local newspaper about community issues. But each night when she went to bed, the first thing she saw when she closed her eyes was the image of her son hanging from the tree.

While Anne struggled to look ahead, Giles seemed unable not to look back. Each morning at seven he would start into Justin's room to wake up his son for school, and then he'd remember. Each evening when he came home from work and heard the neighborhood children playing in the yard, he waited to hear his son's voice. Although he tried to keep control, he felt broken with pain and confusion. "I was angry at Justin for not feeling comfortable enough to talk with me or with Anne. I was a little angry at Leah and Anne for not noticing it. And I was angry at myself because as a counselor, as a professional, I'm supposed to be able to pick up on things like that." Occasionally his anger exploded. Conflicts that had existed in his marriage all along were brought to the surface by Justin's suicide. Three months after their son's death, Giles and Anne began seeing a counselor, who told them that 60 percent of the parents of an adolescent suicide eventually divorce.

Leah had sessions with the school psychologist and with Anne and Giles in their therapy. She didn't talk much to her parents about her brother's suicide, and they didn't force the issue. But Anne and Giles tried to watch her more closely without making their worry obvious. They went out of their way to chauffeur her to meetings and friends' houses whenever possible. They didn't like her to be alone at home, and since her brother's death, neither did she. Anne felt uncomfortable in the house, too. "When I got off work late at night or went out on a call at midnight, I didn't like seeing the damn trees in the dark. I guess I've sort of turned against trees. I've decided I like sky, a lot of sky." Within a year of Justin's death they moved to a house on the other side of Putnam Valley. "Anne and Leah didn't want to stay in the old house because the memories of Justin were so strong," says Giles. "I would have *preferred* to stay because the memories were so strong."

One of the ways Anne and Giles tried to work through their grief was by talking about it. The week after Justin's death Anne got a call from a television station in New York asking for an interview. She said yes. "I thought I may as well make out of it what I could. Nothing was going to change the fact in this instance, but it might alter future instances." Over the following year she and Giles told their story to *People, Ladies' Home Journal,* the *New York Times, USA Today,* the *Donahue* show, the BBC, and more than sixty local newspapers and radio and television stations. They spoke at suicide prevention centers, churches, and high schools. Anne became a member of the New York State Council on Youth Suicide Prevention. At one presentation Giles was asked what advice he would give to parents. "Many teens don't like to be held, to be touched. But I encourage parents to hold, to show love physically. Touch the head," he said, almost involuntarily reaching out with hands that had been still for nearly an hour. "Put an arm around the shoulders—whatever seems comfortable. And even if it doesn't feel comfortable, do it anyway. Because the more you practice, the easier it gets."

Anne's and Giles's efforts in suicide prevention had a peculiar effect on the town of Putnam Valley. Despite the outpouring of concern immediately following Justin's suicide, the community seemed to put it quickly in the past. Two nights after the death, the meeting called by Richard Brodow at Putnam Valley Junior High was attended by more than 250 people. Two months later, when Anne Spoonhour called for a meeting on adolescent suicide prevention, only a dozen parents showed up. As Anne became increasingly involved in suicide prevention, some people in the community resented her efforts. In conversations at the library or at the grocery store there was talk that "enough is enough" and "let's not call attention to ourselves." Some worried that the Spoonhours were making Putnam Valley "the suicide capital of the world." A friend of Anne's who had helped her with her prevention work was stopped on the steps of the church one day by a prominent local citizen. "What are you people trying to do?" he demanded. "Win an Academy Award for Justin Spoonhour?" Although the Putnam Valley Mental Health Department beefed up its programs for adolescents, two years after Justin's death Putnam Valley still had no suicide prevention program in its classrooms. "What are we waiting for?" asked one mother. "Are we just going to sit back and wait till the next suicide?"

But something curious took place at the same time. Several years before Justin's death there had been another teenage suicide in Putnam Valley. A high school junior had walked into the woods and shot herself. Like every other suicide in Putnam Valley before Justin's, the death had been hushed up. "Nothing was said in school although everybody knew," recalled Lora Porter, whose son had been in the girl's class. "It was almost as if the entire town conspired to pretend it hadn't happened. Then when Anne and Giles chose to handle Justin's suicide by talking openly about it, I think they effected a catharsis for Colleen's group. As people began talking about Justin, Colleen's friends began talking about Colleen for the first time, saying that it was too bad she didn't have anyone to talk to, too bad no one saw what was happening to her. They had never had a chance to talk about it before. I don't know whether I would have had the courage to speak out the way Anne and Giles did, but I have often thought they did a very great service for this group of young people."

Two years after Justin's death the Spoonhours' house in Lookout Manor was empty. The grass was overgrown and the swing set was rusting in the backyard. An orange TOTFINDER sticker still clung to one window. On the mailbox the name SPOONHOUR was crossed out. Anne's father, who owned the house, was trying to sell it. He talked of going into the woods across the street and cutting down the tree from which Justin had hung, but Anne and Giles said no. They did not want to destroy a living thing.

# 2

# HISTORY

———◆———

# I

# PRIMITIVE ROOTS: THE ROCK OF THE FOREFATHERS

―――――

*Lo, my name reeks*
*Lo, more than carrion smell*
*On summer days of burning sky . . .*

*Lo, my name reeks*
*Lo, more than that of a sturdy child*
*Who is said to belong to one who rejects him . . .*

*To whom shall I speak today?*
*Brothers are mean,*
*One goes to strangers for affection . . .*

*To whom shall I speak today?*
*I am burdened with grief*
*For lack of an intimate . . .*

*Death is before me today*
*[Like] a sick man's recovery,*
*Like going outdoors after confinement . . .*

*Death is before me today*
*Like a man's longing to see his home*
*When he has spent many years in captivity.*

WRITTEN FOUR THOUSAND YEARS AGO in the first intermediate period
of the Middle Kingdom in Egypt, these lines are part of the first recorded reference to suicide. In "The Dispute Between a Man and His *Ba*," a man who is
tired of life and buffeted by bad luck considers killing himself. Angered by his
complaints, his soul, or *ba*, threatens to leave him. The man implores his *ba* to
remain, since to be abandoned by his soul would deprive him of an afterlife.
His *ba* urges him to enjoy life, to surrender himself to pleasure. These lines are
taken from the man's final answer, four poems in which he deplores the
greed and injustice of the times, laments his isolation, and speaks longingly of
death. In the end his *ba* agrees to stay; it is not clear whether the man goes on
to kill himself.

The seven sheets of papyrus that make up "Dispute" describe an interior
landscape not unlike that of almost any lonely, despairing person considering
suicide today. Just as Dana Evans invented insults to reinforce her self-
loathing, the anonymous Egyptian sings out his own curses: "Lo, my name
reeks / Lo, more than carrion smell." Just as Justin Spoonhour was overwhelmed by the cruelty of the world around him, the Egyptian is stung by the
indifference of society: "I am burdened with grief / For lack of an intimate." His
final words to his *ba*, in fact, perfectly articulate the internal journey of a suicidal person: from loss of self-esteem, to despair of finding surcease from pain,
to a conception of death as a refuge—"Like a man's longing to see his home
/ When he has spent many years in captivity." From these seven sheets we can
trace an unbroken line of loneliness, dejection, and hopelessness that has been
common to suicidal people for four thousand years.

Yet if the interior landscape of the suicidal person has changed little over
four millennia, the way we view the act of suicide has varied widely. Today in
the Western world we think of suicide primarily as a psychiatric problem. We
study it, search for its causes, and struggle to prevent what we consider a tragic
and sometimes shameful act. The ancient Egyptian would have found this attitude puzzling. In his time and place earthly existence was considered a mere
prelude to blissful afterlife. Death was not an end but a beginning. There were
no social or religious prohibitions against suicide, and the Egyptian would certainly not have been considered mentally ill. For him suicide was not only an
acceptable escape from an intolerable life but a path to blessed immortality.
"Truly, he who is yonder will stand in the sun-bark," he tells his *ba*, "making
its bounty flow to the temples." During the turbulent period when "Dispute"
was written, suicide seems to have been frequent. In "The Admonitions of a
Sage," a popular story of the time, a wise man observes that suicide is so com-

mon the crocodiles are glutted with despairing people who have hurled themselves into the river.

Since the beginning of man, in all times and in all places, there has been suicide, but the way a culture judges its suicides varies from place to place and time to time, largely depending on how that culture views death. Attitudes have ranged from fierce condemnation and hostility to mild disapproval and tolerance, to acceptance, encouragement, and incorporation into the sociocultural system. If our ancient Egyptian had killed himself in pre-Christian Scandinavia, for example, he would have been guaranteed a place in Viking paradise. If he had taken his life during the Roman Empire, his death would have been honored as a glorious demonstration of his wisdom. If he had cut open his stomach in feudal Japan, he would have been praised as a man of principle. If he had killed himself in fifteenth-century Metz, however, his corpse would have been crammed into a barrel and floated down the Moselle. In seventeenth-century France his corpse would have been dragged through the streets, hanged upside down, then thrown on the public garbage heap. In seventeenth-century England his estate would have been forfeited to the crown and his body buried at a crossroads with a stake through the heart.

According to Christianity suicide was a sin against God and a crime against the state, and such punishments were designed to deter despairing people from its evil. These penalties (often waived if the suicide was deemed insane) gradually disappeared during the eighteenth and nineteenth centuries. The last recorded crossroads burial of an English suicide took place in 1823, when a man named Griffiths was interred at the intersection of Eaton Street, Grosvenor Place, and King's Road, London. By that time the scientific study of suicide had begun, and the question became not whether suicide was a sin or a crime but why it occurred. Gradually, suicide was seen not as a moral issue but as an act of pathology. Still, the rationality of science hardly dispelled the opprobrium attached to the act: In England, confiscation of a suicide's property was not abolished until 1870, and as late as 1955 a man was sentenced to two years in prison for trying to kill himself. Punishment for attempted suicide was finally abolished in 1961 when Parliament passed the Suicide Act. Even after that, moral outrage found legal approval. In 1969 an Isle of Man court ordered a teenager who had attempted suicide to be flogged.

———————

When John Roscoe, an English missionary, lived among the Baganda of central Africa for several years in the late nineteenth century, he found that the lives of the Baganda, like those of most primitive tribespeople, were circumscribed by an elaborate web of myths. "The Baganda were very superstitious about suicides," wrote the Reverend Mr. Roscoe. "They took innumerable precautions to remove the body and destroy the ghost, to prevent the latter from causing further trouble." Some of those precautions must have seemed familiar to the Englishman. After a suicide the body was taken "to a distant place where cross-roads met" and burned, in an attempt to destroy the ghost, using as fuel the tree or hut from which he had hanged himself. (People would not live in the hut in which a suicide had taken place for fear they might be tempted to follow suit.) When women passed the spot, they threw grass or twigs on the site to prevent the suicide's restless ghost from entering them and being reborn.

Contemporary historians suggest that Christian punishments of suicide echoed the purification rituals of primitive tribes. But the law that condemned Mr. Griffiths to burial at a London crossroads in 1823 was born of moral disgust, while the Baganda custom was born of fear that the suicide's ghost would return to impregnate young tribeswomen. (The same precautions were taken with the corpses of twins and of children born feetfirst.) In the former instance it was the act itself that provoked horror; in the latter it was the consequence of the act.

Primitive fear of the suicide's ghost stemmed in part from a general fear of the dead, especially of those who met a sudden or violent death. Their ghosts were considered particularly restless because of the desperate state of mind in which they left life. The soul had not made a smooth break; it was considered "unclean." Extensive purification rituals were performed to expiate the "blood guilt," to appease the ghost of the slain, and to dissuade it from haunting the living. Such precautions were crucial in the case of suicides, whose ghosts were notoriously malevolent. Not only had the suicide spilled blood, he had spilled family blood, which was even more "powerful." And while the ghost of a murdered man haunted only his murderer, the ghost of a suicide might seek revenge against an entire tribe, an entire world that had troubled him. In various cultures a suicide's ghost was believed to cause tempests, famine, hailstorms, or drought, or to make barren the earth that it touched.

Some tribes, therefore, like the Baganda, buried a suicide's corpse at a crossroads so that the ghost might not find its way home. In other tribes the corpse was mutilated or burned so that the suicide's spirit would be unable to "walk." In others the body was buried far from the graves of his kinsmen so that his soul might be quarantined. The Bannaus of Cambodia buried suicides in a corner of the forest; natives of Dahomey left the bodies of suicides in the fields to be devoured by wild beasts. And Alabama Indians threw them into the river. Among the Wajagga of East Africa, after a man hanged himself a goat was sacrificed with the same noose in hopes of mollifying the dead man's soul.

Such measures, it was hoped, would isolate the suicide's soul and render it unable to cause mischief. The Jakuts believed that the soul of a suicide never came to rest; the Omaha Indians believed that a self-murderer was excluded from the spirit world; the Paharis of India believed that the suicide's ghost hovered eternally between heaven and earth. Both the Iroquois and Hidatsa Indians maintained that the souls of suicides occupied a separate village in the land of the dead because their presence made other dead souls uneasy. The Dyaks of Borneo said that suicides went to a special place where those who had drowned themselves lived forever up to their waists in water and those who had poisoned themselves lived in houses built of poisonous wood, surrounded by plants that emitted noxious fumes. The Dakotas believed that a suicide's ghost was forever doomed to drag behind him the tree on which he had hanged himself—hence women hanged themselves from the smallest trees that would bear their weight.

The belief that a suicide's ghost might return to pester the living went hand in hand with the notion of revenge suicide. In some primitive societies suicide was committed as a direct act of vengeance, in the belief that as a ghost one was more easily able to persecute his persecutors. "Man has an enemy whom he cannot fight successfully," observed an ancient proverb. "He can successfully disgrace his enemy by hanging himself in his enemy's front yard." An ancient Chinese law placed responsibility for the death on the person who had supposedly caused it, and people frequently killed themselves to entangle an adversary in legal proceedings, to embarrass him, or to ensure his harassment by the suicide's angry ghost. The ghost was believed to haunt the place where the act had been committed, trying to persuade others to follow his example and attempting to strangle those who chose to live.

Some revenge suicides worked more directly. The Tshi-speaking peoples of Africa's Gold Coast believed that if, before committing suicide, a person blamed his act on another, that person was required to kill himself using the same method unless the suicide's family was financially compensated. For many years India had several accepted forms of revenge suicide. In certain areas of southern India, if a man plucked out his eye or killed himself after a quarrel, his adversary was required to do the same either to himself or to a relative. An eye for an eye, a suicide for a suicide, was the rule. A woman who had been insulted might smash her head against the door of the woman who insulted her, whereupon that woman had to do the same. If a woman poisoned herself, the woman who "drove her to her death" followed suit; if she refused, her house was burned down and her cattle stolen. Until recently a legal method of debt collection in India was to sit at the debtor's door and refuse food or drink until the charge was paid. If "sitting *dharna*," as it was called, ended in starvation, the creditor believed that public opinion would avenge him upon his enemy. When one of the Rajput rajas levied a war tax on the Brahmans, a number of the wealthiest, having argued in vain, stabbed themselves with daggers in front of the raja while cursing him with their last breaths. Thus denounced, the raja was shunned even by his friends.

The notion of revenge suicide or "killing oneself upon the head of another" may seem archaic, but the primitive tribesman who hangs himself on his enemy's doorstep provides a literal illustration of Freud's theory that suicide is a sort of inverted murder in which anger meant for another is turned inward on the self. Today, revenge, conscious or unconscious, remains a powerful motive in many suicides, although the punishment exacted is, of course, more psychological than physical. A particularly cruel example, pointed out by English historian Henry Romilly Fedden, is that of the nineteenth-century Frenchman whose mistress was unfaithful. Before killing himself he told his servant that after his death a candle should be made of his fat and carried, lighted, to the woman. To accompany it he composed a note telling her that as he burned for her in life, so, too, he burned for her in death.

Among most tribes, primitive fear of suicide was not based on moral judgment, although precautions taken to assuage vengeful ghosts might eventually have given birth to the idea that the act of suicide was in itself, like murder, something "wrong." (And precautions may have evolved into punishments.) In fact, certain cultures tolerated and even encouraged suicide. The Goths believed that those who died naturally were doomed to languish eternally in caves full of venomous creatures; therefore, old men threw themselves off a precipice called the Rock of the Forefathers. The Iglulik are among several Eskimo tribes who believed that a violent death ensured a place in paradise, which they called the Land of Day; those who died by natural causes were confined to the Narrow Land. In some cultures elderly suicides were provoked by the belief that a man entered into the next world in the same condition as he left this one; consequently, it behooved him to take his own life before he grew feeble. The ancient Celts considered natural death shameful, and men who threw themselves from cliffs were celebrated with song. "They are a nation lavish of their blood and eager to face death," wrote the Roman poet Silius Italicus of the Spanish Celts. "As soon as the Celt has passed the age of mature strength, he endures the flight of time impatiently and scorns to await old age; the term of his existence depends upon himself." Among the Chukchee of Siberia, those who died voluntarily were said to have the best abode in the afterlife: "They dwell on the red blaze of the aurora borealis and pass their time playing ball with a walrus-skull." In pre-Christian Scandinavia only those who died a violent death were permitted to enter Valhalla, where they fought mock battles and drank from the skulls of their enemies; Vikings unlucky enough not to die in combat often slew themselves with swords or threw themselves from cliffs. Odin, the Viking god of war, was himself said to be a suicide. As death approached, he assembled his followers and stabbed himself in nine places, declaring that he would join the gods at their immortal feast, where he would welcome all those who died with weapons in their hands.

Recommending violent death as a path to paradise was a way of promoting a properly bellicose spirit in warrior societies. Elsewhere, "economic suicide" by the elderly and infirm was encouraged during periods of hardship so that there would be sufficient rations for the tribe to survive. In some cultures sacrificial suicides were carried out to honor the gods or to ensure a good harvest.

Among the Aztecs, a young man was selected each year to impersonate the god Tezcatlipoca. He received the homage of his people for one year, at the end of which he offered himself up to death at the altar, and his living heart was cut out. Each year, in the mountains of Tien-tai in China, several Buddhist monks sacrificed their lives, hoping to obtain nirvana for themselves and protection from evil spirits for their community. On the appointed day the monk, observed by a crowd of spectators, entered a furnace and sat on a wooden seat. The door was shut and the fuel lit. Afterward the ashes were collected, washed, and revered as the relics of a saint.

Such suicides were ostensibly voluntary, but social custom rendered them all but compulsory. In India, when sacrificial suicides were, on occasion, rescued by the military, the victims escaped whenever possible and returned to embrace death. Similarly, according to an old custom in Malabar, people who were taken ill prayed to their idol for recovery. Once healthy they fattened themselves up for a year or more and then on a festival day gratefully cut off their heads before the idol who had saved their life.

Some contemporary suicides kill themselves in the fantasy that their death may reunite them with a lost loved one. In primitive societies such suicides were common, but the act was compelled less by grief than by cultural tradition. "There is another world, and they who kill themselves to accompany their friends thither will live with them there." This Druid maxim expresses the motivation behind a custom dating back to ancient Egypt, where wives and servants took poison and were buried with their pharaohs, along with weapons, furniture, perfumes, combs, tools for grinding corn, and anything else that would make life in the next world comfortable. As Egyptian civilization progressed, the corpses of wives and servants were replaced by symbolic figurines; in other societies, however, the practice persisted. In Siam, after the king's corpse was laid in his grave, his wives, concubines, and ministers of state drank poison and were placed next to him along with six horses, twelve camels or elephants, and twenty hunting dogs, thus providing the king with means of diversion in the afterlife. In Scythia, Herodotus tells us, a king was buried with his cook, butler, groom, steward, chamberlain, and one of his concubines—all of them strangled—who were expected to wait on their master in the next world as they had in this. A year after the king's death fifty of his servants and fifty of his horses were strangled, stuffed with chaff, and mounted on scaffolds around his tomb, each dead servant riding a dead horse, ever prepared to fight for his dead master. At the interment of the king of Benin in western Africa, the ruler's favorite lords and servants leaped into his tomb, vying for the honor of being buried alive with their master's corpse. According to Herodotus, the death of a Thracian man triggered a "keen competition" among his wives to determine which among them he had most loved. The winner was slain over the grave and buried with her husband.

The custom of a widow or concubine taking her life on the death of her husband has been practiced in nearly every part of the world. (The gender reverse of this has seldom been observed, although in one tribe on the Gold Coast a man of low rank who married a sister of the king was expected to kill himself on the death of his wife. "Should he outrage native custom and neglect to do so," noted one anthropologist, "a hint is conveyed to him that he will be put to death, which usually produces the desired effect.") The best-known example of wifely suicide is suttee, named for a heroine of Hindu mythology who threw herself onto her husband's funeral pyre to prove her devotion. Historically, the act has been a blend of choice and coercion. A Hindu wife is expected to dedicate herself to her husband—no matter how miserably he may treat her—even after his death. The *Padmapurana,* an eleventh-century religious text, outlined a virtuous woman's duties to her husband—"whatever his defects may be, a wife should always look upon him as her god"—and instructed her that when her husband dies, she should "allow herself to be burnt alive on the same funeral pyre; then everyone will praise her virtue." Hindu widows are bypassed by inheritance laws; they are forbidden to attend wedding or birthday celebrations or to wear jewelry, makeup, or bright clothing. The alternative is suttee, for which a widow is honored above all other women, bringing respect to her memory and to her family.

Suttee was already in vogue when Alexander the Great invaded India in 327 BC, and when the English arrived two millennia later, they were horrified to find it still practiced widely; in 1821 there were 2,366 reported cases. Outraged by this "primitive act," the British declared it illegal in 1829—only six years after they abolished stake-and-crossroads burial in their own country. But the custom persisted in remote areas well into the twentieth century. In 1987, in the village of Deorala, several days after her husband's death from a ruptured appendix, eighteen-year-old Roop Kanwar climbed onto his funeral pyre and cradled his head in her lap. The pyre of sandalwood and coconuts soaked with clarified butter was set ablaze and she burned to death. Twelve days later, more than one hundred thousand Rajputs gathered in Deorala to glorify her act. The village took on a carnival atmosphere; booths were set up to sell pictures of the dead couple, vendors sold refreshments, and a loudspeaker system was installed to help locate lost children. Kanwar's suicide also inspired international outrage, protests by Indian feminists, and the enactment of federal legislation providing the death penalty for anyone convicted of abetting suttee. Fifteen years later, when a sixty-five-year-old woman burned to death on her husband's funeral pyre in the village of Tamoli, her sons were accused of forcing her into suttee because they wanted her property and were arrested for murder. "The government of Madhya Pradesh will not tolerate a few demented people dragging the entire state into prehistoric times," said the minister for rural development in the central Indian state.

Scholars of self-destruction classify such acts as "institutional" or "ritual" suicides—deaths that are all but demanded by cultural tradition—as if they were embarrassing anachronisms that had nothing in common with suicides in the "civilized" world. They are thus dismissed as the acts of primitives. Yet in Japan for thousands of years suicide has been an acceptable, often honorable, way out of intolerable situations. "The Japanese calendar of saints," wrote one nineteenth-century Western historian, "is not filled with reformers, almsgivers and founders of hospitals or orphanages, but is overcrowded with canonized suicides and committers of *hara-kiri*. Even today, no man more . . . surely draws homage to his tomb, securing even apotheosis, than the suicide, though he may have committed a crime."

The Japanese attitude toward suicide is, in large part, based on a Buddhist tradition that places less value on life in this world than on life in the next. Existence on earth is ephemeral, the body is merely a temporary lodging of the soul, and biological life is not only meaningless but filled with suffering. Death is the point at which a person makes contact with the eternal world. If a person acquits himself well at the moment of death, offenses committed during his earthly life are forgiven. In some cases suicide can be the most exquisite death of all.

Historically, suicide in Japan has enjoyed not only religious tolerance but state approval. The romantic aura that surrounds suicide grew out of the development of seppuku, a traditional form of suicide better known outside Japan as hara-kiri, or "belly-cutting." It was practiced by the samurai, or military class, who followed an ethical code known as Bushido—"the way of the knights." At the heart of Bushido was the creed of loyalty to one's lord or to any matter of principle. When a *bushi,* or knight, was forced to choose between two courses of action, one of which involved the sacrifice of principle and the other the sacrifice of life, he unhesitatingly chose the latter. At the same time a man raised in the samurai tradition was taught from an early age that a samurai's most important trait was to suppress outward displays of emotion, be it pleasure or pain. The supreme test of a samurai's self-discipline and devotion to principle was the act of seppuku.

Seppuku originated about a thousand years ago during the beginning of Japanese feudalism as an honorable way for a soldier to avoid the humiliation of capture. By the seventeenth century it was widely used as a death penalty for the samurai. While common criminals were hung in the town square, a member of the military class condemned to death might be allowed to expiate his crime by his own hand. Thus, obligatory seppuku was a privilege granted by the feudal lord, saving the samurai the shame of being handed over to the public executioner. Members of the military class were trained to prepare for the possibility of voluntary death by self-disembowelment, and warriors frequently rehearsed the seppuku ceremony, in which every step was prescribed by custom.

A noble suspected of misconduct or of disloyalty would receive a letter from the emperor politely hinting that he must die. The letter was often accompanied by a jeweled dagger. On the appointed day, clothed in ceremonial dress, the doomed man knelt on a red mat on a small platform built for the occasion in his baronial hall or in the temple. Friends and officials formed a silent semicircle around him. After prayer the emperor's envoy handed the dagger to the noble, who publicly confessed his wrongs. The noble stripped down to the traditional loincloth, plunged the dagger into the left side of his abdomen, drew it across to the right, then turned the blade and cut upward. As he fell forward, the *kaishaku,* a friend of the noble, severed the noble's head with a long sword. The bloodstained dagger was taken back to the lord as proof of his noble's fealty.

Often, a disloyal noble anticipated the wishes of his lord and committed seppuku without prompting. There was incentive for this: if death had been demanded by the lord, only half the samurai's property was forfeited to the state; if voluntary, his dishonor was erased and his family inherited his full fortune. Over the years voluntary seppuku became common in a variety of circumstances: to follow one's dead lord into the next world; to avoid beheading by the enemy in a lost battle; to restore injured honor in a situation where revenge was impossible; to protest the conduct of a superior; to admit an error; to keep a secret; to turn one's lord from a course of action that might injure his reputation. Whatever the motive, seppuku ensured the samurai a traditional burial and a respected memory.

Seppuku eventually extended beyond the military class and became the national form of honorable suicide. It is believed that during the feudal ages some fifteen hundred cases of seppuku occurred each year, more than half of them voluntary. "The Japanese are an obstinate, capricious, resolute and whimsical people," observed Montesquieu. "They have a natural contempt of death, and rip open their bellies for the least fancy." In 1868, twenty samurai involved in the murder of a French officer were condemned to commit seppuku before the French ambassador. The latter found it difficult to appreciate this gesture, and after eleven of the soldiers had proved their remorse, he reprieved the remaining knights. While the practice appalled foreigners, it remained sacred to the Japanese; the following year a member of the Japanese parliament proclaimed seppuku "the very shrine of the Japanese national spirit and the embodiment in practice of devotion to principle."

Although obligatory suicide was prohibited by law in 1873 and the frequency of voluntary seppuku declined, it continued to be practiced—and acclaimed—as a noble death. In 1891, protesting the failure of the government to take action against Russian encroachments on Japan's northern border, Lieutenant Ohara Takeyoshi became a national hero by disemboweling himself in front of the graves of his ancestors in Tokyo. After the Japanese-Chinese War, when Japan allowed Port Arthur to be occupied by the Russians, more than forty Japanese army officers committed seppuku in protest. But seppuku has often been chosen under less ostensibly heroic circumstances. In 1929, for instance, the almost 250 recorded cases of seppuku included rebels making political protests, railway watchmen atoning for accidents resulting from their negligence, and teenagers reprimanding their drunken fathers. That same year a Japanese naval captain at the Moscow embassy, taunted by his Russian teacher about his unflinching loyalty to the emperor, lost his temper and threw a chair at the woman, striking her on the hand. The mortified captain saw only one way to redeem his honor. He gave three thousand rubles to the teacher, wrote his will, and, kneeling in front of a photograph of the emperor, committed seppuku.

Seppuku is, of course, only one of many methods of suicide used in Japan. It is not the method that distinguishes Japanese suicide, however, so much as its central role in the national tradition. There exists, in fact, a special vocabulary to describe various social genres of suicide. The naval captain who killed himself following the quarrel with his teacher was committing *kashitsu-shi*—suicide to admit failure or to atone for a mistake. Such suicides are a frequent occurrence in a country that places a premium on competition. In one recent year, for example, 275 company directors killed themselves after business disappointments or corruption scandals. Studies have attributed the high rate of Japanese adolescent suicide to fierce competition in schools. Failure to pass the exam for entrance to a university—or failure to be admitted to a prestigious university—brings shame to both student and family and is often an occasion for *kashitsu-shi*. The boys who committed seppuku to protest their father's drunkenness were committing *kangen-shi*—a way of criticizing a superior in a society where few modes of criticism are available. A well-known example of *gisei-shi*—sacrificial suicide—was practiced by the kamikaze pilots of World War II, about twenty-two hundred of whom plunged to their deaths shouting, *"Tenno heika banzai"*—"Long live the emperor!" And though the compulsory suicide of wife, retainers, and slaves following a lord's death was outlawed in AD 59, *junshi*—suicide following a master's death—persisted. In 1912, all of Japan was inspired when sixty-three-year-old General Kiten Nogi, beloved hero of the 1904–5 war with Russia, and his wife committed seppuku following the death of Emperor Mutsuhito. "He mingles with the gods on high, my mighty sovereign lord," wrote Nogi, "and, with intensely yearning heart, I follow heavenward."

Suicide committed by more than one person is called *shinju* (literally "inside the heart"). *Jyoshi shinju*—love-pact suicide—became widespread toward the end of the seventeenth century, when increasingly rigid class stratification and strict codes of behavior forbade love between unmarried people. Kabuki and Bunraku (puppet) drama is full of love-pact suicide, usually involving a commoner and a geisha. Their union forbidden in this world, they kill themselves, often by tying themselves together with a rope and drowning, to ensure their union in the next. With arranged marriages the rule until recently, *jyoshi shinju* continued to flourish. In 1954 there were almost one thousand cases, and a few years later, in a poll asking teenagers what to do about a love that parents opposed, 45 percent answered that the "most beautiful" solution was double suicide. In 1985, when their marriage plans were forbidden by their families because they were said to be too old, a seventy-year-old man and a sixty-nine-year-old woman, both widowed more than twenty-five years, committed *jyoshi shinju* by hanging themselves in a hotel room.

*Oyako shinju*—parent-child suicide—is still common. Plagued by poverty, unable to pay back loans, or humiliated by spouses, some parents kill their children and then kill themselves. In Japan, being an orphan has traditionally been considered a fate worse than death, and *oyako shinju* is often portrayed as an act of devotion. The majority of cases involve the mother, often under threat of impending divorce. In Japan, where women are trained to show obedience, divorcées often have difficulty finding respectable jobs, and in some instances, even their own families will not take them in. Some four hundred examples of *oyako shinju* are believed to occur each year. In several recent cases a mother, despondent because her sixteen-year-old son was depressed about his forthcoming school entrance exams, murdered her son and attempted to gas herself; an unemployed man and a woman who suffered from heart disease strangled their eighteen-year-old daughter and then gassed themselves; a woman suffering from stomach trouble strangled her two daughters, aged eight and ten, who had light cases of asthma, then attempted to gas herself. "My daughters and myself are so weak physically that we have caused you so much trouble," she wrote her husband. "Please allow us to go ahead of you."

---

Although it still occupies a central role in the Japanese cultural imagination, since World War II, suicide, like many other Japanese institutions, has become "westernized." In retrospect, the turning point may have occurred in 1970 with the suicide of Yukio Mishima.

One of Japan's most celebrated twentieth-century writers, Mishima was born into an aristocratic samurai family. Mishima deplored what he saw as the materialistic decadence and moral decay of Japan's postwar westernization, and in both his writing and his life he urged a return to the purer values of imperial Japan and the samurai tradition. Mishima took up bodybuilding at thirty and became an expert in karate and kendo, the ancient sword-fighting art practiced by samurai warriors. He organized the Shield Society, a private, eighty-five-man army dedicated to restoring the samurai spirit. All his life he was infatuated with suicide. "If you want your beauty to endure," he wrote at age thirty-four, "you must commit suicide at the height of your beauty." In one of his most famous short stories, a young army officer and his wife commit seppuku after a night of passionate lovemaking. Mishima subsequently made the story into a film in which he played the lieutenant.

On November 25, 1970, at the age of forty-five, after sending his publisher the final portion of *The Sea of Fertility,* a quartet of novels he had been working on for many years, Mishima and four members of the Shield Society raided the Tokyo headquarters of Japan's Self-Defense Forces. From a balcony overlooking the courtyard, Mishima harangued a crowd of twelve hundred servicemen, accusing the Self-Defense Forces of impotence, denouncing Japan's United States–imposed constitution, and urging them to restore the prewar Japanese state based on rule by the emperor. The soldiers hooted and called Mishima a fool. Realizing the futility of continuing, Mishima walked inside, shouting, *"Tenno heika banzai,"* then performed the ancient ritual of seppuku. His chief lieutenant served as *kaishaku,* severing Mishima's head with a sword before committing seppuku himself and being beheaded in turn.

Although a few right-wing groups called Mishima a hero, for the most part, both in Japan and abroad, his death was seen as an example more of histrionic posturing than of protest, a pathetic gesture rather than a noble act. (The Japanese prime minister suggested Mishima was mad.) The three young disciples who survived the raid were sentenced to four years in prison on charges that included "murder by request"—the first time in Japanese history that the venerable custom of beheading a friend as he committed seppuku was made the basis for criminal charges. In articles appraising Mishima's life and death, Japanese and Western writers alike focused on his domineering grandmother, his homosexuality, his narcissism, his obsession with death. A book reviewer for the *New York Times* described Mishima as "a sadomasochistic homosexual for whom death was the ultimate act of exhibitionism and self-gratification. It would not be too much to see Mr. Mishima's suicide as a fatal form of masturbation."

Mishima's suicide may have stemmed as much from his sexual psychoses as from his loyalty to the samurai principle; more accurately, the two were inextricably linked. But in the rush to psychoanalyze Mishima, we may have lost sight of his death as being his own, as having meaning beyond the aberrant motives others assigned to it. As after any suicide, Mishima's entire life was reinterpreted in light of his death. Even his literary output was reevaluated; reviewers found weaknesses they had apparently not noticed before, the psychosexual elements were highlighted with knowing remarks, and his stock as a writer dipped. The postmortem seemed an ironic illustration of what Mishima's suicide was ostensibly protesting. The suicide of a man who had killed himself to protest Japan's westernization was viewed from a distinctly Western perspective. Today, most Japanese regard Mishima with embarrassment.

Because of suicide's honored place in Japanese culture, it has often been assumed that the Japanese suicide rate dwarfs that of Western countries. Yet despite Durkheim's contention that "the readiness of the Japanese to disembowel themselves for the slightest reason is well known," for many years suicide in Japan was no more prevalent than in the West, its rate of about 19 per 100,000 higher than that of the United States but lower than that of many northern or eastern European countries. In the last decade, however, the rate has risen precipitously. In 1998, Japan's rate of 26.1, more than twice that of the United States, was among the highest in the world. The rising rate has been blamed primarily on Japan's decade-long recession, which has spawned widespread layoffs, bankruptcy, and homelessness. A great many of the suicides are those of middle-aged businessmen who have been let go by the companies for which they've worked for decades.

The rising rate, perhaps not coincidentally, comes at a time when the traditional Japanese conception of suicide has been changing. Seppuku, of course, has all but disappeared; Japanese suicides now choose pills, gas, or hanging. Press accounts of suicides are followed by familiar-sounding discussions of economic strain, psychological crisis, and the breakdown of the nuclear family. The Japanese, it is said, now kill themselves for the same reasons people kill themselves in the West. The military official who takes his life in shame over a security leak and the man who takes his life to protest a political action are now likely to be discussed as psychological misfits. Although the National Police Agency continues to sort suicides by traditional causes (health, financial worries, and so forth), Japanese psychiatrists invariably cite depression as the underlying culprit.

The rising rate has met with an increasingly Western response. The country's first suicide prevention hotline, formed a year after Mishima's death, now has fifty branch offices. A Japanese Association for the Prevention of Parent-Child Suicide has been formed. In 2001, the Japanese government allocated money to suicide prevention for the first time, funding suicide awareness programs, publishing a booklet listing the warning signs of suicide, and advising companies to offer counseling to troubled employees. Three years later, the Japanese Medical Association distributed a "Suicide Prevention Manual" to physicians and medical students, instructing them how to detect and treat depression and urging them to get troubled patients into psychiatric care, where they are more and more likely to be treated with antidepressant medication.

These developments reflect a conceptual change in how depression is viewed. Acceptance of suffering is at the center of traditional Buddhist thought; for centuries, Japanese saw sadness as an inevitable human condition, not a medical problem. Only in the most extreme cases was depression considered to be abnormal, and treatable in institutions; the notion of mild depression was unknown. Then, in 1999, in a rather dramatic illustration of the chicken-or-the-egg conundrum, a Japanese pharmaceutical company decided to introduce SSRIs to Japan and came up with the phrase *kokoro no kaze*—a soul that has caught a cold—to describe mild depression and suggest the need for its alleviation. The American pharmaceutical giants quickly followed. "People didn't know they were suffering from a disease," a Japanese product manager for Paxil said. "We felt it was important to reach out to them." Between 1998 and 2003, sales of antidepressants in Japan quintupled. Whether the Japanese are happier is not yet clear. Perhaps not surprisingly, an increasing number of Japanese are found to suffer from *kokoro no kaze*. In 2004, in a public admission that would have been unthinkable a decade ago, the imperial family acknowledged that Crown Princess Masako was on antidepressants and in counseling for depression and an "adjustment disorder."

Despite these symptoms of westernization, suicide in Japan remains in transition—a blend of traditional and contemporary attitudes that have tragically been entwined over the past few years in a rash of "Internet suicides," in which strangers browse the Web in search of a date not for love but for death. In Japan, the Internet is chockablock with suicide-related Web sites, chat rooms, and bulletin boards on which lonely young people can read about suicide in history, debate the pros and cons of various methods, and advertise for suicide partners. One such site offers a slide show of "proper" places to kill oneself—forested spots with views of Mount Fuji are particularly popular—and rates ten suicide methods for such considerations as "pain," "chance of success," and "annoyance to other people." In 2003, thirty-four Internet suicides were reported. The following year, a thirty-four-year-old mother of two advertised for suicide partners on the Net and within days recruited six young volunteers: four men and two women, all strangers to each other, who traveled from as many as six hundred miles away. When they met for the first time, they drove a rented van to a mountainside parking lot west of Tokyo, sealed the van from the inside with tape, took sleeping pills, lit charcoal stoves, and tied themselves to each other. Next to the mother of two, who was sitting in the driver's seat, the police found a note: "Mother is going to die, but I was happy to give birth to you." Japanese clinicians suggest that these Internet suicides are carried out by aimless, despairing, emotionally crippled people who seek in death something they are unable to find in life. And yet these suicides represent a sort of high-tech gloss on the venerable tradition of *jyoshi shinju*—love-pact suicide. "One single suicide seems quite awful and wrong," Yukio Saito, a Methodist minister who founded the country's first suicide prevention hotline, told a reporter. "But a double suicide has, in a sense, affection and peace, solace."

# II

# THE CLASSICAL WORLD: "HE IS AT LIBERTY TO DIE WHO DOES NOT WISH TO LIVE"

WHERE DID CONTEMPORARY Western attitudes toward suicide come from? In ancient Greece, the birthplace of Western civilization, suicide was considered a respectable option. It is true that a few taboos surrounded the act; for instance, in Athens, the corpse of a suicide was buried outside the city, the offending hand cut off and interred separately to prevent the suicide's ghost from attacking the living. But these were the products less of moral judgment than of the ancient Greeks' abhorrence of any violent or untimely death—murder, stillbirth, abortion—and their horror of shedding kindred blood. Suicides from starvation, which were bloodless and slow, were rarely denied ordinary rites; there was no sudden wrenching of the soul from the body, which the Greeks most feared.

In fact, the histories and literature of ancient Greece brim with suicides, which are usually described without shock or blame. They seem to aspire to one quality: honor, whether originating from pride, patriotism, shame, or grief. The first Greek suicide on record is Jocasta, who, on discovering that she had married her son Oedipus, "steep down from a high rafter, throttled in her noose, she swung, carried away by pain." Homer recorded her suicide without comment, as a natural, even inevitable, response to an intolerable situation. Leukakas

144

jumped from a rock into the sea to avoid being raped by Apollo. Dido preferred to stab herself on her husband's funeral pyre rather than remarry. Erigone hanged herself from a tree when she discovered the body of her murdered father, touching off an epidemic of suicide among Athenian women. Charondas, the lawgiver of Catana, a Greek colony in Sicily, decreed that no armed men should enter the assembly under pain of death. Returning to the assembly in haste one day, he forgot to remove his dagger, thus breaking his own law. He quickly drew his weapon and killed himself.

Suicide to avoid capture was almost de rigueur among the ancient Greeks. At ninety, the Athenian orator Isocrates starved himself to death rather than submit to Philip of Macedon. Demosthenes took poison to avoid falling into the hands of Antipater. Entire regiments or towns committed suicide rather than surrender. In 425 BC the oligarchs of Corcyra, trapped in a temple and condemned to death, took their own lives, according to Thucydides, "thrusting into their throats the arrows shot by the enemy, and hanging themselves with the cords taken from some beds that happened to be there, and with strips made from their clothing; adopting, in short, every possible means of self-destruction." It is perhaps not surprising that Pantites, one of two survivors of the battle of Thermopylae, found hanging himself the only way to redeem his reputation on his return to Sparta.

Only the most extravagant suicides were attributed to insanity. Herodotus informs us that in 490 BC, Cleomenes, king of Sparta, "went quite mad" and "began to mutilate himself, beginning on his shins. He sliced his flesh into strips, working upwards to his thighs, and from them to his hips and sides, until he reached his belly, and while he was cutting that into strips he died." Cleomenes' suicidal delirium was blamed by some on the drinking of unmixed liquors, a nasty habit he had picked up from visiting Scythians.

In classical Greece, suicide was not the province of physicians but of philosophers, who introduced most of the ethical arguments, pro and con, that would be used for the next two millennia. The Pythagoreans disapproved of suicide. They taught that man is a stranger in this world, and his immortal soul, imprisoned in the body, undergoes atonement and purification, the success of which dictates whether at death it will return to its divine origin or transmigrate into another body and start over from scratch. Suicide, therefore, interfered with that process, and the Pythagoreans forbade men "to depart from their guard or station in life without the order of their Commander—that is, of God." Reinforcing their antisuicide stance was Pythagoras' theory of numbers, which hypothesized that a fixed number of souls were available for use in the world at any given moment. Suicide skewed the spiritual mathematics, for it was possible that no other soul was ready to fill the gap caused by such an abrupt exit from life.

In Plato's *Phaedo,* Socrates, condemned to death by the state, refined this theme. Mortals are the soldiers of the gods, he said, and a man's life is akin to a soldier's watch. Suicide, therefore, was desertion. We may leave our station only on orders from above. Furthermore, he said, man belongs to God, and suicide was therefore destruction of divine property. "If one of your own possessions, an ox or an ass, for example, took the liberty of putting himself out of the way when you had given no intimation of your wish that he should die, would you not be angry with him, and would you not punish him if you could? . . . Then, if we look at the matter thus, there may be reason in saying that a man should wait, and not take his own life until God summons him, as he is now summoning me." Socrates explained that in *his* case he had been called by God, and calmly swallowed the hemlock.

The *Phaedo* provoked disparate reactions. While the Greek orator Libanius claimed that the arguments in the *Phaedo* kept him from committing suicide after the death of the emperor Julian, the young Greek philosopher Cleombrotus was so fascinated by Socrates' description of the souls' immortality that he flung himself into the sea and drowned. Plato himself was divided on the subject. In the ninth book of his *Laws* he reiterated his general condemnation of suicide but admitted certain circumstances in which it may be justified— extraordinary sorrow, unavoidable misfortune, intolerable disgrace, or compulsion by the state. On one cause he was adamant: those who commit suicide "in a spirit of slothful and abject cowardice" shall be buried "in deserted places that have no name."

Plato's student Aristotle borrowed the Pythagorean notion of responsibility beyond the self but asserted that we belong not to God but to the state. Suicide weakened the city economically by depriving it of a citizen. In a discussion of courage Aristotle sparked a debate that continues to this day: "To kill oneself to escape from poverty or love or anything else that is distressing is not courageous but rather the act of a coward, because it shows weakness of character to run away from hardships, and the suicide endures death not because it is a fine thing to do but in order to escape from suffering." Nevertheless, when Aristotle died in exile at sixty-two, there were persistent rumors that he had killed himself.

While Plato found suicide justifiable when external conditions became intolerable, the Epicureans turned the argument inside out, making the choice of suicide an internal process. Plato's "objective" circumstances under which suicide was permissible became subjective. Suicide was no longer an involuntary act dictated by outward circumstances but a voluntary assertion of freedom. Epicureans held that pleasure should be the guiding principle in life: whatever produced pleasure was good, and whatever produced pain was evil. Death, they believed, was neither good nor evil, and they professed to be as indifferent to it as to life. "The many at one moment shun death as the greatest of evils, at another yearn for it as a respite from the evils in life," said Epicurus. "But the wise man neither seeks to escape life nor fears the cessation of life, for neither does life offend him nor does the absence of life seem to be any evil." While pointing out the folly of killing oneself through fear of death, Epicurus urged men "to weigh carefully, whether they would prefer death to come to them, or would themselves go to death." Lucretius, the Roman poet and Epicurean who killed himself at forty-four, put it more seductively: "If one day, as well may happen, life grows wearisome, there only remains to pour a libation to death and oblivion. A drop of subtle poison will gently close your eyes to the sun, and waft you smiling into the eternal night whence everything comes and to which everything returns."

For the Stoics, "to live consistently with nature" was the ideal. When the conditions essential to that ideal no longer existed, suicide was a reasonable choice. Zeno, founder of the Stoic school, lived to the age of ninety-eight without encountering a reason sufficient to depart life. Then one day, upon leaving his school of philosophy, he stumbled, put a toe out of joint, went home, and hanged himself. The suicide of his successor, Cleanthes, seems only slightly less arbitrary. Suffering from a gum boil, he was advised by his doctor to refrain from food for two days. The remedy was effective, and he was told he could resume his normal diet. Cleanthes declined, saying that "as he had advanced so far on his journey towards death, he would not retreat," and he starved to death. It is said that Timon of Athens grew a fig tree so that he might never lack a branch from which to hang himself.

At certain times, in ancient Greece, suicide even enjoyed official sanction. As early as 500 BC, in the Greek colony of Ceos, citizens who were over the age of sixty or incapacitated by sickness were allowed, even encouraged, to take their own life. After crowning their brows with floral garlands they drank state-provided hemlock or poppy juice. (The custom may have been introduced during a famine.) At the Greek colony of Massilia (modern Marseille) magistrates kept a supply of poison on hand for those who, pleading their case before the senate, obtained permission to kill themselves. (Acceptable reasons included illness, sorrow, and disgrace.) The law was intended to prevent hasty, impulsive suicides and to make reasonable, state-approved suicides as rapid and painless as possible. "Such a discussion is tempered with a manly benevolence; which does not suffer anyone to quit life rashly, but affords means of accelerating the end of him, who has wise reasons for his departure," wrote Valerius. "Any one for instance may thus make an approved and honourable exit, who experiences the extremes of good and bad fortune; either of which affords sufficient grounds to covet a termination of life—the former lest it should forsake us or the latter continue with us." This type of rationality seemed irrational to Libanius. Referring to a similar state-sponsored suicide program briefly practiced in Athens, he wrote sarcastically of a man who pleaded permission to kill himself to escape from his garrulous wife; a man distressed because his neighbor's wealth had outstripped his; a man who preferred to part with his life rather than to part with a treasure he found.

Such excess anticipated the Roman Empire. For if the Greeks rationalized suicide, the Romans made it a fashion, even a sport. Like Greece, the Roman
Republic had its share of suicides and for much the same reason—to avoid dishonor and disgrace. Indeed, the death of Marcus Porcius Cato has been cited
as a model of rational suicide through the ages. A just, scrupulous man, Cato
dressed simply, never rode when he could walk, and "even from his infancy,"
wrote Plutarch, "in his speech, his countenance, and all his childish pas-
times, he discovered an inflexible temper, unmoved by any passion, and firm
in everything." Cato had placed his life at the service of the Republic, and when
Caesar crossed the Rubicon in 49 BC, Cato followed Pompey into Greece.
After Pompey's defeat, Cato fled to Utica, where he tried to rally the Republican party. But when several defeats put an end to his hopes for the survival of
the old virtues of liberty and republicanism, he decided to die rather than live
under Caesar. Cato spent the last evening of his life arguing favorite philosophical questions with his friends, then retired to his chamber to read Plato's
*Phaedo.* Glancing up, he noticed that his sword was missing from its usual
place. His son, suspecting his plans, had removed it. Confronting his friends,
Cato accused them of forgetting their Stoic ideals, asking them to "show cause
why we should now unlearn what we formerly were taught." His friends
wept. The sword was sent to him, carried by a child. "Now I am master of
myself," said Cato, who, after testing the sword's point, returned to the
*Phaedo,* reading it through twice before falling into a sleep so deep the men
outside could hear him snore. Near midnight he sent one of his men to the port
to make sure the transports had left safely. Plutarch wrote:

> Now the birds began to sing, and he again fell into a little slumber. At
> length Butas came back, and told him all was quiet in the port. Then
> Cato, laying himself down, as if he would sleep out the rest of the
> night, bade him shut the door after him. But as soon as Butas was gone
> out, he took his sword, and stabbed it into his breast.

When his friends heard Cato fall from his couch, they rushed in to find him
in a pool of blood, alive. As a physician began to sew up the wound, Cato
regained consciousness and, according to Plutarch, "thrust away the physician,
plucked out his own bowels, and tearing open the wound, immediately
expired."

Cato was acclaimed as a hero. "The people of Utica flocked thither," wrote
Plutarch, "crying out with one voice, he was their benefactor and their saviour,
the only free and only undefeated man." His suicide impressed even Caesar,
who, on receiving the news, exclaimed, "Cato, I grudge you your death, as you
have grudged me the preservation of your life." Horace composed an ode in

his honor. His act also won the approval of antisuicide writers such as Cicero, who declared that death may sometimes be the least of evils, for "when God himself shall give a just cause, as formerly to Socrates, lately to Cato, certainly every man of sense would gladly exchange this darkness for that light." Valerius Maximus called it "a noble lesson to mankind. How much superior in the opinion of all honest men is dignity without life to life without dignity." Seneca declared, "Jupiter himself could not have seen anything more beautiful on earth."

Seneca was the most prominent teacher of the Roman Stoics, who would raise suicide to an art form during the Roman Empire. For the Stoics, suicide was a final resource, an ultimate weapon against the vicissitudes of life. Whether the complaint be incurable illness, insufferable pain, or taedium vitae—the boredom and purposelessness of life—the Stoic attitude was *Mori licet cui vivere non placet:* "He is at liberty to die who does not wish to live." The Stoics did not condone irresponsibility, however. Suicide was not to be a rash, impulsive act but accepted or rejected after a careful weighing of pros and cons. Praising an ill friend's extensive deliberations, Pliny the Younger wrote, "A resolution this, in my estimation, truly arduous, and worthy of the highest applause. Instances are frequent enough in the world of rushing into the arms of death without reflection, and by a sort of blind impulse: but calmly and deliberately to weigh the motives for life or death, and to be determined in our choice as reason counsels, is the mark of an uncommon and great mind." Pliny the Elder maintained that the option of suicide was proof of man's superiority to the gods—man at least has the power of escaping to the grave. Conversely, he considered one of the greatest proofs of the bounty of Providence was that it had filled the world with herbs by which a sinner might procure a rapid, painless death. For the Stoics, suicide was the ultimate proof of man's freedom. The human spirit need never be broken, for, as Seneca observed, death was only a moment away.

> Foolish man, what do you bemoan, and what do you fear? Wherever you look there is an end of evils. You see that yawning precipice? It leads to liberty. You see that flood, that river, that well? Liberty houses within them. You see that stunted, parched, and sorry tree? From every branch liberty hangs. Your neck, your throat, your heart are all so many ways of escape from slavery. . . . Do you enquire the road to freedom? You shall find it in every vein of your body.

Seneca's own death was consistent with his teachings. When his friends wept upon being informed that Emperor Nero, his former pupil, desired his death, Seneca chided them. "Where had their philosophy gone, he asked, and that resolution against impending misfortunes which they had devised over so many years?" wrote the historian Tacitus. Seneca bade farewell to his wife,

Paulina, but she insisted on sharing his fate. "I will not grudge your setting so fine an example," he said. "We can die with equal fortitude. But yours will be the nobler end." They each cut their arms, but the aged Seneca bled slowly. A Stoic to the last, he had his wife carried into another room because "he was afraid of weakening his wife's endurance by betraying his agony—or of losing his own self-possession at the sight of her sufferings." Paulina survived; the emperor insisted on her rescue and treatment. Nero, who over the years demanded the suicides of dozens of his subjects, would himself commit suicide three years later, stabbing himself in the throat while fleeing a revolt.

The Romans' approach to suicide was reflected in their laws, which denied the *liber mori* only to criminals, soldiers, and slaves. A man accused of a crime committed another crime if he took his own life to avoid trial. Roman criminals often took their own lives because felony was usually punishable by death and the confiscation of property. Suicide *before* trial saved the suicide's goods for his family. Roman law also forbade the suicide of slaves because a Roman slave was his master's property—to kill himself, therefore, was to steal from his master. In fact, slaves came with a six-month antisuicide guarantee: any slave who attempted to kill himself within a half year of purchase could be returned to his former master. A soldier's suicide was likened to desertion and regarded as a weakening of the legions that, if unpunished, might spread and become a threat to Roman security. Suicide by a private citizen, according to Justinian's *Digest* of AD 533, was not punishable if caused by "impatience of pain or sickness, some grief" or by "weariness of life . . . lunacy, or fear of dishonor." This left a great deal of leeway. Suicide was a crime only if it was "without cause"—an irrational suicide—the premise being that a man capable of killing himself for no reason might be just as apt to kill someone else instead.

In Imperial Rome, therefore, the only objections to suicide were not moral but economic; suicide was a crime only in proportion to its effect on state finances or stability. Otherwise the morality of a "Roman death," as the poet Martial called it, was beyond dispute. The question was no longer *whether* but *how*. Suicide was a final test of character, to be carried out with dignity, courage, even bravado. When Caecina Paetus was condemned to death for his part in an unsuccessful conspiracy against Emperor Claudius, he knew that suicide was his only honorable option, but fear made him hesitate. His wife, Arria, seized his dagger and stabbed herself. Dying, she handed his weapon back to him, saying, "It does not hurt, my Paetus." The fact of death seemed almost irrelevant; the manner of dying was the thing. Convinced that Nero sought his death, Petronius Arbiter, a celebrated voluptuary whose exquisite manners earned him his nickname "the Arbiter of Taste," determined to evade the emperor by taking his own life. Calling his friends about him at his villa, he opened and closed his veins at will, prolonging his death as he arranged his affairs, took naps, or engaged in conversation. Unlike Cato, he spent his final hours not in contemplating philosophical questions but in cheerfully exchanging epigrams, songs, and gossip. Finally, he opened his veins for the last time, and in the middle of a sumptuous banquet Petronius Arbiter died as elegantly as he had lived.

For sheer exhibitionism the suicide of Peregrinus is unsurpassed. A wealthy native of Propontis, Greece, Peregrinus spent many years wandering through Palestine and Egypt and, after flirtations with Christianity and Eastern mysticism, found his niche in the doctrines of the Cynics. Preaching the vanity of pleasure and a contempt for death, he grew in reputation as he traveled along the Mediterranean coast. Expelled from Rome for insulting Emperor Antoninus Pius, he decided to solidify his position among the early Cynics by ending his life in a manner illustrating that school's disdain for death. He announced that he would die on a flaming pyre at the Olympic games in AD 165. Vast crowds gathered to witness the spectacle. Telling them that he was about to bring "a golden life to a golden close," Peregrinus doffed his Cynic's robes, threw incense on the burning pyre, and, invoking the spirit of his ancestors, walked into the flames and disappeared as the moon rose. It is said that a brilliant phoenix flew upward from the fire.

One had to go to extremes to be noticed at a time when thirty thousand people a month were sacrificed for sport in the arenas and pet fish were fed the blood of slaves. The Stoic enthusiasm for suicide was a reflection of the general Roman attitude toward death, a nonchalance perhaps unrivaled in history. Scottish anthropologist Sir James Frazer reported that in Rome at the time of the Punic Wars, volunteers offering to be beheaded for public sport for five minae—payable to the dead man's heirs—were so plentiful that many people, to improve their chances of getting the job, offered to be beaten to death rather than beheaded because that was a slower, more painful death and hence more appealing to spectators. With the barbarousness of the arena, the casual cruelty of the emperors, and the turmoil into which the Empire was frequently thrown by intrigues and civil wars, indifference to death may have been an important survival skill. It is in the moral chaos of the later Roman Empire, however, that the roots of Christianity's fervent antisuicide sentiment can be found.

---

Considering Christianity's nearly two thousand years of intense opposition to suicide, it is surprising that neither the Old nor the New Testament directly prohibits the act. There are six suicides in the Old Testament. They earn neither blessing nor condemnation. Saul, wounded by the Philistines, fell on his sword to avoid capture, whereupon his armor bearer did the same. Abimelech also killed himself to avoid dishonor. During his siege of the tower of Thebes, he was mortally wounded by a millstone thrown by a woman; he commanded his armor bearer to kill him so that it could not be said that a woman had slain him. When Zimri realized that his siege of Tirzah was doomed, "he went into the citadel of the king's house, and burned the king's house over him with fire, and died." Praying, "Let me die with the Philistines," Samson pulled down the walls of the temple of Dagon, destroying both his enemy and himself. After deserting his master King David, Ahithophel, his advice rejected by Absalom, "saddled his ass, and went off home to his own city. And he set his house in order, and hanged himself." Even Ahithophel's suicide is recorded without criticism, and he was provided a ritual burial in his ancestral tomb. In the New Testament, Judas Iscariot's suicide after his betrayal of Jesus Christ is viewed as a natural gesture of repentance; it is simply observed that "he went and hanged himself."

In the succeeding two millennia, pro-suicide writers cited the Bible's matter-of-fact treatment of self-destruction as evidence of Christian tolerance of the act. Antisuicide forces interpreted it as an implied condemnation, suggesting that suicide is so atrocious as to make specific written prohibition unnecessary. "In the same manner," wrote one eighteenth-century minister, "I do not recollect in Scripture a single word against man-eating." More probably the scarcity of suicide resulted from the strong commitment to life felt by Jews of the Old Testament period. An oft-cited example is Job. Although his sheep, oxen, camels, servants, and children had been destroyed and his body afflicted "with loathsome sores from the sole of his foot to the crown of his head," Job refused to lose faith. When his wife suggested that he give up in the face of such adversity, bidding him "curse God, and die," Job was outraged. "You speak as one of the foolish women would speak," he told her. "Shall we receive good at the hand of God, and shall we not receive evil?" Ever since, Job has been employed as a role model for antisuicide moralists who find in his patient fortitude the proper attitude toward suffering. However, his was an example not often followed by early Christians.

In fact, by teaching that man's earthly existence was merely a grim prelude to the eternal afterlife, Christianity offered an unmistakable, if unintentional, incentive to suicide. The longer one's life, the more opportunity there was to sin and the less chance of eternal bliss. Suicide—in the form of martyrdom—became the quickest ticket to heaven. Baptism wiped the slate clean of original sin; martyrdom erased the transgressions of a lifetime. Not only was the martyr guaranteed redemption, but he earned posthumous glory, annual commemoration in the church calendar, and an income for his family from church funds.

Christians had ample opportunity to sate their appetite for martyrdom. Anti-Christian mobs roamed the streets, and each day the authorities fed hundreds of Christians to the lions. More often than not the Christians met the Romans halfway. Aedesius slapped the governor of Egypt; he was tortured and thrown into the sea. The centurion Marcellus threw down his arms in the middle of a parade and cried, "I am a soldier of Jesus Christ"; he was executed. The histories of the first three centuries AD overflow with what we now call "indirect" suicides but at the time were described as "the splendid martyrs of Christ" who "everywhere astounded the eyewitnesses of their courage."

The Christian martyrs received moral support from the church hierarchy. Even Clement, bishop of Alexandria, one of the few early Christian writers to attack voluntary death, condemned it not because suicide is sinful but because the martyr tempts the pagan to commit the sin of murder. Tertullian forbade his flock even to attempt to escape persecution. Like a football coach before the big game, he exhorted imprisoned Christians to die heroically, citing celebrated pagan suicides such as Lucretia, Dido, and Cleopatra as role models, and pointing out that Jesus Christ on the cross had given up his spirit voluntarily before crucifixion could kill him. Invoking the primitive notion of "killing oneself upon the head of another," Tertullian promised posthumous revenge: "No City escaped punishment, which had shed Christian blood."

And so the Christians rushed the pagan judges, confessing their faith and begging for martyrdom. Eusebius, bishop of Caesarea, described a woman who celebrated her death sentence by "rejoicing and exulting at her departure as if invited to a wedding supper, not thrown to the beasts." Once condemned, the Christians leaped into the flames, hugged the lions, and baited the pagans. Three young Christians who had destroyed pagan idols turned themselves in and were ordered to die on gridirons. As the execution began they called to the governor, "Amachus, give orders that our bodies may be turned on the fire if you do not desire to be served with meat cooked only on one side." Ignatius, bishop of Antioch, en route to Rome and a date with the lions in the arena, was giddy with anticipation: "Let fire and cross, encounters with wild animals, tearing apart of bones, hacking of limbs, crushing of the whole body, tortures of the devil come upon me," he wrote, "if only I may attain to Jesus Christ!"

Death by lion was the easy way out compared to the chosen fate of St. Simeon Stylites, who is said to have stood on a sixty-foot pillar near Antioch for thirty years, exposed to wind, rain, and snow. For one of those years he stood on one leg while the other was covered by hideous ulcers. His biographer was delegated to retrieve the worms that fell from St. Simeon's body and to replace them in his open sores, as the saint urged the worms, "Eat what God has given you." St. Simeon was one of many early Christian monks and hermits whose stupefying asceticism often led to madness, early death, and sainthood. One lived for thirty years on crusts of barley bread and muddy water; another carried 150 pounds of iron and lived in a dried-up well. To contemporary psychiatrists, such "chronic suicide" would be traced to masochism, but to the early Christians it was a blessed ending, perhaps even more praiseworthy in the eyes of God than being killed in the arena. "Lo! For these thirty years and more I have been dwelling and groaning unceasingly in the desert!" boasts St. Anthony in Flaubert's *The Temptation of Saint Anthony* ". . . And those who are decapitated, tortured with red hot pincers, or burned alive, are perhaps less meritorious than I, seeing that my whole life is but one prolonged martyrdom."

Clearly, things were getting out of hand. It is not known how many martyrs died all told during the early years of Christianity. Contemporary estimates range from ten thousand to one hundred thousand. While there is no way to compute how many of these martyrs were voluntary, by all accounts the percentage was high. Yet there was evidence that some of the suicides were not religious zealots but impoverished Christians who found martyrdom the only way to secure food for their families. Others pursued self-sacrifice as far as prison in order to receive the alms and gifts that were often showered on prospective martyrs; then, well before their appointments with death, they recanted and were freed. In the fourth and fifth century, as the Roman Empire crumbled and the Church grew more powerful, ecclesiastical writers began to voice their disapproval. Gradually, suicide under persecution was no longer recognized as martyrdom, extreme asceticism was disparaged, and even suicide to preserve one's chastity was no longer unanimously praised. Disapproval calcified to denunciation. "If it is base to destroy others," declared St. John Chrysostom in the fourth century, "much more is it to destroy one's self." To St. Augustine, writing in the early fifth century, suicide was "monstrous."

In *City of God,* Augustine set forth the arguments that would become the cornerstones of the Christian view of suicide, a position that, on the whole, remains that of the Catholic Church today. Realizing that Christianity contained a logical dilemma—if paradise is achieved by avoiding sin, the most sensible step following baptism is suicide—Augustine tried to demonstrate that suicide itself was a sin greater than any that it could atone for. He took his arguments not from the Bible but from Plato's *Phaedo.* Life is a gift from God, explained Augustine, and suffering is sent by God to be endured. To bear suffering is a test of a soul's greatness; to evade it is an admission of weakness and an act against the will of God. To reject God's gift is to reject him—which is a sure path to eternal damnation. Furthermore, if a man kills himself to *atone* for his sins, he sins, for no private individual has the right to kill a guilty person; and if an innocent man kills himself to *avoid* sin, he has innocent blood on his hands—a sin worse than any he might have committed by living, for a suicide has no time to repent. Finally, Augustine maintained, a man who takes his own life kills a man and thus breaks the Sixth Commandment. Suicide, according to Augustine, was murder.

Augustine's arguments against suicide, devised to restrain the mania of martyrdom, were based on a respect for life that contrasted sharply with the barbarity of the Roman Empire. Nevertheless, they triggered an unexpectedly barbaric reaction. Though Augustine himself did not recommend punishment for what he called "a detestable crime and a damnable sin," his pronouncements, combined with the growing tide of public opinion, resulted in the first Christian edicts against suicide. In AD 452, the Council of Arles, declaring suicide to be caused by diabolical possession, reaffirmed the Roman slave clauses prohibiting suicide by servants. In 533, the Council of Orleans denied funeral rites to anyone who killed himself while accused of a crime. "The oblations of those who were killed in the commission of any crime may be received," they wrote, "except of such who laid violent hands upon themselves." Not only was suicide a crime, they implied, it was the worst of crimes; ordinary criminals were still allowed Christian burial. In 563, the Council of Braga denied funeral rites to all suicides; and in 693, the Council of Toledo declared that even attempters would be excommunicated.

The Church could not have made itself clearer. Suicide was a mortal sin. In a few centuries it had gone from being a passport to paradise to being the shortest route to hell. When the Albigenses of southern France sought martyrdom in droves in the thirteenth century, they were following in the footsteps of the early Christian martyrs. Near Narbonne, 140 of the group's spiritual elders cheated the executioner by throwing themselves on a burning pyre; elsewhere, seventy-four knights chose hanging over recantation and freedom. While the early Christian martyrs had earned sainthood for such acts, the Albigensians had compounded their sins by suicide and thus, it was said, deserved the savagery with which some five thousand of them were put to death in 1218. Suicides were no longer martyrs for God; they were, according to the eleventh century's St. Bruno, "martyrs for Satan." In this ecclesiastic revisionism, Judas, theologians claimed, was more damned for killing himself than for betraying Christ. Rather than being the ultimate proof of faith, suicide was now conclusive proof of faithlessness; the suicide had despaired of God's grace. When Joan of Arc, imprisoned at Bouvreuil in 1431, threw herself from her cell window to avoid falling into the hands of the English, her suicide attempt was used by the bishops at her trial as further proof of demonic possession.

By then a curious transformation had taken place. The Church had reversed its position on suicide so forcefully, it seemed to jar loose the primitive superstitions surrounding suicide that had been submerged through the classical age. In medieval England, custom dictated that a suicide must leave the room in which he died not by the door but through a hole bored under the threshold. In Danzig the corpse was lowered by pulleys from the window and the window frame subsequently burned. The corpse was then hanged from a gallows. Each town had its own variations; in some areas the bodies of suicides were burned, in others they were buried on the beach below the high-water mark. In Zurich a suicide who had killed himself by jumping from a height was buried under a mountain whose weight would press upon his restive soul. While these customs had their origins in the primitive rituals designed to placate the suicide's ghost, the ghost was no longer the primary target; now the act itself was the object of punishment, and the rituals began to be defined by fury more than by fear.

What started at Arles as canonical legislation was soon reinforced by civil law. Feudal lords had an economic stake in seeing that their workers didn't kill themselves. In 967, England's King Edgar gave state sanction to the ecclesiastical penalties. Gradually, the connection between suicide and murder that the Church had forged by its interpretation of the Sixth Commandment found secular approval. The suicide was a self-murderer, subject to similar punishment. In England, the first civil mandate against suicide was probably imported by the Danes during their invasion in 1013: "Let him who hath murdered himself, be fined in all his goods to his lord: let him find a place of burial neither in the church nor church yard; unless ill health and madness drove him to the perpetration." The thirteenth-century legal authority Henry de Bracton recorded that the ordinary self-murderer forfeited his goods; the person who killed himself while awaiting trial forfeited both goods *and* land. There were exceptions: "The madman, or the idiot, or the infant, or the person under such acute pain as to produce a temporary distraction, who kills himself, shall forfeit neither lands nor chattels, because he is deprived of reason." Suicide was (self-) murder unless the perpetrator was insane—the loophole by which Catholic and Jewish suicides have been allowed burial to this day.

In *Summa Theologiae* (1267–73), a codification of ecclesiastical teachings, Thomas Aquinas, summing up the Church's position on suicide, reflected the changes since Augustine. Augustine had based his antisuicide stance on spiritual arguments; Aquinas reinforced the religious objections with secular rationale. He reiterated Plato's "life as a gift from God" argument as filtered through Augustine. "Life is a gift made to man by God," wrote Aquinas, "and it is subject to him who is *master of death and life.* Therefore a person who takes his own life sins against God, just as he who kills another's slave injures the slave's master, or just as he who usurps judgement in a matter outside his authority also commits a sin. And God alone has authority to decide about life and death." Aquinas went beyond this familiar reasoning to raise two secular objections. First, he maintained that suicide is unnatural; it goes against man's instinct for self-preservation and is contrary to the charity that a man ought to bear to himself. Second, borrowing from Aristotle, Aquinas said that by killing himself a person injures the community of which he is a part. Furthermore, he asserted that anyone who commits suicide to avoid punishment is a coward.

By combining secular and religious arguments Aquinas offered an intellectual justification for civil penalties against suicide. An act that had been a rational end to the Greeks, an honorable end to the Romans, and a means to heaven to the early Christians was now damned by God and despised by man. Suicide, concluded Aquinas, was "completely wrong."

In Canto XIII of the *Divine Comedy,* written at the start of the fourteenth century, Virgil leads Dante below the burning heretics, below the murderers in their river of blood, to a dark, pathless wood. Dante hears human voices weeping all about him; frightened, he reaches out and snaps off a twig. "Why dost thou rend me?" cries the trunk, turning dark with blood. "Men we were and now are turned to trees." Dante is in the forest of suicides. Every tree and bush in the wood harbors the soul of a self-killer. The tree whose twig he plucked holds the soul of Piero delle Vigne, once chief counselor to Emperor Frederick II of Sicily. In 1249, unjustly accused of treason, imprisoned and blinded, he smashed his brains out against the walls of his cell. Now delle Vigne tells Dante that when the soul tears itself from its own body, it is cast into the seventh circle of hell where it grows into a gnarled, thorny tree. The Harpies, winged creatures with human faces and sharp claws, nest in the trees and pick at their leaves, causing the branches to bleed and the souls to cry out in pain, thus repeating the violent action of suicide every moment for eternity.

# III

# RENAISSANCE
# AND ENLIGHTENMENT:
# "IT IS HIS CASE,
# IT MAY BE THINE"

———

LIKE A KNIFE THROWER'S TARGET, medieval man was circumscribed by Christian dogma, which taught him that life was hell, death was torture, and hell was worse. In this scheme of things suicide was unspeakable. Against this joyless landscape the Renaissance blew in like a cool breeze, bringing an awareness of the world's beauty and a renewed faith in man's possibilities. *Memento mori,* the somber slogan of the Middle Ages, became *memento vivere.* Earthly life was once again valued for itself and not merely as a transition to the hereafter. Renaissance scholars rediscovered classical art, literature, and philosophy, and the Greek and Roman ideals of self-reliance and self-determination were reborn. In his "Oration on the Dignity of Man," Pico della Mirandola imagines God addressing humanity: "Thou, constrained by no limits, in accordance with thine own free will, in whose hand We have placed thee, shalt ordain for thyself the limits of thy nature . . . as though the maker and molder of thyself, thou mayest fashion thyself in whatever shape thou shalt prefer." And if man's life was his own, so was his death. The decaying flesh, voracious worms, and eternal torment that filled the medieval vision of death gave way to a serene new view:

*Death is a remedy against all evils:* It is a most assured haven, never to be feared, and often to be sought: All comes to one period, whether man make an end of himselfe, or whether he endure it; whether he run before his day, or whether he expect it: whence soever it come, it is ever his owne, where ever the threed be broken, it is all there, it's the end of the web. The voluntariest death, is the fairest. *Life dependeth on the will of others, death on ours.* In nothing should we so much accommodate our selves to our humours, as in that.

In his essay "A Custome of the Ile of Cea" (referring to state-sponsored suicide in the ancient Greek colony of Ceos), Michel de Montaigne, whose skeptical essays questioned prevailing attitudes on almost any subject, based his defense of suicide, written in the 1570s, on classical notions of free will. But Montaigne was less interested in endorsing suicide than in demystifying death. "All the wisdom and reasoning in the world boils down finally to this point," he once wrote, "to teach us not to be afraid to die." And in the end Montaigne's arguments were leavened with Renaissance optimism. He found suicide not immoral but a bit foolish. "The opinion which disdaineth our life, is ridiculous," he wrote, "for, in fine, it is our being. It is our all in all." He introduced a practical argument that would become a staple of modern suicide prevention: "Moreover, there being so many sudden changes, and violent alterations in humane things, it is hard to judge in what state or point we are justly at the end of our hope. . . . I have seene a hundred Hares save themselves even in the Greyhounds jawes."

"A Custome of the Ile of Cea" was the first significant discussion of suicide to question the Church's blanket prohibition. After eight centuries suicide was once more a topic for debate. Even those who argued against it, like the fourteenth-century humanist Petrarch, disdained religious intimidation in favor of balanced argument. In *The Funeral,* Erasmus explained that God meant death to be dreadful "lest men far and wide commit suicide. And since, even today, we see so many do violence to themselves, what do you suppose would happen if death weren't horrible? Whenever a servant or even a young son got a thrashing, whenever a wife fell out with her husband, whenever a man lost his money, or something else occurred that upset him, off they'd rush to noose, sword, river, cliff, poison." Yet in *The Praise of Folly,* Erasmus described those who killed themselves in disgust at the miserable world as "people who lived next door to wisdom." In Renaissance literature suicide was once more a conversation piece. Less than a century after Dante condemned suicides to the seventh circle of hell, Chaucer used Thisbe, Dido, Lucretia, and Cleopatra as models in his *Legende of Goode Women;* Lucretia became a heroine of Tudor and Elizabethan poetry and a popular model for Renaissance painters. And as early as 1516, Thomas More's *Utopia* offered what may have been the first

Christian consideration of voluntary euthanasia. In More's ideal republic, although provided the best possible medical care, the terminally ill were permitted, even encouraged, to end their lives.

> But yf the dysease be not onelye uncurable, but also full of contynuall payne and anguyshe, then the priestes and the magistrates exhort the man, seynge he ys not able to doo annye dewtye of lyffe, and by ouer-lyuing hys owne deathe is noysome and yrkesome to other, and greuous to himself; that he wyll determyne with hymselfe no longer to cheryshe that pestilent and peynefull dysease: and, seynge hys lyfe ys to hym but a tourmente, that he wyll nott bee unwyllynge too dye, but rather take a good hope to hym, and other dyspatche hymselfe owte of that paynfull lyffe, as owte of a pryson or a racke of tormente, or elles suffer hym selfe wyllynglye to be rydde owte of yt by other. And in so doynge they tell hym he shal doo wyselye, seynge by hys deathe he shall lyse no commodytye, but ende hys payne.

Renaissance writers would most affect the discussion of suicide not by introducing any fresh philosophical angle but by beginning to describe what, centuries later, would be called the psychology of a suicidal person. In Edmund Spenser's *The Faerie Queene,* Despair, his cave littered with the corpses of suicides, presses a dagger upon the Red Cross Knight. Suddenly, a familiar-sounding iteration of the traditional arguments for and against self-destruction gives way to the magnified heartbeat of a true suicidal crisis: ". . . his hand did quake / And tremble like a leafe of Aspin greene, / And troubled bloud through his pale face was seene / To come, and goe with tydings from the hart, / As it a running messenger had beene."

It would be Shakespeare, of course, who most fully explored the suicidal person's internal landscape. In his eight tragedies there are fourteen suicides. Shakespeare examined what were known as honor suicides—to avoid capture, to rejoin a lost loved one, and so on—and saw them not as types but as individuals with complex motives. Cassius, for instance, who orders his servant to run him through with his sword, is not simply the traditional "suicide to avoid capture" but a proud man undone by his refusal to compromise his lofty self-concept. Othello, too, values his good name more than his life. He stabs himself not so much out of guilt for killing Desdemona but as a way of reviving his reputation. As M. D. Faber has pointed out in an essay on Shakespeare's suicides, Othello kills the bad part of himself (the jealous monster who killed innocent Desdemona) so that the good part (the just, noble warrior) may live on posthumously. Faber suggested that Romeo's suicide is less a romantic attempt to rejoin his lost loved one, Juliet, than an impulsive act of rage, spite, and frustration. " 'I defy you, stars,' cries Romeo just as he decides to die, and in that cry we have much of what is driving him," wrote Faber. ". . . His suicide is, in large part, an obscene gesture directed toward the world and the world's authorities." Hamlet, the melancholy Dane, unable to express his anger at his mother for marrying his uncle, turns his rage inward and contemplates suicide. In his famous soliloquy he moves from the religious prohibitions, his dismay that God had "fix'd his canon 'gainst self-slaughter," to a practical consideration of the pros and cons. Although he admits that exchanging "a sea of troubles" for the "sleep of death" is "a consummation devoutly to be wished," he hesitates, worried that what comes after death might be even worse than his troubled life.

In 1608, seven years after *Hamlet* was first produced and published, John Donne summed up the arguments for and against suicide in *Biathanatos*, subtitled: *A Declaration of that Paradoxe, or Thesis, that Self-homicide is not so Naturally Sinne, that it may never be otherwise. Wherein The Nature, and the extent of all those Lawes, which seeme to be violated by this Act, are diligently surveyed.* The first defense of suicide in the English language was as formidable as its title. Its three parts, devoted to demonstrating that suicide does not contradict the laws of nature, of reason, or of God, were a witty, erudite dismantling of the traditional arguments against what Donne called "the disease of head-long dying."

Donne concluded his vast and detailed survey of suicide by observing that "in all ages, in all places, upon all occasions, men of all conditions, have affected it, and inclin'd to doe it." Suicide is universal, as much a part of us as the instinct of self-preservation it seems to deny. Donne's conclusion rendered the moral question less absolute, affirming that "no law is so primary and simple . . . but that circumstances alter it. In which case a private man is Emperor of himselfe. . . . And he whose conscience well tempred and dispassion'd, assures him that the reason of selfe-preservation ceases in him, may also presume that the law ceases too."

Donne's insistence that each case must be judged individually was probably the result of his own "circumstance." In the preface to *Biathanatos* he explained his reasons for writing the book. After describing a man "eminent and illustrious, in the full glory and Noone of Learning," who was prevented from throwing himself off a Paris bridge, Donne confessed that he had considered suicide himself. "I have often such a sickely inclination," he wrote, although he could not explain exactly why. "Whensoever any affliction assailes me, mee thinks I have the keyes of my prison in mine owne hand, and no remedy presen's it selfe so soone to my heart, as mine own sword."

In *The Savage God*, A. Alvarez explored the reasons for Donne's "sickely inclination." Donne wrote *Biathanatos* at the age of thirty-six, when his brilliant career as poet and courtier was at low ebb. Having been dismissed from his post as private secretary to the Lord Keeper of the Privy Seal, Donne lived with his wife and children outside London. Unable to write or to find a job, Donne thought of death. In a 1608 letter to a friend he wrote of the "thirst and inhiation after the next life" that often overtook him. But Donne admitted that his suicidal thoughts were not wholly due to his reduced circumstances "because I had the same desires when I went with the tyde, and enjoyed fairer hopes than now."

Whatever kept him from "head-long dying" is not known, but that same year Donne wrote *Biathanatos.* Alvarez has suggested that the book itself saved Donne. "I wonder if *Biathanatos* didn't begin as a prelude to self-destruction and finish as a substitute for it," he wrote. "That is, he set out to find precedents and reasons for killing himself while still remaining Christian—or, at least, without damning himself eternally. But the process of writing the book and marshaling his intricate learning and dialectical skill may have relieved the tension and helped to re-establish his sense of his self." Although Donne, who took vows to enter the Church in 1615, continued to be preoccupied by death in his sermons from the pulpit as dean of St. Paul's and in his divine poems, he forbade publication of *Biathanatos* "because it is upon a misinterpretable subject." When it was finally published in 1646, fifteen years after his death, it created a storm of comment. But despite its learned discussion of suicide, the book's main contribution may have been in the simple confession of the preface. Suicide, Donne explained, may be neither a heroic, rational choice nor a sin and a crime, but "a sickely inclination" that can overwhelm a person.

Donne's "sickely inclination" sounds like depression. In the seventeenth century it was known as melancholy, a catchall term that described a variety of moods and symptoms. In the Middle Ages it existed as *accidie,* a sinful malaise born of despair of the grace of God. In "The Parson's Tale," Chaucer described how *accidie* made a man "hevy, thoghtful, and wrawe." A different sort of melancholy was found in the ballads of medieval troubadours, who sang of dying lovers and the supreme value of love on earth. That romantic seed bloomed in the Renaissance when melancholy stemmed not from the sinner's horror of death and eternity but from a realization of the brevity of life. In literature and drama, melancholy would become associated with sensitive, thoughtful, superior minds, even genius, and it threatened to become a fashionable affliction.

To Robert Burton melancholy was far too painful to consider fashionable. "If there be a hell upon earth, it is to be found in a melancholy man's heart," he wrote in 1621 in *The Anatomy of Melancholy,* a chatty, rambling field guide to the species. According to Burton, melancholy was near-ubiquitous, and the fact that his book went through seven editions in forty years may support his claim. A parson and Oxford don who lived, he admitted, "a silent, sedentary, solitary life," Burton himself suffered from persistent melancholy, which he could sometimes alleviate by going down to the Isis to listen to the shouts and curses of the bargemen. But many melancholics, he wrote, found relief only in death. (Burton was rumored to have hanged himself.)

Though the parson in Burton dutifully repeated the antisuicide arguments and quoted the laws and penalties against the act, the humanist in him seems to have realized that suicide, like the melancholy from which he suffered, may not be a matter of choice: "In extremity, they know not what they do, deprived of reason, judgment, all, as a ship that is void of a pilot, must needs impinge upon the next rock or sands, and suffer shipwreck." He questioned the Church's damnation of suicide and suggested that man himself is in no position to pass judgment. "What may happen to one may happen to another. Who knows how he may be tempted? It is his case, it may be thine."

If the Stoics, with their ultrarational approach, had made suicide seem heroic, icy, and a little impersonal, Christianity, by damning and degrading it, had made it seem foul and inhuman. With the Renaissance, Shakespeare, Donne, and Burton managed to humanize suicide, treating it as an object of sympathy rather than of worship or horror. This change was even reflected in the work of several ecclesiastical writers, who, while condemning suicide, admitted to certain exceptions. "There be two sorts of voluntarie deaths," observed Reverend Tuke in *A Discourse on Death* in 1613, "the one lawful and honest, such as the death of Martyrs, the other dishonest and unlawful, when men have neyther lawfull calling, nor honest endes, as of Peregrinus, who burnt himselfe in a pile of wood, thinking thereby to live forever in mens remembrance." Saint Cyran's "Casus Regius" listed thirty-four situations in which the self-murderer was innocent, and theologians and philosophers of the school of Grotius and Pufendorf condoned suicide when committed to avoid dishonor or sin, to save oneself from death by torture, or to offer up one's own life to save that of a friend. In 1613, alarmed by a rash of suicides near Rothenburg ob der Tauber, Protestant minister Johannes Neser preached three sermons in which he reiterated that those who committed premeditated suicide when sane were damned. But men who were driven to suicide by intense vexations, chronic sickness, or extreme pain were not damned, he said, because they did not know what they were doing. When in doubt as to a suicide's sinfulness—as in cases of gout, bladder stone, and urinary gravel, where acute pain might cause temporary derangement—he concluded that the verdict must be left to God.

In 1637, concerned by an apparent increase in suicide, an English country clergyman named John Sym wrote *Lifes Preservative Against Self-Killing*. While agreeing with prevailing seventeenth-century opinion that suicide was the devil's work and "utterly unlawful," Sym compiled what may have been the first collection of warning signs: "gastly lookes, wilde frights and flaights, nestling and restlesse behaviour, a mindlessnesse and close dumpishnesse, both in company and in good imployments; a distracted countenance and cariage; speaking and talking to, and with themselves, in their solitary places and dumps; reasoning and resolving with themselves about that fact, and their motives to it, in a perplexed disturbed manner, with the like." If these signs were present, said Sym, the melancholy man must take precautions to keep the devil at bay: "shunning to go upon lawfull calling into solitary retired places; over waters, bridges, upon battlements of houses; or neere steepe downe places . . . shunning to be alone, or in dark places." Drawing on his experience counseling potential suicides, Sym concluded, "Self-murder is prevented, not so much by arguments against the fact; which disswades from the conclusion; as by the discovery and removall of the motives and causes, whereupon they are tempted to do the same: as diseases are cured by removing of the causes, rather than of their symptoms."

Sym's conclusion—treat the causes and not the symptoms—was ahead of its time. Despite—or perhaps because of—sympathetic consideration for the suicide in Renaissance philosophy and literature, there remained a vast gap between enlightened opinion and the law. Whether a man be pushed to suicide by melancholy, by fever, or by the devil, he risked a variety of punishments. Even the benevolence of More's *Utopia* extended only so far: unauthorized suicides were to be "caste unburied into some stinkyng marrish." Their fate was mild compared to that of suicides in the real world. Facing what they believed to be a rising toll of suicides, courts invoked stiffer penalties in the hope that if fear of eternal damnation was not enough to deter the potential suicide, concern for his property, family, reputation, and corpse might be.

In fifteenth-century France the body of one Louis de Beaumont was to be dragged through the streets "as cruelly as possible, to set an example for others." An ordinance of 1670 reaffirmed that suicide was treason against God and king. The suicide's corpse was hauled through the streets of the city, hanged upside down, then thrown into a sewer or the town dump. His property was forfeited to the king. If the deceased was a nobleman, he was declared a commoner. His forests were razed, his castle demolished, his shield and coat of arms broken, and his memory defamed *ad perpetuam rei memoriam*—to the end of memory. If the corpse of a suicide could not be found, a sentence of defamation was brought in against his name. In 1582, in Scotland, where according to the law "self-murder is as highly criminal as the killing of our neighbor," the Kirk Sessions of Perth refused to allow the corpse of a man who had committed suicide by drowning to be "brought through the town in daylight, neither yet to be buried among the Faithful—but in the little inch [island] within the water." In 1598, in Edinburgh, the body of a woman who drowned herself was "harled through the town backwards, and thereafter hanged on the gallows." In Finland, suicides judged insane were buried outside the churchyard without traditional ceremonies; if "of sound mind," the corpse was burned on a pyre in the forest. Those who attempted suicide were imprisoned with a diet of bread, water, and flogging. In Italy, suicides were hanged; if the corpse could not be found, it was hanged in effigy. In Austria, a person who attempted suicide was imprisoned "until he be persuaded by education that self-preservation is a duty to God, the State and to himself, show complete repentance and may be expected to mend his ways."

In 1601 the lawyer William Fulbecke matter-of-factly described the English punishment of the day: "The body is drawn out of the house, wherein the person killed himself, with ropes; not by the door, for of that he is unworthy, but through some hole or pit made under the threshold of the door; and is thence drawn by an horse to the place of punishment or shame, where it is hanged on a gibbet; and none may take it down, but by order of the magistrate." Suicides were tried posthumously in the coroner's court. The usual penalty for *felo de se*—property confiscation and burial at a crossroads with a wooden stake through the heart—could be avoided if the jury ruled the deceased had acted from insanity. To secure a proper burial, friends and relatives of the dead man had to persuade the court that their loved one was a madman. If the deceased was a man of wealth or position, he was more apt to be found insane and allowed burial; less fortunate suicides were usually awarded the stake and crossroads. Thus, in Shakespeare's *Hamlet,* although Ophelia is allowed burial in sanctified ground, she is denied full rites; the priest explains to Laertes, "We should profane the service of the dead / To sing a requiem, and such rest to her / As to peace-parted souls."

The Colonies appear to have been no less stringent. The Puritans, who fled England, in part, as a repudiation of the social changes taking place there, believed suicide to be "the worst kind of murder," as the Reverend Increase Mather described it in his treatise *A Call to the Tempted. A Sermon on the horrid Crime of Self-Murder.* A man, said Mather, "cannot disgrace himself more than by committing such a sin." Melancholy was no excuse; Satan was behind each and every suicide. (Tormented by "Hypocondriacal affection," Mather had himself been tempted toward self-destruction but, armed only with his faith, had kept the devil at bay.) In Mather's Massachusetts, a 1660 edict outlawing "Self-Murther" proclaimed that those "who lay violent hands on themselves" shall be buried "in some Common High-way . . . and a Cart-load of Stones laid upon the Grave as a Brand of Infamy, and as a warning to others to beware of the like Damnable practices." (The suicide's property, however, was not confiscated. Attempted suicides were whipped, imprisoned, and held liable for court costs.) Thus in the spring of 1707, one Abraham Harris of Boston, a young whitewasher, having "felloniously and willfully Murthered himself, by Hanging himself with a Neckcloth—Contrary to the Peace of Our Soveraign Lady the Queen," was buried at a crossroads near the gallows on the Roxbury Highway, and a cartload of stones was laid on his grave. The burial cost the county sixteen shillings, including one shilling for "money lay'd out in drink" for the constable and six gravediggers.

"Wheresoever you finde many and severe Lawes against an offence," observed Donne in *Biathanatos,* "it is not safe from thence to conclude an extreame enormity or hainousnesse in the fault, but a propensnesse of that people, at that time, to that fault." Clergymen were convinced that a loosening of morals during the Renaissance inspired an increase in suicide. The act, wrote an anonymous observer in 1647, "is now growne so common, that selfe murther is scarce accounted any newes." The evidence is not conclusive. The nature of suicide, however, seems to have changed. In the early years of the Renaissance numerous suicides aspired to the classical mode. In 1538 the Florentine patriot Philip Strozzi, accused in the assassination of Alessandro de Medici, was captured; fearing that under torture he might betray the names of fellow conspirators, he decided on suicide. After carving a line from Virgil— "Arise from my bones, avenger of these wrongs!"—on his cell wall, he stabbed himself, leaving behind a note in which he asked that he be permitted to have his place with Cato of Utica and other great suicides of antiquity. In the late seventeenth and early eighteenth centuries, the stage abounded with classical suicides. In France there were plays about Lucretia, Brutus, Cassius, and at least two on Cato. In England, Joseph Addison's *Cato* was a hit in 1713. Alexander Pope, who wrote the prologue, observed to a friend that "Cato was not so much the wonder of Rome in his days, as he is of Britain in ours." Twenty-four years later Addison's cousin and protégé Eustace Budgell loaded his pockets with stones and threw himself into the Thames, leaving behind a note: "What Cato did and Addison approved cannot be wrong."

But Budgell's suicide was hardly in the tradition of Cato's. A writer and scholar, he had lost twenty-two thousand pounds in the South Sea Bubble speculation and died a failed, lonely man. If his death lacked the classical touch, it hinted at something more complex and more human. By the end of the Renaissance, suicides could no longer be seen simply as the result of honor, black bile, or the devil. They were the product of human struggle, of pride, loneliness, melancholy—and especially poverty. Between 1597 and 1644, of three hundred suicides in three English counties, more than half left no goods at all. The suicides included twenty-nine laborers, thirty-seven spinsters, and assorted shoemakers, tinkers, hostlers, bricklayers, and so on. Far more characteristic than the showily heroic suicide of Philip Strozzi was that of Richard and Bridget Smith in 1732.

Smith was a bookbinder who had fallen into debt after a series of losses and disappointments. He and his wife, agreeing that a life of numbing poverty had little to offer, decided to commit suicide. After cutting their daughter's throat, they hanged themselves from the bedpost, leaving a note addressed to the public:

*These actions, considered in all their circumstances, being somewhat uncommon, it may not be improper to give some account of the cause; and that it was an inveterate hatred we conceived against poverty and rags, evils that through a train of unlucky accidents were become inevitable. For we appeal to all that ever knew us, whether we were idle or extravagant, whether or no we have not taken as much pains to get our living as our neighbours, although not attended with the same suc-*

*cess. We apprehend the taking our child's life away to be a circumstance
for which we shall be generally condemned; but for our own parts we
are perfectly easy on that head. We are satisfied it is less cruelty to take
the child with us, even supposing a state of annihilation as some dream
of, than to leave her friendless in the world, exposed to ignorance and
misery. . . . We are not ignorant of those laws made* in terrorem, *but leave
the disposal of our bodies to the wisdom of the coroner and his jury, the
thing being indifferent to us where our bodies are laid. . . .*

*Richard Smith*
*Bridget Smith*

The Smiths were buried at the crossroads near the Turnpike at Newington.

---

To Enlightenment thinkers like Montesquieu, Rousseau, and Voltaire, Richard
and Bridget Smith's decision to end their lives was perfectly reasonable, and
to punish it with a stake through the heart was an outrage. In an age that
scorned anything hinting of medievalism and put a premium on the rights of
the individual, suicide seemed an essential human liberty. "To be *happy* or not
to be at all," wrote Jeremy Bentham, the founder of utilitarianism, reworking
Hamlet. "Such is the option which nature has given to every human being."
Suicide, insisted the Rationalists, was not a mortal sin or a crime against the
state—to elevate an essentially private act into a cosmic blow against the universe seemed absurd.

"When I am overcome by anguish, poverty, or humiliation, why must I be
prevented from putting an end to my troubles, and harshly deprived of the
remedy which lies in my power?" wrote Montesquieu in 1721. In *Persian Letters* the Oriental traveler Usbek, writing from Paris to a friend in Smyrna, is
astonished by the "ferocity" of the European laws against suicide. "They are
put to death for a second time, so to speak; their bodies are dragged in disgrace
through the streets and branded, to denote infamy, and their goods are confiscated." He argues that if life is a gift, if the gift ceases to give pleasure, why is
one not free to part with it? The body is destined to perish in any case, he concludes, and the soul to live on, so how is the order of Providence disturbed? In
the vast scheme of things, the persistence of a person in bearing the agonies of
a hopeless illness seems merely vain. "All such ideas, my dear Ibben, originate
in our pride alone."

Fifty years later another letter discussing suicide stirred controversy. In
Rousseau's novel *La Nouvelle Héloïse,* Saint Preux, a young man disappointed in love, writes an impassioned letter to his English friend Lord Bomston, explaining that suicide is neither a crime nor inconsistent with belief in
God. "Every man has a right by nature to pursue what he thinks is good, and
avoid what he thinks evil, in all matters which are not injurious to others," he

writes, echoing the Stoic argument. "When our life becomes a misery to ourselves, and is of advantage to no one, we are thus at liberty to put an end to our being." God gave man reason to enable him to choose between good and evil, says Saint Preux, and reason tells us that an unhappy life must be remedied as much as a diseased body: "If it is permitted to seek a cure for gout, why not for life?" He compares the man who does not know how to relieve an unhappy life by seeking death to the man who allows his wound to gangrene rather than summoning a surgeon. As for theologians who insist that suicide disqualifies us from Providence, Saint Preux maintains that in killing ourselves we merely destroy our bodies but bring our immortal souls, in death, closer to God. Saint Preux admits exceptions: people who have duties to others should not dispose of themselves. But, he concludes, since he is not a magistrate, has no family to support, and for friends has only Lord Bomston, nothing stands in his way.

"Young man, a blind ecstasy leads you astray," Lord Bomston begins his reply, in which he discusses the importance of remaining at one's post and stresses the cowardice of despair. He suggests that his friend might find relief in helping others. "Each time thou art tempted to quit life, say to thyself, let me at least do one good action before I die, then go in search for one indigent person, whom thou mayest relieve; for one under misfortune, whom thou mayest console; for one under oppression, whom thou mayest defend." While Rousseau followed this prescription in his own life, readers of *La Nouvelle Héloïse* felt that the passion of Saint Preux's arguments overwhelmed the elegance of Bomston's and indicated where Rousseau's sympathies lay. Preachers accused him of spawning suicides; Saint Preux would become a model for Goethe's *Werther,* which would in turn be blamed for a rash of self-killing. In a letter to Voltaire, Rousseau wrote that the wise man will sometimes give up his life when nature and bad fortune give a distinct order to depart. Rousseau's own unhappy life was increasingly haunted by madness, and after his death in 1778 there were rumors that he had killed himself.

Voltaire's position on suicide was not unlike that of many twentieth-century liberals. On one hand, as a passionate opponent of superstition and injustice, he opposed laws that degraded a suicide's corpse and deprived his innocent family. Calling confiscation of the suicide's property "brigandage," Voltaire, with characteristic acidity, noted that in practice "his goods are given to the King, who almost always grants half of them to the leading lady of the Opera, who prevails upon one of her lovers to ask for it; the other half by law belongs to the Inland Revenue." In his novels and plays Voltaire attacked dogmatism and oppression and proclaimed the individual's mastery over his own destiny. If "self-murder" was a wrong against society, he argued, are not the voluntary homicides committed in war and sanctioned by the laws of all countries far more harmful to the human race? Like Donne, he believed that circumstance, not dogma, must be our guide in judging suicide. Every case must be weighed on its own merits—"Each one has his reasons for his behavior." To Voltaire some reasons were better than others. He teased the hypersensitive melancholics and suggested that young girls who drown themselves for love should not be hasty—change is as common in love as it is in business. Voltaire complained that eighteenth-century suicides could learn a thing or two from the old masters: "We kill ourselves, too," he wrote, "but it is when we have lost our money or in the rare excess of a wild passion for an object which isn't worth it." As for himself, the antisuicide laws made his own suicide improbable, he jokingly confessed in a letter to his friend the Marquise du Deffand: "It is a decision that I shall not take, at least not yet, for the reason that I have got myself annuities from two sovereigns and I should be inconsolable if my death enriched two crowned heads."

The arguments of the eighteenth-century Rationalists were summed up by Scottish philosopher David Hume in his essay "On Suicide." With the confidence of a sharpshooter he set up his targets—"If suicide be criminal, it must be a transgression of our duty either to God, our neighbour, or ourselves"—and then picked them off one by one.

> Were the disposal of human life so much reserved as the peculiar province of the Almighty, that it were an encroachment on his right for men to dispose of their own lives, it would be equally criminal to act for the preservation of life as for its destruction. If I turn aside a stone which is falling upon my head, I disturb the course of nature; and I invade the peculiar province of the Almighty, by lengthening out my life beyond the period, which, by the general laws of matter and motion, he has assigned it.
>
> A hair, a fly, an insect, is able to destroy this mighty being whose life is of such importance. Is it an absurdity to suppose that human prudence may lawfully dispose of what depends on such insignificant causes? It would be no crime in me to divert the Nile or Danube from its course, were I able to effect such purposes. Where then is the crime of turning a few ounces of blood from their natural channel?

If all events proceed from God, said Hume, then so, too, does suicide: "When I fall upon my own sword, therefore, I receive my death equally from the hands of the Deity as if it had proceeded from a lion, a precipice, or a fever." To those who insisted that suicide was a crime against nature, Hume pointed out that man alters nature in many acceptable ways: building houses, cultivating land, sailing upon the ocean. "In all these actions we employ our powers of mind and body to produce some innovation in the course of nature; and in none of them do we any more. They are all of them therefore equally innocent, or equally criminal."

Turning to the argument that suicide is a crime against society, Hume maintained that "a man who retires from life does no harm to society: he only ceases to do good; which, if it is an injury, is of the lowest kind." Furthermore, like Montesquieu, Hume believed that citizenship is a two-way responsibility; when man withdraws himself from society, is he still bound any longer? In any case, wrote Hume, "I am not obliged to do a small good to society at the expense of a great harm to myself: why then should I prolong a miserable existence because of some frivolous advantage which the public may perhaps receive from me?"

To Hume the flaw in the "crime against self" argument seemed self-evident. "That suicide may often be consistent with interest and with our duty to ourselves, no one can question, who allows that age, sickness, or misfortune, may render life a burden, and make it worse even than annihilation." In any case, he wondered, why was the rest of the world so wounded by suicide? "The life of a man is of no greater importance to the universe than that of an oyster."

Written at least twenty years before Hume's death, "On Suicide" was not published until 1777, the year after he died. It was promptly suppressed and was later published from the apparently more tolerant grounds of Basel. But Hume's "oyster" did not go down easily; he and his fellow eighteenth-century "apologists" for suicide, as their enemies referred to them, provoked a fresh torrent of rhetoric from antisuicide moralists. (One London minister, remarking that "On Suicide" had reportedly inspired a friend of Hume's to shoot himself, suggested that Hume should have practiced what he preached.) From pulpits and printing presses across Europe they redoubled the volume of hellfire and brimstone against what they variously described as "a pusillanimous escape," "that miserable insanity," "the foul offspring of vile progenitors," "The Certain Characteristic of a foolish, weak Mind," "An Atrocious Offense Against God and Man," "the offspring of hell," "a crime of the deepest dye," "the most sordid and unworthy selfishness," and "the act of cowards, poltroons, and deserters." As for the causes of this act, they compiled an impressive list of culprits: "gambling," "government," "vanity," "modern philosophy," "intemperate drinking," "licentious novels," "want of benevolence," "want of ambition," "Habits of Idleness," "the examples of profligates," "Indulgence of Criminal Love," "a criminal love of the world," "A Gloomy and Misguided Imagination," "a weakness and timidity of mind," "the difficulty of procuring a livelihood," "the great number of authorized lotteries," "a base, corrupt, loathsome sinful State of Mind," "the fatal insanity of commercial speculation and the irrational desire of becoming wealthy on a sudden," "the mistaken fashion in education which has latterly prevailed, [in which] the superficial shewy and frivolous accomplishments are almost universally preferred to solid science and modest virtue," and above all, "want of submission to the Judge and Arbitrator of human affairs," or as another preacher put it, "Godlessness."

To stem what they believed to be a growing tide of self-destruction, they called for increased church attendance, fewer insanity verdicts in coroners' courts, and stricter antisuicide penalties. "The carcass should have the Burial of an Ass, and the utmost Marks of Reproach cast upon it," suggested one writer, "in order to deter others from giving way to, or falling into the like Snares and Wiles of the Devil." Another proposed that these "sons of perdition" be hanged in chains head down and every minister required to preach against the crime once a year. Another suggested that the bodies of self-murderers be dissected publicly on stages in marketplaces and the skeletons handed over to surgeons to "contribute somewhat to the advancement of *anatomical knowledge.*" One minister favored a combination of all of the above. "It might not only be refused all rites of burial, but be exposed naked to public view, be dragged on an hurdle in the most ignominious posture, and undergo every disgraceful mark of shame, contempt and abhorrence," he wrote. "The populace on these occasions might be harangued with energy on the foulness of the crime, and then the carcass delivered over (like that of the common murderer) for the purposes of public dissection; so that he, who had voluntarily withdrawn himself from being further useful to society in his life, might become so in his death."

Buried in the bombast were important arguments—duty to the state, the virtue of suffering, responsibility to family—but their shrillness obscured their logic. "Many of those who have maintained the criminality of Suicide have indulged an intemperance of zeal, a bitterness of expression, which are ill suited both to the teacher and the investigator of moral science; and which tend to cast unfavourable suspicions, as well upon the Reasoning as upon the Reasoner," observed Richard Hey, a graduate student at Cambridge, whose dissertation on suicide won a university prize in 1783. "It is time that we cease to injure our cause by an injudicious defence of it." Hey noted that a softer touch was also more effective with would-be suicides. "There is a singular impropriety in using a severity of address to the persons whom we would retain from the commission of Suicide," he wrote. "The state of mind in which this crime is *usually* committed, requires gentleness of treatment; as far as may be consistent with an open and full representation of the truth. Wherefore all unnecessary harshness is to be studiously avoided, as tending in a peculiar manner to defeat our principal purpose." While Hey's approach was sympathetic, his conclusion was familiar: "Suicide must stand *universally* condemned."

While preachers reiterated familiar theological objections, the reasoning of antisuicide philosophers became increasingly secular. They focused their arguments on an idea first raised by Aquinas that suicide goes against human nature. In 1690, John Locke published his *Second Treatise on Government,* a manifesto based on the assumptions that life is an "inalienable right" and "life-preservation" a primary law of nature. To the pro-suicide Rationalists the option of suicide was a mark of man's freedom. To Locke freedom was based on self-preservation, which ruled out suicide: "Freedom, then, is not . . .

for everyone to do . . . as he pleases. . . . Freedom . . . is so . . . closely joined with a man's preservation, that he cannot part with it. . . . Nobody can give more power than he has himself, and he that cannot take away his own life cannot give another power over it." Immanuel Kant took the argument one step further. Kant, who believed that Hume's skepticism signaled the end of philosophy, proposed an absolute moral code in which "duty" occupied a central position. Man's first duty was self-preservation; suicide was therefore a vice. "The rule of morality does not admit of it under any condition because it degrades human nature below the level of animal nature and so destroys it." Although his argument was largely secular, Kant's "categorical imperative," which declared that individual behavior ought to serve as an example for all mankind, prohibited suicide no less rigidly than did religion.

In *Reflections on Suicide,* published in 1813, Madame de Staël maintained that there could be no blanket judgment. "The causes of misery, and its intensity, vary equally with circumstances and individuals," she observed. "We might as well attempt to count the waves of the sea, as to analyze the combinations of destiny and character." Her main quarrel was with the idea that suffering was an excuse for killing oneself: "The greatest faculties of the soul are developed only by suffering." But for the majority of suicides her attitude was one of sympathy: "We ought not to be offended with those who are so wretched as to be unable to support the burden of existence, nor should we applaud those who sink under its weight, since, to sustain it, would be a greater proof of their moral strength." This was a factor that writers on both sides of the debate had largely overlooked: would-be suicides were unhappy and in pain. The discussion of suicide could not be limited to a moral debate of right or wrong, cowardice or bravery, sin or honor; the suffering that may lead to the act must be acknowledged. Indeed, at one point in her essay de Staël seemed to be overwhelmed by feeling. "Oh!" she wrote. "What despair is required for such an act! May pity, the most profound pity, be granted to him who is guilty of it!"

While opposing suicide on moral grounds, many writers argued against the antisuicide laws. The Italian jurist Cesare Beccaria pointed out that in economic terms the state was more wronged by the emigrant than by the suicide since the former took his property with him, whereas the latter left his behind. Confiscations inflicted injustice on a man's family, and punishment of the corpse, he observed, was as futile as beating a statue. Only God, he concluded, could punish a suicide. Under attack by the eighteenth-century Rationalists, antisuicide laws gradually fell into disuse. In Geneva, indignities to the corpse were abolished in 1770 after the body of an "innocent" man was dragged through the streets. In southern France, armed citizens stormed a prison to seize the body of a suicide and prevent its being hauled through the town. The following year, in the same district, a crowd gathered to halt the execution of a sentence against a suicide's corpse; police called to the scene made numerous arrests. In 1770, degradation of the corpse was also officially abolished in France; legal action was to be taken only against the suicide's name. In 1790 the French National Assembly, on the motion of Dr. Joseph Guillotin, who would become famous for championing a swift mode of execution, repealed all sanctions against suicide. In the new penal code of 1791, it was not even mentioned. Suicide was legal.

In England, although there was no change in the law through the eighteenth century, coroners' juries made increasing use of the insanity loophole to spare the suicide's corpse and his innocent family. Between 1770 and 1778, coroners in the county of Kent investigated 580 possible suicides and returned only 15 verdicts of *felo de se*. Such leniency dismayed legal purists. "The excuse of not being in his senses ought not to be strained to that length, to which our coroner's juries are apt to carry it," grumbled the celebrated jurist William Blackstone, "viz. that the very act of suicide is evidence of insanity; as if every man, who acted contrary to reason, had no reason at all: for the same argument would prove every other criminal non-compos, as well as the self-murderer." Lunacy, however, remained largely an upper-class prerogative; the verdict of *felo de se* was apt to be applied only to lower-class suicides. "A penniless poor dog, who has not left enough money to defray the funeral charges, may perhaps be excluded the churchyard," observed *The Connoisseur,* a satirical magazine, "but self-murder by pistol genteelly mounted, or the Paris-hilted sword, qualifies the polite owner for a sudden death, and entitles him to the pompous burial and a monument setting forth his virtues in Westminster-Abbey."

England's stubborn refusal to relax its official position on suicide may have been partly the result of its reputation. During the eighteenth century it became generally accepted—by everyone but the English—that as a people they were particularly prone to self-destruction. "We do not find in history that the Romans ever killed themselves without a cause; but the English are apt to commit suicide most unaccountably; they destroy themselves even in the bosom of happiness," wrote Montesquieu in *The Spirit of Laws* in 1748. "This action among the Romans was the effect of education, being connected with their principles and customs; among the English it is the consequence of a distemper." Other reasons put forth for "the English malady" ranged from religious decay, rationalism, licentiousness, and lack of exercise to the people's fondness for butcher's meat, rich foods, sea coal, gambling, and tea. The most frequently cited culprit was the weather. An anonymous eighteenth-century French novel begins, "In the gloomy Month of November, when the people of England hang and drown themselves . . ." In 1805, in a letter to a friend, Thomas Jefferson reflected that his country's clear skies would offer protection against any predilection for hanging that Americans might have inherited from their ancestors. In a satirical essay Boswell suggested that freezing might be a useful suicide prevention device. As November approached, "the English, instead of hanging or drowning themselves, will certainly prefer having themselves frozen up . . . and when it is fine weather, up they will spring like swallows to the enjoyment of happiness."

Some Englishmen were unamused. "Self-murder! Name it not; our island's shame; / That makes her the reproach of neighb'ring states," lamented Robert Blair in his poem "The Grave." "O Britain, infamous for suicide! / An island in thy manners!" cried Edward Young in "Night Thoughts." "It is a melancholy consideration, that there is no country in Europe, or perhaps in the habitable world, where the horrid crime of self-murder is so common as it is in England," thundered John Wesley, founder of Methodism, proposing that the tide of English suicide would turn if self-murderers were hanged upside down in chains. Others questioned whether England's notoriety was deserved. An entry on suicide in the 1797 *Encyclopaedia Britannica* attributed it to rigorous newspaper reporting of suicide—a point Voltaire had made when he remarked that if Paris newspapers kept statistics as accurately as England's, France's reputation for suicide would rival its neighbor's. In an 1804 travel book Thomas Holcroft wrote, "I doubt if as many suicides be committed through all Great Britain in a year as in Paris alone in a month."

The intercontinental competition raged throughout the eighteenth century. Although the numbers were debatable, the nature of suicide had unquestionably altered. A century that began with the suicides of Richard and Bridget Smith would conclude with the deaths of two French soldiers, twenty and twenty-four, who shot themselves out of ennui on Christmas Day, 1773. "No urgent motive has prompted us to intercept our career of life except the disgust of existing here a moment under the idea, that we must at one time or other cease to be," they explained in their note. "We leave our parts to be performed by those, who are silly enough to wish to act them a few hours longer." Accounts of such blasé suicides filled newspapers and drawing room conversations: the Englishman who hanged himself "in order to avoid the trouble of pulling off and on his clothes"; the Frenchman who, when asked to dine by a friend, replied, "With the greatest pleasure—yet, now I think of it, I am particularly engaged to shoot myself." Suicide had become decadent, trivial; one could not take it too seriously. "There are little domestic news," complained Horace Walpole, whose correspondence was spiced with world-weary references to self-destruction, in a letter to Richard Bentley. "If you insist upon some, why, I believe I could persuade somebody or other to hang themselves; but that is scarce an article uncommon enough to send cross the sea."

This nonchalance surrounding the subject of suicide would become even more flagrant in the Romantic Age. If eighteenth-century Enlightenment thinkers made the act philosophically defensible, the Romantics of the early nineteenth century made it positively seductive. The Romantic movement began as a reaction to the rationalism of the Age of Reason. If a man's life was indeed of no more importance to the universe than that of an oyster, to the

Romantics a man's death was everything, a transcendent reunion with nature and with God. "How wonderful is death," wrote Shelley. "A quiet of the heart," Byron called it. Keats longed to "cease upon the midnight with no pain." Taking the Renaissance combination of creativity and melancholy one step further, the Romantics coupled genius and premature death. The poetic sensibility was too good for this world; best to burn brightly and die young, like a shooting star. Some did. Keats died in 1821 at twenty-five, Shelley a year later at twenty-nine, and Byron two years after that, at thirty-six.

If dying young was glamorous, suicide was the ultimate thrill. The act showed an enviable, even heroic refusal to accept the banality of the world. In their preoccupation with suicide the Romantics had two early models. Thomas Chatterton, the precocious son of a schoolmaster, had begun publishing his brilliant poems at age sixteen. At nineteen, penniless, starving, and unappreciated, he swallowed arsenic in his lodging house garret. The details of Chatterton's suicide in 1770 were hardly romantic. What was distilled from them, however—a combination of genius and early death—was irresistible to the Romantics. "The marvelous Boy, the sleepless Soul that perished in his pride," as Wordsworth called him in his "Monody on the Death of Chatterton," became the model of the doomed poet for several generations of Romantic poets and would-be poets.

Four years after the death of Chatterton, Goethe's *The Sorrows of Young Werther* offered a second lethal symbol in the lovesick young hero who shoots himself. As a young man Goethe himself had longed for a glorious death. He had admired Emperor Otto's suicide by stabbing and decided that he would kill himself like Otto or not kill himself at all. "By this conviction, I saved myself from the purpose, or indeed, more properly speaking, from the whim, of suicide," he later wrote. "Among a considerable collection of arms, I possessed a costly, well-ground dagger. This I laid down nightly by my side; and, before extinguishing the light, I tried whether I could succeed in sending the sharp point an inch or two deep into my heart. But as I truly never could succeed, I at last took to laughing at myself, threw away all these hypochondriacal crotchets, and determined to live." Writing *Werther*, it has been suggested, kept Goethe from becoming Werther.

Like Goethe, most of the Romantic writers confined their intoxication with death to literature. Those who followed their own prescription hardly "cease[d] upon the midnight with no pain." Poor, lonely, rejected, and nearing fifty, the poet Thomas Beddoes took curare in Basel. German playwright Heinrich von Kleist, who had proposed suicide pacts to friends for a decade, finally found an accomplice in an incurably ill young woman. After shooting her, Kleist killed himself. Gérard de Nerval, tormented by insanity, used a frayed apron string to hang himself from a lamppost in Paris at age forty-six. More often, like Goethe, the Romantics merely toyed with suicide. The young Chateaubriand brought a shotgun to a lonely forest on his father's estate with the stated intention of killing himself, but his suicide was interrupted by the unexpected arrival of a gamekeeper. He died of old age at seventy-nine. The twenty-year-old de Musset, shown a beautiful view, cried, "Ah! It would be a beautiful place to kill oneself in!" Although de Musset asserts that twice he laid the point of a dagger against his heart, he never drew blood and eventually died at forty-six of a heart attack.

These celebrated writers stopped short of the act itself, but many young men who lacked the talent to express the Romantic ideal in prose expressed it with their death. Life imitated art: *Werther,* of course, was said to have inspired suicides all over Europe for decades, and numerous deaths were blamed on Byron's *Manfred,* Chateaubriand's *René,* and Lamartine's *Raphael.* Alfred-Victor de Vigny's play *Chatterton* was said to have doubled the annual rate of suicide in France between 1830 and 1840, when young men "practised it as one of the most elegant of sports," according to one historian. Suicide clubs flourished. In his letters, Flaubert, writing nostalgically of the friends with whom he'd spent his youth, captured the essential spirit of the Romantic flirtation with suicide: "We swung between madness and suicide; some of them killed themselves . . . another strangled himself with his tie, several died in debauchery in order to escape boredom; it was beautiful!"

# IV

# SCIENCE: MORAL MEDICINE AND VITAL STATISTICS

WHAT SEEMED BEAUTIFUL to Flaubert—and to other victims of what German poet Clemens Brentano called "hypertrophy of the poetic organ"—would soon be attributed to brain lesions, excess phosphorus, heredity, liver disease, madness, and masturbation. The assault of Enlightenment writers on the Church's condemnation of suicide had cleared the way for a secular approach to the subject, while the rapid growth of science and medicine in the seventeenth century laid the foundations for the systematic study of suicide. For the first time self-destruction was discussed not primarily as a philosophical or moral dilemma but as a medical and social problem. The question was not whether suicide was right or wrong but why it happened. The scientific study of suicide had two strands. The statistical model, which would provide the basis for a sociological approach, located the cause of suicide in society. The medical model, forerunner to the twentieth-century psychobiological approach, located the cause of suicide in the body.

Under the impression that suicide was primarily an English phenomenon, physicians explored the effects of climate on the body. Many believed that changes in temperature and precipitation affected the brain. In *The English Malady: or A Treatise of Nervous Diseases of All Kinds, as Spleen, Vapours, Lowness of Spirits, Hypochondriacal, and Hysterical Distempers, etc.*, published in 1733, George Cheyne found that the English had more "nervous distemper" leading to suicide because they ate too many rich foods, did not exercise, and lived in large cities choked with pollution. In 1758, in *A Treatise on Madness,* William Battie, physician to St. Luke's Hospital for Lunaticks, discussed weather and suicide: "Whatever may be the cause of Anxiety, it chiefly discovers itself by that agonising impatience observable in some men of black *November* days, of easterly winds, of heat, cold, damps, etc. . . . In which state of habitual diseases many drag on their wretched lives; whilst others, unequal to evils of which they see no remedy but death, rashly resolve to end them at any rate."

Like most eighteenth-century physicians who wrote on self-destruction, Cheyne and Battie seasoned their scientific theories with antisuicide bias. The first to separate completely the medical argument from the moral was a Frenchman named Merian, who, in 1763, in *Mémoire sur le Suicide,* stated that suicide was not a sin or a crime but a disease. All suicides are in some degree deranged, he said, otherwise they would not so completely contradict the law of nature. As for the cause of that derangement, each physician had his favorite culprit, according to his own theories of insanity: climate, the change of seasons, heredity, cerebral injuries, physical suffering, liver disease, melancholia, hypochondriasis, insanity, suppressed secretions, intoxication, gastritis, unnatural vices, and derangement of the *primae viae,* among others. Physicians conducted autopsies of suicides in search of physical clues. Some discovered lesions on the brains of suicides and suggested this was the cause. The French physiologist Pierre-Jean-Georges Cabanis believed suicide was caused by excess phosphorus in the brain. Franz Joseph Gall, the founder of phrenology, believed that the shape of the skull indicated specific characteristics: composers had a special bulge around the ear; suicides, he asserted, had thick craniums.

More than a few physicians located the cause in another part of the anatomy. "Few, perhaps, are aware how frequently suicide results from the habit of indulging, in early youth, in a certain secret vice which, we are afraid, is practiced to an enormous extent in our public schools," wrote one London physician. "A feeling of false delicacy has operated with medical men in inducing them to refrain from dwelling upon the destructive consequences of this habit, both to the moral and physical constitution, as openly and honestly as the importance of the subject imperatively demands." Perhaps suffering from a chronic case of false delicacy himself, the good doctor continued, "The physical disease, particularly that connected with the nervous system, engendered by the pernicious practice alluded to, frequently leads to the act of self-destruction. We have before us the cases of many suicides in whom the disposition may clearly be traced to this cause."

While most physicians searched for a specific physical source of suicide, Jean-Étienne Esquirol, chief physician at the Royal Asylum at Charenton, maintained that suicide was not a disease per se. In his 1838 book, *Des Maladies Mentales,* he wrote, "Suicide presents all the characteristics of insanity of which it is but a symptom. . . . There is no point in looking for a unique source of suicide, since one observes it in the most contradictory circumstances." Esquirol had reached a conclusion generally accepted by the medical profession today: Suicide is a symptom, not a disease. Accordingly, "the treatment of suicide belongs to the therapy of mental illness," he wrote, ". . . and one has to have recourse to treatment proper to each kind of insanity in order to treat an individual who is propelled toward his own destruction." In the early nineteenth century that might involve a variety of remedies. In his 1840 book, *The Anatomy of Suicide,* Forbes Winslow, a member of the Royal College of Surgeons in London, shared the following prescriptions:

A lady, shortly after her accouchement, expressed, with great determination, her intention to kill herself. Her bowels had not been properly attended to, and a brisk cathartic was given. This entirely removed the suicidal disposition.

Disease of the stomach and liver frequently incite to suicide; hepatic affections notoriously disturb the equilibrium of the mind. Many a case exhibiting an inclination to suicide has been cured by a few doses of blue pill.

In certain diseases of the nervous system, particularly when associated with morbid conditions of the mind leading to suicide, the influence of music may be had recourse to with great advantage to the patient. . . . The monotony of the sound is supposed to have a soothing influence over the mind, similar to what is known to result from the gurgle of a mimic cataract of some mountain rill, or to a distant waterfall.

Every physician had his pet cure. Leopold Auenbrugger suggested drinking cold water: "A pint every hour; and if continuing pensive and taciturn, forehead, temples, and eyes sprinkled with it until more gay and communicative." While numerous physicians swore by this treatment—a Dr. Schonheyde even made his suicidal patients eat salt herring to work up a thirst—others urged temperance. "Once in a while this was hard on the patient, particularly if he had tried to drown himself," noted Esquirol's pupil Jean-Pierre Falret. "But one patient who had been cured by the copious use of water continued to drink it both through gratefulness and habit to the point that at the age of eighty he was drinking twenty-four to thirty pounds of water a day!"

Some physicians found the plunge bath—sudden immersion into cold water—particularly effective in driving suicidal thoughts from the mind. (The plunge bath was discovered, according to Esquirol, when an insane carpenter threw himself into a pond; he was fished out half-drowned but fully sane.) Van Helmont advocated holding the patient under almost to the point of death, to ensure that self-destructive ideas were nipped at their root.

Goethe's physician Hufeland cited the benefits of the douche—buckets of cold water thrown from a height onto the patient's head—in driving such thoughts from the mind. Johann Reil, known in Germany as the father of psychotherapy, suggested the insane and possibly suicidal patient be suspended by ropes from a considerable height "between heaven and earth," while hospital attendants discharged firearms beside him or threatened to scorch his body with flames. In his 1803 *Rhapsodies on the Application of Psychic Therapy Methods to Mental Disturbances,* Reil also outlined a sort of psychodrama in which asylum personnel would act as a celestial jury; the preview of life in the next world was intended to shock patients into their senses in this one.

Most suicidal patients, of course, received less dramatic treatment: bleeding, purging, and cupping, as well as drafts of mercury, bark, quinine, mineral waters, whey, and, occasionally, wine—"but its employment exacts much prudence," warned Joseph Guislain in 1826. Some doctors swore that large doses of opium would restrain self-destructive urges; others preferred morphia. What success these narcotics had with suicidal patients may have resulted from keeping them too drugged to act on their impulses. Tartrate of antimony, another popular remedy, kept them too nauseous. The rotary chair, a contraption in which the patient was whirled in circles as on an amusement park ride, led to copious vomiting and a submissive patient; the chair was recommended for those with "mental alienation with a suicidal propensity."

To restore the mind as well as the body, physical remedies were supplemented with "moral" treatment. Winslow suggested that "travelling, agreeable society, works of light literature, should be had recourse to, in order to dispel all gloomy apprehensions from the mind." Falret, however, cautioned that gay spectacles tend to dampen the spirits of the suicidal. Maintaining that suicidal people think too much, Esquirol said that it was necessary to hinder them from reflection or to force them to think otherwise than they do think. Reasoning, he said, is of no avail. A protégé of Philippe Pinel, whose unchaining of the inmates at Bicêtre marked the beginning of the modern asylum, Esquirol advocated the use of gentle remedies, preferring warm baths and drinks to bleeding and the plunge bath. Of the latter he remarked, "I should as soon think of recommending patients to be precipitated from the third story of a house, because some lunatics have been known to be cured by a fall on the head." He suggested that suicidal persons lodge on the ground floor in a cheerful setting where they could be watched by vigilant persons. He concluded that a little kindness goes a long way. "How many females have come to the Salpêtrière, whom misery or domestic grief has decided to end their days," he wrote, "and who are cured by affectionate attention, consolations, the hope of a better future, and by good nourishment!"

While the new view of suicide as a medical problem brought attention to the plight of suicidal people, it introduced a troubling theme. When the discipline of medical psychiatry emerged in the eighteenth century, it preserved the medieval assumption of a close relationship between insanity and suicide. The increased use of the insanity defense to avoid forfeiture and degradation of the corpse in suicide cases, however charitably intended, reinforced that link. Although Enlightenment writers had fought to establish the right to suicide as a moral, rational act, the argument in the nineteenth century was not whether suicide was moral but whether suicide could *ever* be rational. Physicians attempted to calculate what proportion of suicides were mentally ill. Estimates ranged from Brierre de Boismont's 14 percent to the 100 percent of Esquirol and Falret. "As no rational being will voluntarily give himself pain, or deprive himself of life, which certainly, while human beings preserve their senses, must be acknowledged evils," wrote a Dr. Rowley, "it follows that every one who commits suicide is indubitably *non compos mentis.*" Thomas Chevalier, professor of anatomy and surgery at the Royal College of Surgeons in London, came to slightly less sweeping conclusions: "I am far from supposing that all suicides are lunatics; but I must contend that from the facts I have stated, the *onus probandi* lies on those who *deny* the existence of insanity in such a case." A suicide was a lunatic until proven rational.

The insanity debate had terrifying implications. In nineteenth-century medicine, many types of mental illness were believed to be inherited, and some physicians maintained that suicide was the most hereditary type of insanity. Medical texts and histories of the period are studded with examples of intergenerational suicide. "Two cases have occurred, one in Saxony, the other in the Tyrol, in each of which seven brothers hanged themselves one after another," reported one journal in 1891. The mere existence of such cases was accepted as proof that suicide was an inherited trait. "We know, as a fact, that there is no abnormal constitutional state more commonly transmitted from parent to child than this tendency to self-destruction," asserted Samuel Strahan, a respected physician and lawyer, in *Suicide and Insanity,* published in 1893, "and that the major part of the annual increase of suicide, as well as of other degenerate conditions of which we have spoken, is due directly to propagation is absolutely certain." Maintaining that self-preservation is the first law of nature, Strahan declared "the absence of this fundamental instinct . . . is *per se* irrefragable proof of unfitness to live." He cited eleven family trees (many from his own practice) "showing how the offspring of the suicide and his contemporary relatives often sink so low in the scale of vitality that the stock becomes extinct." Pursuing the thought to its ugly conclusion, he wrote, "The practical lesson to be drawn from these family histories is: that the unfit cannot be propagated indefinitely. If the experiment be persisted in, infantile death, sterile idiocy, barrenness and self-destruction will appear and extinguish the stock."

Over the course of the nineteenth century a new stigma emerged. "All the superstitious fear of the queer and the mad attached itself to suicide; the instinctive withdrawal of the sane from the tainted extended itself to cases of the calmest and most rational suicide," wrote Henry Romilly Fedden in *Suicide*. "Finally, these new medical ideas hardened family prejudice against suicide: a suicide in the family became tantamount to insanity in the family, a stigma not confined to one member, but attaching jointly to the whole group and its descendants." With the birth of the medical approach to suicide, self-destruction was no longer viewed primarily as a sin and a crime but as something abnormal and sick.

---

While physicians searched for the cause of suicide by examining the body, social scientists searched for it by sifting statistics. The state had begun keeping track of the number of suicides in the Middle Ages, when the king of England needed to account for his taxpaying citizens. In 1215 the Magna Carta charged "the guardian of the crown's pleas," or coroner, with keeping written records of births and deaths in his area. The coroner was, of course, particularly interested in deaths by murder or suicide, in which case the dead man's property was forfeited to the crown. The coroner's "rolls" were the sole source of such information until 1527, when Bills of Mortality, periodic lists of deaths and their causes, were published in London. Thus, the bill of August 27, 1573, in the parish of St. Botolph Without Aldgate, finds that "Agnis Miller wieff of Jacob Miller who killed selfe with kniff was putt in the ground." Common folk studied the bills for morbid tidbits of gossip, while the wealthy kept an eye on increases in death during times of plague to help decide whether it might be prudent to leave the city for a while.

The first attempt to use these bills for anything more scientific was in 1662, when John Graunt, a London tradesman, published his *Observations made upon the Bills of Mortality,* in which he sorted the information into various categories, including cause of death. Thus, Graunt told us that 1,306 died of apoplexy, 998 of jaundice, 829 drowned, 279 of grief, 243 dead in the streets, 158 of lunatique, 136 of vomiting, 86 murthered, 74 of falling sickness, 67 of lethargy, 51 of head-ach, 51 starved, 26 smothered, 22 frighted, 14 poysoned, 7 shot, and 222 hanged themselves, among others. Graunt pointed out that while certain causes of death—plague, spotted fever, measles—claimed a varying toll from year to year, others—"consumption, dropsies, grief, men's making away themselves"—remained fairly constant. Like an oddsmaker he estimated the likelihood of a person dying from a particular cause. "I dare ensure any man at this present, well in his Wits, for one in the thousand, that he shall not die a *Lunatick* in *Bedlam* within these seven years, because I finde not above one in about one thousand five hundred have done so," he wrote. "The like use may be made of the Accompts of men, that made away themselves, who are another sort of Mad-men, that think to ease themselves of pain by leaping into *Hell;* or else are yet more Mad, so as to think there is no such place; or that men may go to rest by death, though they die in *self-murther,* the greatest Sin."

During the eighteenth century writers tabulated "moral statistics" in an attempt to measure social ills such as crime, divorce, illegitimacy, and suicide. In one of the most ambitious early studies, Brierre de Boismont gathered data on 4,595 French suicides between 1834 and 1842. He also interviewed 265 people who had planned or attempted suicide. While admitting that many suicides were caused by mental illness, de Boismont denied that all suicides were insane. In his list of causes he attributed 652 to mental illness, 530 to alcoholism, 405 to painful or incurable disease, 361 to domestic troubles, 311 to sorrow or disappointment, 306 to disappointed love, 282 to poverty and misery, 237 to ennui, 99 to indolence and want of occupation, and so on. Among the victims de Boismont noted a higher proportion of males, alcoholics, unmarried people, and the elderly. Like many investigators he remarked on the increasing suicide rate, which he attributed to the pressures of urban life. Suicide, he proposed, was a consequence of societal changes that led to disorder and alienation.

This conclusion was shared by the swarm of statistical studies published over the following four decades, examining the distribution of suicide in relation to age, sex, marital status, occupation, social class, place of residence, education, degree of culture, race, religion, height, skull size, skin color, disease, intemperance, topography, weather, and lunar cycle.

One of the first arguments these studies attempted to settle was that of nationality. Despite the assumption that suicide was "the English malady," the statistical microscope revealed that England had no more suicides than Belgium and far fewer than France. Paris, in fact, had one suicide for every 2,700 people in 1836, compared to London's one in 27,000 during 1834–42. (The purveyor of these suspiciously symmetrical statistics, it must be confessed, was an Englishman.) Berlin dwarfed both cities with one suicide for every 750 persons. At the opposite end of the scale, Palermo had only one in 180,000. Summarizing studies of suicide and nationality in his 1881 book, *Suicide and the Meaning of Civilization,* Thomas Masaryk, a philosopher who went on to become the first president of Czechoslovakia, concluded, "The evil frequently appears among the Danes, Germans, French, and Austrians, seldom among the Spaniards, Portuguese, Yugoslavians, Irish, and Scottish, moderately in England, Sweden, Norway, and the United States."

The effect of climate on suicide was another controversial subject. After analyzing dozens of studies, Italian professor of psychological medicine Henry Morselli posited the existence of a suicide belt between 47 and 57 degrees north latitude and between 20 and 40 degrees east longitude. "On this area of about 942,000 square kilomètres are found the people who of all others in the civilized world manifest the greatest inclination to suicide," he wrote. Morselli attributed this inclination to the temperate climate they shared. Another writer agreed, observing that "extremes of heat and cold lessen the prevalence of self-destruction." But others suggested that extremes of temperature increase suicide by adversely affecting the nervous system. Still others believed that the crucial factor was not the temperature but a sudden change in weather. Boudin concluded that when the thermometer rises, so does the suicide rate. Fodéré and Duglas identified twenty-two degrees Reaumur (approximately 82°F) as the boiling point for suicidal despair. Others linked fluctuations in suicide to the phases of the moon or to the effect of the west wind—perhaps influenced by the popular superstition that strong winds rose whenever someone hanged himself. Villemair maintained that exactly nine-tenths of suicides occur on rainy or cloudy days; Cabanis asserted that a rainy autumn following a dry summer is particularly conducive to violent death. But the long-held belief that gloomy November was the month of suicide was debunked. Suicide was most frequent in the spring. "Suicide and madness are not influenced so much by the intense heat of the advanced summer season as by the early spring and summer," explained Morselli, "which seize upon the organism not yet acclimatised and still under the influence of the cold season."

Nineteenth-century studies left few statistical stones unturned. They tabulated method: "Nationality has a noticeable effect on the choice of means," observed Masaryk. "The French and Romantic peoples, in general, often shoot themselves; the Scandinavians, Germans, and Slavs frequently hang themselves. The Parisians—men—choose drowning more often than shooting. In Italy, men shoot themselves most frequently; women drown themselves; but hanging is less frequent than in all other lands." They explored occupation: "A very low suicide frequency appears among clergymen of all forms of worship; poets, artists, and men of genius are often seized by the tendency to suicide," asserted the author of an early German study. "Crowned heads commit suicide not infrequently; professional beggars almost never." They explored place of death: a study of Prussian suicides from 1872 to 1875 found that 918 ended their lives in the woods, 639 in rivers, 419 in the streets, 284 in gardens, 220 in jails, 144 in hotels, and 21 in trains, carriages, or ships. They examined height: "The frequency of suicide in the various parts of Italy generally is in a direct ratio with stature," wrote Morselli, "and the inclination to self-destruction increases from south to north as the stature of the Italians gradually increases." They explored time of day, day of the week, and weeks of the month: in 1833, M. A. Guerry reported that of 6,587 cases, suicide was committed most frequently on Monday, least frequently on Sunday, while de Boismont found that a majority of suicides occurred during the day and that the suicide rate was highest during the first ten days of the month. Morselli was at a loss to account for this finding. "From whence this fact proceeds is not clear," he commented, "unless it be that in the first days of each month debauchery, dissipation, orgies, especially in large cities, are more numerous."

Although their statistics were admittedly inaccurate—data collection methods varied widely, and then, as now, suicide tended to be underreported—nineteenth-century social statisticians, or sociologists, as they were now called, uncovered several patterns that remain true today: that males kill themselves far more frequently than females; that suicide rates rise with age; that single or divorced people are more apt to kill themselves than married people, Protestants more often than Catholics; that suicide occurs more often in spring than in fall and winter; that it declines in time of war and rises in periods of rapid economic change, political crisis, and social instability. And no matter what variations were found from country to country, one thing on which they concurred was that the number of suicides was soaring. (At century's end a German priest calculated the total number of nineteenth-century suicides to be more than one and a half million.) Almost all agreed on the cause: "The certainty of the figures and the regularity of the progressive increase of suicide, from the time when statistics were first collected to now," wrote Morselli in 1881, "is such and so great even in respect to countries different in race, religion, and number of inhabitants, that it is not possible to explain it otherwise than as an effect of that universal and complex influence to which we give the name of *civilization*."

It was clear that society played a role in suicide, but no one knew exactly how. For all the dogged statistical digging, no overarching social theory made sense of the confetti of numbers until the publication of Émile Durkheim's *Le Suicide* in 1897. Durkheim, a lecturer at the Sorbonne, was not primarily concerned with suicide. He was interested in establishing the new discipline of sociology as a science. Like many of his peers, however, he had been struck by the fact that industrialization and economic progress seemed to be accompanied everywhere by a rise in suicide, and the trove of suicide statistics afforded him an ample data base from which to formulate and test his sociological theories.

In *Le Suicide,* Durkheim analyzed European suicide statistics for the last half of the nineteenth century and, like his predecessors, noticed that suicide occurs with varying frequency in different populations. Durkheim then examined the impact of race, heredity, imitation, humidity, and temperature on the suicide rate and concluded that they had little effect. To understand suicide, he said, it was necessary to examine social forces rather than isolated individual motives. Suicide was explicable only by the state of the society to which the individual belonged. While a certain number of suicides were inevitable in every society, some societies were more conducive to self-destruction than others. In societies where social ties were strong, there would be little suicide; where they were weak, there would be more. The more an individual was integrated into social groups—religion, family, community—the less likelihood of suicide.

Durkheim suggested that every suicide could be classified as one of three types—egoistic, altruistic, or anomic—according to its social context. Egoistic suicide occurs when an individual is left to his own resources instead of being well integrated into a social group, whether it be family, religion, or community. This, said Durkheim, helped explain why the rate of suicide by Protestants was higher than that of Catholics although both religions condemn the act. Protestantism, which encourages the spirit of free inquiry and emphasizes free will, may tend to encourage suicide, while the traditional, strictly ordered belief system of the Catholic Church offers a more tightly stitched social community. Similarly, the traditional family life of grandparents, parents, and children living under one roof offered stability in a world in which divorce and transience were increasingly prevalent. Thus the suicide rate of unmarried people was higher than that of married people of similar age. Children offered added protection; the more children in a family, the lower the rate of suicide for the parents. So, too, rural communities offered greater opportunity for social contact than did big, impersonal cities and therefore had lower suicide rates. The egoistic suicide is often the lonely, the unemployed, the single, the divorced person living alone, who has no one or nothing to which to belong. One way of belonging, oddly enough, is war. Observing that suicide rates tend to dwindle during wars and other national emergencies, Durkheim reasoned that in times of crisis, society literally rallies round the flag, and personal problems are dwarfed by concern for family and country.

The opposite of egoistic suicide is altruistic suicide, in which an individual is *excessively* integrated into a social group. In some cases society's hold is too strong on certain individuals, who sacrifice their own identities and goals, and even their lives. Such suicides, said Durkheim, result from insufficient individuation. Many Greek and Roman suicides, Indian suttee, and Japanese seppuku are examples of altruistic suicides. Durkheim noted that altruistic suicides are more common in primitive societies where under certain circumstances suicide is encouraged (the aging Eskimo who walks off into the snow rather than burden his community), and in rigidly structured groups like the military, where certain suicides have a sacrificial element: the soldier who tosses himself on a grenade to save his platoon. As notions of suicide have changed over time, altruistic suicide is said to have become rare in the Western world, but each culture has its examples. The Eskimo is not unlike Captain Lawrence Oates, who wandered off to die in the antarctic snow believing his weakness made him a hindrance to Scott's 1912 polar expedition; the Hindu woman who throws herself onto her husband's funeral pyre is not unlike the captain who goes down with his ship; the 967 Jews who killed themselves at Masada rather than surrender in AD 73 are not unlike the 912 who swallowed cyanide-laced Kool-Aid at Jonestown in 1978; the kamikaze pilots of World War II who crashed their fighters into American aircraft carriers are not unlike the contempory Palestinian and Al-Queda terrorists who serve as human bombs. Many people resist thinking of these sacrificial deaths as suicides. But in recent years psychiatrists have pointed out that many "altruistic" suicides are not entirely selfless but arise from a complex tangle of motives that may include the need to give one's death—and life—a higher meaning.

Anomic suicide, Durkheim's third category, occurs when a person's life changes so abruptly that he is unable to cope. Like a man in a dream who finds himself in a strange town, he feels lost, his accustomed way of life seems useless, his normal supports are gone. He is overwhelmed by anomie. The change might be triggered by a death in the family, a painful divorce, a sudden financial reversal, or even unexpected wealth. Or it might be provoked by a more general disturbance—a plague, a decline in religious beliefs, or a stock market crash—that jars a society's equilibrium. At these times an entire society may experience anomie. Thus, suicides increased when the Black Death disrupted the stability of the Middle Ages, just as centuries later the U.S. suicide rate peaked during the Great Depression. Durkheim demonstrated a correlation between the economy and suicide, which tends to rise steeply during a depression—as well as during a boom. At these times the wealthy were more likely to turn to suicide than the poor. "Lack of power, compelling moderation, accustoms men to it. . . . Wealth, on the other hand, by the power it bestows, deceives us into believing that we depend on ourselves only. . . . The less limited one feels, the more intolerable all limitation appears."

*Le Suicide* was a landmark book. Not only did it establish the field of sociology but it marked the beginning of the modern study of suicide. It offered the first comprehensive social theory of suicidal behavior—that "suicide varies inversely with the degree of integration of the social groups of which the individual forms a part." Since its publication in 1897 (an English translation did not appear until 1951), *Le Suicide* has been analyzed, refined, and criticized. Subsequent sociologists have challenged Durkheim's conclusions as being based on unreliable data. They have pointed out exceptions to his general rules—Catholic Austria, for instance, has long had one of the highest suicide rates in the world. Studies using more advanced statistical techniques have found that suicide may be as common among the poor as among the rich; as common in rural areas as in the cities. Still other critics assert that Durkheim's typology is too broad and that the distinction between anomic and egoistic suicide is often blurred. (Durkheim admitted that egoism, anomie, and altruism "are very often combined with one another, giving rise to composite varieties; characteristics of several types will be united in a single suicide.") But no one has ever seriously challenged Durkheim's basic theory, and his work has served as the foundation for all subsequent sociological investigations of the subject.

While *Le Suicide* was a milestone in the study of suicide, it did not explain why some people who were Protestant, widowed, or divorced killed themselves when most did not. Durkheim's belief that "social facts must be studied as things, that is, as realities external to the individual," made the psychology of the individual suicide virtually irrelevant to his theory. Without a psychological understanding of suicide, however, the work of Durkheim and his predecessors was incomplete. "When we learn that the most densely populated parts of the world have the highest incidence of suicide, and that suicides cluster in certain months of the year, do we thereby learn a single adequate, explanatory motive?" asked psychoanalyst Alfred Adler in 1910. "No, we learn only that the phenomenon of suicide is also subject to the law of great numbers, and that it is related to other social phenomena. Suicide can be understood only individually, even if it has social preconditions and social consequences."

Adler was speaking at the Vienna Psychoanalytic Society's special session on suicide in children, thirteen years after the publication of Durkheim's masterpiece. The focus of the discussion in Freud's living room was light-years away from the social determinism of Durkheim and his disciples. The talk was not of religious affiliation, marital status, or amount of annual rainfall but of revenge, inferiority, and sexual repression. Each analyst explained suicide according to his own theoretical perspective. Adler emphasized the strength of the aggressive drive and the desire of the suicidal person to inflict pain on surviving relatives. "Thus the unconscious creates a situation in which sickness, even death, is desired," he said, "partly in order to hurt the relatives, and partly to show them what they have lost in the one they have always slighted." Isidor Sadger asserted that "the decisive factor here is erotic. . . . The only person who puts an end to his life is one who has been compelled to give up all hope of love." The psychoanalyst Wilhelm Stekel emphasized the role of aggression and murderous impulses: "No one kills himself who has never wanted to kill another, or at least wished the death of another."

Freud's input that evening was limited to a few general remarks. Although his theories of depression and aggression would provide the framework for a psychoanalytic understanding of suicide, he never developed a comprehensive theory of suicide or wrote about it as a subject in itself. Freud brought the 1910 meeting to a close by urging, "Let us suspend our judgment till experience has solved this problem." And yet, as psychiatrist Robert Litman has pointed out in his paper "Sigmund Freud on Suicide," the fifty-three-year-old Freud had had ample experience—both clinical and personal—with suicide. In 1883, Freud wrote his fiancée, Martha Bernays, about the suicide of a friend, a young doctor named Nathan Weiss, who hanged himself shortly after an ill-advised marriage. In 1885, a year before their stormy four-year courtship ended in marriage, Freud alluded to suicide in another letter to Martha: "I have long since resolved on a decision, the thought of which is in no way painful, in the event of my losing you. That we should lose each other by parting is quite out of the question. . . . You have no idea how fond I am of you, and I hope I shall never have to show it." The twenty-nine-year-old Freud, like some lovesick teenager, exemplified an observation he would make many years later in a discussion of melancholia: "In the two opposed situations of being most intensely in love and of suicide the ego is overwhelmed by the object, though in totally different ways." Although Freud suffered periods of depression throughout his life, this was the only time he is believed to have mentioned suicidal thoughts of his own.

Freud's case histories contain numerous descriptions of suicidal behavior. The only sister of the patient known as the Wolf Man committed suicide by poisoning. Plagued by hallucinations, the paranoid Dr. Schreber made frequent attempts to drown himself in his bath. The eighteen-year-old patient known as Dora forced her parents into obtaining treatment for her by leaving a letter threatening suicide in a place where they were sure to find it. Freud noted the attention-getting aspects of her act, and in analysis, when Dora spoke of her father's suicidal threats, Freud commented on the significance of the suicidal child's identification with the suicidal parent. In 1898 a patient of Freud's killed himself. "A patient over whom I had taken a great deal of trouble had put an end to his life on account of an incurable sexual disorder," he wrote in *The Psychopathology of Everyday Life,* in which he described his own unconscious efforts to repress the memory of the suicide.

In *Totem and Taboo* (1913), Freud returned to a consideration of the murderous component in suicide. "We find that impulses to suicide in a neurotic turn out regularly to be self-punishments for wishes for someone else's death," he wrote. In *Mourning and Melancholia* (1915), Freud restated his belief that murderous impulses turned inward could lead to suicide, but how did the mechanism function? Freud had based his work on his conviction that human behavior is ultimately shaped by instinctual drives. At the time of the meeting he believed that these drives were libido and self-preservation. How did suicide satisfy these drives? How could the ego consent to its own destruction?

Freud suggested that in both mourning and its pathological cousin, melancholia, when an object of love is lost, the ego re-creates an image of the loved one inside the self. Thus, the lost love object lives on in the ego in what Freud compared to a shadow. This identification, or "shadow," is not fully integrated into the personality, thereby enabling part of the ego to "split off" and observe. In this "ego splitting" a part of the ego may sit in judgment on the rest of the ego, criticizing it, attacking it, even condemning it to death. Suicide is the ultimate expression of this dynamic. In other words suicide originates in the wish to kill someone whom the suicide has loved or identified with; because he cannot kill this person, he "kills" him by destroying the internalized image of him. Psychologically, suicide is thus a kind of inverted murder or, as psychologist Edwin Shneidman has put it, "murder in the 180th degree."

At the time he wrote *Mourning and Melancholia,* Freud believed that all aggression had a sexual origin. In 1920 he proposed the existence of another primal drive. "After long hesitancies and vacillations we have decided to assume the existence of only two basic instincts, *Eros* and *the destructive instinct*," he later wrote. "The aim of the first of these basic instincts is to establish ever greater unities and to preserve them thus—in short, to bind together; the aim of the second is, on the contrary, to undo connections and so to destroy things. In the case of the destructive instinct we may suppose that its final aim is to lead what is living into an inorganic state. For this reason we also call it the *death instinct*." Most aspects of human behavior, Freud believed, could be understood as the product of the struggle between the sexual drive and the death instinct, Eros and Thanatos, love and hate.

While Freud's primary purpose in proposing the death instinct was to explain the phenomenon of masochism, it also provided an explanation for suicide. While the death instinct exists in everybody, Freud said, in suicidal people it prevails over their instincts for love and life. "We find that the excessively strong super-ego which has obtained a hold upon consciousness rages against the ego with merciless violence," he wrote in *The Ego and the Id*. "What is now holding sway in the super-ego is, as it were, a pure culture of the death instinct, and in fact it often enough succeeds in driving the ego into death." Ten years after adjourning the Vienna Psychoanalytic Society's special session on suicide, Freud had devised a theory that, in part, suggested that every death is, to an extent, psychological self-murder.

# V

# FAITH, HOPELESSNESS, AND 5HIAA

---

NEARLY A CENTURY LATER, a growing number of people believe that the key to the enigma of suicide may lie in a glassy, contemporary six-story building overlooking the Hudson River in Upper Manhattan, where, in the second-floor neuroanatomy laboratories of the New York State Psychiatric Institute, twenty-seven stainless-steel deep freezers preserve, at minus eighty degrees centigrade, some two hundred brains. Although harvested from people of various ages, sexes, and ethnicities, these brains have one thing in common: they all come from people who killed themselves. Psychiatrist John Mann and neurobiologists Victoria Arango and Mark Underwood, of the NYSPI's Mental Health Clinical Research Center for the Study of Suicidal Behavior, are studying these brains to find out what else they have in common, and how they might differ from the brains of those who die by other causes.

Donated by grieving families in hopes that their tragedies might benefit others, these brains are said to constitute the country's finest collection of specimens from suicide victims. They are, therefore, treated as gingerly as Tiffany diamonds. Each freezer is equipped with a computerized warning system so that if its interior temperature rises to minus sixty degrees centigrade, liquid carbon dioxide will automatically be discharged to cool its contents. Each freezer is also linked to Arango's cell phone, to her home, and to the home of a technician who lives near the institute so that someone will know immediately if anything goes wrong. Until a few years ago, the specimens were donated by families in Pittsburgh, where Arango, Underwood, and Mann previously

191

worked, and in New York City. When, for political and bureaucratic reasons, it became impossible to collect in New York, NYPSI found another collaborator, and recent additions to the collection have all been imported, oddly enough, from upper Macedonia. Several times a year, NYSPI pathologist Andrew Dwork travels to southeastern Europe to pick them up. The specimens must be obtained and flash-frozen within twenty-four hours of death (otherwise they deteriorate); the donors must have died suddenly (a prolonged death increases the brain's acidity and makes it harder to study); and they must not have been taking medications (the chemical complications would confound the findings). Each brain is accompanied by a "psychological autopsy," a collection of interviews with friends and family, in an attempt to gather information— method used, clues left behind, previous attempts, history of aggressive behavior, and so on—that may shed light on the physical evidence, as well as provide the basis for a psychiatric diagnosis.

In New York, each brain is prepared for study by being divided into its left and right hemispheres, each of which is then subdivided into ten or twelve blocks. Using a microtome, a machine that looks and works something like a meat slicer in a butcher shop—but with infinitesimal precision—a technician can pare a slice thinner than a piece of paper. Transferred to a glass slide, the tissue is examined using autoradiography, which maps chemical alterations in brain regions. It is then compared to a similar sample from the brain of a person of the same age and sex who had no psychiatric disorders and who died suddenly of a cause other than suicide. By reassembling the slides by computer, researchers can also construct a virtual model of how those chemical alterations might interact to affect mood or behavior.

Since the 1970s, researchers have been exploring the link between depression and serotonin, one of the more than a hundred kinds of neurotransmitters identified thus far. Neurotransmitters are the brain's chemical messengers— molecules that jump the narrow gaps known as synapses between neurons to carry information from the signal-sending (presynaptic) neuron to the receiving (postsynaptic) neuron. Receptors on the postsynaptic neurons bind to the serotonin and register biochemical changes in the neuron. The presynaptic neurons eventually reabsorb the serotonin using molecular sponges called transporters. (The antidepressants known as SSRIs work by binding to serotonin transporters and preventing presynaptic neurons from reabsorbing the secreted serotonin too quickly, allowing it to linger in the synapse.)

Neurobiologists have long been aware that serotonin seems to exert a soothing effect on the mind. Over the years, low serotonin levels in the brain have been linked to depression, aggressive behavior, and impulsivity. At the NYSPI—as at several other cutting-edge laboratories in this country and in Europe—Mann, Underwood, and Arango, who have worked together since 1985, have been homing in on how serotonin may more specifically be involved in suicide. Studies at the NYSPI and elsewhere of people who attempt suicide have found evidence of serotonin depletion in the cere-brospinal fluid—the liquid that bathes the brain and spinal cord. Postmortem studies of completed suicides have found lower-than-normal levels of sero-tonin in the brain. That the low serotonin levels in suicide victims is similar in degree regardless of psychiatric diagnosis suggests that the serotonin deficit is associated with the suicidal behavior and not with the psychiatric disorder.

Over time, the NYSPI researchers have zeroed in on the frontal cortex. Using autoradiography, they have found that in depressed patients, serotonin activity is reduced throughout the frontal cortex, whereas in patients who have attempted suicide, the reduced serotonin activity is confined to the orbital pre-frontal cortex, the portion of the brain that sits immediately above the eyes and is the source of our ability to control our impulses—"the emotional seat belt," as Mann has described it. ("Depression affects more parts of the brain," observes Arango. "Suicide appears to be more local.") Postmortem studies, too, have suggested that not enough serotonin seems to be reaching this key part of the brain.

Arango assumed that the reason there was less serotonin in the cortexes of suicide victims was that they had fewer serotonin neurons. But when Under-wood, using a video-based computer imaging system attached to a microscope, manually identified, counted, and analyzed every serotonin-synthesizing neu-ron—some tens of thousands—in the brain stem, he found that the brains of suicide victims had more serotonin neurons than did control brains. Arango and her colleagues narrowed it down still further. The prefrontal cortex has two parts; the upper part (the dorsal prefrontal cortex) appears to be more affected in depression, while the lower part (the orbital prefrontal cortex) appears to be more affected in suicide. In 2001, Arango found that the brains of completed suicides contained fewer neurons in the orbital prefrontal cortex than control brains did, but a normal number in the dorsal prefrontal cortex. Furthermore, the orbital prefrontal cortex had one-third the number of presynaptic serotonin transporter sites than that of control brains, but some 30 percent more postsy-naptic serotonin receptors, suggesting that the brains of people who kill them-selves are trying to make the most of what serotonin they have, by attempting to increase their ability to receive serotonin while decreasing the number of transporters that reabsorb it.

Arango has turned her attention to the brain stem, the part of the brain that leads to the spinal cord, where serotonin is made and subsequently projected to the rest of the brain. Doing more "neuron counting," Arango has found that there is *more* of the enzyme that makes serotonin in the brain stems of com-pleted suicides than in control brains. "So the problem is *not* in the brain stem," she says. "There seems to be a disconnect between the brain stem and the pre-frontal cortex. The cortex is behaving as if it doesn't have enough serotonin. The brain stem is working overtime to make up the deficit, trying to make more serotonin, but somehow it is getting lost on its way to the cortex." Arango and her colleagues are now studying the middleman, so to speak—the amygdala, an almond-shaped part of the brain located in the anterior portion of the temporal lobe and associated with fear and aggression.

---

The idea that suicide is rooted in the brain dates as far back as the fifth century BC when Hippocrates suggested that an excess of black bile led to a condition whose symptoms included "sadness, anxiety, moral dejection, tendency to suicide," and which was treatable with mandrake root and hellebores, a plant whose leaves contain a toxic alkaloid. The link between suicide and the brain, however, would, for the most part, lie dormant during the following two millennia, as suicide was blamed on the devil, the weather, and civilization, among other scapegoats. In the eighteenth and nineteenth centuries, with the rise of "scientific" medicine, physicians once again turned to the brain; some pathologists claimed to find organic lesions in the brains of completed suicides, others an excess of phosphorus. Although the shadows of Durkheim and Freud dominated the discussion of suicide through the first half of the twentieth century, the suspicion persisted that depression and other forms of mental illness could be traced to physical aberrations in the brain. This was reflected in a variety of treatments: insulin coma therapy, in which patients were deliberately put into a coma up to sixty times over two months; Metrazol convulsive therapy, in which injections of a synthetic preparation of camphor induced explosive seizures; electroconvulsive therapy, in which patients were strapped to a table and shocked with 125 volts; and prefrontal lobotomies, in which two holes were drilled through the skull and a dozen or more nerve fibers were severed in the frontal lobes. These treatments, which worked by damaging the brain, were—among physicians, at least—wildly popular. A 1937 *New York Times* article extolling the virtues of the lobotomy pronounced it to be "surgery of the soul."

In *Mad in America,* journalist Robert Whitaker cites some of the less mainstream somatic "treatments" inflicted on mentally ill patients during the first half of the twentieth century. They were injected with malaria-infected blood, arsenic, manganese, cesium, horse serum, and extracts from animal ovaries, testicles, pituitaries, and thyroids. They wore "blankets" coated by refrigerant, which dropped their body temperatures into the seventies and kept them in "hibernation" for up to three days. They were forced into ice-packed cabinets and refrigerated for a day or two. Their teeth were pulled one by one (in the belief that insanity could be cured by removing potential hiding places for bacteria), and if that didn't work, their tonsils, colon, gallbladder, appendix, uterus, ovaries, cervix, and seminal vesicles were removed (in that order) until they were sane or dead. (Forty-three percent of patients given what was called the "thorough treatment" died.) In the course of these therapies, which were often administered without the patient's consent and often without warning, many patients died, many more were irreparably damaged, and some were said to be cured—which usually meant they had been dulled into a state of bovine tractability.

Then, in the early 1950s, a number of tubercular patients at the Sea View Sanatorium in Staten Island were treated with a new compound called iproniazid, which was intended to help them breathe more easily. Although iproniazid proved to be a red herring in the treatment of tuberculosis—it not only failed to ease breathing but caused jaundice—the drug had an unexpected and fortuitous side effect: despite their grim medical prognosis, the patients grew surprisingly animated, even happy. (A 1953 newspaper photograph shows a semicircle of Sea View patients clapping hands as two residents dance.) The compound, which evolved into imipramine, was quickly pressed into service as the first modern antidepressant.

If altering brain chemicals was part of the solution to depression, it stood to reason that brain chemicals were part of the problem. Working backward, researchers learned that the drug was effective because it inhibited the action of monoamine oxidase, an enzyme that inactivates the neurotransmitters serotonin, norepinephrine, and dopamine after they have been released into the nerve synapses. It gradually became clear that the proper functioning of certain neurotransmitters was vital to the expression and regulation of mood. When something went wrong in this communication system, certain forms of depression might occur. Over the following decades, researchers focused their attention on one of those neurotransmitters, serotonin. When serotonin levels were low, depression was more likely; when serotonin levels were elevated, depression in many patients was relieved. Many disorders once regarded as purely psychological were now thought to be caused by chemical imbalances.

The connection between suicide and serotonin was made almost by happenstance. In the early 1970s, a Swedish psychiatrist named Marie Åsberg and her associates at the Karolinska Institute in Stockholm were searching for chemical markers in the cerebrospinal fluid of severely depressed patients. By identifying some of the markers, they hoped to describe some of the subgroups of depression. One thing they found was that about a third of the sixty-eight patients in the study had especially low levels of a chemical called 5-hydroxyindoleacetic acid—5HIAA for short—a metabolite, or "breakdown product," of serotonin.

In 1975, Åsberg's research team learned that one of the depressed patients in the study had completed suicide by taking an overdose of his antidepressant medication. When told the news, one psychiatrist remarked, "All these low 5HIAA patients kill themselves." She explained that not only had this man had a low level of 5HIAA in his cerebrospinal fluid, but so had another recent suicide, a woman who had drowned herself in a lake. When Åsberg checked the case records, she found low 5HIAA among more than two-thirds of those who had attempted or completed suicide. Furthermore, many of the low 5HIAA suicides had chosen violent methods.

Åsberg organized a study of forty-six suicide attempters, sixteen of whom suffered from severe depression, the rest from a variety of psychiatric illnesses. Although some had normal levels of 5HIAA in their spinal fluid, the group as a whole had an abnormally low level—an average of 3.5 nanograms (a nanogram is one billionth of a gram) per milliliter less than the forty-five healthy volunteers in the control group. Within one year, six people in the study had committed suicide. All of them belonged to the low 5HIAA group.

Since then, some two dozen studies have confirmed an association between suicide risk and low serotonin. Whether suicidal patients suffered from depression, schizophrenia, alcoholism, or personality disorders, low serotonin, or its metabolite, seemed to be a common denominator in those who had made suicide attempts or who had completed suicide. Low serotonin may predispose people to act impulsively, aggressively, and perhaps violently while under stress or in emotional turmoil. Indeed, in 2003, the NYSPI's John Mann, in a study of attempted suicide, reported that those attempters who had used the most lethal means had the least serotonin-based activity in their cerebrospinal fluid—"the more lethal the suicide attempt, the bigger the abnormality," he observed.

The link between serotonin function and aggressive and impulsive behavior has been reinforced by animal research. Mice with low serotonin attack faster and acquire addiction more readily; rats with low serotonin are more likely to attack and kill other rats; monkeys with low serotonin are more likely to attack other monkeys, to increase their alcohol intake, to take risks, to be ostracized by their peers, and to die a violent death. If levels of serotonin are increased in these animals, their aggressive and impulsive behaviors decrease. Although low serotonin is believed to be heritable, it may also be affected by environment: a strong maternal influence can improve serotonin functioning in rhesus monkeys, as can a rise in group status. But when monkeys are isolated in cages, their serotonin level drops by 50 percent. It has been suggested that with humans, too, a stressful event—the death of a family member, the loss of a job, physical or sexual abuse—may disrupt the serotonergic system and increase the chances of depression and, possibly, suicide. Substance abuse, stress, and even low cholesterol may lower serotonin levels. On average, men have lower serotonin levels than women, which may be a clue to why they are statistically far more likely to complete suicide, although many more women attempt.

Although serotonin may hold the key to the enigma of suicide, serotonin dysfunction does not inevitably lead to self-destruction. Low serotonin levels are also found in people whose poor impulse control manifests itself differently—in cruelty to animals, in impulsive arson or murder, in alcoholic aggression—as well as in people who merely get highly frustrated or depressed. Furthermore, not all people who kill themselves have low serotonin; although the number varies from study to study, about 20 percent of the suicide brains

Arango and her colleagues have examined have no sign of serotonin dysfunction. Furthermore, the serotonin study samples have been small, the studies have not been entirely consistent, and the results may apply to only a small segment of the population at risk for suicide—those with a history of impulsive, aggressive behavior. The evidence is not clear regarding people who complete suicide using less violent means, such as carefully hoarding sleeping pills. Given that serotonin research has been limited largely to adults, it is not yet apparent whether the connection between low serotonin and suicide extends to children and adolescents. It is also likely that the link between serotonin and suicide may be part of a larger, more intricate biochemical picture yet to be mapped. Finally, the biochemical research may help explain individual suicides, but it cannot explain fluctuating rates of suicide among different cultures and demographic groups. Few would suggest, for instance, that the nearly 300 percent rise in adolescent suicide rates from the fifties to the mideighties was due to a sudden change in the neurochemistry of children's brains during the Eisenhower administration—or that serotonin levels are lower among the Lithuanians, with their lofty rate of suicide, than among the Greeks, with their perennially low rate.

However incomplete the evidence, the biology of suicide clearly holds great possibilities for prevention. Although we can't directly measure serotonin in the spinal fluid, by measuring the level of serotonin metabolites (5HIAA), it may be possible to determine who might be especially vulnerable to suicide. If those metabolites are low, Mann has suggested, the risk of suicide over the following year is four to six times higher than if those metabolites are at normal levels. But suicide is a statistically rare event. Only about one in a thousand people attempt suicide, and the number who would have to be tested to screen out those few is enormous. In addition, measuring 5HIAA requires a painful, expensive, and time-consuming spinal tap. Researchers at NYSPI are trying to develop a test that, by monitoring serotonin functioning in the prefrontal cortex, might help doctors determine which of their depressed patients are at higher risk. It is also possible that a blood test could eventually be developed that might calculate one's chance of suicide. Such biological tests will undoubtedly aid suicide prevention efforts—and will spur the development of ever more specifically targeted medications—but they will also introduce ethical questions about how the results of those tests might be used, as well as about the psychological consequences for those who are tested.

---

There are other ways of parsing the relative contributions of nature and nurture to suicide. More than thirty studies in the past several decades have found a higher rate of suicidal behavior in the family members of those who complete suicide or make a serious attempt. In a massive Danish study, published in 2002, 4,262 people between the ages of nine and forty-five who had completed suicide were compared to more than 80,000 controls. Those with a family history of suicide were two and a half times more likely to take their own lives. Furthermore, a family history of psychiatric illness increased suicide risk by some 50 percent for those without psychiatric problems; at highest risk were those whose family histories included both suicide and psychiatric illness. (Nevertheless, "suicide families" accounted for only 2 percent of all suicides, while family psychiatric history accounted for 7 percent.) As for attempted suicide, a 2002 study by psychiatrist David Brent reported that the offspring of people who attempt suicide have six times the risk of people whose parents have never attempted. The mere existence of what have been called suicide families, of course, does not establish a genetic basis for suicide. If indeed something is being passed along biologically, it may be a genetic predisposition to depression, alcoholism, or schizophrenia, all of which are strongly linked to suicide risk, rather than a genetic predisposition for suicidal behavior.

A 1985 study of the Old Order Amish of southeastern Pennsylvania, however, suggested that what is being passed in such families might be more than vulnerability to psychiatric illness. The Amish are ideal subjects for suicide research: alcoholism, divorce, violence, unemployment, and a solitary old age, all of which are factors that have been linked to suicide, are virtually unknown among a people who live in close-knit communities governed by a strict moral code. Suicide itself is still referred to as "that awful deed" or "the abominable sin," and until recently, Amish who killed themselves weren't permitted burial in the community cemetery. Combing through records, Janice Egeland, a medical sociologist from the University of Miami, found that there had been twenty-six suicides among the Old Order Amish during the previous hundred years. Retrospective studies suggested that twenty-four of them could have been diagnosed with depression or manic depression—some, admittedly, on the basis of such culturally inappropriate symptoms as "racing one's horse and carriage too hard" or "excessive use of the public telephone." What caught Egeland's attention was that four families accounted for 73 percent of the suicides. Interestingly, the families with the most serious cases of depression were not necessarily those with the most suicides, suggesting that some of the clustering of suicide could not be explained solely by the clustering of mood disorders.

Another way of examining possible genetic factors is to look at twins. Identical twins, coming from the same egg, share identical genetic material. Fraternal twins, coming from two eggs, share only half their genes, making them no more similar, genetically speaking, than nontwin siblings. If there is a genetic contribution to suicide, one might expect more pairs of suicides among identical than among fraternal twins. Reviewing all the published twin studies, psychiatrist Alec Roy found nearly four hundred pairs in which at least one twin had completed suicide. Of the 129 identical pairs, 13 percent of the surviving twins completed suicide; of the 270 fraternal pairs, less than

1 percent did. Looking at attempted suicide, Roy found that nearly 40 percent of identical twins whose co-twin had completed suicide had themselves attempted suicide. No surviving fraternal twin had done so. Although suggestive, the findings fell short of proving a genetic link; the evidence for genetic influence in suicide in the twin studies was much less strong than for genetic influence of mental illness. Then, too, identical twins may share more intense psychological bonds than fraternal twins and thus, after losing a twin to suicide, might be more likely to follow suit out of either grief or the long-standing habit of parallel behavior.

Distinguishing environmental and psychological effects from genetic contributions, however, is tricky. As with twins, the clustering of suicides within families could also be explained by modeling: when exposed to a certain behavior within a family, other members can perceive it as an option. One way to try to control for such influences is to study adoptees, who share their genes with their biological parents but their environment with their adoptive parents. If suicide has a strong genetic influence, one would expect a significantly higher suicide rate in the biological parents of adoptees who complete suicide than in the adoptive parents—which is what Danish researchers found when they examined all adoptions in Copenhagen between 1924 and 1947 and learned that fifty-seven of the adoptees eventually committed suicide. There was a significantly greater incidence of suicide in the biological relatives of suicides than in the adoptive relatives. The researchers also found that these suicides were largely independent of the presence of psychiatric disorders, leading them to suggest that there may be a genetic factor in suicide separate from the genetic transmission of mental illness.

The Holy Grail of biological suicide research is, of course, a specific candidate gene for suicidal behavior. Researchers are currently investigating polymorphisms in three genes that play critical roles in the regulation of serotonin, but have thus far found nothing conclusive.

---

"Reducing suicide to a biological basis is to ignore the psychological pain which drives it," psychologist Edwin Shneidman has said. "There can be no pill that salves the human malaise that leads to suicide." Shneidman is among the most vocal of the mental health professionals who worry that the emphasis placed on the biology of suicide over the last few decades has slighted the psychological and sociological aspects. They don't contest that the brain chemistry of some suicides may be skewed; it stands to reason, they say, that if someone is depressed to the point of considering suicide, his or her brain chemistry will reflect it. They suggest, however, that neurobiologists who identify serotonin dysfunction as the cause of suicidal behavior are mistaking a symptom for a disorder. "What is being measured is *concomitant* and not *causative*," writes Shneidman. "If one (unethically) effected low levels of

5HIAA in prisoners, would they then automatically commit suicide? These biochemical values reflect inner physiological states; they are not necessarily precursors of specific behaviors." Shneidman suggests that "what is being measured (with such precision) is general *perturbation,* and not specifically suicide." The fact that suicide tends to "run" in families does not necessarily point to a genetic etiology. "French runs in families," Shneidman has observed. "Common sense tells us that French is not inherited."

Indeed, the biological explanation of suicide can seem dismayingly reductive. I recall attending a conference for suicidologists in San Francisco at which Susan Blumenthal, a psychiatrist and then director of the short-lived Suicide Research Unit at NIMH, was presenting a slide show to give "an overview of our knowledge base" about adolescent suicide. Because of time restrictions, she had been asked to squeeze a presentation for which she normally allotted forty-five minutes into a fifteen-minute slot. Blumenthal spoke briskly about chemical markers, affective disorders, Marie Åsberg's studies, and low 5HIAA as colorful slides crammed with data flashed across the screen, often so quickly that the audience was able to focus only briefly on a yellow bar here, a group of red dots there. The slides flashed faster and faster until they seemed a kaleidoscopic blur, while Blumenthal struggled to keep up, rattling off statistics with the fervor of a baseball fan reciting batting averages. I was able to decipher only scraps of her commentary: "Males would be the straight line. . . . Six times greater incidence in the biological relatives of adopted young people. . . . By no means would I suggest that all suicides are genetic. . . . People who have this finding are at twenty times greater risk of killing themselves. . . . The squares are the violent attempts by suicide, and the circles are the suicide attempts by poisoning. . . ." As I watched this hectic son et lumière, I realized I had nearly forgotten that we were talking about human beings. I thought of Justin Spoonhour and Brian Hart, of Cato and Hamlet, of Richard and Bridget Smith. I thought of the ancient Egyptian trying to convince his *ba* to accompany him into death, which lay before him "like the fragrance of myrrh / Like sitting under sail on breeze day." And I wondered with some discomfort at the possibility that the answer to the question of "to be, or not to be" might all boil down to a matter of 3.5 nanograms of 5-hydroxyindoleacetic acid.

The neurobiologists, however, reiterate that biological characteristics do not determine suicidal behavior; they merely make some individuals more susceptible to impulsive, aggressive, and possibly suicidal acts. Whether those impulses are acted on depends on a variety of social and psychological factors. "I'm not saying that suicide is purely biological," says Arango, "but it starts with having an underlying biological risk. Having a low level of serotonin isn't by itself enough to lead to suicide. But when mixed with other factors—psychiatric illness being foremost, but also life experience, stress, and other psychological elements—it may lead to suicide. Suicide is multifaceted. But we believe that if a person doesn't have that biological predisposition, if he or she doesn't have

that low level of serotonin, even if all those other psychological and social factors are there, that person won't kill himself." In their paper "Serotonin Chemistry in the Brain of Suicidal Victims," Arango and Underwood describe how
the interaction of these ingredients might play out:

> Taking all evidence together, it is likely that suicide is not the result of a
> single factor but, rather, the outcome of several factors operating simul-
> taneously at a given moment in life. For example, an individual (male)
> born with the biological risk for suicide (i.e., low levels of serotonin)
> later suffers a major depressive episode which leads to the loss of his job,
> heavy alcohol drinking, and marital problems. When his wife begins
> divorce proceedings, he becomes isolated and hopeless and kills himself.
> In such an example, the biological risk is present from birth, but that
> alone is not enough to lead the person to suicide. A psychiatric disorder
> (depression in this case) followed by the stressful life events (the loss of
> his job and the disintegration of his family), all on top of the biological
> risk, operates simultaneously at that specific point in time, culminating
> in suicide.

"Suicide is a three-dimensional problem involving psychology, sociology,
and biology," says Herman van Praag, chairman of the department of psychiatry at the Albert Einstein College of Medicine in New York City, and a pioneer in linking low 5HIAA to severe depression and suicidal behavior. "All
three are important and continuously interacting. Biology is not the sole
answer. Biochemistry, for instance, cannot explain why Rembrandt is a great
artist. It might explain the colors and materials he uses. It's the same with suicide. To find out why someone is depressed, it's very important to look at biology. But given a state of increased suicidality, the reasons why one picks up
a gun, another takes a pill, and another suppresses the intention are very
much caused by that person's personality and what kind of environment he
lives in. The exploration of suicide must be three-dimensional."

---

With the "medicalization of suicide," as it has been called, some of those other
dimensions have faded into the background. Nearly a century after William
James—in an 1895 address to the Harvard Young Men's Christian Association
titled "Is Life Worth Living?"—called suicide a "religious disease" and its
cure "religious faith," I attended the fifteenth annual meeting of the American
Association of Suicidology. On the second morning, I wandered into a workshop called "Suicide: The Challenge to the Clergy." The panel consisted of an
articulate young rabbi, a middle-aged Catholic priest, and a quiet, white-
haired Episcopal minister. Each gave a short presentation on how his faith had
viewed suicide throughout history. Afterward, the question-and-answer ses-

sion evolved into a discussion of whether suicide was a sin. "None of us is willing to label it as a sin or crime," said the rabbi, pointing out that in Jewish law only people who kill themselves "calmly and with clear resolve" are considered suicides, a diagnosis that allows all others to be buried. The three clergymen agreed that if people who took their own lives were declared mentally ill, they were not suicides and could therefore be buried. "An enlightened point of view," murmured the minister.

Several people in the audience, however, questioned the necessity of declaring a person mentally ill in order to bury him. The priest responded that "the thinking is basically for someone to act *that* contrary to the drive of life, they must be crazy." There was a murmur of discomfort in the audience, which grew when he added, "Even with the terminally ill suicides, deep down you'll find disturbance in makeup of personality." A college chaplain in the audience maintained that some of the suicides he'd known had made calm, rational decisions. The priest replied quickly, "I don't think anybody who is perfectly normal will commit suicide." The Episcopal minister, sensing contention, pointed out that the presumption that a suicidal person is not in his right mind is born of compassion. But the debate continued for ten minutes. The priest became increasingly insistent. "I don't know of anybody who has committed suicide that wasn't a schizophrenic," he said. A voice from the back shouted, "I don't think it has anything to do with insanity." The priest's face reddened. "I'm making a judgment and you're making a judgment," he said, his voice digging in, "but my judgment is backed by empirical evidence." The voice in the back replied softly, "My judgment is backed by personal experience. It happened in my family."

The priest's insistence on describing suicide as proof of mental illness was unsettling; were he not wearing his clerical collar, he could have been mistaken for one of the psychiatrists presenting papers at the convention. But his stance was a reflection of how much the theological discussion of suicide has changed. As the twentieth century progressed, suicide was seen far less as a moral, ethical, or theological issue than as a medical-psychological problem. "Have we a right to commit suicide? Is it selfish to kill one's self? Is suicide cowardly or courageous?" asked psychiatrist Gregory Zilboorg as early as 1937. "It is almost too obvious to say that whatever drawing-room or academic philosophical interest these questions may have, a scientific study of suicide must disregard them and their possible answers." Thirty years later an editorial in the *Journal of the American Medical Association* asserted, "The contemporary physician sees suicide as a manifestation of emotional illness. Rarely does he view it in a context other than that of psychiatry." The entry on suicide in the *Encyclopaedia of Religion and Ethics* notes, "Perhaps the greatest contribution of modern times to the rational treatment of the matter is the consideration . . . that many suicides are non-moral and entirely the affair of the specialist in mental diseases."

With this "rational treatment," the antisuicide laws were finally erased. If suicide was the product of psychological disturbance, punishment was obviously inappropriate. In England, although a statute prohibiting burial of suicides in the highway was passed in 1823, confiscation of property was not abolished until 1870, and attempted suicide was punishable by up to two years in prison well into the twentieth century. When attempters regained consciousness in the hospital, they usually found a policeman at their bedside, waiting to interview them. Until World War I, suicide attempters were often sent to prison, particularly after a second or third attempt. The sentence was considered to be, as one prosecutor observed, "in the interests of the defendant's health"—behind bars he might be prevented from trying again. By the 1950s, prosecution and imprisonment were rare "unless there is some outstanding feature only a prosecution might cure, or if there have been repeated attempts at self-destruction," as Lilian Wyles explained in her 1952 book, *A Woman at Scotland Yard*. "A severe lecture on their stupidity is mostly delivered to the offenders by a senior officer." In 1955, of 5,220 attempted suicides known to the police, only 535 came to trial. Most of these were discharged, fined, or placed on probation. Forty-three were sentenced to prison, the majority for less than six months. In 1961, under pressure from doctors, lawyers, and clergymen, the Suicide Act was passed, abolishing the law that made suicide a crime and attempted suicide a misdemeanor. Shortly afterward, London's Ministry of Health declared that attempted suicide was to be regarded as a medical and social problem, and cases were to be referred to a psychiatrist. In the United States, only Texas and Oklahoma retain laws against attempted suicide, and these have not been enforced for many years.

Suicide remains a sin in Roman Catholic canonical law. "Intentionally causing one's own death, or suicide, is therefore equally as wrong as murder; such an action on the part of a person is to be considered as a rejection of God's sovereignty and loving plan," reiterated the Vatican's 1980 Declaration on Euthanasia. "Furthermore, suicide is also often a refusal of love for self, the denial of the natural instinct to live, a flight from the duties of justice and charity owed to one's neighbor, to various communities or to the whole of society—although, as generally recognized, at times there are psychological factors present that can diminish responsibility or even completely remove it." Except for the last phrase, the declaration essentially echoes the words of St. Augustine fifteen centuries earlier. But the verdict of insanity that is still invoked to ensure suicides a Christian burial now seems a firm belief rather than a tender mercy. (And even that verdict is not always sufficient. A few members of the clergy still refuse to officiate at funeral services for a suicide, and as late as 1969 a pregnant woman who killed herself in Chicago was denied full religious rites.) The fierce moral debate that dominated the discussion of suicide for centuries has quieted. The handful of twentieth-century theologians who have written on suicide plow familiar ground—duty to God, state, and family—although most tend to emphasize the spiritual value of suffering rather than the sin of suicide.

"There is but one truly serious philosophical problem, and that is suicide," began Camus's *The Myth of Sisyphus,* published in 1940. "Judging whether life is or is not worth living amounts to the fundamental question of philosophy." Apparently, few agree. In a 2,100-item bibliography on suicide covering the years 1897 to 1957, only twenty-five entries were listed under the category "Religious-Philosophical." The rest were psychological, sociological, or medical titles. Yet the sociological study of suicide, too, has become increasingly muted. Although hundreds of studies have been published since Durkheim's *Le Suicide,* the majority of them are reformulations of Durkheim's work. In a variation on his theme of anomie, for example, Andrew Henry and James Short examined fluctuations in rates and concluded that people who are deeply involved with others are at low risk for suicide, while people who are isolated from meaningful relationships are at high risk. Sociologists Jack Gibbs and Walter Martin refined Durkheim's concept of "social integration" into what they called "status integration." Every individual, they said, belonged to several categories in which he played a clearly defined role. For instance, a man might belong to these statuses: male, black, plumber, married, and parent. The more frequently a person's combination of statuses conformed to the combination common in the population to which he belonged, the higher his "status integration"—and the lower his chances of suicide. Departing from Durkheim, Jack Douglas, in *The Social Meanings of Suicide,* questioned the accuracy of suicide statistics, pointing out that suicide has many different definitions and meanings, and insisted that rather than sift through statistics to find those meanings, we try to "determine the meanings to the people actually involved."

The psychological study of suicide, too, has gradually been eclipsed by the biological. After Freud's exploration of the unconscious, it was no longer possible to attribute suicide to simple causes such as poverty, loss of a job, or disappointment in love. Suicide was instead understood to be the end result of a complex variety of forces, conscious and unconscious. In *Man Against Himself,* psychoanalyst Karl Menninger offered an illustration:

A wealthy man is one day announced as having killed himself. It is discovered that his investments have failed, but that his death provides bountiful insurance for his otherwise destitute family. The problem and its solution, then, seem simple and obvious enough. A man has bravely faced ruin in a way that benefits his dependents.

But why should we begin our interpretations only at this late point in such a man's life, the point at which he loses his wealth? Shall we not seek to discover how it came about that he lost it? And even more pertinently, shall we not inquire how he made it, why he was driven to amass money, and what means he used to gratify his compulsion, what unconscious and perhaps also conscious guilt feelings were associated with it and with the sacrifices and penalties its acquisition cost him and his family? And even those who have money and lose it do not in the vast majority of cases kill themselves, so we still do not know what this man's deeper motives were for this particular act. All we can really see from such a case is how difficult and complex the problem becomes as soon as we take more than a superficial glance at the circumstances.

As for the "deeper motives," different theorists have emphasized different components. In *Man Against Himself,* Menninger cataloged a multitude of self-destructive activities from "chronic" or "partial" suicides such as alcoholism, asceticism, and antisocial behavior, to "focal suicides"—self-mutilation and purposive accidents. He interpreted all of these as expressions of the death instinct described by Freud. Menninger believed that three elements must be present for someone to express the most extreme self-destructive behavior by committing suicide: the wish to kill, the wish to be killed, and the wish to die.

Freud's "death instinct" has not been widely accepted by psychiatrists, however, and as an explanation for suicide it is so broad as to be virtually useless. "To say that the death instinct gains the upper hand over the life instinct," observed Zilboorg, "is merely an elaborate way of stating that man does die or kill himself." Freud's formulation of depression, on the other hand, has become the basis for the psychoanalytic understanding of suicide, with the result that subsequent therapists—in the attempt to cast suicide as inverted murder—have underestimated other possible factors: grief, love, fear, hopelessness, rigid thinking, frustration, low self-esteem, magical belief in immortality, desire for reunion with a lost loved one. Even Zilboorg conceded that most suicides combine a strong unconscious hostility with an unusual inability to love others.

Trying to reduce all suicides to a psychological common denominator has provided some far-fetched results. Psychiatrist Maurice Farber concocted a mathematical formula describing the likelihood of suicide for a given person, in which *DEC* represents Demands for the Exercising of Competence, *DIG* represents Demands for Interpersonal Giving, *TS* is Tolerance of Suicide, *Su* is Availability of Succorance, and *HFT* is Degree of Hope in the Future Time Perspective of the Society:

$$S = f\left(\frac{DEC, DIG, TS}{Su, HFT}\right)$$

Despite such painstaking logic, suicide remains an enigma. Indeed, despite the strides made in the biological understanding of self-destruction over the past several decades, most suicidologists would undoubtedly agree with Karl Menninger, a lifelong student of suicide who, at a conference in 1984, confessed, "It's a durn mystery, you know, in spite of all we've written about it."

# 3

# THE RANGE
# OF SELF-DESTRUCTIVE
# BEHAVIOR

◆

# I

# WINNER AND LOSER

LIKE RICHARD CORY, the handsome, wealthy gentleman in the Edwin Arlington Robinson poem known to generations of high school English classes, Peter Newell seemed to lead an enviable life. At fifty-four he was a good-looking man with a full head of graying hair and a beard. He was a skier, golfer, and sailor. He held a well-paying job with a major corporation. He had two healthy and loving daughters and a two-year-old grandson. Amicably divorced for five years, he was living with an intelligent, attractive woman whom he planned to marry. Yet, like Richard Cory, who, "one calm summer night / went home and put a bullet through his head," Peter Newell chose to end his seemingly enviable life. One Sunday evening, he sat down in his favorite chair, placed a gun in his mouth, and pulled the trigger. On his desk he left a note, in his careful, boyish hand:

> The world is composed of winners and losers. The winners get stronger and the losers get weaker. As the winners get stronger, the losers just shine their shoes, load their dishwashers, and walk the dog for them. . . . It's innate, it's inborn. It'll never change, ever. Well, right on, winners, go ahead. But here's one loser you won't have to kick around anymore. I'm going to stop right now!

The disbelief that follows almost every suicide was especially pronounced after the death of Peter Newell. The word used most often to describe him was *gentleman*. He had a firm moral sense—what a colleague at his funeral referred to as "the Quaker-like principles that dominated his life." Suicide seemed the antithesis of those principles. Peter was also a truly "gentle" man who could not bear to argue or fight. It was difficult to believe that such a meticulous and considerate person had chosen such a violent way to die. Several people close to him, in fact, insisted that his death must have been a murder and, even after they saw his suicide note, were convinced he had been forced to write it.

And yet, looking back, one can tease out several strands of discord and unhappiness that reached into his childhood. Peter was the second son of well-to-do parents who, he felt, considered him an unexciting "good little boy" as compared to his brilliant and difficult older brother. His father died when Peter was thirteen. Adolescence was an uncomfortable time for him. He was chubby and uncoordinated, and he often preferred to stay alone in his room at boarding school, listening to music and thinking melancholy thoughts instead of socializing with his classmates. At Yale, he was on the verge of flunking out when he enlisted in the navy. This, too, was a disappointment. It was the height of World War II, and Peter dreamed of being a fighter pilot, but he was such a fine aviator that the navy felt he was more valuable as an instructor, and he was sent to Texas to teach cadets how to fly. What was intended as a high compliment was experienced as a crushing blow.

Peter was still in the navy when he married Barbara Spires, whom he had met on the beach in the Connecticut town where her family spent the summers. She was a student at Smith College and he was in the service, so much of their courtship was carried out by letter. They married after Barbara's graduation. After Peter was discharged, he finished at Yale, graduating with a degree in mechanical engineering. Like so many young postwar couples, they settled down to raise a family in the suburbs.

Outwardly, their early years in Darien, Connecticut, seemed an American idyll. They lived in a comfortable house with a half-acre yard in a quiet upper-middle-class neighborhood. Peter commuted to nearby Stamford, where he worked as a graphic engineer for Time Inc., while Barbara settled into her role as housewife and mother. Peter was a playful, affectionate father to their two daughters. At the beach he splashed for hours in the water with his children and later was a patient swimming teacher. His younger daughter remembers how each time she washed her hair, her father would sniff her head and tell her how good she smelled. A gifted carpenter and handyman, Peter loved to work around the house, and as his daughters watched him painstakingly rebuilding a boat, remodeling the den, or taking apart the engine of his MG, they were proud of their father's skill.

Two years after the birth of their eldest child, Ruth, another daughter, Kathy, was born severely retarded and deaf. Peter was devastated. Once when Kathy was very sick and crying uncontrollably, Barbara sat in one room praying for her to live, and Peter sat in another room praying for her to die. When Sally was born, Peter and his wife felt that they could not handle all three children, so when Kathy was five, her father drove her to an institution near Hartford. Peter brought Kathy home for the holidays, but she would pull out all the pots and pans and books and scream through the night. After a few years they no longer brought her home. Although Barbara continued to visit her, Peter refused. "Having a retarded child hit him fifty times harder than it did my mother," Sally would recall, "because he had this thing about failure—he just couldn't tolerate it—and I think he saw this as a failure on his part."

Although Kathy certainly needed help, institutionalizing her was consistent with Peter's character. He preferred things to be as neat and controlled as an engineering problem. "We were not an emotional family," says Sally. "There wasn't much hugging and kissing, and crying was done in private. My father never wanted to hear negative things. If I came to him upset by something at school, he'd never sympathize, he'd always wonder if it was my fault and say, 'Can't you stop complaining?'" Peter himself rarely complained; he seemed to assume that any mishap was his fault. Nevertheless, what mistakes he made, he preferred to hide. "He would never tell us about his failures," says Sally. "It would have been such a comfort if he had, especially when I started having problems at school. He was always on time, always prepared, always conscientious. He was the paragon, the brain, and we could *never* live up to him." Not until she was in her twenties did Sally find out from her mother that her father had had troubles in school himself, that he had, in fact, nearly flunked out of Yale.

One of the things Peter hid from his children was the growing tension in his marriage. He and Barbara had not known each other well before marrying. Gradually, they learned that they had little in common. Peter was active and athletic; his wife was uninterested in sports. On one of their first sailing trips, she got sick and asked to be taken ashore. She never went sailing again. He loved music of all kinds—jazz, classical, Broadway—and spent much of his time in the basement playing the harmonica or listening to records as he worked. She had little feeling for music. He loved to work outdoors; she spent much of her time indoors, reading. Their marriage roles divided along traditional lines. He handled the yard work; she handled the children. He handled the bills; she handled the cooking. He liked a clean house; she tended to be a little sloppy. He believed in disciplining the children; she was more permissive. He was acutely sensitive and occasionally depressed; she had little tolerance for his melancholic moods, and when she found him lying on the living-room floor, listening to sad music, just as he had as an adolescent, she would tell him with annoyance to get up.

This tension, however, was kept under wraps. "I never saw my parents fight," says Sally. "I always thought they deliberately postponed arguments until we were asleep." Although they presented a smooth facade to the outside world, their marriage deteriorated to the point where they were staying together only for the sake of their children. Ruth was a quiet, well-mannered girl, but Sally was as wild and anarchic as her father was orderly and scrupulous. She had never done well in her studies, and in high school she was in danger of being kicked out. She skipped classes and sneaked out of the house at night to go to parties, driving with her friends across the border to New York where the drinking age was lower. She got heavily involved with drugs. At various times Sally was arrested for possession of marijuana, for shoplifting, and for criminal trespassing in a church.

At first her father set curfews, devised elaborate reward systems based on her grades, picked her up at the police station, and paid her fines. He sent her to a psychiatrist, but Sally was sullen and resistant, and after six months she stopped going. When Peter forbade her to drive his car, she took her mother's and immediately had an accident. He grounded her, but she would slip out her bedroom window. He lost his temper with her; she would scream right back. The more he tried to control her, the more out of control she became. It was the suburban parent's nightmare, and Peter felt he was a failure as a father. "I don't think he ever imagined something like this could happen," says Sally. "He had mapped out his life, and this didn't fit in." When Sally turned seventeen, Peter seemed to give up. From then on she came and went as she pleased. When she ate meals with her parents, the air was thick with tension. "Once, my father had to pick me up at the station after the police had brought me in, thinking I was a runaway," says Sally. "When he walked in, he looked like a beaten man." One evening Sally passed her parents' bedroom and saw her father weeping, his head down on the dresser. It was the first time she had ever seen him cry. But communication between them had broken down long ago, and she just walked by.

Peter's younger daughter was not the only source of pain in his life. That year, Time Inc. closed its Connecticut lab. Although he was told the company would find a position for him in its New York office, Peter was devastated. His wife remembers him coming home every night and crying. He became increasingly depressed, which put even more strain on their marriage. Although Peter and Barbara had planned to stay together until Sally finished high school, even that now seemed ludicrous, since she had dropped out. When Sally was eighteen, they divorced. In keeping with his lifelong feelings of guilt and responsibility, Peter asked for so little in the settlement that the lawyer they shared had to urge him to take more. Barbara kept the house and most of their possessions; Peter moved into a nondescript one-bedroom apartment in a modern high-rise in downtown Stamford.

The next few years were a period of change for Peter, in which he seemed to loosen up somewhat. He began to wear brightly striped shirts and jeans instead of white button-downs and tailored slacks. He bought a motorcycle and could be seen riding into town in his business suit with a pipe in his mouth. Once, when Sally gave him a joint, he even tried marijuana. Nevertheless, it was a lonely time. Since his departure Sally had become even more out of control. Although she kept him at a distance, Peter tried to be a dutiful father. When she broke both legs in a car accident, he visited her often at the hospital. She got pregnant at age twenty by a boy she had met at a rock festival. "I told my mother right away, but it took me a long time to get up the nerve to tell my father. He took things so much to heart, I knew it would be a real blow. We talked for two hours, and he sort of begged me to get married for the baby's sake. He really put his heart and soul into that talk. He was so moving and caring that he persuaded me. It had been a long time since we talked that long." Though Peter had always dreamed of giving his daughter a traditional church wedding, he was one of the few witnesses when Sally and Bill were married by a justice of the peace. Four months later he rushed to the hospital in time for the birth of his grandson, Owen. And when Sally and her family moved to California, where they lived on welfare and food stamps, he wrote her faithfully, whether or not he got a reply.

After his divorce Peter joined Parents Without Partners, an organization that sponsors parties and outings for people who are divorced or widowed. Through this group he met Anna, a woman with whom he began a passionate, stormy relationship. They fought, broke up, and made up many times. The breaking up was always painful for Peter, but the making up was so sweet that he stayed with her for nearly two years. The relationship's downs, however, seemed to throw him into despair; after a fight he would call Anna and beg her to come by. Alarmed at how depressed he sounded, she would relent and rush over to comfort him. In a four-page letter to his older brother, Peter matter-of-factly described his job, his golf game, and his carpentry projects. Then he wrote:

The next "event" on my calendar is the breakup of Anna and I in early November. All fall, at my suggestion, we had been seeing each other only every other weekend. I had suggested that we each do a little "outside" dating. She apparently did and I didn't, so finally she said she didn't think we ought to date each other anymore, and we haven't. All this threw me into an absolute panic. I proposed. She refused. Pop's old revolver misfired. And I started dating another lady. All in the space of five days! Boy, do I need psychiatric help!

In the next paragraph he was back to news of mutual friends and a discussion of the weather. "Well, that's about all the news I have," he concluded. "My very best to you both." If the letter was a cry for help, it was characteristically well camouflaged, using offhand remarks and exclamation points to mask his deepest feelings. His brother shrugged off the reference to "Pop's old revolver" as some unfamiliar figure of speech. In any case he did not reply to the letter for eleven months, and Peter did not seek "psychiatric help."

Peter's new "lady" was Jane Freund, a bright, vibrant woman who worked with problem learners in a local elementary school. Eleven years younger than Peter, she had been divorced five years and had three teenage sons. They had met through Parents Without Partners, and a few days after breaking up with Anna, Peter asked her out. After thirteen years of strained marriage, Jane was surprised that a relationship could be so relaxed. Peter was gentle, with a good sense of humor and a miscellany of talents. Unlike Peter's ex-wife, Jane loved the outdoors, and they frequently skied, sailed, and hiked. On a weeklong canoe trip in Minnesota, Jane remembers Peter playing chanteys and hymns on his harmonica in their tent during a rainstorm. She was impressed at how easily he made others happy. They also enjoyed simpler pleasures—movies, the theater, and long walks. "We'd have dinner at his apartment," recalls Jane. "He didn't know how to cook, so we'd put some food on to simmer and then go make love. One of our jokes was that we were going to write *The Lovers' Cookbook*—easy recipes that you could make quickly and then let simmer for an hour or two."

For Peter the relationship offered a real challenge. Jane was far more opinionated and assertive than he. One night early in their affair, Jane ran into a former lover at a party and kissed him warmly on the lips. Peter left the party disturbed. The next day they had planned to go sailing. When the hour came and he had not come by to pick her up, Jane called him. "I'm not going," said Peter in a tight voice. "I can't see you. I can never see you again." Jane was confused. When she drove to his apartment, she found him in a terrible, agitated state. "I just can't talk to you now," he said, weeping. "I don't know what I'm going to do, but I just can't see you now."

Although they smoothed things over, Jane was alarmed by Peter's reaction. She found other aspects of his behavior similarly unsettling, if less extreme. "When we had people over, Peter was a wonderful host for the first ten minutes," says Jane. "He'd extend his hand, hang up coats, get people drinks, sit them by the fire, make small talk. But as the evening went along, he sort of faded into the background." At one party Jane remembers hearing someone ask Peter if he was a commuter. "No," he replied. End of conversation. Later Jane explained to Peter that the woman wanted to know more about him, and asking whether he was a commuter was merely a conversational opening. At another party Peter remained silent during a spirited discussion of single-sex education at college. "Well, Peter, what do *you* think?" asked Jane. "I don't know," he said. "Come on," pressed Jane. "You must have formed some opinions about it." But Peter said no, he didn't have an opinion. Jane, who liked a good discussion, even an occasional argument, found this reluctance exasperating. "Peter was not a passive person," she says. "But in some ways he didn't know how to stand up for himself." Even discussing the relative merits of drip-dry and all-cotton sheets, or the best way to wrap meat for the freezer,

Peter preferred to concede rather than to make waves. "Please tell me how to do it," he'd say, "then I'll just do it that way."

Annoyed by Peter's meekness in minor matters, Jane was troubled by the way he repressed truly important issues. When Peter mentioned that he had a third daughter, Kathy, who was in an institution, Jane asked him how she was. "I don't know," he said. He told her he hadn't seen her in many years. Jane, who worked with autistic children, was appalled. "He didn't want to be involved with anything that would tug at his heartstrings," she says. "He didn't like things that weren't clean and clear, that he couldn't solve. He seemed to block out difficult and stressful things, just pulled the blinders down."

One night after making love they began talking about the worst times they had ever known. Peter said he had once felt so bad that he had put a bullet in a gun, spun the chamber, put the gun in his mouth, and fired. Jane was stunned. She asked how often he had done this, and he said, "More than once." Jane threatened to leave him if he didn't get help, so Peter went four times a week to a psychiatrist, who put him on antidepressants.

They never talked about his suicide attempts again. Though Jane couldn't forget them, she dismissed them because they had happened before he'd met her and because things seemed to be going so well. "One thing that helped me put it out of my mind was that the sex was so beautiful and so loving. It was free and erotic with lots of laughing and tumbling around," she says. "So whenever this little worry came up, I would argue myself out of it by saying that anybody with whom lovemaking is this beautiful can't . . . you know . . ." Her voice trails off.

As Peter continued in therapy, he seemed to be gaining confidence. "He really didn't know how to stand up for himself," says Jane. "But he was learning." She smiles. "We had an argument once, it was something so stupid, it was about which material is warmer, down or Polarguard. We argued all evening long, and I kept thinking, 'Gee, he's not quitting.' Next morning I apologized, and he said, 'You know why I kept that argument going? I've never really been able to argue. Before this my stomach used to tie itself into knots, and this time my head kept sending messages down to my stomach saying, 'Everything all right down there?' and my stomach kept saying, 'I'm fine down here, keep it going up there!'"

When her youngest son, Andy, went away to boarding school, leaving Jane alone in her four-bedroom house, Peter moved in. Jane's children liked him, not only because he was pleasant and easygoing but because they saw how happy he made their mother. "He changed her a lot—she was not on edge so much," says Andy, who was fifteen at the time. "She seemed *much* happier with him than she'd ever been with anyone else." Peter grew especially close to Andy, a shy, introverted boy who, like Peter, had had problems in school. Peter taught him how to sail and how to work the rotary mower. He took him on the back of his motorcycle on errands into town or on Sunday-night trips to get ice cream. Once, Andy asked Peter, "When are you and my mother going to get married? Because if you do, I'll like it that you're my stepfather." Moved, Peter had to turn away so Andy wouldn't see his tears.

Peter seemed to enjoy the new domestic arrangement. As always he loved doing yard work, rewiring electrical outlets, repairing old furniture. When Jane tried to teach him how to cook, Peter was initially resistant, but gradually he mastered omelets, hamburgers, and chicken. They soon settled into a period of tranquillity. Jane often thinks of lazy Sunday mornings in her backyard, trading sections of the *New York Times,* sipping coffee. Yet a part of Peter still held back; he continued to maintain his apartment even though he and Jane had begun to talk seriously about marriage.

Peter's work was a source of increasing unhappiness. In the past year he had been asked to join his company's paper-purchasing group, an administrative post that used none of his technical skills. He ended up buying the paper for the subscription cards that fall out of magazines. He realized that he had been kicked upstairs, and he felt demeaned. "I think he worked not because he enjoyed it but because he had to earn people's respect," says Jane. "I think he was terrified of being without a job."

At the same time, Peter's relationship with his own family seemed to be improving. That summer Sally returned from California with two-year-old Owen. She moved in with her mother and got a job cleaning houses. Although life was still difficult—she and her husband were considering separation— she never told her father. "I would have lied rather than tell him how miserable my life was," says Sally. "I guess I saw him as an innocent, and I didn't think he could take it." On the Fourth of July, Peter, Jane, Sally, and Owen watched the fireworks display at the town beach, Peter carrying his grandson on his shoulders. They swam at the pond near Jane's, and Peter held Owen on the surface of the water, just as he had held Sally when he'd taught her to swim so many years before. One night, Peter, Sally, and Ruth, who had come East for a visit, went out to dinner. "I picked a little family-type place because my father always liked this Italian restaurant when we were young," says Sally. The evening was relaxed and pleasant, just the way they might have imagined it before all the troubled years. "He talked some about his personal life, and I felt really touched by that," says Sally. "I wanted to talk to him more like this. I felt I was finally getting to know him."

One night a few weeks later Sally had dinner with Peter and Jane. Her father drove her home. "We took the parkway and got off at Westport, and I said why this exit? He said he wanted to take the long way. He said something about it being a prettier route, but it was unusual for him to go out of his way like that. We didn't talk about anything special, but later it occurred to me that he wanted to drag it out, that he may already have known what he was going to do."

Two weeks later Peter spent the weekend alone. He had told Jane that he missed having time to himself just to read or putter around the house. Jane was due to drive Andy up to his new school in New Hampshire and planned to return Sunday evening. Although she would have liked to have Peter's company, she suggested it might be a good opportunity for him to get some time on his own.

That weekend Peter wrote an eight-page letter to an old friend. By Peter's standards the letter was extraordinarily frank. He told her of his doubts about Jane; of his fear that because he was eleven years older he would end up being a burden to her; that one day he would be "old and tottering" while Jane was "still strong and healthy." He wrote of her forcefulness. "Jane went through five years of psychoanalysis, which has left her overflowing with confidence. I'm just over a year into psychotherapy and, it seems to me, stalled out. The result sometimes is that I feel I am the one out of step." He wrote of sometimes finding it difficult to be with Jane's children, fond as he was of them. "Those absolutely awful years with Sally have undoubtedly left a lot of scars on me. I would much prefer to stay completely out of the business of raising kids. . . . All of this makes me feel very old and very inflexible," he wrote. "Sometimes I think I'm best suited to be a hermit!" He wrote at length of his disappointment in his job:

> The work itself requires care and accuracy but absolutely none of my technical training and experience. In many respects it is clerk's work. For the first time in my years with Time, taking time off for vacations is a real problem and the load when I return is appalling. But I guess more than anything else, it is humiliating! I've been hanging on by my teeth until I can take early retirement at 56½, a whole year and seven months away. But sometimes even that seems an eternity. The early retirement benefits are very appreciable but I sometimes wonder if anything is worth it. It isn't so much that I want to be something else—I don't really know what I want to do—but I very much want to stop what I am doing.
>
> Enough of my troubles! The good news. Ruth continues to live in Boulder, Colorado, with her husband. She spent two days here in Connecticut this summer and . . .

---

Sunday afternoon Jane drove home from New Hampshire in a storm. She stopped off in Springfield to call Peter and tell him she would be home in a couple of hours. Peter sounded a little down—there were awkward pauses in the conversation—but Jane was impatient to get back and didn't press the issue. Rain beat down on the telephone booth. Cars roared past. Jane remembers feeling, "Oh, honey, I miss you, I can't wait to get home and snuggle up into your shoulder." But what she said to Peter was "I can't wait to get home and have a drink."

When she walked in the house, Peter wasn't there. She found a bowl of sliced peaches on the counter and thought perhaps Peter was making peach shortcake, one of his favorite desserts, and had gone to the store to get some whipping cream. Jane told herself he would be home in half an hour. He wasn't. She telephoned his apartment repeatedly, but there was no answer. In the back of her mind she thought of the possibility of suicide, but she couldn't believe it. "I was like a rabbit frozen in car headlights, paralyzed. I just sort of insisted on life as usual. I went to bed thinking, 'He'll come home at three in the morning and sit on the edge of the bed and tell me he's depressed.'"

At 6 a.m. she drove to his apartment and knocked on the door until her hand hurt. She called the police, who broke the door down. "At first I thought he was asleep. He was sitting with his legs crossed and his head tilted, and his hands were in his lap. And then I saw the gun in his hand. I saw that black metal and all the red, and I turned away and said to myself, 'Oh my God, he's done it.' I told everybody—his parents, my parents, his children, my children—that he looked sort of peaceful. But that wasn't true. His mouth was open, and there was a waterfall of blood."

Jane couldn't look anymore. She went into the kitchen. "A big policeman standing at Peter's desk called out that there was a note. I didn't want to go into the room again so I asked him to read it to me." At the morgue they gave her a brown envelope with the contents of Peter's pockets. "There was blood on the money and on his credit cards," she recalls. "I trimmed the edges of the bills where the blood was and washed the credit cards." She drove to New Hampshire to get Andy. She had told him on the phone that Peter had died but said she couldn't tell him how until she saw him. Andy guessed that Peter's commuter train had crashed or that he had been in an accident on his motorcycle. When he got in the car, she told him. Jane recalls, "He looked so sad that I pulled over at a gas station, and we took a walk into a field. We hugged, and he was crying so hard I thought his legs would buckle. I wondered how this man could have done something that would hurt a fifteen-year-old kid so much he's going to fall down if I don't hold him up."

The memorial service took place at the church in which Peter and Jane had planned to marry. "I was in charge of the arrangements, which was probably the most responsible thing I'd ever done," Sally says. "It made me feel like an adult." It was a simple service, as the family agreed Peter would have preferred. They sang the familiar Protestant hymns: "Eternal Father, Strong to Save" and "Abide with Me." The minister read from Ecclesiastes and from the Twenty-third Psalm. Jane spoke, as did Peter's daughters and a friend from work. One of Jane's sons remembers thinking how fragmented the group was. There were friends from different parts of Peter's life—his family, his friends from work, from the navy, and from Parents Without Partners—but none of the different circles seemed to intersect.

In the week after the service Jane, Sally, and Ruth cleaned out Peter's apartment, looking for clues that might help them understand his death. Jane found Peter's letters to his former girlfriend Anna in which he sounded pathetic and groveling. She was so upset by them that she burned them. Sally read a journal her father had kept one summer when Jane had gone to Alaska for a month; he had written of his feelings of rejection. She realized her father had been more insecure and unstable than she had imagined. "He must have been so unhappy all those years," she says, "and it gradually intensified until he couldn't stand it." Sally, who had herself toyed with the idea of suicide during her teenage years, had insomnia and nightmares. "I kept trying to imagine myself in his place, sitting in the chair with a gun in his hand. I just didn't know how he could do it." Andy noticed that there were fifty more miles on the speedometer of Peter's motorcycle than on the night before he had left for school, when he and Peter had driven into town for ice cream. "On Saturday or Sunday," Jane says, "Peter must have taken a long ride somewhere, maybe to try to dissipate that sense of 'My God, it's coming over me again, that black cloud.'"

In their effort to find some answers, Sally and Ruth met with their father's psychiatrist. They talked for half an hour, but the psychiatrist, citing doctor-patient confidentiality, told them little. "We tried to work around that," says Sally, "by making statements like 'He was sensitive, insecure, had a poor self-image, and we wondered whether that might be the reason he committed suicide.' The doctor said yes, that was close. He said my father's death had taken him by surprise, too. But I was annoyed because he didn't seem very remorseful."

Jane, who was hounded for months by bloody nightmares, was bewildered. She knew Peter had been unhappy and depressed at times. She knew he had problems expressing his feelings. She knew that he had always had high standards and principles that perhaps at bottom he felt he could never live up to. She knew enough about psychiatry to realize that Peter had had lifelong feelings of inadequacy, and a part of him had seemed to need to be punished. She knew that he had attempted suicide before he'd met her. But why now? Why that weekend? Why just when it seemed everything was going so well? She wondered if perhaps he had been opening up so fast in therapy that it had scared him. Perhaps his melancholy had come over him at a time when he was vulnerable and no longer had enough defenses to cope. But at bottom there was something inexplicable, like those fifty extra miles on his speedometer.

When Jane met with Peter's psychiatrist, she found that the part of Peter she didn't know was larger than she had suspected. He told her that Peter had made three other suicide attempts before he'd met her. In fact, the psychiatrist had known about the gun and had told Peter that if he did not get rid of it, he would stop treatment. Instead, Peter padlocked the gun in a metal case and put it in his cellar. "I think Peter thought he could always use it if he needed to," says Jane. "I wish the psychiatrist had stepped out of the traditional role and invited me in. It might have diffused the danger that lay in the secrecy of that gun. Peter was not an assertive person, and if he hadn't had access to a weapon, I don't think he would have done it. I think he would have just suffered through whatever black mood he was in.

"I feel I have to keep justifying him because I lived with him and I loved him, and if he came back, I would live with him again. But when I went back to the apartment, I found a velvet-lined case with another small gun and something that looked like a shotgun lying in pieces," she says slowly. "I don't know how to put that together with the man I knew. That's a mystery I'll never solve. There's no one who can tell me why because the person who knows is dead, and even he probably didn't know." Jane folds her hands. "But I know now what I hadn't known before, that it is possible for even the most deeply disturbed and desperately unbalanced among us to be a beautiful person."

# II

# UNDER THE SHADOW

---

FROM TIME TO TIME magazines print articles with titles like "Are You the Suicide Type?" They offer statistics on who is likely to complete suicide: four times more men than women kill themselves; whites complete suicide more than nonwhites; suicide rates rise with age, soaring after sixty; divorced men are three times more likely to kill themselves than married men; two of every three suicides are white males; and so on. Through these demographic factors a composite emerges, like a police artist's sketch, of an older, white, divorced, unemployed male who lives alone and is in poor health—the "suicide type" or "high-risk paradigm," as clinicians call it. As a white male who was divorced and approaching retirement, Peter Newell was in many ways the typical suicide.

Such articles, however, usually conclude that there is no such thing as a suicide type. Suicide cuts across all sex lines, age groups, races, and diagnoses. Just as no two fingerprints are identical, no two lives are identical, and no two suicides are identical. While the vast majority of suicides may be associated with a diagnosable psychiatric illness, focusing on an underlying disorder may divert us from the fact that for the suicidal individual, the act has a meaning, a goal, a motivation. "No one ever lacks a good reason for suicide," observed the Italian author Cesare Pavese. But Peter Newell's reasons were different from Justin Spoonhour's. The man who responds to voices urging him to kill himself is different from the terminally ill man who decides he has had enough of life. The depressed woman who builds up to the act over many years is different from the girl who, rejected by her lover, impulsively flings herself from a bridge.

"Suicide," says psychologist Edwin Shneidman, "is an attempt to solve a problem." That problem is rarely external pain or misery on a large scale. In fact, adversity often seems to strengthen the desire to live. History is brimming with people who, in the face of prodigious bad fortune, poverty, illness, or torture, manage to survive, and with others who, despite being blessed with every possible advantage, such as Peter Newell, take their own lives. This is reflected on a macroscopic level by the higher rates of suicide in industrialized nations than in underdeveloped countries; in the upper classes than in the middle and lower; among whites than among blacks. It is also illustrated by the reported rarity of suicides and suicide attempts in the Nazi concentration camps. In *The Drowned and the Saved,* Primo Levi, noting the low incidence of suicide at Auschwitz, wrote, "The day was dense: one had to think about satisfying hunger, in some way elude fatigue and cold, avoid the blows. Precisely because of the constant imminence of death there was no time to concentrate on the idea of death." Yet many survivors seemed to experience a delayed reaction in which a built-up residue of depression found expression only after the immediate threat of death was gone. Levi was one of only three of his original convoy of 650 prisoners to return alive from Auschwitz. Forty-two years later, at age sixty-seven, suffering from severe depression, the author threw himself down the stairwell of his fourth-floor apartment in Turin, one of numerous death-camp survivors who ultimately took their life.

The internal misery that leads to suicide often involves loss. "It is impossible to think that I shall never sit with you again and hear you laugh. *That every day for the rest of my life you will be away,*" wrote Bloomsbury painter Carrington in 1932, less than a month after her beloved Lytton Strachey died. One month later she killed herself. Three days after his bride died of asphyxiation when he had tried to smuggle her into the United States in a suitcase, a thirty-one-year-old Iranian émigré shot himself in the head with a pistol he had bought the day before after telling a friend, "I'm just dead. I lost everything." Such suicides often involve the conscious or unconscious fantasy that death will bring a reunion with the lost loved one. Not long after his beloved dog Boxer died, one elderly man fell ill, became despondent, and took a nonfatal overdose. When a psychiatrist examined him, the man spoke sadly of his life and physical infirmities. But when he was asked what he had imagined death would be like, he brightened up and said, "Well, I rather thought Boxer would be there."

Suicide is frequently occasioned by the loss or threatened loss of status, career, or power. People often kill themselves when they are on the verge of being exposed or captured, such as Hitler and his lieutenants, who swallowed cyanide as the Allies closed in. One reads of criminals who kill themselves even as the police are knocking on their door. "There is no refuge from confession but suicide; and suicide is confession," observed Daniel Webster, arguing a murder case in 1830. Newspapers often report the seemingly inexplicable suicides of powerful men. Only later does news of some scandal emerge. On January 10,

1986, in New York City, for example, Donald Manes, the popular Queens borough president, was found at the wheel of his car, dazed and bleeding profusely from knife slashes on his left wrist and ankle. At first it was assumed he had been mugged—Manes insisted he had no recollection of the evening—but over the next few weeks, as a vast bribery and graft scheme unraveled around him, it became apparent that Manes had attempted suicide. His world continued to disintegrate. A close friend agreed to testify against him; the mayor, his political mentor, called him a crook. One night in March, while talking on the phone with his psychiatrist, Manes pulled a knife from his kitchen drawer, thrust it into his chest, and died. Months later a former friend and political ally, himself convicted of racketeering, described Manes as "one so corrupt that he chose suicide rather than face the consequences of his crimes."

Like those Japanese who commit *kashitsu-shi*—suicide to admit failure or to atone for a mistake—some people cannot face shame or loss of face. Paul Kammerer, the eminent Viennese biologist, spent most of his professional life attempting to prove the inheritance of certain acquired characteristics in a particular species of toad. In 1926 it was found that India ink had been injected into the paws of some of the toads, producing tainted results. Although it was never ascertained whether Kammerer or his assistant was responsible, his reputation was ruined. Six weeks after being accused, he shot himself in the head in a forest outside Vienna. In 2003, shortly after being exposed as the inadvertent source of a highly publicized leak embarrassing to the British prime minister, David Kelly, a fifty-nine-year-old, government-employed chemical- and biological-weapons expert, known as a careful, rigorous scientist and a deeply private man, walked into a wooded area near his home, swallowed painkillers, cut his left wrist, and bled to death.

The scandal can seem minor to the outside world. In 1956, when French bakers went on a nationwide strike, the mayor of a small town, scorned by citizens who felt he hadn't done enough to get bread supplies, climbed a power line and killed himself by touching a hundred-thousand-volt high-tension wire. In 1980, Lady Isobel Barnett, a wealthy English widow, was convicted and fined the equivalent of $650 for shoplifting a tin of tuna and a carton of cream. "I have only myself to live with, and I can live with myself," she said after the trial. Four days later she electrocuted herself in her bath. In 2003, the celebrated French chef Bernard Loiseau, whose family had a history of bipolar disorder, shot himself to death, apparently despondent over rumors that his restaurant was on the verge of losing one of its three *Guide Michelin* stars.

The suicide may involve the loss of a sense of self, as poignantly evidenced by the high rate of suicide in the Federal Witness Protection Program, in which government informants are literally provided with new identities—names, jobs, homes, and fingerprints. It may involve a threatened loss of status. A depressed psychoanalyst, urged by his therapist to enter the hospital, refused, saying it would hurt his image. When his therapist went on vacation, the psychoanalyst shot himself. Preserving his image was apparently more important than preserving his life. It may involve the loss of a way of life or of an ideal, as when a person fails to fulfill his early promise. Bruce Gardner was voted the most valuable college baseball player in 1960, but after spending four years in the Los Angeles Dodgers farm system, he never achieved the greatness predicted for him. At thirty-two, a high school physical education instructor, he walked out to the pitching mound at his alma mater, the University of Southern California, and shot himself in the head. Clutched in his right hand was his diploma and next to his body lay a plaque commemorating his selection as an NCAA All-American a decade earlier.

Such deaths may, paradoxically, be an attempt to preserve that self-image. "I believe that suicide has a lot to do with the ideal—often unconscious—that one has of oneself based on early relationships," psychiatrist Robert Litman told me. "Suicidal people tend to believe that if they do not live up to it, their lives must be a total failure. Often, then, they kill themselves in order to preserve that ideal, to save the flag, save the halo—in addition to punishing the failed self. You know that song Frank Sinatra sings: 'I did it my way.' Well, I think that the ideal of the hero who does it his way is suicidogenic—it's a breeding concept for suicide because many people think it's either my way or no way, and if it's no way, it's suicide."

For some, loss of sanity—or fear of its loss—may be a spur to suicide. In 1941, Virginia Woolf, plagued much of her life by what would now be called bipolar disorder, stuffed her pockets with stones and walked into a river near her home. She left a note to her husband that began, "Dearest, I feel certain that I am going mad again. I feel we can't go through another of those terrible times. And I shan't recover this time. I begin to hear voices, and I can't concentrate. So I am doing what seems the best thing to do."

On the other hand, suicide is often completed by people who are seemingly on the mend, such as Peter Newell, who was making progress in therapy and on the verge of marriage to a woman he loved. "Paradoxical and tragic suicidal efforts may occur in a patient who is recovering from a psychosis out of a fear of 'getting well,'" wrote psychiatrist Lawrence Kubie, "when 'getting well' means to the patient that he must return to an unacceptable situation from which he can see no escape other than suicide." Kubie also described the common phenomenon of "depressive response to success," in which people whose self-esteem is so low that they feel they do not deserve success or happiness may kill themselves shortly *after* something wonderful has happened or some long-sought goal has been attained.

Many suicides are aggressive acts directed at a particular person or group of people, motivated by conscious or unconscious rage or a desire for revenge and often accompanied by the fantasy of surviving to witness the enemy's suffering. In a graphic illustration of Freud's thesis that suicide is murder turned inward, a policeman under investigation during New York's corruption scandals of the 1930s arranged to meet his sergeant, who he believed had mistreated him, in a bar. While waiting, he told several people there that he planned to kill the sergeant as soon as he saw him. The sergeant never showed up; after a long wait the policeman shot himself, leaving this note: "To whom concerned: Goodbye you old prick and when I mean prick you are a prick. Hope you fall with the rest of us, you yellow bastard."

Of course, the policeman may have planned all along to kill himself after killing the sergeant. Freud was among the first to emphasize the overlap between homicidal and suicidal behavior, which may blur most literally in murder followed by suicide. Although no national statistics are kept, studies estimate that about 5 percent of people who commit homicide also complete suicide, usually immediately following the murder. Murder-suicides fall into a few general types. In one, not unlike Japan's tradition of *oyako shinju,* a parent, usually the mother, murders her child or children and then kills herself, often within the first six months of her child's life, and often in the grip of severe postpartum depression. (One literature review found that of eighty-eight women who had murdered a child, nearly half had also attempted or completed suicide.) In another, an elderly person, usually male and often ailing, kills his chronically ill spouse and then kills himself. (The perpetrator frequently conceptualizes the murder as a mercy killing.) In the United States, however, the overwhelming majority of murder-suicides—as many as three-quarters—involve a man who kills himself after killing his wife or lover, often triggered by the victim's decision to end the relationship, and usually the culmination of years of abuse marked by jealousy.

Less than 2 percent of murder-suicides involve victims who are strangers to the perpetrator. Like the killings at Columbine, these incidents tend to involve more than one victim and are often carried out after long deliberation by disgruntled individuals who believe they have been slighted or humiliated in some way. When their grudge comes to a boil, they lash out at their perceived persecutor—and at anyone else who may be in the vicinity. Murder and suicide are, of course, also combined in terrorist acts, from Samson to the Japanese kamikaze pilots to contemporary Muslim terrorists. "Although such events are murder-suicides, the perpetrator probably does not regard his own death as a suicide, but as a necessary outcome of the successful completion of his mission," point out Matthew Knock and Peter Marzuk in their review of murder-suicides.

Although there are several types of murder-suicide, they have a great deal in common: 93–97 percent of the perpetrators are male; over 85 percent of the victims are female; nearly 90 percent involve only one victim; and 80–94 percent involve firearms. Although alcohol seems to have less of a role than it does in simple suicides, depression almost always plays a part. "One central theme seen in all types of murder-suicide," write Knock and Marzuk, "is the perpetrator's overvalued attachment to a relationship that, when threatened by dissolution, leads him to destroy the relationship." That relationship may be literal—a marriage, a friendship. It may be figurative—a job, a sense of recognition. In either case, the perpetrator may believe that the only way to preserve that relationship is to end it forever.

Many suicidal people unconsciously fantasize that they are killing others. They may even feel that by completing suicide they are not killing themselves but killing the entire world. This is a dynamic described in A. E. Housman's poem "I Counsel You Beware":

> *Good creatures, do you love your lives*
> *And have you ears for sense?*
> *Here is a knife like other knives,*
> *That cost me eighteen pence.*
>
> *I need but stick it in my heart*
> *And down will come the sky,*
> *And earth's foundations will depart*
> *And all you folk will die.*

While suicide is often motivated by loss, real or metaphorical, for many people it also represents, simultaneously and paradoxically, some form of psychic gain. The suicidal terrorist's religion tells him that earthly existence is but a prelude to an eternal afterlife in which he will be revered for his deed. The bereaved widow kills herself in the belief she may rejoin her lost love. Other gains are less conscious. The suicidal person described by Litman kills himself in the hope that his idealized image will live on; the speaker in the Housman poem perceives of suicide as a trump card enabling him to triumph over a world that has rejected him. Like the drowsy person who pinches himself to see if he is awake, some people kill themselves to prove they are alive. Suicide may be the only way they know to assert order or control over a situation in which they feel trapped. "If I commit suicide, it will not be to destroy myself but to put myself back together again," wrote Antonin Artaud, the avant-garde dramatist who spent much of his life in mental institutions. "Suicide will be for me only one means of violently reconquering myself, of brutally invading my being, of anticipating the unpredictable approaches of God. By suicide, I reintroduce my design in nature; I shall for the first time give things the shape of my will." (In the end, Artaud's death was shaped less by his will than by his ailing body; he died of rectal cancer in 1948.)

"Suicide always seeks to achieve something, even if only peace or an end to pain," observes psychiatrist Robert Jay Lifton. In *The Broken Connection* he suggested, "Killing oneself may appear to be the only way to break out of the 'trap' or 'encirclement' and assert whatever it is one feels one wants to, or must, about one's life. One lacks the power to express that assertion in living, or even the power that certain forms of madness, or extreme psychological disorder, provide for alternative forms of assertion that at least keep one's life going." And so suicide seems the only way to survive. Lifton further wrote:

> Despair and hopelessness are associated with perceptions of the future. One's ultimate involvements are so impaired that one is simply unable to imagine a psychologically livable future. Whatever future one can imagine is no better, perhaps much worse, than the present ("However low a man has sunk, he can sink even lower, and this 'can' is the object of his dread" is the way Kierkegaard put the matter.) *More specifically, the suicide can create a future only by killing himself.* That is, he can reawaken psychic action and imagine vital events beyond the present only in deciding upon, and carrying through, his suicide. And for that period of time, however brief, he lives with an imagined future.

The search for self-knowledge is the essential motivation for suicide, according to James Hillman. In *Suicide and the Soul*, the Jungian psychologist argued that we must experience death in order to understand and fully experience life. "The impulse to death need not be conceived as an anti-life movement; it may be a demand for an encounter with absolute reality, *a demand for a fuller life through the death experience.*" The soul can experience death in ways short of suicide: depression, amnesia, intoxication, exaltation, failure, psychosis. Hillman, however, asserted that "for some, organic death through actual suicide may be the only mode through which the death experience is possible."

Although Hillman seems to have gone to an almost absurdist extreme, his basic premise—that suicide almost always involves an attempt at transformation—seems essentially true. Many people who survive a suicide attempt speak of its cathartic effects—a dynamic perhaps analogous to the truism that an alcoholic can begin to recover only after he "hits bottom." "The suicidal attempt may express a fantasy of returning to infancy for the purpose of living life over again," wrote Lawrence Kubie, one of whose patients, after making several attempts, told him, "I wanted to go right back to the very edge of obliteration *but not over the edge.* Then I could start afresh." It is also evident in the calm that many suicidal people feel after making the decision to kill themselves—what the Viennese psychiatrist Erwin Ringel called an "ominous quiet." A twenty-five-year-old man who survived his suicide attempt recalls the triumph he felt when he decided to take his own life: "It was like being in class and everyone around you is giving the wrong answer, but the teacher isn't calling on you. But you know you have the answer. Blowing your head off is the answer. The answer to life, the answer to your identity, the answer to your self-preservation. That gun to your head is the most beautiful answer. And even as you are thinking of killing yourself, you can be full of passion, full of life. I think for many people it's that zest to live that makes them keep wrapping the noose around their neck. They're saying, 'I'll show you how much I want to live.' "

For some, suicide may itself be a kind of achievement. "Is it conceivable to murder someone in order to count for something in his life?" wrote Cesare Pavese. "Then it is conceivable to kill oneself so as to count for something in one's own life. Here's the difficulty about suicide: it is an act of ambition that can be committed only when one has passed beyond ambition." For whatever reason—a father dead when he was six; a strict, demanding mother; the suicides of two close friends in adolescence—Pavese had a lifelong preoccupation with suicide. The idea of self-destruction—he called it his "syphilis"—runs like an underground stream through his diary, *The Burning Brand,* bubbling to the surface at moments of rejection, loneliness, and disappointment. "I know that I am forever condemned to think of suicide when faced with no matter what difficulty or grief," he wrote at age twenty-eight. "It terrifies me. My basic principle is suicide, never committed, never to be committed, but the thought of it caresses my sensibility." Although the "trigger" was a brief, unhappy affair with an American actress—the last of his many failed attempts to achieve an enduring relationship with a woman—his suicide had been percolating for his entire life. "Today I see clearly that from '28 until now I have always lived under this shadow," he wrote in 1950. Ten days later, a month after winning Italy's top literary prize, he took a fatal overdose in a hotel room. In his last diary entry he wrote:

The thing most feared in secret always happens.

I write: oh Thou, have mercy. And then?

All it takes is a little courage.

The more the pain grows clear and definite, the more the instinct for life asserts itself and the thought of suicide recedes.

It seemed easy when I thought of it. Weak women have done it. It takes humility, not pride.

All this is sickening.

Not words. An act. I won't write any more.

———

Although the causes of suicide are infinite and unique, suicidal people share a common denominator of pain. "When I was nineteen, I had my first deep depression," says Anne-Grace Scheinin, a middle-aged author. "I was terrified. Everything—the way I walked, the way I talked—slowed to a crawl. I felt empty, like everything inside me had been cut up and pulled out. It was as if something had died inside me and was disintegrating. I couldn't concentrate. Reading a book, I'd find myself skimming the same passage over and over until I'd realize I had read the same paragraph sixteen times. After eight months I began to wonder whether my depression would ever lift. I envisioned spending my whole life like that. The feeling that it was never going to end is what made me think of suicide." Scheinin made six attempts in two years before being diagnosed with bipolar disorder. By the time I met her, thanks to lithium and periodic hospitalizations, she had not made an attempt in more than a decade.

Some describe that pain as a prison, a tunnel, a blizzard, a desert, the bottom of a well. In *Darkness Visible,* William Styron compared his suicidal depression to "being imprisoned in a fiercely overheated room." In *The Bell Jar,* a fictionalized account of her breakdown and suicide attempt in 1953 at age twenty, Sylvia Plath, in the words of her heroine, Esther Greenwood, described her gathering depression as feeling "as if I were being stuffed farther and farther into a black, airless sack with no way out." After Greenwood's suicide attempt, her patron financed a stay in a private psychiatric hospital. "I knew I should be grateful to Mrs. Guinea, only I couldn't feel a thing," comments Greenwood. "If Mrs. Guinea had given me a ticket to Europe, or a round-the-world cruise, it wouldn't have made one scrap of difference to me, because wherever I sat—on the deck of a ship or at a street café in Paris or Bangkok—I would be sitting under the same glass bell jar, stewing in my own sour air." Her mother suggested they pretend that her breakdown and suicide attempt had all been a bad dream, but as Greenwood observes, "To the person in the bell jar, blank and stopped as a dead baby, the world itself is the bad dream."

In that state the outside world gradually seems irrelevant; the person's focus narrows like the lens of a camera. Clinicians call this tunnel vision. Erwin Ringel called it the presuicidal syndrome, a state characterized by constriction, inhibited aggression turned toward the self, and suicidal fantasies. He described it as "an experience of harassment, of being surrounded from all sides, and of being ever more intensely squeezed into a steadily tightening space." In Edwin Shneidman's *Voices of Death,* a young woman recalls her feelings the moment before she jumped from a fifth-floor balcony: "Everything was like a terrible sort of whirlpool of confusion. And I thought to myself, 'There's only one thing I can do, I just have to lose consciousness. That's the only way to get away from it' . . . everything just got very dark all of a sudden, and all I could see was this balcony. Everything around it just blacked out. It was just like a circle. That was all I could see, just the balcony . . . and I went over it."

A. Alvarez described this stifling condition as a foreign land with its own laws and "its own irresistible logic." The logic, he wrote, is not the kind employed by philosophers.

The logic of suicide is different. It is like the unanswerable logic of a nightmare, or like the science-fiction fantasy of being projected suddenly into another dimension: everything makes sense and follows its own strict rules; yet, at the same time, everything is also different, perverted, upside down. Once a man decides to take his own life he enters a shut-off, impregnable but wholly convincing world where every detail fits and each incident reinforces his decision. An argument with a stranger in a bar, an unexpected letter which doesn't arrive, the wrong voice on the telephone, the wrong knock at the door, even a change in the weather—all seem charged with special meaning; they all contribute.

Alvarez wrote from personal experience. In an epilogue to *The Savage God* he described his own suicide attempt at age thirty-one. He recalled the suicidal threats his parents had made when he was a child, which embedded the idea in his unconscious. Then one day, many years later, following "some standard domestic squabble," he realized that he wished he were dead. "After that," he wrote, "there was only one way out, although it took a long time—many months, in fact—to get there." Once he knew, it seemed an inevitability—"the last slide down the ice slope had begun and there was no way of stopping it." He described that slide: the marital fights, the drinking, the isolation. Inside, he experienced that "presuicidal syndrome." "My life felt so cluttered and obstructed that I could hardly breathe," he wrote. "I inhabited a closed, concentrated world, airless and without exits. I doubt if any of this was noticeable socially: I was simply more tense, more nervous than usual, and I drank more. But underneath I was going a bit mad."

Two months after deciding on suicide, following a Christmas spent drinking and quarreling with his wife, who finally walked out on him, Alvarez swallowed forty-five sleeping pills hoarded for the occasion. He went into a coma for three days but recovered.

The constricted world described by Alvarez and the simultaneous urge for transformation described by Lifton and Hillman are dramatically evident in the unpublished journals of Lisa Courtney, a talented twenty-three-year-old silversmith from Newburyport, Massachusetts. For Lisa, depression was a "fog" that settled over her each fall. One autumn a series of events made that fog even more dense: the end of a relationship, the breakdown of her car, anxiety over getting along with new roommates, concern with her work. In the journal she kept during this time she wrote on one hand about her art, family, and friends, and the possibility of new love, and on the other about her doubts, anxiety, and loss of confidence. In her journal entries one can trace her growing depression, her feeling of numbness—"as if I were encased in foam rubber packing," she wrote—and, at the same time, her need to change her life, "to be a different person."

October 2: . . . September just flew by. I want to slow things down; give me a break! This light fogginess around me prevails, I wish I could control it better. Even in trying to remember the week—there is a dimness about it. . . . God, I hope this mind fog will lift.

October 6: . . . Somehow I find a strength that makes it possible for me to smile for a little while. Then suddenly I feel paralyzed. I can't function. I can't do any of the little chores I want to get done. I started a letter [to an old friend], but too many letters to write and nothing to say (well, I couldn't gather my thoughts) made me stop. I just couldn't think at all to be able to start a sentence. . . . I have so many things to do—list after list, day after day, and they don't get shorter. . . . One thing at a time, I must get these things done. I can't work! I can't think! I have so much designing to do. I can't even begin because I am thinking of everything at once. I can't clear my mind to focus on one thing. . . . I have no physical desire. I feel empty. My body is shut off. I don't WANT. I want to cry. It hurts. . . . Everything just seems so pointless. Nothing is going anywhere. Nothing is *getting done.* Help me, Lisa. Don't lose your strength. Rest now, it's night.

October 16: . . . I fantasize about running away. Why does this fantasy always come to me? What am I running away from? What am I running towards? To change myself, be a different person. Why don't I like myself? I want to know so much more, experience so much more than I do now, force myself into situations that are very difficult that I will find my way out of, become a bit hardened and not so naive. I am so afraid, so cautious. I am in a larger box than I was before, but I still feel walls around me, the walls of fear and self-imposed confinement that I *must* break down. I keep thinking about external changes: dress differently, change my hair, but I know it is what is inside that I want to change. . . . I am afraid I am sick. My body feels weak sometimes. There's something wrong with my voice and my breathing. Sometimes I have to push out words. I am afraid and angry with myself. Almost embarrassed. Cigarettes oh shit. My vagina itches. I get sore from brief intercourse. I don't know what's wrong. I try not to think about this, but I'm afraid. Sometimes I think if I found out I were going to die then I might be able to break through the walls that limit me. Can't I do it now anyway?

November 13: . . . How can you tell people that you can't feel anything? They will hate you. You are no longer alive or worth knowing if you can't feel. HELP ME LISA help me.

Over six weeks, Lisa's handwriting gradually changed from small and neat to large and scribbled. On November 15 she wrote a chronology of her slide:

Fog is getting very deep.
    Work is getting difficult. I don't want to design.
Having trouble concentrating on production. The new girl is learning so fast.
I am quiet at work. Have nothing to say.
Orders to do
car trouble again
don't want to work on new home—barely set up stuff—throw rest in cellar.
    withdrawing from people. Can't think or communicate anything but confusion, panic, lost.
    exhausted from work—just trying to keep from running out of the place and screaming help me God! I'm afraid.
    I can't remember what day it is.
    No relief except sleep.
    morning: panic, can't get out of bed
    work to do
    car to fix
    change addresses
    make wedding presents
    can't remember how to do things at work.
    I feel nowhere
    I have lost my place in time.
    can't make decisions
    I can't design. I have two designs to work on but my hands aren't working right. I can't see how to make the heart symmetrical. I don't want to work. I have to get out of there. Everyone knows I am mixed up. I make bad vibrations. I am hoping they remember I am not always like this. I leave work.
    Eat lunch slowly. Try to rest my mind.
    I don't know where to go. I hate you Lisa. Come back to earth. I hurt. I hurt you Lisa.

That afternoon Lisa stabbed herself superficially in the stomach. She was able to drive herself to the hospital, where she was stitched up and released. "I wasn't trying to die; I just wanted to cut through the fog," she told her parents. One month later the fog hadn't lifted. Lisa cut her wrists and throat with broken glass, then rolled off the roof of a five-story building to her death.

# III

# THE MANNER OF DYING

IN JAMES M. CAIN'S classic whodunit *Double Indemnity,* whose plot hinges on a murder disguised as a suicide, a savvy insurance agent shows an associate a book of statistical tables on suicide. "Take a look at them," he says. "Here's suicide by race, by color, by occupation, by sex, by locality, by seasons of the year, by time of day when committed. Here's suicide by method of accomplishment. Here's method of accomplishment subdivided by poisons, by firearms, by gas, by drowning, by leaps. Here's suicide by poisons subdivided by sex, by race, by age, by time of day. Here's suicide by poisons subdivided by cyanide, by mercury, by strychnine, by thirty-eight other poisons, sixteen of them no longer procurable at prescription pharmacies. And here—here, Mr. Norton—are leaps subdivided by leaps from high places, under wheels of moving trains, under wheels of trucks, under the feet of horses, from steamboats. *But there's not one case here out of all these millions of cases of a leap from the rear end of a moving train.* That's just one way they don't do it."

Although Cain's insurance agent is wrong—people have killed themselves by jumping off the backs of moving trains—his basic point is correct. There are many ways to complete suicide. The National Center for Health Statistics has enumerated at least forty-four general categories. The method one chooses depends on race, sex, occupation, availability, psychology, and, to an extent, fashion. In ancient Greece death by hemlock was popular; hanging, as Euripides observed, was considered "unseemly." In Rome, chic suicides fell on their swords or opened their veins in a warm bath. According to the scholar Servius, Roman suicides by hanging were "cast forth unburied." Such class snobbery persisted into the eighteenth century, when an Englishman, learning of a

233

friend's suicide by that method, remarked, "What a low-minded wretch to apply the halter! Had he shot himself like a gentleman I could have forgiven him." The lower classes usually chose the noose, of which a French author observed, "Hanging is a type of death of which the infamy is so well established that a man who would choose it in despair, unless he were the dregs of society, would be unpardonably dishonored among honest men. One must take poison, shoot oneself, or die by fire. Drowning is another vulgar death." Nevertheless, in Paris, where life centered around the Seine, drowning seems to have been à la mode in the nineteenth century. Downstream at Saint-Cloud, fishermen who found the bodies of suicides in their nets were paid a fee for each corpse they brought to La Morgue.

The introduction of domestic gas in the nineteenth century and the proliferation of prescription drugs in the twentieth brought about a radical change in suicide methods. "Not only have they made suicide more or less painless, they have also made it seem magical," wrote Alvarez in *The Savage God.* "A man who takes a knife and slices deliberately across his throat is murdering himself. But when someone lies down in front of an unlit gas oven or swallows sleeping pills, he seems not so much to be dying as merely seeking oblivion for a while. . . . In suicide, as in most other areas of activity, there has been a technological break through which has made a cheap and relatively painless death democratically available to everyone."

In most countries firearms, hanging, and poison are the most common methods of suicide, but their frequency varies from culture to culture. Only in the United States, where gun control restrictions are minimal, do firearms rank first; they account for some 60 percent of suicides, followed in order of frequency by hanging and overdose. Until recently, American women killed themselves most often by overdose; now firearms account for the majority of female suicides. Availability is a key factor; in England, where gun control laws are stiff, domestic gas ranks first, while firearms are used in a mere 2 percent of suicides. In China, the only major country where a nearly equal number of men and women kill themselves, self-poisoning is disproportionately popular, perhaps because of the easy availability of agricultural pesticides combined with scant access to emergency medical care. But the popularity of any given method is subject to change. In Sri Lanka, for instance, jumping into a well was the preferred way until the introduction of indoor plumbing rendered wells obsolete. Self-poisoning with pesticides now tops the list.

In Norway, a disproportionate number of suicides are by drowning. "Since many Norwegians live and work on the water, it is perhaps not surprising that some of them choose to die in the water as well," observed Herbert Hendin, an American psychiatrist who has made extensive studies of suicide in particular geographic or ethnic groups. In *Suicide in America,* Hendin pointed out that half of all black suicides in New York were by jumping, compared to about 25 percent in the city as a whole and less than 3 percent in the rest of the country. He suggested that just as life in Norway centers on the sea, life in Harlem centers on its rooftops. "Sexual experience, fighting, and drug usage frequently take place on the Harlem rooftops," he wrote. "In this context, it is not surprising that jumping from the top floors or roofs of such buildings is a very common method among black suicides." In the South, where guns are an accepted part of many households and children learn to handle them at an early age, firearms are used in suicide more frequently than in the rest of the country. In some cultures, of course, certain forms of suicide have demanded traditional methods: the belly-cutting of the Japanese samurai; the hurling onto her husband's funeral pyre of the Indian widow; the self-immolation of political protesters, beginning with Buddhist monks in the early years of the Vietnam War.

The popularity of suicide methods also varies according to profession. A study of physicians, who complete suicide at three times the rate of the general population, found that 55 percent of all physician suicides use drugs—to which they have easy access—while only 12 percent use guns. Dentists use anesthetic gas more frequently, chemists tend to swallow cyanide, merchant seamen have a higher rate of drowning, and more miners kill themselves with explosives than any other group. In a rash of ninety-three suicides by New York City policemen between 1934 and 1940, nine of ten killed themselves with their service revolvers. These examples suggest not only that availability is crucial, but that people tend to use methods that relate to how they have lived their lives.

While the majority of suicides die by gunshot, hanging, or poison, less than 1 percent a year in the United States kill themselves by what the National Center for Health Statistics refers to as "unspecified means." This rubric covers a variety of methods that seem as infinite as the variety of causes for suicide. Over the past two centuries people have completed suicide by jumping into volcanoes, vats of beer, crocks of vinegar, retorts of molten glass, white-hot coke ovens, or slaughterhouse tanks of blood; by throwing themselves upon buzz saws; by thrusting hot pokers or broomsticks down their throat; by suffocating in refrigerators or chimneys; by locking themselves into high-altitude test chambers; by crashing airplanes; by jumping from airplanes; by lying in front of steamrollers; by throwing themselves on the third rail; by touching high-tension wires; by placing their necks in vises and turning the handle; by hugging stoves; by freezing to death; by climbing into lion's cages; by blowing themselves up with cannons, hand grenades, or dynamite; by boring holes in their heads with power drills; by drinking boiling water, hydrochloric acid, or Drano; by walking in front of cars, trains, subways, and racehorses; by driving cars off cliffs or into trains; by swallowing poisonous spiders; by piercing their hearts with corkscrews or darning needles; by starving themselves; by swallowing firecrackers; by holding their heads in buckets of water; by beating their heads with hammers; by pounding nails or barbecue spits into their skulls; by strangling themselves with their hair; by walking into airplane propellers; by swimming over waterfalls; by hanging themselves with grapevines; by sawing tree limbs out from under themselves; by swallowing glass; by swallowing hot coals; by swallowing underwear; by stabbing themselves with spectacles sharpened to a point; by cutting their throats with handsaws, sheep shears, or barbed wire; by forcing teams of horses to tear their heads off; by decapitating themselves with homemade guillotines; by exposing themselves to swarms of bees; by injecting themselves with paraffin, cooking oil, peanut butter, mercury, deodorant, or mayonnaise; by crucifying themselves.

Such imaginative methods, which account for only a tiny fraction of suicides, receive wide publicity—they are often used as supposedly "humorous" filler items in newspapers—and contribute to the idea that all people who commit suicide are insane. (Indeed, the use of a more bizarre method may well reflect a greater degree of psychopathology.) Yet on closer inspection such methods may seem unusual but not inexplicable. The man who jumped into a vat of beer was a brewer; the man in the high-altitude test chamber was an air force technician; the man who lay in front of the steamroller was a construction worker; the man who blew himself up with a cannon was a soldier; the man who constructed a guillotine and decapitated himself was an assistant executioner in Corsica.

In his 1920 paper "The Psychogenesis of a Case of Homosexuality in a Woman," Freud described his analysis of an eighteen-year-old Viennese girl who had attempted suicide. The girl had been strolling with an older woman with whom she was infatuated. They encountered the girl's father, who disapproved of the liaison. He scowled at his daughter. The woman told the girl they must separate, and the girl immediately flung herself over an embankment onto a railway line. Freud, pointing out that the German word *niederkommen* means both "to fall" and "to be delivered of a child," believed that the girl's attempt expressed her desire to bear her father's child, and punishment for her murderous rage toward her mother. In a footnote to the paper he wrote, "That the various methods of suicide can represent sexual wish-fulfillments has long been known to all analysts. (To poison oneself = to become pregnant; to drown = to bear a child; to throw oneself from a height = to be delivered of a child.)"

Freud's tidy explication—one wonders, for instance, whether the girl would have run several miles to find a high place from which to jump had there been none at hand—has inspired numerous other attempts to invest suicide methods with universal symbolic meanings. "The choice of the manner of dying is in itself a significant tell-tale feature," wrote Freud's disciple Wilhelm Stekel. "Women who 'have fallen' or who struggle against temptations, throw themselves out of the window and into the street. The man who entertains secret thoughts of poisoning somebody, takes poison; one who yearns after the flames of love, sets fire to himself; he who believes himself surrounded by poisonous thoughts, turns on the gas." Stekel, who was in poor physical health, killed himself at age seventy-four by overdosing on aspirin. It is not known whom he secretly wished to poison other than himself. In *Man Against Himself*, Menninger linked drowning to a desire to return to the womb; psychiatrist Joost Meerloo traced hanging to sexual frustrations and claimed that "jumping out of the window may quite paradoxically signify a wish to grow up." In the late 1970s, psychiatrists Sidney Furst and Mortimer Ostow suggested that suicidal male homosexuals stab or shoot themselves as an expression of their desire to be attacked by another man's penis. As for homosexuals who jump from heights, this was considered an expression of sexual guilt for "phallic erection under improper circumstances."

As far-fetched as such interpretations seem, choice of method is rarely random, as Hendin demonstrated in his fascinating discussion of method and motive in *Suicide in America*. "Some suicides use their control over how they choose to die to express their feelings about why they want to die," he wrote. "A prisoner can hang himself because it is the only method of suicide available to him, but hanging is also used to express a variety of suicidal motivations. Some people hang themselves as punishment for their desire to choke others: one patient who did, used to 'playfully' choke his wife. For other suicidal individuals, hanging represented how choked and 'hung up' they felt. One such young man came from a family that blocked his every independent constructive effort, while constantly holding out hope of what they would do for him in time. No one could have more effectively 'hung up' anyone than this family 'hung up' their son, and his final retaliation was to hang himself." People whose anger, self-hatred, or need for punishment is especially intense may use particularly violent methods, according to Hendin. An enraged man who lost his job, fell into debt, and was deserted by his wife killed himself by sealing off the kitchen, turning on the gas, stabbing himself in the chest, and then hanging himself. Hendin suggested that "the multiplicity of methods helped this man express the intense feeling that he was being attacked on all sides." It was no accident, in all senses, when a man depressed over his impotence blew himself up with a stick of dynamite; a lonely Massachusetts spinster suffocated by locking herself into her hope chest; a woman who felt abandoned by her family shut herself into an abandoned refrigerator in her basement; a talented young climber, despondent over breaking up with his girlfriend, leaped off the cliffs he had so often scaled, executing, as he fell, a perfect swan dive; an elderly opera buff in failing health jumped to his death from the top balcony of the Metropolitan Opera House.

Many suicidal people are impulsive and use whatever method is at hand. A man in traction transferred the pulleys and cords from his fractured leg to his neck and strangled himself. Prisoners hang themselves not necessarily because of sexual frustration, as Menninger implies, but because the only available means are their shoelaces, shirts, or bedsheets. One particularly desperate inmate chewed through the veins in his wrist. Mental hospital patients manage to procure a variety of tools: plastic bags, windows, broken glass, nails, coat hangers. Other suicidal people may plot their death for weeks, months, or even years, making lists of possible exits, sifting through the pros and cons, weighing the merits not of whether to live but how to die. "Suicides have a special language," wrote Anne Sexton in her poem "Wanting to Die." "Like carpenters they want to know *which tools. /* They never ask *why build.*" Sexton thought and wrote about suicide for years before fatally overdosing in 1974. Some suicidal people are extremely choosy—their method must be in keeping with their personality. Women (and some men) may reject shooting, jumping, or stabbing because they don't want to disfigure their face or body. Hospitalized after many attempts with pills, one woman told her doctor, who was concerned at her being placed on a high floor of the hospital, not to worry. She could never jump, she said, because she was afraid of heights. (A young Chilean, slightly less acrophobic, tied a handkerchief over his eyes before leaping from a twelfth-floor ledge.) Some people go to great lengths to kill themselves by a certain method and will accept no substitute. "A man who has attempted to drown himself will not readily be induced to cut his throat, and *vice versa,*" observed one nineteenth-century doctor. A study of six people who survived leaps from San Francisco's Golden Gate Bridge revealed that the bridge had assumed an almost mystical significance for them. All six said they had planned suicide only from the Golden Gate, and no other bridge—or method—would do. This type of insistence—conscious or unconscious—is illustrated by the story of the man on the window ledge. A policeman, drawing his revolver, cries, "Don't jump or I'll shoot!" The man obediently comes inside. This tale, of which several variations are told, may be apocryphal, but it is certainly psychologically accurate.

"It takes a tremendous amount of energy to figure out how you're going to kill yourself," says a forty-seven-year-old woman who tried. "I wanted something that was final and wasn't going to be messy. I didn't want to jump off the roof; I might end up only half-dead, and I wouldn't like that. I didn't want to blow my head off—I didn't happen to feel that physical disembodiment would be a particularly pleasant thing for everybody." She chuckles ruefully. "I kept thinking about what would be easiest for everyone else. Of course the easiest thing would have been if I'd lived." One night she drove to a nearby field, hooked up a vacuum cleaner hose to the exhaust pipe, zipped herself into a sleeping bag, and stuck the hose into her mouth. The police discovered her the next morning, curled in her sleeping bag, unconscious. She was revived at the hospital. No one could figure out how she had survived until a friend realized the car had a catalytic converter that filtered out carbon monoxide. She had taken the wrong car.

Like this woman, some suicides go to great lengths to avoid hurting loved ones by trying to make sure they won't find the body or that they won't find a disfigured corpse. Others, consciously or not, design their suicides to punish, blame, or take revenge—a contemporary form of the oriental practice of "killing oneself upon the head of another." A mother who disapproved of her daughter's fiancé killed herself at the wedding reception. A California woman lay across the tracks in front of the commuter train on which she knew her husband was returning home. One July 4 a thirty-year-old New York man, depressed over breaking up with his girlfriend, stuck a powerful firecracker in his mouth, lit it, and blew himself up on the front steps of her home. In his book *The Undertaking,* Thomas Lynch describes the case of a cuckolded man who lay down beside his sleeping wife and sawed through his throat with an electric carving knife; she was eventually awakened not by the hum of the knife but by the warmth of her husband's blood on her body.

A decision related to choice of method is whether to leave some final word. Only one in five or six suicides leaves a note. Suicide notes have been written or typed on ordinary paper, hotel stationery, prescription slips, therapists' appointment cards, in books of poetry and prayer books. They have been etched in dirt, printed on a mirror with lipstick, written on a blackboard with chalk, scrawled in blood, carved in wood, typed on a computer, and dictated onto audiotape and videotape. While they are usually addressed to spouses, family members, lovers, and friends, suicide notes have also been addressed to psychiatrists, police, coroners, the press, "to whom it may concern," or to the entire world. One man wrote to his dog, "Bow wow and good-bye, Pepper." Almost a third of those who leave notes leave more than one; one man left several notes in every room of his house. Most are left at or near the scene of the suicide, but some are mailed or e-mailed. Some are hastily scribbled, others go through many drafts. Some are written in poetry, in styles ranging from free verse to rhymed couplets. Suicide notes have been as long as dozens of pages and as short as a few words. One man simply wrote, "No comment." Another, "Good-bye, suckers."

For many years researchers believed that notes held a key to understanding motivation for suicide, but several dozen studies have revealed little more than that suicide notes reflect the range of emotions of suicidal people. In one early project, psychologists Edwin Shneidman and Norman Farberow categorized nine hundred notes according to socioeconomic level. They found that more advantaged writers spoke of being "tired of life," while blue-collar suicides were apt to focus on physical illness and the press of details of living. A Philadelphia study of 165 notes found that slightly more than half displayed feelings of gratitude and affection, while 24 percent were openly hostile and negative and 24 percent were "neutral." In a study by psychiatrist Calvin Frederick, five graphologists, five secretaries, and five policemen were shown forty-five sets of suicide notes, each consisting of a genuine note and three verbatim copies in the handwriting of a nonsuicidal person of the same sex and approximate age of the genuine note writer. Asked to select the genuine notes, the secretaries and detectives couldn't tell the difference. The handwriting experts selected the genuine notes more than 60 percent of the time. They found the penmanship of the suicidal individual to be "impulsive, spontaneous, aggressive, agitated, aimless, disorderly, and laden with anxiety." In sum, suicide notes, which would seem to offer a window into the soul on the edge of the abyss, have yielded little of use. Writes Shneidman, "Suicide notes often seem like parodies of the postcards sent home from the Grand Canyon, the catacombs or the pyramids—essentially *pro forma,* not at all reflecting the grandeur of the scene being described or the depth of human emotions that one might expect to be engendered by the situation." Investigation into why more than 75 percent of suicides do *not* leave some final written expression has turned up little. "Whether the writers of suicide notes differ in their attitudes from those who leave no notes behind it is impossible to say," observed psychiatrist Erwin Stengel. "Possibly, they differ from the majority only in being good correspondents."

Many note writers ask for absolution, like the minister who hanged himself in his church after scrawling on the paper wrapper that came around the rope, "God forgive me." Others go out of their way to insist that certain people are not to blame. But as Herbert Hendin has observed, "'You are not to blame' written to a husband, wife, or parent usually turns out to mean the opposite." Some attempt to provoke lingering guilt. After receiving a letter from his girlfriend telling him she was marrying another man, an Illinois man wrote, "Darling, I cannot live without you. I am going to the garage and use the car that is in there. Remember, I loved you so much I died for you." Others are more direct. "I hope this is what you want," wrote one man to his wife. Notes may be frank expressions of anger. A man who gassed himself after learning that his wife had run off with his brother wrote on the back of her photograph, "I present this picture of another woman—the girl I thought I married. May you always remember I loved you once but died hating you." One mother found her teenage son hanging behind the Christmas tree. A note pinned to him said, "Merry Christmas."

Notes may offer literal explanations for the suicide. In Thomas Hardy's *Jude the Obscure,* the title character, whose family had fallen upon hard times, found a haunting note underneath the hanged bodies of his three sons: "Done because we are too menny." Gay activist Michael Silverstein asphyxiated himself at thirty-six, writing, "Help isn't what I want now. I've decided it's alright to stop if I want to. *I'm tired.*" Rarely do notes offer philosophic defenses of suicide or treatises on the moral ramifications of the act. More often they are filled with practical instructions, outlining the disposition of property, guest lists for the funeral, what to tell the children, reminders to "change the spark plugs on the Ford every ten thousand miles," to "please see that Tommy gets a Mickey Mouse watch for his birthday," or "Don't forget to put out the garbage on Thursdays." A thirty-year-old psychiatrist left this note: "Car to Helen or Ray. Needs a tuneup. Money to Max and Sylvia. Furniture to George plus $137 I owe him." A thirteen-year-old Los Angeles girl who shot herself shortly after actor Freddie Prinze's suicide left her parents an eight-page letter detailing which of her toys and clothes to give to whom, and advice on the care of her pets, plus repeated requests to "please let me be buried by Freddie." While such directives may be thoughtful ways to ease a family's burden, they can be subtle attempts to control a friend or relative after one's death. "I would like my sister Frances to have the piano that you have in your apartment," wrote a sailor to his girlfriend. "Do this or I will haunt you. Goodbye Sweets. Be seeing you soon. Love. Joe."

Some notes written after the overdose has been taken or the gas turned on may sound as if the writer is conducting a scientific experiment on the experience of dying. After swallowing a lethal overdose of sleeping pills, a sixty-eight-year-old man played solitaire, pausing occasionally to record his thoughts. At 9 p.m. he wrote, "No one's fault . . . no one to blame," and quoted Sydney Carton's last words from *A Tale of Two Cities:* "It is a far, far better thing that I do than I have ever done; it is a far, far better rest that I go to than I have ever known." Later he wrote, "Thirty-five minutes past nine. It works so slow." At the bottom of the page there was a final, plaintive entry: "I can't win."

Above all, notes reflect their author's unhappiness. A twenty-year-old who gassed herself in a New York City rooming house on July 4, 1931, wrote, "This is my Independence Day—from life. Love and holidays are not for me. I'm tired and no one wants me." The celebrated young Brazilian cartoonist Péricles killed himself on New Year's Eve, 1962. After shaving and putting on his best white suit and silk tie, as if he were going to a party, he spread a blanket and pillow on the floor, turned on the gas jets of the stove, and lay down. He left this note for his mother:

> I'm deeply sorry for you. I spent Christmas Eve alone in this apartment hearing the laughter and joy of neighbors. But it's impossible to go through it again. On a day like this everyone seeks the company of beloved ones. Here I am with nowhere to spend New Year's in anyone's company. It's simply my fault. Forgive me for such a vulgar note.

Fanny Imlay Godwin, the illegitimate daughter of the feminist writer Mary Wollstonecraft, suffered an unrequited love for her half-brother-in-law Percy Bysshe Shelley. In 1816, at age twenty-two, she poisoned herself at an English seaside inn, leaving this note:

> I have long determined that the best thing I could do was to put an end to the existence of a being whose birth was unfortunate and whose life has only been a series of pains to those persons who have hurt their

health in endeavoring to promote her welfare. Perhaps to hear of my death may give you pain, but you will soon have the blessing of forgetting that such a creature ever existed.

A fifty-year-old Massachusetts man simply wrote:

> I'm done with life
> I'm no good
> I'm dead

In the end the lengths to which suicidal people go to communicate their feelings are matched by the difficulty of writing something that can explain or mitigate such an act. David Kinnell was a depressed eighteen-year-old who had been known in his Massachusetts high school as a gifted poet and athlete before his parents started having marital difficulties and his life became centered increasingly around drugs and rock music. Many times he had asked his mother to listen to a particular song. "Can you hear it?" he would say. "Isn't it beautiful?"

Living at home after graduation, David spent much of his time in the basement listening to his albums, copying down the lyrics as the songs played. One day he borrowed his mother's car, saying he had a job interview and wouldn't be home until after midnight. He drove five hundred miles to a park, where, as a child, he had spent many happy times with his family. At an overlook called Inspiration Point he hanged himself from a tree. When the park ranger found him, the tape deck in his car, parked nearby, still blared music by his favorite group, the Grateful Dead.

In the week following his death David's family and friends began to receive packages from him in the mail. His psychologist received a stack of records and a note saying that killing himself was the right thing to do. The youth leader of his church received a book written by Jerry Garcia, the leader of the Grateful Dead, with a note asking him to pass it on to the psychologist after he had read it. A girlfriend received a record and a note saying, "Call my mother. Please come to it." (She did call his mother, and she did go to David's funeral.) David's thirteen-year-old sister received a $100 gift certificate from Laura Ashley for her birthday the following month. David's mother received a six-page letter that consisted largely of song lyrics by the Grateful Dead, Bob Dylan, Pink Floyd, and other groups, strung together, one song after another. "They were almost impossible to understand," says his mother. "But they seemed to say that he'd gone over the edge, and he couldn't come back. I think he felt so out of control, and finally he took control of his own life. . . . Toward the end of the letter there was a song that said, 'Carry on my wayward son / There'll be peace when you are done.' . . . It was a comfort to read that. I regarded it as an affirmative statement, that he was at peace."

David had labored over his farewell packages for several months. All those times his mother had seen him in the basement copying down lyrics from records, he had been composing his elaborate suicide notes. Then he had wrapped his gifts, put them in the trunk of his mother's car, and mailed them en route to the park where he had chosen to die. While so much care, effort, and thought had gone into the packages, it seemed a tragic footnote that the boy who had once expressed himself so well in poetry could only communicate through someone else's music. And even then he was unable to make himself understood. His mother took the note David sent her to a local youth counselor, who identified some of the songs. "But I could research every single lyric, every single song, and I still don't think I'd understand," she says. She recalls all those times David asked her to listen to his music, how he had tried to explain, how she had tried to comprehend. "'Isn't that beautiful?' he'd say, and I'd say, 'I can't understand it. Tell me why you think it's beautiful.' And he'd say, 'You just don't understand.' But now I think he meant much more than that—'you don't understand'—not just the lyrics, but the whole thing, everything."

# IV

# THE NUMBERS GAME

---

AT THE OPPOSITE END of the investigative spectrum from clinicians who look at suicide on an individual basis are the statisticians and sociologists who churn out graphs and charts in pursuit of a broad, external perspective. What they tell us may at first seem esoteric (for instance, that from 1928 to 1932 males in Minneapolis were more apt to kill themselves on Tuesday, females on Thursday) or even trivial (that, in metropolitan areas, the greater the airtime devoted to country music, the greater the white suicide rate). But they are trying to answer the question—why people kill themselves—not by examining case histories of individuals but by examining case histories of entire groups.

According to the World Health Organization, about 1 million people take their own life during an average year: as many as are killed in murders and wars combined. Although no countries or cultures are immune to suicide, some are more prone than others. In the nineteenth century, when statistics were first employed to measure various societal ills, a country's suicide rate served as an index of national pride or embarrassment. So, too, in the twentieth century, when Sweden acquired an international reputation for suicide. In 1960, President Eisenhower provoked a fuss when, during a speech at the Republican National Convention, he attributed Sweden's high rate to the country's liberal welfare policies, intimating that socialism had left its citizens with nothing to struggle for. Eisenhower overlooked the fact that in 1960 Sweden had about the same suicide rate as it had in 1910, long before its welfare policies were introduced. (Today, Sweden ranks thirty-third among the one hundred nations that report suicide statistics to the WHO.)

Scandinavia, however, presents an interesting paradox. While the suicide rates of Denmark and Sweden have long been among the highest in the Western world, Norway, also a welfare state, has consistently ranked far lower. A six-year study undertaken by the four Scandinavian nations suggested that the reasons had little to do with politics. Focusing on Norway and Denmark, the Nordic Planning Group on Suicidology devised a complex system of calculating "social integration" and found that Norwegians had far stronger ties to family, neighborhood, social clubs, and church, bonds that Émile Durkheim and other sociologists have long believed reduce the likelihood of suicide. (During the 1970s and 1980s, the Norwegian rate approached that of its Scandinavian neighbors—boosted by a surge in suicides among young men, whose degree of social integration was reported to be in decline. Over the next decade, however, the rate fell again.) Why are Norwegians more apt than Danes—or Swedes or Finns—to form such bonds? Herbert Hendin, who spent two years studying suicide in Scandinavia, found that suicidal people were psychologically quite different in each of three Scandinavian countries and that the difference reflected their cultural backgrounds. In Denmark, Hendin was struck by how often suicidal behavior was used to arouse guilt. Danish mothers often discipline their children by letting them know how hurt they are by their behavior, and the child learns how to use his own suffering to arouse guilt in others. Young Danes are also taught to suppress aggressive feelings. Dependence on the mother is encouraged far more than in America, Hendin said, making them especially vulnerable to what he called "dependency-loss" suicides.

Swedes encourage their children to be independent, but they also foster an intense concern with competition and achievement. "Among the men, success or failure has a life-or-death meaning," wrote Hendin. "Expectations for performance are rigid and self-hatred for failure is great." At the same time Hendin found that Swedish children are taught not to express emotions; they deal with their anger by withdrawal and detachment. This response is exemplified in a common Swedish phrase, *tiga ijhal,* to kill someone by silence. Their psychological profile encourages what Hendin characterized as a "performance" type of suicide, triggered by a failure to live up to perceived expectations.

By contrast, Norwegian mothers tend to be warm and emotionally involved with their children without having rigid expectations. The child is encouraged to express his feelings, and as he grows, he is less concerned with performance and more able to show his emotions. Norwegians, said Hendin, are better able to communicate their anger and frustration in ways short of suicide.

According to Hendin, to understand suicide we must take a "psychosocial perspective"; that is, we must investigate its meaning within its cultural group, synthesizing psychological, social, and cultural factors. Suicide for a Norwegian differs in meaning and motive from suicide for a Korean. Similarly, within the United States, suicide for an urban black differs from suicide for a suburban white or a Native American. "On some level all suicidal people are united by some common denominator of unhappiness," said Hendin. "But what makes them unhappy and why they want to die is a function of the time and place in which they live."

If the suicide rate is any barometer, Lithuania, with a rate hovering around 45 suicides per 100,000 people—four times the U.S. rate—is the unhappiest nation in the world. It wasn't always thus; indeed, the suicide rate in the former USSR over the last few decades offers a dramatic illustration of psychosocial influences. In its Communist heyday the Soviet Union did not report suicide statistics to the WHO; suicide, Party spokesmen asserted, was a "bourgeois activity." Western suicidologists, however, suspected the rate was high, as is often true of groups experiencing excessive social regulation. In fact, from 1984 to 1990, under the more relaxed policies of perestroika, the suicide rate for Russian males declined by 32 percent, nearly four times the decline for males in other European countries. (The drop was not solely attributable to the life-affirming properties of freedom; it also coincided with a vigorous national antialcoholism campaign.) Following the breakup of the Soviet state in 1990, with its cataclysmic economic, political, and social changes, the Russian suicide rate soared—as did the rates for Lithuania, Belarus, and most other former Soviet states and Eastern European satellites. Many of the victims were middle-aged men unable to readjust and find a new career in the shambles of the Soviet economy. Today, these countries report the highest suicide rates in the world, eclipsing Hungry, Denmark, Austria, Finland, Switzerland, West Germany, Japan, Sweden, and other nations with traditionally high rates.

Among the countries at the other end of the scale are Italy, Spain, and Mexico, which have suicide rates consistently under 10 per 100,000. Although their low rates are often attributed to the preponderance of Roman Catholics in these countries, Costa Rica and Northern Ireland, which are predominantly Protestant, have low rates, while Catholic Austria has one of the highest rates in the world. (For centuries it has been traditional wisdom that Protestants have a higher suicide rate than Catholics, Catholics a higher rate than Jews. Actual figures are difficult to procure—death certificates in the United States do not record religious affiliation—but several European studies show that although the rates for all three groups increased over the twentieth century, the rate for Jews rose more rapidly.) Of course, some of the disparity is the result of reporting techniques. Industrialized countries, which tend to have higher rates, also tend to have more sophisticated methods of gathering statistics and fewer taboos against doing so. Reported rates in predominately Catholic or Muslim countries may be artificially low; greater stigma surrounding suicide usually begets greater reluctance to certify a death as suicide. A few countries may, like the former Soviet Union, underreport—or not report at all—for political reasons. In 1985, for instance, a Nicaraguan newspaper reported that Sandinista censors objected to the publication of a story about a ninety-six-year-old woman who had killed herself. The story, said the Sandinistas, was "an attack on the psychic health of the people and, therefore, an attack against the security of the state."

The United States ranks near the middle of the nations reporting to the WHO. Although its rate of 11.0 in 2002 was close to what it was at the turn of the twentieth century (10.2), it has fluctuated over time. During periods of economic depression there is more suicide; during times of war, when, as Durkheim pointed out, personal woes are overshadowed by the larger conflict, there is less. During World War I the rate dipped from 16.2 in 1915 to 11.5 in 1919 before rising steadily in the twenties. The suicide rate crested during the Depression, reaching its apex in 1932 at 17.4. As the economy stabilized, so did the suicide rate, and by 1936 it had dropped to 14.3. During World War II the rate sank to a low of 10.0. After the war it rose slightly, and ever since it has remained fairly constant, ranging from a low of 9.8 in 1957 to a high of 13.1 in 1977. (Not all wars have an ameliorative effect on the rate. Although the rate of suicide among Vietnam veterans has been high, the war itself had little impact on the country's rate, perhaps because it was so controversial, fragmenting rather than uniting the citizens as did the more "popular" world wars. Similarly, the war in Iraq will likely have little effect on the national rate, although at least twenty army men and women serving in Iraq took their own lives during the first year of the war and seven others killed themselves not long after returning home—a rate of suicide nearly a third higher than the army's historical average.)

Many studies have shown that suicide rates fluctuate according to the economy. When the United States rate is graphed against economic indicators over time, the two lines nearly reverse each other. A growing body of research links unemployment and ill health, suggesting that the stress of joblessness triggers problems in marriages, conflicts with children, and physical and mental difficulties among vulnerable people. Examining data from 1940 to 1970, sociologist M. Harvey Brenner of John Hopkins University estimated that when unemployment rises one percentage point, 4.1 percent more people complete suicide.

Within the United States the suicide rate varies widely. Nevada has long had the highest rate of any state, consistently twice that of the nation as a whole. Las Vegas and Reno are a magnet for the transient, the divorced, and others hoping to reverse their fortunes. Other states with consistently high rates are Florida, Arizona, Colorado, Wyoming, Alaska, Montana, New Mexico, Oregon, and California—all Western states with the exception of Florida, whose high rate can probably be accounted for by its unusually high proportion of elderly citizens. Some attribute high Western rates to the stereotypical image of the Western male as tough, unemotional, and willing to use violence as a solution (and, with the West's high rate of gun ownership, to a speedy, lethal means of effecting it). Others hypothesize an "end of the road" theory, suggesting that people often move West with the expectation of changing their life, but when their problems persist, they may become disappointed, hopeless, and suicidal. Indeed, ever since the early nineteenth century, statistics have shown that Americans who move within the United States are at higher risk of killing themselves. "The suicide rate seems to mirror American migrations," writes psychiatrist Howard Kushner in *Self-Destruction in the Promised Land*. ". . . It is a historical rule of thumb that wherever the in-migration is the greatest as a percentage of the total population, so is the overall suicide rate." (Over the past several decades, in fact, with increased migration to the sun belt, rates in the South and Southwest have been rising, although this is attributable in part to the advanced age of many of those sun-seekers.) Indeed, the lowest rates are generally found in the relatively more stable Northeast. New England has had a consistently low rate, which some credit to "Yankee fortitude," although this explanation has been contradicted by the recent appearance among the states with the highest rates of Vermont, where Yankee fortitude had been thought to be of a particularly potent strain.

Migration affects the suicide rate; immigration may have an even greater effect, adjusting to a country being even more disorienting than adjusting to a new state. First-generation immigrants have rates more proportionate to those of their homelands—albeit two or three times higher—than to those of their adopted country, although the rates converge toward that of the host nation over time. For instance, German, Austrian, and Scandinavian immigrants to the United States have extraordinarily high rates, while Italian, Irish, and Greek immigrants have relatively low rates. Danish psychiatrists have pointed to the high rate of Norwegian emigration to the USA as the cause of Norway's low suicide rate compared to Denmark or Sweden. They have argued that depressed and suicidal Norwegians emigrated and became subsumed in American statistics. Among Scandinavian immigrants, however, the Danish and Swedish rates remain two or three times the Norwegian rate.

Ever since statistics on suicide were first kept, researchers and reformers have suggested that the rate of suicide is lower in the country than in the city, where, as one sociologist put it in 1905, "the struggle for existence is carried on with the greatest keenness, and . . . nervous tension reaches its highest pitch." Chief blame for the rising suicide rates of the nineteenth and twentieth centuries was placed on "urbanization." But in this country the difference between urban and rural rates has become less pronounced in recent decades, and studies from around the world now show higher rates of suicide in rural than in urban areas. (In China, for example, the rate is two to five times greater in rural regions than in cities.) In the United States, the change may in part be due to the increasingly hard-pressed economy in rural areas—dramatically expressed by the rash of suicides among bankrupted farmers in the eighties and nineties—as well as by limited access to mental health services and emergency care, greater availability of firearms, and a reluctance by a traditionally self-reliant population to reach out for help.

Just as it was long assumed that higher suicide rates were to be found in the city, it was also assumed that the larger the city, the higher the rate. This is not always true. As early as 1928, sociologist Ruth Cavan pointed out that the suicide rate depends less on a city's size than on its age. Rates tended to be highest in relatively new cities like San Francisco, Oakland, Los Angeles, and Seattle, where traditional social institutions—church, family, schools—were more fragmented. Indeed, in well-established Eastern cities such as Chicago and Philadelphia, the rates are moderate, and people are often surprised to learn that New York City's rate is far lower than that of the country as a whole, leading some to suggest that the grit of that city cultivates a survival mentality. Rates vary not only from city to city but within cities themselves, being most prevalent in extremely wealthy sections and neighborhoods with shifting populations. A study of Minneapolis suicides from 1928 to 1932 found them concentrated in the center of the city, an area of rooming houses and cheap hotels that the researcher called "a land of transiency and anonymity." Studies of Seattle and Chicago yielded similar results. In his 1955 district-by-district survey of London, Peter Sainsbury found that "social isolation" was a more important factor than poverty in determining high-risk areas. In the poor but close-knit working-class sections of London's East End, the rate was far lower than in prosperous suburbs like Bloomsbury, whose comfortable houses were interspersed with one-room flats, transient hotels, and boardinghouses. He also found high rates around railroad stations and areas settled by immigrants and the newly rich, both of whom, he suggested, faced problems of adjustment. Twenty-seven percent of London suicides had been living alone, while only 7 percent of the general population lived alone. (One cannot, of course, conclude from these results whether suicidal people are drawn to living in lodging houses or whether living in lodging houses drives people to suicide.)

In the nineteenth century, differing rates among countries were often attributed to climate. (As late as 1930, San Diego's high rate was blamed on "too much sunshine"; more likely the real culprit, as in Florida, was the concentration of elderly people.) These days climate's effect is said to be negligible—studies by psychiatrist Alex Pokorny in the 1960s exploring the relationship between suicide and temperature, wind speed, barometric pressure, relative humidity, and seven other meteorological variables found no significant effect. Time of year, however, plays a role. Although Ishmael, in Herman Melville's *Moby-Dick,* described suicidal depression as "a damp, drizzly November in my soul," T. S. Eliot was a more accurate emotional weatherman: for suicides, April *is* the cruelest month, its rate some 12 percent above the average for the rest of the year. In November, in fact, the rate is near its nadir. The winter months generally have the lowest rates, and contrary to conventional wisdom, there is no increase around Christmas, New Year's, or any other major holiday, although a British study found an increase in attempts on Valentine's Day. Perhaps the rate rises in the spring and early summer because a person's despair may be heightened by the regeneration around him. "A suicidal depression is a kind of spiritual winter, frozen, sterile, unmoving," wrote A. Alvarez. "The richer, softer, and more delectable nature becomes, the deeper that internal winter seems, and the wider and more intolerable the abyss which separates the inner world from the outer. Thus suicide becomes a natural reaction to an unnatural condition." (In *Girl, Interrupted,* a memoir of her stay in a psychiatric hospital, Susanna Kaysen put it more drily: "It was a spring day, the sort that gives people hope: all soft winds and delicate smells of warm earth. Suicide weather.") More than two thousand years ago, Hippocrates observed that melancholia was more likely to occur in spring and autumn; contemporary research has found that while many depressive episodes begin in winter, they reach their greatest intensity in spring, with a smaller, secondary peak in the fall. This variation may have biological roots, as there are pronounced seasonal fluctuations in neurotransmitter levels (including serotonin), as well as in certain hormonal activity, which can cause disruptions in mood, energy level, sleep patterns, and behavior.

Ever since 1833, when M. A. Guerry examined 6,587 French suicides and found that a disproportionate number took place on the first day of the work-week, Monday has been the most popular day for suicide—perhaps because people are returning to the "real world" of school and jobs after the exhilaration of the weekend. The beginning of a new week may seem to promise a new beginning, a rebirth; when it turns out to be no different it can be depressing, a dynamic reflected in popular songs such as "Blue Monday" and "Stormy Monday." (In Guerry's time, when the work week lasted six days, Sunday was the least popular day for suicide; today, Saturday is.) Time of day? Though it is commonly assumed that most suicides take place in the dark recesses of the night, they are more likely to occur in the morning, which may constitute a sort of miniature version of spring: The world is getting up and starting anew—why can't I? This pattern, too, may be driven by chemistry: most depression is circadian, and depressed people commonly feel especially anxious on waking.

Conventional wisdom has long held that police, doctors, and dentists kill themselves at abnormally high rates. "If a person works in an occupation which brings him in close contact with death and provides him with convenient means to end his own life, suicide poses a greater danger than in more innocuous professions," wrote the authors of *Traitor Within: Our Suicide Problem,* in 1961, noting that executioners, whose careers are devoted to killing others, also appeared to have a high rate of killing themselves. Early studies of suicide by occupation were confounded, however, by demographic variables, including age, gender, and marital status, all of which affect suicide rates independently. Sociologist Steven Stack points out, for instance, that suicide rates for elementary-school teachers are 44 percent lower than for the working-age population in general, but when one controls for gender—the majority of elementary-school teachers being women and women having a much lower rate than men—there is no significant difference. In his 2001 study, "Occupation and Suicide," Stack controlled for such factors and found health professionals to be at highest risk: dentists topped the list with a rate 5.4 times higher than expected, followed by physicians and nurses. ("Dentists suffer from relatively low status within the medical profession and have strained relationships with their clients—few people enjoy going to the dentist," Stack has suggested.) Mathematicians, scientists, artists, and social workers also appear to be at increased risk, while police have a rate only slightly higher than expected, when compared to other working-age men. (Executioner was not among the thirty-two occupations considered by Stack.)

Other researchers have parsed the medical field still further to find that surgeons, who may feel directly responsible for the life and death of their patients, tend to have high rates, while obstetricians, pediatricians, and radiologists have lower ones. Psychiatrists may have the highest rate of any medical specialty— six times that of the general population, according to some studies. Estimating that one in three psychiatrists suffers from depression—three times the rate in the general population—the authors of a study of psychiatrists and suicide suggest that the field attracts troubled people seeking to understand their own problems. Noting that eight of Freud's closest disciples had killed themselves, the neurologist Walter Jackson Freeman, who, as the gung ho promoter of prefrontal lobotomy in this country no doubt had some complicated reasons for his own career path, called suicide "a vocational hazard for the psychiatrist."

To account for the elevated rate of physician suicide in general, experts point to the high stress level of the work and the tendency of doctors to keep their feelings inside. The type of personality often attracted to the field of medicine, they say, may be especially vulnerable. "It draws workaholics, overly conscientious people who take failure poorly, and idealists, who are frequently disappointed during their careers," psychiatrist Robert Litman has observed. In addition, physician suicide is encouraged by the ready availability of lethal drugs and the knowledge of how to use them. (More than half of physician suicides overdose, while only 12 percent use guns—numbers that are nearly reversed in the general population.) Physicians, who have a hard enough time recognizing depression in their patients, are slow to recognize depression in themselves and, even when they do, may be reluctant to seek help—hardly surprising given that medical licensing boards forbid them from practicing if they are being treated for any psychiatric condition. The suicide rate is especially high among female physicians, lending support to research suggesting that women who enter male-dominated professions, such as female chemists and soldiers, may be at increased risk.

---

The challenges of assimilating into an entrenched culture may also play a part in African-American suicide. For many years it was believed that suicide was, as one researcher put it, "a white solution to white problems." Indeed, despite facing poverty, violence, and two hundred years of oppression, blacks in this country have historically had a suicide rate about half that of whites. Attempts to explain this were based on Durkheim's suggestion that the greater a person's status, the greater the potential fall and the greater the chance of suicide. Suicide, it was said, was a luxury blacks couldn't afford because they were too busy trying to survive. "Black folks have so many problems they don't even have time to think about committing suicide," went the old saw. (Comedian Dick Gregory quipped, "You can't kill yourself by jumping out of the basement.") A more psychologically sophisticated explanation for the low black rate derived from Freud's belief that suicide is the result of murderous impulses toward a lost love object turned inward. In dealing with frustration and aggression, social groups were said to turn either to homicide or to suicide, and rates varied inversely in a given community. Sociologists pointed to the high homicide and low suicide rates among American blacks (as well as to the low homicide and high suicide rates in Sweden and Denmark) as evidence. The generally held—if rarely expressed—opinion was that blacks killed other people while whites killed themselves.

Although the black homicide rate is indeed high—seven to ten times higher than that of whites—suicide is also a significant problem for blacks, particularly among young males. From 1980 to 1995, while the rate for white males age ten to nineteen increased only slightly, the rate for young black males more than doubled. The increase was especially precipitous—233 percent—among blacks age ten to fourteen. (Like the overall adolescent rate, the youthful black rate plateaued and dipped in the midnineties; by 1998, the rate had subsided to what it had been in the early eighties.) Throughout this time, the rate of elderly blacks has remained low, about one-third that of whites, putting in sharp relief the distinctive age pattern of black suicide. The rate peaks in youth (47 percent of black suicides occur among ages twenty to thirty-four, although this group comprises only 22 percent of the black population), then levels off after age thirty-five while the white rate rises. Why is the young black male rate so high? Why is the elderly black rate so low? Until relatively recently these questions went unexplored.

Herbert Hendin's study of youth suicide in Harlem in the late sixties was one of the first close looks at African-American suicide. He learned that the rate for black New York males age twenty to twenty-five was higher—in some years twice as high—than that for white males of the same age. This had been true since 1910, when detailed records were first kept in New York City. His findings contradicted conventional thinking on the relationship between suicide and violence. Interviewing young black men and women who had made serious suicide attempts, he found a direct relationship, not an inverse one, between suicide and homicide. Almost all had a history of violence in their childhoods—fathers who were physically violent or who died violent deaths, mothers who were abusive—and violence became a part of their lives. They had often thought of killing someone else—sometimes it didn't seem to matter whom—before they attempted to kill themselves. "Many of these subjects came to life only through acts or fantasies of violence," wrote Hendin. "In merely talking of past fights or brutality they became far more animated than usual. They see living itself as an act of violence, and regard death as the only way to control their rage."

For suicidal young blacks, parental rejection and abuse are compounded by rejection from society and by the realization that discrimination limits their opportunities for advancement. "It does not seem surprising that suicide becomes a problem at such a relatively early age for the black person," Hendin wrote. "A sense of despair, a feeling that life will never be satisfying, confronts many blacks at a far younger age than it does most whites. For most discontented white people the young years contain the hope of a significant change for the better. The marked rise in white suicide after forty-five reflects, among other things, the decline in such hope that is bound to accompany age." If, as suicidologists say, hopelessness is a central ingredient of the suicidal equation, many young African-Americans are at perpetually high risk. A black man who hanged himself in a juvenile detention center left this note: "I haven't got nothing. And I ain't never going to be nobody. Tell my mother good-bye, if you can find her."

"To be a Negro in this country and to be relatively conscious is to be in a rage almost all of the time," wrote James Baldwin. Statistics can only hint at the sources and consequences of that rage. Adolescents lacking a parent are more likely to attempt suicide; today 68 percent of black children are born to single mothers, more than half of all black children have no father at home, and divorce among blacks is twice as frequent as among whites. Unemployment, as Brenner pointed out, is correlated with suicide; for much of the eighties and early nineties, joblessness among black men hovered around 30 percent, nearly three times higher than among white men; for black teens the rate exceeded 40 percent. Although the boom of the 1990s brought black unemployment down, it is still twice the white rate. In 2002, boom over, one-third of black families were in debt or had no assets, three times the rate of white families. High school dropouts are at higher risk for suicide; some 18 percent of black males drop out of high school. Rates of suicide among the incarcerated are shockingly high; one in three African-American males will be behind bars at some point in their lives. Given that blacks also suffer from poor housing, disproportionately poor education, and poor access to quality health care, it is remarkable that the black youth suicide rate is not far higher.

Perhaps it should not be surprising that many young urban blacks treat violence, including murder, with nonchalance. "They believe they have nothing to lose," social worker James Evans Jr. told *Time* magazine. "Even if they should lose their own lives, they feel as if they will not have lost very much." Homicide or suicide may seem the only way of making a dent in a world that is repressive, contemptuous, or, at best, indifferent to their presence. In *Invisible Man,* Ralph Ellison described violence as a way for blacks to reassure themselves of their existence: "You ache with the need to convince yourself that you do exist in the real world, that you're a part of all the sound and anguish." Social worker Ruth Dennis, who has studied black suicide and homicide for several decades, points out that such violence has become an accepted cultural tradition for young urban blacks. "His group may demand that he prove his manhood by not 'backing down' from a life-threatening encounter even if it means his own destruction," she told the audience at a National Symposium on Black Suicide. "This behavior is demanded by the only group that accepts him." Dennis compared it to the behavior of eighteenth-century European gentlemen who felt obliged to challenge someone to a duel at the slightest insult.

Social scientists suggest that some young urban blacks express a combination of suicidal and homicidal impulses by provoking someone else into killing them. They may consider it a more acceptable form of death than suicide per se, which is perceived as unmanly. And so they engage, kamikaze-like, in shootouts with police against overwhelming odds, often triggering their own death. One young black man, for instance, brandished a pistol he knew to be unloaded at policemen and was shot. It has been suggested that 10 percent of fatal shootings by police in this country may, in fact, be cases of what has been called "suicide by cop." In one of the few studies of the subject, researchers analyzed 437 shootings by police officers in the greater Los Angeles area and determined that, although they had been recorded as homicides, 46 fit the description of what, in a cumbersome but descriptively precise phrase, they dubbed "law-enforcement-forced assisted suicide." Twenty-nine percent of the victims had histories of psychiatric treatment; 65 percent had talked of suicide to family or friends; 100 percent had brandished a weapon and shown evidence that they wanted the police officers to shoot them. A few psychologists have suggested that radical groups like the Black Panthers, one of whose slogans was Revolutionary Suicide, have deliberately courted death at the hands of authorities, or that rioting by African-Americans following incidents of police brutality is a form of collective self-destruction, given that most of the damage is usually suffered by black-owned property. "The problem with such speculations is that they often arise out of unconscious and sometimes conscious attempts to blame the victim for the brutal acts of another," writes psychiatrist Alvin Poussaint, professor of psychiatry at Harvard Medical School. "According to this rationalization, violence among blacks is suicidal behavior, a black who resists a white policeman is trying to commit suicide: so the policeman who murders is morally absolved of homicide. Such assumptions imply that blacks who rise up and rebel against an unjust system are crazy rather than courageous, insane rather than incensed.

Many institutional authorities refuse to acknowledge the willingness of black youth to risk their lives because they want a better life."

In *Lay My Burden Down: Understanding Suicide and the Mental Health Crisis among African-Americans,* Poussaint and coauthor Amy Alexander suggest that suicidal blacks of all ages may suffer from what they call post-traumatic slavery syndrome, a state of low self-esteem and internalized racism inculcated by a system that, long after the end of legal segregation, continues to discriminate against them. They say that many black suicides are what Durkheim called fatalistic. "There is a type of suicide the opposite of anomic suicide," wrote Durkheim. ". . . It is the suicide deriving from excessive regulation, that of persons with futures pitilessly blocked and passions violently choked by oppressive discipline." Durkheim believed that fatalistic suicide was rare, relegating it to a footnote in *Le Suicide* and citing as an example the suicides of very young (and presumably beleaguered) husbands. Nevertheless, he wrote, "Do not the suicides of slaves . . . belong to this type, or all suicides attributable to excessive physical or moral despotism?"

Durkheim's theory was supported by Warren Breed's 1970 study of suicide in New Orleans. He found that more than half of suicides by blacks occurred in the context of conflict with authorities—landlords, lawyers, tax officials, and police—compared with only 10 percent of white suicides. Many had a great (and perhaps justified) terror of the police, like the young man who had always expressed such a fear although he had never been arrested. One night, during an argument, he shot and wounded his girlfriend; when he heard police sirens, he turned the gun on himself. In many cases blacks completed suicide in the face of problems that could easily have been resolved had they had some basic knowledge of community resources—legal aid services, housing authorities, tax agencies, and so on. "The Negro is subject to the imperatives of two communities," wrote Breed, "and when his difficulties extend outside of the Negro sphere, he is faced with authorities who are white—to him an alien force. He bears a double burden of social regulation. A white man can feel trapped, too, but the data demonstrate a much lower frequency of the 'authority' stress factor in white male suicide."

With so much against them, why have blacks had such a low rate of suicide? Ironically, their very history of struggle against discrimination may play an important role, by forcing them to cultivate an inner strength that offers protection against self-destruction. "Their expectations of life have been different from those of whites," says Alvin Poussaint. "Thus, tragedy that might drive a white man to self-murder might be accepted by a black man as one more incident in a life of hard times." ("Black Poets should live—not leap / From steel bridges, like the white boys do. / Black Poets should live—not lay / their necks on railroad tracks, like the white boys do," as poet Etheridge Knight puts it in "For Black Poets Who Think of Suicide.") This may help explain the astonishingly low rate of elderly black suicide. In

2000, the rate for black males over sixty-five was 12 per 100,000—three times lower than that of their white counterparts. The rate for elderly black women has hovered around 2 per 100,000 for many decades—perhaps the lowest rate of any demographic group in this country. Elderly blacks, it is theorized, have made a certain peace with their lives in a racist society, scaling down their hopes to fit reality more closely. (One psychologist offers a more practical explanation, suggesting that the majority of violent black males are removed from the population before they reach old age, having killed themselves, been murdered, or been imprisoned.) In the face of adversity, blacks have developed a strong network of family, religious, and community ties—ties that, as Durkheim pointed out, offer protection against suicide. In a study of marital status and suicide, Steven Stack found that while the divorce or death of a spouse raised the risk of suicide significantly among African-Americans, as it does among whites, being single did not. The association between marital status and suicide was less operative for blacks than for whites, which the author suggested was attributable to traditionally stronger family ties. The extraordinarily low rate among elderly black women may further be encouraged by the matriarchal tradition in African-American families. Black grandmothers play an important role in family life (caring for children, cooking, keeping house), which may give them a sense of purpose that many elderly whites say they lack. Older blacks are also bolstered by their strong sense of spirituality and their immersion in religious traditions with powerful taboos against suicide.

If the bonds forged during segregation offered African-Americans some protection against suicide, what effect has integration had? In 1938, psychoanalyst Charles Prudhomme predicted that as blacks in America entered the white-dominated mainstream, their suicide rate would approach the white rate (just as the rates of immigrants grow more similar over time to those of the majority population and less similar to those in their countries of origin). The black suicide rate has indeed risen since 1938—although no faster than the white rate. Prudhomme's theory was lent credence by a 1965 study that found that while Harlem's suicide rate was half that of New York City as a whole, there were three middle-class Harlem communities in which the suicide rates equaled those of the entire city. Ruth Dennis has suggested there may be two forms of black suicide: the angry urban suicide Hendin described and the suicide of those trying to assimilate, to succeed in a world dominated by whites. Success in the white-dominated world may be a double-edged sword. As blacks move, geographically and socioeconomically, they are less likely to be part of tight-knit communities; indeed, over the past several decades, the involvement of blacks, especially young males, in social and religious organizations, has declined. A 1998 study traced the rise in African-American suicide—of youth suicide in particular—to a decline in religious beliefs and practices. (Given that in-migration has historically led to a rise in the suicide rate, the massive twentieth-century flow of black Americans from the South to the North, from rural to urban areas, where they were exposed to unfamiliar stresses, may in some measure be responsible for the rising rate. Rates are higher for blacks in the North; in the South they have remained traditionally low.) Just as women's suicide rates grew as they entered the mainstream of society, so, too, have black rates risen as their status—and their expectations—has risen. Durkheim was the first to observe that poverty may protect people from suicide because those who expect little are not disappointed when they receive little. Psychologist Richard Seiden writes, "Perhaps these unifying social ties are destroyed as personal aspirations are realized. Could increased suicide be the ticket of admission to the middle-class American dream?" This view was supported by a study by Alton Kirk, a psychologist at Michigan State, who found that blacks who attempted suicide had less racial pride and less sense of black identity than blacks who did not attempt suicide. Kirk believes that black consciousness, in giving one a more positive self-concept, offers a protective shield against suicide. Those who "try to become more assimilated into the contemporary white American society," he says, will "find themselves in 'the ethnic twilight zone,' belonging to neither the white or the black world."

While the rate has risen, it remains comparatively low. The low rate is especially surprising given African-Americans' consistent underutilization of mental health services. Part of the reason is financial: only about 25 percent have health insurance. Part is historical: often denied medical care or offered substandard treatment in segregated facilities or poorly funded and understaffed hospitals, blacks may have an understandable skepticism of the medical community in general and of mental health professionals in particular. Part may be cultural: in a 2000 National Mental Health Association survey, two-thirds of blacks considered depression to be a "personal weakness" treatable by prayer and faith; only a third recognized it as an illness for which they'd take a prescribed medication—nearly the reverse of the figures for the general population. Many African-Americans describe depression as "the blues" or "being down" and may think of it as an almost inevitable part of life—something to suffer through, not something to see a therapist about. "The internal strength which allowed blacks to endure centuries of hardships has, it seems to us, morphed over the decades into a form of stoicism that provides little room for acknowledging and addressing mental health problems," write Poussaint and Alexander. (Poussaint, whose brother died of a heroin overdose, and Alexander, whose brother jumped to his death, cowrote *Lay My Burden Down* in part to break the silence about depression and suicide in the African-American community.) The shame associated with mental illness was poignantly expressed in a suicide note, quoted in *Lay My Burden Down,* left by a twenty-three-year-old black man who shot himself to death: "Mom, don't tell anybody I killed myself. Just tell them somebody killed me because I don't want people to think I'm crazy."

To those clinicians who increasingly tout the link between mental illness and suicide—and promote psychopharmacology as a panacea—the low rate of African-American suicide is baffling. (One can't help playing devil's advocate: Might blacks actually have a *higher* rate if they turned more to medication and mental health professionals? Might whites have a lower rate if they spent less time with pill-dispensing physicians and more with family, church, and community?) Certainly the paradox offers intriguing territory for exploration. Things have changed since I attended the 1985 NIMH Youth Suicide Conference and was surprised to find that of the more than four hundred attendees, only sixteen showed up for the presentation on black youth suicide. Yet there remain relatively few rigorous studies of African-American suicide. (For several years, in fact, the American Association of Suicidology was unable to award its annual prize for research on minority suicide.) Although an increasing number of prevention centers train volunteers, most of whom are white, in how to deal with callers whose ethnic and cultural backgrounds differ from their own, few people could argue with Alton Kirk's observation that "Blacks view suicide among blacks as a rare occurrence; whites see black suicide as a black problem. Too many people, black and white, fail to see that black suicide is symptomatic of more general societal problems—societal problems which we must work together to solve before they destroy us all, both black and white."

One of the reasons that sophisticated research on black suicide has been scarce is that until 1964, the National Center for Health Statistics lumped all "nonwhites" into a single statistical category. At that point, the office began subdividing this group into blacks and "all others," which still left Native Americans, Asians, and dozens of other groups in one category. Until 1997, Hispanic-Americans were buried within the "white" statistical category, ensuring that research on Hispanic-American suicide would be virtually nonexistent. One of the few large-scale studies surveyed the five Southwestern states (Arizona, California, Colorado, New Mexico, Texas) where the majority of all Hispanics in America live and where, since 1975, death certificates have distinguished between Anglos and Hispanics. The study showed that the suicide rate of Hispanics (9.0) was less than the national rate for whites and one-half that of Anglos living in that area. This was true for both males and females. Almost 70 percent of Hispanics who completed suicide were under age forty, and 33 percent were under twenty-five (compared with only 17 percent of Anglos). For women the rate peaked early, then fell off sharply; for men the rates were highest in the twenties and after age sixty but still much lower than for Anglos. (It must be remembered, however, that this study was primarily of Mexican-Americans and did not reflect cultural differences among various Hispanic groups.) In 2002, the rate among Hispanics (which includes persons of Mexican, Puerto Rican, Cuban, and Central and South American origins) was 5.0, slightly less than half the overall national rate. As with black suicide, the Hispanic rate peaks in youth. Hispanic high school students are nearly twice as likely as their white or black classmates to say they have attempted suicide.

Research on Native American suicide is similarly sparse, a fact underscored during a six-week period in 1985 when nine young Native Americans (eight Arapaho and one Shoshone) killed themselves on the Wind River reservation in Wyoming. All were young men, and all chose hanging—using rope, socks, bailing twine, sweatpants, and the drawstring from a sweatshirt. Over the following months, psychologists and counselors held weekly suicide prevention sessions in the reservation schools, discussing clues, warning signs, alcohol abuse, and so on. A task force delivered family counseling. A teen suicide hotline was established. But there was another, less clinically orthodox response. The community's young Arapaho took part in a tribal rite last performed in 1918 to ward off an outbreak of Spanish influenza. Four feathers, each decorated with a red ribbon and blessed with the Arapaho sacred pipe, were placed near the tribal sun-dance ground to mark the points of the compass and purge the unhappiness that might have caused the suicides. Inside a tepee, an elder cleansed members of the tribe by tapping on the ground, painting their faces with scarlet paint, and having them step over a burning herb. Hundreds of young people waited their turn outside. There would not be another suicide for almost six months.

Although the two approaches may have combined effectively in this case, they demonstrate the cultural gap that many say led to the suicides. In pre-reservation days, each Indian tribe developed its own attitude toward self-destruction. Chippewa, for instance, believed suicide was a foolish but not deplorable act; the Alabama tribes considered it cowardly; Creeks were said to kill themselves "after the slightest disappointment." Many tribes released aggression and frustration in other ways. Among the Cheyenne, for instance, suicide was rare but not unknown. When a warrior grew depressed or lost face, a war party was often organized. In battle he would take some heroic risk that resulted either in a renewal of his self-esteem or in his death. Another outlet for masochistic aggression was the sun dance, in which warriors engaged in various kinds of self-mutilation.

"After they were confined to the reservation, the Indians were forbidden to hold their Sun Dance or carry out any other 'primitive and barbaric rituals,'" wrote Larry Dizmang in his study of suicide among the Cheyenne. "They could no longer hunt the nearly extinct buffalo, and of course fighting between tribes was outlawed. A Government program designed to improve health conditions forced the Indian men to cut their long hair, a prized symbol of their strength; and, because the Indian could no longer support himself or his family on the reservation, the Government was forced to set up welfare programs, which only added to the rapid downward spiral of increasing dependency and loss of self-esteem."

Today, the Cheyenne are one of many tribes to have found new ways to vent aggression: alcoholism, homicide, and suicide. The suicide rate for Native Americans is the highest of any racial or ethnic group in this country. In 1995, the rate of 19.3 was nearly twice the rate of the nation as a whole. As with blacks, the rate is especially high for young males: 54.0 for adolescents and a whopping 67 for those aged twenty-five to thirty-four. (Although the rate for young Indian females is substantially lower than for young Indian males, the rates are still about three times higher than for the general population.) But while the suicide rate for American Indians as a whole is high—fueled in part by high rates of drug and alcohol abuse—there is tremendous variation among the nation's four hundred tribal groups. The tribes with the highest rates are generally the ones in which traditional values have been most eroded. Trying to fit into a dominant new culture while maintaining traditional values may result in what social scientists call marginality—the inability to form dual ethnic identification because of bicultural membership.

A similar pattern is found among the Inuit of Alaska, Greenland, and especially Canada, who have one of the world's highest suicide rates. Suicide has always played an important role in Inuit culture, but it used to be the "economic" suicide of the elderly and ill who walked off to die during times of scarcity to conserve the tribe's resources. Today, suicide among the Inuit is largely a problem of the young, especially men between the ages of fifteen and twenty-nine. While the overall Canadian suicide rate is 12.9 deaths per 100,000, rates in the largely Inuit Nunatsiavut, Nunavik, and Nunavut regions average 80 per 100,000. In a 2001 survey in one small arctic community, one in three respondents had attempted suicide during the previous six months.

Over several years in the 1990s, Canada's Royal Commission on Aboriginal Peoples held public hearings in ninety-two communities and concluded, in a widely discussed 1995 Special Report on Suicide, that the causes were numerous and catastrophic: disruptions of family life from enforced attendance at distant boarding schools; drugs; alcohol; brain damage or psychosis from sniffing solvents; poverty; limited employment opportunities; substandard housing; inadequate sanitation; and cultural stress from loss of land, loss of language, suppression of belief system, and the decline of subsistence hunting and fishing. Other researchers have concluded that, like certain American Indian tribes, those Inuit communities that have retained more cultural traditions have lower suicide rates, as do communities that, for various reasons, have been isolated from or resistant to governmental attempts to impose assimilation. In 2003, the Canadian national Inuit organization Inuit Tapiriit Kanatami passed a resolution identifying suicide prevention as the Inuit's number one health priority; in 2004, the National Inuit Youth Council published a National Inuit Youth Suicide Prevention Framework. The NIYC's president, Adamie Padlayat, said, "Inuit culture is rooted in values such as resilience, survival, and adaptiveness. We need to articulate to Inuit that these traditional values are important today for our survival in contemporary Canadian society."

---

Ethnicity has an effect on suicide; so, too, does sexuality. The history of homosexuality is strikingly similar to the history of suicide. Over the millennia both were viewed as a natural act, then as a sin and a crime, then as a disease. Just as suicides were dragged through the streets, hanged upside down, and burned, homosexuals were imprisoned, beaten, castrated, burned at the stake, and hanged in public squares. For centuries, exposure in a homophobic society—and the attendant public humiliation, possible imprisonment, and loss of friends, family, and career—almost literally meant the end of one's life. Many homosexuals saw no option but to make that figurative end literal. Newspapers of the 1940s and 1950s were filled with accounts of men who killed themselves after being arrested on a "morals charge." Many more suicides went unreported, including those who killed themselves after being blackmailed and those who killed themselves in shame as they acknowledged their feelings. "Prior to the development of the gay movement, public identification as a homosexual was, almost by definition, linked to scandal, social ostracism, blackmail and suicide," wrote Eric Rofes in *"I Thought People Like That Killed Themselves"—Lesbians, Gay Men and Suicide,* in which he discusses "the myth of the suicidal homosexual." As the title of Rofes's book suggests, for many years homosexuality and suicide were seen as synonymous. "I remember in the fifties it was almost understood that you weren't really queer if you didn't feel the melancholia that would cause you to attempt self-destruction," observed Pat Norman, director of the San Francisco Gay/Lesbian Health Service, at the 1986 National Conference on Gay and Lesbian Suicide. Novels, plays, and films reinforced that myth, frequently portraying homosexuals as miserable, guilt-ridden individuals who ended up killing themselves. In Lillian Hellman's 1934 play *The Children's Hour,* a schoolteacher accused of lesbianism is driven to suicide by the homophobic citizens of a small Southern town. "Homosexuality used to be a sensational gimmick," Mart Crowley, author of the play *The Boys in the Band,* told an interviewer in 1969. "The big revelation in the third act was that the guy was homosexual, and then he had to go offstage and blow his brains out. It was associated with sin, and there had to be retribution."

For many years the medical profession reinforced that myth. In the late nineteenth century, homosexuality, like suicide, was reinterpreted as a disease to be "cured." As with suicide, homosexuality's evolution from a moral to a medical problem merely changed the nature of the stigma. Well into the second half of the twentieth century, in fact, some mental health professionals insisted that homosexuality was a form of suicidal behavior: "The homosexual act in itself may already represent a suicidal tendency, an inner fury against prolonging the race, or an unconscious need to merge with the stronger person of the same sex," wrote the distinguished psychiatrist Joost Meerloo in 1962. It wasn't until 1973 that the American Psychiatric Association, under duress, dropped homosexuality from its roll call of mental illnesses in the *Diagnostic and Statistical Manual of Mental Disorders.* Nevertheless, it would be hard to disagree with Myron Mohr, former director of the Baton Rouge Crisis Intervention Center, who has observed, "Regardless of what the APA has said, there are still therapists who believe that homosexuality is a disease they must try to cure."

"Have lesbians and gay men internalized the myth of homosexuals as suicidal and engaged in massive self-destruction?" asks Rofes. Not surprisingly, given the highly politicized environment of gay rights and the fiercely territorial nature of mental health research, the answer has been a subject of controversy. Although accurate statistics are difficult to compile because sexual orientation is not listed on death certificates and because many gays, especially during more closeted eras, have chosen to keep their sexual orientation secret, various studies have concluded that gays and lesbians attempt suicide two to seven times more often than heterosexuals. A 2000 survey of 3,648 men between the ages of seventeen and thirty-nine found that nearly 20 percent of those who had same-sex partners had attempted suicide, compared with 3.5 percent of the heterosexuals. Although studies of completed suicide are few, a 1986 study concluded that gay men accounted for 10 percent of male suicides in San Diego County. A study of male twins, one of whom was gay and the other straight, found that the gay twins were nearly four times as likely to have attempted suicide, twice as likely to have considered it.

Several suicide researchers have attacked some of the earlier studies for their alleged lack of scientific rigor and their predilection for political posturing. A 1978 Kinsey report, for instance, which found that 35 percent of gay men had attempted or considered suicide, was criticized for recruiting many of its subjects from bars and bathhouses, a "biased" sample likely to include a disproportionate number of alcoholics. (A gay suicidologist likened this to criticizing "Aborginal American studies for being 'biased' because researchers had only taken their study sample on reservations.") Indeed, in 1978, when the vast majority of gays were still closeted and gays in the streets were still being beaten and arrested merely for being gay, where else might researchers find a population sufficient for their study? If they had confined their search to the usual places—college newspapers and psychology department bulletin boards—suicidology might still be waiting for the first study on gay and lesbian suicide. A few of the critics produced studies of their own, calling the earlier findings into question. Yet this supposedly more rigorous research may itself have been flawed because of their authors' apparent ignorance of gay life. One frequently cited paper that found no significant difference in completed suicide rates for gay versus straight adolescents relied for information about sexual orientation on a parent and a friend, the author apparently being unaware that many closeted gay adolescents live double lives in which parents and "straight" friends are often the last to know the truth, or the least likely to admit it.

Whether or not the data on gays and suicide is airtight, even the most scientifically stringent suicidologists could hardly deny that gay and lesbians face conditions likely to increase suicide risk. Numerous studies show higher rates of depression, panic disorder, and anxiety disorder among gays than among straights, encouraged, no doubt, by the stress of having to live life on the margins of society. Among gays and lesbians, rates of alcohol and drug abuse—risk factors for suicide among any group—are estimated to be about three times higher than in the general population, not surprising given that for many years gay and lesbian socializing revolved around bars: one of the few places where they were able to gather comfortably. (Alcohol and drugs are also, of course, a way of dealing with oppression and social stigma.) Yet why is the suicide rate among blacks, who have also suffered centuries of persecution, lower than that of the general population, while the gay rate seems to be higher? Unlike blacks, gays often lack traditional supports that may act as a buffer against suicide. They are vulnerable to what Durkheim called "egoistic" suicide, the final refuge of those who don't belong to cohesive social groups. Many have been rejected by their families, friends, and religions. In *Is the Homosexual My Neighbor?* a man comments, "Less than two months ago I was told by a sincere Christian counselor that it would be 'better' to 'repent and die,' even if I had to kill myself, than to go on living and relating to others as a homosexual." To attribute gay suicide solely to discrimination, as some gays have done, is absurdly reductive; but to deny that homophobia is a factor, as some mainstream suicidologists have done, is equally ludicrous. And though in recent decades the gay rights movement has made it more acceptable to live openly gay lives, gay men and lesbians still face discrimination in employment, immigration, the military, and the ministry. The National Gay Task Force found that more than 90 percent of two thousand gay males and lesbians surveyed had experienced abuse at some point in their lives because of their sexual orientation.

The problem of gay suicide has been immensely complicated by AIDS. In the 1980s, when a diagnosis of HIV/AIDS was a virtual death sentence, there was almost universal suicidal thinking for persons at risk. One man who was given a tentative diagnosis of AIDS hanged himself in a San Francisco park; the diagnosis turned out to be inaccurate. In 1985, one of the first systematic studies of suicide and AIDS found that AIDS patients in New York City were thirty-six times more likely to kill themselves than other men aged twenty to fifty-nine, and sixty-six times more likely than the general population. Although the development and widespread use of antiretroviral medications have transformed a positive HIV status from a terminal illness into a chronic condition, recent evidence suggests that people with AIDS nevertheless have a risk of suicide up to twenty times that of the general population. A positive test result for HIV has been linked to increased anxiety, depression, suicidal ideation, and suicide attempts, though only a slightly increased risk for completed suicide. Although the new combination therapies have allowed AIDS/HIV patients to live longer, the side effects of those medications (including depression, anxiety, and insomnia), as well as chronic disorders (diabetes, hypertension, and other illnesses and infections that eventually invade an increasingly weakened immune system), often so diminish the quality of life that thoughts may turn to suicide. Gay men may no longer "exchange formulas for suicide as casually as housewives swap recipes for chocolate-chip cookies," as the late gay activist Randy Shilts put it in 1990, but right-to-die groups that once catered primarily to the elderly continue to report numerous calls from young men with AIDS and HIV/AIDS-related complex. In a survey of 113 men over the age of forty-five who had HIV/AIDS, 27 percent had thought of taking their own lives in the previous week; those who reported suicidal thoughts perceived significantly less social support from friends and family than those who hadn't. Indeed, although the stigma of an AIDS diagnosis has lessened, the suffering caused by AIDS is still frequently exacerbated by lack of support. AIDS patients may lose their jobs and their apartments; they may be abandoned by family, friends, and lovers—even by hospital personnel. If loss is a key to suicide, gay men—many of whom can no longer count the number of friends they have lost to AIDS—remain at risk.

Stigma, internalized homophobia, and the specter of AIDS are factors that may be especially daunting for gay and lesbian adolescents, for whom suicide seems to be a particular danger. Although the findings are less clear regarding completion, several recent population-based studies have found increased rates of suicidal ideation and behavior among gay and bisexual young people. A 1999 survey of 3,365 students, for instance, found gay males seven times more likely than heterosexual males to have made an attempt. (Most studies of gay and lesbian suicide attempts document elevated risk in young males, but not young females—the reverse of the general population, in which young females attempt suicide far more frequently than do young males.) A 1998 survey of nearly forty thousand junior high and high school students in Minnesota found that 4 percent of straight males had considered suicide, 28 percent of gay males. In an Indiana University study of 979 gay men and women from the San Francisco area, 20 percent had attempted suicide before age twenty.

Despite these statistics, in the attention to adolescent suicide, gay and lesbian suicide has been relatively neglected. "All of the problems that affect youth suicide in general affect gay youth suicide as well," Paul Gibson, a social worker at a San Francisco shelter for runaways, has said. "But gay young people have the doubly difficult task of not only trying to survive adolescence but of coming to terms with their sexuality and developing a positive identity." Although many adolescent suicide attempts are made in response to a stressful act, like the breakup of a romance, a study by the Los Angeles Suicide Prevention Center of suicidal behavior in fifty-two gay adolescents found that their attempts were more often the result of longstanding anxieties and fears surrounding their emerging homosexuality. (Some counselors believe that many seemingly inexplicable or so-called out-of-the-blue teenage suicides may be the acts of adolescents who are struggling with homosexual feelings, have no one they dare confide in, and decide suicide is the only solution. These deaths, of course, never find their way into studies of gay suicide.) Not surprisingly, the LASPC research found that young gays and lesbians often lacked the social supports generally available to heterosexual teens. "Gay and lesbian youth face total rejection from their family," according to Gibson. "Many of the young people we work with at Huckleberry House were told to leave home when they came out to their parents. Gay and lesbian adolescents also face the prospect of not having any kind of peer group support. Many gay and lesbian young people lose close friends in coming out to them. Frequently they are harassed, ridiculed, and assaulted at school by their peers, either if they're open about who they are or if it's suspected. School becomes a scary place for them." Even when they seek help, they may not have the support of counselors. Gibson says, "Helping professionals frequently worsen the problems of gay and lesbian youth by failing to accept their orientation." The one person who accepts the gay adolescent's sexual orientation may be his or her lover. In that case the relationship can take on a life-and-death intensity. "They put all the energy that's missing from the relationship with the family that doesn't want them and from the peer group that rejects them into their relationship with their lover," says Gibson. "When that relationship ends, they feel as if *everything* is over."

Some of the obstacles faced by gay and lesbian youth are exemplified in the short life of Jim Wheeler, whose story was told in the documentary film *Jim in Bold*. The middle of seven children in a close-knit Quaker family, Wheeler grew up in western Pennsylvania farm country, the son of a family physician and a substitute teacher. From early on, it was clear to his parents that Jim was different—a sensitive child more interested in painting, dancing, and playing with Barbie dolls than in playing football. Jim seemed happy, for the most part, but as he entered high school, his effeminate mannerisms and eccentric preferences made him a target for increasingly vicious teasing. Jim pretended the name-calling—sissy, fairy, faggot, queer—didn't bother him and became only more determined to flaunt what he called his "punk-rock attitude," dyeing his hair orange, showing off his multiple piercings, and polishing his persona as an artist. At sixteen, he told his family he was gay. They were not surprised. His mother told him she loved him but said it would be a hard road ahead. But his family wouldn't know until after his death, when they found the poetry he'd written, just how hard it turned out to be—for instance, that after gym class one afternoon, some of the athletes had pulled him from the shower, thrown him to the floor, and urinated on him. In a rural area where to come out of the closet might well have been considered metaphoric suicide, Jim didn't know anyone else who was gay. "He wanted to be normal," one of his sisters later wrote. "And in his eyes I guess being normal meant not being gay. He could not see any future for himself." When he began to talk of suicide, his family assumed he was being his usual histrionic self. But after Jim cut his wrists, his parents took him to a therapist, who told Jim that homosexuality was an unpardonable sin. The cure? Prayer. In any case, the therapist told Jim's parents not to worry; Jim was a cutter and cutters never kill themselves. Five months after Jim's high school graduation, not long after he had gone into therapy, Jim's mother and older sister found him hanging just inside the door of his apartment. He was nineteen. After his death, they found a sad, defiant poem he'd written describing the shower incident. It ends with words "single gay male that's me."

# V

# BACKING INTO THE GRAVE

IN HIS SURVEY of the etymology of the word *suicide,* linguist David Daube traces the various phrases that reflect a particular culture's attitude toward the subject. The Old Testament has no specific expression for suicide; the act was merely described, as when "Saul took his own sword, and fell upon it." The ancient Greeks had numerous ways to denote self-destruction, most of which emphasized dying rather than killing: "to seize death," "to be delivered from life," "to leave the light," "to carry oneself off," "to consume oneself," "to dispose of oneself," and "to get oneself out of the way," among others. A noun for the act was not introduced until the second century AD when the Christian presbyter Clement of Alexandria observed that philosophers allow the excellent man "a sensible removal." Ancient Rome's vocabulary included the following phrases: "to seek death," "to procure one's own death," "to cause violence to oneself," "to fall by one's own hand." An unsuccessful suicide was "to wound oneself in order to die."

As "wounding oneself in order to die" became a sin and a crime, the vocabulary describing it became increasingly fierce. Someone who in ancient Greece elected "to flee the light," in medieval England was said "to murder oneself," "to destroy oneself," or "to assassinate oneself." *Self-murder* became the most popular way to describe the act, although the law favored the Latin *felo de se.* Others borrowed a term first used by Hamlet when he cried, "Oh that the Everlasting had not fixed his canon 'gainst self-slaughter." Donne, says Daube, introduced the more clinical *self-homicide* in *Biathanatos.* In 1618, Edmund Bolton employed the term *self-killing.* In his *Anatomy of Melancholy,* Robert Burton used a host of sympathetic synonyms: "to free themselves from grievances," "to put an end to themselves," "to dispatch themselves," "to precipitate themselves," "to fall by one's own hand," "to let himself free with his own hands," "to make away with themselves," and so on.

According to the *Oxford English Dictionary,* the word *suicide*—from the Latin *sui,* self, and *caedere,* to kill—was first used in 1651 by Walter Charleton, an English physician, when he said, "To vindicate oneself from extreme and otherwise inevitable calamity by *sui-cide* is not (certainly) a crime." A. Alvarez cites an earlier usage in Sir Thomas Browne's *Religio Medici,* published in 1642: "Herein are they in extremes, that can allow a man to be his own assassin, and so highly extol the end and suicide of Cato." In the 1662 edition of his dictionary, *A New World in Words,* Edward Phillips takes credit for the word: "One barbarous word I shall produce, which is *suicide,* a word which I had rather be derived from *sus,* a sow, than from the pronoun *sui,* unless there be some mystery in it; as if it were a swinish part for a man to kill himself." Today, although there are dozens of slang expressions such as "offing oneself," "taking the pipe," and "hanging it up," and euphemisms such as "to make away with oneself," the word *suicide* is widely used in English. Not surprisingly, our vocabulary continues to reflect our attitude: while the act itself is no longer a crime, most people still speak of "committing" a suicide, as we "commit" crimes, incest, perjury, or faux pas.

Although there is general agreement on the word, there is a great difference of opinion as to what it means. The definition of *suicide* would seem straightforward—"the act or instance of taking one's own life voluntarily and intentionally"—according to *Webster's Third New International Dictionary.* Yet even this description is imprecise. Everyone would agree, for instance, that a man who puts a gun in his mouth, pulls the trigger, and dies is a suicide. But what of the man who puts a gun in his mouth not realizing that it is loaded? What of the man who loses at Russian roulette? Is he a suicide or merely unlucky? A strict interpretation of Webster's definition, in fact, might exclude many deaths that we classify as suicides but that are arguably "voluntary"— that of Socrates, for example, who was ordered to kill himself. And what of the Japanese samurai whose suicide is demanded by cultural tradition? The spy who takes his own life rather than divulge classified information? The terminally ill woman who asks her husband to put a fatal dose of pills on her tongue? The child who swallows poison from the medicine chest? The man who, addicted to nicotine, cannot stop smoking and dies of lung cancer? The people who, on September 11, 2001, rather than be burned to death, jumped from the World Trade Towers?

There is, in fact, little agreement on exactly what constitutes a suicide. Over the years dozens of definitions have been proposed, and entire books have been written on the problem of terminology. For medical examiners *suicide* is a medical-legal classification, one of five modes of death including accidental, natural, homicidal, and undetermined. Many deaths, however, fall through the cracks between these categories. Warned by his doctor that to drink again would kill him, an alcoholic with cirrhosis of the liver continued to drink heavily and soon died. His mode of death was certified as natural. A twenty-five-year-old laborer with a history of mental instability and suicide attempts drove his pickup truck into a wall at dawn, leaving no skid marks. His death was certified as undetermined. A woman took an overdose of barbiturates in the kitchen at 4:30 p.m. She knew that every working day for three years her husband had come home at 5 p.m. and his first act was to get a beer from the refrigerator. This afternoon, however, her husband was delayed and did not get home until 7:30. Her death was certified as suicide.

In 1637, John Sym, the rural English clergyman who was considered something of a suicide prevention expert, pointed out in his book *Lifes Preservative Against Self-Killing,* that there were many ways of killing oneself, not all of them technically suicide. Sym divided suicide into "direct" and "indirect" categories. Indirect suicide included "*eating* to gluttony, and *drinking* to drunkennesse; using *labour* and *recreations* to surfeiting." The commission of a mortal sin, he said, was indirect suicide, as were duels, keeping company with "accursed persons," battle against a mightier adversary ("when *self-conceited,* wilfull, *foole-hardy men* will fight against their *enemies,* upon desperate *disadvantages;* and imminent perill of death"), and "when any doe out of a *bravery,* and gallantry of spirit, goe needlessly with a charge of money, or of men's persons, or errands; *either* in the night, through a place haunted and beset with murderous robbers; *or,* at any time through knowne *ambushments,* and strong *troupes* of enemies."

Sym's "indirect" suicide is the equivalent of Durkheim's "embryonic suicide." Durkheim observed that many people who had no conscious intention of killing themselves acted in ways that imperiled their life. He suggested that "the daredevil who intentionally toys with death," "the man of apathetic temperament who, having no vital interest in anything, takes no care of health and so imperils it by neglect," and "the scholar who dies from excessive devotion to study" had much in common with the "true suicide." "They result from similar states of mind," wrote Durkheim, "since they also entail mortal risks not unknown to the agent, and the prospect of these is no deterrent; the sole difference is a lesser chance of death."

Freud, referring to such examples as "half-intentional self-destruction," said that people found many unconscious ways to express their death instinct. In *The Psychopathology of Everyday Life* he described an officer who, shortly after his mother's death, fell and was severely injured in a cavalry race, and a man who shot himself "accidentally" after being rejected by the army and by his girlfriend. Calling these "purposive accidents," Freud wrote, "I have now learnt and can prove from convincing examples that many apparently accidental injuries that happen to such patients are really instances of self-injury." This held true, apparently, even in the great psychiatrist's own household. "When a member of my family complains to me of having bitten his tongue, pinched a finger, or the like, he does not get the sympathy he hopes for, but instead the question: 'Why did you do that?'" In fact, when one of Freud's children fell ill and was ordered to spend the morning in bed, the boy threw a tantrum and vowed to kill himself, "a possibility that was familiar to him from the newspapers," noted Freud. In the evening his son showed him a chest bruise he'd gotten from bumping against a doorknob. "To my ironical question as to why he had done it and what he meant by it, the eleven-year-old child answered as though it had suddenly dawned on him: 'That was my attempt at suicide that I threatened this morning.'"

In *Man Against Himself,* Karl Menninger wrote that "in the end each man kills himself in his own selected way, fast or slow, soon or late." Menninger cataloged four hundred pages worth of self-destructive behavior, from nail biting to world war, and divided them into three types. In "focal" suicide, the self-destructive urge zeros in on a specific part of the body and results in malingering, "purposive accidents," impotence, frigidity, or self-mutilation. In "organic" suicide certain people lose the will to live and contrive their own illnesses and premature deaths via cancer, heart disease, diabetes, or emphysema. In "chronic" suicide, a person kills himself slowly, through alcoholism, asceticism, martyrdom, neurotic invalidism, antisocial behavior, or psychosis. All of these, said Menninger, were expressions of the death instinct and represented "variant forms of suicide."

In the six decades since *Man Against Himself* was published, researchers have refined and added to Menninger's compendium of what is sometimes called "subintentioned death," "slow suicide," "silent suicide," "suicide on the installment plan," or "suicide by inches." Some examples include smoking, drugs, reckless driving, obesity, high blood pressure, workaholism, procrastination, overexercise, high-risk sports, eating disorders, running away from home, and delinquency. Then there are those people who don't take their medication; terminally ill patients who refuse lifesaving operations; people who continue to eat fatty foods in spite of high cholesterol levels; women who avoid doctors when they find a lump in their breast; gays who continue to engage in high-risk sex, knowing that the odds of contracting AIDS are high. The French writer Henri Barbusse once remarked that two armies at war form one vast mass of humanity committing suicide. Well into his nineties Karl Menninger still traveled the country to decry what he called "the great and growing suicide club America seems to be caught in"—the nuclear arms race.

In his later work Menninger suggested that self-destructive behaviors are often, in fact, ways of postponing or averting true suicide. "The development of symptoms is a struggle for health, a struggle toward recovery, an effort to avert something which is even worse than that to which one must submit in order to escape it," he said. "The organism says, anything rather than suicide, anything rather than give up the most precious thing of all, namely my life.

Sickness, even neurosis, even crime, but not that awful oblivion, that awful nothingness." Thus, according to Menninger, certain forms of self-destructive behavior may serve—paradoxically—as survival techniques. He warned that if substitutes fail, however, they often lead to the ultimate self-destruction of suicide.

A dramatic use of self-destructive behavior as a way of staying alive is self-mutilation, the most common form of which is wrist-cutting, primarily in young females. Some wrist-cutters are diagnosed as suffering from schizophrenia or borderline personality disorder, while others have no diagnosable disorder but suffer from low self-esteem, intense guilt, and an inability to express themselves verbally. Their act is often precipitated by the threat of impending loss or abandonment—the hospitalization of a parent, being left by a lover. Their tension builds, their anger turns inward, and they punish themselves by repeatedly cutting their wrists—or arms, legs, neck, face, or abdomen. Despite such violence, most cutters say they feel not pain but catharsis. As one researcher characterized the meaning of the act, "I bleed; therefore I am alive." (Indeed, wrist-cutting seems to be a self-inflicted cousin of the common nineteenth-century medical technique of bleeding, in which physicians systematically removed small amounts of blood from depressed and suicidal patients.)

This is the sort of affirmation described by Ellen Parker, a thirty-two-year-old hospital worker who had, when I met her, periodically been cutting her wrists ever since she was an adolescent. When Ellen was nine, her father died after a long illness. Her mother, who had spent many years caring for her husband, was also sickly, and Ellen felt ignored. A shy, reclusive teenager, Ellen often felt so much she thought she might explode; and at the same time she was terrified that she felt nothing at all, that she had no relationship to the real world. "At times I would get so frustrated that I would pound the pillow or go outside and throw rocks. Sometimes I'd even bang my head against the wall—but I couldn't do that when my mom was in the house, so I had to find quieter ways to relieve the pressure." The way she found was to cut her wrists, deep enough to bleed but not deep enough to require medical attention. Two decades later, despite years of therapy, Ellen still kept her feelings inside. About once a month, when she felt especially depressed, she went home and made four or five cuts on her arm, from her wrist toward her elbow, about three or four inches long. After washing and bandaging the cuts, she usually had a glass of wine and listened to music before it was time for bed. Ellen didn't think of these incidents—her "ritual" as she called it—as suicide attempts. She had no intention of dying, and she knew the cuts were superficial. "It's a way of relieving the pressure," Ellen told me. "It's kind of like letting out a sigh. I get a peaceful feeling and a kind of self-satisfaction at having hurt myself."

The form of "slow suicide" most likely to lead to the fast kind is alcoholism.

As many as 30 percent of people who complete suicide and 23 percent of people who attempt suicide have alcohol use disorders. Or we can look at it from another statistical angle: an estimated 5 percent of Americans are alcoholic, and about 3 percent of them will die by their own hand. (People who abuse alcohol have a risk of suicide 115 times that of a psychiatrically healthy population.) They are likely to be white, middle-aged, and unmarried, with a history of previous suicide attempts. Alcohol and/or drug abuse is especially likely to lead to suicide when combined with mental illness, particularly with depression. (Two of every three people with manic-depressive illness, and one of every four with major depression, have alcohol or drug problems; the rates for those with schizophrenia are nearly as high.) Those who suffer from a psychiatric illness and abuse alcohol are at far greater risk for attempting or completing suicide. Indeed, the majority of suicides involve a combination of alcohol and depression.

While there is agreement that suicide and alcohol are closely related, there is less agreement on exactly how they interact. Certainly, alcohol and depression may form a vicious cycle: drinking can lead to depression; depressed people often self-medicate by drinking, which may only exacerbate their depression—and may, over time, alter the brain's delicate chemistry. Alcohol and drugs, of course, also promote suicide by reducing inhibitions, encouraging impulsive and risk-taking behavior, and keeping the depressed person from seeking help. Some researchers believe alcoholism and suicide are different consequences of the same underlying causes. They agree with Menninger, who says that alcoholism is "a form of self-destruction used to avert a greater self-destruction." Alcohol may be used as an escape, and when it fails to put sufficient distance between the drinker and the source of his unhappiness, the ultimate escape of suicide may be chosen. Others dispute Menninger's hypothesis, pointing out that many alcoholics eventually kill themselves outright. They suggest the opposite progression—that alcoholism leads to social difficulties that lead to suicide. In a study of 147 suicidal male alcoholics, three-fourths of the sample reported that prolonged drinking led to rejection by friends, disruption in social relationships, and job difficulties, which precipitated suicidal thinking. Another study found that nearly one-third of alcoholic suicides had experienced the loss of a close relationship within six weeks of their death. Certainly, no matter what the sequence, increased drinking often leads to loss of control, and suicide can be a way of reasserting control. Alcoholism, like depression, can be a way of stopping one's life at a certain point; suicide can be a way of stopping one's life permanently. For some, alcoholism may be suicide in a more acceptable guise. According to his first wife, the writer Jack Kerouac maintained that because he was Catholic, he couldn't commit suicide; he therefore planned to drink himself to death. He died in 1969 of a massive abdominal hemorrhage brought on in large measure by acute alcoholism.

Excessive drinking is one way to kill oneself; insufficient eating is another. An estimated one in every hundred females in this country, most of them young and white, suffer from anorexia nervosa. In a misguided attempt to conform to cultural norms of attractiveness, they may literally starve themselves into illness and even death. The underlying causes of anorexia—low self-esteem, feelings of self-hatred—are not dissimilar to the roots of suicide, and the disorder is often accompanied by traditional suicide attempts. "I didn't think I was worth anything," said one young girl, who dropped from 120 to 80 pounds. "I had no friends, no one to talk to. I was really depressed. I wanted to kill myself. I had thought of taking a knife or pills, but I couldn't. That was suicide, and I knew suicide was a sin. So I just stopped eating." Another young anorexic who was close to death says, "I would rather have died than eaten." Many do. Fifteen percent of acute anorexics will die of what one psychiatrist calls "intestinal suicide."

An even greater number of people in this country suffer from bulimia. Bulimics, who tend to be middle- or upper-middle-class women with high intelligence and high standards, endure recurrent episodes of compulsive eating followed by self-induced vomiting, fasting, or the abuse of laxatives or diuretics. Some bulimics vomit as many as six times a day or take as many as three hundred laxatives a week. Although the ostensible purpose is to develop a more beautiful figure, the effect is a litany of self-destruction not unlike that achieved by the early Christian martyrs. Bulimics may suffer from rotten teeth and receding gums (the result of being bathed in stomach acid each time they vomit), swollen salivary glands, sore throats, abrasions on the esophagus walls, numb or curling fingers and lips (from low potassium levels), and broken blood vessels in the eyes. In her attempts to vomit, one young woman repeatedly jammed her fingers down her throat so forcefully that years later she still has teeth marks on the back of her hand. Occasionally, bulimics die from a severe electrolyte imbalance or from rupture of the stomach or esophagus during a binge. But their self-destructive urges often take a more direct form; in one study one-third of bulimics had made at least one suicide attempt. Perhaps surprisingly, unless one agrees with Menninger that self-destructive behavior is often a way of avoiding true suicide, a recent review of more than thirty studies concluded that about 1 percent of people with eating disorders complete suicide, a figure far lower than that for those who suffer from depression.

Experts suspect that many single-passenger auto deaths may well be suicides in disguise. Some, like Willy Loman in *Death of a Salesman,* who kills himself by driving into a tree, are unequivocal suicides. For Loman "autocide" seemed to be a way of ending his life without forfeiting his insurance premium. Others are somewhat less obvious about their intentions, such as the man who, after an argument with his wife, wrote a note saying, "You'll be sorry when I'm dead," jumped into his car, and sped off down the highway.

Two minutes later he had a fatal crash. The police report concluded, "It looked as if he pointed it into the tree." But suicidal intent is difficult to prove, and such deaths are usually classified as accidents unless a note is found. When a young Massachusetts woman drove on the wrong side of the highway with her headlights off and was killed in a head-on collision, her death was ruled an accident. Researchers estimate, however, that as many as 15 percent of single-car crashes are suicides, and auto accidents have been linked to suicidal behavior in several studies. Psychiatrist Melvin Selzer has demonstrated that suicidal people have more than twice as many auto accidents as nonsuicidal people. In a subsequent study Selzer compared ninety-six drivers responsible for fatal crashes with a control group of drivers. Almost half of the fatal-crash drivers had exhibited depression, violent behavior, and suicidal thinking, compared to 16 percent of the control group. Drivers in crashes were at least four times more likely to have been under severe stress from alcoholism, job problems, or financial troubles. "I don't think there are many overt suicides by auto," Selzer has said, "but the driver may be increasingly depressed, angry, and frustrated until he reaches a state at which it is a matter of indifference to him whether he lives or dies." Young men in particular may drive in careless, risk-taking ways, speeding, racing, driving with their eyes closed, or engaging in games of "chicken" like that played by James Dean in *Rebel Without a Cause*. Reckless driving is often combined with alcohol; in one study more than 50 percent of a group of accident-prone drivers were alcoholics.

The connection between suicide and risk-taking behavior is most dramatically apparent in Russian roulette deaths, which coroners usually classify as accidents. For some people, like Peter Newell, Russian roulette seems to offer a passive-aggressive approach to suicide. For novelist Graham Greene, who suffered from manic depression and toyed with suicidal thoughts throughout his life, Russian roulette seemed to be an attempt to shock himself from numbness. It was one of a number of risk-taking behaviors (drinking, dalliances with prostitutes, travel in war zones) he employed in what he called his "lifelong war against boredom." A study of twenty Russian roulette victims, all but one of them men, found that they were young (many were students) and in good physical health. Half of them were known to have been depressed, however, and nearly 60 percent had a history of drug or alcohol abuse or psychiatric disturbances. "They use risk-taking behavior as a form of self-treatment for depression," observed Dr. David Fishbain, the study's lead author. Although the researchers were unable to conclude whether the victims were "true suicides" or not, the urge for death was clearly evident; more than half of the victims had fired the gun more than once, and 16 percent had loaded more than one bullet in the gun. All had played the "game" with other people present.

The person who plays Russian roulette has a one in six chance of dying; the person who climbs Mount Everest has a one in ten chance of dying. Is it suicidal to attempt that climb? The odds are not good for war correspondents, soldiers of fortune, skydivers, motorcycle racers, daredevils, glacier skiers, climbers who spurn ropes and protective hardware, and others who spend their lives in pursuit of extreme physical risk. Some call them adrenaline junkies and suggest that such people need a high concentration of the stress hormones that are released by fear or excitement. Impulsivity and sensation-seeking have been shown to be associated with the gene for a receptor of the brain chemical norepinephine, suggesting that thrill-seeking personalities are driven, in part, by biology to a life of living on the edge. Edge-livers themselves dismiss the suggestion that they might harbor a "death wish." "I would describe myself as having a life wish," Himalayan mountaineer Gordon Wiltsie has said. "When you do adventurous things, you get a real sense of being alive and enjoying being alive. Life gains value when you realize that it could be extinguished." Freud said as much in a discussion of war: "Life is impoverished, it loses in interest, when the highest stake in the game of living, life itself, may not be risked. It becomes as shallow and empty as, let us say, an American flirtation."

Some people complete suicide by getting someone else to kill them, becoming what Aldous Huxley called a "murderee." Like the Christian martyrs who goaded the Romans into executing them or the angry young men who engage in "suicide by cop," they provoke someone or something else into striking the final blow. Sometimes this strategy is invoked because of the stigma of suicide. Among the Malays, for whom suicide is a sin, if a man wished to die, he ran amok, killing people randomly until he himself was killed. In certain aboriginal tribes of Australia, if a native wanted to die but couldn't get someone to kill him, he might expose himself to a venomous snake. To evade the divine decree against suicide, eighteenth-century Irish Catholic convicts facing torture in Australian prisons drew straws. The man holding the longest straw was killed, thus avoiding prolonged torture; the man who drew the second straw did the killing—whereupon he was executed by the authorities. In war, suicide may be disguised as heroism. "Many soldiers have the fantasy of throwing themselves into the turmoil of battle in order to die," wrote psychiatrist Joost Meerloo. "One of them, who was very courageous indeed, became very depressive after the war because God had not understood his magic gesture and had not used the enemy to kill him." Some would call such men heroes; sociologist Marvin Wolfgang might call them examples of "victim-precipitated homicide." In his 1950s study of murder in Philadelphia, Wolfgang stated that 150 of 588 consecutive homicides were cases of victim-precipitated homicide, many of them husbands who attacked their wives, provoking their wives into murdering them. One drunken man, for instance, beat his wife, then handed her a kitchen knife and dared her to use it on him. She said that if he hit her once more, she would. He slapped her in the face; she stabbed him to death. In a more recent, particularly horrific example, a forty-three-year-old

German man responded to an Internet posting seeking someone willing to be "slaughtered," whereupon he was stabbed to death, carved into pieces, and eaten, over a period of months, by a forty-two-year-old computer technician. After the rejection of a defense request that the defendant be found guilty only of "killing on request" (his lawyers pointed out that the victim had consented, even begged, to be killed) he was convicted of manslaughter and sentenced to eight and a half years in prison.

Many of these people may be unaware of their desire to die, or they may prefer to leave their fate to chance. They may have some magical belief that they cannot take their own life, or they may feel an intense need to be punished by others or to be killed by a symbolic parent. Psychiatrists believe that some people commit murder in the hope of invoking the death penalty. (There are mental health professionals who oppose capital punishment partly because it may encourage violent, suicidal persons to murder.) A twenty-two-year-old babysitter who murdered two small children in her care told police that although she had loved them, she killed them in the belief that if her crime was sufficiently odious, the death penalty would be invoked. She had attempted suicide many times and believed she was incapable of killing herself. (She did not get her wish.) Many death row inmates have tried to insist on their right to the death penalty. In 1977, convicted murderer Gary Gilmore, who demanded to be shot by a firing squad, fought several stays of execution and made two suicide attempts before being executed.

Some forms of suicide are metaphorical. Beset by rumors of marital infidelity, 1988 presidential candidate Gary Hart challenged the press to "put a tail" on him. That very weekend he canceled his campaign appearances to dally with a young model. In the ensuing scandal he resigned from the race, one in a long line of politicians to have committed "political suicide." Such an unconscious need to fail had been recognized by Freud, who said that men who sabotaged their own success were commonly seen in psychoanalysis. In what has been called "pseudocide," some people fake their own suicide, disappear, and start over again somewhere else under a new identity. This is one of many forms of social suicide in which one withdraws from contact with the outside world, essentially declaring the rest of the world dead. In Melville's *Moby-Dick,* Ishmael settles for temporary withdrawal; rather than giving in to "pistol and ball," he ships out for two years on the *Pequod.* Some suggest that various forms of nonaction are essentially suicidal, as in the renunciation of ambition or creativity. The poet Arthur Rimbaud stopped writing at nineteen although he lived almost two decades more. A long-term study of gifted young people found that some had been conspicuous failures in their adult lives, accepting what one psychologist called a sort of "partial death" in lieu of overt suicide. Joost Meerloo believed that such resignation is widespread: "Most people are no longer alive after their entrance into maturity," he wrote. "They commit a partial and token suicide by stopping their growth and stopping the pleasure of expansion. They bury themselves in old accepted habits and customs, drowning their sense of curiosity regarding new inner and outer experiences. Contented apathy and the ending of inquisitive curiosity may be looked at as the early intrusion of death." Ernest Hemingway referred to such behavior as "backing into the grave." Hemingway himself went headfirst, shooting himself when he felt his creative powers had deserted him.

Some theorists seem to believe that almost every action we take—or don't take—may represent some form of self-destructive behavior. In *How to Stop Killing Yourself,* a sort of layman's version of *Man Against Himself* published in 1950, Dr. Peter Steincrohn found examples of self-destruction almost everywhere—"exercisitis" (exercising after age thirty), "vacationitis" (being too relaxed on vacation), and even "disbelief in the philosophy of self-destruction" (a refusal to recognize that we are all suicidal in some way). But not all behavior having possible self-destructive consequences is necessarily motivated by a desire for punishment or death. Merely getting into a car could be considered suicidal behavior, given current accident rates. Some psychiatrists call entering a convent a form of suicide; others call it enlightenment. "One must be careful and not fall into the trap that Menninger did," writes French sociologist Jean Baechler. "Biting one's nails is a form of self-mutilation so removed from total suicide that there is something arbitrary about keeping it in a study of suicide. As ever, it is a question of degree."

Exploring the extent and variety of self-destructive behavior may, however, help us understand that within each of us there is the capacity for self-destruction that may emerge in various forms at various times. "There is a little murder and a little suicide dwelling in everybody's heart," wrote Menninger. "Give them a powerful weapon like a car, inflame their inhibitions or irritations or frustrations, and diminish their suppressive control by means of alcohol or fatigue, and the murder or suicide may get committed." Although few of us pick up the gun, much less pull the trigger, we all engage in activities that have within them a germ of self-destruction.

Several writers on suicide propose that self-destruction is best conceptualized as a continuum of behavior ranging over a broad spectrum. On one end there is the person who puts a bullet through his brain, the completed suicide. On the other, the person who lives a full, healthy, loving, creative, positive life. Located along that continuum are various forms of self-destructive behavior, from suicide attempts to alcoholism to reckless driving to cigarette smoking to the tiny acts of self-sabotage we engage in daily. We all lie on that continuum somewhere between those two extremes, moving along the scale in either direction as circumstances change. In *The Winter Name of God,* author and priest James Carroll wrote:

A thousand people are "officially" dead of suicide every day, but they are not the only ones who are faced with the constant choice between life and death. We all are. . . . We might lack the nerve to commit the final act, and we may not recognize our "sinful" tendencies for what they are, but day in and day out we confront the problem of our innate attraction to self-destruction. We live in a world that encourages the small daily acts of negation that prepare us for the great one. There are meanings of suicide that neither the courts nor the dictionaries admit, but that make it impossible for us to regard those thousand people a day who do themselves in as very different from us. They are not necessarily "sick" or "sinners," but simply our sisters and brothers. And who are we? We are the resigned housewives, the compulsive playboys, the despairing priests, the addicted teenagers, the reckless drivers, the bored bureaucrats, the lonely salesmen, the smiling stewardesses, the restless drifters, the walking wounded. . . . It may be nothing more than the steadfast commitment to sameness. The simplest form of suicide is the act of refusing the adventures and challenges that offer themselves to us every day. "No thanks," we say. "I prefer not to," we murmur, like Melville's Bartleby, preferring to stare at the wall outside the window. Preferring, as I do on especially bad days, to stay in bed.

# 4

# PREVENTION

# I

# CONNECTIONS

————

AT 10 P.M. ON A TUESDAY NIGHT in April, the phone rang in a small room in a one-story building in Los Angeles. Pat, a trim, forty-three-year-old woman wearing sneakers, jeans, and a sweatshirt, picked up the receiver and, in a warm, gentle voice, said, "Hello, may I help you?" As she listened to the answer, she grew still. "Nine Percodans? I don't know," she said. "I'm not a doctor. . . . Did you take nine Percodans? Did someone you know take them?" After each question Pat listened intently before asking the next. "How old is your friend? . . . Nineteen? . . . Is she there with you? . . . No? How frightening." Pat spoke slowly, her voice comforting but firm. "Your friend should get some help. Do you have anyone to call who can help you with this? . . . Maybe you should call the paramedics. Did you call her house? . . . She has roommates? . . . Might they know where she is? . . . Might she call you back? . . . No? . . . She just called you to say good-bye?"

Pat put on her glasses as if they might help her focus even more closely on the caller. If she felt any tension, her voice didn't betray it. "Do you have any idea where she might be, places she might go? . . . Does she have a car? . . . Does she have any family? . . . Have you called them? . . . They're looking for her? . . . What's your friend's name?" Pat's voice softened. "Is it that you don't want to give her last name? . . . If she calls us, can we call you?" Pat paused a moment. "Are you frightened? . . . What of? . . . We're not the police. And even if we were, it's not against the law to kill yourself. . . . Is there anything I can do to help *you*?" Pat's head bowed over the desk. "If you *are* Susan or if you have taken the Percodan, you need to get to the hospital immediately." There was a brief silence and then the sound of weeping spilled from the phone. "What has happened?" said Pat tenderly. "Why do you want to die?"

Pat was sitting on the edge of a plastic swivel chair, leaning over a desk in a corner of the "telephone room" at the Institute for Studies of Destructive Behaviors and the Suicide Prevention Center, commonly known as the Los Angeles Suicide Prevention Center, the oldest and most famous of the country's suicide prevention centers. (In 1997, the Institute was dissolved; since then, the Suicide Prevention Center has operated under the auspices of the Didi Hirsch Community Mental Health Center.) Pat was a volunteer on its twenty-four-hour crisis line. She was alone in the room, but two other counselors were handling calls in nearby offices. Otherwise, the building was empty. On the desk in front of Pat were the tools of her trade: a telephone with four incoming lines, an array of directories, and two Rolodexes with nearly three hundred referral options organized by category: Alcohol, Battered/Rape, Bereavement, Child Care, Employment, Food, Free Clinics, Incest, Pregnancy, and so on. Next to the telephone lay a pack of cigarettes. Pat never smoked during a call, but her hand sometimes closed over the pack during stressful moments. Above the desk, a bulletin board was covered with schedules, newspaper clippings about suicide, notices of workshops on adolescent suicide, and a half dozen messages: "Steve, Ruth called back to say she now has a volunteer job and is feeling much better" and "Erica called to thank us; she's feeling real good now" and "Vivien called to thank everyone for helping her son Rick. She said he'd called here a lot over the past 18 months."

The other half of the room had the look of a college dormitory lounge. A television set and a sheaf of magazines sat on a round wooden table. In the far corner were two brown couches where volunteers on the one to seven a.m. shift catnapped during lulls. A large map of Los Angeles County hung on one wall. The room had one window, whose venetian blinds were closed. The sound of traffic seeped in. The building, a former convalescent home, was in an ethnically mixed neighborhood on the edge of downtown Los Angeles. (These days the center occupies two slightly spiffier rooms at the Didi Hirsch offices in Culver City.) To the east, the neon of bars and fast-food joints gave way to the lights of houses glittering against the Hollywood Hills. To the west, beyond the downtown area, lay the Pacific Ocean. Somewhere in between was a nineteen-year-old girl who sat in her bedroom sobbing, telling the woman in this room that she wanted to die.

As Pat tried to comfort the girl, she gathered information that might help her assess how lethal the situation was and what supports the girl might have to see her through this crisis. Like a climber struggling for a foothold on a steep rockface, she searched for a way to establish a connection. Though the girl sounded timid, despair made her stubborn: She kept coming back to her first question—would the nine Percodans kill her or leave her a cripple?

"*Any* medication could kill you; I don't have that information," Pat said.

"Where is your pain coming from? Is it physical? . . . Have you spoken to any-one about it? . . . Does your therapist know how you're feeling? . . . You called her? She's away? . . ." Pat shook her head. "I don't know. I don't have that kind of training—and even a doctor won't give you that information over the phone. . . . Do you live with your family? . . . Are you close to your father? . . . How about your mother? . . . Have you talked to her about this? . . . Why not? . . . What would she say if you told her? . . ." Pat twisted slightly in her chair. "It must be hard when those you love are so far away from how you're feeling." She was silent for a moment, listening to the girl's quick, anxious breaths. "You don't trust me at all, do you?" said Pat kindly. "I won't hurt you—I promise that."

This was the eleventh call Pat had taken since beginning her shift at 6:30 p.m. The crisis line at the SPC receives an average of fifty-five calls a day from people who are lonely, depressed, angry, and perhaps suicidal. The lines are open twenty-four hours a day, 365 days a year. The SPC is the only suicide pre-vention center or twenty-four-hour general-purpose crisis line in Los Angeles County. When other hotlines and therapists close up shop for the day, many of them leave the SPC number on their answering machines for callers in crisis after office hours. Although the SPC has four incoming lines, the phone company has told the center that during its busiest hours, 7 p.m. to 1 a.m., callers must sometimes dial five or six times before they can get through.

The SPC keeps careful records of who calls and why. (After each call, the counselor types a summary of the call into the computer database and assigns it a lethality score on a one-to-five scale, with one denoting "thoughts only, no prior attempt," and five being "potential or imminent attempt or attempt already in progress.") They have learned that calls come from as wide a range of people and problems as seem to exist. The vast majority are from the troubled person himself. The rest are from third-party callers—concerned rel-atives and friends not knowing what to do about a despairing loved one, physicians or therapists seeking advice on how to handle a suicidal client. Nearly two-thirds of the calls are from women. While most calls are from the Los Angeles area, they have come from as far away as Iowa, Florida, and France. In 2003, one-third of the SPC's calls were from people under the age of eighteen—a 300 percent jump over fifteen years earlier. Once, an eight-year-old boy called. He was lonely, he told the counselor. His mother traveled a lot on business, and he worried that he was the reason she was never home. Later, the counselor called the boy's mother. She was initially outraged at the intrusion, but when she realized that her son had been upset enough to call a suicide prevention center, she listened.

Although the notion of a suicide prevention center may conjure images of heroic volunteers talking desperate people into putting down a loaded gun, the majority of calls are much less dramatic. Most callers to the SPC or to any of the more than six hundred suicide prevention and crisis centers in the United

States are not in immediate danger of killing themselves. This has led some critics to suggest that most people who call a prevention center don't really want to die. The SPC agrees. They believe that even the most desperately suicidal people are ambivalent—a part of them wants to live, and a part of them wants to die. By calling the center they have issued a "cry for help." Nevertheless, many of those who call the center are at risk for suicide. A previous attempt is the most accurate predictor for subsequent suicide, and nearly half the people who call the SPC have made previous attempts. Three percent of the calls are considered emergencies—either the caller is believed to be in imminent danger of making an attempt, or she has already swallowed pills or cut her wrists and may die unless the SPC gets her immediate help.

Although contemplating suicide is not a prerequisite for calling the crisis line, counselors are trained to ask specifically about suicide on every call. "And we don't ask whether they're 'thinking of hurting themselves' or 'thinking of doing something to themselves,'" Karl Harris, a burly ex-policeman who directed the crisis line for several years, told me. "We ask, 'Are you thinking of killing yourself?'" It can be a difficult question to get used to asking. When Harris worked with thirteen streetwise hostage negotiators, who manned the lines as part of their training, he couldn't get them to ask the question without pussyfooting around—they were afraid of putting the idea in the caller's mind. But it won't, according to Harris. "People will lie about everything else on the phone, then you'll ask, 'Are you thinking about killing yourself?' Instant truth. If they're not, you'll hear, 'Good God, no way.' If they are, you'll hear a sigh of relief: 'Yes, I am.'"

About a third of the calls to the SPC are suicide-related. The rest are crisis-intervention inquiries not necessarily related to a suicide threat. The calls Pat had taken so far that night included an elderly widow who lived alone and said she wanted to kill herself ("What is life if you have no friends and your children don't give a shit about you?" she sobbed); a woman worried that her teenage son, who was terrified that he might be gay, was considering suicide; an alcoholic who was drunk and said he wanted to die; a gay man who wanted and didn't want to take the Valium he said he had, and had tried thirteen other hotlines that night, all of which were busy or had shut down for the evening; a seventy-three-year-old man who was drinking and "thinking of doing himself in"; a brain-damaged, middle-aged "chronic" caller who telephoned almost daily for an emotional boost; a forty-six-year-old woman who had just swallowed seven sleeping pills; a psychotic twenty-three-year-old man who was brilliant, incoherent, and angry. The callers seemed to have little in common except that they felt the world was closing in on them and they had no alternative but to depend on the kindness of strangers.

Karl Harris liked to compare the crisis lines to a hospital emergency room. "We're an ER for people with emotional problems," he told me. "They come to us, and like an ER, we do triage; some just need aspirin or a Band-Aid, some need to be seen again, and others need extensive patching and follow-up." With each caller Pat was trained to assess the immediate risk of suicide, listen to the person's story, focus on the problem, and discuss possible options. Each caller had a different need, and it was up to Pat to help the caller decide what might best fill that need. To the infirm, elderly widow, Pat provided several names and numbers and said, gently but firmly, "Tomorrow, *call* the seniors group, and go to the doctor and get some answers about your physical condition. If you need to call us before you go to the doctor, please do. Now get yourself a Coke and a book and try to relax tonight." To the mother of the gay youth, she interspersed her sympathetic remarks with urgent suggestions; the boy needed professional help, she said, giving her the number of a gay community service group and urging her to persuade her son to call the crisis line. "Put a card with our number on it by his bed," she said. To the elderly alcoholic she gave a referral to the nearest Alcoholics Anonymous meeting and some reassurance ("We're here," she said kindly when he fretted she had left the line. "We're not going anywhere"). To a lonely, middle-aged woman she described the kinds of counseling available and patiently gave her directions to a local clinic. "Sally, are you going to be okay tonight?" she said. "If you feel worse, will you give us a call back? . . . I'll be thinking of you."

Pat tailored her approach to fit each caller. With the older woman she was motherly. With the psychotic young man she patiently absorbed his anger. With the man who, like certain other "chronic callers," had a time limit on his calls, she was gentle but firm. "Well, my friend, I'm going to have to hang up now," she said when his ten minutes were up. With the young gay man she was supportive but forceful: "You don't sound like you mean it," she said after he agreed to call back if he needed to. "You sound as if you're saying it because you think that's what I want to hear." Pat's voice inspired trust and confidence; even when the risk seemed high, she never seemed anxious herself, although in a moment of extreme stress she might sigh and say, "Oh, mercy." Every caller was taken seriously, even one who apologized for dialing the wrong number, to whom Pat said warmly, "I'm glad you did"—in case he had the right number and was too scared to talk. Pat took nothing for granted; each caller was unique, each call its own world. And although she seemed so relaxed and sure, at one point after a difficult call she turned to me and admitted, "The longer I'm here, the more questions I have—and the less I know."

The girl was no longer crying, but her breathing was heavy. Slowly, Pat had established a thin ledge of trust. "Did something happen tonight?" she asked. "Can you tell me what that was? . . . Was it something someone said? . . . Who?" After each question Pat let the girl's answer settle for a moment before continuing. "What did he say? . . . Have you talked to him about it? What kind of compromises? . . . Sexual things? . . . Is this the person you want to spend your life with? . . . You care for him too much to leave him, but you have a hard time staying with him?" Pat paused. "You know, suicide is a permanent solution to a temporary problem. . . . Is your fiancé in counseling? . . . Do you think you're ready to share your life with someone who thinks he's perfect? . . . Would it be so terrible to end your relationship with him rather than end your life? . . . Why? . . . How do you know you can't live without him? . . . You tried? . . . Maybe a month isn't enough. . . . Everything changes. Nothing stays the same." Pat hunched over, her elbows on her knees. "Have you ever told him you were thinking of killing yourself? . . . What does he say? . . . He doesn't believe you? . . . Have you talked to him tonight? . . . How did you end the conversation?" Pat listened to the answer, then repeated it softly to herself: "Sweet dreams."

Pat, who makes a living raising orchids, had worked on the crisis lines for ten years when I met her. Like many of the center's 130 volunteers, she became involved after suicide touched her own life when her nephew killed himself. A friend told her about the Suicide Prevention Center. Pat had never heard of it. But she called the center and enrolled in their support group for family and friends left behind after a suicide. When she finished the program, she decided she wanted to work on the telephone lines. Like many of the volunteers, Pat thought she would be getting into the business of saving lives. At her first interview she was asked why she wanted to work on the lines. "Because I want to help people," she said. Pat laughed, remembering. "I wanted to be the Band-Aid queen. I thought I'd save the world. Of course I found out it wasn't quite like that."

Although many of the crisis line volunteers are graduate students in psychology or social work, many, like Pat, have full-time jobs and work at the SPC in their spare time; among the center's volunteers are a mailman, a screenwriter, an actor, a UCLA professor, a massage therapist, a computer programmer, an FBI agent, a retired stockbroker, and several full-time parents with time to spare during the day when their kids are in school. Training for the lines is rigorous. If the volunteer passes the initial interview, she (three out of five volunteers are female) attends seven all-day training sessions over two months. About half the training is devoted to lectures and discussions by the SPC staff and guests on suicide risk-assessment, mental illness, substance abuse, domestic violence, teen suicide, gay and lesbian youth, chronic callers, and survivors after suicide. The other half is spent role-playing in small groups where the trainee handles simulated calls from a variety of clients: gay callers, abusive or obscene callers, alcoholic callers, help-rejecting callers. There is homework: required reading of selected papers and articles on suicide. The prospective volunteer must also put in at least three sessions of "observation," listening in while an experienced counselor handles actual calls. "We look for volunteers who know how to listen—which is not as easy as it seems—and who are flexible, open-minded, and able to empathize with callers from a wide variety of backgrounds," says crisis line coordinator Sandri Kramer. Applicants who have been depressed or suicidal are not automatically rejected—in fact, says

Kramer, they often make good counselors because they know whereof their callers speak—but they must show evidence that they are strong enough to handle the work. Those who have recently lost a family member or close friend to suicide are encouraged to wait a year or so, until the wound isn't quite so fresh. Of every fifty applicants, about thirty-five complete training and are invited to work on the lines. Once accepted, volunteers agree to work a four-hour shift each week for a minimum of one year.

Most suicide prevention lines base their work on "active listening," a technique generally attributed to the psychologist Carl Rogers, founder of "client-centered therapy." In "active listening" the listener affirms what the caller is feeling. If the caller says, "I feel really awful," the listener might say, "It sounds as though you're feeling pretty awful." As the caller vents, the volunteer listens actively until the crisis has passed, then perhaps offers a referral. In fact, the SPC's "active listening" has become a little more active. The staff has found that an increasing number of their callers are chronic, and counselors are urged to make sure that these callers have followed through on previous recommendations. At other centers, volunteers are "workers," "listeners," or "befrienders"; at the SPC they are "counselors." The SPC counselor is trained not merely to listen but to probe, to ask questions, to solicit information, to sort through options, and to help the caller come up with a plan of action. But counselors must not make decisions, give answers, or pass judgment. Above all they are forbidden to play God or therapist. Former crisis line coordinator Beverly Kalasardo recalls one counselor who was dropped from the lines: "He wanted so badly to help the callers that he almost wanted to change their lives. He heard someone needing help and thought, 'Quick, we have to fix it!' When he couldn't, he sometimes got angry. . . . Most of our callers would *like* us to fix their lives, they'd like to drop their problems in our lap. They tell us there's nowhere to turn, but there usually is. And we have to help them find that person or place. I think if we had a motto, it would be to help the callers help themselves."

Occasionally, a caller is in a crisis in which he cannot be helped to help himself, and more direct action is needed. While some prevention centers, to preserve confidentiality, do not trace calls or mediate with third-party callers, the SPC does both. (In recent years, the counselors' task has become harder because an increasing number of callers use cell phones, which are difficult, although not impossible, to trace. Another telephonic advance, caller ID, has made their job easier by enabling them to recognize previous clients.) Although "we try to avoid it as much as possible because it can be so traumatic," says Sandri Kramer, about once a week a counselor must send the police or an ambulance to a caller's home. In keeping with the SPC's philosophy of helping the clients to help themselves, the counselor will first try to get the caller or someone else in the home to take such action or at least agree to let the counselor do so. If the caller refuses to give his address, the counselor will try to keep him on the line long enough to trace the call (which can take several hours) and dispatch emergency help.

More often, however, a counselor will maneuver behind the scenes. Beverly Kalasardo was on the line when a fifteen-year-old girl in tears called from her high school. Her boyfriend had just received his grades and realized he was going to fail. Making her promise not to tell anyone, he told the girl he had a shotgun and was going to kill himself. Kalasardo calmed the girl as they tried to find a solution. They couldn't talk to the boy's parents; his father was an abusive alcoholic, and his mother wouldn't have cared. They couldn't talk to her parents; they didn't like the boy either. Kalasardo asked the girl if she would feel comfortable talking to the school counselor. The girl said no. "I asked her if I could, and she said yes," recalls Kalasardo. "So I called the counselor and explained the problem. Meanwhile, the girl talked to their friends, who walked the boy from class to class. The counselor called the boy in, and without letting him know he knew about his plans for suicide, told him he had been looking at his grades, and while it was a shame that they were low, he could go to summer school and pull them up without hurting his record. The boy hadn't thought of this option and was relieved. He told the girl. She called me. Later, she wrote me a nice thank-you letter."

Endings are not always so happy. The SPC has estimated that between 1 and 2 percent of its callers eventually commit suicide. Although they don't make a point of reading the obituaries, the staff members occasionally find out. When this happens, they meet to share their grief and to talk about how the caller had been handled, what might have been done differently, and what might be done in the future. One of the most disturbing deaths occurred when a shy, young, unemployed accountant who had worked as a volunteer on the lines became depressed and suicidal. One day he called and told a volunteer he was going to kill himself. He asked the volunteer to call the police because he was terrified that his body might lie undiscovered for a long time. Keeping the young man on the line, the volunteer had another volunteer call the police. While the volunteer was still on the phone, the man shot himself the moment he heard the police knock on the door.

Such incidents explain why SPC staffers stress the importance of recognizing one's limits. "A lot of you came here thinking, 'I'm going to give these people something magic,' " Kalasardo used to tell each new class of trainees. "I know I did. And it was a rude awakening to realize I couldn't. Please understand your limitations. You're going to want to take them by the hand and lead them to a new life. But you can't. There is no special magic that will give a caller a new life or that will keep a caller from committing suicide if he really wants to. All you can do is listen, really listen. That's what people need when they're hurting. You may think that listening's not very much, but you may be the first person to ever listen to them. And you may be the last."

It was past eleven. As the city of Los Angeles began to fall asleep, the volunteers at the center were trying to put people to bed, like air traffic controllers trying to talk pilots down through heavy storms for a safe landing. But some did not want to come down and ended up circling, circling. As the call continued, Pat leaned still lower over the desk and held the phone even tighter against her ear, as if by sheer will she might be able to squeeze across Los Angeles to some unknown room and sit beside this nineteen-year-old girl. They had been talking for more than an hour. Pat could feel the girl, like a fish on a line, pull away, then come closer, then pull away again. Pat was trying different approaches, her voice now a little softer, now probing, nudging, but never losing its concern. She asked fewer questions and offered more suggestions. Although the girl had opened up a little, her voice was still a small, thin monotone, and she kept coming back to the Percodan and whether nine would be enough.

"Are you determined to take those nine Percodan?" Pat asked. "I can't stop you. I hope you don't do that. . . . I think you're making a mistake. . . . It's going to take a little more strength to choose a different option." Her voice became firmer. "No, you haven't. You have *not* tried everything. . . . I suspect you're stronger than you sound. . . . I think you deny your strength." Pat sensed the girl retreating. "I can't give you anything you don't already have. But I don't want you to hurt yourself. I don't want you to kill yourself. Do you think you can get through tonight?" Pat paused. "You may be moving into a place where you are going to have to grow, and that may feel very threatening to you. But you need to share this with your therapist. Will you call her tomorrow? . . . Would you let *me* call her tomorrow? . . . Have you thought about changing your therapist? . . . Why don't you ask your psychology teacher to suggest a therapist? . . . Why would it embarrass you? . . . But you're *not* crazy." Pat was silent for a moment. "Go to that teacher and ask for a therapist." Pat listened. "One more thing: If you're thinking of killing yourself at any point again, will you call us first? . . . Will you? . . ." As the girl apologized for taking up so much of Pat's time and thanked her for listening, Pat imperceptibly shook her head, then said softly, "Thank you for calling."

After the girl hung up, Pat held the phone in midair, staring at it as if more words or tears might still pour out. Then she gently set it in its cradle. She let out a deep sigh. "Oh, mercy," she said. It was 11:20, and she had been on the phone for eighty minutes. "I think she's going to kill herself," she said, "or at least make an attempt." For the first time since she'd taken the call, she sounded tired and a bit defeated. "I told her I can't keep her from killing herself, but also you have to remember you can't make her kill herself." She shrugged. "You have to hold on to that, working here." Pat nodded her head slowly, sadly. "She hung up crying, and when I picked up the call, she was crying."

Another counselor who had also just finished a call walked in and plopped down on the couch. The SPC stresses the importance of talking over each call afterward to give oneself time to recover before the next and to help forestall burnout. (The average volunteer works on the lines for about two years.) "I really felt I took it as far as I could," Pat said to her colleague, "that if we went any further, we'd get redundant." She began to write up the call, then looked away. "She was the most fragile caller I've ever had," she said. "It was like trying to hold water in your hands. It just keeps slipping through." Pat was quiet. For eighty minutes she had been aware only of the girl, of the sound of their voices meeting in the phone. Now the world began to come back. The sound of traffic spilling through the venetian blinds was softer now, almost soothing. It was 11:30. The phone rang. Pat put on her glasses, picked up the receiver, and in a warm, gentle voice said, "Hello, can I help you?"

# II

# SUICIDOLOGY

SUICIDE PREVENTION is not a new idea, but the use of kindness, care, and patience, as demonstrated by Pat and the SPC, is by and large a twentieth-century development. The first recorded instance of suicide prevention occurred in 600 BC when Roman soldiers, forced to cut drains and sewers, considered the work beneath a warrior's dignity and threw themselves off the Capitoline Rock. The epidemic abated only when the king, Tarquinius Priscus, ruled that soldiers who killed themselves would be crucified in public and abandoned to the birds and beasts of prey. For the next two millennia desecration of the corpse, confiscation of property, exorcism, and sermons enumerating the tortures of hell were what passed for suicide prevention. Although an occasional clergyman earned a reputation for his ability to rid suicidal people of their demons, or an asylum director gained renown for the efficacy of his "moral treatment," the notion that suicidal people should be helped rather than terrorized didn't take root until 1906, when Henry Marsh Warren founded the National Save-A-Life League.

Warren was a thirty-nine-year-old Baptist minister who left his New Hampshire parish to go to New York City, where he became pastor at the Central Park Baptist Church. He also held regular services in hotel lobbies around the city for what he called The Parish of All Strangers. One evening a twenty-year-old girl staying at a Broadway hotel called the manager and asked to speak to a minister. The manager was unable to reach Warren that night. The following morning a maid found the woman unconscious, an empty bottle marked POISON nearby. She was rushed to Bellevue Hospital, where Warren went to her bedside. The girl told Warren she was from a small West Coast town, had been jilted by her boyfriend, and had come to New York, where nobody knew her, to kill herself. She had wanted to talk to a minister first, she said, but had been too miserable to wait. "I think maybe if I had talked to someone like you," she told Warren, "I wouldn't have done it." Not long afterward she died.

If in its many retellings over the years the story of the young woman and the minister has gained a suspiciously smooth veneer, the result of their meeting is indisputable. In his next sermon to The Parish of All Strangers, the shaken Warren described the girl and cried, "I wish that all who believed that death is the only solution to their problems would give me a chance to prove them wrong." He placed an ad in the newspaper urging anyone considering suicide to call on him. In the following week eleven people appeared. All of them admitted they had decided to kill themselves, yet all were eager to pour out their despair. Warren listened. All eleven eventually abandoned their plans. Warren gave up his pastorate, set up an office in his home on Washington Square, and devoted himself to what he called the National Save-A-Life League.

The idea that someone might *welcome* dealing with suicidal people was novel, and ministers, doctors, and social workers were delighted to send these troublesome people to the league. (At the turn of the century many physicians, in fact, refused to treat suicidal people, who were believed to be insane or doomed to suicide by heredity; suicide was a crime and a sin, and the medical profession did not wish to contaminate itself with such cases. Suicidal people were scorned, ignored, or locked up in mental hospitals.) Newspaper stories and word of mouth drew others, and soon about eight people a day were arriving at the league's offices, where they were treated with what Warren described as "human sympathy and understanding," by himself or one of several volunteers. While one-third of the cases required more than that and were referred to psychiatrists, Warren found that merely by giving troubled people a chance to talk confidentially to a stranger, he could help them get through a crisis. Although Warren believed "the one sure remedy lies in Paul's message to his Philippian jailer, 'Believe in the Lord Jesus Christ and thou shalt be saved,'" he did not proselytize and in a pinch was quick to offer more earthly aid: money to tide them over, a square meal, a train ticket home, or an invitation to rest at his twenty-one-room home in Hastings-on-Hudson, ten miles north of the city.

Warren didn't wait for would-be suicides to come to him. He arranged with churches, hospitals, and the police to interview attempted suicides and scanned the newspapers for stories about suicide and suicide attempts. Local attempters were visited by a league fieldworker. Out-of-towners received letters advising them against the futility of their act and, where possible, referring them to a league volunteer in their city. (Eventually, the league had representatives in thirty-five cities and received two thousand letters a year asking for help.) Families of New York City suicides were visited as soon after the death as possible, to be comforted, counseled, and, if necessary, helped financially. Children of suicides were sent to summer camp for a week at the league's expense, to help them "forget." At one time the league, which did not charge for its services and was funded by private donations, sponsored its own Saturday-morning radio show in which it presented dramatizations of its cases and invited public support. In 1932, league volunteers interviewed 2,816 would-be suicides or their friends at its offices and visited 1,084 families in which suicides had occurred and 2,168 homes where suicide had been attempted. According to Warren, the National Save-A-Life League more than lived up to its name; he claimed the league saved one thousand people a year. By 1940, when Warren died and his son Harry Warren Jr. took over the operation, the league, by its own estimation, had saved thirty-four thousand lives.

By then several other suicide prevention organizations were in operation. In 1906, the same year in which the league began, the Salvation Army founded the London Anti-Suicide Bureau, offering free consultation, sympathy, and advice. During its first year, 1,125 men and 90 women applied to the London Bureau, more than half of whom, according to Salvation Army founder General William Booth, had been driven to the brink of suicide by financial problems. Branches were established in Berlin, New York, Chicago, and Melbourne. Elsewhere, Zurich established its Anti-Suicide League, and Berlin a Suicides' Aid Society. In Budapest, after a wave of 150 suicides by drowning in April and May 1928, a "suicide flotilla" patrolled the Danube and managed to save nine of ten would-be suicides. In Odessa an antisuicide museum displayed firearms, knives, and poison bottles left by people who had killed themselves, as well as grateful letters from those dissuaded from their plans.

Vienna offered the would-be suicide a smorgasbord of services. All suicide attempts that came to police attention were reported to the welfare department. A written summons was issued to the attempter, and if it was ignored, a social worker made a house call. The social workers helped the attempters find housing, employment, and financial assistance. The Ethical Society Agency for Suicidal Persons, founded in 1927, tried to reach the despairing *before* they made an attempt. From six to eight each evening, lay volunteers and social workers were available to listen and provide advice, referrals, and occasionally financial aid to troubled people. Trained workers interviewed relatives, friends, and employers and acted as mediators in family disputes and housing squabbles. To promote an esprit de corps among its clients, the center organized an annual banquet at which leading Viennese stage performers provided entertainment. To help prevent adolescent suicide, Vienna opened a youth counseling service in 1928, in which about thirty lawyers, teachers, physicians, social workers, and priests offered advice in their own homes. Unfortunately, these organizations disbanded when their leaders were forced to flee during the Nazi occupation.

One suicide prevention agency still going strong traces its roots to 1935, when a recently ordained twenty-four-year-old Anglican minister named Chad Varah officiated at the funeral of a thirteen-year-old girl who, menstruating for the first time, didn't understand, had no one to ask, and killed herself. Her death made a deep impression on Varah, who had always been more interested in counseling than in other kinds of parochial work. In 1953, in response to a magazine article he had written on "the new morality," he received fourteen letters from people who said their problems had driven them to the verge of suicide. "They didn't need professional help," Varah recalls. "They needed someone to talk to, someone to listen. They needed a friend." Varah read that there were three suicides a day in London. He imagined them "dying miserably in lonely hotel rooms." Varah took out a newspaper ad that invited people contemplating suicide to telephone or visit him, and on November 2, 1953, he set up shop in the crypt of his church, St. Stephen, Walbrook, in London's business district. A newspaper article later gave Varah's service its name—the Samaritans.

In the beginning Varah and his secretary manned the telephone, but soon so many people were calling and coming in to talk to him that volunteers were recruited to make tea for the troubled as they waited in line. By the time they reached Varah, many didn't need to see him—they already felt better after talking to the volunteers. Varah decided to use the volunteers to talk to the clients and found that caring contact between two people reduced the client's loneliness and despair. The concept of "befriending," as Varah called it, had been born. Befriending might mean a volunteer and a client talking on the phone, meeting for tea, or visiting at the Samaritan office or in the client's home. Befriending was not counseling or therapy; volunteer and client met on equal ground. The recruiting slogan for volunteers was "Are you ordinary enough to be a Samaritan?"

Befriending was not intended to obviate professional help, but Varah's hunch that fear kept many people from seeking that help was justified. The Samaritans befriended one hundred clients that first year; today, there are 203 Samaritan branches in the United Kingdom, staffed by eighteen thousand volunteers, that receive nearly 5 million calls each year. Troubled people can call Samaritans in fifty countries, including Armenia, Egypt, Israel, Russia, the United States, and Zimbabwe. Despite their extraordinary expansion—they have become a veritable McDonald's of suicide prevention—the Samaritans have retained their intimacy and efficacy by clinging to their original formula. Over the years, erudite researchers have made many attempts to analyze the essence of befriending, but as one Samaritan volunteer put it, "In its purest form, befriending is love."

For many years the National Save-A-Life League was the only prevention group in the United States. Other organized efforts to help the suicidal disappeared almost as quickly as they began. In 1936, for example, Robert Rehkugel, a sixty-four-year-old Methodist pastor in Oakland, announced plans for the Suicide Prevention Society of America, in which retired pastors would counsel potential suicides. Rehkugel planned a Suicide Prevention Sunday, a Suicide Prevention Week, and a Suicide Prevention Patrol of men and women to intercept would-be suicides and restore them to their families. The society's motto, he said, was Prevent, Seek, and Save; its goal, a 50 percent decrease in suicide by 1940. Beyond the fact that this goal wasn't met, it is not known what became of the project. Fifteen years later Julia Shelhamer, a seventy-year-old minister's widow, distressed by reading of the suicide of a prominent Washington, D.C., man, placed a classified ad in the newspaper: "Discouraged? Call DI0614." Her phone rang steadily—one Sunday she received 110 calls. Her remedy was to listen to callers' problems, then ask them to pray with her. In 1935, department store tycoon Marshall Field financed the Committee for the Study of Suicide. Under the direction of prominent psychiatrist Gregory Zilboorg, it collected in-depth data on more than fifteen hundred suicides, but work was suspended shortly after the United States entered World War II.

Beyond these isolated examples, the field of suicide and suicide prevention was primitive and taboo in the first half of this century. Indeed, there was no "field." "Prior to the 1950s, except for the efforts of a few courageous practitioners, suicide went untreated as a mental health problem and was hardly ever discussed," psychiatrist Calvin Frederick has written. "It was rarely a point of focus in the media, or in professional literature." Although an occasional sociologist flung a statistical net at suicide, the subject was not considered a respectable research topic. The word itself seemed distasteful to professionals. (As late as 1955 a Veterans Administration project on suicide was tactfully named the Central Research Unit for the Study of Unpredicted Deaths.) The few papers to be found in the professional literature consisted of a handful of case histories or brief vignettes. No one had attempted to systematically examine the psychological characteristics of suicide and to use that research in prevention. Then, in November 1949, a thirty-one-year-old psychologist found himself alone in a room with hundreds of suicide notes.

———————

Edwin Shneidman was a precocious young man who entered the University of California at Los Angeles at the age of sixteen. He earned his master's degree in psychology before serving as a captain in the U.S. Army Air Force. After the war he received his Ph.D. from the University of Southern California and began work at the Veterans Administration Neuropsychiatric Hospital in Brentwood. In November 1949, he was asked to draft letters of condolence to the widows of two former VA patients who had committed suicide. To find out more about the men, he visited the Los Angeles County coroner's office one rainy afternoon. In a basement vault lined with dusty folders, Shneidman found the folder for one of the men, which contained copies of the man's suicide note. He looked in another folder and another and realized that the coroner's office had been filing suicide notes in this room for decades. Shneidman spent the afternoon rummaging through the folders. Though Shneidman's interest in suicide until then had been tangential, he realized that the study of suicide was "a virgin field." "I felt," he says, "like a Texas millionaire coming home and stumbling into a pool of oil."

Shneidman called Norman Farberow, a VA psychologist who had written his doctoral dissertation on attempted suicide, and told him about the notes. Like Shneidman, Farberow was thirty-one, had attended UCLA, and had been a captain in the army air force. Following the war he and Shneidman were fellow trainees in the new VA clinical training program, where they became friends. While their backgrounds were similar, the two men were vastly different in appearance and temperament. Shneidman, a short, compact man, sizzled with energy like water on a frying pan; Farberow was a slim, neat, almost elegant man with the manners and bearing of a diplomat. Shneidman's feisty, restless drive could be grating; the word used most often to describe Farberow is *gentleman*. For many years the two of them would make ideal collaborators.

With their cache of 721 notes, Shneidman and Farberow believed they might discover the key to suicidal motivation in the last words of people who kill themselves. They decided to compare the notes with a control group of simulated suicide notes—"pseudocide notes," as Shneidman dubbed them—composed by nonsuicidal people. Visiting labor unions and fraternities, they asked members to write the note they would write if they were about to take their own life. While some of the longshoremen were skeptical—"You could see them smirking, thinking to themselves, 'What are these crazy people doing?'" Farberow remembers—they complied. The genuine and simulated notes were typed on index cards, numbered, and shuffled. Then Shneidman and Farberow analyzed them blindly. When they broke the key, they found that the pseudocide notes showed no particular personality patterns; the real notes betrayed various but recognizable characteristics. Fifteen percent, for instance, were written by what they called surcease suicides—older people seeking a release from pain. Many notes reflected a marked ambivalence—it seemed that part of the writer wanted to live, part to die. One note succinctly illustrated this: "Dear Mary: I hate you. Love, George."

The suicide-note study was just the beginning. Working out of a cramped basement room in the VA hospital, Shneidman and Farberow began a massive examination of attempted, threatened, and completed suicide. From the coroner's office they collected the names of eight thousand people who had killed themselves over a ten-year period. Then they combed through two hundred thousand files at hospitals and clinics for the names, collecting the suicide notes, case histories, psychological test results, diaries, and therapy records of these suicides. From physicians they gathered data on 501 attempted suicides. They wandered the wards of Los Angeles County General Hospital interviewing people who had attempted or threatened suicide. And from the local VA hospital they assembled a sample of nonsuicidal patients.

Their findings contradicted several widely held beliefs. Though it had long been assumed that people who threatened suicide never committed it, they found that three-fourths of suicides followed previous threats or attempts. Though it had long been assumed that "you have to be insane to commit suicide," they found that only 15 percent of suicides were psychotic. The vast majority were depressed. They discovered that almost half of those who killed themselves did so within ninety days after an emotional crisis, and at a time when they seemed to be recovering; one-third had seen a physician within six months of their death; most suicides were neither crazy people hell-bent on death nor people whose suicide came "out of the blue." These depressed people didn't really want to die; they left clues to their plans, and if family and friends had been alert to those clues, they might have been able to prevent the suicide. As Shneidman put it, it was possible for a person "to cut his throat and cry for help at the same time."

Shneidman and Farberow intended to confine their efforts to research, but as they prowled hospital wards gathering data, they developed a reputation among the staff as suicide experts. Nurses began asking them to speak with patients who had been admitted following an attempt. The two psychologists politely refused; they were doing research, not therapy. "They'd say, 'This man came in last night; he drank some cleaning fluid. Would you talk to him?' or 'This man cut his throat. Would you speak with him?' But we said, 'We can't talk to him, we're here on research,'" recalls Shneidman. "Our access to patients dried up. Then someone advised us to buy candy for the nurse, and when she asked us to see a patient, say yes. 'But we know nothing about suicide,' I told him. He said, 'You know more than she does.'" Shneidman chuckles. "And willy-nilly we were in the treatment business."

That Shneidman and Farberow were accepted as clinical experts on suicide merely because of their interest in the topic is not surprising. If the subject of suicide was ignored by researchers, it was anathema to clinicians. "There wasn't much known or written about the suicidal patient—treatment was very hit-or-miss," recalls a social worker. "Most professionals did not want to deal with them. They were afraid of the responsibility. Social workers and psychologists referred—or deferred—to psychiatrists because they were able to hospitalize." Psychiatrists were no better equipped. "I was taught *nothing* about suicide in medical school and virtually nothing in my residencies," says one psychiatrist. "It was just something that you prayed wouldn't happen, and if you had a suicidal patient, you put him in the hospital." The hospital was equally unenlightened. "There was very little specific treatment of the suicide problem and very little understanding of why a person might be suicidal," says a social worker. "The standard procedure was to put all suicidal patients on one ward and just watch them a little more closely." Fear and ignorance were compounded by the anger many physicians felt at the suicidal patient, especially at those who were rushed to the hospital after an attempt. "Medical staffs were overworked, and many doctors resented spending their time and talents on the suicidal," says a social worker. "Some doctors while sewing up someone's wrists would say, 'You didn't do that right—next time you have to cut *this* way to do the job.'" Follow-up care was rare. "The idea was to pump them out, patch them up, and get them home as soon as possible," says Shneidman. "Nobody wanted the responsibility."

Eventually, Shneidman and Farberow began to discuss combining clinical and research activities in a service for suicide attempters. "We thought of it as a suicide prevention referral service," says Farberow. "The idea was to evaluate and help suicidal people while they were in the hospital, then make sure they got to some kind of resource in the community." They called Robert Litman, director of the psychiatric unit at Cedars-Sinai Hospital, a bright young clinician who had written a paper on how to deal with suicide on a hospital ward. "They had been working with notes and charts, and now they wanted to work with people," recalls Litman, whose interest in the subject of suicide had been sparked when his former college classmate Thomas Heggen, author of *Mr. Roberts,* had taken an overdose and drowned in a bathtub. "They took me to a restaurant in Beverly Hills and literally plied me with liquor. Then they said, 'What do you think about the idea of a suicide prevention center?' I said, 'You're kidding.' They said, 'We'll put an ad in the telephone book saying suicide prevention, and suicidal people will get in touch with us. You'll take care of them, and we'll study them.'" Litman chuckles, remembering. "I thought it was crazy," he says. "I thought we would attract all the crazy people in town, and we wouldn't be able to handle them."

With the help of Harold Hildreth, a psychologist at the National Institute of Mental Health who believed that NIMH should be exploring taboo areas, Shneidman and Farberow were awarded a five-year, $377,000 demonstration grant, an extraordinary sum considering the time and the subject matter. Meanwhile, Shneidman, Farberow, and Litman discussed names for their service. They agreed that the title should include the word *suicide.* "It was time for the taboo problem and its attendant stigma to be brought out into the open where it could be acknowledged and dealt with openly and constructively," they wrote. "We were also aware that what we were planning to do was not *prev*ention, it was *inter*vention," recalls Litman. "But Suicide *Inter*vention Center?" He shrugs. "Didn't have a ring to it. Sounded lofty. So we decided to call it Suicide Prevention Center as a challenge rather than hide behind a less provocative title." On September 1, 1958, the Los Angeles Suicide Prevention Center opened with one phone line and a staff of five.

From its earliest days the LASPC had an improvised, informal quality. The center was located in an abandoned and condemned tuberculosis ward on the grounds of the Los Angeles County General Hospital. The dilapidated, eight-story redbrick building, ringed with creaky wooden porches where TB patients had taken the sun, had a rococo appeal; television crews filming a story on the center would inevitably drift off to examine the architecture. The center was on the fourth floor, accessible by a clanging, wheezing, often out-of-order elevator. The rooms were high-ceilinged and dimly lit; some were tiled and held bathtubs twice the size of humans. Although a fresh coat of paint and shipments of secondhand desks and chairs from the VA made their corner of the building livable, the setting was bleak. Even as they moved in, the structure was being vandalized by community agencies for plumbing and electricity. One morning a Hollywood film crew arrived; the LASPC's home, it seemed, made an ideal bombed-out building for their latest World War II movie. "We were concerned that the building would make our clients even more depressed," says Sam Heilig, a social worker who joined the center in 1960, "but when we'd ask patients if it depressed them, they said no, it sort of fit their mood." The hospital used a system of colored lines painted on the floor to guide patients to various departments from the guard station at the street. It seemed fitting that the line leading to the LASPC offices was painted blue.

In its first year the LASPC worked with fifty patients. Each Monday morning Litman would walk over to the county hospital and scout the wards for people who had been admitted over the weekend for a suicide attempt. Usually, there would be at least a half dozen, from which one would be selected as the center's "case of the week." Litman conducted a full psychiatric interview, a psychologist gathered test information, and a social worker interviewed the patient's family and friends. At Friday-morning staff meetings the case was discussed in detail, and treatment recommendations and referrals to appropriate agencies were made. The goal was to examine each case intensively, to learn as much as possible about why that person had tried to kill himself. "None of us knew anything at that time, so we went very slowly," recalls Farberow.

"That was our intention," says Litman. "But what happened was that these people told their friends and their friends told their friends, and pretty soon people were calling us and literally saying, 'I'm just about to make a suicide attempt—do I have to take these pills or jump off a building before I can talk to you? Or could I shortcut it and come in directly?'" The LASPC became a magnet for suicidal people. Calls came from distressed people, concerned friends and relatives, and therapists happy to refer their difficult cases. One early call came from a teacher who walked into her classroom during recess and found a student hiding behind the blackboard with a plastic bag over his head. When she yanked the bag off and brought the boy around, his first words were "That's all right. I have a knife at home." The boy was seven. He was referred to a psychiatric service. Another call came from a frantic psychiatrist. His patient was in the next room behind a locked door with a gun. What should he do? The staff member on duty calmed the psychiatrist, then talked him through the crisis, telling him not to call the police but to take his time, talk to the man, and bring in his friends and family. The psychiatrist followed the advice. Eventually the door opened, and his patient emerged and surrendered the gun.

Because no rules or guidelines existed for dealing with suicidal people, the LASPC improvised techniques as they went along. Though most of the staff had been trained in Rogerian or Freudian models, these strategies seemed impotent in a suicidal crisis. When a person was out on a ledge, metaphorically or otherwise, it seemed feckless merely to repeat back to him what he was saying and too time-consuming to take five years on the couch to find out why he was up there. "Both of those have given way to better clinical common sense," Shneidman wrote. "That is, we became directive, assertive, straightforward, even authoritarian—anything that it takes to keep a person from becoming a case in the coroner's office." To fulfill its mission the LASPC went to lengths unheard of in traditional therapeutic circles: the staff made house calls, met clients in restaurants, escorted suicidal people to the hospital, brought in family and friends, phoned across country to get one man's estranged wife to come and see him, dispatched ambulances or police, and traced calls. One day a client ran out of the offices onto the roof with several LASPC staff members in hot pursuit; they grabbed her and wrestled her back inside before she could jump. Another time a suicidal young woman was brought in by her family; halfway through the consultation she ran out of the building. An LASPC staffer tackled her, put her in a car, and told her brother to sit on her while he drove her to the hospital.

Like polar explorers, the LASPC staff probed the boundaries of the vast, uncharted territory of suicide and its prevention. Shneidman skittered out on the edge, mapping and naming the new field, inventing its vocabulary, sparking ideas, giving speeches, and writing papers. His wild, often abrasive brilliance was complemented by Farberow's meticulous organization, dependable scholarship, and attention to detail. As clinical director, Litman was the glue that held the center together, as he saw his own patients, oversaw everyone else's caseload, and assumed the responsibility for medication and hospitalization. On the rare occasions when a client committed suicide (of the center's first three hundred patients, there were two), Litman led the painful meeting at which the case was discussed; the staff tried to comprehend what had led to the person's decision and what else might have been done to prevent it. Litman had some of the imagination of Shneidman and the affability of Farberow and worked well with both of them. His genial, quirky manner and enthusiasm helped give the staff the feeling of a team. Suicide prevention, in fact, tended to scramble the mental health pecking order that placed psychiatrists at the top, followed by psychologists and then social workers. At the LASPC *everyone* was involved, and there were few rules about who did what. One of the most adept at handling desperate callers, in fact, was the receptionist, Alice

Arnold, an outgoing woman who had never worked in the mental health field before. "She was supposed to take business calls, but when none of us was available, she had to take a lot of suicide calls," remembers Litman. "And she was great on the telephone. . . . When all else fails, you can fall back on being motherly and probably be right."

For many years suicide had been a subject no one talked about. On the fourth floor of the old TB building, people talked of little else. "People used to ask us wasn't it depressing, but it was very lively," says Sam Heilig. "We had a great camaraderie, and we had a lot of laughs." And because no one had ever before made this kind of intensive effort to study suicide, there was a feeling among the staff that they might solve the enigma. "I really thought that within a few years we would unravel some of the mysteries of why a person takes his life," says David Klugman, a psychiatric social worker who joined the staff in 1960. "I believed that by analyzing each event in depth as it happened, we'd find some key or clue that would explain it. Maybe I was a little naive, but I thought we were going to find the answer."

While they did not find the answer, they developed many of the concepts and techniques that are now standard in the field. (And published them. Between 1956 and 1966, Shneidman, Farberow, and Litman alone authored, coauthored, or edited four books and more than eighty papers on suicide, ranging from "Suicide Among General Medical and Surgical Hospital Patients with Malignant Neoplasms" to "Sex and Suicide.") They developed the concept of clues. They developed the concept of lethality, described by Shneidman as "the probability of an individual killing himself in the immediate future." Previously, a person was thought to be suicidal, or he wasn't. The LASPC proposed that some suicidal people are at higher risk than others, and for each person the degree of risk or "lethality" fluctuates over time. They devised a Suicide Potential Rating Scale, a fifteen-item questionnaire based on demographic and psychological factors, to measure that risk. They developed the idea of "the suicidal crisis"—that most people are acutely suicidal for a relatively short time and, if helped through that time, will survive. During that crisis the LASPC stressed the importance of active intervention, constant contact with the patient, calling in the family, and breaking confidentiality if necessary. They described suicide as a "dyadic" event and suggested involving a person's "significant other" in treatment whenever possible. And for those who work with suicidal people, they stressed the importance of frequent consultations, sharing the burden, and working as a team.

In 1958, after giving a speech at the VA hospital, Shneidman and Farberow were approached by Theodore Curphey, chief medical examiner–coroner for Los Angeles County, whose office was responsible for determining the cause (heart attack, gunshot, and so forth) and mode (natural, accident, homicide, or suicide) of all deaths in the county. Each year some one hundred deaths were regarded as equivocal—the coroner was unable to determine whether the death was an accident or a suicide. Curphey suggested that the LASPC might be able to help. Just as pathologists and toxicologists ascertained the cause of death by examining physical evidence, the LASPC staff might collect psychological evidence, interviewing relatives and friends of the victim to reconstruct his state of mind preceding his death. LASPC staff members were made deputy coroners, and the Death Investigation Team annually performed more than one hundred "psychological autopsies," as Shneidman named them. Their most celebrated case was number 435: Marilyn Monroe. When she died of an overdose of barbiturates on August 4, 1962, Curphey asked Farberow and Litman to investigate. By interviewing Monroe's friends and associates they learned that she had attempted suicide twice before and that she had been deeply depressed before her death. Their recommendation was for "probable suicide." (Psychological autopsies are now commonly used to help determine cause of death as well as in suicide research.)

In the media glare following Monroe's death the "professional suicide workers" of the center's "suicide team" received nationwide attention, and the LASPC caseload grew exponentially. "By this time we knew that we needed to expand our services," says Farberow. "We had been conducting ourselves like a clinic, with regular office hours, eight to five. But people were calling us after hours. We knew that because the lines continued to ring whenever one of us was working late. It was usually somebody looking for help." Before long, they were in what Litman calls "the telephone business." They started by hiring a telephone exchange to transfer calls to staff members' homes. But the staff was small, and after a few weeks they realized that they were losing too much sleep. So they trained professionals—psychiatric interns, graduate students in psychology or social work—and paid them $10 a night to take the calls at home. With the Night Watch program, help was now available twenty-four hours a day.

But the volume of calls continued to mount, and in 1964 the center decided to use trained nonprofessionals on the telephone. Although at the time the National Save-A-Life League and England's Samaritans used lay volunteers, the LASPC prided itself on its professional approach. "I had a lot of reservations," admits Klugman. "By 1960 I had a master's in social work and seven years of field experience, yet I felt ill-prepared and inadequate to handle some of the situations I was dealing with on the phone. So how were we going to train middle-aged housewives to do this?" Once they started, however, the LASPC learned the lesson the Samaritans had learned—that trained laypersons can do as well as professionals, even better in some ways. "They didn't let their professional guard get in the way," says Farberow. "They were able to interact on a very direct, personal basis with the suicidal person." The volunteers even began to see an occasional patient in the office and to provide counseling in selected cases. The LASPC caseload continued to grow. In 1966 the center was contacted by nearly seven thousand people.

Not only was the center's caseload expanding, but their single-minded devotion to suicide lured other professionals out of the woodwork. In 1963, having received a major increase and extension of its NIMH grant, the center moved out of the old TB ward and into a two-story building near downtown Los Angeles. Their new home on Pico Boulevard became a hub for the study of suicide and its prevention. Requests for advice, consultations, reprints, and speeches poured in from around the country and eventually from around the world. Staff members traveled the nation, teaching evaluation and treatment techniques to physicians, nurses, police, clergy, and mental health profession-als. The center produced films for police and for physicians on how to handle suicidal people. Twice a year the center offered three-to-five-day training insti-tutes for people from all over the country interested in starting a suicide pre-vention center in their own community.

The center's diversity gave it the atmosphere of a small university. Clergy, sociologists, and psychologists visited the center to study suicide or to study how the LASPC studied suicide. Graduate students and interns spent semes-ters training at the center. Visiting professors gave speeches on suicide and self-destruction. Friday-morning "case of the week" seminars were renowned for their spirited intellectual discourse. Shneidman organized a program in which distinguished scholars, including sociologist Erving Goffman, philoso-pher Stephen Pepper, and psychologist Elsa Whalley, spent several months at the center "to contemplate suicide and to think about death." Farberow, who spent 1964 abroad studying prevention organizations in London, Berlin, Paris, and Vienna, became active in the fledgling International Association for Suicide Prevention, and the LASPC's stream of visitors gained a global flavor. Ten years earlier no one had talked about suicide in the professional commu-nity; now the LASPC had become a sort of international think tank devoted solely to the study of suicide and its prevention.

Although their work had begun as a research effort and had only by serendipity come to include clinical work and the use of trained volunteers, Shneidman and Farberow now felt that their most important task was to dis-seminate the knowledge they had gathered. Comparing the suicide prevention center to "a lifeguard station on a dangerous beach," they believed that every city of any size across the country should have its own center. "Shneidman had no doubt in his mind that suicide prevention should be a movement," says a colleague. "When we talked about a suicide prevention center in every com-munity, he carried it to the extreme—that *every* person should be a one-man suicide prevention center, should know the signs and be able to help in a sui-cidal crisis."

In 1965, Stanley Yolles, the director of NIMH, announced the establishment of a national center for research and dissemination of information on suicide. He asked Shneidman to head the project. Shneidman was ready to move on. He had become restless at the LASPC. For more than a decade he and Farberow had been partners and coauthors; one name was rarely seen in print without the other. In the public mind they were linked together as Shneidman and Farberow, suicide's Siamese twins. Shneidman was anxious to be on his own. The Center for Studies of Suicide Prevention, as it would be called, was an opportunity to advance both his own career and the growing suicide prevention movement. The following year he moved to Washington.

---

If suicide was still a taboo subject, suicide prevention had taken a giant step forward with the formation of the CSSP. The fifties and early sixties were a time of government largesse toward mental health, and in their 1966 reorganization NIMH designated five high-priority areas: alcoholism, drug abuse, child and family mental health, crime and delinquency, and suicide. For suicide, which only ten years before could not even be mentioned as a problem, it was an achievement of sorts. Now it had official recognition as a federal target, a social ill to be attacked, like poverty and crime, with good old American know-how and money. The CSSP could dispense grants for research, training, and demonstration projects, but the bottom line was clear. As Shneidman wrote not long after his arrival in Washington, "The goal of the NIMH Center for Studies of Suicide Prevention is to effect a reduction in the suicide rate in this country."

Suicidology—a word coined by Shneidman to describe the study of suicide and its prevention—had been born, and the movement's peripatetic ringmaster was everywhere, preaching prevention, inventing concepts, and fizzing with ideas. Identifying the dissemination of clues as "the most important single item for effective suicide prevention," Shneidman, who became known as Mr. Suicide, called for a program in "massive public education"—and carried it out almost single-handedly by writing pamphlets, organizing symposia, and giving hundreds of interviews. "The 'early signs' of suicide must be made known to each physician, clergyman, policeman, and educator in the land—and to each spouse, parent, neighbor, and friend," he declared. Toward this end the CSSP funded the *First Training Record in Suicidology,* in which actors dramatized calls to a prevention center; it commissioned *Quiet Cries,* a play highlighting the ambivalence shown by people experiencing suicidal crises; it assembled a "basic library on suicidology" of ten books and twelve pamphlets, available for $40 a set; it published a journal, the *Bulletin of Suicidology,* that kept people abreast of developments in the field. It promoted the First National Conference on Suicidology, at which Shneidman was voted founding president of the American Association of Suicidology, an alliance of mental health professionals, sociologists, clergy, and prevention center volunteers. It sponsored a postgraduate fellowship program in suicidology at Johns Hopkins University, in which social workers, sociologists, and psychologists took courses in crisis intervention, the psychology of suicide, biostatistics, suicide and the law, and the epidemiology of mental illness; worked in acute treatment clinics; performed psychological autopsies; did fieldwork in prevention centers; and acted as an expert witness in moot trials involving suicide. Suicide prevention now had not only federal sanction but academic credentials as well.

The most visible evidence of the CSSP's work was the proliferation of prevention centers. "Just as there are fire stations throughout our country, there ought to be suicide prevention centers in every part of the land," wrote Shneidman. There were fifteen when he arrived in Washington. A year later there were forty-seven, and by the time he left the CSSP in 1969 there were more than one hundred, with names like We Care, Dial A Friend, Learn Baby Learn, Life Line, Help, and Rescue, Inc. The suicide prevention movement coincided with the spirit of altruism and activism that marked the sixties, and saving lives seemed like the ultimate in caring. Magazines offered histrionic accounts of tearful calls and heroic rescues; movies like *The Slender Thread,* starring Sidney Poitier and Anne Bancroft, and *Dial Hotline,* with Vince Edwards and Kim Hunter, dramatized the risks and rewards of volunteering at a prevention center. Would-be lifesavers learned the ropes in articles that promised to teach them "How to Set Up a Suicide Prevention Center."

While the LASPC served as the prototype—many center directors trained there or used its manual—there were wide variations. Some centers were autonomous, others were affiliated with hospitals or community mental health centers. Some were organized by the clergy, others by physicians, social workers, psychologists, or nurses. While the common denominator was a twenty-four-hour phone line staffed by nonprofessional, trained volunteers, some centers offered face-to-face contact as well. A few offered group therapy. Some had outreach teams for emergencies; at one center volunteers accompanied policemen to the homes of attempters. San Francisco Suicide Prevention placed an ad in the newspaper inviting those too shy to call to write; a Gainesville, Florida, center encouraged suicidal pen pals. A prevention center in Buffalo hosted a weekly television and radio show on which the agency director interviewed people who had once attempted suicide and were now leading productive lives. One center served as an alternative service placement for conscientious objectors.

The CSSP did not fund centers for direct service, and most programs were dependent on community support. Budgets ranged from $500,000 yearly at the Buffalo center to $26.25 per month (the cost of a telephone and a listing) reported by a center in Bismarck, North Dakota. Centers raised funds with walkathons, dances, plays, dinners, rock concerts, house tours, and bingo. When donations fell short, volunteers often passed the hat among themselves. They publicized their services through interviews, telephone directories, brochures, bumper stickers, bookmarks, and newspaper, radio, and television ads. They posted flyers in banks, bars, barber shops, beauty parlors, bus stations, airports, motels, libraries, schools, factories, emergency rooms, police stations, and trailer parks. Some centers enclosed brochures with bank statements, industry paychecks, phone bills. The message was clear: suicide prevention was everyone's business. Shneidman even pointed out that suicide prevention was cost-effective; he calculated that every averted suicide saved as much as $1 million in lost wages and taxes as well as ambulance and coroner's costs.

But the growth of knowledge about suicide wasn't keeping pace with the zeal to prevent it. The movement's accomplishments were measured in quantity: the proliferation of centers, the number of articles written. In a bibliography covering 1897 to 1970, Farberow noted that more papers and books on suicide had been published in the last thirteen years (2,542) than in the previous sixty-one. But a review of these publications reveals few rigorous studies, more groping than exploration, and little of practical use. A sample of journal articles includes "Lunar Association with Suicide," in which the authors found a slight increase during the new moon, which they were at a loss to explain, and "Suicide in the Subway," which discovered "important differences" between those who lay in the train's path ("traumatic death") and those who touched the third rail ("nontraumatic death"). "One of the problems in the study of those who kill themselves is that the subject of the study is deceased and hence not available for study," began the article "Spiritualism and Suicide," which therefore suggested that mediums be used to contact suicides for research purposes. "If communication is established with a deceased suicide, it seems mundane to administer an MMPI or a Rorschach," observed the author, referring to two common psychological tests. "However, a psychoanalyst, for example, might well be able to conduct an interview that would illuminate the psychodynamics behind the act. Occasionally, though, spirits have their own agenda for communicating and object to questions."

The author had a point: research in suicide *is* limited by the fact that studies are ex post facto. "Individuals correctly determined to be suicides are not available for study," notes one psychologist. "They are at the morgue." Other methodological problems have frustrated suicidologists. Because suicide is a statistically rare event, it can take many years to accumulate a significant sample. There have been few long-term studies using sizable control groups. Some of the research is based on as few as two or three subjects, and the same case studies are trotted out again and again like prize pupils, often to illustrate different points. A 1972 summary of research findings since 1882 concluded that the vast majority of suicide research was monotonous, uninspired, and scientifically inept.

Meanwhile, there were mounting concerns about suicide prevention centers. By 1972 there were more than three hundred, but the feverish growth had been haphazard, and there were no accepted standards for service or training. The authors of a survey of 253 centers were "struck by the wide variability in training, efficiency, and effectiveness of the services." Callers to some centers had problems just getting through. When psychologist Richard McGee placed seventy-six calls to nineteen agencies in the Southeast, he was confronted by eight different types of answering and referral services—message machines, patch systems, callbacks, and so forth—and often experienced long delays before reaching a human being. A 1970 CSSP-sponsored task force, calling for the establishment of minimum standards for centers, admitted, "The establishment of suicide prevention programs was entered into by many who were serious and dedicated but, also, by others who were capricious and ill-advised. The result is a mixture of services which as a whole lack purpose, direction, commitment, and involvement."

Even more distressing was the growing evidence that suicide prevention centers were not preventing suicide. While centers often publicized their efforts by claiming their work "saved lives"—the National Save-A-Life League, for example, asserted that since 1906 they had saved one thousand lives per year—they offered no real proof. Few centers evaluated their services, and their assumption that the application of care and support prevented suicide was based on letters and calls from grateful clients. When a 1968 study found that the suicide rate in fifteen English towns with a Samaritan branch had fallen, the declining English suicide rate was credited to the Samaritans. But a subsequent, more carefully controlled study found no difference in the rates of comparable communities that had a Samaritan branch and those that did not. In the United States, psychologist David Lester compared eight cities that had prevention centers in 1967, eight with centers in 1969 (but not in 1967), and eight without centers during those years and found that the centers made no significant difference in the suicide rate. While centers provided a "needed and useful service" in counseling the distressed, Lester concluded that suicide was "relatively immune" to prevention programs. Other statistics seemed to support this. Between 1960 and 1970 the number of centers in California grew from one to nearly thirty; the suicide rate grew from 15.9 to 18.8. In Los Angeles, site of the movement's flagship prevention center, the rate jumped from 17.5 to 21.3. And in the United States as a whole it rose from 10.6 to 11.6.

The exaggerated hopes kindled by prevention programs underscored their apparent failure. The centers were discredited as quickly as they had been embraced. By 1969, Shneidman had left the CSSP for academia. Citing surveys that claimed only 12 to 15 percent of the calls to centers dealt with suicide, his successor, psychiatrist Harvey Resnik, advised centers to change their names to "Suicide Prevention and Crisis Intervention Center" to reach a broader base. The shift at CSSP reflected not only disappointment with the centers' failure to subdue the suicide rate but also the changing agenda of the federal government. During the late 1960s there was increasing pressure to do something about runaways, teenage pregnancy, and "the drug epidemic." When Bertram Brown became NIMH director in 1970, he designated child mental health as the institute's top priority. Child mental health was in, drug abuse was in, minority groups were in. Suicide was on its way out. The government, which in ten years had spent more than $10 million on suicide research, decided it was a bad investment. In 1972 the CSSP was disbanded, and the concept that had launched the Los Angeles Suicide Prevention Center more than a decade earlier—that suicide was a proper and necessary research topic, that suicidal people could and should be helped—had been diluted. Fifteen years after Shneidman, Farberow, and Litman insisted that the word *suicide* be a part of their new center's title, a sign on the bulletin board at the UCLA meditation center printed the LASPC's telephone number above this all-purpose encomium: "Need a place for a good rap? Call the Los Angeles Suicide Prevention Center."

---

Why didn't all this time, money, and sheer good intentions have a measurable effect? Research shows that most calls to prevention centers are not from the severely suicidal. In a study of ten centers, 33 percent of their callers had been considering suicide, and the percentage of seriously suicidal callers was far smaller. More than half of the four thousand calls received monthly at the Suicide Prevention and Crisis Center in Buffalo, for example, were from crank callers, pranksters, or people who hung up immediately. The majority of suicides are older white males; the majority of prevention center callers are young white females. Although some suggest that most people are simply not aware that prevention centers exist, a study by San Francisco psychiatrist Jerome Motto found that while 80 percent of a group of depressed and suicidal persons had heard of the local prevention center, only 11 percent had used it. Suicidal people, reasons sociologist Ronald Maris, are simply too isolated to call a stranger.

Yet prevention centers clearly get many high-risk callers. At the LASPC, several follow-up studies showed that about 1 percent of callers killed themselves within two years. Although these figures may be interpreted several ways, they indicate that prevention centers work with a high-risk group: callers represent about one hundred times as great a risk of suicide as the general population.

Some say prevention centers do not offer enough. "They don't take responsibility for the patients," says psychiatrist Douglas Jacobs. "People call up and get referred, but research shows that follow-through is at best fifty percent. Many patients may never make it—they may feel they've already *made* a connection." Centers may be better suited to helping the "situational suicide," a caller whose stability has been upset by specific events, than the chronic suicidal caller. In his follow-up studies of LASPC clients, Litman found that most subsequent suicides were by high-risk callers who were suicidal over a long period; they need more than just a patient ear and a referral. However, when the LASPC experimented with an eighteen-month follow-up program of callbacks and home visits to high-risk cases, there were seven suicides in the group that got extra care and only two in the control group. The specially trained volunteers felt "overwhelmed" by the demands of continued contact and wanted to turn over more difficult cases to the professional staff. The continuing relationship offered by the volunteers was "too little too late," concluded Litman.

Concerned by the unsupervised growth of centers in the late sixties and early seventies, the American Association of Suicidology has tried to impose minimum standards for prevention centers. But whether because of cost, excessive criteria, or simply because it's not necessary, only 172 of the 626 suicide prevention and crisis intervention centers currently listed in the AAS handbook have been certified. This reinforces the skepticism felt by some mental health professionals about the centers' efficacy. Although attitudes have come a long way since 1965, when the San Francisco coroner referred to the staff of the local center as "a bunch of clowns," some psychiatrists disparage the "amateurism" of the volunteers and dismiss their work as "hand-holding." Others worry about the danger to callers who get busy signals or an answering machine, or who are put on hold. (While such annoyances may further depress a caller, one suicidal woman who called a center and got an answering machine burst out laughing at the absurdity of the situation. The tension of her despair was pricked, and she survived the night.) A few analyze the motives of the volunteers; several studies have suggested that suicide prevention work may attract emotionally troubled people seeking to work out their own problems while attempting to help others. Nevertheless, therapists often refer their patients to prevention centers when they don't want to be disturbed. Centers report a boom of calls in August from people whose therapist has gone on vacation, leaving the local prevention center's number.

At the same time, while admitting that they are no substitute for professional help, some prevention center volunteers harbor distrust and resentment of mental health professionals. (At one point, in fact, the rift between professionals and volunteers threatened to split the AAS in two.) "It's nothing but doctors figuring out how to protect themselves from suicidal patients," scoffs the head of one center, walking out of an AAS seminar. Hearing that a suicidal patient shows "strong cathexis of the self with superego aggressive energy and inadequate cathexis with narcissistic libido," a volunteer wants to know how to use that "on the firing line." As a result of such mutual antipathy the possible benefits of therapist-volunteer cooperation have not been fully explored.

Meanwhile, prevention centers continue to refine their services. In an attempt to reach a greater number of high-risk callers, centers have developed programs for specific target groups. Some operate special lines for AIDS, child abuse, rape, the homeless, gays and lesbians. Some offer group therapy for the suicidal or support groups for bereaved family and friends left behind after a suicide. Others run training and education programs for the police, the military, or high school and college students. San Francisco Suicide Prevention spawned the Friendship Line, a twenty-four-hour suicide hotline for the elderly, including regular callbacks and home visits. For many years, the Samaritans of Boston organized a suicide prevention program at a local jail, in which inmates befriended other inmates. Perhaps the most important innovation was the establishment, in 1999, of the National Hopeline Network, a single, easy-to-remember, toll-free number (1-800-SUICIDE), through which calls are routed to the nearest AAS-certified crisis line. By 2005, the Hopeline had received more than 1 million calls.

In the past several years, government attention has returned to suicide, with a fanfare of federal activity that brings to mind the heyday of the CSSP. In 1999, Surgeon General David Satcher issued a "Call to Action to Prevent Suicide," which outlined the need for broader public awareness of the problem, increased research and development into treatment and prevention strategies, and reduction of stigma associated with mental illness and suicidal behavior. This, in turn, led to the National Strategy for Suicide Prevention, in which a coalition of clinicians, researchers, and survivors designed a comprehensive blueprint for reducing suicide and self-destructive behaviors. Its eleven goals and sixty-eight objectives range from standardizing protocols for death-scene investigations to improving firearm safety design to increasing the number of TV programs, movies, and news reports that follow recommended guidelines for depicting mental illness and suicide. The NSSP initiative is ambitious. But without sufficient funding at the federal, state, and local level, it won't get far. Indeed, an Institute of Medicine Report, published by the Academy of Sciences as part of the NSSP initiative, pointed out that suicide, which is responsible for more than thirty thousand deaths a year, receives one-tenth the federal funds given to the prevention and treatment of breast cancer, which takes the lives of some forty thousand women each year. "The committee finds that this is disproportionately low, given the magnitude of the problem of suicide," they concluded. "A substantial investment of funds is needed to make meaningful progress." Whether that investment will ever be made— or whether federal attention to suicide will last any longer than it did during the glory days of the CSSP—remains to be seen.

How these initiatives will affect suicide prevention centers also remains to be seen. They will likely continue with business as usual. Although they no longer make exaggerated claims of efficacy, evidence suggests that suicide prevention centers do, in fact, save lives. A University of Alabama study, comparing suicide rates in Alabama counties that had a center with those that did not, found that the centers were associated with a reduction of suicides by young white females—the demographic group to which most callers belong. Extrapolating their calculations to include the entire nation, they estimate that suicide prevention centers save the lives of 637 young white females each year.

With or without statistical reinforcement, the value of prevention centers should not be assessed solely by the suicide rate. While the word *suicide* is prominent in their advertising and an estimated one-third of their callers are suicidal, suicidality is not a prerequisite for calling the SPC or any other suicide prevention center. But if what keeps people alive is connection, centers may provide a small dose of caring that may prevent someone's sadness from spiraling into suicide months or years down the line. "Most callers are lonely, frightened, desperate people who don't know where to turn, and when they call the center, at least they get some sort of answering voice," says Robert Litman. "That's not necessarily suicide prevention, but it does play a part in stabilizing society. It is a little bit of society's answer to the chaos that society creates." Just as Nietzsche said the thought of suicide "helps one through many a dreadful night," the thought of a suicide prevention center has gotten many thousands of people through their own dreadful nights. David Klugman remembers one of the first calls he handled at the LASPC. When he picked up the phone and said "Hello, may I help you?" there was a silence. Then a timid voice on the other end said, "I can't talk now . . . I just needed to know someone's there."

# III

# TREATMENT

---

THE VAST MAJORITY of people who attempt or complete suicide never come in contact with a prevention center. Even for those who do, the prevention center is only a first step. There are two parts to suicide prevention—identifying the person at risk and deciding how to help him. Most of the work of the prevention movement has focused on finding the suicidal person. Shneidman is one of many suicidologists who believe that suicidal people communicate their intentions through the kinds of "clues" described earlier—giving away prized possessions, making statements like "You'll be sorry when I'm gone"—but that most people don't know how to listen. "Education is the single most important item in lowering the suicide rate," he says. "I don't mean suicide prevention classes. I mean a general heightening of awareness, so that if I give you my watch, you won't simply take it and thank me. You ought to say, 'Ed, sit down, tell me what's happening.'" Shneidman advocates mass media campaigns like the one that helped 46 million Americans give up smoking in the past several decades.

Even to suicidologists, however, clues are often recognizable only in retrospect—and in hindsight almost anything can look like a clue. "I'm sure if you or I went out the window right now, somebody might say, 'I knew that was going to happen someday,'" psychologist Douglas Powell told me. While working at Harvard University Health Services, Powell counseled the friends of a student who had run through a dormitory window to his death shortly before final exams. For weeks afterward the boy's friends wondered why, agreeing there had been no apparent cause, no clue. Then his roommate recalled a singular detail: Nick had always set ashtrays, mugs, and postcards on his win-

312

dowsill. For several weeks before his death, each time Nick sat in front of that window, he had removed another item. "People say, 'Well, how can these things happen to your children and you not notice them?'" the father of a sixteen-year-old boy who attempted suicide told a reporter. "Well, all I can say is you can sit in a house and the sun goes down and you never see it go down, and the next thing you know it's dark."

Even when people recognize clues they may fail to respond, through ignorance, denial, indifference, or even hostility. Psychiatrist Leon Eisenberg told me about a college student who was having a turbulent affair with a classmate. "He said, 'If you don't go steady with me, I'll jump off this building.' She said, 'You don't have the guts.' He did. He ran right up the steps to the eighth floor, out on the roof, and jumped off," says Eisenberg. "And I might add that the young lady showed no remorse at all." It is not known what proportion of people who leave clues go on to kill themselves. "All the students come in at some point and talk about suicide," a high school social worker says. "I can't put them *all* in the hospital."

How should one respond to a cry for help? The most important thing is to listen, to show empathy, and to take the problem seriously. Too often, because of uneasiness or fear, a friend may laugh off a plea or ignore a clue. "Anybody who talks about suicide is serious," says psychiatrist Michael Peck. "It's not up to us to make a judgment about whether he or she will do it or not." Although you may suspect the person is talking of suicide just to get attention, it is vital to take the person at his or her word. One of the biggest myths about suicide, as the LASPC learned, is that people who talk about it won't do it. While there are no statistics on how many of those who threaten suicide go on to attempt it, it's far better to overreact than to underreact. Avoid being judgmental. Telling the person to "snap out of it" is like telling someone with two broken legs to get up and walk. And the common response "But you have everything to live for" may only deepen the person's feelings of guilt and inadequacy. Questions like "Are you very unhappy?" and "How long have you felt this way?" give a person the chance to vent his feelings and perhaps reduce his anxiety. Although people often worry that asking about suicide will plant the idea in the distressed person's head, this is not true. Asking about suicide demonstrates concern and shows a willingness to discuss anything he or she might be feeling. Experts suggest being direct: "Are you thinking of suicide?" If the answer is yes, ask if he has planned how he might do it. If he has a plan, this indicates imminent danger and the need for immediate professional help.

But even when the signs are recognized and the person is brought into treatment, it is only the beginning. Every day in hospitals, emergency rooms, outpatient clinics, private offices, and suicide prevention centers, clinicians must make quick decisions about the risk of suicide, sifting the highly suicidal from the suicidal from the nonsuicidal. These decisions are usually made by observing the patient's appearance, body language, and discernible mood—and by asking about self-destructive thoughts, sleep disturbance, alcohol use, access to lethal means, sources of stress, and other factors associated with suicide. Clinicians have long wished for a more "objective" assessment tool—test chestnuts like the Rorschach, TAT, and MMPI have proved to be of little help—and over the years they have devised dozens of scales and questionnaires that purport to quantify suicide risk. Perhaps the most widely used is the Beck Scale for Suicide Ideation (SSI), which measures the intentions of people who are thinking of suicide with nineteen questions, beginning with "Wish to Live" (scored "moderate to strong," "weak," or "none") and "Wish to Die" (same options). Developed by University of Pennsylvania psychiatrist Aaron Beck, the founder of cognitive behavior therapy (and of the Beck Hopelessness Scale, the Beck Depression Inventory, and the Beck Anxiety Scale), the SSI is one of the few tests shown to have some predictive value. A twenty-year follow-up study of seven thousand depressed patients who had taken the SSI identified forty-nine suicides; those who had scored above 3 on the SSI were nearly seven times more likely to have completed suicide.

Psychologists at the University of Washington decided to focus on why people *don't* kill themselves; their Reasons for Living scale scores forty-eight factors connected to a patient's coping skills, fear of social disapproval, moral objections to the act, and concern for family. And while most scales are intended for those who may be *thinking* about suicide, the Risk-Rescue Rating, devised by Boston-area therapists Avery Weisman and William Worden, computes the lethality of an actual attempt by assigning points to five risk factors (which include actual damage inflicted, and method—pills get one point, jumping and shooting, three) and five rescue factors (which revolve around the chances of being found in time to survive). The rating is tabulated by dividing risk score by risk plus rescue scores and multiplying by one hundred. Thus, it is demonstrated that a thirty-eight-year-old unmarried waitress who ingested sedatives, then went to a movie theater, where she was found in a coma and subsequently died, received an eighty-three, the highest possible score.

While these scales provide useful checklists for clinicians, playing "the numbers game," says psychiatrist Douglas Jacobs, can be dangerous. "You have to be careful. On a percentage basis, young people are less likely to kill themselves, but if one of them does, for that person it's one hundred percent." Jacobs points out that the risk factors used in most scales may change. The dramatic increase in adolescent suicide has subsided; the rate for the elderly has gone down. (It has been suggested that different scales be developed for specific populations: for young females, for Native Americans, for middle-aged alcoholics, for patients in psychiatric hospitals.) Suicidal feelings fluctuate over time, and a rating that may be valid one day may be invalid the next; like the weather, points out psychiatrist Robert Simon, suicide risk must continuously be monitored. And no matter how specific the scale, no matter how frequently applied, there will be exceptions to the rule. University of Alabama researchers, declaring that most assessment tests are "too complex or cumbersome for practical and routine use," devised the SAD PERSONS scale, an acronym for ten risk factors. Scoring one point for each, the patient's probability of making an attempt is rated from one to ten. Suggested treatment is based on score, ranging from "send home with follow-up" (0–2) to "hospitalize or commit" (7–10). The researchers concede that some people may slip through the statistical net. "For example, a fourteen-year-old girl who attempted to hang herself 'because the devil came and told me to' might score only three points on the scale."

Some believe the patient may be the best judge. In their 1973 paper "Patient Monitoring of Suicidal Risk," a group of California therapists suggested that clinicians simply ask the depressed patient how long and under what circumstances he will stay alive. The patient is then asked to make a pledge: "No matter what happens, I will not kill myself accidentally or on purpose at any time." The authors wrote, "If the patient reports a feeling of confidence in this statement, with no direct or indirect qualifications and with no incongruous voice tones or body motions, the evaluator may dismiss suicide as a management problem." Claiming that in five years none of the six hundred patients who had made "no suicide" decisions had broken their pledge, the authors declared that their technique was "suitable for use by inexperienced nonprofessionals as well as by experienced professionals."

"Patient Monitoring of Suicidal Risk" may smack of a certain inmates-running-the-asylum naïveté, but over the decades it has evolved into the widespread and controversial practice of "no-suicide contracts," in which a patient promises, verbally or in writing, not to kill himself, and to keep his therapist informed of any self-destructive impulses. Although studies have shown that under the temporal and financial pressures of managed care, clinicians increasingly rely on no-suicide contracts as a form of risk management, no studies have shown whether they actually work. A survey at Harvard Medical School found that 86 percent of psychiatrists and 71 percent of psychologists worked in settings where no-suicide contracts were regularly invoked, yet fewer than 40 percent had been trained in their use. Many clinicians find them helpful; others point out that signing a contract may make the therapist feel safer but is no guarantee the patient won't kill himself. "Indeed, the use of such contracts flies in the face of clinical common sense and may in fact increase danger by providing psychiatrists with a false sense of security, thus decreasing their clinical vigilance," wrote Marcia Goin, president of the American Psychiatric Association, in 2003. ". . . We can make contracts with builders, insurers, and car dealers, but not with patients." Arguing that no-suicide pacts cannot substitute for comprehensive risk assessment, psychiatrist Robert Simon concludes, "The contract against self-harm is only as good as the soundness of the therapeutic alliance."

What assessment scales and no-suicide contracts prove most convincingly, it seems, is that our ability to predict suicide is negligible. "Although we may reconstruct causal chains and motives after the fact, we do not possess the tools to predict particular suicides before the fact," concluded psychiatrist Alex Pokorny after his scale for suicide risk proved unsuccessful in a prospective study of forty-eight hundred inpatients at a Texas VA hospital. Says Robert Litman, "Even for someone in a high-risk category, the chances of suicide within a year are much less than the chance that he will *not* have committed suicide within that time. In twenty-five years, I can remember perhaps three cases where I felt the chance of a certain person committing suicide within the next year was more than ten percent."

Even the most effective scales are intended to be a supplement to clinical judgment, not a substitute for it. "You can know all the statistics and scales and still not have any ability to assess a patient," says one psychiatrist. But if the scales haven't proved their worth, neither has clinical intuition. In one study a computer was shown to be more accurate than experienced clinicians in predicting suicide attempters. Adding insult to injury, half the patients preferred the computer to the therapist as interviewer.

For some of these reasons, a number of mental health professionals scoff at the "clues" approach to suicide prevention. "We've reached the point of no return in defining vulnerable populations," says psychiatrist Herbert Hendin. "It amounts to looking for the proverbial needle in a haystack." Hendin knocks Shneidman's proposed educational blitz. "I don't follow the logic of putting millions into educating the lay public in something that psychiatrists haven't proven *they* can identify. It makes more sense to do something for the people you *do* find. A lot of seriously suicidal people present themselves to us in ways nobody can miss—they jump from five-story buildings—and nobody does anything for them." The highest predictor of suicide risk is a previous attempt; between 25 and 40 percent of completed suicides have tried before, and 2 percent of those who attempt will complete within one year, 10 percent within ten years. Yet most attempters are returned to the community after being stitched up or pumped out, without provision for further treatment. (In one study, half of all adolescents brought to emergency rooms after a suicide attempt did not receive follow-up care—surprising until one learns that 70 percent of emergency-department physician training programs offer no instruction in the management of psychiatric problems.) "If you could identify twenty percent of the seriously suicidal from those who make attempts and cure ten percent," declares Hendin, "you could literally change the suicide rate."

———

Can clinicians "cure" suicidal people? The question is rarely asked. The bottom line at most prevention centers and in most prevention literature is to get the suicidal person to professional help. Although getting the person to that help can be difficult—reluctance by the person or his family to admit there is a problem, the stigma of being in treatment, and the high cost of quality care are a few of the obstacles—it is often assumed that once we do, the problem is solved. Yet professional help is no guarantee against suicide. Clinicians often point out with alarm that slightly more than half of people who kill themselves have never seen a mental health professional; the flip side—that nearly half of people who kill themselves *have* seen a mental health professional—should be considered nearly as disturbing. Indeed, people who have made attempts and entered treatment have the highest suicide rate of any patient group. Yet the focus of suicide prevention has been on assessment and prediction of suicide risk; treatment has largely been ignored.

How do clinicians treat suicidal people? A therapist's first task, of course, is to address the crisis and decrease the risk of suicide, just as counselors are trained to do on the SPC phone lines. "The immediate goal of a therapist, counselor, or anyone else dealing with highly suicidal people should be to reduce the pain in every way possible," writes Shneidman. "Help them by intervening with whoever or whatever is causing their distress—lovers, parents, college deans, employers, or social service agencies. I have found that if you reduce these pressures and lower the level of suffering, even just a little, suicidal people will choose to live." In his book *Definition of Suicide,* Shneidman described a counseling session with a distraught college student. Pregnant, single, profoundly religious, and overwhelmed by shame and guilt, the girl had decided to kill herself. Shneidman's initial task was to help her to realize that alternatives existed.

I did several things. For one, I took out a single sheet of paper and began to "widen her blinders." Our conversation went something on these general lines: "Now, let's see: You could have an abortion here locally." ("I couldn't do that.") . . . "You could go away and have an abortion." ("I couldn't do that.") "You could bring the baby to term and keep the baby." ("I couldn't do that.") "You could have the baby and adopt it out." ("I couldn't do that.") "We could get in touch with the young man involved." ("I couldn't do that.") "We could involve the help of your parents." ("I couldn't do that.") "You can always commit suicide, but there's obviously no need to do that today." (No response.) "Now, let's look at this list and rank them in order of your preference, keeping in mind that none of them is perfect."

The very making of this list, my non-hortatory and non-judgmental approach, had already had a calming influence on her. Within a few minutes her lethality had begun to de-escalate. She actually ranked the list, commenting negatively on each item. What was of critical importance was that suicide was now no longer first or second. We were then simply "haggling" about life—a perfectly viable solution.

Once the immediate danger has passed, how does a therapist treat a suicidal patient? Ask almost any therapist and he or she is likely to answer, "Suicide is a symptom, not a diagnosis." (Although "suicidality" is included as one of nine symptoms of a depressive episode in the *Diagnostic and Statistical Manual of Mental Disorders,* suicide itself is not listed as an illness.) Nor is suicide dependent on a specific disorder. "Suicidal behaviors may be generated in the presence of practically any diagnostic entity, and at times in the absence of pathological states," says psychiatrist Jerome Motto. Because a clinician can't treat suicide as directly as he might treat, for example, strep throat—there is no antibiotic for suicide—he must treat the patient's closest diagnosable ailment, which is, more often than not, some form of depression. Many clinicians believe that if they successfully do so, they've treated the suicidal patient, as if suicidality were simply a nasty side effect of the underlying illness. Yet some suicidal patients, albeit a minority, have no diagnosable underlying illness, and patients often kill themselves shortly after coming out of a depression—or long after a depression has lifted. "Suicide proneness is primarily a psychodynamic matter; the formal elements of mental illness only secondarily intensify it, release it, or immobilize it," psychiatrists Dan Buie and John Maltsberger have written. "The urge to suicide is largely independent of the observable mental state, and it can be intense despite the clearing of symptoms of mental illness."

How is the "underlying illness" of the suicidal patient treated? Although there is no pill for suicide, there are scores for depression and other psychiatric conditions. Over the past several decades, growing emphasis on the role of mental illness in suicide has combined with extraordinary advances in the development of psychotropic medications to effect a sea change in the treatment of suicidal people. Twenty or thirty years ago, depressed and possibly self-destructive people were likely to be treated with psychotherapy, supported, where indicated, by medication. By the new millennium, drugs were the treatment of choice—in most cases the only treatment—for depression as well as nearly every other psychiatric condition, with psychotherapy occasionally playing a supportive role. As journalist Daphne Merkin wrote in the *New York Times,* "In our age the triumph of the pharmaceutic has overtaken the triumph of the therapeutic; for all but a select few the cost-effective discussion of dosages has replaced the expensive discussions of dreams."

What is now referred to as the "drug revolution" had its roots in the late 1940s, when French naval surgeon Henri Laborit was looking for something to calm his patients before administering anesthesia. He found that chlorpromazine, a sedating antihistamine, induced a "euphoric quietude." He recommended the drug to his psychiatrist colleagues, who tested it on a variety of mentally ill patients and found it effective in the treatment of manic depression and schizophrenia. In 1954 it was introduced to the United States. Thorazine, the brand name by which chlorpromazine would be known, achieved remarkable results. Patients who had been unruly and assaultive were suddenly docile. In some hospitals the use of straitjackets, wet packs, and seclusion was virtually abandoned. Many patients were able to return to the community. Described—admiringly—by some as a "chemical lobotomy," Thorazine became the drug of choice in American mental hospitals. Although many therapists believed Thorazine would be a panacea for suicidal patients, the drug offered control, not cure. In 1954, the year tranquilizers were introduced at Metropolitan State Hospital in Norwalk, California, the inpatient suicide rate more than doubled. Investigators suspected that the staff might have relaxed their vigilance because of the drugs' efficacy in controlling symptoms. (Indeed, Thorazine rendered patients "immobile" and "waxlike," as described by the lead investigator for the pharmaceutical company that manufactured it. He meant this as high praise.)

Over the following decades, Thorazine was followed by a succession of seemingly ever more miraculous medications: lithium, a naturally occurring salt, proved effective in moderating the roller-coaster mood swings of manic depression; clozapine helped quiet the nattering voices of schizophrenia; monoamine oxidase inhibitors and their successors, the tricyclic antidepressants, such as Tofranil, had a leavening effect on severe depression. Perhaps the biggest change came in 1988, when fluoxetine (better known by its brand name Prozac) was introduced in the United States, the first in a new class of antidepressants known as selective serotonin reuptake inhibitors (SSRIs), which, as their name suggests, act by blocking the removal of serotonin at the synapses, thus increasing the availability of serotonin in the brain while leaving other neurotransmitter levels unaffected. Prozac and its cousins—Zoloft, Paxil, and so on—were so successful in providing relief to depressed men and women, as well as in giving a lift to millions more mildly unhappy people, that by 2000, one in ten Americans was taking antidepressants. An increasing number of citizens of Prozac Nation, as it has been dubbed by the writer Elizabeth Wurtzel, are young; in 2002, nearly 11 million children and teenagers were prescribed antidepressants, accounting for 7 percent of all antidepressant prescriptions, more than triple the number ten years earlier.

Despite their success in relieving the symptoms of psychiatric illness in millions of people (and, in the process, doubtless keeping many of them from killing themselves), these medications have had a more complicated relationship to suicide than might be expected. Among all the psychopharmacological treatments, the only one clinically proven to reduce suicide risk is lithium. In 2001, Harvard Medical School psychiatrists Leonardo Tondo and Ross Baldessarini analyzed thirty-three studies conducted over the previous thirty years and found that patients with major depression or bipolar disorder who *hadn't* taken lithium were thirteen times more likely to have completed or attempted suicide than those who *had* taken it. (The suicide rate of those who *had* taken lithium was, nevertheless, nearly three times higher than that of the general population.) In a German study, 378 psychiatric inpatients, half with bipolar disorder, half with major depression, were randomly assigned to lithium, an anticonvulsant, or an antidepressant on their release from the hospital. Over the following two and a half years, four killed themselves and five made serious attempts; none were in the group taking lithium. The study's author suggested that lithium may have a direct effect on suicidal behavior, independent from its effect on depression, perhaps by reducing aggression and impulsivity. Unfortunately, not all patients respond well to lithium, either because their systems won't tolerate it, or because of its possible side effects—blurry thinking, weight gain, tremors, lethargy. Others may balk because of the hassle: lithium treatment requires monitoring of blood levels every few months. Or, like Brian Hart, they may consider lithium stigmatizing and stop taking it, either periodically or permanently. (Nearly one-half of all patients with bipolar disorder fail to adhere to their medication regimens at some point.) If there is anything more dangerous than a bipolar patient not being on lithium, it is a bipolar patient going off lithium; Tondo and Baldessarini found that suicidal acts rose sixteenfold in the first year after discontinuing treatment.

The tricyclic antidepressants, on the other hand, while enormously helpful in relieving depression, are also potentially lethal; many people have ended up killing themselves with the very medication prescribed to keep them from killing themselves. Knowing that a mere six or seven pills might mean the difference between an effective dose and a fatal one, clinicians faced a catch-22 —they couldn't prescribe antidepressants without the risk of the patient using them to kill himself, but it was difficult to treat clinical depression without prescribing antidepressants. Patients near the beginning of treatment may experience what has been called rollback, in which the antidepressant gives them sufficient energy to act on their suicidal feelings—as well as supplying them with the means to do it—before their depression lifts completely.

The introduction of the SSRIs seemed to resolve these issues. Although they are about as effective as the tricyclics, the SSRIs are less expensive, have fewer side effects (lowered libido being the most prominent), and are easier to administer. They are also far less toxic; used in intentional overdoses, they are rarely fatal. Indeed, many researchers suggest that the only problem with SSRIs is that not enough people take them and those who do don't take enough. Studies of completed suicides reveal that only 8–17 percent were being treated with antidepressants or other prescription psychiatric medications, and only 6–14 percent of depressed suicide victims had dosage levels sufficient to be of any help. (Some of these low dosages, of course, can be attributed to patient noncompliance: one in four victims of suicide fail to adhere to their medication schedule in the month before death.)

Given that they reduce depressive symptoms and decrease aggressive, impulsive behavior, it would seem to follow that the SSRIs might have a measurable effect on suicide. Indeed, the massive increase in the number of prescriptions written for SSRIs in the United States and several other countries over the 1990s correlated with a decline in suicide rates in those countries. At the same time, most controlled studies have failed to find that SSRI treatment has made statistically significant differences in suicidal behavior on an individual level. (It is difficult to gauge accurately the effect of medications on self-destructive behavior, because suicidal people are systematically excluded from clinical trials by drug companies hoping to demonstrate the superiority of their products and because it would be unethical to withhold treatment from them during a controlled prospective study.) Indeed, evidence of their efficacy in treating depression has also proved elusive; in half of all adult studies, SSRIs have proved no better than placebos.

Nevertheless, the SSRIs were so popular that when reports began surfacing in the early 1990s suggesting that Prozac itself seemed to *make* some people suicidal, they were dismissed by pharmaceutical companies and federal regulators as vigorously as if someone had tried to discredit motherhood and apple pie. Those concerns resurfaced in 2003, however, when an FDA drug safety analyst reviewed the results of fifteen clinical trials evaluating the effect of various antidepressants on pediatric depression. Few of the trials showed that drugs relieved depression any better than placebos. (Indeed, of all the SSRIs, only Prozac has been shown to be effective in treating depressed pediatric patients.) Far more troubling, however, he found that children and teenagers given antidepressants were almost twice as likely as those given placebos to become suicidal. The risk was small—of one hundred pediatric patients given antidepressants, two or three might be expected to think about or attempt suicide who would otherwise not have—yet statistically significant. (None of the children in the trials completed suicide.) Perhaps most troubling of all, the results of many of these trials had been kept secret for years by the drug companies that had sponsored them.

The news was so shocking that, seemingly in denial, the FDA initially disputed their own analyst's findings and hired a team of researchers from Columbia University to reassess the data. The Columbia researchers, however, agreed with the FDA analyst. In October 2004, following hearings in which dozens of devastated parents blamed their children's suicides on the drugs, the FDA required the makers of ten antidepressants (including Prozac, Zoloft, and Paxil) to include "black box" warnings on the labels attesting that they "increase the risk of suicidal thinking and behavior" in children and adolescents. (No one is yet certain whether SSRIs trigger suicidal behavior or whether, like the tricyclic antidepressants, they may supply patients with sufficient energy to act on their suicidal feelings before their depression lifts completely.)

Given that both lives and money were at stake—$12 billion of antidepressants were sold worldwide in 2002—it was a difficult and contentious decision. Some therapists suggested that the efficacy of SSRIs and the ease of prescribing them had allowed physicians to become cavalier about dispensing them and expressed hope that the warnings would discourage indiscriminate and inappropriate use. Others worried that the warnings would scare therapists off from prescribing potentially lifesaving drugs for children in need. As it is, said psychiatrist John Mann of the New York State Psychiatric Institute, only 20 percent of the four thousand adolescents who kill themselves each year have ever taken antidepressants, and NIMH estimates that 15 percent of teenagers with untreated depression will eventually kill themselves. "It is probably the case that antidepressants both cause and prevent deaths," wrote Andrew Solomon, author of *The Noonday Demon,* a study of depression, in the *New York Times.* "But it is also clearly the case that they prevent more deaths than they cause. The danger is that in seeking to prevent antidepressant-related suicide, we will increase depression-related suicide."

---

The ascendancy of the SSRIs has tipped the scales in the long, bitter turf war between biologically oriented and psychodynamically oriented therapists. These days, few clinicians would suggest that psychotherapy alone, without medication to address the underlying illness, is enough to prevent profoundly suicidal individuals from killing themselves. Yet many would maintain that medication alone is enough to deal with depressed and possibly suicidal individuals. Indeed, in most so-called therapy, the only contact the doctor may have with a patient following an initial assessment and prescription are brief follow-up visits to discuss side effects and to ascertain whether the dosage needs adjustment—a procedure quicker and, in many cases, no more personal, than an automobile's three-thousand-mile oil change. Discussions of treatment issues in the literature revolve around medication, monitoring, and compliance; psychotherapy, if mentioned at all, is usually described only as an aid in encouraging adherence to the pharmaceutical schedule.

The recent controversy over SSRIs and suicidal behavior suggests, however, that while psychopharmacology has changed the way we treat suicidal people, it may not, by itself, be enough. Despite their extraordinary success, medications have proved to be something of a red herring in the treatment of suicidal patients. They may relieve the symptoms of psychiatric illness, but they do little to alleviate the stresses—family problems, loss, trauma—that may have triggered or exacerbated the illness. And, says psychiatrist John Maltsberger, "While they are no doubt important in preventing a great many suicides, they do not necessarily alter the underlying vulnerability to suicide." Indeed, the excitement over antidepressants has obscured the fact that depressed and suicidal patients are best served by a combination of medication and psychotherapy. When a recent NIMH study of 439 depressed teenagers concluded that Prozac was far more effective than talk therapy in treating depression, it was hailed as a triumph of medication over psychotherapy; all but ignored was the finding that the most effective treatment of all was Prozac *and* talk therapy.

Numerous other studies have demonstrated better outcomes in depressed, bipolar, or schizophrenic patients who receive both medication and psychotherapy rather than drugs alone. Yet most insurance companies cover the costs of brief medication visits but not of more than a few sessions of psychotherapy, which is often dismissed as expensive, complicated, time-consuming, and even irrelevant. "Medicine alone is not sufficient for treatment of suicidality," concluded a comprehensive report on suicide by the Academy of Sciences in 2001. ". . . Psychotherapy provides a necessary therapeutic relationship that reduces the risk of suicide."

What kind of psychotherapy? Because the field is itself fragmented by turf battles, there is little agreement on how to treat any mental illness. A person suffering from depression may be treated with yoga, Reiki, massage, hypnosis, sleep-deprivation therapy, homeopathy, magnets, Saint-John's-wort, Qigong, acupuncture, or any of the more than 250 types of psychotherapy practiced today. (Of them, only psychoanalysis is agreed to be inappropriate for suicidal patients: "Most are too anxious, too depressed, or just not well enough put together to stand it," says Herbert Hendin, himself a psychoanalyst.) Although suicidal patients come with different diagnoses with different needs, they are likely to get whatever the therapist practices. "One would hope that clinicians had a number of strings to their therapeutic bow and would change depending on the nature of the problem," says psychiatrist Leon Eisenberg. "Unfortunately, this field is characterized by people who do the same type of treatment for every customer that comes along." A therapy that may work with suicidal patients will be ignored by most clinicians if it is not their modus operandi.

Although evaluations of long-term therapeutic interventions on suicidality are rare—too difficult, too expensive, too risky, too ethically iffy—a few approaches appear to be helpful in reducing suicide risk. Beck's cognitive behavior therapy, a short-term treatment that helps depressed patients to reinterpret their negative, distorted thoughts in a more realistic, positive light, seems to reduce the feelings of hopelessness that lie at the core of many suicides. Studies have shown it may reduce suicidal ideation and attempts more effectively than nondirective psychotherapy. Dialectical behavioral therapy, developed by University of Washington psychologist Marsha Linehan specifically for use with chronically suicidal people, helps the patient to develop alternatives to self-destructive behavior, and to find ways to handle the intense surges of emotion that characterize borderline and bipolar patients. In weekly psychotherapy sessions, a problematic behavior or event from the past week is discussed in detail; in weekly group therapy sessions, coping skills and mindfulness techniques adapted from Buddhist meditation are taught. Between sessions, therapist-client telephone contact is encouraged. "The emphasis is on teaching patients how to manage emotional trauma rather than on reducing them or taking them out of crises," Linehan has written.

Group therapy with suicide attempters has been valuable in reducing stigma and isolation. "The person realizes she's not alone—that everyone else in the room has had suicidal thoughts, so there's no need to maintain secrecy," Chrisula Asimos, a San Francisco psychologist who worked with groups of suicidal people for many years, told me. The group, in fact, tends to reduce the focus on suicide. "The issue of suicide loses its impact," says Asimos. "We talk openly about suicide, but we focus on other options. In a group, people can see how other people who have been there longer have moved away from suicidal behavior and explored healthier alternatives." Bonding among group members (who are encouraged to be in individual therapy as well) extends beyond meetings; they organize group dinners and birthday parties, and like members of Alcoholics Anonymous who call each other when they have the urge to take a drink, they share home telephone numbers to be available to each other in times of crisis. When one group member who was acutely suicidal worried about jumping from her apartment window, the entire group helped her move from her lonely twentieth-floor rooms to a cheerful residence club on the ground floor.

But while group therapy seems to make suicidal patients more comfortable, the thought of working with a roomful of high-risk patients can be daunting. "Group therapy for suicidal patients hasn't caught on because therapists are afraid of it, and I can well understand why," says Norman Farberow, who pioneered therapy groups for suicidal people at the Los Angeles Suicide Prevention Center. "Most suicidal people are insatiable in their need for care and support, and when you get a half dozen depressed and severely suicidal people together, it's very draining." There has been no conclusive research on the efficacy of groups for the suicidal, but of hundreds of high-risk patients who were in Farberow's groups, none completed suicide while in the group, although two former members took their lives after they had left the group against staff advice. When I met Chrisula Asimos, she had been running groups for sixteen years; during that time, no member had completed suicide. At one meeting, however, an older member suffered a fatal heart attack while in the bathroom. It was a traumatic experience for the group, but, said Asimos, "I'm convinced he came there to die—that we were his family."

In some therapeutic approaches the therapist himself seems to serve as a substitute family. In their work with suicidal patients over several decades, Boston psychiatrists John Maltsberger and Dan Buie have evolved what they call the "psychodynamic formulation" of suicide. "This approach looks at suicide in terms of developmental failures that make it impossible to maintain a sense of self-worth," says Maltsberger. "Many people who grow up suicide-vulnerable have failed to get the love they ought to have had from their mothers. Others have received good mothering but for little-understood reasons cannot make use of it." In normal development, he explains, capacity for autonomy increases with age, enabling one to endure degrees of loneliness, depression, and anxiety. Suicide-vulnerable people fail to develop sustaining inner resources; they must depend on external supports. When those supports fail, suicide is a danger.

Though Maltsberger's theoretical approach to suicide is heavily influenced by Freud, in practice the psychodynamic formulation is quite practical. "It boils down to finding out what a person has to live for," says Maltsberger. "Most people live for all sorts of things—friends, a special person, work—and if they lose something on one front, they pick it up on another. But suicidal people are quite deficient in any capacity to keep themselves afloat on the basis of inner resources. Once somebody threatens suicide, you start looking at what resources the person has."

Maltsberger and Buie specify three areas people live for: other people, work, and their body. "Obviously, when someone who is dependent and depressive loses a girlfriend or a husband, it can precipitate a suicidal crisis," says Maltsberger. "Then there are people who never have relationships, who lock themselves in the library and devote themselves to scholarship. But when they retire or can't work anymore, they may kill themselves. A surgeon may live only to operate; if he loses the use of his hands, he may do away with himself. And there are people who are very dependent and depressive, but as long as they can jog and look in the mirror and say 'Gee, I'm in great shape,' they can go on.

"So if someone has relied all his life on some capacity to work at Sanskrit, and he goes blind, the task becomes to find what this person can substitute as a lifesaving activity." Just as Shneidman worked to "widen the blinders" of the pregnant young woman on a short-term basis, Maltsberger, in the psychodynamic formulation, tries to help the patient expand his long-term reasons for living. "It isn't always possible. Many people are quite indifferent to the love of others, for instance. Others may be indifferent to success at work. Suicidal people are very specialized in what they will accept as a reason for living." At first, says Maltsberger, the therapist himself may have to constitute that reason "until the patient can regain his balance and stand up again."

The psychodynamic formulation offers therapists a practical way to help decide *when* someone is suicidal, what to do for treatment—which, in many cases, may involve medication—and whether hospitalization is indicated. It also requires a therapist to know a patient's history thoroughly and to spot events in a patient's daily calendar that might heighten suicide risk. "Treating suicidal people means being available—intensively—from time to time when they're between supporting figures or research projects," says Maltsberger. "I might call them on the telephone every day. You have to be waiting there like a net, hoping that as time goes on the person can widen his repertoire and make room for other sustaining influences."

Even the psychodynamic formulation, however, offers only temporary relief. Can vulnerability to suicide be altered? Maltsberger sighs, like the Wizard of Oz after giving out heart, brains, and courage only to find that Dorothy still needs to find her way back to Kansas. "That's most ambitious," he says slowly. "That means helping the patient restructure his mind, which is very, very difficult and, in some cases, impossible." He pauses. "Often psychiatrists don't want to try."

In part because they are the only mental health professionals allowed to prescribe medication, psychiatrists have long been regarded as the last word for suicidal patients. "We all use psychiatrists as backups for these cases," a Boston social worker told me. "The psychiatrist is the bottom line." One would therefore expect psychiatrists to know a good deal about suicide. They don't. In fact, they score no better then radiologists on tests determining their knowledge of suicide risk factors; other mental health professionals score only slightly higher than college students and the clergy. A 1983 survey of more than three hundred training institutions found, on average, no more than a half day's formal education devoted to suicidology by any of the mental health disciplines. Fifteen years later, a survey of 166 psychiatry residency programs found that while most now offered training in the treatment of suicidal patients, such training was often "relatively superficial in nature" and was usually delivered in the context of supervised clinical work. Only one-quarter offered workshops devoted specifically to suicide. (Forty percent of graduate programs in clinical psychology offer formal training in treating suicidal patients.) What suicide training there is is increasingly devoted to pharmacology; discussions of family dynamics, interviewing techniques, and unconscious forces have given way to discussions of dosages and blood levels. Indeed, many clinicians feel that no specific training for suicide is needed. "Experience is the best teacher," insists one psychiatrist. (Residents *are* likely to acquire experience; a majority of patients on training wards are there because of a suicide attempt or severe ideation.)

Others disagree. "Residents are trained as they get cases, by supervisors who were treated in the same haphazard way," sociologist Donald Light told me. Light spent two years in the 1970s studying psychiatric residency training at the Massachusetts Mental Health Center in Boston, one of the most highly regarded psychiatric training programs in the country at the time. "So a lot of homemade ideas about suicide care are perpetuated from one generation of psychiatrists to the next." Light recommended a specific training module to the American Psychiatric Association, in which each residency would have an in-house expert through which all suicide cases would be routed. Residents would be required to work at a crisis phone service and to attend regular seminars in suicide care, stressing availability, the need to relax confidentiality, the necessity of involving friends and family, and the importance of working in clinical teams. The APA's response, according to Light, was "polite."

Alan Stone has been another advocate of specific training in suicide care. Years ago, after a rash of suicides at McLean Hospital, an elite, private psychiatric institution near Boston, where he was director of residency training, Stone concluded, "During the course of that epidemic, it became painfully apparent that many psychiatrists possess no systematic or comprehensive approach for dealing with suicidal patients." In a series of papers, Stone and the late Harvey Shein, his successor and former student, proposed that "suicidal risk must be *monitored* in a way that is analogous to the current hospital management of acute coronary artery disease." They suggested that suicidality be made an explicit focus of treatment and that the patient's family be brought in and told. "Once the patient's suicidal thoughts are shared, the therapist must take pains to make clear to the patient that he, the therapist, considers suicide to be a maladaptive action irreversibly counter to the patient's sane interests and goals; that he, the therapist, will do everything he can to prevent it." (Ironically, Shein, who campaigned for openness about suicide, couldn't follow his own prescription; several years after the last of those papers was published, he took a fatal overdose of sleeping pills at the age of forty-one. The embarrassed hospital was hardly forthcoming itself; it reported that its promising young psychiatrist had "died suddenly" and persuaded the local newspapers to call the death a heart attack. At the next staff meeting, the hospital director didn't mention Shein's suicide until a grieving employee insisted on broaching the subject.)

It is clear that some training is needed. There are therapists who still share with laymen simple misconceptions about suicide—for instance, that if you ask a person about suicide, you'll plant the seed in his mind, or, conversely, that if he talks about suicide, he won't do it. Or that if a patient really wants to kill himself, you can't stop him. The most common fallacy may be the supposed distinction between serious and nonserious attempters. While it is tempting to assume, for example, that wrist-cutters are manipulators who don't intend to die, they should always be taken seriously. Writes Maltsberger, "Some patients almost ready for suicide but as yet undecided may betray their ambivalence through a minor attempt. . . . We know of one young schizophrenic woman who ingested six Stelazine tablets, an event misunderstood at the time as a negativistic gesture of little significance. A few days later, her indecision resolved, the patient fired her father's pistol through her head."

Sometimes, specific types of therapy may be harmful. One such approach involves what children call reverse psychology; while most therapy concentrates on the part of the patient that wants to live, "paradoxical technique" plays the flip side. The patient says life isn't worth living; the therapist agrees. Light remembers a psychiatrist who claimed never to have lost a patient with this risky technique. He came close. "One girl had a blade at her wrist and he kept saying, 'Go ahead, go ahead.' He was pushing her down the hallway and she went screaming out of the hospital." She made a small cut but recovered. Such brinkmanship requires an experienced therapist. Impressed with the jocular, Jewish-mother approach his supervisor used, a young resident tried it himself. "So already you should die" came out sounding like "you should die." Two months into treatment his twenty-two-year-old patient put the plastic slip of a record jacket over his head and suffocated.

Another therapist took the opposite tack. On learning that one of his patients, a businessman, had slashed his wrists, he rushed to the emergency room where the patient was being sewn up and gave him a right hook to the jaw. "How dare you do anything so stupid?" he yelled. "If you ever do anything like that again, I'll kill you!" Perhaps encouraged by his therapist's concern—or stunned by his Sunday punch—the patient did in fact get better.

When Maltsberger was a resident, he had a patient who repeatedly slashed her wrists. "I was getting fed up," he recalls, "and one day I said, 'If you're not interested in changing, we can arrange for you to be someplace else.' I think that remark was motivated by hate. My basic message was 'We're tired of you; get off your ass or get out of here.'" On the next attempt the patient nearly killed herself. It was the first time Maltsberger had confronted countertransference hate—an emotional response therapists may have to certain patients. Such reactions can be particularly intense with suicidal patients. Extraordinarily demanding, they may attack the therapist, verbally or physically; they may shadow him or make anonymous phone calls. (Maltsberger knows of two instances in which patients telephoned suicide threats at the moment they correctly guessed their doctor was eating Christmas dinner.) The mere passivity— "almost a sucking quality," says Alan Stone—of some suicidal patients is likely to inspire boredom, malice, even hatred, in a therapist. "When you deal with suicidal people day after day after day, you just get plain tired," says James Chu, a psychiatrist at McLean Hospital. "You get to the point of feeling, 'All right, get it over with.'"

In one of the few papers on the subject, Maltsberger and Buie describe how therapists may repress such feelings. A therapist may glance at his watch, feel drowsy, daydream—or rationalize referral, premature termination, or hospitalization just to be rid of the patient. Sometimes a frustrated therapist will issue an ultimatum. Maltsberger recalls one therapist who, treating a chronic wrist-cutter, "just couldn't stand it, and finally she said, 'If you don't stop that, I'll stop treatment.' The patient did it again. She stopped treatment, and the patient killed herself." Reviewing the treatment of thirty men and women who killed themselves as inpatients or within six months of discharge, William Wheat isolated several patterns that he believes contributed to the suicide: the therapist's refusal to tolerate a patient's immature, dependent behavior; the therapist's pessimism about treatment progress; and the therapist's inability to recognize an event or crisis of overwhelming importance to the patient. "All of these processes," wrote Wheat, "can lead to a breakdown in the therapeutic communication resulting in the patient's feeling abandoned or helpless, thus setting the stage for the disastrous result of suicide."

Light contends that only certain therapists are able to withstand the demands of suicidal patients. "We should be candid about the fact that most psychiatrists are not built for suicide care. Let's select about ten percent who have the stomach for it, who can handle the high anxiety, who might even *like* it, who have a kind of Green Beret outlook, and give them special training and then make it clear to other psychiatrists that when they get a suicidal case, they refer it to this person." The late Bruce Danto, a psychiatrist who founded the Suicide Prevention and Crisis Intervention Center in Detroit, liked to talk about what he called the "psychiatric suicidologist," which, in his description, seemed to be part social worker, part psychologist, and part cop. (With degrees in sociology, social work, and medicine, and a deputy sheriff's badge, Danto was all of the above.) "The psychiatric suicidologist must have skills over and above those of psychiatrists in general," he told me. "With these problems you can't simply sit back in your chair, stroke your beard, and say, 'All the work is done right here in my office with my magical ears and tongue.' There has to be a time when you shift gears and become an activist." Support might involve helping a patient get a job, attending a graduation, visiting the hospital, even making house calls. "I would *never* send somebody to a therapist who has an unlisted phone number," said Danto. "If therapists feel that being available for telephone contact is an imposition, then they're in the wrong field, or they're treating the wrong patient. They should treat only *well* people." The psychiatric suicidologist must also pay attention to "the tools of self-destruction." Danto kept a collection of guns and knives belonging to suicidal patients, who held receipts. "Once you decide to help somebody, you have to take responsibility down the line."

While many psychiatrists find such suggestions too gung ho, they admit that not all psychiatrists are equally fit to deal with suicidal cases. "There are many psychiatrists who don't necessarily have great experience in treating people who have made suicide attempts," Ari Kiev, a Manhattan psychiatrist, has said. "I would much rather have my social worker or even the receptionist deal with some suicide-prone patients than just any psychiatrist." Herbert Hendin gets many referrals from uncomfortable colleagues. "A lot of people who do reasonably well with other patients cannot deal with suicidal patients," he says. "The bigger tragedy is if somebody is *not* comfortable, you shouldn't spend ten years trying to analyze his discomfort—let him treat someone else." Robert Litman interviewed more than two hundred therapists shortly after the suicide of a patient. They expressed fears of being vilified in the press, of being sued, of being investigated, of losing professional standing, and of inadequacy. (Suicide is, in fact, the most common cause of malpractice litigation against mental health professionals.) Litman points out that therapists must understand that no treatment—psychopharmacology, psychotherapy, electroshock, hospitalization—can guarantee that suicide will not occur. When he lectures residents about suicide, he tells them that it is important to realize that they will undoubtedly have a suicide at some point in their practice. Indeed, it is part of psychiatry's folklore that one is not a full-fledged therapist until one has had a patient who completed suicide.

"These doctors who get so anxious when a patient threatens suicide haven't settled in their own lives the question of who's responsible," says Maltsberger. "If there's any blame to be assigned, it would be on the person who brought the patient into that plight in the first place. That might be the patient, the patient's parents, or it might be God. Who knows? But it isn't the poor therapist!" In forty-five years of practice Maltsberger has never had a suicide. Doesn't that make him nervous? "All the time," he says quickly. "But at this stage of the game if a patient of mine did away with himself, I would be very sad, but any self-reproach would have to do with how well I applied my art. It's like surgery. If you operate on somebody and you don't make any mistakes, and you tie off all the bleeders and the patient doesn't make it, it's sad, but that's probably the way the ball bounces."

"I had a patient a couple of years ago who dropped out of treatment to go back to school, but he continued to come in periodically," says Ari Kiev. "One night I got a message that he'd called at nine. I called back at ten, and whoever answered said he was asleep." Kiev speaks slowly. "Next day his girlfriend called me and said she hadn't been able to locate him. She'd tried at home and nobody had answered. I put two and two together and called 911. They went up there and he was dead. He'd gotten drunk and taken an overdose. So I was having second thoughts—since it wasn't like him to call me, maybe I should have acted on the call and insisted that whoever answered the phone wake him up, which is when I would have found he *couldn't* be wakened and called the police." He riffles through the appointment calendar on his desk. "I don't think I'm responsible, but you feel responsible. . . . I can answer these things from the point of view of the psychiatrist's way of BS-ing the world and BS-ing himself—'It's the patient's responsibility'—but you're caught up with people, and it's not as easy as all that."

Certainly, some suicides may be resistant to any intervention. In a study of schizophrenic hospital patients, Shneidman and Farberow describe a man who received psychotherapy but remained acutely suicidal. He was given a steady barrage of electroshock treatments for several years, but he repeatedly tried to hang himself. He was given a lobotomy. He was calmer, but remained suicidal. One day, despite the vigilance of hospital staff, he finally succeeded in hanging himself.

Amid a glossary of possible techniques, clinicians sometimes overlook simpler approaches. "I had a slasher my first year in the hospital," recalls one psychiatrist. "She kept cutting herself to ribbons—with glass, wire, anything she could get her hands on. Nobody could stop her. The nurses were very angry.

They hate these patients, and they get very angry at the resident whose patient it is. I didn't know what to do, but I was getting very upset. So I went to the director and in my best Harvard Medical School manner began in a very intellectual way to describe the case. To my horror I couldn't go on but began to weep. I couldn't stop. He said, 'If you showed the patient what you showed me, I think she'd know you cared.' So I did. I told her that I cared, that it was distressing to me. She stopped. It was a very important lesson."

Psychiatrists may be the bottom line for suicide care, but the ascendancy of HMOs and the proliferation of SSRIs have made it likely that most depressed and suicidal patients will never see a psychiatrist—or any other mental health professional. Between 50 and 75 percent of those seeking help for a psychiatric disorder are treated in a primary care setting; up to 10 percent of primary care patients suffer from major depression. Yet general practitioners, who are thus best positioned to help suicidal patients, are perhaps least prepared. Medical education is dominated by illnesses of the body, and the mind is relegated to a few lectures in psychology plus a four-to-six-week psychiatric rotation. Commenting on his 1997 survey, which found that fewer than half of primary-care-physician-training programs collaborated with departments of psychiatry—and that those that did, didn't collaborate much—former APA president Jerry Wiener suggested that the current position of GPs as the frontline providers of psychiatric care "leaves them in the role of the emperor who rides naked through the streets while managed-care and cost-cutting health-policy gurus ask that we admire the emperor's new clothes." In another survey, 3,375 primary care physicians reported widespread lack of knowledge about the diagnosis and treatment of depression—which may help explain why more than half of patients with depression seen by primary care physicians are misdiagnosed. (NIMH data suggest that as many as 30 percent of people who walk into a general practitioner's office use physical complaints as a smoke screen for depression and other mental health problems and that GPs miss 90 percent of those cases.) Even when depression is accurately diagnosed, the majority of patients are undermedicated, receive inadequate follow-up, and often fail to be given appropriate medication adjustment. Depressed children may be most at risk; a survey of pediatricians and family physicians found that 72 percent had prescribed SSRIs for a child or adolescent, yet only 8 percent felt they had received sufficient training in treating youthful depression.

If few GPs are equipped to diagnose and treat depression, fewer still are equipped to assess and treat suicidal patients. The knowledge base has no doubt improved since 1967, when a survey of Philadelphia medical schools found that half the students believed that if a person talks about suicide, he will not commit it. (Half also believed that masturbation frequently causes mental illness; it is not clear whether this was the same half.) Yet in a recent poll reported in the *Journal of the American Medical Association,* 91 percent of physicians felt their knowledge of suicide assessment and treatment techniques was inadequate. One-third of people who kill themselves see a primary care provider in the week before their suicide; more than half in the month before, and nearly 75 percent in the previous year. "Many people go to physicians hoping to be asked about suicide," says psychiatrist Alan Stone. They're not likely to be. A 2000 study found that many physicians still believe the old canard—that if they ask a patient about suicide, it will plant the idea in his head. This may be why only slightly more than half of primary care physicians directly question patients about suicide during routine depression evaluation. Although the 2001 Academy of Sciences Report recommended that medical and nursing schools incorporate the study of suicidal behavior into their curricula, there is institutional reluctance. "We don't pay enough attention to psychiatric aspects of medical education, so I welcome anything in that direction," says psychiatrist Leon Eisenberg. "But specifically for suicide?" He shrugs. "We don't even teach our medical students how to deal with stress in themselves." Even if GPs *had* the training to assess suicidality, few have the time; the average visit to a primary care physician lasts 16.3 minutes, during which patients bring an average of six problems to discuss. "The worst thing about HMOs is that there's no longer any time to spend with the patient," says a GP with thirty years' experience. "The drugs came along and really worked, but they're so easy to abuse—a patient comes in depressed, and when you look out and see fifteen or twenty people in the waiting room, you don't have time to do anything other than toss prescriptions at the fellow."

------

Among the most difficult decisions for any medical professional, whether psychiatrist or family physician, is whether to hospitalize when a patient is, as Ari Kiev puts it, "hot." Increasing attention to patients' civil rights has barbwired the issue; a clinician may be sued for putting a patient into the hospital or for keeping him out. "People often send people to hospitals not because they think they'll do better there but because they're afraid there will be a suicide for which they'll be held responsible," says Hendin. Such buck-passing is based on the belief that the hospital, where access to potential tools of self-destruction is limited, is the safest place for suicidal patients. "We tend to think we've solved the problem by getting the person into the hospital," says Norman Farberow, "but psychiatric hospitals have a suicide rate more than five times greater than in the community." (They are, admittedly, working with a high-risk group; the majority of inpatients are admitted because they have threatened or attempted suicide.) While acknowledging that hospitalization may be the only answer to a severe suicidal crisis, Farberow calls it "an expensive, frequently crippling, stultifying experience." In the opinion of some psychiatrists, the hospital may literally be the last resort. "I rarely put suicidal patients in the hospital anymore," says Maltsberger. "People need the hospital when they have nothing else to sustain them. If they can get a good therapist without going in, they're better off. The hospital is the absolute end of the line."

Certainly, even at the finest hospitals and despite the most stringent controls, patients find ways to kill themselves. Some 5 percent of all suicides take place in mental hospitals, nearly half of them within a week of admission. David Reynolds, an anthropologist who entered a California VA hospital under an assumed name and condition found "hundreds of ways"—nails; windows; razors; plastic bags; broken glass; high places; coat hangers; tonguing and accumulating pills; stuffing toilet paper down one's throat; even clogging a sink, filling it with water, then banging one's head against a faucet until, unconscious, one drowns. In a study of hospitalized patients who had completed suicide, more than 40 percent had been on fifteen-minute "checks" at the time of their death. Paradoxically, some in-hospital suicides may be a sign of a healthy environment; an exceedingly low rate of suicide in a hospital may mean restrictive measures are excessive. "Very often hospitals are dominated by the same mentality that may have brought the patient there in the first place," says Hendin. "They don't want to be blamed for a suicide, so they devote their efforts to monitoring the patient—preventing and controlling." There is little evidence that seclusion rooms, surveillance cameras, twenty-four-hour observation, or removal of "sharps" and other ingredients of "suicide watch" are effective. Half of all suicides at Metropolitan State Hospital in Norwalk, California, over forty-two years took place in seclusion rooms. In fact, a study attributing a decline in suicides at Baltimore's Sheppard Pratt Hospital to a decrease in such measures concluded that protective restrictions may increase suicide by calling attention to it. Susanna Kaysen, whose memoir, *Girl, Interrupted,* describes her stay at McLean Hospital, told me that after months of unshaven legs and plastic spoons, "people started thinking about committing suicide because the hospital makes such a big deal about *keeping* people from committing suicide." Hendin shakes his head: "That's what the problem is! Suicidal people are into control, the hospitals are into control, and it becomes a power struggle in which no therapy can take place."

Therapy may not be the most important service a hospital can offer a suicidal patient. When William Styron, suffering from depression and beset by suicidal thoughts that seemed only to be exacerbated by the medication his psychiatrist prescribed, inquired "rather hesitantly" about hospitalization, his psychiatrist said he should avoid it "at all costs," because of the stigma. When his condition worsened, however, Styron was admitted. Although he scorned the therapeutic agenda—group therapy was "a way to occupy the hours"; art therapy was "organized infantilism"—Styron believes that the hospital saved his life.

. . . it is something of a paradox that in this austere place with its locked and wired doors and desolate green hallways—ambulances screeching night and day ten floors below—I found the repose, the assuagement of the tempest in my brain, that I was unable to find in my quiet farmhouse.

This is partly the result of sequestration, of safety, of being removed to a world in which the urge to pick up a knife and plunge it into one's own breast disappears in the newfound knowledge, quickly apparent even to the depressive's fuzzy brain, that the knife with which he is attempting to cut his dreadful Swiss steak is bendable plastic. But the hospital also offers the mild, oddly gratifying trauma of sudden stabilization—a transfer out of the too familar surroundings of home, where all is anxiety and discord, into an orderly and benign detention where one's only duty is to try to get well. For me the real healers were seclusion and time.

Time, however, is a luxury that few patients can afford. Styron was fortunate in being able to finance a seven-week stay in one of the best psychiatric facilities in the country. Most insurance policies cover only five days of inpatient care—down from thirty in the late eighties, ninety in the late sixties—hardly long enough to get started on a course of medication, let alone in-depth psychotherapy. (Medications are the primary—and, often, only—form of treatment in psychiatric hospitals today.) Hospitals across the country are under increasing pressure from insurance companies to make patient stays shorter, and under pressure from all sides to get patients "cured," or at least functioning, before their coverage runs out. (The American Psychiatric Association boasts that most hospitals "begin planning for discharge on the first day of admission.") Over the last several decades, with growing reliance on drug therapy and increased pressure to cut costs, the average psychiatric hospital stay has dwindled to twelve days. At private hospitals like Styron's—of which there are not many left—inpatient treatment can run more than $1,000 a day, a rate at which extended care is available only to a select group. The alternative is a state hospital, where levels of staffing, training, funding, and treatment are far lower, making it "extremely difficult for state hospital staff to provide a true rehabilitative program to their patients," according to psychiatrist Robert Okin. "Moreover, these conditions lead staff to conclude that they are neither expected nor required to do much more than provide a safe place for patients to spend their time."

Today, even a "safe place" for patients to spend their time is difficult to obtain. When advances in psychopharmacology, press exposés of state hospital "snake pits," and the Community Mental Health Centers Act of 1963 led to deinstitutionalization in the late sixties, the move was applauded as a reform in the tradition of Pinel striking off the chains at Bicêtre two centuries earlier. Beyond the great expectations, however, there was little planning. Thousands of patients were discharged annually to community facilities that were inadequate or nonexistent. The state hospital population plummeted from 558,600 in 1955 to 54,000 in 2000, setting adrift a flood of mentally ill people to fend for themselves amid a patchwork quilt of services that had neither the time, training, nor funds to cope with them. Many of the deinstitutionalized ended up wandering the city streets. Experts estimate the number of America's homeless to be as high as 3.5 million—as many as 35 percent of whom suffer from untreated psychiatric illness. Many others ended up in prison, having committed petty crimes, acted threateningly, or just caused trouble once too often. Some 250,000 mentally ill Americans live behind bars—78 percent more than a decade ago and nearly five times the number in state psychiatric hospitals.

There has been no research on the effect of deinstitutionalization on suicide, but while state hospitals are crying out for qualified therapists (who can make three times more money in private practice), patients are crying to get in. "These days it's easier to get admitted to Harvard than into the state hospital," observes one psychiatrist. In most states, a person must be judged to be at risk of doing "serious harm to himself or to others"—homicidal or suicidal. But admission is often decided on the basis of bed availability rather than need. "They take only the most violent, the most psychotic," fumes a community mental health center director in New York City who admits he has coached suicidal patients on how to act sufficiently disturbed when they present at a hospital. Suicide ideation no longer guarantees admission; people commonly *attempt* suicide to get in. Even then they may be refused. Investigating the suicide of a Los Angeles woman, a social worker learned that on the last day of her life she had tried to commit herself into three large hospitals with psychiatric units. She was turned away at all three. That night she killed herself.

Even if a person manages to get into a public psychiatric hospital, stringent admission standards have changed the hospital milieu. "You used to be able to send a depressed patient to the hospital for R and R," says an Oakland therapist. "Now people in the hospital are *very* crazy, and if you are able to get hospitalized, you're surrounded by psychotic patients. It can be very scary." If a patient isn't "crazy" enough, the hospital isn't apt to let him remain. "You get into unfortunate situations because the state hospitals often don't keep people who are suicidal unless they are incredibly suicidal," says Stanford University psychiatrist Alan Schatzberg, who worked at McLean Hospital for nearly twenty years. "It becomes a kind of dangerous game of chicken."

The patient is usually the loser. Repeated studies have shown that the suicide rate jumps in the weeks immediately after patients leave the relative safety of the hospital and return to the stressed environment they'd left, frequently without provision for follow-up care, and with the increased likelihood that they will stop taking their medications. "Often caught in the dilemma of being too well to be in the hospital but not well enough to deal with the realities and stresses of life outside, as well as having to contend with the personal and economic consequences of having a serious mental illness, patients sometimes feel utterly hopeless and overwhelmed, and kill themselves," writes Kay Jamison in *Night Falls Fast.* Yet something as seemingly trivial as a piece of mail may help. A study by San Francisco psychiatrist Jerome Motto and epidemiologist Alan Bostrom of 843 suicidal people who refused follow-up treatment after discharge found that sending them regular letters expressing concern—as simple as "we hope things are going well for you"—resulted in a lower rate of completed suicide.

With treatment decisions increasingly based on legal or financial considerations rather than on patient need, the suicidal person is caught in the middle. At a time when the percentage of mentally ill people in this country has swollen, according to NIMH estimates, it is increasingly difficult for them to get care. The inability of the mental health system to cope with the demand has led to a practice that seems an unsettling symptom, as it were, of an underlying illness in the system. In the past several decades, more than a few overcrowded clinics and hospitals, frustrated by a particularly troublesome patient, have bought him a ticket and put him on a bus bound for a distant city, where he arrived homeless, friendless, and alone. "Greyhound therapy," as it has been dubbed, seems a chilling end point to the humanism that, in part, inspired deinstitutionalization. It makes one wonder how far, despite our 250 different psychotherapies and our armamentarium of wonder drugs, we have come since the medieval days when townspeople loaded irksome madmen onto a boat and shipped them downriver in what became known as a ship of fools.

---

Because so much emphasis has been put on psychotherapists and dispensers of medications, it is easy to forget that suicide prevention has long had another genre of gatekeeper: the clergy. Modern suicide prevention programs were originated by religious groups, but despite strong evidence that religion plays a protective factor, with the medicalization of mental illness suicide has been secularized and the clergy's role consequently underestimated and ambiguous. Studies say that 50 to 80 percent of people with mental health problems come first to the clergy. "Often the clergy are not aware of the problem and pass it off," says Monsignor James Cassidy. "Most clergymen don't realize their limitations and the importance of getting professional help." Earl Grollman, a rabbi in Belmont, Massachusetts, and the author of numerous books on death and suicide, says, "I have to laugh when I read Ann Landers telling suicidal people to 'speak to your clergyperson.' There might be three people in all of greater Boston that I consider to be knowledgeable in this field. Clergypeople feel they have to give a religious orientation, not understanding that prevention consists of listening, caring, and touching." Grollman pauses. "There's a story told about Martin Buber. He is praying when someone knocks at the door and says, 'Can I see you?' Martin Buber says, 'I'm busy. Come back later.' The person never comes back—he commits suicide. And Martin Buber says, 'Here I had a chance to be with God, but I lost God in prayer.'"

"I don't think doctors appreciate the role of the pastor in counseling," the Reverend Robert Utter of the Church of the Nazarene in Cambridge told me. "But that may be changing. They've come to realize we're available every hour of the night or day, and we don't charge a fee." For the parishioner in crisis Utter prescribes a list of scriptures, extra prayer, perhaps an outing with the church singles group, and in emergencies the counseling center at nearby Eastern Nazarene College. "We believe in hell, so our people would think twice before taking their life," says Utter. "There is an expression I use when counseling people who talk about suicide. I tell them, 'You think you have problems now; wait until you end up in hell. You'll just be out of the frying pan and into the fire.'" Prescribing the Bible rather than antidepressants can be a risky therapeutic approach. In 1980, a California church and its pastor were sued by the parents of a twenty-four-year-old man, in the first prominent clergy-malpractice lawsuit. After a previous suicide attempt, Kenneth Nally had been in pastoral counseling with the Reverend John MacArthur Jr. of Grace Community Church of the Valley, who referred to suicide as "one of the ways that the Lord takes home a disobedient believer." Nally shot himself. Although Nally had been seen by several physicians and a psychiatrist, his parents claimed that MacArthur had tried to dissuade their son from seeking secular help and had made his condition worse by telling him that his depression was the result of his sinning.

Although the $1 million suit was eventually dismissed by the California Supreme Court in 1988, which ruled that as "non-therapist counselors," the clergy had no legal duty to save lives, it underlined that in their response to suicide, clergy are often torn between viewing the person as a patient and viewing him as a parishioner. Religion and psychiatry work in an uneasy truce, as if psychological and spiritual dimensions inhabited different halves of the person. While counseling in the emergency room of the Cambridge Hospital, psychologist Nancy Kehoe, who is also a nun, realized that religion never came up in patient assessments. Kehoe sent a questionnaire to local clinics and found that of fourteen hundred suicidal cases, religion was broached in fewer than three hundred, more often than not by the patient. "In the face of suicide, which is a person's ultimate statement about life and death, why do we separate mental health and belief?" asks Kehoe. Clinicians have found numerous reasons to do so. "Many of them were taught that science and psychology should be separate from religion," says Kehoe. "Some are very uncomfortable with the subject. Others don't know what to ask beyond 'Are you Protestant, Jewish, or Catholic?'" Kehoe's definition goes beyond what she calls "God talk"; it means thinking about a person's spiritual life as part of the total picture. "Then when a person is talking about suicide, it's natural to say, 'What do you think you're going toward? What kind of spiritual things keep you going?'" Clinicians in Kehoe's study who did bring up religion found it useful. Says Kehoe, "Some even felt that if a person had lost faith, it was an indicator of suicidal risk." (One wrote, "Highly religious people do not commit suicide.") She sighs. "All I'm asking is whether we'd learn something about a person if we brought up his spiritual beliefs, without judging whether or not it's going to save lives."

Kehoe's findings are troubling. If suicide is purely a biological and psychological problem, then treatment is clearly the undisputed province of the physicians and mental health professionals. But the strands that combine to prevent a suicide are as numerous as those that combine to push someone to suicide. In the twenty-first-century perspective of suicide from the medical model, we risk excluding not only the religious or spiritual dimension of self-destruction, as Kehoe points out, but the social and existential dimensions as well. "Suicide can best be understood in terms of concepts from several points of view," wrote Edwin Shneidman in *Definition of Suicide.* "It follows that treatment of a suicidal individual should reflect the learnings from these same several disciplines." Shneidman suggested that optimum treatment might be effected by a "Therapeutic Council." "Such a council would be concerned with the biological, sociological, developmental, philosophical, and cognitive aspects of its patients. It might include a biologically oriented psychiatrist, a psychoanalytically oriented therapist, a sociologist, a logician-philosopher, a marriage and family counselor, and an existential social worker." While Shneidman's proposal is, of course, impractical, the concept is sound. If suicide is caused by a variety of factors, suicide prevention should address each of those elements.

Even further, true suicide prevention might address the problem *before* people reach the point of crisis, before they call the hotline or appear in the emergency room. While not thought of primarily as suicide prevention measures, there are many steps that might help reduce the suicide rate: further developing our understanding of alcoholism, depression, and schizophrenia; routine screening for problem drinking in all patients; tackling such societal ills as unemployment, divorce, homelessness, violence, inadequate education, unwanted children, and neglect of the elderly; improving medical and social services and making them accessible and affordable to all; finding ways to promote ethical and spiritual values; and reducing the threat of terrorism. In short, one might lower the suicide rate by giving people more reasons to stay alive. Years ago psychologist Pam Cantor appeared on the television news show *Nightline* to discuss the causes of suicide. At the end of the program, host Ted Koppel said, "All right, we have half a minute left. You've described the litany of ills that exist. Is there anything that can be done short of changing our society inside out?" "Well, I don't think you should say 'short of,'" answered Cantor. "I think that's what's necessary."

# IV

# SOCIAL STUDIES

---

ONE AUGUST DAY in 1937, a forty-seven-year-old bargeman and World War I veteran named Harold Wobber took a bus to the Golden Gate Bridge, paid his way through the pedestrian turnstile, and began to walk across the mile-long span. He was accompanied by a tourist he had met on the bus, Professor Lewis Neylor of Trinity College in Connecticut. They had strolled across the bridge, which stretches in a single arch from San Francisco to the hills of Marin County, and were on their way back when Wobber tossed his coat and vest to Professor Neylor. "This is where I get off," he said quietly. "I'm going to jump." As Wobber climbed over the four-foot railing, the professor managed to grab his belt, but Wobber pulled free and leaped to his death.

Less than three months after the Golden Gate Bridge had opened to great fanfare, Wobber became its first known suicide. Since then more than twelve hundred others have jumped, making it, as one researcher observes, "the number one location for suicide in the entire world." As with most suicide statistics, the numbers are conservative. Only those who have been seen jumping or whose bodies are recovered are counted as bridge suicides. One expert suggests that several hundred others may have leaped unseen, in darkness, rain, or fog, been swept out to sea, and their bodies never found. A leap from the bridge is easy, quick, and lethal; one merely steps over a chest-high railing. At seventy-five miles per hour, the 240-foot drop lasts four seconds. If the force of the fall doesn't kill the jumper instantly, crushing his internal organs, the current will sweep him out to sea to drown or be devoured by sharks. Of all the people known to have fallen or jumped from the bridge since it opened, only twenty-six have survived.

The Golden Gate Bridge is not the only location to exert a particular fascination for suicidal people. Throughout history certain cliffs, churches, and skyscrapers have earned reputations as suicide landmarks: Niagara Falls, the Cathedral at Milan, St. Peter's, the Eiffel Tower, the Empire State Building, the cliffs at Beachy Head, and Giotto's Campanile on the Duomo in Florence are among them. Not all settings are so grand. In 1813, in a French village, a woman hanged herself from a large tree; within a short time several other women followed her example, using the same branch. In New York's Bowery there was a saloon in whose back room so many vagrants killed themselves, it became known as Suicide Hall. And, of course, most towns have their "lover's leap." In Japan, where self-destruction has found institutional acceptance, many suicides choose a spectacular natural setting for their death—"almost any place in Japan that is famous for its scenery is also famous for its suicides," observed an American visitor in 1930.

Three years later, a Japanese place famous for its scenery—Mihara-Yama, a volcano on the island of Oshima—would provide a dramatic case study of the roles of culture, imitation, and social policy in suicide. On January 7, 1933, Mieko Ueki, twenty-four, and Masako Tomita, twenty-one, classmates at an exclusive Tokyo school, bought tickets on the small steamship that made three trips weekly to the island. After the six-hour, sixty-mile passage the young women scaled the three-thousand-foot peak. When they reached the crater, which boiled and sputtered with sulfur clouds, Mieko told Masako that she had visited Mount Mihara the previous year and been enchanted by the legend decreeing that the bodies of those who jumped into the crater were instantly cremated and sent to heaven in the form of smoke. This was a beautiful, poetic form of death, said Mieko, and she intended to jump. Masako protested but eventually agreed not to intervene. The two girls bowed to each other. Then Mieko leapt into the smoking crater.

The story of the maiden and the volcano quickly became legend. Japan was in the midst of an economic depression, and the volcano was a national attraction for both tourists and suicides. In the remaining months of 1933, 143 people followed Mieko's example; on one April day there were six suicides, while twenty-five more were forcibly prevented. The deaths kindled a mixture of horror and fascination. The steamship company bought two new ships and made daily trips to accommodate the rubberneckers; company shareholders made a profit on their investment for the first time in four years. Along the harbor, fourteen hotels, twenty restaurants, and five taxicab companies opened within two years; the number of island photographers increased from two to forty-seven; a post office was built at the crater's edge; three camels were imported to carry tourists across the mile-wide strip of volcanic desert that surrounded the crater; horses ferried them to the summit. And a twelve-hundred-foot "shoot the chute" was built to spice up the return trip down the slope for those who chose to make it. Suicide had become a spectator sport; on a day when several hours had passed without a death, a tourist laughingly shouted, "I dare someone to jump!" A man ran forward and threw himself into the crater.

Eventually, the embarrassed government intervened. It was made a criminal offense to purchase a one-way ticket to Oshima, and plainclothes detectives were instructed to mingle with passengers on the boat, arresting anyone who looked bent on self-destruction—their criteria are not known. Tokyo police patrolled the crater; by the end of 1934, policemen and civilian onlookers had restrained 1,208 people from jumping. A barbed-wire fence was erected and a twenty-four-hour watch was posted. The hastily formed Mount Mihara Anti-Suicide League even devised an elaborate arrangement of mirrors to give would-be suicides a terrifying view of the volcano's interior. Despite these efforts at least 167 more men and women leaped to their death in 1934, and 29 who had been restrained dove off the steamship returning them to Tokyo. By the time access to the mountain was closed in 1935, an estimated 804 males and 140 females had found their death in the volcano. (Today, the country's leading suicide spot is Aokigahara-Jukai, a dense forest at the foot of Mount Fuji, where about seventy people a year take their life, usually by hanging or overdose, many of them coming from far away. A study of 116 people who attempted suicide in the forest found that most believed it to be "a sanctuary where suicide was allowed," a setting that would "purify" or "beautify" their death.)

Although the authorities acted tardily in the case of Mount Mihara, elsewhere, when certain locations seem to beckon the suicidal, steps have been taken to discourage them. In 1850 an American physician traveling in Europe wrote, "At one time there seemed to be a growing propensity to jump from the Leaning Tower at Pisa; three persons—as I learnt from my guide while on a visit to it—having thus put a period to their existence; on which account visitors could no longer ascend it without an authorized attendant." In 1881 the column in Paris's Place Vendôme was closed following a wave of suicides. In the early twentieth century a lake near Kobe, Japan, was drained because of the number of people who drowned themselves in its waters. Fences and barriers have greatly reduced the number of suicides at St. Peter's, the Eiffel Tower, and the Arroyo Seco Bridge in Pasadena. In the first sixteen years after the Empire State Building opened in 1931, sixteen people jumped to their death; not until 1947, when a man landed on a woman in the street below, critically injuring her, was a seven-foot, spiked fence installed around the eighty-sixth-floor observation deck. In the nearly six decades since then, only fifteen others have jumped. In many other instances in which barriers, window stops, or emergency phones have been installed, suicides have been eliminated or greatly reduced. Nevertheless, despite more than twelve hundred deaths and six decades of debate, no barrier has been erected at the Golden Gate Bridge.

Even before Harold Wobber leaped to his death, there was concern about the

Golden Gate's potential for suicides. Although the bridge was designed to accommodate benches for pedestrians, the bridge's board of directors feared they might be used as stiles, making it even easier for people to climb over the rail. The benches were never installed. Over the years, as the death toll mounted, various measures were considered: electric fences, barbed wire, safety nets, a twenty-four-hour motorcycle patrol, signs advising THINK BEFORE YOU LEAP, and legislation prohibiting jumping from the bridge. As early as 1953 a barrier was proposed. An engineer told the bridge board that the existing railing could be raised to seven feet for $200,000. All of these proposals were rejected as being either too expensive, too dangerous to workers on the bridge, too foolish, or merely ineffective.

In the face of increased publicity and rising public concern, a few precautions were taken. In 1960 the bridge board ordered pedestrian sidewalks closed between sunset and sunrise. By 1970 a closed-circuit television system had been installed in the toll office, enabling workers to scan the pedestrian walkway and dispatch officers to restrain possible jumpers. A two-man tow truck roved the bridge. Patrolmen were taught to be on the lookout for women without purses, people edging away from their tourist group, or people staring intently at the surface of the water. Bridge personnel were trained in suicide prevention by a local prevention center. Thirteen telephones, from which concerned people can contact the control tower, have been placed at intervals along the span. California highway patrolmen and bridge personnel conduct random patrols by car, motorcycle, bicycle, and on foot. Over the years, bridge workers, patrolmen, toll officers, passing motorists, and pedestrians have talked down or pulled back hundreds of would-be jumpers, often at risk to their own lives. One state highway patrolman alone claimed to have prevented 217 suicides in nine years on the job. Indeed, it is estimated that for every suicide from the bridge, two others are prevented.

During the suicide prevention movement of the late sixties and early seventies, the debate over an antisuicide fence came to a head. A committee was formed to lobby for a barrier, and the argument raged in editorials and letters to the editor. The bridge battle was a microcosm of discussions about personal freedom and the value of life that have taken place around the country wherever antisuicide barriers have been proposed. How far should we go to prevent suicide? Bridge directors received hundreds of letters, about two-thirds opposing the barrier. Some argued that it would spoil the view: Why destroy the view for so many for the sake of so few? Some suggested it was a waste of money: Why spend money on someone who wants to die? Others felt the money would be better spent on free mental health care. Many defended a person's right to suicide. "If and when I decide to die I would prefer the bridge as an exit point and I don't want to be kept from it by a high, jail-like railing," one woman wrote to the San Francisco Chronicle. "There are worse things than death and one should be able to make that personal choice if necessary." A few even argued that an unfettered bridge saved lives by acting as a magnet to which disturbed people were drawn and could more easily be intercepted and delivered to treatment. The most popular argument against a barrier was that it simply wouldn't work; common sense said that suicidal people would simply go kill themselves somewhere else.

Arguing in favor of the barrier, suicidologists pointed out that suicide is often an impulsive act, and the impulse, once thwarted, is frequently abandoned. They cited studies showing that only 10 percent of those who attempt suicide go on to kill themselves. They pointed out that 90 percent of bridge suicides jump from the side of the bridge facing San Francisco—facing what they're leaving behind—as an indication of their ambivalence. They explained that suicidal people are apt to choose a highly personal method, and if that method is unavailable, they may abandon their plans rather than switch to another. In a suicidal crisis, people often lack the flexibility to generate alternatives when foiled. The suicidologists pointed to other locales in which barriers had decreased the number of suicides without spoiling the view. They indicated that the lethality of the method and the impulsiveness of many suicides made the bridge an especially deadly combination. "The bridge is like having a loaded gun around," said psychiatrist Jerome Motto at a 1971 hearing. "I think it is the responsibility of those in control to unload the gun." Although the bridge board authorized a $20,000 preliminary study and a sample of the winning design was constructed, the debate dragged on and the barrier went unbuilt.

Then Richard Seiden, a pro-barrier Berkeley psychologist, gathered the names of 515 people who had been restrained from jumping from the bridge dating back to its opening day. Checking their names against death certificates, he learned that only twenty-five had gone on to take their own life. Although his research proved that people did not inexorably go on to commit suicide using another method, critics argued that people restrained from jumping were not truly bent on death. What about those who had jumped and lived? In 1975, psychiatrist David Rosen interviewed six of the eight people known to have survived leaps from the Golden Gate Bridge. None of the eight survivors had gone on to kill themselves; the six he interviewed all favored the construction of an antisuicide fence. They all said that had there been a barrier, they would not have tried to kill themselves some other way. Their plans had involved only the Golden Gate Bridge; like those who attempted suicide in the forest of Jukai, they spoke of an association between its beauty and death. For them, Rosen said, the bridge was a "suicide shrine."

A second study by Seiden supported the notion that the Golden Gate Bridge had a "fatal mystique." Comparing Golden Gate suicides to San Francisco–Oakland Bay Bridge suicides, he found that although the two spans were completed within a few months of each other and are about the same height, five times as many people had completed suicide from the Golden Gate Bridge as from the Bay Bridge, its homely sister. Unlike the Golden Gate, the

Bay Bridge does not allow pedestrian traffic. Yet even when pedestrian suicides were omitted, the Golden Gate still spawned three times as many suicides. The Golden Gate Bridge, said Seiden, had become "a suicide mecca"; while its suicides usually made the front page, Bay Bridge suicides were rarely publicized. Seiden found "a commonly held attitude that often romanticizes suicide from the Golden Gate Bridge in such terms as 'aesthetically pleasing,' and 'beautiful,' while regarding Bay Bridge suicide as 'tacky' and 'déclassé.'" His statistics supported this: half of the bridge suicides who lived east of San Francisco had chosen to drive over the Bay Bridge and across the city to the Golden Gate Bridge to end their life.

Although Seiden's and Rosen's research seemed to put to rest the notion that if people were kept from killing themselves at the bridge, they would simply "go someplace else," the campaign for a barrier became a moot political issue. "The bottom line is money," says Seiden. "If it costs money, the bridge directors don't want to do it." Yet in 2003, a fifty-four-inch-high steel fence was built between the bridge walkway and the automobile lanes to prevent bicycles from accidentally drifting into traffic. The $5 million project was deemed a necessity—"it's a public safety issue" was the refrain.

Clearly, more than money is involved. In one recent poll, 54 percent of city residents continued to oppose a suicide barrier. Seiden believes that San Franciscans like to think of their city as a tough-living, hard-drinking town and may take a perverse pride in the bridge's reputation. Gray Line tour bus drivers recite the bridge's suicide statistics in their tourist spiel; guidebooks describe its fatal allure. In 1981, workers at a local lumberyard organized a sports pool in which players bet on which day of the week the next Golden Gate suicide would take place. For many years, the city's newspapers kept a kind of running box score in which news of each new jumper concluded with the observation that it was the bridge's $n$th suicide. In 1995, as number 1,000 approached and the publicity crested, a disc jockey promised a case of Snapple to the victim's family. Under pressure from various suicide prevention agencies, however, the local media was persuaded to downplay bridge suicides; indeed, the California Highway Patrol stopped its official public tally at 997. Lack of publicity couldn't stem the tide. In July 1995, a twenty-five-year-old man became the bridge's unofficial thousandth suicide. And the number continues to climb; when Seiden sends out his research papers, he pencils in the updated statistics.

But the line between pride and embarrassment is thin. In January 2005, shortly after a filmmaker shooting a documentary about the Golden Gate's "grandeur" revealed that cameras he had set up on the bridge had captured more than a dozen people jumping, the suicide barrier issue was rushed onto the agenda of the bridge's building and operations committee. Two months later, the bridge's board of directors voted to seek $2 million to study the issue. (The filmmaker says that his documentary will now focus not on the bridge's "grandeur," but on "the human spirit in crisis.")

One breezy autumn morning Seiden and I drove from downtown San Francisco toward the Golden Gate Bridge. Just before the tollbooths on the bridge's south side he directed me onto a narrow road on the right marked RESTRICTED ACCESS. About fifty yards down the road there was a deserted, weedy lot littered with ladders, broken window casings, and confusions of chicken wire. In the midst of this, like an abandoned sculpture, stood a curious metal structure, an eighteen-foot section of steel fence painted the same russet red as the Golden Gate Bridge. Its pencil-thin spires rose about eight feet into the air. On one-half of the fence the spires pointed toward the sky; on the other half they curved gently inward at the top, like the fingers of a cupped hand. Through the graceful spires there was a stunning view of the Golden Gate Bridge as it leaped more than a mile over the bay into the soft green hills of Marin County. "Winning design number sixteen," said Seiden quietly. "It's been sitting here for years."

---

Bridge barriers, nets on observation decks, signs and emergency telephones on bridges, windows that don't open wide—these are only some of the ways in which "environmental risk reduction," as Seiden calls it, might help prevent suicide. "There is more than one approach to suicide prevention," says Seiden. "You can try to get inside people's heads and work with their self-esteem. You can work with parenting and with early recognition of depression, but you can also try to do something about the lethal agents of suicide—the guns, the pills, the bridges. It's the same as automobile safety. You can do driver training and you can make the car safer. You can change the environment as well as change the individual." With suicide seen almost exclusively from the medical model, however, the possibilities of environmental and social change have been neglected. Critics say that these are superficial measures, that Seiden is treating symptoms, not causes. "Sometimes that's all you can treat," says Seiden. "Frankly, we haven't had a good record in treating suicidal patients from the inside out."

For many years the most popular method of suicide in Great Britain was asphyxiation—sticking one's head in the oven and turning on the gas. After the discovery of oil and natural gas deposits in the North Sea in the fifties and sixties, most English homes converted from coke gas, whose high carbon monoxide content made it highly lethal, to less toxic natural gas. From 1963 to 1978 the number of English suicides by gas dropped from 2,368 to 11, and the country's overall suicide rate decreased by one-third. By the mideighties, however, the suicide rate had rebounded to its previous level, suggesting that potential suicides were substituting other methods. But the evidence indicated that taking away one method can have a remarkable effect. Indeed, British and Australian studies show that restrictions on prescribing barbiturates have reduced the number of attempted or completed barbiturate suicides without increasing the number of suicides by other means. Suicidologists have called for tighter regulation of potentially lethal medications and for training physicians and pharmacists in clues to depression and suicide. They propose the universal use of blister packaging, which requires single capsules to be punched out individually, allowing more time for emotions to cool or rescuers to intervene.

"Much could be gained if we tried to make suicide more difficult for the potential candidate. . . . Opportunity makes the suicide as well as the thief," observed David Oppenheim at the 1910 meeting of the Vienna Psychoanalytic Society devoted to suicide. "An opportunity for self-destruction is offered to anyone who is in the position to bring about his death by some swift and easy action that is painless and avoids revolting mutilations and disfigurement. A loaded pistol complies so well with all these conditions that its possession positively urges the idea of suicide on its owner." Far more urging takes place now than in Oppenheim's day. There are 200 million civilian-owned guns in the United States (more than twice the number thirty-five years ago), including 65 million handguns. During that time, numerous studies have linked increased gun ownership not only to increased rates of crime, armed robbery, and homicide, but also, unarguably, to suicide.

Only in the United States, among all the countries in the world, are guns the primary means of suicide. They are the most frequently used method in every age group, except ages ten to fourteen, in which they have recently been eclipsed by hangings. In a landmark 1983 study, NIMH researcher Jeffrey Boyd scrutinized suicide rates for 1953 to 1978 and found that the firearm suicide rate had steadily risen while the rate by all other methods had declined. In 1953, firearm suicides accounted for 46 percent of all suicides; in 1978 they constituted 56 percent. (Today, they account for 57 percent.) The jump in the firearm suicide rate accounted for an overall increase in the suicide rate from 12.4 in 1953 to 13.3 in 1978. Suggesting that the rise in suicide by firearms was related to the rise in gun sales and noting that handguns were used in 83 percent of all suicides by firearms, Boyd concluded, "It is conceivable that the rise in the suicide rate might be controlled by restricting the sale of handguns."

Subsequent research has supported this hypothesis. One study found that the strictness of state gun-control laws was significantly correlated with suicide rates; states with the toughest gun control laws had the lowest suicide rates. The rates in the ten states with the weakest handgun laws were more than twice as high as rates in the ten states with the strongest laws. A study of suicides in Los Angeles, as well as throughout California, during a three-year period found that citywide, countywide, and statewide the suicide rate by firearms rose and fell in near perfect harmony with the volume of gun sales. A Harvard School of Public Health study found that access to firearms has a much higher correlation to suicide than does suicidal ideation or major depression. Areas of the country in which there are more handguns—the

South and the mountain states—had higher rates, even after controlling for depression and suicidal thoughts. "Where there are more guns, there are more suicides," observed David Hemenway, the study's coauthor.

"If guns are outlawed, only outlaws will have guns," a favorite National Rifle Association homily, implies that ordinary citizens need guns to protect themselves. Yet a gun in the house is eleven times more likely to be used to attempt or complete suicide than to be used in self-defense; only 2 percent of gun-related deaths in the home are the result of a homeowner shooting an intruder, while 83 percent are the result of a suicide—often by someone other than the gun owner. In a study of eighty-two consecutive suicides in Cuyahoga County, Ohio, thirty-five were by gunshot. Only three of the guns had been purchased for the purpose of self-destruction; the majority had been acquired to protect the family. In a King County, Washington, firearms study, there were thirty-seven suicides for every self-protection homicide. Some 35 percent of American households have guns, making them five times more likely to experience a suicide than homes in which there are no guns present. "Guns don't kill—people do," another pro-gun-lobby mantra, is technically correct, yet guns make a suicide attempt five times more likely to be fatal; 90 percent of suicide attempts by firearm result in death, compared with 2 to 3 percent of attempts using drugs. "If some persons would use slower methods of self-destruction, some lives might be saved," concluded a National Violence Commission report. "The possibility that the presence [of firearms] is in some instances part of the causal chain that leads to an attempted suicide cannot be dismissed. With a depressed person, the knowledge of having a quick and effective way of ending his life might precipitate a suicide attempt on impulse."

Despite these studies, and while therapists commonly advise families of suicidal patients to "get the guns out of the house," little has been done on a broad scale to reduce firearm suicides. At the least, suicidologists recommend an enforced waiting period between purchase of a gun and the right to possess it, since the suicidal impulse might fade during that time. Although few of the guns used for suicide (according to one study, about 10 percent) are specifically purchased for that purpose, a study of 238,000 people who legally acquired handguns in California found that suicide was the leading cause of death among recent buyers. In the week following a handgun purchase, gun buyers are fifty-seven times more likely to kill themselves—and they remain at risk for years afterward. (The impact of the Brady Bill has yet to be fully determined. Although one study found a significant reduction in suicide rates following its enactment, the study's methodology has been questioned.) Suicidologists further suggest that the guns we do have should be fully child-proofed. In any case, while many more Americans kill themselves with guns than are murdered with them every year, suicide is rarely mentioned by either side in the gun control debate. In an editorial accompanying Jeffrey Boyd's research in the New England Journal of Medicine, Richard Hudgens admitted,

"It is unlikely that the suicidal use of guns will be an important factor in any eventual decision to limit their availability, for suicide is not high on the list of America's political concerns." When approached with the idea that a soaring firearms suicide rate might justify a call for tighter gun control, a National Rifle Association spokesman responded, "The NRA is not for gearing laws to the weakest element of society."

This Darwinian reflection speaks to the heart of the question of how far we should go to prevent suicide. Clearly, we cannot and should not make the world "suicide proof" nor our lives a twenty-four-hour suicide watch. Even if we could, suicides would of course still occur. But even if bridge barriers and gun control legislation were to have no effect on the suicide rate, there may be compelling reasons why such measures should nevertheless be taken. To put up or not put up a barrier says something about the way we feel about suicide and suicidal people.

I remember discussing the proposed Golden Gate Bridge barrier with a San Francisco friend. "Ninety-nine percent of us don't need it," she said. "Is it fair to ruin the view for the sake of a few? If they want to die so much, why not let them?" I found this attitude shared by many people. Their view often seemed based less on respect for individual freedom than on ignorance of the psychodynamics of self-destruction and discomfort with the subject of suicide in general. Whatever their reasons, it troubled me that so many otherwise kindhearted people should object to preventive measures. For how far is it from this passive condoning to the voices one sometimes hears when a crowd has gathered at the base of a tall building, to watch the weeping man on the ledge high above, shouting, "Jump, jump, jump"?

Fortunately, in answer to the voices who cry "Jump," many other voices cry "Live"—not just the voices of family, friends, therapists, and prevention center volunteers but the voices of strangers. When the twenty-year-old manager of a Brooklyn clothing store began receiving telephone calls for a now defunct suicide prevention hotline, he took time to listen to their problems. "They just start talking," he said. "I tell them they have the wrong number, but I ask them if I can help. . . . I believe in helping people out." When a twenty-six-year-old Austrian threatened to jump from the 446-foot steeple of St. Stephen's in Vienna, a thirty-four-year-old priest whose hobby is mountain climbing scaled the steeple and persuaded the man to descend. When an eighteen-year-old girl stood on the ledge of a seven-story building in Mexico City, Ignacio Canedo, an eighteen-year-old Red Cross male nurse, inched out toward her. Canedo was tied to a long rope, held on the other end by a squad of firemen. "Don't come any nearer!" shouted the girl. "Don't, or I'll jump!" Canedo grabbed for her and missed. The girl screamed and jumped. Canedo jumped after her, caught her in midair, and locked his arms around her waist. They fell four floors before the rope snapped taut. Canedo's grip held, and he and the girl were hauled back to the roof. "I knew the rope would save me," said Canedo. "I prayed that it would be strong enough to support both of us." There are hundreds of similar stories of potential suicides saved by strangers who instinctively reached out.

As a term project for "The Psychology of Death," a course taught by Edwin Shneidman at Harvard, one student placed an ad in the personals section of a local alternative newspaper: "M 21 student gives self 3 weeks before popping pills for suicide. If you know any good reasons why I shouldn't, please write Box D-673." Within a month he had received 169 letters. While the majority were from the Boston area, others came from as far away as New York, Wisconsin, Kentucky, even Rio de Janeiro. They offered many reasons why he should stay alive. Some wrote of music, smiles, movies, sunny days, sandy beaches. Some quoted Rod McKuen, e. e. cummings, or Dylan Thomas. They suggested he spend time with others less fortunate than he; implored him to think of those he would leave behind; called him a coward and dared him to struggle and survive. Some referred him to a therapist. Others offered friendship, enclosing their phone number or their address. A few enclosed gifts: two joints of marijuana; an advanced calculus equation; a Linus doll; magazine clippings on the subject of kindness; a photo of apple blossoms with the message "We're celebrating Apple Blossom Time." Some simply broke down in the middle of their letters and pleaded "Don't" or "You just can't."

The student was not actually contemplating suicide, but the answers he received were real. Whether they might have persuaded someone truly suicidal to stay alive is impossible to say. But if the forces that lead someone to suicide are numerous, those forces that combine to prevent someone from killing himself may be equally complex, whether they be SSRIs, a prevention center volunteer, a barrier on a bridge, a Linus doll, or the voice of a stranger saying "I care." "There is no magic bullet that goes right to the heart of suicidality," says Robert Litman. "Many, many things together bring a person to suicide, and many, many things together prevent a suicide. But if you have, say, twenty suicidal things and you can relieve just one, leaving only nineteen, you're probably going to get a sense of improvement and a little more hopefulness. And if you can maybe relieve parts of two or three others and get it down to seventeen, to sixteen, you're going to get another little increment of hopefulness, and you're on your way."

---

It was the last day of the fifteenth annual meeting of the American Association of Suicidology. More than five hundred suicidologists from dozens of states and countries had gathered at the Vista International Hotel in New York City for a four-day smorgasbord of workshops on "Suicide: Problems in the Big City," "Demographic Factors in Suicidal Behavior," "Fundraising: Effective Strategies and Methods for Suicide and Crisis Centers," and fifty-five other topics.

A who's who of suicide had assembled. Norman Farberow was there. So were Herbert Hendin, Ari Kiev, Bruce Danto, and Nancy Allen, the public health worker who was instrumental in organizing the first National Suicide Prevention Week in 1974. And everywhere you looked there was Edwin Shneidman, speechifying, kibitzing, or just standing in the back of the room watching the proceedings like a proud father. Heady company; at one point twelve past presidents of the AAS sat at the dais. Their combined efforts represented more than a hundred books, a thousand articles, and two hundred years of experience in the study of suicide and its prevention.

Now, while volunteers took down posters in the lobby (a photograph of a blank brick wall—SUICIDE IS A DEAD END), and the silver-haired proprietor of the Thanatology Book Club closed up shop, the day's first meeting was getting under way downstairs in the Nieuw Amsterdam Ballroom. It was nine o'clock. Fewer than a third of the registrants were in attendance. Some were recovering from a "Backstage on Broadway" tour arranged by the entertainment committee, while others opted for last-minute sightseeing or for confirming flights home, rather than this session on "Borderline Personality Disorders and Suicidal Behavior."

Grisly fare for a Sunday morning. Several people in back slept through presentations by mildly eminent psychiatrists. (My notes are hieroglyphs: "central organizing fantasy of narcissistic union" and "objective scrutiny of object relations.") As Otto Kernberg, who pioneered the study of the borderline patient, read a dense theoretical paper, a group of psychiatrists in front gazed up with adoration and a prevention-center volunteer in back joked about marketing the speech as a sedative.

When Kernberg finished, the moderator, a young psychiatrist who had been alternating pensive nods with glances at his watch—it was his job to herd everyone upstairs in time for "Is There Room for Self-Help in Suicide Prevention?"—invited questions. Hands shot up in front, and their owners raised progressively complex issues. But a hand in back, belonging to a shabby fellow in a ponytail, persisted. And the moderator finally gave in.

The man stood. His jeans and flannel shirt were worn but not dirty. His ruddy face couldn't decide on a beard or a shave, and his eyes were as cloudy as his question, a stammering ramble proposing meditation as a panacea for suicide. Eyes started to roll in the audience, and there were tolerant chuckles. The moderator flashed the panel an embarrassed collegial smile. When the ponytailed man slowed for a moment, the moderator broke in, "That's an interesting question, but let's move on. We have time for one more." He looked for another hand; the man remained standing. The moderator began his thank-you-very-much-I'm-sure-we-all-learned-a-lot speech, and the man was beginning to sit, bewildered, when Kernberg reached for the microphone and said, "I'd like to answer that question," and in his textbook Viennese accent began responding with care and respect.

# V

# LIFE OR LIBERTY

————

MOST SUICIDOLOGISTS are governed by a simple rule: when a life is in danger, one does whatever one can to save it. Some disagree. "Suicide is a fundamental human right," Thomas Szasz has written. "This does not mean that it is morally desirable. It only means that society does not have the moral right to interfere, by force, with a person's decision to commit this act." In numerous books, articles, and speeches, Szasz, a professor of psychiatry at the State University of New York in Syracuse, has articulated his belief that mental illness is a fiction invented by psychiatrists to justify coercive interventions and, in the process, trample on the rights of individuals. Not surprisingly he is vehemently opposed to such staples of suicide prevention as third-party intervention, physical restraint, call tracing, and, above all, involuntary commitment. The relationship between suicide preventer and suicidal person, which suicidologists liken to that of parent and child, Szasz views as something far less benign: "If the psychiatrist is to prevent a person intent on killing himself from doing so, he clearly cannot, and cannot be expected to, accomplish that task unless he can exercise complete control over the capacity of the suicidal person to act. But it is either impossible to do this or it may require reducing the patient to a social state beneath that of a slave; for the slave is compelled only to labor against his will, whereas the suicidal person is compelled to live against his will."

Szasz does not believe that society should support or encourage suicidal people in their desire to kill themselves; he considers counseling, therapy, or any other voluntary measures desirable. In his own practice Szasz readily offers help when and if requested. "In fact, I firmly believe that psychiatric help,

352

including help concerning suicide, can be given more effectively if there is no threat of coercion overhanging it," he observed in a spirited debate with Edwin Shneidman. "I think I can be more effective in my work with persons who are suicidal because they know that they can talk as freely about suicide as they can talk about the stock market or divorce, and I will not intervene in the one any more than the other. I do not get uptight about it. And the ultimate decision remains in their hands." (It is hard not to wonder whether Szasz got uptight in 1994, when he agreed to pay $650,000 to settle a lawsuit filed by the widow of one of his patients. The suit charged that Szasz had advised his patient, a physician suffering from bipolar disorder, to stop taking his lithium; six months later, the doctor hanged himself with battery cables.)

Suicidologists insist that the opposition of Szasz and other civil libertarians to suicide prevention is based on a misunderstanding of suicidal thinking. They note that right-to-suicide advocates ignore the ambivalence and impulsiveness of most suicide attempts. They point to the many people who have attempted or contemplated suicide and survived to live productive lives, including such well-known figures as the pianist Arthur Rubinstein, who tried to hang himself with his belt at age nineteen (the belt broke); the philosopher Bertrand Russell, who considered suicide as a teenager; and Abraham Lincoln, who was suicidally depressed after breaking off his engagement to Mary Todd. "The 'right' to suicide is a 'right' desired only temporarily," writes psychiatrist George Murphy. "Every physician should feel the obligation to support the desire for life, which will return even in a patient who cannot believe that such a change can occur." Over the years Herbert Hendin has interviewed four people who survived six-story jumps. Two changed their minds in midair, two did not, and only one attempted suicide again. In another instance, a depressed twenty-eight-year-old who survived a leap from the Golden Gate Bridge in 1985 recalled the moment he left the rail: "I instantly realized I had made a mistake. I can't tell you how frightening that was." One thinks of Tolstoy's Anna Karenina jumping in front of the train and trying to get up—"Where am I? What am I doing? What for?"—even as the train crushed her.

In any case, say suicidologists, someone prevented from killing himself can always try again. Research shows that 10 percent of attempters will complete suicide within ten years. Most suicidologists believe that if someone is truly determined to kill himself, he will. "The right to kill oneself can be exercised quietly, without involving society, by anyone sufficiently determined to do so," writes Hendin. "Someone on the window ledge of a tall building threatening to jump or someone who is found unconscious after swallowing sleeping pills has forced society to notice him, whether or not he is hoping to be saved or helped. Surely confinement for a limited period for the purpose of evaluation with a view to providing help is indicated." Edwin Shneidman puts it more pungently: "Suicide is not a 'right' any more than is the 'right to belch.' If the individual feels forced to do it, he will do it."

Additionally, suicidologists point out that in exercising the "right to suicide," one may violate the rights of others. People who jump from high places occasionally land on innocent passersby, injuring or even killing them. Carbon monoxide may seep from garages into adjoining houses or apartments, poisoning family or neighbors. People who use an automobile to complete suicide often injure or kill passengers in other cars. Suicide also inflicts psychological injury, most deeply on surviving relatives and friends but also on bystanders. "Although such cases have not been studied, individuals have been severely traumatized by seeing another person kill himself or herself," writes sociologist Samuel Wallace. "Do people in public places, in train stations, or on sidewalks beside tall buildings have a right to be free of the grotesque spectacle of public suicide?"

Although most right-to-suicide arguments describe suicide as a voluntary expression of free will and "rational" choice, most suicidologists insist that suicide is not an act of free will at all. They would argue that it was not Szasz's physician who had made the decision to die, it was the physician's bipolar disorder calling the shots. "Suicidal persons are succumbing to what they experience as an overpowering and unrelenting coercion in their environment to cease living," writes sociologist Menno Boldt. "This sense of coercion takes many familiar forms: fear, isolation, abuse, uselessness, and so on." If we accept that suicide is not voluntary, says Boldt, "the ethical question of the right to suicide becomes largely academic." Because the suicidal person is psychologically coerced, Boldt implies, physical coercion is justified as a protective measure taken on behalf of someone incapable of protecting himself—the same reasoning by which parents assume responsibility for their children.

At the bottom of such arguments is the widespread opinion that, as the medical historian Ilza Veith has put it, "the act [of suicide] clearly represents an illness." Finding suicidal people mentally ill has practical implications. Although standards vary from state to state, most involuntary commitment statutes specify that the individual must be considered dangerous to himself or to others and also mentally ill—criteria to be determined by the admitting psychiatrist. Although efforts by civil libertarians to abolish involuntary commitment have made it more difficult, suicidal persons are the only people who may be held against their will for weeks, months, or even years on the sole basis of what they "might" do in the future rather than what they have done in the past—and not to others but to themselves. One Arizona woman spent fifty-eight years without comprehensive review in a state mental hospital after a suicide attempt. "If a sociologist predicted that a person was 80 percent likely to commit a felonious act, no law would permit his confinement," comment the authors of the article "Civil Commitment of the Mentally Ill: Theories and Procedures" in the *Harvard Law Review*. "On the other hand if a psychiatrist testified that a person was mentally ill and 80 percent likely to commit a dangerous act, the patient would be committed." Szasz offers another analogy:

"If a middle-aged lady goes to the doctor with a terrible gallbladder and says, 'I really don't know what to do. Should I have it out or shouldn't I have it out?' and the doctor can't stand it, restrains the patient, takes her to the hospital, and has the gallbladder out, you know what will happen to the doctor!"

To Szasz the logic of suicide prevention is flawed from the start; he believes that mental illness is a myth invented by the mental health professions to consolidate their power and to justify coercive interventions. But even if one accepts the existence of mental illness, the difficulty of drawing the line between sickness and health is strikingly illustrated by the "expert" testimony of opposing psychiatrists in court trials. While one attests to the defendant's sanity, the other may just as persuasively insist that the defendant is insane. "If everyone who evinces some abnormality is to be regarded as mentally ill, there would hardly be a normal person left among the educated; all of us carry a secret fragment of a neurosis (and perhaps even the makings of a psychosis)," wrote psychiatrist Wilhelm Stekel in 1910. "I think it is the lazy way out to say, in order to relieve our consciences, that all suicides are ill, psychologically inferior persons who are no great loss anyway."

Ever since 1763, when the French physician Merian asserted that all suicides were deranged, there has been a running debate over exactly what percentage of suicides might be considered mentally ill. As previously mentioned, current thinking maintains that about 90 percent of completed suicides suffer from some sort of psychiatric disorder, a figure that to a good many clinicians seems high, but is, perhaps, not surprising, given that our definition of mental illness has steadily expanded over the past half century. The increasing association of suicide with mental illness has had the salutary effect of largely removing it from the realm of sin or volition—and may thus help reduce the stigma associated with the act. Yet calling suicidal behavior "sick" may also be an attempt to make ourselves feel better, by distancing us from an act that strikes a disturbing chord. "I remember dealing with my first suicidal patient. I found it very difficult to understand that a person could really choose this," says psychologist Nancy Kehoe. "I had to go out for a long walk and try to take in how much pain that person must feel to want to take his own life." Now, dealing with suicidal patients, "I let myself get in touch with the times I've felt pretty desperate, the fleeting moments of driving down the turnpike and wishing a truck would hit you. We've all had those moments where we say, 'Enough—I can't take it anymore.'"

The diagnosis of mental illness is especially suspect when it comes to self-destruction. "The argument connecting suicide and mental illness is tautologically based upon our cultural bias against suicide," Zigfrids Stelmachers, director of a Minneapolis prevention center, has said. "We say, in essence, 'All people who attempt suicide are mentally ill.' If someone asks, 'How do you know they are mentally ill?' the implied answer is 'Because only mentally ill persons would try to commit suicide.'" For many years the Los Angeles Suicide Prevention Center reflected this bias, listing one of the symptoms of mental illness as "functional changes in which there is less achievement than usual of life-preserving and other valuable goals." A Harvard University study giving doctors edited case histories of completed suicides found that the highest estimate of mental illness when a sample had been diagnosed *before* suicide was 22 percent. Afterward the highest estimate was 90 percent.

"Suicide is pre-judged by the medical model of thought," wrote Jungian analyst James Hillman in *Suicide and the Soul.* "It can be understood medically only as a symptom, an aberration, an alienation, to be approached with the point of view of prevention." The analysts's goal, he stated, was not to be for or against suicide but to explore "what it means in the psyche." Believing suicide to be an attempt at transformation, Hillman observed that the analyst who tries to prevent suicide with tranquilizing drugs or confinement might be depriving the person of what might be the most significant experience of his or her life. "The analyst cannot deny this need to die. He will have to go with it. His job is to help the soul on its way. He dare not resist the urge in the name of prevention, because *resistance only makes the urge more compelling and concrete death more fascinating.*" This emphasis on the soul rather than on the body, on the spiritual rather than on the medical, on exploration rather than on prevention, "may release the transformation the soul has been seeking. It may come only at the last minute. It may never come at all. But there is no other way." Paradoxically, implied Hillman, *not* preventing suicide is the most effective form of suicide prevention. "By preventing nowhere, the analyst is nevertheless doing the most that can be done to prevent the actual death. By his having entered the other's position so fully, the other is no longer isolated. He, too, is no longer able to break freely the secret league and take a step alone."

The notion that a "death experience" or even death itself may provide a necessary "transformation" for the patient fascinates a few therapists, disgusts others, and, in either case, is dismissed as irrelevant in the clinical situation, an attitude expressed by one therapist who, scoffing at the right to suicide, points out, "No therapy can work with a corpse." In a review of Hillman's book, Robert Litman maintained that if philosophical and ethical theory are to have any relevance to the clinician, they cannot be developed apart from the clinical setting. Yet can clinical practice be developed apart from philosophical and ethical issues? Szasz writes:

> In regarding the desire to live, but not the desire to die, as a legitimate human aspiration, the suicidologist stands Patrick Henry's famous exclamation, "Give me liberty, or give me death!" on its head. In effect, he says, "*Give him* commitment, *give him* electroshock, *give him* lobotomy, *give him* life-long slavery, but *do not let him choose* death!" By so radically illegitimizing another person's (but not his own) wish to die, the suicide-preventer redefines the aspiration of the Other as not an aspira-

tion at all: the wish to die becomes something an irrational, mentally diseased being *displays* or something that *happens* to a lower form of life. The result is a far-reaching infantilization and dehumanization of the suicidal person.

Perhaps in an ideal world people would not want to die, but as Stelmachers says, "Some of the things that happen in these people's lives give them pretty rational reasons for ending their lives." If the cry for help can be translated "help me live," it can also be translated "help me die." "A totally open therapeutic relationship must make room for everything, including suicide," writes philosopher Peter Koestenbaum. "Only in such a way can the freedom of the patient be recognized and nurtured." Making room for suicide does not mean a clinician must set up suicide facilitation services in a prevention center or refuse treatment to a ten-year-old who has tried to hang himself—or encourage a patient with bipolar disorder to wean himself from lithium—but that he must acknowledge the possibility of suicide at least as much as he fears it. "If the person says, 'I'm going to kill myself,'" says Stelmachers, "one way to respond is to say, 'Well, maybe suicide *is* the best way out for you, but let's talk about it first.' This says many things to the person. . . . It says, 'I really am interested in you and your problems. Even more than in preventing suicides!' It also negates a sneaking suspicion he might have had about himself that he must be crazy to even consider such an act." Psychiatrist Herbert Brown, commenting on the physician's responsibility to the suicidal patient, says, "Our responsibility might be seen as an obligation to genuinely engage the patient and then to help to open him or her to a truly free choice as a whole and separate person, a choice that may be suicide."

I recall attending a conference on suicide sponsored by Harvard Medical School and the Cambridge Hospital, when the ethics of prevention came up: "Do we have the right to say no?" wondered an audience member. There were appreciative chuckles; it is among the oldest and, by clinicians, least seriously discussed topics in suicide. "Tough question," commented the late psychiatrist John Mack. "Shall we refer that one to God?" More chuckles. "We have a right to take a different position," continued Mack. "Our responsibility as clinicians is to choose life." Another panel member spoke up: "I think the philosophical answer is different from the clinical one." Until they are part of the same answer, the study of suicide and its prevention may never be complete.

# 5

# THE RIGHT TO DIE

# I

# A Fate Worse
# Than Death

---

AFTER MOST SUICIDES, friends and family may feel guilt because they could not prevent the death. Billie Press felt guilty that she could not help her father kill himself. After most suicides, friends and family grieve because their loved one chose to die. Billie grieved because her father wanted to end his life but couldn't. After most suicides, friends and family believe their loved one died too soon. Billie believed her father died too late. In most suicides the tragedy is that someone died an "unnatural" death; for Billie the tragedy was that her father died a "natural" death.

When Billie's father, Bill, retired as head proofreader of the *New York Times* at eighty, he could look back on a full life. He had worked on newspapers for more than fifty years. A well-read man, he was fond of quoting Shakespeare and had an old-fashioned, courtly manner of speaking. He loved to sing—in the shower, in the car, or with the barbershop quartet of *Times* employees he had organized. After his retirement he moved in with his eldest daughter, Billie, a child development specialist, and her family in a Boston suburb. He read books, watched television, and worked in the garden. He joined a Golden Age club and went on excursions to museums and the theater. "He was so gallant," Billie, who was named for her father, told me. "He was one of the only men in the club, and on trips he always allowed all the women onto the bus first. By the time he got on, the only seats left were in the back, and his guts would get jounced up until his stomach hurt."

Although Bill had had a heart attack when he was fifty-eight, at a checkup at age seventy-five his doctor had marveled at what excellent shape he was in. But now his eyesight, hearing, and memory grew weaker. Cooking on the gas stove, he couldn't see well enough to tell when the flame was low; bending over for a closer look, he often singed his eyebrows. Scissors and tape would disappear, and when his daughter asked him where they were, Bill could never remember where he had left them. "His physical condition declined," recalled Billie, "but he still had a wonderful brain and a marvelous sense of humor." Although he was often lonely, Bill worked to keep up his spirits. One day his teenage granddaughter asked, "Poppy, isn't it terrible to be old?" Bill shook his head. "Oh, no," he said. "Not when you live with people you love."

At the age of eighty-five, the night before his granddaughter's wedding, Bill had a stroke and a heart attack. After six months of rehabilitation he was hopeful of a complete recovery when a second stroke left him paralyzed on his right side, unable to walk, and incontinent. Although he wanted to come home to live, his daughter and son-in-law could not afford round-the-clock nursing care. After much discussion and with great reluctance, Bill was moved from a cozy bedroom in his daughter's house to a cramped, drab room in a local nursing home.

Although the nursing home had a good reputation, it proved to be a torment. Unable to shift position or to move in any way, Bill was wholly dependent on the staff. But the staff rarely attended to his needs, and he soon developed bedsores. "I'd come over every day after work, and my father would be lying in his own feces," said Billie. "I'd clean his bottom, wiping off the shit they'd left." But things were no better at either of the two nursing homes they tried next. "What really makes me angry is that when my father went into a nursing home at age eighty-five, he had every tooth in his head. But they never brushed his teeth. In two years his teeth rotted and fell out one by one. Finally he could eat nothing but gruel—my father, with teeth like a horse, who at age eighty could eat McIntosh apples." Billie shook her head angrily. "You know that line from Shakespeare—'sans teeth, sans eyes, sans everything'? My father got like that."

Finally they found a home that provided acceptable care, but a series of small strokes left Bill increasingly immobile. He had no control over the left side of his face, and saliva dripped from a corner of his mouth. "Am I leaking?" he would nervously ask. Bill also suffered excruciating pain from osteoarthritis. "They gave him only three aspirin every four hours, and for three hours he'd be okay, but the last hour he was in agony," said Billie. "He kept telling me that they didn't control the pain." Perhaps even more harrowing was the lack of stimulation, the sheer numb routine of his days. Roused from bed each morning, Bill was strapped into a wheelchair and left on his own, face to the wall. When his position grew painful, he was unable to shift himself, and unless he shouted, aides checked on him only once every four hours. Most of the other nursing home residents were mentally as well as physically impaired, so although Bill's mind was sharp, there was no one to communicate with. It was all the more frustrating for him to be aware of his situation, yet powerless to change it. "My dad kept saying, 'I must have done something very bad in my life to deserve this,'" recalled Billie.

One day Bill, ever the scholar, said to his son-in-law with a sad smile, "Why can't I shuffle off this mortal coil?" He had occasionally joked about suicide; now he told Billie that he was serious about wanting to end his life, but he had no access to pills, no gun, no rope, and he could hardly jump out the window or walk off the roof when he couldn't even shift position in his wheelchair. He fantasized about ripping his bedsheet into strips, knotting them into a rope, and hanging himself from the door. When he told Billie of his plan, she tried to change the subject. But in the following weeks Bill continued to bring up suicide. "I would hold his hand, and we would weep when he talked about it," Billie told me. One day he looked up at his daughter. "Sweetheart, can't you bring me the means for my demise?" he begged her in his characteristic, elegant manner of speech. Each night Billie lay in bed unable to sleep. "All I thought about was Dad," she said. "I loved him so much, and I hated to see him miserable. I felt he was entitled to end his life, and I knew that if I were in his position, I would want to die, too. I was determined that somehow I would help him. But how would I get the pills? How would I give them to him? She discussed it with her husband, who feared that she would be arrested for aiding and abetting a suicide, and pointed out that even if she was acquitted, her teaching license would almost certainly be revoked. When she told her father that if she helped him she might lose her job, he was adamant. "Sweetheart, you mustn't do it then," he said. "I must suffer to the end."

As his condition steadily declined, her father continued to say wistfully that he wished he could end his life, although he knew it was impossible. The nursing home staff did little more than keep him alive. "They never put on his glasses or his hearing aid," Billie said. "I bought him a radio, but they wouldn't tune it for him, so he just sat there with static crackling, unable to see or hear." Gradually, he lost even his ability to talk. Said Billie, "Like an autistic child, he could just repeat the sounds he heard—my brilliant father, who had been head proofreader at the New York Times—he'd just rock and babble." When she visited, it took a great effort to get him to recognize her: "I'd get in front of him and take his hands and say, 'Daddy, Daddy, it's me. It's me.'"

Each time she saw her father, he was worse. "In the last year there was some mercy, because with each small stroke he was more out of it, and eventually he was no longer aware of what he was going through." When Billie visited, she would wheel her father outside, and they would sit in the sun. "I'd always bring him bananas. He loved bananas, which were one of the few things he could eat by himself. I'd peel the banana, and he was just able to hold it in his one good hand." She talked to her father, but only rarely was she able to understand a word he said. "He looked terrible," she said, "so shrunken and wasted." One day

Billie wheeled her father into town. She left him for a moment outside a variety store while she ran across the street to run an errand. Her father sat in his wheelchair, silent, impassive. When Billie came back a few minutes later, the owner of the store was standing angrily over her father. "How could you leave him here, lady?" he said. "He's scaring all the customers away."

One month before his ninetieth birthday, Bill got pneumonia, slipped into a coma, and died. "It was such a relief," Billie recalled. "My father had been suffering so much, and now he'd finally escaped." It was almost three years after he'd first asked his daughter to help him commit suicide. When I met her more than a decade later, she still wrestled with her frustration at not having been able to help him die, and she found it difficult to talk about his death without bursting into tears.

Her father's prolonged death also made Billie think hard about her own future. She worried that one day, like her father, she might be hopelessly debilitated and want to die but be unable to do anything about it. "I am scared of going my father's route," she said firmly. "I don't want to repeat what my father went through." A few years after her father's death, she began to read books and attend conferences on the right to die with dignity. She joined the Hemlock Society, a national organization advocating the legalization of voluntary euthanasia for the terminally or incurably ill. "I think the worst thing that could happen in life would be to lose the ability to take one's own life," she told me. "I can't imagine killing myself—ever—but it is such a comfort just to know that I have that option. For me the bottom line is that people should have choices. And when the quality of life is gone—whether because of terminal illness or extreme age—one of the choices should be the option of leaving this life. And if, like my father, one wants to but is unable to carry it out himself, one should be allowed to have help. To die a less painful death is a human right." She rapped the table with her knuckles for emphasis. "Why did my father have to go on suffering for two and a half more years when he wanted so much to end it?"

---

In those cultures in which death is accepted as a natural part of life, the image of Bill Press strapped into his wheelchair, face to the wall, wanting to end his life but unable to, might seem absurd. They would consider his daughter's desire to help him end his suffering not as a sin or a crime but as a sign of respect. In many primitive societies, including some in which the act is otherwise taboo, suicide is common in the case of extreme age or incurable illness. Anthropologist Paul Bohannan's study of six tribes in Nigeria, Kenya, and Uganda found that all of them considered suicide evil except for people who were hopelessly ill. "Among the Karens of Burma," wrote anthropologist Edward Westermarck, "if a man has some incurable or painful disease, he says in a matter-of-fact way that he will hang himself, and he does as he says."

Although their religion forbids suicide, it was common in India for Hindus suffering from leprosy or other incurable ailments to bury or drown themselves with appropriate religious rites. When an elderly Aymara Indian of Bolivia is terminally ill, friends and relatives keep a death vigil by her side. The invalid may ask for help, in which case the family withholds food and drink until she succumbs. Studies suggest that such deaths are caused not by starvation but by the will to die.

In Western civilization the concepts of a "right to die" and of "death with dignity" are also venerable. The word *euthanasia,* in fact, is derived from the Greek words *eu,* meaning "well," and *thanatos,* meaning "death." In ancient Greece it meant just that: a good or easy death. "Thus was he blessed with an easy death and such a one as he had always longed for," wrote Suetonius of Caesar Augustus. "For almost always on hearing that any one had died swiftly and painlessly, he prayed that he and his might have a like *euthanasia,* for that was the term he was wont to use." For the Greeks, of course, a good death was often achieved by suicide. Even philosophers who generally frowned on suicide felt that killing oneself to escape intractable pain or hopeless illness was not only excusable but honorable. Plato, who condemned suicide when motivated by sloth or cowardice, admitted that "if any man labour of an incurable disease, he may dispatch himself, if it be to his good." Pliny the Elder believed suicide was justifiable when one suffered from gallstones, stomach pains, or "diseases of the head." The Stoic Musonius said, "Just as a landlord who has not received his rent, pulls down the doors, removes the rafters, and fills up the well, so I seem to be driven out of this little body when nature, which has let it to me, takes away, one by one, eyes and ears, hands and feet. I will not, therefore, delay longer, but will cheerfully depart as from a banquet." The most eloquent classical spokesman on the subject, quoted by right-to-die advocates through the centuries, was Seneca:

> I will not relinquish old age if it leaves my better part intact. But if it begins to shake my mind, if it tears out its faculties one by one, if it leaves me not life but breath, I will depart from the putrid or tottering edifice. I will not escape by death from disease as long as it may be healed, and leaves my mind unimpaired. I will not raise my hand against myself on account of pain, for so to die is to be conquered. But if I know that I will suffer for ever, I will depart, not through fear of the pain itself, but because it prevents all for which I would live.

Such sentiments were often met with sympathy by classical physicians. In his essay "The Arts," Hippocrates, the father of modern medicine, wrote that the physician was required to "do away with the sufferings of the sick, to lessen the violence of their diseases, and to refuse to treat those who are overwhelmed by their diseases, realizing that in such cases medicine is powerless."

Physicians who believed a case was hopeless routinely suggested suicide and often supplied the lethal drugs with which to accomplish it.

During the Middle Ages and the Renaissance, when suicide was perceived as the worst of sins, terminal illness was often accepted as a mitigating factor. Charles Moore, an eighteenth-century English clergyman who penned a six-hundred-page attack on suicide, conceded that "the most excusable cause seems to be an emaciated body; when a man labours under the tortures of an incurable disorder, and seems to live only to be a burden to himself and his friends." As medical treatment became increasingly sophisticated, scientists and philosophers debated the responsibility of doctors to such patients. "I esteem it the office of a physician not only to restore health, but to mitigate pain and dolors," wrote Francis Bacon, "and not only when such mitigation may conduce to recovery, but when it may serve to make a fair and easy passage." Benjamin Franklin, like Bacon, was fascinated by life-prolonging technology but deplored painful, extended deaths. "We have very great pity for an animal if we see it in agonies and death throes," he observed. "We put it out of its misery no matter how noble the animal." In 1798 in *Medical Histories and Reflections,* British physician John Ferriar cautioned against overweening devotion to duty. The physician, he wrote, "should not torment his patient with unavailing attempts to stimulate the dissolving system, from the idle vanity of prolonging the flutter of the pulse for a few more vibrations. . . . When things come to the last and the act of dissolution is imminent . . . he should be left undisturbed."

Over the following century, with the development of analgesics and anesthetics that could not only relieve the suffering of dying patients but also hasten death, there were appeals for more radical measures. In an essay entitled "Euthanasia," published in England in 1872, S. D. Williams claimed that "in cases of incurable and painful illness the doctors should be allowed, with the patient's consent, and after taking all necessary safeguards, to administer so strong an anaesthetic as to render all future anaesthetics superfluous; in short, there should be a sort of legalized suicide by proxy." In 1906 a bill proposing legalization of euthanasia for incurable sufferers who wished to die was introduced into the Ohio legislature. Though the bill was rejected, it triggered intense debate. Many protested that such a law would be an invitation to people who wanted to get rid of burdensome relatives, to fortune hunters who wished to hasten an inheritance, and to physicians who wished to disguise their mistakes. A *New York Times* editorial compared the practice of euthanasia to "practices of savages in all parts of the world." In 1935 such savages as H. G. Wells, George Bernard Shaw, Julian Huxley, and A. A. Milne became founding members of the Voluntary Euthanasia Society in London. "Vast numbers of human beings are doomed to end their earthly existence by a lingering, painful, and often agonising form of death," said founding president C. Killick Millard, a physician. "Voluntary euthanasia should be legalised for adults suffering from an incurable, fatal, painful disease." In 1936 a bill sponsored by the society that would allow terminally ill people to apply for euthanasia was defeated in Parliament. The following year, as the debate reached a crescendo, G. K. Chesterton wrote, "Some are proposing what is called euthanasia; at present only a proposal for killing those who are a nuisance to themselves; but soon to be applied to those who are a nuisance to other people."

Chesterton's acerbic prophecy was already being fulfilled in Germany, where discussions of humanitarian euthanasia similar to those in Great Britain and the United States had been raised earlier in the century. In 1920, in their book *The Permission to Destroy Life Unworthy of Life,* psychiatrist Alfred Hoche and attorney Karl Binding introduced the concept of *lebensunwertes Leben*—"life unworthy of life." These distinguished professors argued that there were situations in which killing was consistent with medical ethics. Those who suffered from brain damage, retardation, and certain psychiatric illnesses were already "mentally dead," and ending their lives was not murder but "an allowable, useful act." This line of reasoning was adapted and further twisted by the Nazis. When they took power in 1933, one of the first laws they enacted was compulsory sterilization of people with hereditary illnesses. It was only the beginning. What the Nazis called "euthanasia" was mass murder, decreed by Hitler—an admirer of Hoche and Binding's book—and carried out by prominent German physicians and psychiatrists. None of the victims were voluntary; none, in fact, were aware of what awaited them as they were shipped to one of six "liquidation institutions." From September 1939, when the program began, to August 1941, when it ended in response to public criticism by German clergymen, approximately one hundred thousand mentally and physically handicapped German men, women, and children were put to death. Not long afterward, of course, the Nazis began applying their mass murder techniques to millions of Jews.

---

Gradually, the meaning of the word *euthanasia* had changed. In ancient Greece it simply referred to a good death, whatever the cause. By the end of the nineteenth century it referred to the taking of life to end suffering. By the end of World War II it had come to mean the taking of life without permission. Since then the word has been avoided by many right-to-die advocates who prefer phrases like *self-deliverance, accelerated death, death by design, hastened death, self-termination, elective death,* and *the final freedom.*

Whatever terminology is used, however, the last several decades have seen extraordinary developments in the debate on euthanasia and the right to die. This is in large part because the nature of old age and illness has dramatically changed. In 1900, the average life expectancy in America was forty-seven. By 2005, it was seventy-eight. In 1900, the three leading causes of death were pneumonia and influenza, tuberculosis, and diarrhea, for all of which cures have since been found. (Pneumonia, once known as "the old man's friend" for bringing a peaceful death to many elderly sufferers, is now routinely treated with antibiotics.) Today, half of all deaths are due to heart disease, while one-fifth are caused by cancer. Respirators, heart-lung machines, intravenous feeding systems, heart bypasses and transplants, pacemakers, and sophisticated antibiotics have enabled many to live longer, more productive lives, but these technological advances have been a mixed blessing. "For every illness, there is some procedure that can delay the moment of death," physician Morris Abram, who chaired a presidential panel on medical ethics, has observed. "The question is: For how long, at what cost, at what pain, at what suffering?" In 1900, most Americans died at home; nine of ten now die in hospitals or nursing homes. "The classical deathbed scene, with its loving partings and solemn last words, is practically a thing of the past," wrote the late ethicist Joseph Fletcher. "In its stead is a sedated, comatose, betubed object, manipulated and subconscious, if not subhuman." Asked Fletcher, "Where can we draw the line between prolonging a patient's life and prolonging his dying?"

Right-to-die advocates worry that physicians may be ill-equipped to draw that line. Doctors have traditionally been trained to regard preservation of life as their highest goal. In doing so, they may ignore death and dying. "I do not remember a single mention of it in the medical school curriculum," writes Marcia Angell, a physician and former editor of the *New England Journal of Medicine.* "It was as though dying were a medical failure and thus too shameful to be discussed. As doctors, we were to succeed, not fail, and success was measured by our ability to stave off death." The Hippocratic oath, once a staple of medical school graduation ceremonies, says in part, "I will give no deadly medicine to anyone if asked nor suggest any such counsel." Although the oath is rarely pledged these days, it decorates the wall of many a physician's office, and doctors are, for the most part, still conditioned to preserve life with unquestioning allegiance. One oncologist vows, "I'll treat my patients as long as they're still wiggling; that's my job." Some people worry that doctors' dedication to life at any and all cost—reinforced by fear of malpractice suits—may blind them to considerations of the quality of that life. At a hearing called by the Senate Special Committee on Aging, Warren Reich of the Kennedy Institute of Ethics at Georgetown University said, "The terminal patient may desperately want rest, peace, and dignity, yet he may receive only infusions, transfusions, a machine, and a team of experts busily occupied with his pulmonary functions but not with him as a person." Such myopia often leads to miraculous recoveries—but sometimes to unintentionally sadistic scenes: a man suffering from terminal cancer, down to sixty pounds, was resuscitated fifty-two times in one month though he repeatedly begged, "For God's sake, please just let me go."

An increasing number of people have realized that they don't want their life to end this way, that there indeed may be fates worse than death. They propose that the quality of a life may be as important as its quantity. "The dignity starts with . . . choice," says a character in *Whose Life Is It Anyway?,* a play by Brian Clark about an artist paralyzed from the neck down who asks to be released from the hospital and allowed to die. "Without it, it is degrading because technology has taken over from human will. My Lord, if I cannot be a man, I do not wish to be a medical achievement." Joseph Fletcher wrote, "We are discovering that saving life is not always saving people. And that death may not always be an enemy to be fought off, but sometimes a friend to be helped and invited." Some people suggest that in their use of life-support systems, doctors may be prolonging not life but death. It is commonplace to hear elderly people say, "I don't fear death, but I fear dying." One terminally ill seventy-eight-year-old, who was intubated and connected to life-support systems despite repeated requests to be left alone to die, switched off his own ventilator during the night. He left a final message for his attending physician: "Death is not the enemy, doctor. Inhumanity is."

Such scenes have become increasingly rare over the past few decades with the growing acceptance of passive euthanasia—a concept pithily and poetically described by nineteenth-century poet Arthur Hugh Clough, who wrote, "Thou shalt not kill; but need'st not strive / Officiously to keep alive." It was a concept with which few Americans were familiar until 1975, when, a few weeks after turning twenty-one, a New Jersey woman named Karen Ann Quinlan swallowed a number of tranquilizers before drinking several gin and tonics with some friends at a local tavern, whereupon she fell to the floor, unconscious. Rushed to the hospital, she was given oxygen and put on a respirator, but she went into a coma.

Her parents, devout Catholics, kept constant vigil over their daughter. Every examining doctor agreed that Karen had suffered irreversible brain damage and had no hope of recovery. After three months the Quinlans, with the support of their parish priest, asked the doctors to disconnect the respirator and let their daughter "pass into the hands of the Lord." When the doctors refused, the Quinlans went to court, seeking permission to withdraw the respirator and allow their daughter to die "with grace and dignity." No American court had ever authorized the withdrawal of life-support equipment. The Quinlans' lawyer argued that Karen had a constitutional right to die and that keeping her alive "after the dignity, beauty, promise, and meaning of earthly life have vanished" constituted cruel and unusual punishment. A court-appointed guardian for Karen insisted that removal of the respirator would be an act of homicide and a violation of both the law and the medical code of ethics. A lawyer for the doctors claimed that no court could determine whether Karen might still recover.

The superior court judge ruled against the Quinlans, but the New Jersey Supreme Court reversed the decision on appeal, observing that "ultimately, there comes a point at which the individual's rights overcome the state's interests." On May 17, 1976, Karen's respirator was turned off. However, she did not die. She lived in what neurologists call a "persistent vegetative state" in a New Jersey nursing home. Fed a combination of high-calorie nutrients and antibiotics through a nasogastric tube, her 70-pound body (she had weighed 120 before her coma) lay curled in a fetal position. Nurses turned her every two hours to prevent bedsores. Her father visited Karen each morning on his way to work; her mother visited several times a week, and a radio in her room played twenty-four hours a day. On her birthdays her family held a bedside mass, and cards arrived from all over the world. But Karen remained completely unaware of the outside world. She died of pneumonia in 1985, ten years after she had lapsed into a coma.

The image of Quinlan in that irreversible coma imprinted itself onto the national consciousness, personalizing an issue that was easy to ignore in the abstract. Many people realized that they didn't want to "end up like Karen Quinlan." They argued that choices about end-of-life care should be made by the patient or the patient's family rather than by doctors, signaling a move away from the paternalism, in which all-powerful physicians withheld information and made unilateral treatment decisions, that had dominated medicine for so long. In a 1950 Gallup poll, 36 percent of Americans believed doctors should be permitted to stop treatment at the request of a dying patient. By 1984 the figure had grown to 73 percent. Doctors got the message. That same year, in an article in the *New England Journal of Medicine,* a group of prominent physicians suggested guidelines for the treatment of hopelessly ill patients. "Basic to our considerations are two important precepts: the patient's role in decision making is paramount, and a decrease in aggressive treatment of the hopelessly ill patient is advisable when such treatment would only prolong a difficult and uncomfortable process of dying." About patients who, like Quinlan, are in a persistent vegetative state, they wrote, "It is morally justifiable to withhold antibiotics and artificial nutrition and hydration, as well as other forms of life-sustaining treatment, allowing the patient to die." According to a study reported in the *Journal of the American Medical Association* in 1985, doctors issued DNR (do not resuscitate) orders three times as often as they had ten or twenty years earlier. A 1988 poll of the American Medical Association found that eight of ten members favored withdrawal of life-support systems from hopelessly ill or irreversibly comatose patients if the patients or their families requested it. For the most part, the Church grudgingly made its peace with passive euthanasia. Pope John Paul II, while condemning euthanasia in a 1980 Vatican declaration, said, "When inevitable death is imminent in spite of the means used, it is permitted in conscience to take the decision to refuse forms of treatment that would only secure a precarious and burdensome prolongation of life." (Twenty-five years later, as he lay dying of heart failure and septic shock in his simply furnished bedroom in the Vatican, John Paul II declined to return to the hospital for more aggressive treatment, choosing to let nature take its course.)

The sea change in attitude following the Quinlan case was reflected in a series of court decisions that established the right of patients or their families to withdraw life-sustaining treatments. In January 1985, five months before Quinlan's death, the New Jersey Supreme Court ruled that feeding tubes, like respirators, could be withdrawn from a terminally ill patient when requested by the patient or the patient's guardian. In 1990, the Cruzan case—in which the family of a comatose twenty-five-year-old woman sought to have her feeding tube removed—reached the United States Supreme Court, the first right-to-die case to do so. Although its decision recognized a "constitutionally protected liberty interest in refusing unwanted medical treatment" and ruled that feeding tubes constitute medical treatment and could be withdrawn, the court essentially left such decisions up to individual states. Laws vary from state to state, however, and court rulings have been contradictory. Doctors have been sued, and in some cases arrested, for withdrawing life support, as well as for *not* withdrawing life support. With no clear guidance from the law, it is hardly surprising that physicians are apprehensive about making the life-and-death decisions they are confronted with daily. Most hospitals have hired staff lawyers to give legal counsel on right-to-die cases; many also have ethics committees that act as sounding boards and help review treatment decisions; a few employ in-house philosophers. The vast majority of cases never reach the courts. In these "negotiated deaths," doctors and hospital administrators meet with the patient's family to discuss comatose or terminally ill cases and whether, when, and how to withdraw life-support equipment—or to refrain from starting it in the first place. (Decisions must, however, frequently be made in emergency settings where extended consultation or philosophical deliberation is impossible, and many hospitals lack defined procedures for recording the wishes of dying patients.) The American Hospital Association estimates that 70 percent of the six thousand or so deaths that occur in this country each day are in some way timed or arranged.

In an attempt to ensure that their wishes concerning end-of-life care are respected, a growing number of Americans have signed living wills, in which they specify the conditions under which they would prefer not to be kept alive by life-sustaining technology, or a health care proxy, in which they assign another person to make their medical decisions in the event of incompetency. In 1991, in the wake of the Cruzan decision, the federal government enacted the Patient Self-Determination Act, which required that hospitals and nursing homes inform patients and their families of their right to sign such documents. By 1992, all fifty states had legalized an advance directive of some kind, theoretically enabling patients or their families to refuse the sort of protracted treatment Quinlan had received. Fewer than one in five Americans, however, have signed an advance directive, and those who have often find that such documents may be ignored in the hubbub of emergency rooms. A 1995 survey revealed that 66 percent of physicians believed there was nothing wrong with overriding a patient's advance directive. In another survey, 70 percent of physicians said they would like to leave a living will with their own doctors, while 65 percent said they would *not* obey a living will with which they disagreed. "I've talked to physicians who say that if they are working in the emergency room and in the pocket of a patient who comes in they find a duly executed living will, they will take it out and throw it in the wastebasket," says a philosophy professor who leads hospital discussion groups on medical ethics. Small wonder that a study of some nine thousand terminally ill patients found that those who had signed living wills, health-care proxies, or DNRs were just as likely to be resuscitated as those who hadn't. In many cases, their doctors were unaware of these preferences; in some cases, they simply ignored them.

That the issue of passive euthanasia is far from resolved became painfully apparent in 2005, when the case of Terri Schiavo reopened the national debate over when and how medical treatment can be withdrawn. A twenty-six-year-old insurance company clerk whose heart had stopped briefly one February night in 1990 because of an undiagnosed potassium deficiency, Schiavo had been in a persistent vegetative state for eight years when her husband went to court for permission to remove the feeding tube that kept her alive.

In the Quinlan and Cruzan cases, family members were united in wanting life-sustaining treatment withdrawn. In the case of Terri Schiavo, however, the family was divided. Although his wife had left no written directive, Michael Schiavo maintained that Terri had told him several times that she would not want life-prolonging measures. He requested that her feeding tube be removed. Though doctors testified that their daughter had suffered irreversible brain damage and was incapable of thought or emotion, Terri Schiavo's parents, Robert and Mary Schindler, insisted that she was responsive to their voices and might improve with therapy. They wanted the feeding tube kept in place. (A patient in a persistent vegetative state may appear to smile or grimace spontaneously, but neurologists say these are involuntary reflexes, not responses to specific stimuli.) The judge accepted Michael Schiavo's testimony, ruled that Terri would not have wanted to be kept alive by artificial means, and, since Florida law gives spouses primacy in making decisions for incapacitated patients, ordered the feeding tube removed.

Thus began what one medical ethicist described as "the most extensively litigated right-to-die case in the history of the United States," a seven-year battle in which Schiavo's parents fought to protect what they called their daughter's right to life, while her husband fought to protect what he called his wife's right to die. The Schindlers' cause was taken up by religious conservatives and abortion opponents who saw the Schiavo case as part of the wider right-to-life battle. Michael Schiavo's cause was taken up by right-to-die advocates who saw three decades of legal rulings in jeopardy.

After years of litigation in Florida state courts, during which time Terri Schiavo's feeding tube was ordered removed and reinserted twice, the case came to a boil in the spring of 2005, when, prodded by conservative lobbyists, Congress attempted to intervene, setting off a furious and unseemly rondo of sanctimonious sound bites (House majority leader Tom DeLay called removal of the feeding tube, variously, "murder," "an act of medical terrorism," and an "act of barbarism"); sub-rosa communiqués (a memo encouraging Senate Republicans to take up the cause noted "the pro-life base will be excited that the Senate is debating this important issue"); armchair doctoring (several members of Congress with medical degrees rendered their own diagnoses of Schiavo's condition after viewing an edited, three-year-old videotape of her, whereupon a Democratic representative who is a psychiatrist accused them of "legislative malpractice"); and political grandstanding (in a backdoor strategy to block removal of the feeding tube through a law intended to protect people called to testify before Congress, a House committee issued a subpoena for Terri Schiavo).

Some nine hundred miles south, outside Woodside Hospice House in Pinellas Park, Florida, where forty-one-year-old Terri Schiavo lay in her bed, unaware that she had become a political prize in the struggle between liberals and conservatives, the scene was no less histrionic. Protesters, many of them veterans of antiabortion and stem-cell-research battles, prayed, chanted, wore tape over their mouths printed with the word *life*, and brandished signs (MUR-DER IS LEGAL IN AMERICA; YOU WOULDN'T LET A DOG DIE OF THIRST; NEXT THEY COME FOR YOU). One man blew a ram's horn; another paraded a figure of Jesus on the crucifix up and down the block on a trailer. There were scores of arrests, several death threats, an anonymous bomb threat, a last-minute appearance by Jesse Jackson in a white limousine, and a tent city of television crews to capture it all. It might have seemed fodder for a Preston Sturges screwball comedy had the case not been so tragic, and the stakes, on both a personal and a political level, so high. That it took place during the Easter season heightened the drama. (Some right-to-life advocates referred to the unfolding events as "The Passion of Terri.") Meanwhile, across the country, a new generation of Americans, too young to remember Karen Ann Quinlan, were having dinnertable discussions about what they would want to happen if they ended up "like Terri Schiavo." (According to one poll, 78 percent of Americans wouldn't wish to be kept alive in her condition; in another, 67 percent thought elected officials were trying to keep Schiavo alive more for political gain than from concern for her or for the principles involved.)

Despite Congress's attempts to subvert the judicial process, a Florida circuit court judge, saying Congress had no jurisdiction in the matter, once again ordered the feeding tube removed. Another appeal to the Supreme Court was rejected. On March 18, the feeding tube was removed for the third time.

But what one congressman called "a national political farce" was not yet over. Although the case had already been heard by nineteen judges in six courts and had been appealed unsuccessfully to the Supreme Court three times, Republican congressional leaders hastily called Congress back from its two-week Easter recess for an emergency session in which they rushed through a special bill allowing "any parent of Theresa Marie Schiavo" to sue in federal court to keep her alive. (President Bush's return from his Texas ranch to sign the bill was the first time in five years he had interrupted a vacation to return to the capital.) The Palm Sunday Compromise, as its supporters called it, out-raged even some conservatives, who accused Congress of violating a corner-stone of constitutional philosophy by interfering with the ruling of a state court. After another legal flurry, however, the federal appeals court in Atlanta refused to order the tube reinserted. Once again, the Supreme Court declined to intervene. On the morning of March 31, 2005, nearly two weeks after the removal of her feeding tube, Terri Schiavo died. By then, the only thing on which it seemed all could agree was that nearly thirty years after the Karen Ann Quinlan case, Americans remained deeply conflicted about right-to-die issues.

---

The furor over Terri Schiavo surprised most right-to-die advocates, because these days, doctors routinely practice passive euthanasia in ways that go beyond withdrawal of life-support systems. They may call for a DNR or a "no code" order, in which case a dying patient will not be given "heroic measures." They may hasten the death of a terminally ill patient by not treating an infec-tion or by failing to prescribe antibiotics for pneumonia. Some doctors go fur-ther, into an even more hazy legal area. They may put a bottle of pills on the table of a terminally ill patient who has asked to die. "Take two if you can't sleep," they may say. "But don't take them all, or they will kill you." Some doctors may increase a patient's intravenous dose of morphine until he stops breathing. Or they may practice "terminal sedation"—administering enough painkilling drugs to push suffering patients into unconsciousness, withhold-ing nutrition and hydration until death occurs. The late Christiaan Barnard, the South African surgeon who in 1967 performed the first successful heart trans-plant, admitted that he had practiced passive euthanasia in a variety of forms for many years. "I have learned from my life in medicine that death is not always an enemy," he wrote in Good Life/Good Death. "Often it is good med-ical treatment. Often it achieves what medicine cannot achieve—it stops suf-fering." Many patients, however—especially in the age of managed care, which limits their choice of providers and often forces them to switch from doctor to doctor—do not have the kind of intimate relationship with their physician that allows these issues to be raised. And by the time a patient needs end-of-life care, the "family doctor" has usually been replaced by a team of specialists, often strangers to the patient.

Some right-to-die advocates claim that passive euthanasia merely means allowing people to die the way they did a century ago, before the advent of what Barnard called "rampant technology." They believe that in some cases more direct action is necessary—that it should be legal for physicians to provide a lethal dose of medication for terminally ill patients who request it. Others suggest that physicians should be permitted to give such patients a lethal injection—what is called voluntary euthanasia. "Can doctors who remove the feeding tubes from patients in a persistent vegetative state really believe that there is a huge gulf between this, and giving the same patients an injection that will stop their hearts beating?" wrote ethicist Peter Singer in his 1994 book, *Rethinking Life and Death.* "Doctors may be trained in such a way that it is psychologically easier for them to do the one and not the other, but both are equally certain ways of bringing about the death of the patient." Wrote cardiologist Thomas Preston in the *Wall Street Journal,* "the morphine drip is undeniably euthanasia, hidden by the cosmetics of professional tradition and language." Joseph Fletcher has asked, "What, morally, is the difference between doing nothing to keep the patient alive and giving a fatal dose of a painkilling or other lethal drug? The intention is the same, either way. A decision *not* to keep a patient alive is as morally deliberate as a decision to *end* a life."

Legally, however, those decisions are vastly different. While in most states it is licit in most instances to withdraw life-support systems, thirty-nine states have statutes explicitly prohibiting assisted suicide, while in six other states the practice is implicitly prohibited by common law. With or without legal sanction, people have long been helping their suffering loved ones die. In 1920, thirty-six-year-old Michigan farmer Frank Roberts was convicted of murder and sentenced to life imprisonment in solitary confinement, and with hard labor, for supplying poison to his wife, who suffered from multiple sclerosis, had previously attempted suicide by swallowing carbolic acid, and had begged to die. (The governor later commuted Roberts's sentence and he was released from prison after three years.) In 1983, Betty Rollin helped her seventy-six-year-old mother, terminally ill and often in agony from ovarian cancer, obtain a lethal dosage of barbiturates, then sat with her while she died. A television journalist and author, Rollin described her mother's death in *Last Wish,* which became a best seller and generated thousands of letters, the vast majority of them praising her act.

Despite such a change in reception, assisted suicide remains risky, although judges and juries tend to be lenient. In one recent case, Huntington Williams, a seventy-four-year-old emergency medical technician in rural Connecticut, helped his longtime friend, sixty-six-year-old John Welles, who was dying of prostate cancer, complete suicide by cleaning his revolver, carrying it outside while Welles used a walker, and giving him advice about where to aim. (Williams walked to the end of his friend's driveway before Welles pulled the trigger.) Charged with second-degree manslaughter under a state law prohibiting assisted suicide, which carries a maximum prison sentence of ten years, Williams was given a year's probation. The courtroom, packed with friends of the two men, burst into applause when the decision was announced. One right-to-die advocacy group, studying newspaper clippings, has estimated that the incidence of double suicides and assisted suicides involving the terminally ill has increased forty times since Frank Roberts helped his wife to die. These admittedly unscientific findings probably represent only a small fraction of the actual cases, since few come to court or surface in newspapers or books. The vast majority are carried out in secret. Says a woman who obtained a lethal dose of barbiturates for her terminally ill mother, then sat with her while she swallowed it, "What makes me sad and a little angry is that because what I did is against the law, for the rest of my life I will have to keep secret something that I feel so good about."

But even with the help of a friend or a family member, suicide can be difficult. Lethal medications aren't easy to obtain, and without knowledge of what constitutes a lethal dose, people can easily find themselves worse off. Other methods, such as gunshot and hanging, may be more certain to end in death, but are extraordinarily traumatic for both the protagonist and the loved ones left behind. That is why an increasing number of people believe that it should be legal for physicians, who have the technical expertise, to assist terminally ill people to take their own life. Although no physician in America has ever successfully been prosecuted for assisting a suicide, every major national medical organization in this country opposes the practice, and over the years, only a few cases of physician-assisted suicide have come to public attention. That would change in June of 1990, when an unemployed sixty-two-year-old Michigan pathologist hooked up a fifty-four-year-old English teacher from Oregon to a homemade suicide machine in the back of his 1968 Volkswagen van.

---

If assisted suicide advocates had had a choice, they would not likely have chosen Jack Kevorkian as the standard-bearer for their cause. A short, skinny man whose hawkish face, close-cropped white hair, and porkpie hat made him look more like a racetrack tout than the television ideal of a physician, Kevorkian had evinced a fascination with the end of life that had earned him the nickname Dr. Death long before he hooked up Janet Adkins to his suicide machine. The only son of Armenian refugees who had come to this country to escape the Turkish genocide, Kevorkian had, over his career, become increasingly marginalized by the medical profession for his controversial proposals: that lives might be saved by performing battlefield transfusions directly from corpses to wounded soldiers; that doctors might calculate the optimal time for organ harvesting by photographing the retinal blood vessels of dying patients to determine the exact moment of death; that organs be harvested from consenting death-row inmates; that medical experiments be performed on consenting death-row inmates during executions to advance our understanding of the dying process—and thereby help to avoid killing innocent animals in the name of science.

As an intern, Kevorkian had been outraged by the plight of elderly patients allowed to suffer prolonged deaths; in his thirties, he had watched his mother die slowly and painfully of bone cancer. But the primary motivation that led him to assisted suicide was his interest in medical experimentation on the dying. When he heard that physician-assisted suicide and euthanasia were widely practiced in the Netherlands, it occurred to him that patients who opt for euthanasia might be ideal subjects. In 1987, he flew to Amsterdam and met with leaders of the Dutch euthanasia movement, who found his proposal so radical they feared it might damage their cause. Kevorkian returned home, determined to perform assisted suicides himself, though his goal of experimentation on the dying would eventually fall by the wayside. He passed out business cards that read:

Jack Kevorkian, M.D.
Bioethics and Obitiatry
Special Death Counseling by Appointment Only

(*Obitiatry*—from the Latin *obitus*, "death," and the Greek *iatros*, "doctor"— was a word Kevorkian had invented to describe his specialty, the treatment of death and dying.) When the oncologists to whom he distributed his cards refused to refer patients to him, he inserted classified ads in local newspapers: "Is someone in your family terminally ill? Does he or she wish to die—and with dignity? Call Physician Consultant." Only two people called, neither of whom Kevorkian felt would make an appropriate case: a man phoning from out of state on behalf of his comatose brother, and a young woman who was clearly mentally disturbed. Kevorkian published an article in which he described his plans for suicide clinics ("obitoria") in which terminally ill patients might be assisted to their deaths "under controlled circumstances of compassion and decorum." When his obitoria idea failed to catch on, he decided to act on his own. Working at his kitchen table, with an electric drill, a soldering iron, and $30 worth of parts scavenged from flea markets, garage sales, and hardware stores, he built his first suicide machine: a frame of scrap aluminum, a trio of intravenous lines connected to three inverted bottles—one containing a harmless saline solution, the second sodium pentothal, and the third a mixture of succinylcholine (a muscle relaxant) and potassium chloride (a poison)—and a simple on/off switch that triggered a small electric motor salvaged from a toy car. After an article about Kevorkian and what he dubbed his Mercitron appeared in a local Michigan newspaper, he started getting calls from around the country—from reporters wanting to interview him and from suffering people wanting to use his machine.

In the fall of 1989, Janet Adkins read about Kevorkian in *Newsweek*. Married thirty-three years, the mother of three, an English teacher at a community college in Portland, Oregon, and a member of the Unitarian Church and of the Hemlock Society, Adkins had been diagnosed with early-stage Alzheimer's. As medical treatments failed and her mind continued to falter, she decided that, rather than risk waiting until she was unable to make any decisions at all, she would end her life. She considered taking pills or jumping from a tall building, but feared she might botch the job. Besides, she wanted a more dignified death. After reading about Kevorkian's machine, she asked her husband to telephone Kevorkian, who encouraged her to take part in an experimental drug trial she was considering. But the drug didn't work, her condition deteriorated, and the following April, her husband called Kevorkian again. After reviewing Janet Adkins's medical records, Kevorkian decided he had found his first case.

On June 1, a few days after playing tennis with one of her sons (she could still beat him but she could no longer keep score), Adkins and her husband flew to Detroit and met with Kevorkian in their room at the Red Roof Inn. Later, they went out to dinner. (In the preceding weeks, Kevorkian had frantically contacted doctors' and dentists' offices, funeral homes, hotels, churches, and friends, in an effort to find a site for the assisted suicide. Everyone refused him. Adkins told him that his van would be fine.) On June 4, 1990, three days after Adkins and Kevorkian had met, Kevorkian's two sisters drove Adkins to a wooded public campground outside Detroit, where Kevorkian, who had rented a campsite, was waiting in his van. Adkins lay down on the built-in bed next to the suicide machine. The windows were draped with yellow curtains Kevorkian had sewn to give them some privacy. Kevorkian hooked up Adkins intravenously to the saline solution. At Adkins's request, Kevorkian's older sister, Flora, read the Twenty-third Psalm. When she was ready, Adkins pushed the switch, shutting off the saline solution and opening the adjoining line of sodium pentothal, which would put her to sleep. Adkins said, "Thank you, thank you." Kevorkian replied, "Have a nice trip." After one minute, a timing device triggered the flow of potassium chloride. Within six minutes Adkins was dead.

At the time, Michigan had no laws that specifically addressed assisted suicide; the act was covered under statutes prohibiting murder and manslaughter. Kevorkian was arrested and charged with first-degree murder. The charge was eventually dismissed. Over the following eight years, Kevorkian would assist in at least 130 more "medicides" (Kevorkian shorthand for "medically assisted suicides"). Some took place in parks and motels, some in the homes of friends, some in the back of Kevorkian's rusted white VW bus. (Afterward, Kevorkian always notified the authorities and let them know where the body could be found. For convenience—and so his vehicle wouldn't be impounded when the police arrived—he often left the corpse in a wheelchair, an explanatory note pinned to the clothing, outside a hospital door.) Some used the Mercitron, or a variation incorporating the minor improvements Kevorkian made, Rube Goldberg–fashion, over time. After Kevorkian's medical license was suspended, and he could no longer easily obtain potassium chloride, some used a second Kevorkian creation, in which the patient released a clip on a tube to deliver carbon monoxide through a plastic mask. Over the years Kevorkian was helped in his work by a Dickensian cast of characters: his younger sister, Margo Janus, who was often behind the camera, videotaping the proceedings, until her death in 1994; Neil Nicol, a salesman of medical supplies, who had been the experimental subject when Kevorkian had first transfused blood from a corpse (a stroke victim) to a live human being (Nicol) in the sixties, and who now assisted with logistics and transportation, furnishing the carbon monoxide as well as providing his living room's foldout sofa for the site of several Kevorkian-assisted suicides; and Geoffrey Fieger, a flamboyant local lawyer and former rock band roadie, known for winning huge settlements in medical malpractice suits, who kept his client from being convicted during an eight-year game of cat and mouse with local prosecutors determined to prevent Kevorkian from turning Michigan into what they called "the suicide capital of the world."

The defacto manager for Kevorkian's jury-rigged operation was an energetic older woman named Janet Good, former district manager for a company selling home permanents, active feminist, and founder of the Michigan chapter of the Hemlock Society. Good met Kevorkian in 1989 after she saw his ads, offering to help the terminally ill, in her local newspaper. "I was getting calls from all these poor, suffering people who were saying, 'Please send me a Hemlock pill,' " Good recalled when I met her in 1997. "I thought Dr. Kevorkian could give me narcotics to help them out of their misery." He couldn't, but he told Good about his suicide machine.

Their relationship got off to a difficult start when Good's husband, a retired police captain, refused to let their home be the scene of the Janet Adkins "medicide." But Good soon made herself indispensible: screening applicants ("I think of them as patients, but we call them clients, so we're not thought of as practicing medicine without a license"); getting release forms signed; scheduling assisted suicides; suggesting hotels and plane flights for out-of-town clients; and taking notes at Kevorkian's hearings and trials. Indeed, if the Kevorkian operation could be said to have an office, it was the family room of Good's suburban redbrick ranch house, which sat on a half-acre plot of carefully clipped lawn bordered by purple impatiens. In the shadow of a large television and a glass-fronted bookcase filled with *Reader's Digest* condensed books, Kevorkian met Good almost every other day, occasionally playing hooky on the local golf course. Sitting in two well-worn pink recliners, with a jar of chocolate-covered graham crackers (Kevorkian's favorite cookies) between them and the Goods' spaniel at their feet on the lavender wall-to-wall carpeting, they sorted the mail Kevorkian had lugged there in a large shopping bag. (Good's husband, who tolerated but did not smile on these proceedings, usually retreated outside to weed the garden.) The letters were divided into three piles: those thanking Kevorkian for his work ("I call them 'the love letters' "); those from people Kevorkian couldn't help either because they were insufficiently sick or serious or because they were depressed; and those from potential "candidates." Good or Kevorkian called every candidate, interviewed them, and requested their medical records. Good was also, occasionally, present at the end, when, she says, Kevorkian often wept. She explained to me, "People say, 'It's so macabre—you're there when people die.' But it's so personal, so private, so gentle, so nonsuffering, so easy, that all you feel is calmness for the family. I admire the doctor for putting his life in jeopardy, but I admire him even more for the caring and concern he gives people in the final hours and minutes of their lives." (Several months after I met her, Good, suffering from pancreatic cancer, was herself helped to her death in her home by the man she called "the doctor" or "Doc" or, occasionally, "my Doctor Kevorkian.")

Even today, it would be difficult to overestimate the grip that Kevorkian had on the national imagination. His name recognition in the nineties was second only to Bill and Hillary Clinton's. He was called a devil, a monster, a loose cannon, a lunatic, a madman, a psychopath, a sicko, a kook, a publicity hound, a vigilante, a serial killer, Jack the Ripper, the Antichrist, Doctor Arrogance, and Doctor Death. He was also called a hero, a saint, a savior, a visionary, a crusader, a prophet, a pioneer, an angel of mercy, and Doctor God. Right-to-life protesters and disability rights advocates picketed his court appearances; strangers approached him on the street to bless him or encourage him to "keep up the good work." His critics called him callous and controlling; his "patients" said he was far more caring than the other doctors they'd encountered during their suffering. In court, family members of people Kevorkian had assisted to their deaths wore buttons that read I BACK JACK.

Kevorkian's notoriety was doubtless reinforced by his personal eccentricity. A lifelong bachelor who lived on his pension and Social Security benefits— he never accepted payment for his services—Kevorkian subsisted largely on a diet of Velveeta-on-white-toast sandwiches, bought his threadbare clothes at the Salvation Army (he favored cardigan sweaters and clip-on ties), worked at a plywood desk on a manual typewriter purchased for $2 at a garage sale, and slept on a single mattress on the floor of his rented second-floor apartment in Royal Oak, a suburb of Detroit. He loved puns, wrote risqué limericks, was a passionate golfer, and played cards every other week with a small circle of acquaintances. (He was said to have a good poker face.) He played the flute, organ, and piano. He composed music. (In 1976, after quitting his job as a pathologist, he drove his van to Los Angeles, where he spent his meager savings on making a film—never released—based on Handel's *Messiah*.) He was an amateur painter whose canvases depicted severed heads, maimed bodies, internal organs, skulls, cannibalism, and genocide. By all accounts, he was a shy, cocky, witty, vulgar, opinionated man with a profound disdain for authority. His few friends and associates admitted he could be prickly and abrasive, but said these qualities were more than compensated for by his brilliance and his courage. Kevorkian likened himself to Margaret Sanger, Sigmund Freud, Rosa Parks, Dr. Martin Luther King Jr., and the fictional Dr. Frankenstein. He showed up for a television interview dressed up in cardboard stocks, with a ball and chain on one leg, to dramatize his persecution; for a court appearance, he wore a colonial costume—tights, powdered wig, shoes with oversize buckles—to protest being tried under a centuries-old common law. He gave the family members of his early medicides gold chains engraved with a number indicating their loved one's chronological place in the order of those he had assisted.

"The medical profession made a mistake when they ostracized me," said Kevorkian. "I have no career anymore. This is the substitute." Though motivated partially by revenge and partially by his love of the spotlight, he was also a principled man who believed, as he put it, that "personal autonomy is the highest right." And his work tapped into a reservoir of genuine pain and need that conventional medicine had been unable or unwilling to deal with. Each week he received dozens of letters, phone calls, and e-mails. His waiting list eventually numbered in the hundreds. People traveled to Michigan from California, Colorado, Pennsylvania, and Massachusetts to take advantage of his services. Kevorkian did not help everyone who importuned him. He tried to weed out those with mental illnesses. He counseled many ailing people, terminally ill and otherwise, who went on to die a natural death. As his caseload grew, however, his evaluations grew more cursory, his definition of incurable increasingly flexible. In addition to patients suffering from cancer, lung disease, heart disease, and AIDS, he assisted people with multiple sclerosis, rheumatoid arthritis, osteoporosis, Parkinson's disease, fibromyalgia, Huntington's disease, emphysema, Crohn's disease, quadriplegia, chronic fatigue syndrome, and "miscellaneous intense pain." According to a Wayne State University study, 70 percent of Kevorkian's patients were not terminally ill—that is, not predicted to die within six months—but were suffering from chronic diseases and disabilities. Indeed, some seemed not to be suffering from anything at all. In several cases, including that of a woman who had claimed she had MS, autopsies revealed no physical evidence of any disease.

Early on, Kevorkian had argued for a one-month waiting period between his first meeting with a prospective patient and the appointed death date. And in an article called "A Fail-Safe Model for Justifiable Medically-Assisted Suicide (Medicide)," he had suggested that each applicant undergo extensive consultations with a psychiatrist, a neurologist, and a priest. But these careful plans eroded under time and pressure. He often assisted people he'd barely met, like the forty-five-year-old woman with breast cancer whom he'd first encountered the previous day. Consultation was almost nonexistent, unless one counted casual conversations with a Kevorkian associate. (Kevorkian's "psychological evaluation" of Adkins, which consisted of his assessing "her moods as well as the content and quality of her thoughts" over dinner—"There was absolutely no doubt that her mentality was intact and that she was not the least depressed over her impending death," he concluded—was one of his more thorough examinations.) There was ample evidence that some of his cases might have benefited from further evaluation: a forty-two-year-old nurse with chronic fatigue syndrome and a history of marital difficulties and psychiatric problems; a fifty-eight-year-old woman with seemingly inexplicable pelvic pain and major depression; a forty-three-year-old with MS who was experiencing no physical pain but, according to a friend, "a lot of emotional pain," no doubt exacerbated by the fact that her husband had recently divorced her and taken their children. Often the assisted suicides seemed arranged not for maximum thoroughness but for maximum convenience. In several instances, Kevorkian performed double assisted suicides, in which the participants had never met before their rendezvous with the doctor.

Despite Kevorkian's slapdash methods, Michigan prosecutors seemed unable to put him behind bars. After he escaped three assisted-suicide convictions, they grew increasingly reluctant to try; it seemed no jury would convict him. Kevorkian, however, *wanted* to be put on trial to keep the assisted-suicide issue onstage. (He may also have wanted to keep himself onstage; his medicides were occurring so frequently that they no longer routinely made the front page.) And so he looked for a case that might force the law's hand and propel the issue to the Supreme Court. He found Thomas Youk, a fifty-two-year-old former accountant, air force veteran, restorer of vintage cars, and amateur race-car driver, who suffered from advanced amyotrophic lateral sclerosis (ALS), a progressive neuromuscular disease for which there is no cure. Unable to move his arms or his legs, Youk was confined to a wheelchair; barely able to swallow, he was fed through a gastrostomy tube. "I don't want to die," he told his brother, "but I don't want to live like this." He found Kevorkian's address on the Internet and dictated a letter to his wife. Kevorkian visited Youk on September 15, 1998—less than three weeks after the enactment of a revised Michigan law making assisted suicide a felony. But Kevorkian had something more than assisted suicide in mind. Because Youk couldn't flip the switch on the suicide machine himself, Kevorkian would administer a lethal injection, thereby crossing the line from assisted suicide to euthanasia.

The following day, Kevorkian videotaped himself injecting Youk with potassium chloride. Kevorkian mailed the tape to *60 Minutes,* a television newsmagazine show. On the program, acknowledging that he had helped at least 130 other people to die, Kevorkian challenged prosecutors to charge him with murder. Three days later, they did. Kevorkian, who insisted on acting as his own attorney—in order to propel the case to the Supreme Court, Kevorkian would have to lose in Michigan, which Fieger refused to help him do—tried to convince the jury that he had committed not murder but an act of mercy. The prosecutor tried to demonstrate that Kevorkian was less concerned with his patient's well-being than with advancing a cause. Kevorkian was found guilty of second-degree murder and sentenced to ten to twenty-five years in prison.

Today, the seventy-seven-year-old Kevorkian is prisoner #284797 in the Thumb Correctional Facility, a minimum security prison in rural Michigan, where he reads, does crossword puzzles, listens to classical music, calls friends from the pay phone outside his cell, and signs an occasional autograph for a guard or a fellow inmate. In 2004, he wrote an "Open Letter to Michigan Legislators," in which he pressed for lifting the state's ban on capital punishment—so that condemned men could undergo medical experimentation before their deaths. He will be eligible for parole in 2007. The newspapers that only a few years earlier couldn't get enough of him rarely mention his name, other than to note that his health is failing.

---

Though Kevorkian's notoriety has faded, it is likely that had all those front-page stories on his medicides never been printed, the assisted-suicide debate would not have moved so quickly and definitively into the nation's consciousness. Most of those who advocated its legalization argued that Kevorkian's modus operandi demonstrated the importance of regulating the practice to protect both patients and physicians, of bringing it out into the open to ensure that no abuse occurred. Dying in the back of a VW van, homemade curtains notwithstanding, wasn't the "death with dignity" for which they were fighting. Opponents of physician-assisted suicide said the specter of Kevorkian was a good reason never to legalize the practice. Either way, it was no longer possible to ignore the subject. And either way, support for physician-assisted suicide was rising. "When a person has a disease that cannot be cured, do you think doctors should be allowed by law to end a patient's life by some painless means if the patient and his family request it?" asked a Gallup poll in 1947. Thirty-seven percent of respondents said yes. By 1973, that number had risen to 53 percent. By 1990, it was 65 percent; by 1996, 75 percent.

One of the most interesting aspects of the discussion has been the revelation of how frequently physician-assisted suicide takes place. Pre-Kevorkian, the practice had been underground. Yet studies repeatedly show that a great many physicians support assisted suicide for the terminally ill—and that a surprising number of them have been doing in private essentially what Kevorkian was doing so publically. A 1995 study of oncologists in Kevorkian's home state found that 18 percent had participated in physician-assisted suicide and 4 percent in voluntary euthanasia. A 1996 study of physicians in Washington

State discovered that 16 percent of respondents had been asked by patients for physician-assisted suicide or euthanasia. Of those who requested physician-assisted suicide, 24 percent received prescriptions; of those who requested euthanasia, another 24 percent received lethal injections. A 1997 *New England Journal of Medicine* report revealed that more than half of San Francisco Bay Area physicians treating AIDS patients had assisted at least one completed suicide. A year later, the same journal reported that when suffering patients asked for lethal prescriptions, 16 percent of doctors complied. Assistance is not limited to physicians. A 1996 survey of 852 intensive care nurses found that nearly one in five had, almost always at the request of the patient or his family members, hastened a dying patient's death, usually by administering a high dose of morphine.

Despite these figures, many doctors who support physician-assisted suicide don't believe it should be legalized; they say they are handling things well enough on the sly. Those who favor legalization point out that not all patients have close relationships with doctors willing to help. They argue that if physician-assisted suicide is kept secret, more people will risk putting their friends, family, and health care providers in legal jeopardy, and more people will be forced to take matters into their own hands and risk botching the job.

If Kevorkian had offered the only model of physician-assisted suicide, the course of the right-to-die movement might have been different. But in 1991, less than a year after Kevorkian had helped Janet Adkins die, another American physician admitted to helping a patient to her death. Writing in the *New England Journal of Medicine,* Timothy Quill, a primary care physician and former hospice medical director in Rochester, New York, described how he had given a patient with end-stage leukemia a prescription for a lethal dose of barbiturates, knowing that she would take them when she felt it was time to die. Three months later, she did. Quill explained that he was motivated not only by compassion but by his concerns about what might happen if he failed to provide the prescription. "I feared the effects of a violent death on her family," he wrote, "the consequences of an ineffective suicide that would leave her lingering in precisely the state she dreaded so much, and the possibility that a family member would be forced to assist her, with all the legal and personal repercussions that would follow."

If Quill's article had been published a year or two earlier, it might have occasioned more controversy. As it was, compared with Kevorkian's rushed and emotionally ambiguous medicides, Quill's example seemed quite civilized. A bearded, avuncular-looking man with an impeccable résumé, Quill had been the patient's physician for nearly eight years; he had suggested hospice and other alternatives; he had discussed the matter with her over several months. Quill believed that his assistance was a natural part of the doctor-patient relationship, in keeping with the principle of "nonabandonment," in which physicians are ethically bound to respond to the needs and desires of their suffering patients, even—and perhaps especially—when those patients are dying. Although his essay provoked criticism from a few physicians who asserted that Quill hadn't sufficiently assessed his patient for depression, most people—doctors and suffering patients alike—voiced support. He received more than a thousand letters, all but a handful praising what he had done. The *New York Times* commended his "courageous act." A grand jury refused to indict him. Quill, pointing out that many other doctors did in secret what he had openly described, said that his only regret was that because the law criminalizes the practice, he had not been with his patient when she died.

---

Without Kevorkian (as a role model to avoid) or Quill (as a role model to emulate), it is difficult to imagine that, only three years after Quill had published the story of the patient he called Diane, physicians in Janet Adkins's home state would be authorized to do what Quill had done, with the full protection of the law. In 1994, spurred by a coalition of physicians, lawyers, ethicists, and grassroots organizations, Oregon voters narrowly approved ORS 127.800-897, the Death with Dignity Act, making theirs the first state to legalize physician-assisted suicide. (Ballot initiatives including both assisted suicide *and* euthanasia had recently failed in California and Washington State. Some blamed the Washington failure on negative publicity from a recent Kevorkian double assisted suicide in which neither of the patients was terminally ill.) Blocked by legal measures for three years, the Oregon legislation was eventually repassed by a wider margin. It took effect in November 1997.

The Death with Dignity Act stipulates that physician-assisted suicide is available only under certain conditions: the patient must submit a written request signed by two witnesses, as well as two oral requests separated by a fifteen-day waiting period; the patient must be competent to make independent decisions about health care; there must be a "reasonable medical judgment" that the patient will die within six months of an "incurable and irreversible disease"; the diagnosis and prognosis must be confirmed by a consulting physician; the physician must present alternatives to suicide such as hospice and palliative care; and the drugs must be administered by the patient himself rather than by a doctor or a family member. In the spring of 1998, a woman in her eighties suffering from breast cancer that had recently spread to her lungs became the first person to die under the protection of the act when, surrounded by family members, under the guidance of the physician who had prescribed the lethal dose, she swallowed a mixture of barbiturates and syrup, washed it down with a glass of brandy, and quietly died.

Eight years later, perhaps the most surprising aspect of the Death with Dignity Act is how seldom it has been used. Although its opponents had predicted that if the act was passed, a flood of ailing, elderly Oregonians would take advantage of its provisions, by 2005, according to the Oregon Department of Human Services, 208 people had used the Death with Dignity Act to die. Of the some 30,000 Oregonians who die each year, about 34 complete physician-assisted suicide.

Supporters of the act point to the fact that so few people have availed themselves of it as an indication that its safeguards are working. They say that the mere knowledge that physician-assisted suicide is available keeps some people from using it; they suggest that most terminally ill patients wish not for death but for the comfort of knowing that they could end their lives on their own terms if they chose to. This is supported by data showing that more than a third of those who obtain the means to die under the act do not use them; they die of their underlying illnesses. "For many people, the simple act of asking for the prescription and getting it—having it in their hands—satisfies whatever it is that's driving them to do this," state epidemiologist Mel Kohn told the *Oregonian*. Said a seventy-nine-year-old retired country doctor dying from inoperable kidney cancer who requested and was given a lethal dose of barbiturates, "I don't know if I'd ever take it, but I'd like to have the option." He put the drugs in his desk drawer—where they stayed until after he had died of natural causes, his family and his hospice team at his side.

From the accounts that have emerged so far, it appears that the vast majority of Oregonians who do use the act to end their lives succeed in getting the "death with dignity" they seek. They are able to decide the manner and timing of their death, put their affairs in order, say good-bye, choose whom they'd like to be with them when they die, and in the end have experiences not unlike those peaceful (if perhaps overidealized) late-nineteenth-century deaths described by Joseph Fletcher, in which the suffering patient died at home surrounded by his intimate circle. Just as Socrates gathered his students around him when he drank his hemlock more than two thousand years earlier, dying Oregonians usually invite family and friends to be with them at the end. The people in attendance sometimes include the prescribing physician and often include volunteers from Compassion in Dying, a nonprofit group dedicated to helping terminally ill people explore their end-of-life options, that has been involved in more than 75 percent of the suicides completed under the act.

The deaths have been gentle, even sociable. (Only one person has thus far died alone—by his own choice.) A fifty-four-year-old former health care aide suffering from terminal liver cancer spent her last day packing up her belongings, calling family members to say good-bye, and compiling a memory book of words and photographs for her sister. That evening, surrounded by eighteen friends who had received hand-drawn invitations to attend her death, she sat on her bed, swallowed antinausea medication, and then drank from a Pyrex beaker of water in which a Compassion in Dying staff member had dissolved the ninety capsules of Seconal her physician had prescribed. A man dying of AIDS organized a communion service attended by sixty relatives and friends, after which he went to his bedroom with his family and his partner, said his good-byes, prayed, drank the medication, and died in his partner's arms. A fifty-six-year-old author-sailor-songwriter swallowed his medication and drank from a pint of Southern Comfort while his son played guitar. A group of friends and relatives who had gathered outside his house lit candles when they were told that he had stopped breathing. A seventy-eight-year-old World War II veteran with end-stage pancreatic cancer died in his bed, surrounded by his wife, daughters, and nine-year-old granddaughter. Before drinking the lethal dose, he said, "If I had any more love, I'd have to keep it in Fort Knox."

In 2000, Peggy Sutherland, a sixty-seven-year-old divorced mother of five, was told that fourteen years after smoking her last cigarette, she had lung cancer again. Over the following year, she underwent two surgeries (one lung was removed entirely), intensive chemotherapy and radiation, and seemingly never-ending rounds of CT scans, bone scans, PET scans, and MRIs. Her strength declining, her thick, dark hair gone, she tried to keep up with the opera nights and jazz concerts she loved, to attend the board meetings of her many community interests, to continue with her Friday-morning bridge group, and to visit her nine grandchildren. But as the cancer spread to the bone and ate away a rib, the pain grew so great that she had to be hospitalized several times. In August, her doctors told Sutherland she had less than six months to live. Around that time, one of her sisters was diagnosed with the same kind of cancer, and Sutherland watched her suffer a lingering death. During one of her better periods, the week before Thanksgiving, Sutherland went with her family to their cottage on the Oregon coast, where they had often gone when the children were young and their mother had taught them how to sing their favorite songs in harmony.

One morning in December, when Sutherland woke, she could hardly sit up, so intense was the pain. Rushed to the hospital, she spent three weeks tethered to tubes, a morphine pump implanted in her spine, her mind so fogged by painkillers she could barely carry on a conversation. She was coughing up blood, losing control of her bowels, and having difficulty breathing without an oxygen tank. She would never walk again. On Christmas Day, with her family around her hospital bed, she gave her grandchildren their gifts. After a desultory New Year's Eve in the hospital with her family, she was sent home and provided with hospice care. Sutherland, who had herself worked as a hospice volunteer, knew the end was near. "She didn't see any point to staying alive that way for another six weeks," said her daughter Kathleen. The day after she came home she told her children that she was ready to die.

Sutherland's children talked about her experience, as well as their own, in *Compassion in Dying: Stories of Dignity and Choice* (a book by Compassion in Dying president Barbara Coombs Lee from which this description is largely drawn). According to them, their mother's decision was in keeping with her lifelong belief in independence and self-sufficiency, a resolve that had been tested when her husband of four decades had divorced her six years earlier. Indeed, that year, when Oregon's Death with Dignity Act was first passed, she had talked approvingly about the right to choose one's own death. A philosophy major in college, she had always valued speaking openly about difficult subjects. Over the previous months, she and her children had talked about life and death in general and about her life and death in particular. Now her children moved quickly to help their mother carry out her wishes. Her longtime internist referred Sutherland and her family to Compassion in Dying, who sent them the paperwork necessary to apply under the Death with Dignity Act and made available their team of palliative-care experts and volunteer counselors. Although her children, two of whom are physicians, supported her decision, they occasionally played devil's advocate, raising objections just to make sure she had no second thoughts, and that if she did, she'd feel comfortable voicing them. But she remained firm.

On the morning of January 25, 2001, one year after the return of Sutherland's cancer, her best friend, her sister, her nephew, her physician, and her five children and their spouses gathered in her apartment in Portland, overlooking the Willamette River. The previous night had been difficult. "She was waking up in these weird morphine states, half-awake and half-asleep, crying out, having bowel movements," recalled daughter Ellen Baltus, who had slept on the floor next to her mother's bed. Once her family had assembled, however, she seemed relaxed. "I remember feeling surprised at how clear-minded Mom seemed the morning of her death, lucid and happy," said Baltus. Downstairs in the kitchen, a Compassion in Dying volunteer opened ninety capsules of secobarbital, a fast-acting barbiturate, and mixed them in water. Upstairs, as Peggy Sutherland had requested, passages from Shakespeare and a poem by Annie Dillard were read. "I watched her take it in, seeming so relaxed and ready," said Baltus. "I could see in her face the relief she felt in being able to finally end the suffering." But Sutherland remained her independent self to the end; when her son read the Twenty-third Psalm, she interrupted him partway through to insist on the King James version. Her friends and family held her and said their good-byes. When the glass containing the barbiturate was placed beside her, she drank the liquid and fell asleep. Twenty minutes later, she was dead.

––––––

Some say the Oregon Death with Dignity Act doesn't go far enough. They point out that even when a physician is involved, assisted suicide is not always foolproof. In Oregon, although most patients die within thirty minutes of swallowing the lethal medication, in a few cases the patient has lasted as long as twenty-four hours; in one instance, a forty-two-year-old man dying of lung cancer consumed the prescribed dose, went into a coma, and woke up nearly three days later. "David said he came back to suffer like Jesus," said his wife. "And he did." Two weeks later, he died of natural causes.

Some also claim that the act discriminates against those people, like Tom Youk, who can't bring hand to mouth to take the pills or who can't swallow them or who can't keep them down. They point to the Oregon man who applied for physician-assisted suicide, received his lethal dose in the mail, but had difficulty downing the medication; his brother-in-law had to prop up his head to enable him to drink all of it through a straw. Discussing the case, the Oregon deputy attorney general suggested that once assisted suicide is accepted, lethal injection may also need to be accepted, because the Death with Dignity Act does not provide equal access to people who cannot swallow—and may thus violate the Americans with Disabilities Act. "To confine legalized physician-assisted death to assisted suicide unfairly discriminates against patients with unrelievable suffering who resolve to end their lives but are physically unable to do so," wrote a group of six ethicists, lawyers, and physicians, including Timothy Quill, in the *New England Journal of Medicine,* contending that it should be legal for doctors to bring about death in terminally ill patients, at the patient's request, using lethal injections. Although the vast majority of doctors reject active euthanasia as a violation of medical ethics and an abuse of the doctor-patient relationship, some ethicists, as we have seen, maintain that there is no real moral distinction between physician-assisted suicide and voluntary euthanasia. They cite the case of Sigmund Freud, who suffered from cancer of the mouth for the last sixteen years of his life. Refusing painkillers so that he could continue to work with an unclouded mind, Freud made a pact with his physician, Max Schur, that when his condition became unbearable, Schur would help him die. In 1939, when the pain became so great that he was unable to read or write, and necrosis of the bone gave off an odor so foul that even his beloved chow kept his distance, Freud asked his physician to keep his promise. Schur gave him two injections of morphine, and Freud died quietly, at the age of eighty-three.

Voluntary euthanasia—actively causing a person's death at his or her request—is against the law throughout most of the world (although that has not stopped doctors in various countries from practicing it and, like Jack Kevorkian in the case of Thomas Youk, in some cases admitting it). There is, however, one country in which euthanasia, as well as physician-assisted suicide, has been widely practiced since 1973, when a physician gave her ailing seventy-eight-year-old mother a lethal injection. Although Article 293 of the Dutch criminal code called for twelve years' imprisonment for anyone who "takes the life of another at his or her explicit and serious request," a Dutch court found her guilty but gave her a short, suspended sentence. Public opinion strongly supported the physician's act. Over the following decade, a series of court cases established conditions under which physicians in the Netherlands might perform "aid-in-dying," as it was called, without fear of

prosecution. The patient must be experiencing unbearable suffering that cannot be relieved in any other way; the patient must make a voluntary, well-
considered, and persistent request; the physician must consult with another
physician in making the decision; the case must be reported to the coroner. In
1984, the Royal Dutch Medical Association announced its support for the
practice, provided that guidelines were followed. (Physicians opposed to
euthanasia split off and formed a separate medical group.) In 1993, a statute
explicitly stipulated that a physician following the guidelines would not be
prosecuted. In 2001, the Dutch parliament formally legalized physician-
assisted suicide and euthanasia. For several decades, Dutch doctors have
quietly helped more than five thousand terminally ill patients to end their lives
each year—nearly 4 percent of all deaths in the Netherlands—either by providing drugs to be taken orally or, far more often, by lethal injection.

"Every patient, every human being, has the right to see his suffering as
unbearable and has the right to ask a doctor for euthanasia," says Pieter
Admiraal, a Dutch anesthesiologist and author of *Justifiable Euthanasia: A
Manual for the Medical Profession.* "Every doctor has the right to do euthanasia. And every doctor has the right to refuse to do euthanasia." At a 1986 conference sponsored by the Hemlock Society in Washington, D.C., I heard
Admiraal, a portly, bearded man who was, and is, the most well-known practitioner of euthanasia in the Netherlands, describe one of the hundreds of
patients he had helped to die at his hospital in Delft. "She was twenty-four
years old and she was in a nursing home," he said. "I had a phone call from her
doctor that she wanted to speak to me about euthanasia. I said that she wanted
to speak to me. That's not true. She couldn't. She hadn't been able to speak for
a long time because she had cancer of the tongue. She couldn't swallow, and
they had put a tube in her stomach, through her skin, to feed her. That also
means that she couldn't swallow her saliva. People produce between one and
two liters of saliva each day. She was a very, very nice and handsome girl, and
she was sitting there, in one hand a tissue to remove continuously her saliva,
and with her other hand to write down what she wanted to say to me. But I
knew already what her problem was because that tumor was growing, very
slowly but growing. The next step was a tracheotomy to open her trachea, to
enable her to breathe if it closed. And that's what she refused. So she wrote
down that she refused this kind of tube. And she asked me to assure her that
I would give her euthanasia just before she should suffocate. And I agreed, of
course.

"After a few weeks she came to our hospital because the tumor was bleeding. We all thought that she would bleed to death, but she didn't. She remained
in our hospital for the next two days, and we discussed when we should do the
euthanasia. It was, of course, always a group decision, never a decision on my
own. We talked long with the priest, nurse, and doctor on the case. And she was
writing to us or knocking her head when it was time to do it. And we agreed

we should wait until the last moment because we were all there so we could do it immediately if something went wrong.

"And then two days later it proved that it was necessary to do so. First she saw her parents. Although usually the family are in the room at the moment of giving euthanasia, they refused to be there. In this case, then, the nurse, the priest, her doctor, and myself were there.

"She wrote on her paper a farewell. I kissed her and said, 'Have a very good journey.' And I gave her an injection and she died.

"I have two simple questions for you. I am always with my patients when they are dying, whatever the cause of their death, and if they have tongue cancer or cancer of that sort, then should not the doctor be there available to assist?

"And the second question is, if a doctor is there and he's standing in the back of the room with his hand on his bag and watches this patient suffocate, should not *this* doctor be liable to prosecution?"

# II

# "Your Good End in Life Is Our Concern!"

───────

DESPITE POPULAR BELIEF to the contrary, unless one lives in Oregon, the Netherlands, or Belgium, suicide is not easy—particularly if one is old, infirm, or terminally ill. Under current laws, those without access to lethal drugs are often driven by desperation to more secretive, violent, and lonely deaths, deaths that can be horrifically traumatic for friends and family left behind, like that of the terminally ill cancer patient, immobilized in a Stryker frame and partially paralyzed, who doused his chest with lighter fluid and set himself on fire. Furthermore, when knowledge of proper dosages and methods is lacking, suicide attempts often fail, and bad situations are replaced with even worse ones. Many intended suicides by gunshot leave the person alive but brain-damaged; drug overdoses that are not fatal may have the same effect. One eighty-three-year-old woman obtained an insufficient number of pills and lost consciousness but did not die; her daughter ended up smothering her with a plastic bag.

"There is only one prospect worse than being chained to an intolerable existence: the nightmare of a botched attempt to end it," observed Arthur Koestler. In 1983, two years after writing these words, the seventy-seven-year-old author, suffering from Parkinson's disease and leukemia, made sure he did not botch it: he took a fatal overdose of barbiturates. His wife of eighteen years, Cynthia, although in good health at the age of fifty-five, decided she could not endure life without him and took an overdose at the same time. Their maid arrived one morning to find a note pinned to the door: "Please do not go upstairs. Ring the police and tell them to come to the house." Police found Koestler sitting in his armchair, his wife on a nearby sofa. On the coffee table in front of them were a glass of whiskey and two wineglasses with a residue of white powder. Koestler's suicide note, written ten months earlier and addressed "To Whom It May Concern," said, among other things, "After a more or less steady physical decline over the last years, the process has now reached an acute state with added complications which make it advisable to seek self-deliverance now, before I become incapable of making the necessary arrangements." In a footnote appended to her husband's farewell, Cynthia concluded, "I cannot live without Arthur, despite certain inner resources."

Over the years, a number of organizations have gone to great—and often legally dubious—lengths to ensure their members a death more like that of Arthur Koestler than that of the cancer patient who set himself on fire. Although right-to-die groups date back to 1935, with the founding of Britain's Voluntary Euthanasia Society, they came to wide public attention in the 1980s when an English journalist helped his wife to die and wrote a book about it.

Like many who become involved in right-to-die activism, Derek Humphry was drawn by personal experience. In 1972, while they were living in London during Humphry's years as home affairs correspondent for the *Sunday Times,* his forty-year-old wife, Jean, discovered a lump in her left breast. Tests proved it to be malignant. Despite a mastectomy, chemotherapy, and radiation treatments, the cancer spread to her lymph glands, spine, and bones. In May of 1974 the doctors predicted she would die before the end of the year. Although Jean struggled to maintain a semblance of normal life, she was often in pain so excruciating that she had to be rushed to the hospital. After a particularly harrowing episode she asked her husband to make her a promise: when the pain became too great and she decided that she had had enough, he would supply her with the means to end her life. Humphry promised.

Although Jean's wits were as sharp as ever, her physical condition steadily deteriorated. Eventually, she was forced to stay in bed, drugged into semiconsciousness and using a wheelchair to get around the house on the rare occasions she was up to it. A physician told Derek that the bones in Jean's legs were so brittle that they might snap if she tried to walk. One morning she broke a rib when she bent over too rapidly. When there was another outbreak of cancer at the top of her spine, the doctors at the hospital admitted that little could be done beyond making Jean comfortable. She would probably die within a few weeks. The morning after she returned from the hospital, when her husband brought her medication and her breakfast, Jean asked him if he had been able to procure a drug. Derek, who had obtained a lethal dose of Seconal and codeine from a sympathetic physician, said that he had. She told him that she would die at one o'clock.

Humphry and his wife spent their remaining hours talking about their twenty-two years of married life. Shortly before one o'clock he prepared a cup of coffee for Jean, into which he stirred the lethal mixture. Returning to her room, he placed the mug on the nightstand. They hugged each other and said good-bye. Jean drank the contents, leaned back on the pillow, closed her eyes, and fell into a deep sleep. Derek sat by her side until, fifty minutes later, she died.

Humphry let few people beyond the immediate family know the circumstances of Jean's death. One of those he eventually told was his second wife, Ann Wickett, an American Ph.D. candidate in English literature who was twelve years his junior. She encouraged Humphry to write about his experience. Three years later, in 1978, *Jean's Way,* an account of his wife's last years and how Humphry had helped her die, was published. The book's first printing sold out within a week. Humphry received scores of letters from all over the world, some from terminally ill people asking for help in killing themselves, others from people who wanted to be prepared in case they ever became hopelessly ill. Some revealed that, like Humphry, they had helped someone die but had never told anyone. Others wrote that a terminally ill loved one had begged for assistance with a suicide but that, fearing prosecution and stigma, they had been unable to carry out what Humphry called "an act of love."

What Humphry considered an act of love could legally be considered an act of manslaughter. In 1961, when Britain's Suicide Act decriminalized suicide and attempted suicide, it added a law that made aiding and abetting a suicide a felony, punishable by up to fourteen years in prison (thus making it a crime to help someone commit an act that was itself not a crime). When a journalist asked the police what they intended to do about Humphry, who in the book and in television and newspaper interviews freely admitted he had helped his wife kill herself, an investigation was launched. Eventually, the public prosecutor dropped the case for "lack of evidence." Privately, he admitted that he had been moved by the book and thought Jean had been extremely brave.

In 1979, when *Jean's Way* was published in the United States, where Humphry and Wickett had moved, there was an even greater furor. Humphry told his story on *Donahue, 60 Minutes,* and *Good Morning America.* He received hundreds of letters, many from people who wanted to know what drugs Jean had taken and how to procure them. Humphry was struck by how many people faced situations similar to the one he and Jean had faced and who had nowhere else to turn. He combed through newspaper clippings at the library of the *Los Angeles Times,* where he now worked. "I saw case after case just as compassionate and loving as mine, where people had been prosecuted for aiding and abetting a suicide," he recalls. Humphry felt there should be some sort of organization to help these people. He resigned from his job and organized a meeting of twenty experts in the field of death and dying: professors, lawyers, doctors, social workers, and nurses. He described his goal of a society dedicated to legalizing active voluntary euthanasia for the terminally ill and asked who would be willing to join. "They were all in favor in principle, but they said they couldn't get involved," says Humphry. "They were afraid of how it would reflect on their professional practices." Some feared for their safety. "My God, they firebomb the houses of pro-abortion people," said one attorney. "What do you think they'll do to us?" Nevertheless, on August 21, 1980, Humphry held a press conference to announce the formation of the Hemlock Society, named for the poison that Socrates used to commit suicide. There were four members: Humphry, Wickett, lawyer Richard Scott, and Gerald Larue, a professor of religion at USC. The fledgling organization would operate out of Humphry's Santa Monica garage.

Ten years later, operating out of an office in Eugene, Oregon, and boasting a staff of eight, the Hemlock Society had forty-six thousand members and eighty-one chapters across the United States. Dedicated, as its letterhead said, to "supporting the option of active voluntary euthanasia for the terminally ill," the society had two goals: to educate the public about right-to-die issues and to change U.S. laws to make it legal to assist the terminally ill to take their own lives. To that end, the society published books (including *Common-Sense Suicide,* an apology for elderly suicide by Hemlock member Doris Portwood, and *Double Exit,* Ann Wickett's study of double suicides); edited the *Euthanasia Review,* a scholarly journal; issued the *Hemlock Quarterly,* a newsletter keeping members abreast of the movement; produced a thirty-minute educational video on euthanasia, available for sale or rent to colleges as well as to Hemlock members "for home use"; distributed more than 1 million copies of the Living Will and Durable Power of Attorney for Health Care; issued a wallet-size card on which members could specify their medical wishes in case of an accident; and advertised its work in such diverse publications as the *New York Times Book Review, Science Digest, Lancet,* and *Hustler.* (Only two publications, the Gray Panther newsletter and *Modern Maturity,* refused to run Hemlock ads.)

As its executive director and the public face of the organization, Humphry spent much of his time spreading the word. Lugging a briefcase crammed with Hemlock books, brochures, and membership applications, he spoke wherever he was invited: high school and college classes, retirement communities, hospices, nurses' training courses, and professional conferences. (For a time Hemlock employed a Hollywood publicity agent to book Humphry on radio and television shows.) As a former journalist, Humphry knew the power of the press and how to court it. He published a collection of news clippings on right-to-die cases and sent journalists yellow Rolodex cards, their tabs labeled DEATH/DYING, with a list of topics, from "Pulling the Plug" to "Double Suicide," on which he was prepared to give "background and quotes." Humphry admitted that his efforts may have appeared overly gung ho. "I'm a street fighter, not a philosopher," he told me. "I'm trying to change public opinion." As he addressed Hemlock members in a fund-raising letter, "Your good end in life is our concern! Please help us to help you achieve it." He promised that as soon as the laws changed to permit doctors to help terminally ill people take their lives, Hemlock would, as he put it, "commit corporate suicide."

At its height, Hemlock received some 230 letters and phone calls each day, most of them requests for membership applications, living wills, and books. Not surprisingly, Hemlock also received desperate appeals from people in harrowing circumstances: a man whose wife was dying of cancer and wanted the name of a pharmacist who would supply her with a lethal dose; a woman who had just been told she was terminally ill with pancreatic cancer and said she must know where to get drugs immediately; a woman who had hoarded a supply of barbiturates and wondered whether such and such an amount was enough to kill her. Callers frequently offered Humphry money to help them end their suffering. "I've been offered as much as ten thousand dollars to go into their home and sit with them while they die," Humphry told me. "One woman offered me her Cadillac if I would help her. It's a measure of their desperation. They say, 'Jean had you, I've got nobody, you *must* help me.'"

When such help was requested, Humphry never actively intervened or provided specific information about dosages. Not only was he mindful of the legal danger—in giving such information he could have been charged with aiding and abetting a suicide—but it went against his moral grain. "I never tell anybody what to do or what not to do, but I will discuss with them the pros and cons of their situation," he told me. "How serious is their illness? Does their spouse know? Have they told their doctor of their plans? How long do they think they can hang on? Are they willing to go into the hospital again? Most people appreciate being able to talk this over with somebody. But it is for the individuals and their associates to make the decisions and carry out whatever actions they choose." Humphry often referred callers to local hospices for palliative care, or to lawyers for legal advice. Occasionally, people who appeared emotionally disturbed called or wrote. "We tell them we can't help them, and they would be wrong to join this society," said Humphry. "We suggest that they seek help from a therapist or a crisis intervention center because mental illness can be curable. In addition, a mentally ill person can go and kill himself whereas a terminally ill person is often physically incapable of taking his own life." In 1988, the year before inventing his Mercitron, Jack Kevorkian approached Humphry and offered to open a clinic in Los Angeles to which terminally ill Hemlock members might be referred for assistance in dying. Humphry told Kevorkian he preferred trying to change the law to breaking it.

Many people assumed that Hemlock members must be radical leftists, lonely depressives, or morbid weirdos. But according to membership surveys, Hemlock members represented an average cross section of Americans except that they were apt to be older, wealthier, better educated, and whiter. They ranged in age from nineteen to ninety-eight, with an average age of sixty. Two out of three members were women—not surprising, given that in the United States there are four times as many widows as widowers. The membership included more than two hundred doctors. Only one in twenty Hemlock members was terminally ill. Some joined because of a philosophical belief in the right to die. Others joined to obtain practical information about euthanasia in the event that they became incapacitated. "Hemlock is my insurance policy against pain, senile old age, and loneliness," wrote one member. The majority joined because they had seen someone close to them die in extreme pain and suffering and were determined not to let it happen to them.

Hemlock members also joined because the society acted as a support group. Members could attend not only their local chapter meetings but Hemlock's biennial national conferences, which had the pep and can-do atmosphere of any professional convention, as I found when I attended Hemlock's Second National Voluntary Euthanasia Conference in 1985. In the Starlight Room of the Miramar Sheraton Hotel in Los Angeles, a ballroom-size space accustomed to hosting bridal shows and car dealers' conventions, 240 Hemlock members who had come from as far away as New York, Chicago, and Fort Lauderdale sat at tables draped with gold tablecloths, listening attentively (some taking notes in Hemlock-provided notebooks) to two days of speeches and workshops on such topics as "Memorial Societies and Funeral Prearrangement," "How Euthanasia Was Legalized in Holland," "The Law and Euthanasia," and "The Sexual Needs of the Terminally Ill Person." Anyone expecting Hemlock to behave like a typical special-interest group with an ax to grind would have been surprised by the roster of speakers, which included several opposed to suicide. Edwin Shneidman pushed suicide prevention in the keynote address. Stephen Levine, a Buddhist therapist, meditated before the audience in the lotus position before urging them to "meet pain with love instead of fear" and to resist the temptation to leave their bodies "in an angry, self-hating manner." At the pro-suicide end of the spectrum, German surgeon Julius Hackethal screened a videotape that showed him giving cyanide to a sixty-nine-year-old woman suffering from terminal cancer. In his presentation, "Medical Questions in Euthanasia," Colin Brewer, an English psychiatrist, said, "I want to urge upon you the values of the humble plastic bag. People seem to feel it has certain aesthetic objections. But in combination with even a smallish dose of sedative drugs, it does in fact form a very effective method of ending life because it's essentially a belt-and-braces policy."

As Brewer's advice suggests, the emphasis at Hemlock conferences was not on the philosophical but on the pragmatic. During coffee breaks members were apt to be discussing the shelf life of certain drugs, the optimal wording of living wills, the names of medical textbooks containing tables of lethal dosages, and the ingredients of what some called the "recipe"—what drugs to take for a swift, painless death. Although there was also talk of active, happy lives—it was not uncommon to see people proudly showing photos of their grandchildren or discussing upcoming vacations—each person had come to the conference with a story and a need to tell it. "I have lymphoma of the bones," said a man in a wheelchair. "I'm forty-four. The average age of the patients in my nursing home is seventy. There are people dealing with me that have no training. People are allowed to be in pain. They are put in positions that are painful, and their pleas for medication are often ignored. I came here because I was thinking of ending my life, and I don't know how to do it."

The man with lymphoma could have found out how to end his life by buying one of Hemlock's "how-to" manuals. Although Humphry would have preferred that doctors be allowed to supply the information and assist in the death, since that was—and is—illegal in all but a few corners of the world, he believed that people who took the matter into their own hands were in need of some practical guidance. In 1981, Hemlock published *Let Me Die Before I Wake,* a hundred-page "book of self-deliverance" for the dying, in which Humphry told the stories, down to the specific drug dosages used, of seven terminally ill people who had taken their own lives. Burying the dosages within the stories, Humphry said, forced a person to read the book and partake of Hemlock's message of nonviolence, advance planning, and sharing. It also lessened the likelihood of legal problems. (*Let Me Die* was addressed to terminally ill people. Those contemplating suicide for other reasons were urged to speak to their family, friends, physician, counselor, minister, or suicide prevention center.) When *Let Me Die* was first published, its sale was limited to Hemlock members of three months' standing. In 1982, spurred by appeals from people who said they needed the book immediately, and knowing there had been no evidence of misuse, Hemlock decided to make the book available to the public. Eventually, *Let Me Die Before I Wake,* described by *60 Minutes* as "the bible of the euthanasia movement," would sell some 150,000 copies. Doctors and hospice administrators called Hemlock to request copies for patients who asked about euthanasia, and the book was a popular item at libraries. The Los Angeles Public Library told the author it was their most frequently stolen book; eventually, Humphry noted proudly, they were forced to keep it "under lock and key." Among those who took their lives with the help of *Let Me Die Before I Wake*—Humphry estimates the number to be in the thousands—was an elderly Florida gentleman with a brain tumor who ended his life after several months of keeping the book under his pillow.

Many readers, however, grumbled that they had to do too much *reading.* "The biggest complaint about the book comes from little old ladies who don't want to dig through all the words to find the information," Humphry told me. "They skim the book and say, 'It's too difficult—all I want is the little pill.' I tell them there is no such thing as The Pill. I tell them to read the book again, take notes, underline the important bits. Or I'll say, 'Page sixty is what you want.' I don't say what's on the page, I just say read page sixty." Prodded by such complaints, Hemlock finally printed a brief, easily understandable toxicity chart in the *Hemlock Quarterly* with lethal dosages listed for seventeen drugs. "Only for the information of terminally ill, mature adults," it warned. "Keep this document in a secure, private place."

Eventually, Humphry decided to take things, as he put it, "one step further," by writing *Final Exit: The Practicalities of Self-Deliverance and Assisted Suicide for the Dying*. Following a poetic epigraph from Keats—"Now more than ever seems it rich to die, / To cease upon the midnight with no pain"—*Final Exit* cut to the chase, albeit in fourteen-point type for the convenience of readers with failing eyesight. In a no-nonsense fashion that called to mind Dorothy Parker's poem "Resume" ("Razors pain you / Rivers are damp . . ."), Humphry evaluated more than a dozen possible methods, including shooting ("messy"); hanging ("ugly and extremely traumatic for your loved ones"); car exhaust ("high chance of discovery"); poisonous plants ("risky and painful"); household chemicals ("painful in the extreme"); charcoal cooking fires ("too uncertain"); freezing ("a method for which I have respect"); nonprescription drugs ("a prescription for disaster"); self-starvation ("not as easy as it sounds"); cyanide ("difficult to secure"); injecting air into the veins ("most unsatisfactory"); and electrocution ("Unless you are an ingenious and accomplished engineer . . . definitely not advised"). The book's recommended technique? An overdose of barbiturates ("the drug of choice in self-deliverance") accompanied, just to make sure, by a plastic bag. "If you are repulsed by the addition of the plastic bag, then you must accept a ten percent chance that by some quirk you will wake up, and will have to try again," Humphry wrote. "With the bag, it's 100 percent certain." In a chapter forthrightly titled "Self-Deliverance Via the Plastic Bag," Humphry offered not only practical advice ("It is very important that it be firmly tied around the neck with either a large rubber band or a ribbon. No more air must come in"), but personal philosophy as well ("Should you use a clear plastic bag or an opaque one? That's a matter of taste. Loving the world as I do, I'll opt for a clear one if I have to").

To obtain the drugs, Humphry suggested asking one's physician directly, or requesting two separate barbiturate prescriptions on different dates. He also offered advice on how to shop for a sympathetic doctor; gave tips on how to store lethal drugs; warned readers to check their insurance policies; outlined a suggested suicide note; and weighed in on miscellaneous matters of protocol. "If you are unfortunately obliged to end your life in a hospital or motel, it is gracious to leave a note apologizing for the shock and inconvenience to the staff. I have also heard of an individual leaving a generous tip to a motel staff." The book concluded with a checklist for potential self-deliverers, from (1) "Be sure that you are in a hopeless condition. Talk it over with your doctors one more time" to (16) "Make the preparations for your end extremely carefully and with consideration for others. Leave nothing to chance."

Published in March 1991, nine months after Kevorkian had hooked up Janet Adkins to his suicide machine, *Final Exit* created a sensation, spending eighteen weeks on the *New York Times* best-seller list, selling over a million copies (Katharine Hepburn had two, one for each nightstand), being translated into ten languages, and inspiring numerous letters of thanks from survivors of those who had taken their lives with the book's help.

But *Final Exit* also reached a subset of readers whose friends and families were not so grateful. In 1993, in a report published in the *New England Journal of Medicine,* researchers compared the number of asphyxiation deaths by plastic bag in New York City for one-year periods immediately before and after the publication of *Final Exit.* The number jumped from eight to thirty-three, an increase of 313 percent. A copy of *Final Exit* was found at the scene of nine of the suicides; in six other cases, there was clear evidence that the deceased had taken their own lives with the information from the book. In most of the fifteen cases linked to *Final Exit,* there was no evidence of terminal illness; in six cases, an autopsy could find no illness of any kind. Nationwide, the number of cases of asphyxiation by plastic bag rose from 334 to 437, an increase of 31 percent. Although the total number of suicides did not increase over that time, suicide prevention experts worried that, despite the book's warning, on page 123, that "this information is meant for consideration only by a *mature adult who is dying,*" it would, inevitably, be misused by depressed, impulsive, suicidal people who were not terminally ill—such as the young California woman whose thirteen-year-old daughter found her dead, a plastic bag over her head and a copy of *Final Exit,* pertinent passages highlighted, nearby. Humphry seemed to consider such deaths a kind of collateral damage. "This misuse I regret but can do nothing about," he wrote in *Final Exit*'s third edition, published in 2002. "Suicide has always been endemic in mankind; some of us do not have the emotional and intellectual equipment to cope with a lifetime of troubles—real and imagined—and elect to die. Self-destruction of a physically fit person is always a tragic waste of life and hurtful to survivors, but life is a personal responsibility. We must each decide for ourselves."

---

Hemlock was not the only right-to-die society to publish instructions on how to take one's own life. The first such manual had been promised in 1979 by the Voluntary Euthanasia Society. After decades of quiet respectability, the British group had been invigorated by a recent influx of younger members, including general secretary Nicholas Reed, a brilliant, energetic Oxford graduate. One of the steps taken under his leadership was to change the society's name to Exit, a name more in tune with its upbeat new image. With increased visibility, Exit received a growing number of letters and calls from desperate people seeking information on pain-free suicide methods. Under the Suicide Act of 1961, Exit could not advise those people without risk of prosecution for aiding and abetting a suicide. Although many right-to-die advocates were aware that information on lethal dosages had long been available in certain medical textbooks, no one had ever written a book on how to commit suicide. In October of 1979, Exit announced plans for a ten-thousand-word *Guide to Self-Deliverance*. To avoid possible abuse, Exit said that the booklet would be available only to members of three months' standing. Within several months of this news, membership—a matter of three pounds' dues annually, ten for foreigners—jumped from two thousand to nine thousand. But these anxious new members were forced to wait longer than the required three months. Fearing prosecution, Exit postponed release of the booklet. Meanwhile, in Scotland, where laws against assisted suicide were more lenient, a branch of Exit seceded and published its own guide, *How to Die with Dignity*, in September 1980, not long before Hemlock released *Let Me Die Before I Wake*. Since then, manuals have been published in France, Belgium, Switzerland, Germany, and the Netherlands.

The guides constitute an intriguing cross-cultural study. Exit's *A Guide to Self-Deliverance*, a thirty-one-page booklet to which Koestler, a vice president of the society, wrote the introduction, was finally published in 1981. Like *Let Me Die* and *Final Exit*, it is intended for the terminally ill and not for the merely depressed. "Before considering Self-Deliverance," the book's inside cover cautions, "HAVE YOU RUNG THE SAMARITANS?" Like *Let Me Die* and *Final Exit*, it urges the reader to consider alternatives (hospice care, second opinions, pain clinics, other methods of treatment), to make sure the distress is not temporary, and to consider the effect of the death on family and friends. Suicide, it stresses, is not a decision to be taken lightly but a matter to be pondered over a period of months, time permitting. This said, the manual recommends how *not* to commit suicide. It advises against shooting, jumping, wrist-cutting, and hanging, methods that are especially traumatic for friends and relatives and may leave the victim alive and brain-damaged rather than dead. The manual advocates peaceful, nonviolent methods, suggesting that "the body when found should look simply dead and not disgusting."

To achieve this end the guide outlines five bloodless techniques, most of which combine drugs with a supplementary method—car exhaust, alcohol, drowning in a bathtub, plastic bags—to ensure lethality. "A combination of sedative drugs and a plastic bag should both shorten the process of dying and minimise unpleasant sensations," advises the manual. Written by a committee of Exit members, including several doctors, the guide is disarmingly matter-of-fact, as when it counsels the reader, "You need two plastic bags approximately three feet (one metre) in length and 18 inches (50 cm) in width. Bags smaller or very much larger than this should not be used. Kitchen bin liners are an obvious possibility." A "postscript" written by psychiatrist Eliot Slater strikes a lone lyrical note: "It is the sovereign right of the individual, absolute and inalienable, to say, 'I have thought well what my duties are to all those who love me, and to all others. I have thought also of the rights I owe to myself. Fate has called to me, and I say to you, Farewell.'"

Dedicated "To the memory of those many millions who lived for a while in agony and eventually died in torment because of cruel laws and the prejudices of bigots," the forty-four-page Scottish manual, *How to Die with Dignity,* is even more pragmatic. "I think that already-distressed people can do without long-winded paragraphs," George Mair, a retired surgeon, chairman of Scottish Exit, and author of the manual, told a reporter. "My book is more like a recipe for scones—you add a pinch of this and half a pinch of that." Mair's "recipe" stresses dignity and courtesy. In the section "Methods of Self-Deliverance Which Should Not Be Used," the author advises that jumping off a ship is "highly inconvenient for the ship's crew and passengers," while jumping onto a live train rail is "not in any way dignified and is a great offence to witnesses." Those intending to die by dropping an electric cable in their bathtubs are advised to leave behind "a large notice instructing no one to touch 'anything' without first switching off the mains current." Dr. Mair adds, "It is a matter of personal choice as to whether or not some form of bathing suit is worn." The plastic bag is dismissed with the comment "This is not dignified." Mair outlines the recommended procedure—a lethal dose of barbiturates—in a seventeen-step list of instructions that concludes, "Take soda and spirits and drugs to bedside. Swallow the drugs as rapidly as may be convenient and sip both soda and spirits while doing so." Mair adds that if the place of "deliverance" is a hotel, it is advisable to ask the front desk to hold all calls, to hang the DO NOT DISTURB sign outside the door, and to leave a short letter "to thank the manager and apologise for abusing hospitality." Available only to members, the booklet sold some five thousand copies over fifteen years.

In April 1982, another how-to guide appeared that made the manuals of the right-to-die societies seem relatively innocuous. *Suicide, Mode d'Emploi* ("Suicide: Operating Instructions"), the work of two young Parisian journalists, proposes suicide as a revolutionary act—not merely for the terminally ill but for anyone and everyone. The book contains a section listing fifty recipes for "cocktails" that will ensure a "gentle" death, giving precise lethal dosages and advice on how to forge prescriptions. "I feel no remorse," said the book's publisher, responding to news that *Suicide* had been used by several physically healthy young people to end their lives. "This is a book that pleads for life. But it also recognizes that the right to suicide is an inalienable right, like the right to work, the right to like certain things, the right to publish. What use is a right without the means to execute it?" Others were less appreciative. *Suicide* provoked the outrage of French psychiatrists, clergy, politicians, suicide prevention agencies, and the Association pour le Droit de Mourir dans la Dignité (a French right-to-die society). Although a number of bookstores declined to stock it, and several newspapers, magazines, and radio stations refused to carry advertisements, the French parliament, despite repeated attempts, could not put a stop to the book until 1987, when it passed a law banning all how-to suicide manuals. By then, *Suicide* had sold almost two hundred thousand copies in

France, been translated into seven languages, been the subject of eighty criminal complaints and four court cases, and served as a blueprint for the suicides of at least fifteen people, none of them terminally ill, most of them young and unemployed. In one case a depressed young woman from Nice killed her eight-year-old son, then killed herself. An annotated copy of *Suicide* was found on her bedroom table.

Though right-to-die societies around the world denounced the book, pointing out that *Suicide* had been aimed not at terminally ill people but at everyone, even some of the more responsible manuals encountered difficulties. Among the more than twenty suicides linked to England's *Guide to Self-Deliverance* was a physically healthy twenty-two-year-old music student with a history of psychological problems who was found dead in a London hotel with the booklet at his bedside. Although it was ostensibly available only to members over the age of twenty-five, the boy had simply lied about his birth date. In 1983, *Guide* was withdrawn.

By that time Exit had run into even more serious trouble. In 1980, following the suicide of an elderly Exit member, police raided Exit's cramped basement offices in Kensington and arrested general secretary Nicholas Reed. Soon thereafter, sixty-eight-year-old Exit volunteer Mark Lyons was also arrested; both were charged with various counts of aiding and abetting suicide. Over the following months an extraordinary and unsettling story emerged in court. Moved by heartrending calls from dying people who begged for help, Reed, without the knowledge of anyone else at Exit, had dispatched Lyons to their homes. Carrying a bag containing brandy, barbiturates, and plastic bags, and pretending to be a doctor, Lyons, a bearded, shabbily dressed retired taxi driver, supplied his "patients" with the means for suicide, then sat with them until they died.

Most of the victims were tragic cases: a woman suffering from terminal cancer who had only a short time to live; a victim of spinal osteoarthritis; a man who had been an invalid for three years and who for the last six months had worn an oxygen mask twenty-four hours a day. In each case the victim had repeatedly begged to die. But Reed and Lyons had intervened in less extreme situations. In one, Lyons helped a physically healthy, middle-aged agoraphobe to die. In another, a twenty-five-year-old army veteran told the court that he suffered from depression, drank heavily, and had attempted suicide several times. He had called Exit, met with Reed, and described his miseries. Reed notified Lyons. When Lyons telephoned and demanded thirty pounds for traveling expenses, the man grew suspicious and dropped the matter. And a bedridden woman suffering from severe spinal injuries testified that Lyons was "furious" when she changed her mind about wanting to die. She said that Lyons told her, "You are the only person to disobey me."

After a two-week trial, Lyons was found guilty of five charges of aiding and abetting suicide, and one of conspiring to aid and abet suicide. Taking into consideration the 325 days Lyons had spent in jail awaiting trial, the judge gave him a two-year suspended sentence and the admonition, "No more meddling with pills and plastic bags." Reed, found guilty of two charges of aiding and abetting suicide and one of conspiring to aid and abet, was sentenced to two and a half years (later reduced on appeal to eighteen months). As he was led from the dock of London's Old Bailey Criminal Court to begin his sentence, Reed shouted, "That shows the idiocy of the present law!"

The image of the erudite Reed and the eccentric Lyons with his "suicide kit" taking matters into their own hands was chilling. Although a few radical right-to-die advocates maintained that the ends justified such means, the majority of euthanasia groups were appalled. Exit, which knew nothing of Reed's and Lyons's extracurricular activities until their arrest, was dubbed a "suicide club" by the tabloids, and its credibility was tarnished. Exit subsequently expelled Reed, changed its name back to the Voluntary Euthanasia Society, and assumed a decidedly lower profile for the next several years.

---

*Final Exit* would be Derek Humphry's swan song at Hemlock. He was weary of managing the rapidly expanding organization, which was spending most of its resources trying to change legislation to permit physician-assisted suicide and euthanasia. His personal life, too, had entered what he would later refer to as "that black time." In 1986, Humphry and Wickett had assisted Wickett's parents in a double suicide, using prescription drugs obtained by Humphry. Humphry had been in one room attending to Wickett's ninety-two-year-old father, who was suffering from congestive heart failure, while Wickett was in another room with her seventy-eight-year-old mother, who was recovering from a stroke. When her mother's breathing had grown agitated after swallowing the pills, Wickett had panicked and covered her mother's mouth with a laundry bag. The experience would haunt Wickett and eventually lead her to question her belief in Hemlock's mission. In 1989, Wickett was diagnosed with breast cancer. Three weeks after her mastectomy, one day after she had started chemotherapy, Humphry left her. Wickett claimed Humphry was so unnerved by having to deal with a second wife with breast cancer that he was unable to act rationally. Humphry said the marriage had been troubled for several years and accused his wife of mental instability. They divorced. Wickett, a cofounder of Hemlock, was forced out of her position as deputy director; Humphry ordered the office locks changed. Humphry remarried in early 1991. In October of that year, while *Final Exit* was topping the best-seller lists, Wickett, depressed, lonely, and emotionally exhausted, rode her horse into the hills near her home and took a fatal overdose of barbiturates. In her suicide note, she accused Humphry of doing "everything conceivable to precipitate my death." In 1992, saying he was "temporarily burned-out," Humphry left Hemlock.

Although Hemlock would live on, its position of influence in the right-to-die movement would be eclipsed by two other developments, both of which were, in some way, godfathered by Hemlock. *Final Exit* had sold so well that Hemlock was able to donate nearly a million dollars to support ballot initiatives in California, Washington, and Oregon. (Indeed, without Hemlock's financial resources, the Oregon Death with Dignity Act would likely not have passed— or would, at least, not have passed so soon.) And in 1993, eleven AIDS activists and caregivers, including a physician, a hospice nurse, and several members of the clergy—many of them ex-Hemlockers who had worked on the unsuccessful 1991 Washington initiative—formed Compassion in Dying, the first organization in this country devoted to providing information, consultation, and emotional support for mentally competent, terminally ill adults who wished to end their life. Although Compassion in Dying's support would not extend to providing lethal medications, its volunteers, if requested, would be present at the very end so that clients would not have to die alone. In Compassion in Dying's first thirteen months, three hundred people requested the organization's help; forty-six qualified for their services, of whom twenty-four were helped to their death.

Over the years, the group refined its protocol, which, with some alterations, provided the blueprint for Oregon's Death with Dignity Act. In 1997, shortly after the act went into effect, Compassion in Dying formed a chapter in Oregon. Since then, while continuing to work with clients across the country, the organization has served as a clearinghouse for the vast majority of Oregon's assisted-suicide cases. In recent years, Compassion, which does not charge for its services and is supported by grants and contributions, has responded to inquiries from some four thousand people annually. In most cases, that might mean something as simple as sending them a copy of the Compassion pamphlet "A Gentle Death," which describes end-of-life options; putting them in touch with various social service agencies; or referring them to the Compassion in Dying Web site, from which they can download a letter to give to their physician that will help "start a conversation between patient, family and doctor that can lead to better care and better dying."

But for some five hundred people each year, Compassion in Dying provides "full-scale counseling services." For those who live in Oregon, Compassion in Dying will help them fill out the paperwork required by the Death with Dignity Act, guide them through the legal and medical system, and recommend physicians sympathetic to assisted suicide. The group's medical adviser, a retired oncologist, will shepherd physicians through their legal responsibilities. For clients who live out of state, where physician-assisted suicide is illegal, Compassion in Dying might send a protocol outlining strategies for accumulating and self-administrating a lethal dose of medication. Wherever the clients may live, Compassion in Dying, which is staffed by doctors, hospice workers, social workers, ministers, and twenty-two trained "client support" volunteers, will help them to sort through their options, to deal with conflicting feelings, and to explore their views on dying.

Volunteers might help clients prepare advance directives or, by speaking to their doctors or visiting their nursing homes, help them get those directives enforced. They might drive clients to doctors' appointments, sit with them in the hospital while awaiting a surgical procedure, or, like the volunteer whose client had advanced breast cancer and no one to care for her, take them on a tour of the local hospice. They might get a Compassion in Dying physician to advise a client's doctor about alternative pain medication strategies. When a woman from a small town in the Midwest, for instance, began to experience the gasping breathlessness known as air hunger and her hospice staff appeared to be unaware that small doses of morphine could relieve it, her volunteer coordinated a phone consultation between the hospice staff and a palliative-care expert in that state. They might counsel a client's family, as in the case of a man who asked for help explaining to his teenage son and daughter that their mother, who had terminal brain cancer, was planning to end her life. They might share information on lethal dosages. When a thirty-two-year-old man dying of AIDS asked his physicians for medication to end his life, the doctors were willing to prescribe but weren't sure which medication and what dosage might be reliable. Compassion in Dying managed, through a friend of the patient's, to share that information with his physicians, and the patient took the lethal dose with family, friends, and physicians in attendance. Finally, they might help in such simple but important ways as bringing high-quality bathroom tissue to a client in a medical foster home who, when asked what might make her more comfortable, said what she really wanted was softer toilet paper.

Compassion in Dying takes pains to point out that its work does not inevitably end in assisted death. "Compassion is not an advocacy organization for physician-assisted death, it is an advocacy organization for choice," writes Michaele Houston, a "client support" volunteer for more than forty people since joining the group in 2000. "If that choice is a hastened death, we do not flinch or turn away." Four out of five clients who get full-scale counseling do not end up killing themselves. Some never even get the pills. A sixty-seven-year-old man dying of cancer called Compassion in Dying and insisted that he had to have the lethal medication right away. A volunteer talked to him, visited him regularly, and supported him through several surgeries. Because he had no friends or family to help him get to his doctor's appointments, Compassion volunteers shuttled him to his radiation sessions five mornings a week for two months. Shortly after he finished treatment, the man developed pneumonia. His volunteer sat with him in the hospital for three days until he died—nine months after he had contacted Compassion in Dying.

Some get the medication but never feel the need to use it. A policeman and avid hunter with neck cancer, told by his doctor that the disease would soon invade an artery and cause him to bleed to death, talked of shooting himself. His volunteer described the effect such a violent death might have on his family and persuaded him to try hospice care. The man stopped talking about shooting himself. Although he eventually obtained the lethal medication through the Death with Dignity Act, he died without taking it, in his own bed, with his wife and son at his side—one of fifty-nine potential violent suicides Compassion in Dying estimates that it helped avert during its first five years in Oregon. (Most of those fifty-nine died naturally of their illness; twenty took medication to end their life.)

Those who do end up choosing suicide almost always want Compassion volunteers with them when they die, not only to ensure that everything goes smoothly but because they have grown so close. The volunteers are used to hard-to-ask questions: How does the medication taste? How long will it take to slip into a coma? Will I lose control of my bowels? Compassion in Dying prefers that two volunteers be present so that they can support both the person who is ending his or her life and the family members and friends in attendance. Although the organization never provides the medication, in some cases a volunteer will prepare the lethal dose, dissolving the barbiturates in water and handing the glass to the client. As of 2003, Compassion in Dying had helped 291 clients to what its staffers call "hastened deaths."

----

Compassion in Dying has not been the only group to offer such tangible support. After Derek Humphry left, the Hemlock Society continued to fight for assisted-suicide legislation. But when other states failed to follow Oregon's lead, the organization decided to take matters into its own hands. In 1999, Hemlock launched Caring Friends, a program in which trained volunteers offered "personal support and assistance in dying" to terminally ill members. (Although the Caring Friends service was available to members only, with the help of a fax machine one could—and some did—join Hemlock and initiate a request for Caring Friends services the same day.) Applicants for the program sent in their medical records, a copy of their advance directives, and a personal statement describing "how the illness has impacted his or her life, [and] why a hastened death would be considered." After reviewing the documents, a Caring Friends "counselor" contacted the applicant for an interview. If the counselor determined that the applicant fulfilled the program requirements, the Caring Friends' Senior Committee discussed the case and decided whether to proceed. (Hemlock refused to accept people into the program if their loved ones opposed their plan, in part because disgruntled family members might go to the press or to the police.) If so, one of more than a hundred trained volunteers around the country was assigned to the case. The volunteer visited the client—by airplane if necessary—a number of times "to establish a relationship as a caring friend," by listening, discussing the situation, and exploring issues and options. If the client still wished to end his or her life, the Hemlock volunteer and the client settled on a time and a method.

In the first few years of the Caring Friends program, most clients used barbiturates, but as it became increasingly difficult to obtain lethal dosages, there was a shift to plastic bags filled with helium. (Helium provides a quicker death than plastic bags alone, because the gas forces air out of the bag, depriving the person of oxygen.) Some considered it a less aesthetically pleasing method than a barbiturate overdose, Hemlock admitted, but it was no less effective and was "the one volunteers are trained to understand." (Although Caring Friends drew on the advice of physicians, the plastic-bag-and-helium method enabled it to carry out its work without a doctor's assistance. "This isn't rocket science—you don't need four years of medical school," Hemlock executive director Faye Girsh told the audience at a right-to-die conference in 2002.) Like Compassion in Dying, Hemlock did not supply the means to the end; its newsletter, however, carried advertisements for an "EXIT BAG" whose special features, according to the information sheet that accompanied each order, included "adjustable Velcro strip for snug but comfortable fit with sewn-in elastic and flannelette collar; large size to minimize discomforts of overheating and breathing difficulties." As the information sheet further noted, "The customized EXIT BAG takes the guesswork out of the use of plastic bags. Instead of using bags that are too small, faulty in some way, fastened too tightly with elastic or tape, the customized EXIT BAG allows you to make personal adjustments for safety and comfort." (Although a model specifically designed to be used with helium was eventually made available, Hemlock's newsletter advised that one should say good-bye *before* the bag is pulled over the head since "the helium makes the voice sound like Donald Duck."

On the appointed day, the Caring Friends volunteer and a "senior volunteer"—usually one of four physicians associated with the program—were in attendance. Richard MacDonald, a retired family-practice physician and medical director of Hemlock, who personally presided at more than eighty-five Caring Friends planned deaths, described his function thusly: "I'm sort of a midwife to ensure that we depart safely and surely and as peacefully as possible." As of 2004, more than 150 Hemlock members had departed with the assistance of Caring Friends.

By then, Hemlock had undergone a transition of its own. In 2003, acting on the advice of political strategists and public relations experts who worried that the group's obscure name and rough-and-tumble reputation might hinder its ability to help get physician-assisted-suicide legislation passed, the society changed its name to End-of-Life Choices, a name only a focus group could love. (In a bit of revisionist history, Socrates, who poisoned himself rather than getting a doctor's help, was now considered something of an unsavory character.) Hemlock softened not only its name but its image. Its familiar logo, a sprig of hemlock inset with the words *Good Life, Good Death*, was replaced by a generic drawing of a sun, although whether the sun was rising or setting was a matter of interpretation. The End-of-Life Choices Web site, which featured photos of fortyish couples strolling in a wooded landscape, clearly in the springtime of their lives—even the leaves on the trees were green—had the warm ambience of television ads for Viagra. But its new name and new look were short-lived. In November 2004, End-of-Life Choices joined forces with Compassion in Dying to form Compassion & Choices. (Caring Friends and the Compassion in Dying support program have been combined under the rubric Client Services, making it sound as if it were part of a brokerage house and not an organization that specialized in "hastened deaths.") Derek Humphry had always joked that once its mission was accomplished, Hemlock would commit "corporate suicide." Instead, he wryly noted, the organization had suffered "death by takeover."

---

At the age of seventy-five, Derek Humphry might well be content to act as a sort of rabble-rouser emeritus of the right-to-die movement, feeding the occasional pithy quote to the media and holding forth on the history of the struggle to the high school and college students who approach him for help with their research papers. But though he no longer gets up at 3 a.m. to drive hundreds of miles to give a speech at a nursing home, he continues to speak out on assisted suicide and euthanasia. He still supports right-to-die legislation, but spends less of his time working for it. "I'm more interested in the practical side of assisted suicide," he says.

From his home near Eugene, Oregon, where he lives with his third wife, Humphry runs the Euthanasia Research and Guidance Organization (ERGO), a bare-bones, nonprofit operation devoted to offering information on end-of-life choices and furthering investigation into suicide techniques. He keeps a blog about right-to-die issues. He oversees ERGO's online store, which markets, among other right-to-die-themed items, the third edition of *Final Exit* (containing a description of the helium bag technique); *Final Exit: The Video; The Good Euthanasia Guide 2005* ("The only desk reference book for planning to die well"); and "Self-deliverance from an end-stage terminal illness using a plastic bag," a four-page pamphlet in which Humphry outlines a thirteen-step guide to asphyxiation, illustrated with photographs of a woman demonstrating the correct method. (In the manner of a teen magazine describing a pop star, the ERGO Web site also lists Humphry's "personal favorites": visitors to the site are informed that his favorite flower is the daffodil, his favorite car is the Volvo 740 turbo wagon, and—make of this what they will—his favorite hero is Charles Darwin.)

ERGO is also one of the main backers of the New Technology in Self-Deliverance Group (NuTech), a loose-knit coalition of twenty-four physicians, anesthesiologists, engineers, and laypeople from around the world, devoted to finding alternative methods for ending one's life without the help of a physician and without breaking the law. "We're not very active," says Humphry. "We only call a meeting when someone's got an idea that needs to be assessed, weighed, and tested." NuTech was the organization responsible for developing the helium-and-plastic-bag technique. Its most controversial member is Philip Nitschke, a physician and physicist who is the head of Exit Australia, an assisted-suicide advocacy group. A few years before NuTech was formed in 1999, he invented a computer program called Deliverance, which was rigged to administer a deadly dose of barbiturates if three questions were answered in the affirmative. (The final question: "If you press this button, you will receive a lethal injection and die in fifteen seconds. Do you wish to proceed?") The device was used by four people in Australia's Northern Territory during a nine-month period in 1996–97 when assisted suicide was legal there. Nitschke, who has said that a painless suicide should be available for anybody who wishes it, runs "euthanasia clinics" across Australia in which he offers the latest information on how to take one's own life. To skirt laws against assisted suicide, he has suggested chartering a ship so that those seeking euthanasia might sail beyond the Great Barrier Reef into international waters, where assistance might legally be given. In 2002, he developed the COGEN, a device that produces lethal carbon monoxide—up to a liter per minute—and pumps it through a nasal breathing tube. (The device can be made at home, Nitschke has said, for about thirty-five Australian pounds. It is based on a chemical reaction between sulfuric acid and formic acid. "If you can't get your sulfuric acid," he notes, "you can go and get it out of your car battery. For formic acid you can go crush some ants.") "Scientifically it worked," says Humphry, "but practically, it was difficult to figure out how to make it work. What would the little old lady in the Bronx do with it?" NuTech's Holy Grail is the so-called Peaceful Pill, a nonprescription lethal dosage. To that end, Nitschke has been trying to find a way to manufacture Nembutal at home.

Humphry's preference for the practical is evident in his most recent enterprise. Disillusioned with the buttoned-down direction taken by Hemlock, culminating in its merger with Compassion in Dying, and frustrated by the organization's failure to persuade states other than Oregon to pass assisted-suicide legislation, Humphry and a number of Hemlock and Caring Friends veterans started the Final Exit Network in 2004. In Humphry's words, the group is setting up "a network of people all over the country who will go and help people die under certain circumstances." Unlike Compassion & Choices, the Final Exit Network will be purely practical. ("We applaud the work of organizations that seek legislative action to strengthen our right to die a peaceful and painless death at the time and place of our choosing," reads a Final Exit statement. "However, we feel that legislative change will not come soon enough for the many people who need help NOW and in the interim!")

Says Humphry, "During the nineties, we kept quiet—even myself—about who would give help, in order not to get the Oregon initiative and other legal efforts in trouble. But now that we're at a political standstill, that's out the window."

An all-volunteer organization, the Network has no staff and no offices and conducts business as much as possible by telephone, e-mail, and fax. When a member ($50 annual dues for one, $75 a couple) seeking its services contacts the Final Exit Network, a "First Responder" explains the Exit Guide Program. The Evaluation Committee, consisting of the medical director, a hospice worker, and a veteran Hemlock volunteer, examines the applicant's medical records and discusses the case. If the applicant is accepted, a trained Exit Guide will contact him and arrange a personal interview. The guide may encourage hospice care or suggest a consultation with an oncologist or a psychiatrist. The guide will also provide "information on all alternatives for care at the end of life, including all legal methods of self-deliverance that will produce a peaceful, quick, and certain death." Ideally, a death is attended by one of several doctors associated with the Final Exit Network, but that is not always possible. Says Humphry, "We have trained guides around the country who, in the absence of doctors—we can't have doctors everywhere—will go sit with them, talk with them, be with them, as they carry out their own self-deliverance. . . . There's no need for Kevorkian anymore."

Unlike Compassion in Dying, which will assist only terminally ill people, the Final Exit Network will consider not only terminally ill applicants but, according to their literature, those with ALS, Parkinson's disease, multiple sclerosis, muscular dystrophy, Alzheimer's disease, congestive heart failure, and emphysema, among other incurable illnesses. ("We will serve many whom other organizations may turn away," its Web site boasts.) Unlike Compassion in Dying, whose method of choice for "hastened death"—what Humphry terms "the medical way"—is a dose of barbiturates, the Final Exit Network recommends the helium-and-plastic-bag method, although its volunteers will also aid patients who have managed to obtain lethal medications. "Drugs are hard to get and a bit risky," Humphry points out, while the ingredients for the helium-and-plastic-bag technique are readily available. Although the Final Exit Network will not supply the means, by calling a telephone number listed in the newsletter, a member can purchase an Exit Bag manufactured by a network member in Montana especially for use with helium. "You don't really *need* to buy a special bag—you can get the materials and put together a plastic bag adapted for helium yourself," says Humphry, "but it's typically American that if there is something ready-made available, you get it. People always want the best and the newest."

Like Hemlock twenty-four years ago, the Final Exit Network seems to have gotten up and running with great speed. The first crop of fifteen new Exit Guides from across the country were trained in November of 2004. The two-day session was held in a conference room at the Marriott Airport Hotel in St.

Louis, beneath a "Wall of Fame"—photos of assisted-suicide pioneers including Derek Humphry and Jack Kevorkian. The guides listened to speeches outlining the group's procedures and philosophy, learned about the status of assisted suicide around the world, and were instructed by the network's medical director in the helium-and-plastic-bag technique. "Then—the highlight of the weekend—the Exit Guides each got to participate in a hands-on training with a Senior Guide," reported volume 1, number 1, of the Final Exit newsletter. "We all exchanged opportunities at being the ailing member, the guide, and the senior. These rehearsals were with real helium, real exit bags, and real dialog. Each person got to show how they would handle a similar situation. The group was through by noon in time to catch their flights back home." A second group of guides was trained in March of 2005. The Network's goal is to train enough guides around the country so that no guide will have to travel more than three hundred miles to be with a member when he or she "self-delivers."

The Network's second newsletter reported that in the group's first three months of existence, the guides "served" two people. The newsletter added, "We have 33 cases on our clipboards right now, all awaiting the Member's go/no go decision." Says Humphry, "We hope to build a reputation like that of the Red Cross or Doctors Without Borders—although not on that scale, of course—to be known as people of humanity who are concerned with suffering and will do whatever they can to help."

# III

# "The Limits Are Obscure . . . and Every Errour Deadly"

AT THE HEMLOCK SOCIETY'S Second National Voluntary Euthanasia Conference, I had been impressed by the pep and can-do attitude of the Hemlock members. I had also been impressed by the vitriol that those Hemlock members inspired. Outside the hotel, a dozen chanting protesters marched in a tight circle at the entrance to the hotel driveway. They carried placards that read THIS HOTEL LOVES NAZIS and PULL THE PLUG ON THE HEMLOCK SOCIETY and passed out leaflets urging passersby to help halt the "international celebrations of Hemlock's death cult." On the sidewalk a folding table was adorned with a plastic milk bottle marked JONESTOWN KOOL-AID. To guests entering the hotel the protesters shouted, "Don't go in—the water is laced with cyanide." One man faked a German accent, drawing laughter from the others. Occasionally, a protester called out a rhyming couplet; the others hooted with delight, then took up the chant.

> Derek Humphry killed his wife;
> Now he wants your granny's life.
> If your granny's old don't keep her;
> They say euthanasia's cheaper.
> Hemlock Society you can't hide,
> We still hang Nazis for genocide.

*Euthanasia is a crime.*
*At least it was in Hitler's time.*
*Take 'em to Nuremberg and hang 'em high.*
*There's no such thing as the right to die.*

The protesters were members of the Club of Life, a radical right-wing organization that, over the years, had staged numerous demonstrations against the Hemlock Society. On the first morning of the conference in Santa Monica, as Hemlock members settled back into their seats at the end of a coffee break for a panel discussion of "Ethical Dilemmas in Euthanasia," a young man walked up to the podium and announced, "I'm here to indict Derek Humphry and Gerald Larue for murder." There was a moment of stunned silence before Humphry and Larue wrestled the microphone from the man and escorted him gently but firmly from the podium. At that moment a dozen other Club of Life members who had sneaked in during the coffee break to sit in the back of the room began to chant, "Let him speak! Let him speak!"

It was a curious scene: the protesters, mostly young, well-scrubbed, clean-cut men and women, chanting stolidly, staring straight ahead, while an angry flock of neatly dressed gray-haired women circled around them, half-shouting, half-pleading, "Get out, get out." "Did you pay?" an elderly lady in a red sweater asked one of the protesters, who ignored her. The elderly lady began to beg, "Please let us have our conference." A young woman in a raincoat the color of a robin's egg, her face pinched with passion, whirled around and shouted, "Why don't you commit voluntary euthanasia? It's what you're all about!" It soon became a rhetorical free-for-all, the demonstrators hurling slogans, Hemlock members trying to reason with them. "Never again!" shouted a balding young man with glasses at a white-haired woman who implored, "Please leave. Just please leave." Some Hemlock members wept in frustration because the protesters refused to budge or even to discuss their beliefs. A middle-aged man with a trim brown beard tried to talk quietly to a young man about the dignity of choice, but the young man refused to meet his gaze. "You're killing your grandmother," he suddenly shouted at the bearded man, who replied earnestly, "I *love* my grandmother." Meanwhile, reporters waded into the crowd to ask the protesters sensible questions about their philosophical stance. ("We're against euthanasia and genocide" was their standard response.) Hotel security men finally escorted the protesters out, still shouting, leaving behind a ring of dazed, angry, elderly people.

———————

Whether a suicide is completed by an elderly person in failing health or by a terminally ill person with or without assistance, a wealth of passionate arguments condemns the act. Christian fundamentalists say that suicide is a sin—a violation, as Augustine maintained, of the Sixth Commandment, "Thou shalt not kill." Right-to-die advocates point out that exceptions have been made for self-defense and capital punishment, and that the Church itself has often supported killing in battle. John Donne wondered "whether it was logical to conscript a young man and subject him to risk of torture and mutilation in war and probable death, and refuse an old man escape from an agonizing end." According to Albert Schweitzer, even Mahatma Gandhi, who literally wouldn't hurt a fly, saw fit to go beyond his proscription against killing. Moved by the prolonged agony of a dying calf, Gandhi gave it poison to end its suffering. (His act is doubly significant because cows are held in special veneration by the Hindu religion.) Ethicist Joseph Fletcher, who told the story in *Morals and Medicine,* commented, "It seems unimaginable that either Schweitzer or Gandhi would deny to a human being what they would render, with however heavy a heart, to a calf."

Right-to-die advocates also contend that suicide is not murder because one's body belongs to oneself. "Their argument turns on the proposition that since my life is my own, I can take it without committing murder in the same way that I can take my own money without being a thief," wrote the Russian émigré philosopher Nicholas Berdyaev in his 1962 "Essay on Suicide." "But this argument is false and superficial. My life is not solely my own, it does not belong to me absolutely, it belongs to God first. He is the absolute owner; my life also belongs to my friends, to my family, to society, and finally to the entire world which has need of me."

Berdyaev has summarized what some ethicists call the property arguments. Those who believe we are God's property insist that in completing suicide or performing euthanasia we are "playing God." Some right-to-die advocates argue that if shortening our lives interferes with God's will, so too does lengthening them with life-support equipment. "If it is for God alone to decide when we shall live and when we shall die," wrote philosopher James Rachels, paraphrasing David Hume, "then we 'play God' just as much when we cure people as when we kill them." As one elderly woman says, "When I can't digest my food, when I can't breathe on my own, when my heart can't beat on its own, it could just be that God is trying to tell me something."

In response to those who, like Aristotle, hold that our lives belong to society as a whole, right-to-die advocates question how useful to the state a terminally ill person can be. "Human life consists in mutual service," wrote the author and socialist Charlotte Perkins Gilman in her 1935 suicide note. "No grief, no pain, no misfortune or 'broken heart' is excuse for cutting off one's life while any power of service remains. But when all usefulness is over, when one is assured of an imminent and unavoidable death, it is the simplest of human rights to choose a quick and easy death in place of a slow and horrible one." Gilman worked in the labor and women's suffrage movements until the age of seventy-five when, suffering from cancer, she ended her life. "The time is approaching when we shall consider it abhorrent to our civilization to allow a human being to lie in prolonged agony which we should mercifully end in any other creature," she wrote. "Believing this choice to be of social service in promoting wider views on this question, I have preferred chloroform to cancer." The following morning the headline in the *New York Times* read, "Charlotte Gilman Dies to Avoid Pain."

Many antisuicide authors have argued that to shorten or avoid suffering is cowardly. In 1642, Sir Thomas Browne observed, "When life is more terrible than death, it is the truest valor to live." According to Christian teaching, there is intrinsic value in suffering—especially during the last moments of life—because in doing so one emulates the suffering of Christ on the cross. Terminal illness is thus an opportunity for spiritual enrichment. "The final stage of an incurable illness can be a wasteland, but it need not be," wrote British lawyer Norman St. John-Stevas, a longtime foe of euthanasia. "It can be a vital period in a person's life, reconciling him to life and to death and giving him an interior peace." Fletcher, however, pointed out that if suffering were truly ennobling, we would be bound to withhold *all* anesthetics and medical relief. While some may find the last stages of terminal illness spiritually rewarding, ethicists question whether it is a person's duty to stay alive because others insist that pain is good for him.

Some maintain that to choose death is wrong because a cure might be "just around the corner." While there is life, they say, there's hope. Responding to this argument, Seneca wrote, "Even if this is true, life is not to be bought at all costs." With the biomedical advances of the last century, however, the odds of that hope being rewarded have improved. In 1921, physician George R. Minot was told that he had severe diabetes, for which there was no cure. For two years Minot fought a losing battle against the disease. In 1923, insulin was discovered, and he was saved. Eleven years later Minot won the 1934 Nobel Prize for Medicine for research that led to a cure for pernicious anemia. And there are instances in which apparently "hopeless" cases have recovered. In the spring of 1986, a forty-four-year-old Maryland woman suffered a cerebral hemorrhage and fell into what doctors called a persistent vegetative state, not unlike that suffered by Terri Schiavo. The woman had often told her husband that if she ever became comatose, she wanted him to pull the plug. After forty-one days, her husband, a Presbyterian minister, went to court to stop treatment. The judge refused. Six days later, the woman woke up, smiled, and kissed her husband. Three months later she was able to get around with the help of a walker, and her memory was returning. "Miracles can and do occur," said her husband. "I guess we've muddied the waters surrounding the question of a person's right to die." (Clinicians usually wait several months before considering withdrawing life-support equipment; beyond that time, they say, someone in a persistent vegetative state has virtually no chance of recovery.)

For physicians, patients who choose death may present an agonizing ethical challenge. Many doctors categorically reject physician-assisted death, be it assisted suicide or voluntary euthanasia, as a violation of medical ethics and an abuse of the doctor-patient relationship. Says one oncologist, "How could my patients' trust in me survive if they could never be quite sure whenever I approached their bed that I hadn't come to deliver the coup de grâce?" Radiation oncologist Kenneth Stevens, president of Physicians for Compassionate Care, a group opposed to physician-assisted suicide, says that while people have a right to choose death, they don't have the right to a doctor's help. "People say they want the right to die, but what they're really saying is 'I want someone to kill me,' " he has observed. Other physicians, like Timothy Quill, contend that helping a patient to die may be a rare but organic part of a healthy doctor-patient relationship. Sherwin Nuland, the surgeon whose 1993 book *How We Die* graphically demonstrated that dying is rather more painful and messy than peaceful and neat, believes that a small number of terminally ill patients—"perhaps only a couple in a physician's career"—will remain unresponsive to even the best palliative care. If those patients are persistent in requesting physician-assisted suicide, and all possible relief measures have been tried, he believes that it is the physician's responsibility to relieve his patient's suffering, even if it means knowingly causing his death. "I consider it an issue of morality," says Nuland, who, twice in his own career, has helped suffering, terminally ill patients to die by injecting a lethal dose of narcotic. "Just as others would consider me immoral for considering helping a patient die, I believe it would be immoral to turn my back on the patient."

One of the main justifications for suicide prevention among the young is that their problems are usually temporary and their assessment of them often skewed by depression. For the older person considering suicide, however, depression may be temporary, but loss of movement, vision, hearing, friends, and career is often irreversible. In 1919, German psychiatrist Alfred Hoche introduced the notion of *Bilanz-Selbstmord,* or balance-sheet suicide. He suggested that it was possible for clear-thinking, competent individuals to weigh the pros and cons of living and to decide in favor of death. More recently, the philosopher Richard Brandt compared the choice of rational suicide to the decision of a firm's board of directors to declare bankruptcy.

But at an annual conference of the American Association of Suicidology, during a panel discussion of suicide manuals, a Minnesota counselor and stepmother of a girl who had killed herself stood up. "Rational suicide is a contradiction in terms," she said. "I don't care how paternalistic it is, I think suicide ought to be against the law for everyone. I think life is all there is." The woman was expressing a common belief that suicide, even in terminal illness, is per se irrational. "There's a tendency in the medical profession to think that anyone who doesn't want to prolong life even a tiny bit longer must be incompetent and therefore cannot refuse treatment," Curt Garbesi, former legal counsel for the Hemlock Society, has said. Some believe that terminal illness itself makes people irrational; as one doctor was heard to comment in bioethics rounds, "No dying patient is sane." Certainly, older people are capable of impulsiveness and flawed judgment: more than a few right-to-die cases are complicated by depression, anger, and hostility. One study holds that those who prefer suicide tend to be not only elderly and terminally ill but also depressed. Some psychiatrists suggest that some of the people who carry out so-called rational suicides may be death-oriented men and women waiting for an excuse to take their lives. Lending credence to this notion is a study that found that more people take their own lives because they wrongly believe themselves to be suffering from cancer than do those who actually have cancer. In fact, the suicide rate among terminally ill cancer patients is low: "They tend to cling to what life they have left," says psychiatrist Calvin Frederick. Clearly, a plea for "rational suicide" cannot always be taken at face value. In the *New England Journal of Medicine*, David Jackson and Stuart Youngner described six cases in which right-to-die issues masked feelings of depression and abandonment.

University of Chicago philosopher Leon Kass suggests that the very nature of terminal illness renders patients virtually incapable of true autonomy.

How free or informed is a choice made under debilitated conditions? . . . Truth to tell, the ideal of rational autonomy, so beloved of bioethicists and legal theorists, rarely obtains in actual medical practice. Illness invariably means dependence, and dependence means relying for advice on physician and family. This is especially true of those who are seriously or terminally ill, where there is frequently also depression or diminished mental capacity that clouds one's judgment or weakens one's resolve.

Kass is among those who worry that patients in such a state are not only incapable of true autonomy but susceptible to manipulation. "With patients thus reduced—helpless in action and ambivalent about life—someone who might benefit from their death need not proceed by overt coercion," he writes. "Rather, requests for assisted suicide can and will be subtly engineered." Mental health professionals point out that motives in mercy killings are often mixed—showing "mercy" as much for the killer, who may find caring for an incapacitated person an oppressive responsibility, as for the victim—and that suicide pacts are rarely as mutual as they seem. A study of uncompleted suicide pacts found that one partner—apt to be the male—is usually the aggressor, conceiving the idea and then pressuring the other to go along. After the double suicide of Arthur and Cynthia Koestler, several writers pointed out that the eerie decorousness of the death scene camouflaged a more complex psychological scenario. They suggested that Cynthia had been emotionally coerced into joining her husband in death. ("I'm going to kill myself, aren't we?" is how Edwin Shneidman mocked Koestler's message.) Cynthia had been dominated by Koestler since the beginning of their relationship, when she was a shy young secretary and he a famous author twice her age. She called herself his "slavey." "She was his appendix," wrote a Koestler friend. "That was her role in life. She was content with that role." Her suicide was an obvious and perhaps inevitable extension of their thirty-three-year relationship. "It is hardly an exaggeration to say that his life became hers, that she *lived* his life," wrote Harold Harris, editor of *Stranger on the Square,* the Koestlers' joint autobiography. "And when the time came for him to leave it, her life too was at an end."

Right-to-die groups often hold up Greek heroes or terminally ill patients in excruciating pain as examples when arguing their case. Prevention experts usually cite the depressed, impulsive teenage suicide when rejecting the right to die. The majority of suicides, however, lie somewhere between these extremes. "Some writers opposed to suicide in general would have us believe that all euthanetic suicides are . . . acts of cowardice and fear," University of Utah philosopher Margaret Pabst Battin has written. "I think this is false, but I think it is equally wrong to assume that all suicide in the face of terminal illness is a rational, composed, self-dignifying affirmation of one's own highest life-ideal." Whether they call it "aid-in-dying," "hastened death," "assisted dying," or "the final freedom," right-to-die advocates go to considerable semantic lengths to avoid the dreaded *s*-word. Indeed, under Oregon's Death with Dignity Act, the death certificate must state the cause of death as the underlying illness, rather than suicide, not only to ensure that life insurance claims can't be denied under a suicide clause, but to avoid suicide's association with mental illness and violence. "Activists draw an obsessively careful distinction between 'rational' and all other suicides," writes Andrew Solomon, who, along with his brother and his father, helped his fifty-nine-year-old mother, suffering from ovarian cancer, die by an overdose of Seconal, an event he eloquently describes in *The Noonday Demon.*

> In fact a suicide is a suicide—overdetermined, sad, toxic in some measure to everyone it touches. The worst and the best kind lie at either end of a continuum; they differ more in degree than in essential quality. . . . When we speak of a rational suicide and distinguish it from an irrational one, we are sketching out the details of our own or our society's prejudices. Someone who killed himself because he didn't like his arthritis would seem suicidal; someone who killed herself because she couldn't bear the prospect of a painful and undignified death from cancer seems perhaps quite rational. . . . What is rational for one person is irrational for another, and all suicide is calamitous.

---

Many mental health professionals and suicide prevention experts are sympathetic to the idea of suicide in the face of terminal illness on an individual basis—especially for themselves—but refuse to condone right-to-die groups and legislative changes for fear that they will invite abuse and encourage people to minimize the importance of life. "From an intellectual standpoint I can appreciate the importance of liberty and freedom in a truly democratic society," writes Richard Seiden. "On a deeper emotional level . . . I wonder whether the advocacy of suicidal deliverance does not act as an end of hope for those depressed persons fighting a psychological battle of life and death, a struggle to be or not to be." At Hemlock conferences I attended, each member had a compelling personal story that seemed to clinch the case for legalizing assisted suicide or voluntary euthanasia, yet many seemed unaware that the changes they proposed had implications beyond their own circumstances. They were, in fact, seeking to alter sanctions that have existed for four thousand years. "You are pioneers in the modern advocacy of suicide," Joseph Piccione, a policy analyst at the Child and Family Protection Institute, reminded his audience at a Hemlock Society national conference. "You are sociologically important. And I ask you to consider the risks in the possible and unintended outcomes of your work. Suicide is one of the last taboos. Will the destruction of that taboo open it up to other persons who are not terminally ill but are liable to persuasion? I feel that it is the maintenance of the taboo that may be one way to protect them." Daniel Callahan, director of the Hastings Center, a think tank for biomedical ethics, writes:

> Physician-assisted suicide is mistakenly understood as only a personal matter of self-determination, the control of our own bodies, not to be forbidden since it is only a small step beyond our no longer forbidding suicide. But unlike unassisted suicide, an act carried out solely by the person, physician-assisted suicide should be understood as a social act. It requires the assistance of someone else. Legalizing physician-assisted suicide would also provide an important social sanction for suicide, tacitly legitimizing it, and affecting many aspects of our society beyond the immediate relief of individual suffering. It would in effect say that suicide is a legitimate and reasonable way of coping with suffering, acceptable to the law and sanctioned by medicine. Suicide is now understood to be a tragic situation, no longer forbidden by the law but hardly anywhere understood as the ideal outcome of a life filled with suffering. That delicate balance would be lost and a new message delivered: Suicide is morally, medically, legally, and socially acceptable.

In *Biathanatos,* John Donne defended voluntary euthanasia as a form of suicide. Nevertheless, he refrained from proposing guidelines or laws because "the limits are obscure, and steepy, and slippery, and narrow, and every errour deadly." Donne was articulating an argument known as the slippery slope, which cautions against taking a certain action—even if the act is morally permissible in itself—for fear that it will lead to other actions that are impermissible. (This argument is also called the thin edge of the wedge, the domino theory, or, more colorfully, the camel's nose under the tent.) Opponents of euthanasia believe that to permit a single instance of it will inevitably lead us down a slippery slope of abuse, at the bottom of which lies Nazi-style mass murder. In his oft-quoted 1949 essay, "Medical Science Under Dictatorship," psychiatrist Leo Alexander, an American consultant at the Nuremberg trials, traced Nazi atrocities committed under the banner of "euthanasia" on the rapid journey down that slope. It started with a campaign to promote a utilitarian attitude toward the chronically ill. Propaganda included films such as *I Accuse,* in which a woman suffering from multiple sclerosis was killed by her doctor husband "to the accompaniment of soft piano music rendered by a sympathetic colleague in an adjoining room." A popular high school mathematics textbook included problems detailing the cost of caring for the disabled and chronically ill. One question asked students to calculate how many housing units could be built and how many loans could be made to newlyweds with the amount of money spent by the state on "the crippled, the criminal, and the insane." Alexander wrote:

> The beginnings at first were merely a subtle shift in emphasis in the basic attitude of the physicians. It started with the acceptance of the attitude, basic in the euthanasia movement, that there is such a thing as life not worthy to be lived. This attitude in its early stages concerned itself merely with the severely and chronically sick. Gradually the sphere of those to be included in this category was enlarged to encompass the socially unproductive, the ideologically unwanted, the racially unwanted and finally all non-Germans. But it is important to realize that the infinitely small wedged-in lever from which this entire trend of mind received its impetus was the attitude toward the non-rehabilitable sick.

Although few suggest that right-to-die advocates have a hidden agenda of Nazi-style euthanasia, for many people the specter of the Third Reich is sufficient to justify opposing any change. They point to recent polls and court decisions favorable to the right to die, to the activities of Jack Kevorkian, to the legalization of euthanasia in the Netherlands, and to the passage of Oregon's Death with Dignity Act as weigh stations along the slippery slope. "I think there is no way in which the right to die isn't going to very soon become the duty to die," warned Dame Cicely Saunders, founder of the hospice movement, in a discussion of right-to-die groups. "If you had an illness which made you fairly dependent upon other people, and somebody gave you the possibility to have a quick way out, would you really feel you could go on asking for that care? Human nature being what it is, euthanasia wouldn't be voluntary for very long." In *The Right to Live, the Right to Die,* former surgeon general C. Everett Koop warned that acceptance of euthanasia will invite deception and abuse; people will use it as a loophole to hasten the death of burdensome elderly relatives or to get at a legacy more quickly. "Once any group of human beings is considered fair game in the arena of the right to life," wrote Koop, "where does it stop?" Yale Kamisar, a professor of law at the University of Michigan, opposes changes in the law because the benefit to a few might be outweighed by the danger to many. "Miss Voluntary Euthanasia is not likely to be going it alone for very long," he has written. "Many of her admirers . . . would be neither surprised nor distressed to see her joined by Miss Euthanatize the Congenital Idiots and Miss Euthanatize the Permanently Insane and Miss Euthanatize the Senile Dementia." The German physician Auer has said, "I have seen the true wish for death among my patients . . . one must be able to say to them, 'I have listened—but the consequences for humanity are such that though I could open the door and let you out, others may then be thrown out.'"

Derek Humphry admits that the slippery slope hypothesis is the strongest argument against euthanasia. But he points to Oregon's Death with Dignity Act as an example of how safeguards protecting against abuse can be written into legislation. "What happened in Nazi Germany was a lesson to mankind, but that was in a brutal, murderous dictatorship, whereas we live in a democracy under the rule of law," he says. "I believe we can design laws that draw the line at mature, competent terminally ill people." In any case Humphry maintains that the possibility of abuse is not sufficient reason to abridge the rights of suffering individuals. "Where is the sense . . . in telling a person dying of throat cancer that euthanasia cannot be made available because Nazi Germany murdered thousands of people in the 1940s using a method labeled 'euthanasia'?" he asks in *The Right to Die.* "The lessons of history are there to be learned, and the Nazi experience has taught society how not to let government slip into the hands of an irresponsible minority." Despite Humphry's confidence in our ability to avoid the slippery slope, one doesn't have to look far for slippage. The Hemlock Society itself underwent a rapid evolution in its attitude toward divulging information on lethal drugs, from restricting the purchase of *Let Me Die Before I Wake* to members, to making it available to the public, to printing up a handy one-page list of lethal doses, to describing and evaluating more than a dozen ways to kill oneself in *Final Exit,* to offering "personal support and assistance in dying" to terminally ill members—an evolution apparently based less on firm ethical conviction than on calculating what society had become willing to accept.

---

In the Netherlands, where assisted suicide and euthanasia have been practiced since 1973, a 1990 government-sponsored study, largely replicated five years later, found no evidence that physicians "are moving down a slippery slope." Critics, on the other hand, suggest that the Dutch slippery slope has been more of a slippery crevasse. Poring over these reports, they conclude that safeguards intended to protect against abuse have been "routinely ignored." Although physicians are required to report cases of assisted suicide and euthanasia to the government, only 41 percent of Dutch physicians complied in 1995—an improvement over the 18 percent who did so in 1990, yet still distressingly high, particularly given that 30 percent of the doctors who didn't report their cases admitted that their reason for not doing so was that they had failed to observe the requirements for permissible euthanasia. Although patients seeking assisted suicide and euthanasia must be experiencing "intolerable suffering," in one-quarter of all cases fear of *future* suffering or loss of dignity was cited as the impetus for seeking assisted suicide. Although assisted suicide and euthanasia were originally intended as a last resort, in 17 percent of cases the assisting physicians admitted that alternative treatments were available. (In almost all these cases, the patients refused the alternative treatments, and euthanasia was performed.) Although the patient seeking assistance must make a voluntary, well-considered, persistent request to the physician, more than half of Dutch physicians considered it appropriate to bring up the subject of euthanasia with their patients. (They worried that the patients might be inhibited about introducing the subject themselves—yet didn't seem to worry that suggesting it might suggest to the patients that their situations were hopeless.) Although consultation is required in all cases, it was procured in only about half. Even then, it frequently seemed to be pro forma; in 12 percent of cases in which there was consultation, the "consultant" never actually met the patient. Indeed, the most important reasons given by doctors for consulting a particular physician were that physician's views on life-ending decisions and how nearby he lived. Perhaps that's why consulting doctors disagreed in only 7 percent of the cases.

The studies' most alarming finding was that 25 percent of Dutch physicians admitted to practicing "termination of the patient without explicit request"—the report's way of saying that in about a thousand cases each year, physicians had performed euthanasia without the patient's clear directive. In about 13 percent of such cases, the doctors justified their actions by pointing out that they had previously discussed the subject with their patient. In other instances, physicians explained that their patients were incompetent and unable to give informed consent. Yet the 1990 study indicated that 37 percent of individuals terminated "without explicit request" were competent. (In 1995, the figure dropped to 21 percent.) In 15 percent of the cases in which there was no discussion even though the patient was competent, the doctor didn't bring up the subject because he thought that euthanasia was clearly in the patient's best interest. Among the reasons given by physicians for performing nonvoluntary euthanasia were the patient's "low quality of life" and "relatives' inability to cope." (Defenders of the practice point out that a recent study suggests that the Netherlands, in fact, has a lower rate of ending life without the explicit request of the patient than several European countries in which euthanasia is illegal.) In recent years, the phrase "termination of the patient without explicit request" has been replaced by "life-ending acts without the explicit request of the patient," a slightly less businesslike euphemism.

"Virtually every guideline set up by the Dutch to regulate euthanasia has been modified or violated with impunity," writes Herbert Hendin, one of three foreign observers to have studied firsthand the practice of assisted suicide and euthanasia in the Netherlands. During the five years he spent on the project, Hendin made four lengthy visits to the Netherlands to interview euthanasia's practitioners. "I think they believed that the more I heard and saw, the more I would approve of what they were doing," Hendin told me. In fact, the more Hendin heard and saw, the more horrified he became. "Assisted suicide and euthanasia were supposed to be for extreme suffering, but it had become a routine solution," he says. He was alarmed at how frequently alternatives went unexplored, and at how uninformed some of the physicians were about pain relief. "Palliative care in the Netherlands was even worse than it was here—and palliative care in the United States was awful—and in part it was worse because doctors had this easy option, so they didn't need to make it any better." He was dismayed at how often doctors told him they sought consultations merely to meet the legal requirements. He worried that with only 3 percent of patients seeking assisted suicide or euthanasia referred for psychiatric consultation, psychological or emotional complexities might be overlooked. He was surprised that there were only three hospices in the entire country. (Dutch aid-in-dying advocates point out that the majority of their palliative care takes place in the hospital or in the home.)

While its advocates argue that legalizing assisted suicide and euthanasia will give patients greater autonomy, Hendin found that in the Netherlands, the reverse was true. "In numerous cases, assisted suicide and euthanasia were usually the result of an interaction in which the needs and character of family, friends, and doctor play as big and often bigger role than those of the patient," writes Hendin, pointing out that in a study of Dutch hospitals, doctors and nurses reported that more requests for euthanasia came from the patients' families than from the patients themselves. Hendin cites the case described in a Dutch medical journal of a wife who no longer wished to take care of her ailing, elderly husband; she gave him a choice between euthanasia and admission to a home for the chronically ill. "The man, afraid of being left to the mercy of strangers in an unfamiliar place, chose to have his life ended," writes Hendin. "The doctor, although aware of the coercion, ended the man's life." In another case, the life of a Dutch woman hospitalized with terminal breast cancer who had said she did not want euthanasia was ended because, in the physician's words, "It could have taken another week before she died. I just needed this bed."

Because of cases like these, says British ethicist John Keown, a lecturer at Cambridge University known for his pro-life stance, many elderly Dutch are afraid to go to the hospital; some carry wallet-size cards that say if the signer is admitted, "no treatment be administered with the intention to terminate life." The cards are distributed by the Dutch Patients Association, which will, for a modest fee, writes Keown, "watch over the patient so that euthanasia will not be administered without the patient's consent." Intending to illustrate why it was sometimes necessary for physicians to end the lives of competent patients without their consent, the attorney for the Dutch Voluntary Euthanasia Society described to Hendin the case of a nun whose physician, several days before she would have died, gave her a lethal injection because her religion didn't permit her to ask for death, no matter how excruciating her pain. "If, as its proponents suggest, physician-assisted suicide and euthanasia are about giving patients autonomy," says Hendin, "why wasn't this woman entitled to make her own choice that the pain was less important to her than her feelings about not wanting euthanasia?" When I asked Hendin what he had concluded from such cases, he told me, "After a while, doctors in the Netherlands came to believe that they knew best who should live and who should die. Doctors—particularly young doctors—often think, 'If I were in that situation, *I* wouldn't want to live.'"

Hendin was particularly concerned when a Dutch court ruled in 1993 that a psychiatrist was justified in having assisted the suicide of a physically healthy but severely depressed fifty-year-old social worker. Two months after the death of her twenty-year-old son to lung cancer, the woman had approached the psychiatrist, saying she could not get over the loss of her son and wanted death, not treatment. (Another son had fatally shot himself seven years earlier.) Telling her that he couldn't make such a decision until he knew her better, the psychiatrist saw the woman for a number of sessions over two months, at which point she told him she would stop therapy if he did not help her die. The psychiatrist sent a written description of the case to seven consultants; five agreed that the woman's situation was hopeless and that he should comply with her request. None felt it was necessary to see the patient. About two months after he first met the patient, four months after her younger son had died, the psychiatrist brought a lethal dose of drugs to the woman's home and stayed with her while she swallowed them. The psychiatrist later told Hendin that his patient had said that if he didn't help her, she would kill herself on her own. "He responded to a kind of emotional blackmail, the kind of thing that suicidal patients do all the time," says Hendin. "And he ignored the fact that over time, even without treatment, people do tend to get over the death of a loved one, at least enough so that they can go on. He was annoyed when I suggested that he could have told the patient, 'If you still feel this way in a year and a half, I will do it then.'" Hendin felt the psychiatrist's concern for the patient may have been complicated by other motivations. "His career was going no place. He was looking for a case, so he went to the euthanasia society. I think he wanted to make a name for himself." In 1994, the Dutch Royal Court, while finding the psychiatrist guilty of failing to have the patient seen by a consultant, upheld the lower court's ruling, affirming that mental suffering alone could justify performing assisted suicide and euthanasia. No punishment was imposed.

According to the 1995 report, the woman's case, while rare, is not unique. An estimated 320 psychiatric patients request suicide each year, two to five of whom are ultimately assisted to complete the act. In a recent survey, 6 percent of Dutch psychiatrists surveyed admitted that they had helped a person with a psychiatric disorder to die. (In some cases, the patient also had a terminal illness.) While agreeing that treatment was preferable, two-thirds said that assisted suicide was acceptable in cases of severe mental disorder.

Hendin says that the slippery slope in the Netherlands may be leveling off. A third government study, in 2001, found more physicians reporting their cases, fewer physicians performing "life-ending acts without the explicit request of the patient," and no further increase in the total number of physician-assisted suicide and euthanasia cases. Says Hendin, "Although the Dutch don't concede that they are doing anything wrong, they have responded to criticism in ways I find very hopeful." In the past several years, six centers for the development of palliative care have been established at hospitals in major cities, and more than a hundred new hospices have opened.

Still, it is clear that over the last thirty years, the Dutch guidelines have been stretched. "Given legal sanction, euthanasia, intended originally for the exceptional case, has become an accepted way of dealing with serious or terminal illness in the Netherlands," writes Hendin. Supporters of the Dutch system suggest that if assisted suicide and euthanasia were not available, a great many physically suffering elderly people would commit suicide on their own, in less peaceful, less certain ways—and perhaps end up even worse off. They point out with pride that since the early 1980s, the suicide rate of those over fifty in the Netherlands has fallen by a third—a drop that can likely be ascribed to the fact that older suicidal patients are now asking for euthanasia instead. Maintaining that if any significant proportion of assisted suicide or euthanasia cases had been counted as suicides, the rate would have risen, Hendin told a congressional subcommittee, "It may be more than ironic to describe euthanasia as the Dutch cure for suicide."

---

Hendin is among those who worry that conditions for abuse are even more ripe in the United States, where patient-doctor ties tend to be less intimate than in the Netherlands and access to health care is not equally available to all. Yet there is little evidence to suggest that Oregon has progressed down the slippery slope. Before the Death with Dignity Act was passed, its opponents predicted that overwhelming numbers of sickly Oregonians would kill themselves with lethal dosages provided by physicians. They further predicted an influx of suffering people from out of state—an Oregon Trail of the infirm—to take advantage of the act. Neither scenario has materialized. Through 2004, 208 people—about 30 of the some 30,000 Oregon residents who die each year—had ended their lives with the help of the Death with Dignity Act. (As far as can be determined, only one of them moved to Oregon for the specific reason of taking up residence and thereby gaining access to the act's provisions.) The numbers have fluctuated from a low of 16 in 1998, the first year in which the act was implemented, to a high of 42 in 2003. (At least one supporter has suggested that the law may be *too* restrictive. "I am concerned that so few people are requesting it," said Marcia Angell, the former editor of the *New England Journal of Medicine.* "It seems to me that more would do it. The purpose of a law is to be used, not to sit there on the books.") Opponents of the act also feared that its passage would trigger a domino effect, in which other states would quickly follow suit. Yet that hasn't happened; similar ballot measures have subsequently failed in Michigan and Maine, and a legislative effort in Hawaii was narrowly defeated. Indeed, since the Oregon law was passed in 1994, ten state legislatures have passed statutes making assisted suicide illegal.

While the Death with Dignity Act seems to have been a success thus far, it is difficult to know how well it is really working because so few details have been made available. Although physicians must report assisted-suicide cases to the Oregon Department of Human Services (ODHS), they are required only to check off a list indicating that the requirements—the fifteen-day waiting period, the consultation with another physician, and so on—have been met. They are not asked to provide significant medical information or to describe the patient's reasons for requesting assisted suicide. The ODHS data, therefore, offer only a few basic demographic details: that most patients have cancer, but a few suffer from AIDS or ALS; that their mean age is just under seventy (somewhat younger than Oregonians dying naturally of the same causes); that they are more likely to be women; that they are twice as likely to be divorced as married; that they are likely to be college-educated; that they are overwhelmingly likely to be white.

The scant additional information that has been made public by families or physicians suggests to a few critics that the situation may be more complicated than it seems. The first case, in the spring of 1998, was described by Compassion in Dying as an illustration of how well the Oregon law works; opponents of physician-assisted suicide have described it as an example of why the act is to be feared. Although she had metastatic breast cancer and was enrolled in a hospice program, the patient, a woman in her mideighties, wasn't bedridden; in fact, although no longer able to do her aerobic exercises or to garden, she was mobile enough to do her own housekeeping. Nor was she in great pain. (Unlike the Dutch law, Oregon's Death with Dignity Act does not require patients to be experiencing "unbearable suffering.") Her physician, about to switch jobs, referred her to an internist well versed in care of the dying. He was unwilling to assist her suicide, on the grounds that she was depressed. The patient's family, therefore, contacted Compassion in Dying, and after several "lengthy phone calls," the group's senior medical adviser determined that in fact the patient was not depressed and referred her to a physician willing to help. That physician, who later said that the cancer had spread to the patient's lungs and made breathing difficult, referred her to a pulmonary specialist and to a psychiatrist. The psychiatrist conducted an evaluation and, like the specialist, concluded that she was not depressed and met the qualifications for physician-assisted suicide. The physician to whom she had been referred by Compassion in Dying provided a lethal dose of barbiturates, and two and a half weeks after meeting the patient for the first time, he was at her bedside, along with members of her family, when she died.

Opponents of the Death with Dignity Act raised several concerns. Before the law was passed, assisted suicide activists had assured Oregonians that patients would make their decisions in collaboration with a doctor with whom they had a long-term relationship. Yet when the physician to whom her primary doctor had referred her refused to assist her suicide, his opinion, apparently, was ignored. Indeed, in more than half of the forty-two cases for which information was available in the first two years of the act, the first physician seen by the patient did not agree to assist in the suicide. In some cases, patients had to go to a third or fourth physician until they found a willing helper. None of the physicians who refused to assist were contacted by ODHS, apparently on the assumption that their decisions had been based on a philosophical opposition to physician-assisted suicide and not on reservations about a particular case. (Under the act, physicians are not required to assist in a patient's death; they may refer to another doctor. While 51 percent of Oregon physicians support the act, only 34 percent say they would be willing to write the lethal prescription.) Like a child who, told no by one parent, immediately importunes the other, under the Oregon law, people can simply shop for a physician until they find one who will say yes. "If I get rebuffed by one doctor, I can go to another" is the way Barbara Coombs Lee, a lawyer and former nurse who is executive director of Compassion in Dying, put it. Assisted-suicide applicants are likely to find a physician who will say yes through Lee's organization. In the first fifteen assisted-suicide cases, fourteen different doctors wrote the lethal prescriptions; eleven of the fourteen doctors were associated with Compassion in Dying.

Opponents of physician-assisted suicide wonder whether all options are being fully explored. The physician who assisted in the first case later wrote in a medical journal that the patient was worried primarily about anticipated suffering, a concern that stemmed from having seen her husband experience a lingering death. Although Oregon physicians who agree to assist a suicide are required to point out alternatives such as palliative care and hospice, they are not required to be knowledgeable in those areas, nor are they required to refer the patient to a physician who is. "Under these conditions," write Herbert Hendin and Kathleen Foley, a neurologist at Memorial Sloan-Kettering Cancer Center in New York City, "offering a patient palliative care becomes a legal regulation to be met, rather than an integral part of an effort to relieve the patient's suffering so that a hastened death does not seem like the only alternative." Indeed, according to a taped interview, the assisting physician in the first case had outlined the alternatives—hospice, chemotherapy, hormone therapy—in three sentences. Advocates point out that two of the state's largest health providers have hired ombudsmen to make certain that patients who request physician-assisted suicide don't lose access to other end-of-life treatment options. They also point out that, like the first patient, most of those who receive physician-assisted suicide under the act—86 percent, in fact—were enrolled in hospice. In any case, those not already receiving hospice care are offered it. Although the Oregon Hospice Association initially opposed the Death with Dignity Law, Oregon hospices now work directly with Compassion in Dying—"The fears that we had about not enough safeguards are unfounded," announced the executive director of the Oregon Hospice Association—and hospice patients who seek assisted suicide are told that their wishes will be respected. Indeed, hospice nurses often attend the "hastened deaths" of their patients. Depending on one's point of view, this has been interpreted either as an example of how well the act works or as a mile marker on the slippery slope. In any event, hospice use in Oregon has increased 32 percent since the law went into effect.

Critics of the act are also concerned that those who request assisted suicide may not be sufficiently evaluated for depression. (The psychiatrist who signed off on the first case met with the patient only once.) They point out that anxiety and depression are common in patients with life-threatening illnesses. William Breitbart, a physician who has studied requests for physician-assisted suicide among patients at Memorial Sloan-Kettering, estimates that 25 percent of cancer patients have severe depression; by the disease's end stage, the number has jumped to 77 percent. Studies of terminally ill patients and ambulatory AIDS patients have found that the most significant predictor of support for physician-assisted suicide is depression and psychological distress. (In the first five years of the Death with Dignity Act, 20 percent of requests for assisted suicide came from depressed patients; all of these applications were rejected.) Oregon law, however, requires psychiatric consultation only in cases in which the physician believes the patient might be suffering from a psychiatric disorder "causing impaired judgment"; depression per se is not sufficient. (Critics wonder how many cases there may be in which depression does *not* impair judgment.) As we have seen, studies have repeatedly shown that physicians are not well trained to diagnose depression in patients of any age. Depression is even harder to diagnose in older patients, when its symptoms so often resemble the inevitable symptoms of aging; when patients are physically impaired, the diagnosis is more difficult still. In a survey of Oregon psychiatrists, only 6 percent felt confident that, unless they had a long-term relationship with the patient, they could determine in a single visit whether he or she was competent to make a decision about suicide. In the first six years of the act, 18 percent of assisted suicide cases were referred for psychiatric evaluation. In the absence of such evaluation, some psychiatrists wonder whether the complex influences that factor into a decision to end one's life—whether one is terminally ill or not—can fully be explored. They suggest that, as with suicidal people in general, a terminally ill patient's wish to die can also be a cry for help, and physicians inexperienced in treating suicidal patients may fail to hear this ambivalence.

In a state of ambivalence, a patient may be especially susceptible to outside influence. Under the Death with Dignity Act, at least one of the two witnesses who must sign a patient's written request for assisted suicide cannot be a relative, an heir, or the owner or operator of a health care facility where the patient is receiving treatment. This may help prevent the kind of overt manipulation depicted in Hollywood B-movie melodramas, but it cannot prevent subtler influences of which the protagonists themselves may be unaware and which may, as Kass suggests, be unavoidable in any end-of-life medical situations. (Based on physician interviews in the 2000 ODHS report, 63 percent of patients—compared to 26 percent in 1999 and 12 percent in 1998— expressed concerns about being a burden to their families.) In another Oregon case that provoked controversy, an eighty-five-year-old widow, terminally ill with stomach cancer and experiencing increasing dementia, wanted the option of assisted suicide in case her pain or the indignity of losing control of her bodily functions became unbearable. When her physician referred her to a hospice program, the patient (already enrolled in hospice) and her daughter, a retired nurse who had traveled from Arizona to care for her mother, requested a new physician. The second physician deemed her competent and agreed to participate. According to protocol at Kaiser Permanente, a psychiatric consultation was arranged. Concluding that the patient "did not seem to be explicitly pushing for assisted suicide" and lacked "the very high level of capacity to weigh options about it," the psychiatrist found her ineligible for assisted suicide. He noted that the patient seemed to accept his assessment but that her daughter became angry. He arranged a second consultation, with a psychologist, who observed that the patient's "choices may be influenced by her family's wishes, and that her daughter, Erika, may be somewhat coercive," but nevertheless felt the patient was capable of making her own decision. After meeting with the patient, the medical director of Kaiser Permanente and a palliative care specialist concurred. The patient was given a prescription for a lethal dose of barbiturates. Five weeks later, with her family nearby, the patient took the pills and died.

Although even its opponents admit that there have been no Kevorkianesque abuses under the Death with Dignity Act, they worry that if physician-assisted suicide is allowed, it will, eventually, inevitably, affect certain more vulnerable populations. In primitive tribes elderly suicide has often been accepted, even encouraged, when a person outlived his or her usefulness or during times of extreme hardship and food shortage. The ancient Scythians, for instance, considered it an honor to take their own lives when they became too feeble to keep up with the nomadic lifestyle, saving the tribe the guilt and trouble of killing them. Sociologists call this economic suicide or thrift suicide. Such deaths, however, were often a blend of suicide and murder, in which the elderly had to make a choice between killing themselves or being killed. Of the Massegetae, Herodotus observed, "They have one way only of determining the appropriate time to die, namely this: when a man is very old, all his relatives give a party and include him in a general sacrifice of cattle; then they boil the flesh and eat it. This they consider to be the best sort of death." The Tschuktschi of northern Siberia designated a relative or friend to strangle or stab an old man whose usefulness was over (elderly women remained valuable as midwives or menials); the nomadic Kalmuck Tartars abandoned their sick and lame with provisions in small huts on the banks of rivers; aged Hottentots were served lavish feasts before being abandoned in the wilderness; feeble Ethiopians allowed themselves to be tied to wild bulls and trampled to death; the Congolese jumped up and down on their elderly until they were dead; the Amboyna ate their failing relatives. Well into the twentieth century, in many Eskimo tribes, in time of famine and hardship, the elderly might walk off and freeze to death, hang themselves, or allow themselves to be walled up in an igloo and abandoned.

Such suicides, a sort of self-regulating mechanism for tribal survival in which the population was kept within the limits of the food supply, were often misunderstood by Westerners. The perhaps apocryphal story is told of some missionaries among an Eskimo tribe who discovered this practice and condemned it harshly as a sin against God. The Eskimos were impressed by this argument, and the missionaries departed, promising to come back in a few years to see whether their potential converts were keeping the faith. When they returned, there were no Eskimos left. The obedient tribe had died out, gradually killed off by the imbalance of too many people and too little food.

Some ethicists and demographers believe that the ingredients for such a scenario may soon exist in the United States. And although they do not suggest that we abandon our elderly in igloos, tie them to bulls, or jump up and down on them, they have suggested that they may have a similar "duty" to move on. In 1984, Colorado governor Richard Lamm, referring to the financial and ethical implications of this country's growing medical technology, said, "Like leaves which fall off a tree, forming the humus in which other plants can grow, we've got a duty to die and get out of the way with all of our machines and artificial hearts, so that our kids can build a reasonable life." Lamm's comment, delivered to a meeting of Colorado health lawyers, triggered an uproar. ("Aged Are Told to Drop Dead," screamed the headline in the New York *Daily News.*) Many people were outraged, some called for Lamm's resignation, and one sixty-eight-year-old lobbyist who represented elderly interests likened the forty-eight-year-old Lamm to Hitler. Of the nearly three thousand letters Lamm received, however, the majority praised him for confronting the issue. Meanwhile, Lamm sought to clarify his remarks. "The time is not far off when there will be a direct conflict between the health of the individual and the health of the society," he wrote in the *New Republic.* "We cannot afford all the medical miracles that the profession stands ready to give, and choices will have to be made about the distribution of limited medical resources. Technological immortality is running into fiscal reality." (Several years later, Lamm would provide Derek Humphry with an admiring jacket-copy quote for *Final Exit.*) Thirteen years after Lamm spoke out, philosopher John Hardwig, quoting Lamm approvingly in the *Hastings Center Report,* suggested that "our technological sophistication coupled with a commitment to our loved ones" obligates us to refuse life-sustaining treatment when there is no hope of recovery.

> Which is the greater burden? (1) To lose a 50 percent chance of six more months of life at age 87? Or (2) To lose all your savings, your home, and your career at age 55? I cannot imagine it would be morally permissible for me to ruin the rest of my partner's life to sustain mine or to cut off my sons' careers, impoverish them, or compromise the quality of their children's lives simply because I wish to live a little longer. This is what leads me to believe in a duty to die.

Financial concerns are undeniably a consideration in many right-to-die discussions. "I don't want to be a burden to my children or my spouse" and "Please don't let my life savings be spent on keeping me alive for a few extra weeks" are common refrains among the ailing elderly. As Lamm pointed out, the high cost of health care affects not only the individual but the entire country. One-third of the nation's total health costs are spent on the elderly; one-third of the Medicare budget is spent on patients during their last six months of life. (Medicare and Medicaid combined account for one-fifth of the federal budget.) With the oldest of the 77 million baby boomers entering their sixties, the number of Americans sixty-five and over is projected to double over the next three decades. Elderly Americans comprise 13 percent of the population now; by 2035, they will account for 20 percent. Many economic forecasters fear that we'll go broke long before then. If scientists continue to find cures for diseases, the financial strain will be even worse. As far back as 1984, estimating that it would have cost the federal government an extra $15 billion if Americans who died prematurely of heart disease in 1978 had lived to their full life expectancies, a Washington research group concluded that "the postponement of an individual's death is becoming a Federal affair, and one whose implications we cannot ignore."

Although rationing of health care may seem unthinkable in a nation accustomed to the idea that its citizens are entitled to unlimited medical resources, nearly half of all Americans believe that dialysis and chemotherapy should be rationed at the discretion of a board of doctors and the patient's physician. In his book *Setting Limits,* Daniel Callahan outlined the coming health care crisis and suggested a long-term strategy. His recommendations included restricted Medicare payments for such procedures as organ transplants, kidney dialysis, and coronary bypasses for the aged, along with limited use of feeding tubes and costly antibiotics for the elderly. Although he firmly opposes physician-assisted suicide and euthanasia, Callahan believes the elderly should be "creatively and honorably accepting aging and death, not struggling to overcome them," and suggests that Americans learn to accept a "natural life-span" that might last until the late seventies or early eighties. "How many years do we need to have a reasonably decent life, to raise a family, to work, to love?"

"Any sophisticated doctor would acknowledge privately that rationing on demographic characteristics when resources are tight goes on already," Robert Binstock, a political scientist at Case Western University, has said. This informal rationing can be found in any big city hospital emergency room, "where you have to make a choice of treating a . . . baby or . . . old man and you have only so many people and so much equipment." With increasing pressure on hospitals to control costs, such triage, he warned, could become official policy. Studies show that emergency room personnel tend to devote less time and effort to resuscitating elderly heart attack victims than they do to younger ones, that older women with breast cancer often get less treatment than they need, that hospitals tend to discharge elderly patients "sicker and quicker" than younger patients, and that the elderly are less likely to receive preventive care. "Managed care is rationing by another name," Derek Humphry has commented. Indeed, HMOs so severely circumscribe a patient's choice of doctor, hospital, prescription medications, and home care service that some ethicists wonder whether patients with life-threatening illnesses have enough options to make truly autonomous decisions. Insurance coverage for patients with chronic illnesses like congestive heart failure or ongoing neurological disorders is skimpy. Medicare coverage for palliative services is minimal, and its hospice benefit requires that patients be terminally ill with a prognosis of six months or less to live (a notoriously difficult determination), which virtually eliminates those dying more slowly from chronic cardiac, respiratory, or neurological diseases. An increasing number of hospices are being audited because their patients "live too long."

Pointing out that only 2 percent of Oregonians who end their lives under the

Death with Dignity Act cite financial concerns as a factor, and that the vast majority of those who receive physician-assisted suicide are college-educated and insured, the Oregon Health Department has concluded that economic motives have not influenced the choice of assisted suicide. Yet Portland psychiatrist Gregory Hamilton, cofounder of Physicians for Compassionate Care, says those aren't the only barometers of financial pressure. "The report entirely ignored the fact that Oregon's rationed health plan denies payment for 171 needed services, while it fully funds assisted suicide for the poor," he writes. "Neither did it reveal that over 38 percent of Oregon Health Plan members find barriers to obtaining mental health services." In Maine, when an assisted suicide referendum was narrowly voted down in 2000, it became clear that options for poor people with terminal or chronic illness were severely limited. Maine offered no Medicaid hospice benefit—one of only six states not to do so—and ranked last in hospice use.

As the number and proportion of elderly in this country soar over the next few decades, economic pressure on hospitals, Social Security, and Medicare will increase. While acknowledging the importance of the economic issue, Derek Humphry doesn't want the right-to-die movement supported for the wrong reasons. "This is a very rich country, and it ought to be able to provide proper medical care for everybody," he told me. "It would be deeply repugnant to us to say that people need to take their lives because there isn't enough money to take care of them. I would fight that tooth and nail." He shook his head. "Voluntary euthanasia is an intimate, personal, libertarian decision." Yet in *Freedom to Die,* Humphry and lawyer Mary Clement, while acknowledging that it was "politically incorrect" to cite economics when arguing in favor of right-to-die legislation, write, "One must look at the realities of the increasing cost of health care in an aging society, because in the final analysis, economics, not the quest for broadened individual liberties or increased autonomy, will drive assisted suicide to the plateau of acceptable practice." More than a few rank-and-file right-to-die advocates believe that the ends justify the means. "I believe in triage," says a former Hemlock member. "It's a question of national priorities. Since there's not enough money to accommodate everyone's needs, I don't think the public has an obligation to keep me alive once I start becoming a drain on society." In *Common-Sense Suicide,* a book advocating the right to suicide for the elderly, Doris Portwood concluded a discussion of costs: "Today, the needs of the individual and those of the social community appear to merge, in an economic sense, on the question of old-age suicide. A planned departure that serves oneself, one's family and also the state surely is worthy of decent consideration."

Critics worry that if physician-assisted suicide is sanctioned, certain less privileged groups—the poor, the elderly, the disabled, and ethnic minorities—will be at particular risk in an age of medical cost-cutting, when their already limited choices may become even more constricted. "Assisted suicide and euthanasia will be practiced through the prism of social inequality and prejudice that characterizes the delivery of services in all segments of society, including health care," concluded a 1994 report by the New York State Task Force on Life and the Law, a panel composed of lawyers, bioethicists, health care officials, and the clergy. "Those who will be most vulnerable to abuse, error or indifference are the poor, minorities, and those who are the least educated and the least empowered." Surveys show that the elderly and members of minority groups are less likely to support physician-assisted suicide than the general population.

Members of the disabled community have been particularly active in opposing physician-assisted suicide. The loss of autonomy that right-to-die advocates so frequently cite—the inability to feed oneself, wipe oneself, or carry out other basic daily functions without help—is intimately familiar to many disabled people who find life worthwhile. "When asked to describe the 'indignities' that assisted suicide would help people to avoid, proponents describe disability," writes Diane Coleman, president of Not Dead Yet, an organization of disabled activists who oppose right-to-die legislation. Not Dead Yet, which takes its name from a skit by the British comedy troupe Monty Python, was formed in 1996 after the acquittal of Dr. Kevorkian in the assisted suicide of a forty-four-year-old woman with multiple sclerosis who had been abandoned by her husband and had lost custody of her children. The group's goal is to alter the widespread public image of severe disability as "a fate worse than death." Coleman, who has spinal muscular atrophy and uses a wheelchair by day and a ventilator at night, cites studies showing that pain was not the most significant motivating factor for those who sought assisted suicide under the Death with Dignity Act. "The primary issue was fear of future increased loss of bodily function and the assumption that such loss would mean loss of dignity and autonomy," she writes. "In other words, the issue was fear and prejudice about disability." It was this perspective that motivated many activists in wheelchairs to protest the removal of Terry Schiavo's feeding tube. Outside Schiavo's hospice, they shared their vigil with conservative Christians, a group with whom they might not previously have found much in common but whose deeply held beliefs, while entirely different from their own, had led to a similar anger over the devaluation of Schiavo's life.

But the disabled community is far from unanimous on right-to-die issues. The late attorney Andrew Batavia, a professor of public health policy, helped found a group called AUTONOMY, Inc. to counter the views of Not Dead Yet. "We argue that the disability rights–independent living movement is based fundamentally on autonomy, and people with disabilities should be allowed to make all decisions that affect their lives—including the decision to end their lives, with or without assistance," wrote Batavia, who had been a quadriplegic since injuring his spinal cord in a car accident when he was sixteen. He argued that denying a disabled terminally ill person this autonomy was an example of just the kind of paternalism that disabled activists had fought against for years. Batavia is less certain whether the right to assisted suicide should be extended to people with incurable but nonterminal conditions, but is among those who "conclude in support of the right on the basis of compassion for people who are simply not able to adjust to their disabilities."

Able-bodied advocates of physician-assisted suicide insist that the disabled and other disadvantaged groups have nothing to fear. Yet over the years there has been no shortage of unsettling statements by right-to-die activists that suggest otherwise. Not long after the Euthanasia Society of America was founded in 1938, its second president, Dr. Foster Kennedy, advocated the legalization of euthanasia for "creatures born defective, whose present condition is miserable and whose future . . . hopeless." Another supporter, Dr. Alexis Carrel, went still further: "Sentimental prejudice should not obstruct the quiet and painless disposition of incurables, criminals, and hopeless lunatics." Testifying in favor of a euthanasia bill in the Florida state legislature in 1967, Walter Sackett, a state representative and retired physician who claimed he had assisted "hundreds" of patients to their deaths, pointed out that the state could save $5 billion over the next fifty years if "mongoloids" were permitted to succumb to the pneumonia they frequently contract. Psychiatrist Eliot Slater of Britain's Voluntary Euthanasia Society argued that the right to voluntary euthanasia should extend to the incurably mentally ill: "If a chronically sick man dies, he ceases to be a burden on himself, on his family, on the health services and on the community." Three years after the British psychiatrist Colin Brewer recommended the plastic-bag-and-barbiturates method of self-deliverance at the 1985 Hemlock conference, he pointed out that euthanasia could prevent a severely disabled person from being remembered as "a slobbering wreck." Writing in *Newsweek* in 1992, English professor Katie Letcher Lyle described having her sixteen-year-old cat put to sleep and suggested that a lethal injection might also be the most humane treatment for a severely retarded, occasionally violent forty-year-old man of her acquaintance.

Similarly ominous statements have been made about the elderly. Lawyer Mary Rose Barrington, a past chairman of the Voluntary Euthanasia Society, was concerned that unless people have the option of assisted suicide or euthanasia, "there can be no possibility of an older person, who is a burden to a younger person, feeling a sense of obligation to release the captive attendant from willing or unwilling bondage." I recall being surprised at the 1985 Hemlock conference when a sixtyish woman asked, "With twenty million elderly Americans, shouldn't the Hemlock Society take more liberal action for the elderly nonterminally ill who have lost their zest for life? Shouldn't they at least get physicians to give some nonlethal dosages that the elderly can accumulate and use to end this life?" In *The Good Euthanasia Guide 2005,* citing the high rate of suicide among older Americans, Derek Humphry writes, "These type of statistics are surely telling us of the need to consider setting up responsible physician-assisted suicide for the [ailing] elderly." Philip Nitschke, the Australian doctor who is working to develop the "peaceful pill," has said that it should be made available to all, "including the depressed, the elderly bereaved, the troubled teen."

Such comments are deeply disturbing. The right to comprehensive medical treatment must be as fiercely protected as the right to refuse that treatment. Some people suggest that if we spent as much money and energy on giving the elderly reasons to stay alive as we do on developing technology to *keep* them alive, the euthanasia option might be less appealing. Says psychologist Richard Seiden, "It is realistic to be concerned that sanctioning suicide or self-deliverance may deter society and government from making the difficult and expensive structural changes necessary to improve the life of the sick and elderly." At the 1985 Hemlock conference, during the panel discussion of "Medical Questions in Euthanasia," oncologist Matthew Conolly concluded an eloquent attack on active euthanasia by saying, "My plea to the Hemlock Society is give up this goal of self-destruction. Instead, lend us your energy, your anger, your indignation, and your creativity to work with us to build up such a system of hospice care that death, however it comes, need not be feared. Is this not a nobler cause? And is this not a better way?"

---

In many cultures—including most of those that encourage "thrift" suicide—the wisdom and experience of the elderly earn them respect and veneration. In America, although we strive at all costs to keep them alive, the elderly are more likely to face indifference, impatience, or scorn. "At best, the living old are treated as if they are already half dead," wrote Robert Butler in his Pulitzer Prize–winning book, *Why Survive? Being Old in America.* "Many elders suffer a social death in which they are removed from the mainstream of life," observed sociologists Jack Levin and Arnold Arluke. "They are forced by law or custom to retire, give up leadership positions in their communities and become virtual prisoners in their own homes for fear of muggers and other criminals. Increasing numbers of elders are living in age-segregated housing or nursing homes where many are drugged into dependent states." Within a month after being robbed and assaulted in their Bronx apartment, one couple in their late seventies slashed their wrists and hanged themselves from their bedroom door. They explained in a note that though they had lived in the neighborhood for many years and didn't want to move, "we don't want to live in fear anymore."

Although suicide among adolescents receives the lion's share of attention, the suicide rate of elderly Americans (over sixty-five) is nearly twice as high. And while the rate of elderly suicide has declined somewhat over the last fifteen years, the elderly have accounted for the highest suicide rate for as long as such statistics have been kept. The elderly comprise 12 percent of the population but complete 18 percent of the suicides. As in all age groups, men account for the majority of deaths. (The rate of suicide among women peaks in middle age and declines after sixty.) More than three-quarters of suicides among people over sixty-five are by men, and the vast majority of those are by white men. (Men eighty-five and over are at highest risk; their rate of 54 per 100,000 is five times that of the nation as a whole.) The elderly are also less ambivalent about suicide. While for every adolescent suicide there may be as many as one hundred attempts, among those over sixty-five there are four or fewer. They tend to use more lethal methods—79 percent of elderly men use firearms. "When an old person attempts suicide," concludes an American Psychiatric Association report, "he almost fully intends to die."

It is often said that youth suicide is especially tragic because teenagers have "everything to live for." The elderly, it is implied, have "nothing to live for." Certainly the suffering of the elderly may be more readily apparent. If loss—and one's response to loss—is the root of depression and suicide, the high rate of elderly suicide is not surprising. For most people, old age is characterized by an inexorable accumulation of losses. They face the loss of their jobs, willingly or unwillingly, to retirement. (A disproportionate number of male suicides occur immediately following the retirement age of sixty-five.) Retirement means loss not only of occupation and identity but of income. One in ten elderly Americans has an income below the poverty line. The elderly also face loss of connection. Illness and death claim an increasing number of their family and friends. About one in three Americans over age sixty-five lives alone. In part this reflects a decrease in the strength of family ties. Thirty-five years ago a third of all Americans over sixty-five lived with their children; today, a tenth do. (In contrast, 70 percent of elderly Japanese live with a younger relative.) Not surprisingly, the elderly are more at risk for suicide if they live alone, have lost their spouse, and no longer work. In a landmark study, British epidemiologist Brian Barraclough found that 50 percent of elderly suicides lived alone, compared with only 20 percent of all older people in their communities. In 1998, among males seventy-five and over in the United States, the suicide rate for divorced men was 3.4 times, and for widowed men 2.6 times, that for married men that age. But the factor that puts them at especially high risk for suicide is loss of health. Eighty percent of Americans over sixty-five suffer from at least one chronic illness. Medical problems are a factor in 70 percent of all suicides by people over the age of sixty.

Psychologist Robert Kastenbaum worries that talk of "respect" and "rights" is often used to camouflage our own unwillingness to respond to elderly people in need. "In general, where the 'geriatric case' is allowed to slip away to proper and timely death," he says, "a younger person with similar problems would receive keen attention." Times have not completely changed since Herbert Hendin was a young doctor, when elderly patients were referred to as "crocks" and written off as time-wasters whose cases had disappointing outcomes and little educational value. Physicians are poorly trained not just to deal with end-of-life care, but to deal with elderly patients in general, while most mental health professionals are poorly trained to deal with elderly patients. As a result, although depression remains the most common medical complaint of the elderly, most depressed older Americans go untreated. Even when they are treated, the treatment they get is not all it could be: studies show physicians typically spend less time with older patients than with younger patients. "Since the elderly depressed don't cause much trouble, their plight has been ignored," UCLA psychologist Gary Emery has said. "Their depressed state is often misdiagnosed by health professionals, family members, and the elderly themselves, and the symptoms dismissed as an inevitable result of the aging process. Yet severe depression can be effectively dealt with when recognized in time, and potential suicides can be averted." University of Rochester psychiatrist Yeates Conwell suggests that depression—often undiagnosed, untreated, or dismissed as a "natural" consequence of aging—underlies two-thirds or more of all elderly suicides. And a study of 136 elderly nursing home patients found that one in four who were said to be suffering from senile dementia had severe but potentially reversible behavioral problems. "Too often the old are written off as treatable with pharmacology while younger patients get psychotherapy," said Herbert Hendin, addressing a sparse crowd on "Suicide Among the Elderly" at an AAS conference, while across the hall a discussion of adolescent suicide was standing room only. "The heart of suicide prevention has always been and remains suicide among older people."

Nevertheless, while people over age sixty-five account for 18 percent of all suicides, they account for less than 3 percent of calls to suicide prevention centers. Few centers train volunteers in how to work with elderly callers, and fewer still have programs to encourage elderly clients. There are exceptions. San Francisco's Friendship Line has for several decades operated a twenty-four-hour hotline for the elderly, as well as a program of house calls to depressed elderly clients. The Mental Health Center in Spokane, Washington, reaches out to depressed and suicidal elderly people through its Gatekeeper program, in which meter readers, utility workers, bank tellers, mail carriers, paramedics, and other community workers likely to come into casual contact with the elderly are trained to identify older adults who exhibit signs of distress. Those at risk are referred to the Center's Clinical Case Management Program, which responds with medical and psychiatric assessments, clinical services, and respite care. Life Crisis Services, a telephone hotline program in St. Louis, has trained social work students to offer follow-up telephone counseling to depressed and possibly suicidal elderly callers.

There are numerous changes that might decrease the rate of elderly suicide. Butler's *Why Survive?* is a veritable encyclopedia of the ways we neglect and mistreat the elderly and of the steps we might take to improve their lot. The abolition of compulsory retirement ages, increased Social Security and pension benefits, safer housing, better public transportation, improved nursing-home care, and revitalized senior citizens' programs are a few of the suggestions.

Better pain control is another. In the past few decades, our understanding of the physiology of pain has radically expanded. In fact, palliative care specialists insist that pain management has improved so markedly that in the vast majority of cases—95 percent is the figure most often mentioned—pain can be controlled. This, of course, still leaves a great many cases in which pain can't be relieved by even the most sophisticated methods. Moreover, the 95 percent figure assumes that patients in pain will be treated in the best hospitals with doctors trained in the latest methods of palliative care. But a great many doctors have no training whatsoever in palliative care, and a great many doctors (and patients) are unaware that these ballyhooed advances exist. Although death is the one medical event that every American will face, as of 1996, only 5 of the nation's 126 medical schools had a required course on death and dying, and only 26 percent of 7,048 medical residency programs offered a course on end-of-life care. *The Cecil Textbook of Medicine,* points out Derek Humphry, devotes only 3 of its 2,300 pages to the care of the terminally ill, while *Harrison's Principles of Internal Medicine* asserts, "The discovery and cure of potentially serious disease represents a far greater service to one's patients than ministrations in the course of an incurable condition." In a survey of 1,177 physicians who had treated more than 70,000 cancer patients during the previous six months, 76 percent reported that they didn't know enough about palliative care to be able to control their patients' pain.

Small wonder, then, that despite the advances in palliative care, study after study indicates that a great many Americans die in pain. In 1997, a twelve-member committee of the Institute of Medicine reviewed various studies and found that 40 to 80 percent of patients with cancer, AIDS, and other diseases reported inadequately treated pain. In a study published in the *Journal of the American Medical Association* of some 9,000 terminally ill patients, more than half complained of moderate or severe pain. In a survey of 897 physicians, 86 percent felt the majority of American patients in pain were undertreated, and 49 percent rated pain control for patients in their *own* practice as fair, poor, or very poor. (Thirty-one percent said they would wait until their patients had only six months left to live before using maximum pain medication.) Pain is a problem even at the finest hospitals with the most advanced palliative care techniques. A study of 90 patients at Memorial Sloan-Kettering, perhaps the top cancer care center in this country, found that one in five suffered pain that could be controlled only if they lay perfectly still in bed. Two of those patients killed themselves.

Palliative care does not, of course, consist of managing only physical symptoms. It is commonly observed that those who seek assisted suicide are motivated less by current pain than by fear of future suffering and feelings of despair, hopelessness, dependency, loss of control, and loss of dignity. Yet most physicians are even less well trained to deal with emotional suffering, and few psychiatrists are schooled in the psychological aspects of palliative care. (Indeed, few palliative care services provide ongoing psychiatric care.) Patients are not the only players in end-of-life scenarios whose anxiety about death and dying may influence their treatment. As we saw in part four, many physicians, not surprisingly, experience a sense of failure and helplessness in the face of death. In a survey of oncologists, 25 percent reported that they did not like, or want to care for, dying patients. Hendin and Foley suggest that these anxieties help explain why some doctors may use excessive measures to preserve life—while others may be more ready and willing to help bring it to an end. "Physicians who unwisely prolong the dying process and those who practice euthanasia may have more in common than they realize . . . ," they write. "By deciding when patients die, by making death a medical decision, the physician preserves the illusion of mastery over the disease and over the feelings of helplessness that lack of control induces. The physician, not the illness, is responsible for the death. Assisting suicide and performing euthanasia become ways of dealing with the frustration of being unable to cure the disease." Studies have shown that the less physicians know about palliative care, the more they favor assisted suicide or euthanasia. In a study of oncologists, 20 percent supported assisted suicide; after receiving palliative care training, the number dropped to 9 percent.

Not surprisingly, patients who receive good palliative care are less likely to ask for assisted suicide. "You don't have to kill the patient to kill the pain," Dame Cicely Saunders reminds us. Of some 20,000 patients cared for at St. Christopher's Hospice in London over the years, only three inpatients and two home care patients have taken their own life (none using medication supplied by the hospice). The director of a small Dutch hospice reports that nearly all his patients who initially propose assisted suicide change their mind after being reassured that they'll receive effective palliative care. In Oregon, an anonymous 1999 survey of physicians who had received requests for assisted suicide since the Death with Dignity Act went into effect found that in more than half of the 142 cases for which physicians supplied information, there was no further palliative care intervention of any kind. Of those who did receive such interventions, nearly half changed their mind about seeking physician-assisted suicide. A commission studying the case for euthanasia in England concluded, "If all the care were up to the standards of the best, there would be few cases in which there was even a *prima facie* argument for euthanasia; better alternative means of alleviating distress would almost always be available if modern techniques and human understanding and care of the patient were universally practiced."

Critics of physician-assisted suicide worry that legislation will obviate the incentive for physicians to become properly trained in palliative care. Indeed, until the improvements of the last several years, the Netherlands had fallen behind most other Western nations in palliative medicine and hospice care. In the United States, by contrast, while poor end-of-life care has led to increased support for physician-assisted suicide, that support has, in turn, galvanized physicians to pay more attention to end-of-life care. "Kevorkian and Humphry were a stimulus to medicine," observes Hendin. "It's unfortunate that it took them to frighten the medical profession into doing what it should have done long ago." Medical organizations, foundations, and grassroots groups have sponsored programs to educate health care professionals and their patients about the care of the dying. An increasing number of medical schools are offering courses on end-of-life care, while the number of Medicare-certified hospice programs—both inpatient and home care—has grown from thirty-one in 1984 to well over two thousand. Even so, fewer than 20 percent of all dying patients in this country receive hospice care; fewer than 10 percent of Americans are even aware that hospice care exists; and many regions are underserved.

The problem with many discussions of physician-assisted suicide and palliative care, as with most ethical debates, is that proponents of each side so often reduce them to either/or rather than both/and propositions. This frustrates Marcia Angell, who has said that the two paths "are no more mutually exclusive than good cardiologic care and the availability of heart transplantation." In *Physician-Assisted Dying,* Timothy Quill and Margaret Pabst Battin call these practices "not only compatible but complementary." They point out that the Oregon Death with Dignity Act led not only to physician-assisted suicides but also to "the highest rate of at-home deaths in the nation; high use of prescribed opioids; high referral rates to hospice programs; comprehensive statewide do-not-resuscitate policies; and a high level of public awareness of end of life options." Quill and Battin believe that physician-assisted suicide should be one of the choices available to suffering terminally ill patients—but that care should be so good that it would only be used in rare cases. Like their opponents, they urge improvements in palliative care, social services, and access to quality medical treatment for all. "Where we proponents of legalization part company with opponents is in our belief that it is not fair or justified to postpone legal access to physician-assisted death while we await the solution of these most difficult social problems. Relief of suffering—and with it the freedom to face dying as one wishes—must be available to suffering patients now."

At bottom, perhaps our most important task is to change our attitudes toward the elderly, to celebrate them as valued, integral members of our culture. Although we shrink from the idea of elderly suicide and euthanasia, we encourage it by our neglect and indifference. (Cross-cultural studies demonstrate that societies in which old age brings with it respect and veneration have low rates of elderly suicide.) And if we don't allow them the right to exit this life, we have a responsibility to make this life better for them. "Often people ask whether a human being has a *right* to end his life," says Nico Speijer, a Dutch psychiatrist. "This question is incorrect. We should say rather that everyone has a right to live and *we* have the obligation to make it possible for everyone to live in such a way that he can be a socially integrated member of society to the maximum of his abilities."

In *Common-Sense Suicide,* Doris Portwood compared the decision of an elderly woman to end her life with the decision to leave a party before it's over. "When an older woman leaves a social gathering—perhaps an hour after dinner and when younger guests are settling down to a game or a fresh drink—no one urges her to linger on. Someone may call a cab or offer a lift. She will receive thoughtful words during the process of departure, but no insistence on her staying. There is the assumption that she has, in fact, some good reason for going." (Portwood, who had seen her mother and sister die slow, painful deaths while suffering from Parkinson's disease, took a fatal overdose of Seconal in 1996, by which point her own Parkinson's had rendered her so disabled that she had to dictate her suicide note.) This seems a sad, if understandable, equation. Certainly, the elderly guest must be allowed to leave, but her hosts have a responsibility to make the party more enjoyable so she'll want to stay a little longer. In sum, the right to live with dignity may be as neglected as the right to die with dignity; if more emphasis were placed on the first, the second might not seem so pressing.

---

As early as 500 BC, on the Greek island of Ceos, the law encouraged all inhabitants over the age of sixty to drink hemlock to make room for the next generation. (Average life expectancy at the time was less than thirty years.) In seventeenth-century Brittany, a person suffering from an incurable disease might apply to the parish priest for the Holy Stone. If the priest agreed, the family gathered, prayers were said, and the Stone was brought down upon the sufferer's head, often by the oldest person in the village. Other than these examples, organized suicide facilitation has largely been confined to fiction. In Thomas More's sixteenth-century fantasy *Utopia,* priests and magistrates helped end the lives of terminally ill citizens who wished to die; those who chose death were considered godly and virtuous, although those who refused were provided with continuing medical care. In "The Suicide Club," a short story published in 1878, Robert Louis Stevenson described a leather and mahogany club where for an entry fee of forty pounds dissolute young men draw lots for the right to die. One member wins the right to die; another is obliged to kill him. "The trouble of suicide is removed in that way," explains a club member. In "The Putter-to-Sleep," a short story by Guy de Maupassant, the narrator, scanning a newspaper's suicide statistics, thinks of all the gruesome deaths the numbers might hide. He dreams of an Institute of Voluntary Death where people might chat and gamble before they meet an "easy death."

(In 1892, several years after writing the story, de Maupassant cut his throat in an unsuccessful suicide attempt. He died in an insane asylum a year and a half later of advanced syphilis.) In Kurt Vonnegut's short story "Welcome to the Monkey House," suicide is encouraged as a solution to overpopulation. The World Government establishes a network of Federal Ethical Suicide Parlors staffed by six-foot virgin hostesses; people go there voluntarily to be killed painlessly while lying on a Barcalounger, listening to Muzak. Next door to each parlor is a Howard Johnson's where one is entitled to order a last meal. In the film *Soylent Green,* would-be suicides go to a government building where they can watch movies with idyllic pastoral settings, listen to Beethoven's Ninth, and be painlessly put to sleep.

What these writers proposed in literature, some people have proposed in all seriousness. "What we want, what our grandsons, or great-grandsons will probably have, is a commodious and scientific lethal chamber, which shall reduce to a minimum the physical terrors and inconveniences of suicide, both for the patient and for his family and friends," wrote William Archer, the British drama critic, in 1893. Alfred Nobel, inventor of dynamite and patron of the Nobel Prize, envisioned a "suicide institute" on the Riviera where sufferers could be put to sleep with a view of the Mediterranean, to the strains of beautiful music played by a first-class orchestra. In 1919, Binet-Sanglé, a Sorbonne physician, proposed the establishment of public euthanasia parlors where one could choose from electrocution, poison, gases, narcotics, and other lethal methods to attain an "individually styled" death. Jo Roman, a New York artist stricken with breast cancer who took a fatal overdose in 1979 at age sixty-two, drew the blueprints for an Exit House that would assure nonintervention, or assistance if necessary, in a "gentle" suicide for anyone over forty. Roman's imagination placed Exit House next to the United Nations in New York and equipped it with library, lounge, roof garden, swimming pool, public relations department, and well-tended gardens where "small safe animals such as chipmunks and squirrels go about their business of living and dying." Although Jack Kevorkian described his "obitoria" in much less fanciful terms, his goal was the same: a place where people in pain could go to a painless death.

While perhaps based on good intentions, such proposals are nevertheless very much to be feared. For though these fantasies may sound far-fetched, with increasing economic pressure the "bureaucratization" of suicide, as Margaret Pabst Battin calls it, might conceivably be proposed. "The risk is not Nazism," says Battin, "but individual manipulation, which is coercive in effect." Suicide, according to Battin, can be manipulated in two ways. In "circumstantial manipulation," a person may be given shoddy care, inadequate pain medication, and so forth, so that suicide becomes an obvious choice. In "ideological manipulation," a social group's way of thinking may slowly be altered so that suicide seems preferable. "At bottom," she says, "I think the fear we should all think about is that we may become a society in which the normal, ordinary, expected thing is to do your dying relatively early and easily rather than pro-long it and impose a burden on family and on medical personnel." She com-pares this to the kind of expectation we have that people will marry, usually in their early twenties. "How easy is it to not marry?" she asks. "How easy would it be to resist this expectation about dying? . . . I can envision an elderly per-son's family and friends gathering round her and saying, 'It's time to think about how to bring this to a close, Granny. But don't be frightened, we'll be supportive.'" Despite such troubling scenarios, Battin believes that the individ-ual's right to die must be protected. "Even if the kind of choice it favors might calcify into an expectation," she says, "it still is not a reason to abridge the rights of those who choose to exercise that choice in the first place."

Basically, it is a question of how simple it should be to complete suicide. In de Maupassant's story, the secretary of the Institute of Voluntary Death explains what he calls the "annihilations." "Why should death be gloomy?" he asks his bewildered visitor. "It should be indifferent. We have lightened death, we have made it blossom, we have perfumed it, we have made it easy." William Archer suggested that one day there would be machines by which a man could kill himself for a penny. "In a rational state of civilization," he said, "self-effacement should cost us no more physical screwing up of courage than a visit to the barber's, and much less than a visit to the dentist's."

But even those who advocate the right to die under certain circumstances warn that suicide should not be made too easy. "Robert Lowell once remarked that if there were some little switch in the arm which one could press in order to die immediately and without pain, then everyone would sooner or later com-mit suicide," wrote A. Alvarez. "People are going to help each other die," observed A. J. Levinson, the former director of Concern for Dying, a right-to-die group. "But there are risks—legal, moral, psychological. And I think those risks should stay there." John Arras, former philosopher-in-residence at Montefiore Medical Center in New York City, has frequently advised doctors on ethical dilemmas in medicine. "I believe that the classical philosophical argument for suicide or assisted suicide is very strong," he says. "But I'm wary of the popularization of suicide. It's one thing to stake out the abstract right to die, another thing to parade this before depressed people who may take advantage of it. . . . These are decisions that should be made in fear and trem-bling." Battin concludes her essay "Manipulated Suicide" by stating, "I myself believe that on moral grounds we must accept, not reject, the notion of rational suicide. But I think we must do so with a clear-sighted view of the moral quicksand into which this notion threatens to lead us; perhaps then we may discover a path around."

# IV

# A MODEL HEMLOCK COUPLE

I FIRST MET FRED AND HOLLY ISHAM at Hemlock's Second National Voluntary Euthanasia conference in Los Angeles. They were introduced to me by a friend who had described them as a model Hemlock couple: articulate and attractive people in their eighties, they were planning a double suicide. When the time came, my friend said, they planned to take a fatal overdose on a mountaintop at sunset.

I liked the Ishams immediately; they were the kind of people one might choose for grandparents. Holly was charming, talkative, and as alert as a squirrel. A beautiful woman with neat gray hair and a luminous smile, she had turned eighty-three the day before I met her, but she looked much younger. Fred, a youthful eighty-four, was a small, balding, handsome man with a neat mustache, a shy, almost deferential manner, and a sheepish, endearing grin. Married fifty-nine years, they still looked into each other's eyes, they still touched each other with affection, they still seemed very much in love.

Six years earlier, Fred had learned he had cancer of the prostate. Although a bilateral orchiectomy—the removal of both testicles—slowed the growth of the cancer, two years ago a subsequent bone scan found bone cancer. "Fred had the option of radiation and chemotherapy, but he was told that his quality of life would be greatly impaired, so he refused it," Holly, who did most of the talking, told me. "So for the last two years we've been living it up. But we know there will come a time when the pain will be too great, and we want to be ready." Fred nodded assent. "We've seen so many of our friends and family go the hard way, and we don't want to go through that ourselves," he said. "I don't fear death, but I do fear dying." Holly shook her head. "As long as we have some control over that, I have a comfortable feeling," she said. "We've lived a long and happy life, and we do not want to be dependent on our children. After eighty-three years we feel it doesn't matter when it happens—we've already surpassed the average life span, so *que sera, sera.*" She gave a gay laugh. "I don't see why death has to be a fearful thing. I don't see why it can't be as happy and euphoric as our wedding day."

---

Fred and Holly were married in 1926, two years after they'd graduated from college. In the sixty years since, they'd experienced a full share of highs and lows: the Depression; the house they designed and built in 1931 and still occupied; their three children; their trips around the world. While Fred worked as a commercial artist until his retirement, much of Holly's adult life was devoted to caring for the youngest of their three daughters, whose life was spent in and out of hospitals. At the age of seventeen, surgery to remove a malignant tumor of the spinal cord left her a paraplegic. But in her late twenties the cancer spread, and her life became a nightmare of radiation, medication, and surgery until her death at age thirty.

Seeing their daughter's harrowing final years encouraged the Ishams to be more in control of their own deaths. When I met them, however, Holly and Fred seemed far from the end. They talked with excitement of tours they had taken to Nova Scotia, Tahiti, and Europe; of traveling around the United States to visit their two children, five grandchildren, and two great-grandchildren; of hiking near the cabin they had built in the mountains. They went to movies, concerts, and dinner parties. ("For twenty-two years we've spent New Year's Eve with the same group of friends," Holly told me. "But we're dying off. Our group started with fourteen. Now we're down to seven.") Holly's datebook was crammed with lectures, bridge parties, community service meetings, and garden club get-togethers, most of them sponsored by the local women's club. Fred often drove her to meetings and helped her make place cards and posters for club functions. "I don't have a social life of my own, really," said Fred. "My activities are mostly related to Hol's." Fred seemed content to be in his wife's shadow; he was proud of her, and his quiet strength complemented her high-strung energy. Her devotion to him was evident even when she teased him about his passivity. "I've lived with him fifty-nine years, and I still don't know what he thinks about some things," she said. "He's so agreeable. He'll agree with you, he'll agree with me, he'll agree with everybody." She laughed and gazed at Fred with affection. "And it would take a man like that to put up with me."

As in most of their activities, Holly was the impetus behind their interest in Hemlock. They had joined two years earlier, after she'd seen Derek Humphry interviewed on television. "I'm the aggressor in these things," she admitted. "Fred goes to these meetings to satisfy me." Holly had read *Let Me Die*

*Before I Wake* and *Common-Sense Suicide,* and she studied the *Hemlock Quarterly.* "I talk to friends at the club about it if I feel they're ripe," she said. "I've circulated Hemlock books and membership applications, and I think I've gotten at least six members." At the Hemlock conference Holly was quite active, introducing herself to other members, exchanging stories and phone numbers, asking questions about insurance and death certificates, jotting down ideas in her brown Hemlock notebook. Fred, who hadn't read the Hemlock books, agreed in principle with much of the Hemlock philosophy but was uncomfortable contemplating its practice. "I think that self-deliverance, in connection with the two of us . . ." His voice trailed off. "I haven't sorted it out enough to definitely put me in the position or her in the position, but as an idea, I accept it." Said Holly, "He shares my interest but not my enthusiasm, I would say." Fred nodded: "That's probably it."

As we talked, I realized that the mountaintop-at-sunset suicide scenario was Holly's, and her enthusiasm had made it seem as if it were shared by her husband. Holly had clearly thought a great deal about contingency plans. "If we don't have a pact to go together, if Fred died and I were the survivor, I would just weed out the house, get my affairs in shape, get the pills by some means or other, and have a kind of indefinite date as to when I'd use them," she said. "And if I felt deterioration in the quality of life or became dependent on others to the point that I wanted out, I would take my own life." Holly didn't have the pills yet and was anxious to find a source. "The only fear I have is of not being successful," she said. "And if I woke up and found I was unsuccessful, I hope I'd have a plastic bag handy and be able to finish it off with that." Despite her extensive planning for death, Holly talked with as much excitement about their upcoming sixtieth anniversary as she did about the possibility of a double suicide. "I'm not going to give up any sooner than I have to," she said. "We've had such a good life for fifty-nine years."

Fred, when pressed, said he didn't think about what he'd do without Holly because he was sure he'd die before her. If he didn't? "For the foreseeable future I would go on living here in this home," he said slowly. "Even though I'm sure our daughters would invite Hol or me to live with them, we don't want to be a burden. But I don't know what my life would be because so much of my life concerns her activities." Fred admitted that the Hemlock conference intrigued him. "Those meetings were so thought-provoking that I do want to read some of those books now." Holly beamed. "You can start reading *Jean's Way* this evening to me," she said. They looked at each other fondly.

---

Over the following year I received several notes from the Ishams written by Holly, who had signed both their names. In December I received a Christmas card, a Chinese watercolor titled *Flight* in which two people were hiking through mountains. "We have a few more aches and pains as the years rush by," Holly wrote in her neat, energetic hand, "but we try to ignore them and are keeping *very* busy with family, friends, and club activities. Who says eighty-four and eighty-five is old? Old is a state of mind."

When I saw Holly at the next Hemlock conference, in Washington, D.C., she was with her elder daughter, a nurse. Fred had stayed home. "It's not good," said Holly anxiously. "Things have deteriorated." Fred had undergone radiation treatments in February and again in August. "It's made him quieter and depressed," she said. "He just agrees with everyone—he always has—and he takes every treatment and every medication the doctors recommend." Over the summer he was hospitalized for congestive heart failure; his lungs filled with fluid. Holly and Fred asked the doctors to issue a no-code order. Fred recovered. "The doctors say he probably won't die of the cancer but of heart or kidney failure." As Holly talked, frustration and bitterness seeped into her voice. Although she cared deeply for Fred, she was clearly exhausted by the demands of caring for him. She said that there had been few conversations about suicide; she didn't want to push it. "But at one point I reminded him about the idea of going out together," she said. "I told him that I'd go to Mexico, get the drugs, and we could have a cocktail hour and go out together. He didn't say anything." Holly looked down. "I feel terribly guilty, but sometimes I feel as if I'm just waiting for him to die. He's so down about things. . . . I think he will hang on as long as he can. . . . So I guess my dreams of going out together are . . ." Holly raised her hands in a gesture of despair.

---

Two months later in Los Angeles, I arranged to see Fred and Holly. On the phone Holly told me the doctors had estimated that Fred had between six months and a year to live. For several months Fred had been confined to the house except for trips to the hospital. He slept up to sixteen hours a day and spent most of the rest of the time staring at the television set. The last time he and Holly had visited their cabin was many months earlier, and their last golf game was almost a year ago. Although her doctor and her daughters had urged her not to worry so much about Fred and to maintain her own activities, Holly, who spent most of her time caring for her husband, clearly felt hampered by the restrictions Fred's condition imposed on her life. And yet her voice had little of the anxiety that had been so evident in Washington.

When I arrived at their house, Fred was sitting in an armchair in a corner of their bedroom, in pale blue pajamas, watching television. He looked much older and more frail than when I had last seen him almost two years before. His face had sagged, and rather than promising a smile as it once did, the corners of his mouth turned down as if in fear. His voice was even softer and slower than before, and his hand shook as he sipped from a glass of water. His mind was still sharp. I was delighted to see him. He told me about his chemotherapy. "I've been lucky," he said. "It hasn't given me any discomfort." But he couldn't move around as much as he used to, he said, and he suffered from diarrhea. His right leg had been bothering him, and he worried that the cancer had spread there. When I asked him how his spirits were holding up, he gave a rueful smile. "I take it a day at a time," he said. "Sometimes I feel down, sometimes I feel okay."

One reason why Holly seemed less anxious emerged when Fred got up and walked slowly to the bathroom. Holly leaned forward and spoke even more urgently than usual. "I have a source where I can get drugs," she said. "Fred knows I have a source, but he doesn't know where. One night we were having a cocktail, and he asked if I was stockpiling drugs. I said yes. And he said, 'Well, get enough for me, too.'" Holly was pleased. "I told him that even though I was in good heath and would probably live a long time, I don't want to. When he's gone, I'm sure I could *live* without him, I'm sure I could learn to adjust, but I would feel that my function in life was gone. I wouldn't be needed. So I'd just like to put my things in order and go. Or I'd like to go with him—if I'm lucky enough to get all we need, I'd just like to have a nice little cocktail party for the two of us."

Fred returned. "I've been telling George about how I feel about self-deliverance and about the talk we had," Holly said. Fred was silent for a moment. "I think we understand each other," he said as he trudged back to the couch. "I think we do," said Holly. Although they had discussed the relative merits of hospital, hospice, and home care for Fred, they hadn't talked about suicide since their brief conversation over cocktails. Holly would have liked to, but she didn't want to appear pushy. The presence of a third person seemed to make it easier. Holly talked about it with intensity; Fred was still a bit frightened and embarrassed by the subject. "I think our feelings on this will change from day to day," he said. "I know mine do. Some days I feel okay, and sometimes I feel I'd like to just get it over with. I'm uncomfortable with the idea [of suicide], but it's a matter of deciding whether life is worth living at that time. I wish it were legal and you could have a doctor give a shot."

Holly brought out the photograph album from their sixtieth anniversary celebration, which had brought Fred and Holly, their two daughters, five grandchildren, and two great-grandchildren together for two days. As Holly turned the pages, proudly pointing out her grandchildren, Fred stood behind the couch, smiling. "She's just a ball of fire . . . so energetic," said Holly of a grandchild. "I love her." Fred chuckled with pleasure. "Oh yes, oh yes," he said slowly, softly, and his hands moved from the couch to his wife's shoulders.

When it was time to say good-bye, I kissed Holly, shook Fred's hand, and squeezed his bony shoulder. Then I realized it might be the last time I would see them, and our bodies came closer in an awkward hug. "I hope to be back in L.A. soon," I said, then suddenly realized I meant, "I hope I'll be back in L.A. before one or both of you die." I was filled with sadness. I wanted to say,

"Live, please live," to both of them. But I didn't. As I drove across the city, I wondered how I would react to the very real possibility of one or both of them completing suicide—or self-deliverance, as Holly called it. Would I think it had been a "right" or "good" or "rational" choice?

––––––––––

In December I received a letter from Holly.

> . . . *It became necessary for us to place Fred in a hospice. Our two daughters concurred with the decision, because I could no longer handle 24-hour nursing duty. Naturally it was a painful and tearful decision to make. He updated his Living Will with Durable Power of Attorney. Now his desires are: 1) No resuscitation 2) No intravenous 3) No intubation 4) No injections except for pain or sleep. Simply put, no life supports. Just let nature take its course. . . . I have just talked to Fred's doctor and to him. He called me. He has improved so much. He wheels himself around the hospital and is alert instead of sleeping 16 out of 24 hours. His doctors said there is some lung involvement now, but he may linger quite a while. C'est la vie! . . . Warmest wishes from*
>
> *Fred and Holly*

The following June I received a letter from Holly that began, "I thought that you would like to know that my gentle husband of 61 years died peacefully in his sleep at two a.m., May 1st."

Fred, I learned later, had prospered his first few months in the hospice. He played bingo, was elected president of the council, and was crowned King of Hearts on Valentine's Day. But as his health declined, he lost interest in the organized activities, and he wept whenever Holly visited. One day he asked Holly about Hemlock. "He wanted to know how to do it, where to get it, how much to take," Holly recalled in a telephone conversation with me. "I said, 'Fred, if you had read all the material I'd put in front of you over the years, you'd know.' But I told him, 'I have enough pills saved up for us both, and we can take them and die a peaceful death, but you have to come home to do it. So you just tell me when you want to come home and we'll do it.' But Fred never gave me the high sign."

In April, Fred was bedridden for three weeks. "Finally, at the end, when he was having a very bad time, he said he guessed it was too late for Hemlock. I said, 'Yes, because I couldn't get you out of the hospital now.'" Holly paused. "Fred was miserable because he was so weak, and he had trouble breathing. But the doctors provided enough painkillers so I think he was pain-free." At the end of April, Fred slipped into unconsciousness. He died three days later. "I saw him the night before," said Holly. "I couldn't rouse him, so I went home. At two in the morning they called and told me he had died. It was a blessing. He was at peace. The anxiety and suffering were over. It was the first day of May, one month shy of our sixty-first wedding anniversary."

In the months following Fred's death, Holly sorted through his belongings and talked with her family and to a counselor, trying to forgive herself for the resentment and anger she had felt during her husband's last years. "I'm doing very well," she told me. "I'm not lonely. My philosophy is that grief is a selfish thing so I've gotten right back into my activities and club life." When I asked about her own future, she said, "I know quite positively when I want to make my exit, so I'm making plans. I feel a burden to the kids. I was prepared for a double suicide. I had my notes all written out. Now all I have to do is change the *we* to *I*." I encouraged her to use her vast energy to stay alive. I told her I loved her and would be sorry if she were no longer on this earth. But she sounded certain. I made her promise that she would at least say good-bye.

---

Several months later I came home one Friday night to find a letter from Holly, saying good-bye, and a copy of her suicide note that she planned to leave next to her when she made her "exit." The letter had been written on Monday, and she intended to take an overdose on Thursday night, she said. The note, she wrote in her neat, elegant hand, "will capsulize my reasons for wishing to live no longer." It said:

> *To whom it may concern*
> *"The right to die is as sacred as the right to live."*
> *I am ending my life in a planned and deliberate manner. I have a loving and devoted family and friends who know that this act may be a possibility without knowing when it might occur.*
> *I have lived a full and fruitful life, 61 years of which were shared with my devoted husband. . . . Now I have become dependent on others because of increasing incurable loss of vision and painful, crippling arthritis.*
> *All who know me know that I am fiercely independent. I feel that my family and friends deserve freedom from the anxiety which my declining years have caused them.*
> *I will be 86 years old soon. I do not want to overstay my time. I am not depressed, I am sure that this is the right thing for me to do.*
> *Now I choose to die in a peaceful and dignified way.*
> *I have taken 30 vesparex which should be fatal.*
> *Please respect my right to die.*
> 
> *Holly G. Isham*

Fred's and Holly's ashes were scattered near the mountain cabin they had loved and shared for fifty years.

# 6

## SURVIVORS

# I

# MERRYL AND CARL

———

FOR MANY YEARS suicide was known as the victimless crime. But whether the act of an impulsive teenager, a depressed businessman, or a terminally ill cancer patient, each suicide leaves behind a great many victims—wife, husband, parents, children, friends—for whom the pain is just beginning. "There are always two parties to a death; the person who dies and the survivors who are bereaved," wrote historian Arnold Toynbee. ". . . There are two parties to the suffering that death inflicts; and, in the apportionment of this suffering, the survivor takes the brunt." The suffering of survivors is acute after any death, but the grief inflicted by suicide may be the hardest to bear. In addition to shock, denial, anger, and sorrow, the suicide survivor often faces an added burden of guilt and shame. Although the pain is over for the one who died, and his problems, in their way, answered, the survivor is invariably left with questions. "Suicide is the cruelest death of all for those who remain," says a bereavement counselor. "Each day the survivors face the gut-wrenching struggle of asking themselves, 'Why, why, why?'" What makes a suicide so difficult to resolve is that there may be no answers. "I'll never know why," says a man whose seventeen-year-old son hanged himself. "There's only one person who can tell me, and he's dead." After her husband, Carl, killed himself at the age of thirty-three, Merryl Maleska's life was ripped open just when she'd believed it was most secure. It was the beginning of a long, excruciating journey in which she was forced to reexamine every moment of her life since she had first seen Carl sixteen years before.

———

On a September evening not long after she had arrived for her freshman year at Tufts University in Medford, Massachusetts, Merryl Maleska lay on a bed in her dorm room, flipping through the "pigbook," a thin yellow volume containing pictures of everyone in her class. It was her third night of school and there were hundreds of faces to scrutinize, but when Merryl got to the seventh photograph, she stopped. Something in the boy's eyes—a faraway, intense look—drew her in. She studied his picture. His name was Carl, and he was from a small town in Pennsylvania. She looked at the picture next to his: that boy was a standard-issue matinee idol, but she had passed right over him. Carl was handsome, too; even in a photo not much larger than a postage stamp, she was drawn to his smooth face and his thick brown hair, neatly parted on one side and a little windswept on the other in a way that reminded her of the Kennedys. But it was those eyes, looking straight at her yet keeping their distance, that stayed with Merryl. She called to her roommate, pointed at Carl, and said, "I'm going to marry him." They laughed, and then they laughed again because her roommate realized Merryl wasn't kidding.

In the following weeks Merryl often saw Carl walking across campus in a green high school football jacket with cream-colored sleeves. She was thrilled to discover they took the same biology class (he was a premedical student), and she sneaked peeks at him during lectures. In the cafeteria his name came up often. By the end of his sophomore year Carl had accrued four years' worth of honors—president of the Sword and Shield Honor Society, president of the Biology Club, the biology prize, highest GPA in his class. At the most prominent frat on campus, Carl was known as the Golden Tongue because, although he was quiet, almost timid, he was a riveting speaker. To Merryl he seemed everything his picture promised. When friends teased her about having a crush on a man she had never met, Merryl laughed. But she kept her eyes peeled for that green jacket, and when she saw it coming across campus, her stomach knotted. Before she went to sleep she often found herself pulling out the pigbook and turning to the seventh photograph. It seemed inevitable that someday she and Carl would meet.

They did, sort of, during sophomore year when Merryl's lab partner invited her to the annual Sword and Shield dance. Merryl accepted, half because she knew Carl would be there. When they arrived, Carl, as club president, was greeting guests at the door. Next day Merryl swore to her roommate that when Carl shook her hand, he had given her a meaningful smile. Her roommate, reminding Merryl that she had always needed glasses, kidded that her perception had been blurred by myopia, not romance. But all evening as she danced with her lab partner, Merryl was aware of Carl and of his date, who Merryl felt wasn't nearly good-looking enough for him. For the evening's last dance the disc jockey put on "Light My Fire" by the Doors—and while they danced, people mouthed the words. As the song went on, Merryl found that she and her date were dancing in a corner next to Carl and his date, on the fringe of the vibrating crowd. As Merryl danced, sometimes it seemed to her that she was dancing with Carl and then sometimes with her date and then again with Carl, and she was exhilarated, and sometimes she knew Carl was watching her and it seemed he knew she knew he was watching, and yet he kept watching, and though the song lasted only six minutes and fifty seconds, to Merryl it seemed to go on forever.

Merryl spent her junior year in London, studying English literature. Carl studied political science in Sweden. When Merryl returned to Tufts, she decided to write an article for the school newspaper about students who had lived abroad. One day in the cafeteria, with five of her girlfriends watching and praying, Merryl walked over to Carl and asked him for an interview. They agreed to meet Friday evening. Friday afternoon in front of her mirror, Merryl tried on every outfit she owned, finally settling on a gray wool dress that was prim yet flatteringly tight. That night they went to dinner and talked for hours. Carl was everything Merryl had imagined: intense, strong, and sensitive, with a gentle voice that inspired confidence. Merryl didn't bother taking notes—she never even wrote the article—they just talked and talked. Afterward, she asked Carl back to her dorm. When they arrived, she made him wait on the stairs. She ran to her room, spent fifteen minutes stuffing everything under the bed—she had never expected him to come back and had left the place a mess—then ran back downstairs and invited him up. They spent the night together, and the following morning they took a bus down to her family's summer house on Cape Cod, broke in through the bathroom window, and spent the weekend huddled in her parents' double bed. Merryl told Carl about her crush. He was surprised. He didn't remember her from the Sword and Shield dance, and he was sure he hadn't given her a meaningful smile. But now he did, and the next day, on the bus back to Boston, he asked her to move in with him.

Merryl threw herself into the relationship and was happily overwhelmed. Although Carl was shy and retiring by nature, his intellectual curiosity was fierce, and he cared passionately about certain things; he had dropped his premed program, in fact, to devote more attention to political activism. Merryl, warm and gregarious, had always felt a little frivolous, and Carl's intensity lent her a focus she had not yet found. Carl was the teacher and Merryl was his willing student. This imbalance kept their relationship somewhat tilted, and Merryl was often fearful that Carl would leave her. A year after their graduation, at Carl's insistence, they did break up and were apart for two years. But they got back together at the age of twenty-five, and two years later they were married at Merryl's parents' house on Cape Cod. The bride and groom recited vows they had written in secret. Standing in a gazebo built for the wedding, Merryl expressed her belief that "our lives together will be infinitely richer than our lives apart." Carl's voice broke as he promised, "I will be as open and honest with my emotions as I can possibly be."

They set up married life in a cozy carriage house in Evanston, Illinois, a short commute to the University of Chicago, where Carl was a graduate student in developmental psychology. Merryl embarked on a seven-month job search that landed her an entry-level editorial position at Rand McNally. Carl was immersed in his studies but managed to read widely, tend an indoor garden, and bake bread. It was a happy time. Merryl felt secure in Carl's love, and Carl, who had entered therapy, seemed at peace with himself. One Christmas he surprised her with a pillow he had stitched with a favorite scene: Merryl sitting at a picnic table in their backyard, looking up from her writing in delight as Carl serves her iced tea from a tray. Carl had labored over the pillow for months when Merryl was at work, carefully noting where the markers were on the sewing machine, stitching for hours, then restoring the markers to their original position before she came home.

Gradually, however, Carl's frustration with his work began to show. The University of Chicago had not been his first choice. It didn't offer clinical psychology, only developmental psychology, which led to an academic career. But because the academic market was so tight, the only route assuring an eventual job in psychology was the clinical one. Carl felt cornered. Furthermore, the Chicago program emphasized adult and geriatric psychology; the sole faculty member who specialized in child psychology was two years younger than Carl, and he didn't feel she was the mentor he needed. In any case Carl was a perfectionist who hated to ask for help, and rather than admit uncertainty, he preferred to wait until a piece of work was flawless before turning it in. Carl was especially demanding about his dissertation, an analysis of toddlers' cognitive responses. Carl loved children, and he spent five hours a day on his hands and knees performing puppet shows for two-year-olds, taping their reactions, then recording the results in the dozens of spiral notebooks that lined his study. He made the puppets himself from dolls, proudly showing Merryl each painstaking creation: an elephant, a pilot, a truck. But the project seemed to take forever; there was always another paper to read, another reaction to research, another departmental requirement to fulfill. Friends began to joke about whether he would ever finish. At night Merryl would watch him work at his desk. Though Carl was doggedly trying to live up to his marriage vow and be more open with his feelings, Merryl could sense the tension building inside him, and when she probed, it would often turn out that something had been irking him for days.

Meanwhile, after six years of graduate school, Carl was anxious to start earning money. But the résumés he sent out drew no response. He felt inadequate when he compared his stalled career to the smooth successes of the people around him. His brother had landed a job in a psychology lab at Harvard; his sister was winning awards at Harvard Medical School; Merryl was being given increasing responsibility at Rand McNally. Nevertheless, Merryl was prepared to move when Carl found work; she had given him a list of twenty-five states she'd live in. She preferred New England but would live almost anywhere east of the Mississippi. Texas and the Far West were out. Carl applied to schools in those twenty-five states, but he received no offers. As his dissertation dragged on, he typed and retyped his résumé, changing only the date he expected his Ph.D. to be completed. The time was postponed so often that eventually he just used Wite-Out to change the date.

Eventually, they moved back to Boston. Merryl had found work as an editor at Houghton Mifflin, and Carl had been promised a job at a think tank. But Carl's position didn't come through, and though he seemed to make the best of it, the next two years held a series of progressively more galling disappointments. The job search became numbing. Carl followed up every lead, every newspaper ad, every cocktail party conversation, but the only positions available, it seemed, were at junior colleges for sums so low that people apologized as they offered them. Merryl, who was delighted with her work, watched Carl grow ever more depressed. But she still had faith in him. She *knew* he would get a job, she told him, and someday he would teach in a university. So what if it happened at forty instead of thirty? For Carl's thirty-second birthday Merryl had his portrait painted. Important people had their portraits painted, she reasoned, and she wanted to let Carl know that he was an important person. Carl was pleased with the idea of the gift but was anxious about having an artist capture a time of his life when he felt so fragile. In the portrait, Carl, in his green suit, looks young and terribly handsome. Whenever Merryl passed through the living room where it hung, she found herself looking up at him and marveling at how well the artist had captured that faraway look in his eyes.

Merryl's faith in Carl was so absolute that she was stunned when one January morning she was on her way out the door to work and Carl, lying in bed, said, "If I have to go through another job search like this, I'll kill myself." Unnerved, Merryl said, "Well, I don't want to come in this house and find you hanging." Carl's statement was so out of character that she put it from her mind. In any case, a month later Carl got a job. Merryl baked him a cake in celebration.

Carl was the junior member of a three-person team studying the effect of a new drug on learning disabilities in children. He did the paperwork and ferried the youngsters to and from the hospital where a clinical psychologist ran the experiments. But it was a job, and though it paid poorly, Carl drew a salary for the first time in years. His confidence was renewed. At night he worked on his dissertation; his proposal, two years in the writing, had been accepted, and the finish line was in sight. Meanwhile, he and Merryl talked about having children of their own. They filled their bedroom shelves with books on pregnancy and parenting and discussed buying a house. Although they tried for six months, Merryl did not get pregnant.

One night in late October, Merryl and Carl were filling each other in on their workdays. Merryl had chaired an important meeting and was feeling proud. Carl had always helped celebrate her triumphs, but Merryl sensed her success was making Carl's own dreams seem further from him. Later, when they were preparing for bed, Carl suddenly went into a tense, agitated tirade; he was worthless, he said. He hated his job and he hated himself. It disgusted him to be ferrying vials for someone whose job he would have had if only he'd stayed premed in college. As Merryl watched, horrified, he repeatedly punched himself in the temple with his fist. When Carl calmed down, Merryl tried to persuade him to get help from a therapist. Carl refused, saying he didn't want anyone to see him like this.

Although there were no more violent outbursts, things got steadily worse. Carl's job was due to end in June, and he had to start looking all over again. He had several promising interviews, only to be told later that he was overqualified or that the position had been eliminated. In the middle of May, Carl's brother called to say that he had just accepted a good position in the research department of a large corporation. Carl congratulated him but within half an hour of hanging up he was in a panic of self-loathing, muttering, "I'm worthless, I'm worthless," over and over. His face was drained of color, and his skin looked drawn and taut. Merryl was terrified; she hardly recognized him. This time when she insisted he get help, Carl agreed. Next day, Carl met with a psychiatrist, who said he couldn't take on new patients until the end of the summer, but if Carl was ever in crisis, he would fit him in.

Merryl never knew what kind of mood to expect when she came home from work. Night after night she and Carl lingered at the table, dishes undone, trying to unravel what was happening. Carl ruthlessly criticized decisions he had made over the years. Merryl had had no idea how deeply Carl's self-hatred ran. She told him that she still felt he was the greatest. As far as this job search was concerned, she said, he was a square peg where there were only round holes. But someday there would be a square hole. Carl seemed to take heart. One evening he got a call from Temple University. He had been recommended for a good job. "It's finally working," said Carl, hugging Merryl. "It's all going to pay off." On Merryl's thirty-third birthday, Carl flew to Philadelphia for his interview at Temple. He left a card for Merryl on the dining room table. To Merryl the printed words seemed absolutely perfect:

> *Everyone needs someone*
> *to understand and care*
> *Someone to depend on*
> *and count on to be there . . .*
> *Everyone needs someone*
> *to make a dream come true*
> *And I'm so glad my someone*
> *is someone special—you!*

Underneath the ornately scripted "Happy Birthday," Carl had written, "Dearest Merryl, You've been so supportive and so tender to me. I'll always love you for it. Happy Birthday! I'll hurry home to help celebrate it. Love, Your Carl."

And Carl seemed buoyed. He had an interview at Manhattanville College the following week, there was a possible job at a Boston VA hospital, and he was one of the top two candidates for the position at Temple. The chances of his getting the kind of position he wanted seemed better than they'd ever been.

Then one day in early June, Carl announced that a problem in his dissertation was more serious than he had thought. He believed he had asked the children a question in which the pronouns had not been clarified. If this was true, he said, the research was contaminated. Merryl assured him it didn't sound as drastic as he thought, and Carl seemed soothed. But over the following week his doubts escalated, and on June 10 he told her he was certain his dissertation was ruined. Merryl reasoned with him: even if one question was flawed, he could still salvage most of the project. She persuaded him to call his dissertation adviser in Chicago, who told him it didn't sound like a major problem. But Carl spent every spare moment in his study, chair pulled tight against the desk, flipping through his vast files.

On Sunday, June 13, Merryl woke to find Carl in a white-faced panic. "My life is over," he kept saying in a thin voice, staring straight ahead. "My life is over." Merryl reached for him, but he shrugged her off, saying, "Don't touch me—the pain is too great." All day Merryl sat with him, coaxing, cajoling, reasoning. She reminded him of his triumphs at Tufts: the biology prize, Sword and Shield, the highest GPA. Carl snorted; he wasn't smart, he said—if he'd been smart, he would have stayed premed, but he hadn't because he was a loser, he was worthless. Merryl reminded him of all the people who'd looked up to him, but Carl dismissed her. He'd always been the manager, not the player, always the odd man out, the second-class citizen, the chump ferrying vials for the people *he* should be. No matter how she tried, Merryl couldn't reach him—it was like attempting to penetrate a plastic shield—and even if she made some headway, he'd soon fade further into his own world. "How do people do it?" he said at one point. "How do they kill themselves?" He shook his head. "Maybe it's a good sign that I'm talking about it. Isn't it true that when people talk about suicide, they don't do it?" Merryl told him she didn't think that was true.

On Monday night when Carl was no better, Merryl pleaded with him to let her call the psychiatrist. Carl said no, and Merryl couldn't bear the thought of going against his will, of treating him like a child. At 11 p.m. she finally coaxed Carl into letting her call. The therapist wasn't home; Merryl left her name with his answering service. By the time the psychiatrist called back the next day, Carl seemed stronger. Merryl, who had stayed home from work to be with him, heard him tell the doctor that he was okay, and they made an appointment for Thursday. But Merryl couldn't get the previous day out of her mind. For a moment she wanted to grab the phone and tell the psychiatrist he didn't understand how serious this was. But she didn't; it wasn't right, she thought, and Carl did sound better. That afternoon he took a long nap. Merryl looked in on him from time to time and was relieved to see him sleeping peacefully. It was going to be okay. The worst had passed.

But Carl was up and down all week. One moment he'd be in his white-faced panic, calling himself "worthless." He wasn't eating right; he would push away his plate halfway through the meal. Sometimes he would get up suddenly and go for long walks. Merryl, worried, would ask to go along, but he always said no. One night she asked him whether he was going to come back, and a look flickered over his face as if she'd recognized his deepest fear, but then it disappeared and he said of course he was coming back. Carl spoke often of death. Once, he came in from a walk and said he'd seen a hearse going by and imagined he was in it. Another time, when Merryl killed an ant, he grimaced and said he felt that life was squashing him, like that ant. Merryl told him that if he ever killed himself, he'd be killing her, too. Once, in desperation, she suggested they simply walk off into the woods together. "Do you really mean it?" Carl said. Then he reflected on her suggestion and seemed disappointed. "People can live for forty days in the woods without food." Merryl talked to him about hospitalization, and he said no, it would gall him that the people taking care of him would be the doctors he should have been. At times Carl seemed like a stranger to Merryl—he had night sweats and even smelled different to her. At other times she'd walk into the house and the Carl she knew was cooking dinner, commenting on some event in the outside world. Merryl fought to keep in touch with that Carl, but he always ebbed. Merryl began to have a recurring dream: She was standing on a dock while a vast steamship was pulling away in a dense fog, leaving her alone. It seemed as if Carl was on the ship. The night was too hazy for her to be certain. But in the dream and after she woke, Merryl felt utterly abandoned.

On Thursday, Merryl picked up her parents for dinner. Merryl's mother, who had cancer, had just learned that it had spread. As Merryl drove, the whole world seemed on edge; the traffic loomed dangerously, and shapes that seemed to be people were shadows. She nearly hit a bicyclist, and the rest of the way home she squeezed the wheel tightly. When they walked into the house, Carl was in the kitchen making salad. He looked up, and Merryl could see he was in that white state, but it was concealed by a polite mask because her parents were there. When Merryl and Carl had a moment alone, she asked him if he was all right. As he stirred the salad dressing, he looked up at her slowly and, in that thin voice that chilled her to the bone, said, "No." Her mother came into the room, and Carl went back to his stirring.

After dinner Carl said he was going for a walk. Merryl hurried into the kitchen after him and asked if he was sure he was okay. He was sure, he said. He just had to get out. After he left, Merryl's parents asked her what was wrong, and she told them Carl had been under a lot of strain lately. She didn't go into details—she felt it was her and Carl's business. They talked about her mother's illness, and Merryl felt pinned between the two problems. She felt guilty she hadn't had time to comfort her mother; at the same time she was anxious to find out what had happened at Carl's appointment with his therapist that day. Merryl herself had spoken with her gynecologist that morning about her difficulties getting pregnant, and with her own therapist that afternoon all she had talked about was Carl's depression. Yet life spun crazily through these tragedies—her mother, ever practical, pruning the philodendron that Carl, the gardener in the house, had neglected for months; her father noticing that the rug had been cleaned. When Carl came back after half an hour, he went straight into his study and shut the door.

After her parents left, Merryl asked Carl about his appointment with the therapist. Had he talked to the therapist about suicide? Yes, said Carl, he had. But he had said he didn't have the courage to do it, and the doctor had replied that he wasn't worried. Merryl felt a breeze of relief. But it was short-lived. That night Carl talked wildly. He spoke of giving up the dissertation; he was sure it would be exposed as a failure. He had to finish it, he said, but he couldn't. "If I give up the dissertation, I'm giving up my life." His life was much more than the dissertation, Merryl assured him. Carl looked up from his work and said, "What would happen if I didn't finish it? What would you do?" Merryl told him she would still love him, that she would never leave him. Carl managed a tight smile and for a moment seemed calmed, but then he was back inside himself, going back and forth about whether he could finish it. "This is the living out of my worst nightmare," he said. "I always knew I'd be a failure, and now I am." Eight or ten times he got up from his chair to pace, then sat back down, pulling his chair right up to the desk, his face scouring the quilt of papers; then he would push his chair back abruptly, wood screeching on wood, and pace once more. Once he stared at Merryl and said, "You know, today I looked at that portrait of me that you say has such sensitive eyes." Merryl broke in and said, "They *are,* Carl." Carl leaped up, went into the living room, came back, and said, "They're not the eyes of a sensitive person, they're the eyes of a weak person." He stared at her. "I'm frightened of life."

When Merryl woke on Friday morning, Carl was already at his desk poring over his dissertation. Merryl went off to work carrying a pamphlet on infertility. At noon Carl called to say that he had been offered the VA job. Merryl was flooded with relief. He and Merryl talked about his sudden change of luck, and Carl said that he would pick her up at work at six. When they said good-bye, Merryl's last word was "Congratulations!"

That afternoon Merryl felt as if she and Carl had been pulled back from a precipice. She was able to free her mind from worry for the first time in weeks. She could also devote some thought to the upcoming weekend. Carl's brother's son had been born the week before. The baby had been named Carl, and the christening was to be that Sunday. Afterward Merryl and Carl were going to host a small party. Merryl knew Carl wasn't looking forward to it, but maybe now that he had a job offer, he would be less edgy. A woman at work had baked a cake in the shape of baby blocks, with the name *Carl* written across the top. The cake sat on Merryl's desk that evening as she waited for Carl to arrive.

At six o'clock there was no sign of Carl. At six-fifteen Merryl called home. No answer. Maybe he was on his way. She waited ten minutes and called again. No answer. She called their landlord, who said his son had seen Carl leave at six. Carl had seemed agitated. By seven Merryl was frantic. At seven-twenty she left a note on her desk: "Where are you, Carl? What happened?" With the cake melting in her arms she went outside and hailed a cab.

When she got home, she left the cake on the porch and ran inside. The first thing she noticed was a clothes hanger on their bed. She ran to the closet. One of Carl's suits was missing. For a moment she hoped maybe Carl was going to surprise her with a dress-up dinner out because he'd gotten the job. But then she saw that a second suit was missing, and her stomach went sour. She ran into the bathroom; his toothbrush was gone. She ran to the front closet; the suit-cases were gone. Carl was gone; something had gone bad. Merryl fell sobbing to the floor.

She called her parents. They called her brother, who hurried over. She called Carl's therapist, and when Merryl told him Carl had packed suitcases, he said that didn't sound like a man who was going to kill himself. Merryl and her brother explored every possibility. Maybe he was in a hotel in Boston mulling things over, said Merryl. Maybe he was in his car, parked somewhere in confusion, said her brother; maybe he was even on some nearby street. Merryl half-hoped he'd gone to Atlanta or to the sun belt, places he'd talked about where there might be jobs. She and her brother got out maps and traced possible routes to possible destinations. She waited for the phone to ring, and she imagined Carl's familiar voice saying he was in Atlanta, he'd been looking for work, but he was on his way home. Or maybe she'd get a letter with a Texas postmark telling her he'd gotten a job in Dallas. That night while her brother slept on a mattress in Carl's study, Merryl sat up on her bed with the light on. Every five or ten minutes she'd hear a scratch or a whirr and run to the back door, thinking it might be Carl. But it was always a branch creaking or the wind blowing or a car driving down another street. She pressed herself against the door so hard that months later marks from her forehead and fingers lingered on the glass.

When the sun came up, the fullness of the fact hit her: It was Saturday morning and Carl wasn't there. Merryl ran to the mirror and screamed, "Where are you? Where are you?"

At noon Merryl called the police to report that Carl was missing. When a patrolman arrived, he told her that everything was going to be okay, that it happened all the time, that her husband was probably sitting in the car somewhere, just thinking things through. But as he stood in her living room filling out a missing persons report, and she told him Carl's height, weight, and date of birth, Merryl realized that the world she had tried to contain was yawning wide.

On Saturday night Carl's parents arrived from New Hampshire. They had been packing to drive down for their grandson Carl's christening when Merryl had called. They drove to Merryl and Carl's apartment instead. Saturday night became Sunday, and still no word. Merryl and her in-laws scoured the house for notes but found no hints. Carl had left everything neat. He'd taken out the garbage. He'd opened the windows to let in the breeze.

At nine on Sunday night there was a knock on the door. Merryl sprang up to open it. A policeman wearing sunglasses handed her a slip of paper with a number on it and said, "Somebody's been trying to reach you all day." Merryl's mother-in-law told him they'd been in the house all day. "I don't know," said the policeman. "All I know is just call this number." He turned and left.

Merryl went into the kitchen and dialed the number, which had a New York area code. It rang once. A deep, heavy voice answered, "Medical." In the back of her mind Merryl knew from some TV show that this meant "medical examiner," but still hoping she said, "Is this a hospital?" There was a pause and the voice said, "Lady, this is the morgue."

Merryl dropped the phone and screamed. She ran through the kitchen, out of the house, and leaped off the back porch to the gravel driveway, a six-foot drop. She hurled herself repeatedly onto the space in the driveway where Carl's car should have been. Then she crawled under her landlord's car and lay there screaming, wedged between the carburetor and the gravel.

Merryl could see her mother-in-law's face trying to tell her something as she knelt by the car. She could see legs and feet multiplying. She could hear her name occasionally surface from the blur of voices. And still she screamed. Her head felt as if it were on fire. Her face, her arms, and her legs were scratched and bloody. Her shirt was torn. She'd lost her glasses. She felt she couldn't be in a normal space; the world suddenly seemed so unnatural and misshapen and wrong and dangerous that the only place she could be comfortable was between the car and the gravel. If she had had her way, she would have stayed there forever, screaming.

# II

# THE MARK OF CAIN

IN AN EIGHTEENTH-CENTURY French engraving called *The Desecration of the Corpse,* the naked body of a young man is dragged through the streets of Paris by a spirited white horse. He lies facedown on a wooden sledge, his ankles roped together, his arms outstretched behind him, his fingers scraping the cobblestones. A crowd surrounds the body. One woman shrinks from the scene in horror, covering her face with her hand. A curly-haired child on hands and knees watches in openmouthed terror. A bearded man, his fingers in his mouth, cringes in disbelief, and a dog gingerly sniffs the corpse. Even the horse seems to rear back in shock at his load, but a hand at his bridle pulls him on.

The young man has been "convicted" of suicide. We do not know why he took his life, but we know some of the consequences of his act. After he is dragged by his heels through the streets of the city, he will be hanged head down in the public square as an example to all who might contemplate such a crime. His body will be thrown into the common sewer or tossed in the town dump. If he had been a nobleman, he will be declared a commoner. His forests will be razed, his castle demolished, his goods and property forfeited to the king.

In the foreground of the engraving there is a young woman. She is the only member of the crowd who moves toward the body rather than recoiling from it. The bearded man has put his hand on her back as if to draw her away, and a part of her seems to respond to his touch. But her sorrow is stronger than her dread, and her left leg bends toward the sledge as if she were about to kneel. She is the dead man's wife. Behind her, on a balcony overlooking the street, two small children reach for their father. We do not know what will become of this woman and her children. They own nothing but the clothes they wear. And although they cannot afford to leave the city, they cannot afford to stay because they would forever be shamed by the suicide in their family. Most likely the woman will wander until she finds a town where news of the suicide has not spread, where she and her children may live cautiously, telling people her husband died of a disease, praying no one will ever discover her secret.

Like Merryl Maleska two hundred years later, the woman in the engraving is a survivor of suicide. Although survivors of other kinds of death can depend on the rituals civilization has developed to support them in their grief, for thousands of years survivors of suicide have suffered alone and in silence. Today, although suicides are no longer dragged through the streets and their property is no longer confiscated, survivors still face a legacy of antisuicide attitudes that have evolved over centuries.

---

In ancient Greece a stigma was a mark burned into the skin to identify a slave or criminal. Since then the definition of *stigma* has expanded to mean a mark of shame or disgrace whether visible or not. No subject has been more stained by stigma than suicide. In various centuries in various countries in Europe, Asia, and Africa, the corpse of a suicide might by law or custom be "decapitated . . . to render it harmless," "burned outside the city, its hand cut off and buried separately," "hastily removed and dumped outside tribal territories," "burned so it cannot walk among and wreak vengeance upon the living," "beaten with chains," "thrown out into the fields to be devoured by wild beasts," "buried in a corner of the forest far from the graves of his brethren," "lowered by pulleys from the window, and the window frame subsequently burned," "put in a barrel and floated down the Moselle," "buried at a crossroads by night with a stake driven through the heart," or "buried under a mountain whose whole weight shall . . . press down upon his restive soul." Though such special treatment was intended to prevent the suicide's ghost from wandering, one can easily imagine its effect on survivors.

When primitive taboos were adopted into organized religion and the attitudes of the Church buttressed by civil law, survivors were more directly penalized. In effect they were treated as an accessory to what was now a crime. In England the suicide's goods were forfeited to his feudal lord. (It was sometimes possible for an heir to buy back a suicide's confiscated goods. In 1289, it is recorded, the widow of one Aubrey of Wystelesburg redeemed her husband's property for three hundred pounds.) In France, according to a law of 1270, not only were the suicide's goods confiscated, but his widow was forced to surrender her possessions. In some areas the suicide's family paid a fine to the victim's in-laws for the shame the suicide had brought upon them. Such penalties were intended as a crude sort of suicide prevention in which survivors became innocent hostages. "What punishment can human laws inflict on one who has withdrawn himself from their reach?" asked the eighteenth-century jurist Sir William Blackstone in his *Commentaries on the Laws of England.* "They can only act upon what he has left behind him, his reputation and fortune; on the former by an ignominious burial in the highway, with a stake driven through his body; in the latter by a forfeiture of all his goods and chattels to the king, hoping that his care for either his own reputation or the welfare of his family would be some motive to restrain him from so desperate and wicked an act."

To evade these penalties, survivors learned to disguise suicides by destroying notes, hiding weapons, and securing premature burials. To soften the blow of forefeiture they smuggled valuables out of the house. In France, to counter this "abuse" of the law, a royal edict of 1712 empowered judges to investigate all cases in which the cause of death was doubtful, calling in medical evidence when necessary—an early version of the "psychological autopsy" developed by the Los Angeles Suicide Prevention Center more than two centuries later. In 1736 a second edict ordered that in cases of doubtful death no burial was permitted without license from the authorities. Since the Crown was the beneficiary of a suicide's fortune—and the prosecutor was entitled to a percentage of the take—questionable cases tended to be declared suicides.

In England, where suicides were tried posthumously in Coroner's Court, the penalty was waived if it was ruled that the dead man had been insane. Juries had to decide whether a self-killer was an innocent madman or a sinful criminal. While the Crown usually argued that the deceased had formulated a deliberate suicide plan, survivors tried to prove either that the death had been an accident or that their loved one was a lunatic. In the case of Lancelot Johnson, a London merchant whose body was fished from the Thames in the early seventeenth century, the Crown claimed the defendant had been "observed to walk in a very sad, deep, melancholy and discontented manner along the river's side, there where he had no other occasion to be, but only to execute his said ungodly resolution" and that a note "containing the reasons and causes of his discontentment and purpose to destroy himself" had been disposed of by his wife. The widow Johnson, however, argued that her husband's death must have been an accident because he was too pious to have committed suicide: "He lived in good repute and esteem amongst his neighbours and acquaintances and also carried himself in an exceeding honest, upright, godly fashion." The jury's verdict is not known.

During the eighteenth century many of the laws punishing suicide were erased, but the stigma they had helped create for survivors remained. In 1761, Marc-Antoine Calas, a French law student, hanged himself in his father's shop in Toulouse. When his parents discovered his body, they removed the rope from his neck and hid it in an attempt to conceal the cause of death. Their subterfuge backfired: A wave of religious fanaticism was sweeping the town, and when the boy's death became known, his father, a devout Protestant, was accused of murdering his son to prevent him from reverting to Catholicism. Found guilty and condemned to be broken on the wheel, the old man died protesting his innocence. The matter would have ended but for Voltaire, who took up Jean Calas's cause. Four years later the decision was reversed. In the retrial it was learned that the parents had concealed the true cause of death because they'd dreaded the scandal that news of the suicide would provoke.

The self-murderer's legacy of shame was often invoked by preachers in their attempts to seduce the would-be suicide from the path of damnation. "He plants a dagger not merely in his own breast, but in that of his dearest, his tenderest connexions," observed minister G. Gregory at St. Botolph's Bishopsgate in London in 1797. "He wantonly sports with the pangs of sensibility, and covers with the blush of shame the cheeks of innocence. With a degree of ingratitude which excites our abhorrence, he clouds with sorrow the future existence of those by whom he was most tenderly beloved; and (as is alleged by some concerning the first of murderers) he affixes a mark of ignominy on his unfortunate descendants." Eight years later, in New York City, Presbyterian pastor Samuel Miller was even more blunt: "Stay then, guilty man! Stay thy murderous hand! Extinguish not the happiness and the hopes of a family, it may be, of many families! Forbear, O forbear to inflict wounds which no time can heal, and which may tempt survivors to wish that thou hadst never been born!"

A more temperate argument was offered by Richard Hey, an Oxford fellow, whose 1783 dissertation on suicide describes with surpassing empathy the singular effect of a suicide on a survivor:

> The *Sorrow* which arises upon the Loss of a Friend, is heightened to the most pungent distress, if he has perished by his own hand. The most calm and gentle death, attended with every alleviation to the dying person, and even to his friends, is yet to these usually no small shock. Minds of the firmest contexture, and retained in the best discipline, if not void of common sensibility, cannot at once reconcile themselves to the change. Add but the circumstance of *Violence,* either accidental or by the lawless attack of the assassin; and the shock is redoubled upon the survivors: even the robust constitution may long experience its effects; weaker and more delicate frames are sometimes thrown into a state of disorder from which they never perfectly recover. But, if the violence proceed from the hand of him who falls by it, a certain amazement is superadded to the more common sensations: and while sorrow, commiseration, apprehension, abhorrence, contend for possession of the mind, they spread devastation over the scene of their mutual conflict.

In the nineteenth century, as suicide began to be interpreted as an illness rather than as a sin and a crime, there was a change in the nature of its stigma. While permitted to bury their dead in consecrated ground and to retain their property and possessions, survivors were now the targets of all the superstition and prejudice associated with insanity. Most physicians maintained that insanity was hereditary, and that suicide was the most hereditary form of insanity. The English physician Forbes Winslow wrote in 1840:

> With reference to suicide, there is no fact that has been more clearly established than that of its hereditary character. . . . It is not necessary that the disposition to suicide should manifest itself in every generation; it often passes over one, and appears in the next, like insanity unattended with this propensity. But if the members of the family so predisposed are carefully examined, it will be found that the various shades and gradations of the malady will be easily perceptible. Some are distinguished for their flightiness of manner, others for their strange eccentricity, likings and dislikings, irregularity of their passions, capricious and excitable temperament, hypochondriasis and melancholia. These are often but the minute shades and variations of an hereditary disposition to suicidal madness.

Viewing them as potential suicides themselves, the medical profession began to take a keen interest in survivors. Winslow was one of many medical scholars who traced "singular" cases of suicidal reverberations within families in which relatives and descendants killed themselves, sometimes in the same place, sometimes by the same method, sometimes on the anniversary of a previous family suicide. In 1901, at the Annual Meeting of the Medico-Psychological Association in Cork, Ireland, J. M. S. Wood and A. R. Urquhart presented a family tree that in four generations had spawned six suicides, four people with suicidal tendencies, and six with "obvious" insanity. Several years later a certain George P. Mudge constructed a Mendelian pedigree for two English families, evidently attempting to demonstrate that suicides could be bred like prize-winning peonies. "There exists a tradition in the village in which they live that death by means of self-shooting belonged primarily to the B family, and death by self-drowning to the A family," he wrote in the *Mendel Journal*. "The two families have intermarried, and among their descendants three forms of suicide are manifested, namely, the two original forms, by shooting and drowning, and a new form, by taking poison."

The message to survivors was unmistakable: they were doomed to suicide themselves—or at the least to insanity, alcoholism, or feeblemindedness. It is little wonder that some survivors began to regard suicide as an inevitable family fate. "Many are induced to think of suicide from the circumstance of their being conscious that they labour under an hereditary disposition to insanity," wrote Dr. Winslow. ". . . A gentleman, in full possession of his reasoning faculties, and a man of considerable powers of intellect, said to us one day, in a conversation we had with him on the subject of suicide, 'You may probably smile when I tell you that, happy and contented as I appear to be in my mind at this moment, I feel assured I shall fall by my own hands.' Upon our asking him why he thought so, he replied, that a relation of his had killed himself some years previously, and that he laboured under an hereditary predisposition which nothing would subdue."

These hereditary "theories" were especially terrifying for survivors when they intersected with the rise of the eugenics movement at the turn of the century. In his 1893 book, *Suicide and Insanity,* Samuel Strahan presented eleven family trees—the majority traced from his medical practice—as proof that suicides inevitably spawn imbeciles, murderers, epileptics, drunkards, lunatics, and more suicides. "The suicide by his last act places the bar sinister upon the escutcheon of his family," wrote Strahan, "and the man or woman who marries into such a family runs a terrible risk. Just as the appearance of idiocy, epilepsy, or insanity in a family shows that the stock is deteriorating, so suicide points to the fact that the family has wandered from the path of health." Strahan offered his findings to the public "in the hope that people may be induced to use intelligently, in the propagation of the human race some of the knowledge, care, and forethought so successfully exercised in the breeding of the lower animals."

Although possible genetic contributions are still being explored, the notion that suicide itself is heritable had been discredited by the 1950s. But the popular view of suicide as a social disgrace, fanned by the Victorian emphasis on family respectability, brought a new kind of stigma. A passage from James Joyce's *Ulysses* in which Leopold Bloom and two friends are en route to a funeral is characteristic:

> "But the worst of all," Mr. Power said, "is the man who takes his own life."
>
> Martin Cunningham drew out his watch briskly, coughed and put it back.
>
> "The greatest disgrace to have in the family," Mr. Power added.
>
> "Temporary insanity, of course," Martin Cunningham said decisively. "We must take a charitable view of it."

Bloom is silent; Cunningham, aware that Bloom's father committed suicide, discreetly attempts to change the subject. But Mr. Power's remarks reflect the modern notion that suicide was no longer primarily a personal failure but a family failure. A suicide was a black mark that polluted a family's marriage stock and lowered property values. The word itself, with its evil-sounding sibilance, was poisonous—a taunt hurled by neighborhood children, a secret whispered by their parents. Suicide became an explanation for a widow's quirks, for a young man's "madness," for a haunted house. "Nothing lowered the prestige of a family as much as the 'talk' that a suicide was involved," wrote Henry Romilly Fedden in *Suicide*. "It broke the facade presented to the world; the suicide therefore was primarily culpable in relation to his family. He indeed created a *disgrace in the family*, for suicide, instead of chiefly bringing on a soul the wrath of God and the law, now brought to the ears of the family the twitter of malicious tongues." There was a kernel of truth in Cyril Connolly's sardonic observation that some people are afraid to commit suicide for fear of what the neighbors will say.

Whereas in the eighteenth century survivors had camouflaged the cause of death primarily to avoid losing money or property, now they dissembled to avoid losing face. Funerals were hasty and hushed up; servants were discharged "because they knew"; friends and relatives were avoided; and suicides were transformed in family myths into hunting accidents and heart attacks. Children were told the truth years later if they were told at all. Families entered unspoken agreements to avoid mentioning the name of the departed. Suicide was a family secret to be kept at all costs, a skeleton in the closet. Neighbors sifted evidence and assigned blame; phrases like "he drove her to it" echoed in gossip. Shunned by neighbors, families moved out of the house, out of the neighborhood, out of the state, where people "wouldn't know" and they could start over. But just as in primitive cultures the suicide's wandering ghost was believed to haunt the living, so, too, did memories of the suicide pursue twentieth-century survivors. Whether to unhappiness, madness, or suicide, the survivor felt in some way doomed. Reaching back to the Old Testament to describe his feelings of being stigmatized, one man referred to his father's suicide by drowning as the time when "he placed the mark of Cain upon me."

And so survivors went underground, keeping their grief, guilt, and anger locked inside. Even when interest in the subject of suicide and suicide prevention grew in midcentury, survivors were overlooked by the mental health profession. In the traditional psychiatric model, the case was closed when the patient died. The therapist—if the suicide had been in therapy—tended to focus on his own feelings of guilt and grief instead of reaching out to the surviving family. Most survivors were too ashamed to seek professional help themselves. Some survivors eventually developed severe disturbances that forced them into treatment; only after months of therapy did they reveal that there had been a family suicide buried in their past.

Interest in survivors emerged in roundabout ways. When the Los Angeles Suicide Prevention Center began to perform psychological autopsies in 1958, researchers found widespread resistance, suppression of evidence, and mental trauma among suicide survivors. They found something else as well. Although they had been apprehensive about approaching distraught relatives, they discovered that survivors had a great need to talk—about their grief, their guilt, their anger, and often their own suicidal feelings. It was usually the first time the survivors had been given an opportunity to discuss the suicide, and they frequently found the interviews therapeutic. "I believe that the person who commits suicide puts his psychological skeleton in the survivor's emotional closet," wrote LASPC cofounder Edwin Shneidman. "He sentences the survivor to deal with many negative feelings and, more, to become obsessed with thoughts regarding his own actual or possible role in having precipitated the suicidal act or having failed to abort it. It can be a heavy load." Shneidman urged that suicide prevention programs address the psychological needs of survivors by offering counseling and support he called "postvention."

Like the LASPC, other suicide prevention centers soon realized that survivors were a high-risk group in need of their services. A 1967 study of a St. Louis center showed that one in three callers had had a previous suicide in the family. If, as studies have shown, members of families in which there has been a suicide are eight times more likely to kill themselves, helping survivors clearly constituted effective suicide prevention. "Given the present stage of our knowledge about suicide," wrote Harvey Resnik, Shneidman's successor as director of the Center for Studies of Suicide Prevention, "proper postvention seems the most promising avenue toward reducing the large number of suicides that occur annually." For centuries survivors had been penalized in the name of suicide prevention; now they were counseled in the name of suicide prevention.

Gradually, research on suicide widened its focus to include those left behind. A bibliography of publications on suicide dating from 1897 to 1970 lists only fifteen articles relating to survivors; during the following twenty-five years more than five hundred books and articles on survivor issues were published. In *Survivors of Suicide,* the first book to explore the problems of survivors, published in 1972, psychologist Albert Cain categorized a range of reactions: reality distortion, tortured object-relations, overwhelming guilt, disturbed self-concept, impotent rage, identification with the suicide, depression and self-destructiveness, search for meaning, and incomplete mourning. Recent studies, however, suggest that survivors of suicide may be more similar to survivors of certain other forms of death than previously supposed. A 2003 conference summarizing survivor research concluded that suicide survivors were no more likely to suffer psychiatric disability than those bereaved by other forms of violent death—accidents or murder. They were, however, more likely to feel guilt, to experience social discomfort, and to struggle with trying to understand why it had happened. It also concluded that more research was needed: on the efficacy of various interventions, on suicide's impact on family functioning, and on survivors from different cultural, racial, or ethnic backgrounds, among other topics. "Historically, one of the most neglected areas of suicidology . . . has been the issue of the aftermath of suicide and suicidal behavior," wrote Indiana University psychologist John McIntosh, in a 2003 article summarizing the state of survivor research. ". . . Our knowledge of survivors in many ways remains only a few steps beyond the level of understanding that existed 30 years ago when Cain's seminal effort appeared."

In some ways, the research community is struggling to catch up with survivors themselves. Without waiting for mental health professionals to pinpoint their problems, survivors have been reaching out to each other, forming self-help groups, organizing conferences, catalyzing suicide prevention efforts, and writing articles and books about their experiences. In 1980, two hundred survivors from more than thirty states and Canada attended a National Survivors Conference in Iowa City. Today, survivors can choose from dozens of survivor seminars and panels on suicide and grief each year. Prevention centers and suicidologists now provide training to physicians, coroners, funeral directors, policemen, and the media on how to handle families after a suicide. In 1983 the LASPC was unable to persuade a celebrity survivor to speak at their twenty-fifth anniversary banquet; since then actress Mariette Hartley, whose father shot himself when she was twenty-two; actor Peter Fonda, whose mother cut her throat when he was ten; comedienne Joan Rivers, whose husband took an overdose; and singer Judy Collins, whose thirty-three-year-old son poisoned himself with carbon monoxide, have spoken out about their experiences.

Such openness has begun to diminish the isolation that centuries of stigma have encouraged. "When my brother killed himself, I knew *nothing* about suicide," says one woman. "For some reason I thought maybe this happened to three hundred people a year. I don't know where I got that figure, but it made me feel as if I were the only person it had ever happened to." Indeed, there are millions of survivors of suicide in this country. Even using the official figure of thirty thousand suicides annually, the ranks of survivors are swelled by some two hundred thousand a year—a figure that doesn't include extended family, friends, and therapists, all of whom may be devastated by a suicide. (It also leaves out family and friends of those who *attempt* suicide, an unresearched, infrequently addressed—and often devastated—subgroup of survivors.) Like the Japanese soldiers who emerged from their jungle hideouts to find that World War II had ended decades before, some survivors are finding they no longer have to hide. One thirty-two-year-old Minneapolis woman who was four years old when her mother shot herself began only recently to speak about the suicide: "For twenty-eight years my pain was like a rock I carried wherever I went," she says. "When I finally began to grieve, it was as if my tears dissolved that rock."

Over the past few decades, the shame surrounding suicide has been alleviated by the increasing awareness that depression is a disease. "To the tragic legion who are compelled to destroy themselves there should be no more reproof attached than to the victims of terminal cancer," wrote William Styron in *Darkness Visible*. And, by extension, the family and friends left behind by that tragic legion should be treated with the same openness and compassion extended to those whose loved ones died of cancer or were killed in a car accident. But while suicides are no longer buried beneath mountains to trap their restive souls, their survivors are still struggling under the weight of centuries of stigma. More than a hundred years after confiscation of property was abolished, many life insurance companies continue to deny benefits to families of people who complete suicide within two years after buying a policy. More than two hundred years after Jean Calas hid the noose that had squeezed the life out of his son, survivors still conceal notes, suppress evidence, and pressure coroners to rule the death an accident. Some have even submitted petitions signed by an entire neighborhood attesting to a dead man's sterling character as proof he could not have committed suicide. More than fourteen hundred years after the Council of Braga refused burial to self-killers, suicides are still technically denied burial rites by the Roman Catholic Church; priests employ the traditional insanity loophole to justify burial in consecrated ground.

Long after ministers ceased preaching about suicide's "mark of ignominy," many survivors still feel branded. "I used to drive down the street thinking I had a sign on my car that said MY SON KILLED HIMSELF," says Iris Bolton, an Atlanta counselor who travels the country to speak on survivor issues. "Another car would pass me and I would think, 'Now they know.'" The fact of the suicide can become an identity. "You're no longer yourself, you're the widow of the man who killed himself," says a woman whose husband took a fatal overdose. Although some of the stigma may be more imagined than real, research indicates that the families of suicides are often perceived negatively by others and are offered less support. One study compared the reactions of 119 adults to two newspaper accounts: one of a child's death by suicide and one of a child's death by illness. The child's parents were liked less and blamed more for the child's death when that death was by suicide. Several years after the suicide of her sixteen-year-old son, a woman says, "Losing my son was painful enough, but the whispers, feeling like a leper, being avoided, having people not look me in the eye or acting like nothing happened, never mentioning the death, changing the subject, people being afraid it's contagious, as if it may happen to them if they touch me or reach out to me—is almost worse."

Many survivors still feel they have something to hide. Twelve years after his brother's suicide one young man stubbornly insists his brother was murdered, although he offers no suspects and no evidence. His only reason is that *it can't be.* Other survivors selectively edit their revelations. "I tell everyone my husband died of a cerebral hemorrhage," says one woman. "What I don't say is that it was from a self-inflicted gunshot wound." It is all too easy for survivors to find people who will corroborate their sense of shame. In a memoir about the suicide of his son, journalist James Wechsler described how the police offered to suppress the circumstances of the death. "Even in the numbness of those hours we were astonished at the prevalence of the view that suicide was a dishonorable or at least disreputable matter, to be charitably covered up to protect Michael's good name and the sensibilities of his family."

Even the people closest to the survivor are often eager to pretend the suicide never happened. Families may shut down; friends may keep their distance. The night after they found their nineteen-year-old son's body hanging in their vacation house, one couple had dinner with their closest friends. They had accepted the invitation weeks before, and despite the shock of their son's death, they decided it might be comforting to be with the people who knew them best. When they arrived at their friends' home, their hosts said, "Hi, how are you, how have you been?" They took their coats, poured them cocktails, served them dinner, chatted about the weather, sports, and politics, served them dessert, got their coats for them, wished them good-night, and shut the door. The entire evening had passed without a single mention of the boy's death. The friends were afraid to bring it up; the survivors didn't bring it up because they were waiting for their friends to bring it up. Neither couple thought of anything but the suicide.

# III

# MERRYL:
# THE TORTURE CHAMBER

UNDERNEATH THE CAR Merryl Maleska continued to scream. Neighbors, thinking someone was being raped, called the police, and within minutes two squad cars, sirens wailing, pulled up to the house. Merryl could hear the gruff voices of the policemen as they approached the car. Assuming she was on drugs, they shouted that they would arrest her if she didn't calm down and tell them what was wrong. When Merryl's mother-in-law mumbled something in one policeman's ear, they softened their approach. Five minutes later Merryl crawled out.

Supported by her in-laws, Merryl staggered into the house. She couldn't stop writhing. She clawed at her shirt and ripped strands of hair from her scalp. She was dimly aware that this should hurt, but she felt no pain. She howled that she was going to kill herself. The police, whose presence seemed to Merryl to turn the living room blue, said they'd have to take her to the hospital. Merryl screamed that she'd wait three months and then kill herself when no one was watching. The police said they'd lock her in the hospital anyway. Merryl stopped screaming and stared at them stonily.

After the police left, Merryl continued to pace, numbly pulling and scratching at herself. She felt unable to move or speak in customary ways; she hunched over, squatted in corners, and twisted her limbs; she felt her body had been turned inside out. "The world was completely wrong now," she remembers. "How could I stand up and talk and be normal?" When Carl's brother and sister-in-law arrived, Merryl's sadness and anger focused on them. "I hated the sight of them instantly. I didn't want to see them. I had loved Laurie, but now I resented her. She represented everything I didn't have—the baby, the doctorate, the home, the husband." When they touched her, Merryl turned away. She knew she was being unfair, but she couldn't help it. Sometime after midnight they left, and Merryl was alone with Carl's parents.

Carl's parents were, like Carl, quiet, contained, and responsible. They sat on either side of Merryl on the couch and the three of them held one another, swaying and moaning, sometimes just sighing, lulling. Occasionally her in-laws moved about the room as if in a slow-motion dream. Once, Merryl saw them hug and heard her father-in-law murmur, "Our firstborn." She was flooded with the sudden understanding that Carl was their son as well as her husband. For the first time they were realizing that their son had been deeply depressed. They gently asked Merryl questions about Carl. He had kept so many of his painful feelings from them; until that night they had never known he'd been in therapy. At one point Carl's father turned to Merryl and asked, "When was he last happy?" Merryl couldn't respond; the question made her unbearably sad, and she didn't know the answer.

From time to time one of Carl's parents would lie down in the bedroom, but no one slept that night. The sun rose shortly after four. It was June 21, the first day of summer, the longest day of the year. To Merryl the world outside her window seemed strangely garish: "I'll never forget that dawn. The painful light. Monday morning. People getting into their cars, starting their engines, going to their normal lives."

---

The moment she dropped the phone, Merryl had known in her bones that Carl had killed himself. Later, Carl's father, who had retrieved the dangling receiver and finished talking to the man at the morgue, told Merryl that yes, it was suicide. Now it bothered Merryl that she didn't know more. That afternoon in the living room where Carl's and Merryl's families gathered, she wanted to know exactly how Carl had died. Her father-in-law got upset; why did she have to know every detail? Merryl's anger flared. "I knew everything about the way Carl lived," she said. "And I have to know everything about the way he died." Her father-in-law walked to the window and stared out. "He hanged himself," he said quietly.

Wanting to "protect" her, people tried to keep the facts of Carl's death from Merryl, but over the next few days she pieced the story together. Carl had driven to the Greyhound station and taken a bus to New York City. He'd gone to the YMCA, probably looking for a room with exposed pipes, but when he found none, he walked down Thirty-fourth Street and checked into a seedy single-room-occupancy hotel near Pennsylvania Station. Sometime Saturday night or Sunday morning Carl hanged himself from the steam pipe in his sparsely furnished room. The chambermaid found him Sunday morning at ten-thirty, at almost the same moment his nephew Carl had been christened in Cambridge, 220 miles away. When the police arrived at the hotel, they found pieces of paper with the telephone numbers of Manhattan gun stores.

Three months earlier Merryl had noticed an article in *Redbook* on mourning called "Would You Be Prepared?" She had skipped over it. She'd always avoided anything to do with dying. She was terrified of cemeteries. Now she was the eye of a storm of activity focused on death. Funeral arrangements were made, ministers consulted, relatives notified, and through it all Merryl was treated like an invalid by the two families who had last gathered together to celebrate Merryl and Carl's wedding. It was decided that Merryl would be moved to her parents' house on Cape Cod, where she and Carl had spent that first glorious weekend together twelve years before. Merryl's best friend helped her pack. Her three-year-old son had drowned two years earlier, and she seemed to know how to soothe Merryl. But inside, Merryl was frantic. How would Carl's body arrive? When would she see him? What would he be wearing? That night Merryl and her mother slept on the mattress in Carl's study. They had never been physically close, and Merryl was moved and comforted by their silent intimacy.

On Tuesday morning Merryl was driven to her parents' house. That same day Carl's body was shipped from New York City. The following afternoon Merryl visited the funeral home with her mother and two aunts. They stood in the waiting room while final preparations were made. When she heard the case being cranked to tilt the casket into viewing position, Merryl fell to the floor, sobbing. Her mother and her aunts knelt to help her to her feet. Then the door opened and a middle-aged man with a kindly but formal expression beckoned and said, "This way, please." On a platform at the far end of the next room lay a glistening red metal coffin. Merryl kept telling herself it held some stranger's body, that it couldn't be Carl, but as soon as she saw the wavy brown hair, she knew it was Carl. Her mother and her aunts left, and suddenly she was alone with him.

She studied his face. "I made myself aware of every tiny cell and inch of his body that was visible." There was a spot of dried blood behind his ear that Merryl assumed must have been left from the autopsy. There were red marks on his hands as if they'd been clenched. She touched his forehead. His skin was as cold as marble. She noticed the small scar near his right eye where a mole had been removed two years earlier. "He was incredibly well preserved, intact and normal-looking. But he seemed different. His jaw was set, and it gave him a determined, angry expression. His eyebrows looked just the same. I had always loved his eyebrows. They were blond and soft and thick, and they looked exactly the way they'd looked when he was alive. And that made me so sad. I was overwhelmed with the terrible feeling that a week ago this person had been so filled with living, and now there were just the eyebrows. As I looked at him I could remember exactly what he was saying the week before at that exact time. I would go over and over the events of the week and be astonished and horrified that it had come out this way, that it ended in this permanent fixture in this coffin."

Merryl spent two hours with Carl that afternoon and four hours the next. Sitting on a chair by his coffin, she told him all the things she hadn't had a chance to say. She reminded him of moments in their married life. She told him what was happening now, about all the pain she was feeling. They'd been together almost every day for eight years, and so much of what she felt only Carl could understand. Sometimes she was angry at him, but gently. "Why did you have to do it? Didn't you remember *us*?" she asked. "Why, Carl, why?"

At the funeral Carl lay in a closed casket a few feet from where Merryl sat. Merryl had been very involved in organizing the service: discussing what should be said, deciding where Carl should be buried, talking to the minister about the eulogy. She even changed a few lines in a poem her father had written for Carl and planned to read. She wanted to be part of anything that concerned Carl. But Merryl remembered little of the service: A flautist played something she recalled only as haunting; the minister's words were a blur. She sobbed hysterically through most of the ceremony. From the back of the church the cries of Carl's two-week-old nephew seemed to pierce through her own cries into her heart and made her cry even harder. When Merryl stood at the end of the service, her legs shook uncontrollably. A friend, driving away from the church, told her husband that she doubted Merryl was going to make it. Back at her parents' house, while mourners quietly sipped coffee and ate cold cuts, Merryl lay in bed. A psychiatrist friend of Carl's spoke to her gently, expressing his concern and saying he'd had no idea anything was amiss with Carl. During the entire hour he talked to her, Merryl held pillows over her head.

In the following days Merryl began to attend to the loose ends Carl's death had unwound. While her brother searched parking lots across Boston for the Chevy Citation that Carl and Merryl had bought two years earlier, Merryl called the police in New York City, where Carl's belongings had been stored in a vault. To claim them she had to go over a list of what he had had with him when he died: car keys, watch, wallet, glasses, wedding ring. Merryl called her friends, many of whom she hadn't spoken to in months, preoccupied with Carl's depression. "Hi! Where ya been?" they'd exclaim. "You don't understand," Merryl would say. "Carl committed suicide." There was never a question in Merryl's mind whether to tell people Carl's death was a suicide. "Nobody had ever been ashamed of Carl when he was alive, and there was nothing to be ashamed of when he was dead," she says. "It was just sad and tragic." At one point her brother said he was going to tell his tenants Carl died of a heart attack. "If you want to do that, okay," Merryl said, "but if you're doing it to protect me, forget it."

By Saturday, Merryl and her parents were alone. It was Carl and Merryl's sixth wedding anniversary. In the afternoon her father drove her to the cemetery. For over an hour while Mr. Maleska sat in the car, parked a little ways off, watching with tears in his eyes, Merryl lay on Carl's flower-strewn grave, weeping into the newly turned-up earth.

Sunday evening Merryl read from a book of poetry by Emily Dickinson. Her parents were pleased. They thought maybe she was getting better.

Monday, Merryl woke up and remembered: Carl was gone, and her life would never be the same. "I felt as if I had been pulled off the track," she says. "It was the busiest time of year at work, and everything was on a schedule. That very morning I was supposed to send certain books I'd edited to the typesetter. I thought of my colleagues at the office working so hard, and here I was lying in bed. The office seemed a million miles away. It seemed part of another life. Two weeks before, my work had consumed me, and now I didn't care if those books ever saw the light of day. And it hit me that this was the way it would be. I would never be interested in work again. I would never be interested in anything again. Nothing mattered and nothing ever would. I would never get out of this bed."

The bed she lay in was a rollaway sofa in her father's study. Designed for privacy, the study was an ideal haven for grieving. Merryl would spend most of the next four months in this room, which she had always loved but which she now came to think of as her "torture chamber." She would become intimate with its every detail, staring at her father's books on the shelves until she had memorized a dozen titles without realizing it. Most of her time was spent lying in bed, crying. She cried so much that her mother quickly learned Kleenex wouldn't suffice. It just wasn't strong enough. Instead, Mrs. Maleska made sure a fresh roll of paper towels lay on the floor near Merryl's bed. When Merryl wasn't crying, she screamed, sometimes for as long as an hour, until she was sure her head would burst. At first, when Merryl's parents heard her screams, they came running. Sometimes her mother brought Merryl a cup of tea to soothe her ragged throat. But it soon became clear that the screams were a necessary part of Merryl's life, and with the television on and the door shut—which Merryl insisted on—her parents could sit in the living room on the far side of the house and hear only muffled sounds. "They knew I was screaming, and I knew that they knew," says Merryl. "And I knew it hurt them. But I didn't want them sitting in the next room, waiting for me to stop."

For months Merryl kept the blinds drawn in her room. She couldn't stand seeing the sun. And if she opened the blinds, she would see the gazebo where she and Carl had exchanged their wedding vows six years before and the water where they had sailed and swum so often. At night, fearing the dark, Merryl slept with the light on. Soon, day seemed like night and night like day. In her dim cocoon, time became one vast, formless mass to Merryl, unchanging save one thing: night or day, the digital clock on the corner of the bookshelf across the room seemed to print its luminous numbers in her head.

Merryl left the house only for frequent visits to Carl's grave, driven by her father. Sometimes she sat at the kitchen table while her parents had dinner. Merryl rarely ate, although her mother kept fixing her meals, just in case. Afterward she and her mother lingered at the kitchen table for hours, talking about Carl. Merryl went over every detail of that last week; everything she had done seemed to Merryl to be a reason why Carl had killed himself. Every second of that week held a missed opportunity, a moment she could have stepped in and done something to keep him alive. Why hadn't she called fifteen minutes earlier that last day? If she had stayed home from work that day, would Carl be alive now? Why hadn't she stayed home all week? Why hadn't she grabbed the phone when Carl's therapist called? Why hadn't she made him understand how desperate Carl was? Why hadn't she understood when Carl had talked about suicide? How could she have been so blind? Why hadn't she hospitalized Carl? Why had she argued with him? Why hadn't she been more supportive? Why hadn't she loved him more?

Her mother listened, patiently pointing out the many ways Merryl had supported Carl. Mrs. Maleska was a quiet, thoughtful woman—Merryl had always joked that she had married someone like her mother. The Maleskas had loved Carl like a son and had been shattered by his suicide. Mrs. Maleska did not know whether her cancer would let her live five months or five years, but she listened to her daughter, comforting, questioning, persistently offering evidence of Merryl's love for Carl. They would dissect a single moment for hours before Merryl was convinced she had acted responsibly, but then Merryl would dredge up some fresh evidence and they would go over it again, then settle it again—and then reexamine it from yet another angle. Mother and daughter sat at the kitchen table into the night, Merryl's fingers tying and untying the frayed strands on the belt of her pink chenille bathrobe.

Merryl's father often listened from the next room and occasionally joined them. He said little, though what he said was always helpful. But he didn't understand why Merryl needed to talk it through so many times. Eighteen months later when his wife died, he told Merryl that now he understood why she had been unable to let her grief rest.

Every night after talking with her parents, Merryl swallowed a capsule of Xanax, a mild tranquilizer, to help her sleep. But every night at four she would wake up and find herself thinking about Carl. She tried to imagine what he must have felt like in those last days, starting with the six hours between the time she had said "Congratulations" to him on the phone and the time the landlord had seen him drive away. When had he made his decision? When had he gotten up from his desk? Her imagination traced him from their house in Brookline to the Greyhound station, followed him on the bus to New York, and watched him walking the streets looking for a hotel with exposed pipes. And she pictured that final, sad, unfamiliar room. What had he been thinking of? What had he looked like when he was hanging? Merryl replayed that journey hundreds of times and found hundreds of ways to change the ending: she got home before Carl left and was able to soothe him; she raced to the Greyhound station and intercepted him; she ran down Broadway, saw his silhouette in the hotel window, and rushed inside to cut the rope just in time. And for an hour in the middle of the night Carl was alive again, and everything was all right. But by dawn the real story came back to her, and it always had the same ending—Carl hanging from a pipe in New York and Merryl in bed on Cape Cod, alone.

Gradually, Merryl's thoughts moved back in time from that final week, poring over her relationship with Carl like a piece of fine cloth, holding it up to the light and looking for frayed seams and holes in the fabric. She examined every job interview Carl had had; if only he had gotten *this* one; why hadn't he tried for *that* one? Had she pushed him too hard? Had she been too soft? Why had they moved to Boston? Why hadn't they stayed in Chicago? Every second of their shared life was suddenly reflected through the fact of Carl's suicide. Merryl could spend an entire day in bed mulling over something she had said or done two, four, six years ago, a remark or a touch she had all but forgotten but now seemed critical: the time she'd yelled at him one Thanksgiving morning when he had brought home the wrong bread crumbs; the time she'd blamed him for having their apartment exterminated while the kitchenware was uncovered. Maybe if she had been gentler or kinder to him at that distant moment, he would still be alive. "I haunted myself with how I had not been a good enough wife for six years," she said. "I haunted myself with the feeling that maybe at bottom I just wasn't right for him, that maybe I had just reinforced the failure in him." Eventually, she wondered whether anything in their relationship had been real and good and true.

For every reason Merryl found to hate herself, for every clue she uncovered to reinforce her guilt over Carl's death, her parents, Carl's parents, her friends, and her therapist constantly reassured her that it wasn't her fault, that she had done everything possible. The head of Merryl's bed was lined with cards that friends and relatives had sent, which she read and reread as evidence that she wasn't all bad. She also kept the cards she had given Carl by her bed. "I couldn't bear reading the cards he'd written me that told me how much he loved me," she says. "They made me feel guilty that maybe I hadn't done enough, that I didn't love him enough back. So I would read the cards I'd given him that said how much I loved *him,* and that would comfort me." She kept only one card from Carl at her fingertips, the one he had written on her birthday; she read it over and over to herself, often on her daily trips to his grave. Carl had left no suicide note, and Merryl felt that this card was a kind of good-bye. But she still found reasons to disbelieve its grateful message. And even if she managed to let herself off the hook for a second, it didn't matter—Carl was still dead.

Though Merryl raked herself over the coals in her conscious life, her unconscious was less ruthless. She never had nightmares about Carl though she dreamed of him often. In her dreams he was gentle and comforting. "He was

always telling me in a loving sort of way, 'I had to do it, it was the only way.'"
One night Merryl dreamed that because suicide survivors go through such torment, their loved ones were permitted to come back to life for two months each
year, and the survivor could pick the dates. Merryl chose to have Carl returned
to her every weekend so the joy of his presence would be spread out.

But each morning returned her to square one. "Mornings were the worst,"
says Merryl. "When I woke up, it would all come right back. And I would go
into thought whirls about why and how and who he was and what I'd done.
Each morning I was brought up against the fact that nothing would change."
At ten or eleven Merryl's mother would bring her coffee, and they would start
going over it again. "I wanted to talk endlessly about Carl, about what had happened, about the events, about why, why, why," says Merryl. "If I wasn't doing
it out loud, I was doing it in my head. I was never *not* doing it. I thought if I just
talked enough, I'd find the reason and get rid of the pain." About three weeks
after the funeral Merryl decided the answer was to check into a hospital. "All
I thought was that I have to keep talking this through, and at the hospital I'd
get round-the-clock therapy. I had this dream that the hospital would be my salvation—I'd check in, do intensive therapy for six months, and it would be
over."

On a hot, sticky Fourth of July weekend Merryl and her mother drove to
Boston to visit several hospitals her therapist had recommended. It was the
first time Merryl had ventured farther than Carl's grave. Merryl had never
been inside a psychiatric hospital, and she was shaken. "All I saw were men
in pajamas, vacant-looking people watching TV in the afternoon." Her guide
at the first hospital, a pleasant young man, told her she would spend her first
month on a locked ward like this one. When Merryl asked about therapy, he
told her that each patient received three hours a week. The rest of the time
constituted "milieu therapy"; merely mixing with these people was considered
therapeutic. And there was basket weaving. Merryl was not too numb to be
appalled.

At the next hospital the admissions officer advised against hospitalization,
telling Merryl she was grieving, which is not necessarily depression, though
they may feel the same. "If you check in," he said, "they'll treat you like a
patient and you may start feeling like a patient, and then you may *become* a
patient." He talked about grief cycles, anniversary reactions, and other things
Merryl had never heard of. "I know it will be tough," she told him, "but I just
want to do it and get it over with."

At the third hospital Merryl fell apart. "The interviewer was younger than
I was, and she was sunburned and smiling and had clearly come back from a
happy holiday weekend," recalls Merryl. "She kept asking questions—'Now,
how did he die?' 'What did you do after you got the news?'—as if she were
reading from a checklist. I kept thinking, 'This is a nightmare. Why should
this girl be doing it? Carl should be having this kind of job.' And I couldn't

speak a word." Finally, unable to make herself talk, Merryl called her therapist, who calmed her down enough to enable her to get back to Cape Cod to her own bed where she could scream as much as she wanted.

Merryl thought constantly about killing herself or, more accurately, about wanting to die. She had always loved the ocean, but now she thought of it only as a place to drown herself. She even picked out a particular rock, near the marsh behind the house, that she could tie around her neck so she would sink to the bottom. In bed Merryl held a pillow over her face until she felt lightheaded, trying to feel the way Carl must have felt when he was hanging. But she always came up, gasping for air. She took fistfuls of the Percodan pills prescribed for her mother's cancer and spread them on her pillow. "I sort of taunted myself. I thought, 'What would it take to make me take them?' I would try to make myself feel as desperate as he was. I put them near my mouth, but I never swallowed any. I wanted to be dead, but I couldn't kill myself."

One month after Carl's death Merryl returned to work at Houghton Mifflin, two half-days a week. She was put on "short-term disability," a modified work schedule for employees who have had a serious accident or illness. Merryl didn't do much more than stare at the galleys that awaited editing on her desk. "I just sort of punched things through," she says. "I couldn't concentrate for more than fifteen minutes at a time without a break or a breakdown." Almost anything set her off: a conversation across the hall about a movie she and Carl had planned to see; a casual reference to self-confidence or assertiveness; a passage in a book she was editing that mentioned children; a colleague's conversations with an author named Carl; the sight of the woman who had baked the baby blocks cake. Once, her supervisor, referring to an author from Idaho, joked, "God, the places good people have to wind up these days." Merryl burst into tears. Idaho had been on the list of states she had been unwilling to move to.

Merryl spent much of the time crying at her desk. She avoided people's eyes as she shuffled down the halls so she wouldn't have to say hello. She walked with tiny steps, huddled over. At one point she was mistaken for a fifty-year-old. She lost twenty-five pounds in the first two months after Carl's death, and in her stomach she felt a constant ache. "A knot," she says. "A churning in my stomach and lungs, the way you feel before an important interview or exam. Except it didn't go away. Sometimes I would get a real pain in my heart as if all the heart muscles were clenched very tightly. I always felt I was building up to scream, cry, or gag. A wall of nausea separated me from the people around me. I could see people move and smile, but they were in another world. If I had a conversation with someone, I could see he or she was making normal human gestures, but when I tried to react, I felt muffled. I was standing there talking but with the knowledge that something was wrong, all wrong."

Two months after Carl's death, Merryl made a list of what she believed were her options. She carried it with her wherever she went. The list read:

suicide

a hospital

just refusing to move from bed—having them take me away

going to the apt, lying on mattress, taking enough pills to be uncon-
    scious, away from the world indefinitely

quitting job, moving to another city

getting a different kind of job

going on in these endless cycles of working/not working, staying in the
    city/staying at my parents' home—horrible, horrible

# IV

# THE O'ER-FRAUGHT HEART

---

ALTHOUGH SHE DID NOT REALIZE IT, Merryl Maleska's eating and sleeping difficulties, her screaming, her stomach pains, her depression, even her suicidal thoughts, were all normal responses to an abnormal situation. Behavior that has brought many mourners to psychiatrists with the fear that they are "going crazy" is considered within the standard range of grief reactions: "seeing" the dead person, "hearing" his key in the lock, calling out his name, dialing his office number and expecting him to answer. "Although mourning involves grave departures from the normal attitude to life, it never occurs to us to regard it as a pathological condition and to refer it to medical treatment," wrote Freud. "We rely on its being overcome after a certain lapse of time, and we look upon any interference with it as useless or even harmful." To Freud, grief's purpose was clear: "Mourning has a quite specific physical task to perform: its function is to detach the survivors' memories and hopes from the dead."

Described like this, it sounds as clean and quick as a tonsillectomy, but in fact mourning has proved to be one of life's most painful, lengthy, and complex procedures. A study by the National Academy of Sciences (NAS) found that Americans who lose a family member experience significant disturbance in their way of life for at least one year and as many as three. Of widows and widowers, up to 20 percent remain clinically depressed a year after the death of their spouse. The death of a family member may increase a survivor's smoking, drinking, and drug use as well as the chance of serious physical and mental illness. Men who have lost a spouse or a parent are more likely to die from accidents, heart disease, some infectious illnesses, and suicide. For women, who are more apt to seek support, the loss of a loved one is less likely to increase mortality, though there is evidence that death rates from cirrhosis of the liver and from suicide may rise.

Although Freud laid the theoretical groundwork, it is generally agreed that the systematic study of grief did not begin until the Coconut Grove fire in 1942. Following a football game, the Boston nightclub was packed beyond its legal capacity. A busboy accidentally ignited a decorative palm, and by the time the flames had been extinguished, nearly five hundred people were dead. From his work with the bereaved families, Erich Lindemann, chief of psychiatry at Massachusetts General Hospital, wrote a groundbreaking paper, "The Symptomatology and Management of Acute Grief." He found that it was normal, indeed healthy, to experience such reactions as guilt, hostility, physical distress, preoccupation with the image of the lost loved one, and a sense of merely "going through the motions" of daily living. Grief that is delayed or repressed, suggested Lindemann, is morbid or abnormal. Only through the proper "grief work," preferably aided by psychotherapy, can someone emancipate himself from "bondage to the deceased" and move forward with life. Lindemann's observations have served ever since as the psychological model clinicians use to describe and treat grief.

Over the last several decades increased interest in issues of death and dying, spearheaded by the work of Elisabeth Kübler-Ross and her concept of a "good death," has sparked a corresponding interest in bereavement and the concept of "good grief." At "grief institutes" and "bereavement centers" psychologists and social workers offer help to people who have lost loved ones. Researchers study physiological factors in grief and the biochemistry of tears, while clinicians analyze the grief process. Under this renewed scrutiny Lindemann's model of normal grief has been refined. Rather than the relatively straight line Lindemann proposes, the path of grief is now described by various experts as a circle, spiral, double-back, or zigzag. While they agree that mourners go through periods of shock, intense grief, and recovery, they have defined a variety of models. Some have adapted Kübler-Ross's five stages of dying—denial, anger, bargaining, depression, and acceptance—to grief. Others have cataloged as few as three or as many as twelve different stages. "There's a tendency for the novice to take the stages too literally," writes psychologist William Worden. "After her first book, *On Death and Dying,* many people expected dying patients literally to go through the stages she had listed. Some of them were disappointed when the stages were not passed through in some neat order."

Freud was the first to distinguish between grief and depression, which can have nearly identical symptoms. It is indeed difficult to draw the line beyond which mourning slips into depression. Many clinicians have tried to prescribe a length for normal mourning, and their estimates range from three months to six months, to "four full seasons," to two years, to forever. The NAS report suggested that professional intervention may be needed for those who show as much distress a year after the death as they did during the first month. As Lindemann suggested, the only sure sign of abnormal grief may be the *absence* of visible grief. "Sooner or later," wrote English psychoanalyst John Bowlby, "some of those who avoid all conscious grieving, break down— usually with some form of depression." A psychiatrist at Massachusetts General Hospital has estimated that 10 to 15 percent of the people who come to its mental health clinics are suffering from unresolved grief. Mere time, say grief experts, does not heal everything; the feelings must be talked out. "Give sorrow words," as Malcolm advised Macduff. "The grief that does not speak / Whispers the o'er-fraught heart, and bids it break."

Mourning is among the most primal and universal of responses, as researchers have found in observing grief reactions in animals from dolphins to ostriches to gorillas. One of the most haunting evocations of mourning ever written is Konrad Lorenz's description of bereavement in the greylag goose:

> The first response to the disappearance of the partner consists in the anxious attempt to find him again. The goose moves about restlessly by day and night, flying great distances and visiting all places where the partner might be found, uttering all the time the penetrating trisyllabic long-distance call. . . . The searching expeditions are extended farther and farther, and quite often the searcher himself gets lost, or succumbs to an accident. From the moment a goose realizes that the partner is missing, it loses all courage and flees even from the youngest and weakest geese. As its condition quickly becomes known to all the members of the colony, the lonely goose rapidly sinks to the lowest step in the ranking order . . . the goose can become extremely shy, reluctant to approach human beings and to come to the feeding place; the bird also develops a tendency to panic which further increases its "accident-proneness."

Lorenz has succinctly described some of the reactions commonly experienced by grieving humans: denial, searching, panic, loss of hope, vulnerability, social alienation, and isolation.

———————

While any death is traumatic for survivors, some deaths may be more traumatic than others. A sudden death may be more difficult than a death in which there has been some preparation, some chance to say good-bye. A violent death may be even harder. Murder, which is both sudden and violent, is more shattering still. But because it is sudden, often violent, and freighted with the added burdens of guilt and stigma, perhaps the most difficult of all deaths to resolve is suicide.

Suicide survivors pass through many of the responses common to all survivors, beginning with shock, numbness, and denial. Like Merryl they may have difficulty eating, sleeping, concentrating. They may have nightmares or anxiety attacks in which they endlessly replay scenes in their mind—particularly if the death was violent or if the survivor discovered the body. "The amount of blood hounded me," says a woman who found her lover after he had shot himself in the mouth. "I had dreams for a long time about red checkerboards, about typewriters with black and red keys. I had dreams where *I* was the blood pouring out of his head. I couldn't get that image out of my mind."

While survivors may deny that a suicide has occurred by hiding notes or insisting it was an accident, other forms of denial are less obvious. When one man returned home after the funeral of his younger brother who shot himself, he was reluctant to alter anything in any way. "Every time I moved something, even just a dirty dish on the table, I'd think, 'This is the way it was before he died. If I move this chair or make this bed, he'll be even more dead. Everything I do is making him more dead.'" A woman who had not seen her husband's body after his suicide called his office repeatedly without identifying herself. "I needed to hear, 'No, I'm sorry, he's passed away,' because I couldn't believe it."

The pain may temporarily be deadened by shock. Some grief experts compare this phase to the "disaster syndrome" of emotional dullness, unresponsiveness, and sense of worthlessness experienced by survivors of earthquakes, plane crashes, and other mass catastrophes. Psychiatrist Robert Jay Lifton, in his study of survivors of the A-bomb at Hiroshima, described it as "psychic numbing," a turning off of emotions, "in which the survivor's responses to his environment are reduced to a minimum—often to those necessary to keep him alive—and in which he feels divested of the capacity either to wish or will." This sounds much like one Ohio high school teacher's description of the first few months after her son hanged himself: "I was unable to function. I would drive the three miles to school, but I would forget how to get home. I would have to park the car until I could remember. I would go to the supermarket, but when I came out, I could never find my car. Eventually, I gave up going to the store. I was indifferent to stop signs and red lights. I blocked out sound and sight. I became perfectly mute. And no one could penetrate it."

But eventually, like a patient coming out of anesthesia, the survivor awakens to the relentless enormity of the pain. "It was like a fist reaching into my stomach and closing tight," says one. "I feel as if he shot a hole bigger than me," says another. "I felt as if my heart had been torn from my chest and that I was bleeding to death as surely as my husband," says another. Others: "I felt like a skinned animal." "I felt as if my insides were nothing but smashed glass, and if you could peel my skin away, I would sift down into a pile of tinkling shards." "I am curdled with grief."

Feelings of guilt, common after any death, are vastly intensified after a suicide. Like a child poking his tongue in the hole left by a missing tooth, a survivor examines every interaction with the dead person, from the last contact back to the first. In light of the suicide, every moment becomes evidence of failure. The guilt leads to what grief counselors call the "what ifs" and the "if onlys"—the words or actions they feel might have prevented the death: "If only I'd told her I loved her." "What if I hadn't gone out that night?" Survivors may feel guilt if they saw signs and did nothing, guilt if they saw signs and bent over backward to help, guilt if they failed to see any signs at all. Guilt may be especially intense for parents of suicides. Parents are supposed to die before their children. In a society in which the "success" or "failure" of a child is often seen as a reflection of his parents' worth, a suicide may seem the ultimate evidence of bad parenting. Says one mother, "You tend to say, 'I have three children. Two are very successful; they did it all themselves. I have one child who killed himself; that was my fault.' "

If the suicide occurred during a time of conflict between the suicide and the survivor, guilt may be particularly acute. Suicide can be an act of anger directed at others, with the intent of producing remorse. The circumstances of the act—method, location, note—can be indelible expressions of that rage. "There's no way we can resolve it. He had the last word," says a woman whose son left a three-word suicide note: "Fuck you all." Another woman received a series of annoying phone calls from her husband after their separation. One day he telephoned to say he had a gun and was going to kill himself. Exasperated, the woman said before she hung up, "Go ahead." He did. Today, agonizing over the words she can never take back, the receiver she hung up, she says, "I feel as though I put down a revolver."

"Guilt is a way of bringing control back into a situation that seems out of control," says one grief counselor. "It comes from the perception that you could have done something to prevent it. There's something narcissistic about that because it suggests that you could single-handedly have changed the outcome. It's not rational because you don't take that kind of responsibility for anyone's life while he is alive—otherwise, you don't allow him to be a person. But when someone kills himself, you feel you should have been around him every waking minute. Everyone does. Everyone suddenly takes one hundred percent responsibility for that person's life." In an article in the *Village Voice,* Sheila Weller described how after a suicide thirty friends gathered to discuss the death. All thirty admitted that they felt in some way responsible. In that unanimity their guilt was eased, and they were able to realize that no one person can make someone die or stay alive.

Survivors of suicide may feel more anger than other mourners: at the deceased for rejecting and deserting them; at God for allowing it to happen; at themselves, their family, or the mental health profession for not preventing it; and at the world for not coming to a halt. "I see people who had far more problems than my brother did, and I get so angry," says a young man whose brother shot himself. "Why are *they* alive and my brother isn't?" Guilt, in fact, may be helpful, say Edward Dunne and Karen Dunne-Maxim, sibling survivors and therapists who have worked with more than two thousand survivors over the past four decades. "Guilt is a way of making the world less chaotic," they write, "and some guilt is probably important to counteract the feelings of helplessness a suicide may engender."

In the ancient Hebrew ritual of atonement, a live goat was driven out into the wilderness each year, symbolically laden with the sins of the people. Similarly, after a suicide, survivors often select a scapegoat. The target may be unemployment, drugs, alcohol. It may be a psychiatrist, a boyfriend, a clergyman. Or it may be a member of the family. "There is an especially distressing tendency for the survivors of a suicide to look for a scapegoat," wrote Erich Lindemann and Ina May Greer. "And, as is the fate of most scapegoats, the victim is usually one of their own members and frequently the one least able to bear the added burden." Sometimes the scapegoat may even be the suicide himself, who is held responsible for all the family problems.

Anger at the dead person may be the most difficult to express. "I would be so full of rage if somebody killed my brother. And I would be enraged if my brother killed someone. But he's both those people—and I have both those feelings," says a man whose brother shot himself. At a meeting of survivors in Minneapolis a woman whose son killed himself blurted, "I'm so angry at him. . . . I could just kill him." Realizing what she had said, she burst out laughing. A woman whose seventeen-year-old son shot himself five years ago says, "My anger is with myself." She is quiet for a moment, then she adds, "And at God for letting my child die. And at the family for not seeing it . . . and at his friends, who didn't tell me he'd talked of suicide." Her voice begins to boil. "And at the school, who knew he was withdrawing but never called. I *know* it wasn't their fault. I *know* there's no one to blame." Her voice shakes. "But it's one thing to resolve anger in the mind, and it's another to resolve anger in the gut." She pauses, and when she speaks again, she is calm, apologetic. "I guess I need *someone* to place the blame on—anyone but him."

The suicide of an alcoholic, an abusive parent or spouse, a particularly troublesome child, or someone who has made repeated threats or attempts may be the culmination of an exhausting struggle for both the suicide and the survivor. Perhaps it should not be surprising that one in ten family members confesses to a sense of relief that suicide has brought an end to that struggle. "We all felt some relief," says one young man whose older brother's suicide followed four attempts, numerous hospitalizations, and a decade of manic depression that seemed impervious to drug therapy, electroshock, psychotherapy, and the love of his family. "He had been so unhappy, and now he was out of his pain. My mother said, 'He's at peace now.' I felt my brother had finally taken some sort of initiative and been successful at something." Arnaldo Pangrazzi, a hospital chaplain in Milwaukee who leads survivors' groups, writes, "Some feel guilty about experiencing relief, which implies neither a lack of love for the deceased nor happiness that he or she died. Rather, relief is the awareness that the tension, the waiting, the fear are over."

But merely to describe the shock, guilt, anger, and relief is to make them sound as if they were separate emotions with distinct boundaries. In grief they circle back endlessly on one another. A survivor feels angry for feeling guilty, guilty for feeling angry, worthless for feeling guilty, angry for feeling worthless.

Through all these emotions the suicide survivor may be propelled by the question "Why?" Finding a reason for the suicide can become an obsession. Survivors search for notes, read books about depression and suicide, interview friends, talk to therapists, consult fortune-tellers, and endlessly ask themselves questions, trying to make sense of a senseless act, to solve what centuries of professionals have been unable to solve. Survivors often believe that the pain would recede if they could only find an answer. They may latch onto a reason— the lost girlfriend, the unemployment, the alcoholism—but ultimately it dissolves under scrutiny into more questions. Says one grief counselor, "Even if there *is* a reason, that's never answer enough."

In the year following her husband's suicide one young woman looked everywhere for answers: counselors, survivor groups, suicide symposiums, books on suicide, workshops on holistic medicine, and psychics. She studied her husband's journal for an answer and stared at the next blank page, thinking that if she waited long enough, the answer might somehow appear. She drew up a two-page summary of possible factors, as much for herself as for friends who, baffled by the suicide, kept asking her, "Why?" Yet even her synopsis listed more reasons "why not." And she searched for answers in her dreams. "I've had dreams where I couldn't get his attention. I've had dreams where he'd say he was really alive, and I'd say, 'No, you're dead.' I've had dreams where I'm with him, and we have a wonderful time, and afterward I ask, 'But you died—aren't you going to tell me what happened?' But he'd go or I'd wake up. I've had dreams where he told me what happened and I forgot. One week for four nights I asked for favors. The first night I asked that he come and visit me in my dreams, and he did. The second, I asked that he come and talk. He did. The third night I asked that he come and make love to me, and he did. The fourth night I asked that he tell me why he killed himself. He didn't. He refused."

On the other hand, survivors may try to bury their questions and feelings along with the suicide. "A common response to suicide is to say, 'Let the dead lie,'" says family therapist Monica McGoldrick. "And when a suicide occurs, families tend to close down." Families may participate in a "conspiracy of silence," a kind of cold war in which communication is cut off, and each family member suffers alone, behind closed doors, avoiding mentioning the name of the departed, avoiding one another's gaze. After the suicide of one nineteen-

year-old boy, an awkward, troubling silence settled over his parents and surviving siblings. "For months no one talked about him," says the boy's mother.
"It was as if he'd never existed. Christmas came and went, and no one talked
about it. That began to worry us." The family eventually decided to seek help.
"In therapy we found out everyone had wanted to talk about it, but they
didn't want to make other people unhappy."

A family's denial may take physical form. After a suicide some families
build a "shrine" to the deceased, leaving the room exactly as it was, the bed
unmade, the schoolbooks on the desk. When one couple bought a new house
three months after the suicide of their sixteen-year-old son, the mother insisted
on setting aside a bedroom for her dead child. Two years after his son shot himself, one man keeps his son's half-empty cereal boxes in the kitchen cupboard;
in winter he sometimes checks his son's bedroom "to see if it's warm enough."
Others try to erase all traces of the dead one from the house, throwing out all
his possessions, "sanitizing" his room as if he had never been there. In his
poem "The Portrait," Stanley Kunitz, whose father swallowed carbolic acid a
few weeks before he was born, described such denial:

> *My mother never forgave my father*
> *for killing himself,*
> *especially at such an awkward time*
> *and in a public park,*
> *that spring*
> *when I was waiting to be born.*
> *She locked his name*
> *in her deepest cabinet*
> *and would not let him out,*
> *though I could hear him thumping.*
> *When I came down from the attic*
> *with the pastel portrait in my hand*
> *of a long-lipped stranger*
> *with a brave moustache*
> *and deep brown level eyes,*
> *she ripped it into shreds*
> *without a single word*
> *and slapped me hard.*
> *In my sixty-fourth year*
> *I can feel my cheek*
> *still burning.*

At some point almost everyone who has lost someone to suicide wrestles
with suicidal thoughts of his own. To the survivor there is no statistic more
chilling than the research that shows survivors to be at eight times higher risk

for suicide than the general population. At survivor support groups one of the most frequent questions is, "Is suicide inherited?"

As we have seen, there is no convincing evidence that suicide, per se, is genetically transmitted; there are other reasons why survivors have an unusually high suicide rate. First, while people are not born with genes for suicide, some are born with a genetic susceptibility to depression or other psychiatric conditions associated with heightened suicide risk. Second, after a death of *any* kind the risk of suicide increases. Widows and widowers, for instance, during the first year of bereavement have a risk of suicide two and a half times as high as married people in their age group. Third, once a suicide occurs in a family, it introduces itself as an option. "Before, we didn't live in a world where people killed themselves," says a man whose brother shot himself. "Intellectually, we did, but we didn't believe it really happened. Now, we live in that world where it does happen so we're more apt to think of that possibility." Suicidal thoughts may be prompted by an identification with the deceased, a yearning to join the lost loved one, or a desire to atone for feelings of guilt. Those thoughts, however fleeting, may make a survivor even more bewildered and frightened. "When my brother shot himself, I thought the world had gone crazy," says one young woman. "I felt a little crazy myself. In our family I was always 'the wild one' and my brother was 'the quiet one.' That terrified me because I thought, "*He* did it, and he seemed so much more together than me.'" She shakes her head. "I thought of suicide a lot. I was scared to death, but I wouldn't talk to anybody about it. I knew suicide wasn't hereditary, but I was afraid that one day I'd run off and shoot myself just like my brother."

Experts believe that suicide is more likely to occur in surviving families where the first suicide is not talked about and the guilt and anger are allowed to fester. If not dealt with openly, the influence of a suicide may be felt further down the line. Suicide can be a learned reaction to stress, a coping technique that, once used in a family, can act as a sort of role model. Adults tend to repeat the type of violence—or the type of love—they experienced as children. Just as children physically abused by their parents tend to become abusive parents themselves, suicide by a parent may beget suicidal behavior in children. The poet John Berryman never forgave his father for killing himself when the younger Berryman was eleven. "I spit upon this dreadful banker's grave / who shot his heart out in a Florida dawn," he wrote in "Dream Song 384." In 1972, forty-six years after his father's death, Berryman jumped to his death from a Minneapolis bridge. "In a modesty of death I join my father," he had written in one of his later poems. In 1961, thirty-three years after his father had shot himself, Ernest Hemingway shot himself at age sixty-one. Eleven years later his younger brother Leicester, who had been the one to find their father's body, shot himself, too. One year after her father's suicide a thirteen-year-old Illinois girl fatally stabbed herself, leaving a note: "I am drawn toward death like a bee toward honey, like Juliet toward Romeo, like a baby girl toward her Dada."

Long after his suicide attempt, A. Alvarez realized that he had been introduced to the option of suicide in childhood:

> I see now that I had been incubating this death far longer than I recognized at the time. When I was a child, both my parents had half-heartedly put their heads in the gas oven. Or so they claimed. It seemed to me then a rather splendid gesture, though shrouded in mystery, a little area of veiled intensity, revealed only by hints and unexplained, swiftly suppressed outbursts. It was something hidden, attractive and not for the children, like sex. But it was also something that undoubtedly did happen to grownups. However hysterical or comic the behavior involved—and to a child it seemed more ludicrous than tragic to place your head in the greasy gas oven, like the Sunday roast joint—suicide was a fact, a subject that couldn't be denied; it was something, however awful, that people did. When my own time came, I did not have to discover it for myself.

For some survivors the sense of identification with the suicide can become so strong that their own suicide seems almost inevitable, a destiny to fulfill; they don't choose suicide, suicide chooses them. That sense of identification was brought home to me when, at a suicide prevention conference, I met Jean, a chipper, frizzy-haired, middle-aged Michigan woman who works with disturbed adolescents. When I asked what brought her to the conference, she answered brightly, "I come from a suicidogenic family." Seeing my questioning look, she explained, "My family produces suicides. It generates suicides. It passes them on."

Jean was thirty-one when her brother killed himself. Three years later her mother killed herself, leaving a note blaming her daughter. Jean's father was an alcoholic; her grandfather, who was overweight and had heart problems but refused to follow his prescribed medical regimen, "probably killed himself—after all, you don't have to put your neck in a noose to commit suicide." After her mother's death, Jean herself was twice hospitalized for suicide attempts. "Although I didn't want to die, I felt that killing myself was the right thing to do because my mother had done it. I felt it was my fate." After many years in therapy, Jean no longer believes that her suicide is inevitable, but she is convinced that it is part of her legacy. "It's not hereditary, but it's contagious," she says matter-of-factly.

While admiring Jean's frankness, I found her ready acceptance of her "suicidogenic" heritage unsettling and the word itself a bit frightening. The concept of "contagious" suicide may be the only way she can deal with her family's tragedies, but I wonder how thin the line may be between believing in that fate and embracing it.

On the other hand, for some survivors, a suicide can serve a preventive role.

They are steered away from suicidal thoughts by their firsthand knowledge of the pain their death would inflict on others. "Before my brother killed himself, I'd considered suicide myself," says a young musician who was twenty-five years old when his older brother shot himself. "I used to think my suicide would say to the world that life in the modern world is too much to bear. But my brother's death made me see how futile suicide is. It makes no statement, it just gives people grief. And now when I get depressed and thoughts of death come up, they don't continue long because I think, 'How could I put my family through a second suicide?' "

---

While a suicide loss is painful whether the survivor is a parent, child, or spouse, the nature of the loss may have a different quality for each. A parent may feel more guilt, a spouse, more anger. A sibling often feels confusion about his role in the family. Grandparent, friend, teacher, therapist—each role brings its own special pain. But the effect on children may be the most destructive of all. Studies show that the loss of a parent in early childhood plays a key role in subsequent psychological development; if that loss is by suicide, it can be devastating. "For children," concluded the National Academy of Sciences report on grief, "the suicide of a parent or sibling not only presents immediate difficulties, but is thought by many observers to result in life-long vulnerability to mental health problems."

After a suicide children feel many of the same emotions as adults: denial, anger, confusion, and fear. Guilt can be intense. "Kids are apt to take the blame for any death," says Sandra Fox, former director of the Family Support Center at the Judge Baker Children's Center in Boston, which provides counseling for children and families coping with loss. "They feel they might have been responsible for it because of something they thought or wished or said or did or didn't do. And unconsciously, kids can very much wish their parents dead: 'Daddy, why don't you go play in traffic and die so I can carry off Mummy to a castle and marry her.' Now, if Daddy happens to die, the child thinks it's his fault." Children may have had hostile feelings toward the parent; they may have misbehaved immediately before the suicide; they may feel they might have prevented it—if only they hadn't quarreled with their brother, if only they had stayed home instead of going out to play. They may feel guilt because they didn't know whom to call after finding the body or didn't open the windows of a gas-filled room. Or they may feel guilt at merely being alive when their parent is dead. In his work with survivors of the Hiroshima bombings, psychiatrist Robert Jay Lifton described the "survivor guilt" felt by those who were not killed. The suicide of a parent, Lifton believes, may produce similar pangs in a child.

Children are even more apt to be left alone with their grief than adults. Intending to shield them from pain, well-meaning parents rarely level with their children about death. The subject is either avoided or explained in euphemisms, leaving children's imaginations to fill in the blanks. A study of thirty-six children who had lost a parent to suicide found that half of them were never told the truth; some learned the real story only when they overheard adults talking about it or read the obituary in the newspapers. In a study of forty-five children between the ages of four and fourteen who had lost a parent to suicide, therapists Albert Cain and Irene Fast found that more than a quarter knew intimate details about the death yet were told it was from natural causes. One girl saw her father's body hanging in the closet; her mother insisted that he had died in a car wreck. A boy who had seen his father blow himself to pieces with a shotgun was told that he died of a heart attack. Two brothers who found their mother with her wrists slit were told she had drowned while swimming. When the children contradicted their elders, they were made to feel ashamed for making such statements and told they had merely had bad dreams or had confused reality with a television program.

Such lack of honesty following a suicide can be calamitous to a child. Cain and Fast found that distorted communication contributed to a broad range of symptoms: delinquency, running away, psychosomatic disorders, obesity, neurosis, and an incidence of psychosis three times that in other childhood bereavement cases. In addition, because the children had received the message that they should not know or talk about the suicide, they often felt conflict about knowing and talking in general, with resultant stammers, stutters, shyness, and learning disabilities. Other research has described the effect of unresolved grief in later life. Psychiatrist T. L. Dorpat, in a study of seventeen patients he began treating an average of sixteen years after a parent's suicide, found that unresolved grief had left a malignant residue: guilt, depression, arrested development, self-destructive behavior, and preoccupation with suicide.

The suicide of a parent need not be crippling if discussed openly and honestly. "What's mentionable is manageable," says Sandra Fox, who believes that early intervention with bereaved children can help avoid later problems. Fox encourages parents to explain clearly and directly what happened and why, giving honest information (appropriate to age) about the cause, helping children understand that the dead person is not coming back and that the child's sadness and anger are normal. Fox is often asked at what age a child should be told about a parent's suicide. As soon as they can talk? "*Before* they can talk," says Fox. "I don't mean you tell a two-year-old, 'Your daddy hung himself in the basement.' You start by explaining that Daddy died, and dying means we're not going to see him anymore the way we knew him here on earth. His body has stopped working. Then, as kids are ready and ask 'How did he die?' or 'Why did he die?' you add the fact that it was a suicide. Children feel guilt after any death, and it's important to tell the child, 'You may think there's something you said or did that made your dad kill himself, but I want you to understand that's not what happened. Your dad killed himself because he had problems that he couldn't find any way to deal with.'" Fox pauses. "You have to deal with it immediately, although you certainly will have to rework it later, too, as kids understand more. But don't wait."

---

The devastating effect of a parent's suicide on a child—and the kind of communication that may best relieve it—may be seen in the story of Mary and Karen Vitelli. At noon on an exceptionally hot day in early fall, Mary and Karen were sitting with their mother, Linda, at the kitchen table in their apartment in a Boston suburb. Karen was five years old, Mary ten. A shy, intelligent girl who enjoyed helping out around the house, Mary had heated up SpaghettiOs for lunch. Their mother was sewing a patch on a pair of Mary's pants so they would be ready in time for the new school year that began the following Monday. Mary would be entering fourth grade; Karen would be starting kindergarten. As Mary and Karen teased each other over lunch, their mother suddenly stopped sewing, threw the pants onto the table, hugged her daughters, and went upstairs.

After lunch, Karen asked Mary to give her a shampoo. Mary said they had better ask their mother. They went upstairs and knocked on one of the two doors to her bedroom. There was no answer. That was strange—their mother never took naps during the day. They tried to open the door, but it was locked. They went to the other door, and by throwing all their weight against it, they were able to squeeze into the room. A couch had been pushed against the door. "Where's Mummy?" Mary said. Karen pointed to the other door and said, "Why are her feet hanging there?"

Their mother, her belt around her neck, her flip-flops still clinging to her feet, was hanging from the hinge on the door. "Why did you do this?" Mary screamed at her mother. "You promised you'd never leave us. Why did you do this?" She tried to lift her mother down, but she couldn't. Her shoulder ached for weeks. She ran to the telephone, looked up the number of the body shop where her mother's boyfriend, Chris, worked, and called him. "Come home," she said. "My mother's dead."

In fact, Linda was not quite dead. When Chris arrived, he gave her CPR while Mary called the ambulance. At the hospital Linda went into a coma. The children stayed with their grandmother Rose, and the three of them wept together. A few days later the doctors told Rose there was no chance that Linda would live, and it was agreed she would be taken off life-support equipment. When Rose told the children, Mary was furious. "You can't do that," she shouted. "You lied. Everybody lied. You said she was going to get better."

Although some of the family thought it would be needlessly traumatic, Mary and Karen insisted on seeing their mother's body, and the following day Rose took them to the hospital. Linda's body lay on a bed. The life-support systems had been disconnected. A psychiatric nurse was there to answer the children's questions. "Why did you make my mommy die?" Mary screamed. The nurse gently explained what had happened, but Mary continued to sob hysterically. Later, the nurse asked them whether they would like the clothes their mother had worn that day. "No, no, no, no," Mary whispered to her grandmother. "Don't take them." Rose asked the nurse, who was crying by now, to burn them.

Karen and Mary moved in with their grandmother, a compact, brisk, pragmatic woman who worked as a hairdresser. Divorced when Linda was five, Rose had raised three children on her own. She had been close to Linda, her only daughter, who had married at sixteen and endured nine years of her husband's drinking and verbal abuse before getting a divorce. In the past year Linda had found a new boyfriend and a new career, but the pressures of starting over at twenty-seven had apparently overwhelmed her. Though Rose was crushed by her daughter's suicide, her own grief was put on hold as she cared for her daughter's children. Karen seemed to be handling it well, but Mary was torn between her anger at and her love for her mother. Although she agreed to attend the wake, she refused to go to the funeral or to the cemetery, and when Rose tried to tell Mary how beautiful the service had been, she wouldn't listen. She asked Chris whether he would get a new girlfriend and he said yes, someday. "Well, never bring her here," Mary said. In fact, he never did get another girlfriend; a year later he shot himself near Linda's grave.

Over the following months Mary experienced the classic responses of stigma, fear, anger, and guilt. Three days after the funeral the new school year began, and Mary went back to school wearing the new clothes her mother had bought her. When she came home, she told Rose, "Some of the kids are coming up to me and saying, 'Your mother hung herself.' I want to go to a different school." Rose told her to hold her head high and deny it. Both Karen and Mary refused to go upstairs without their grandmother, and for several months the three of them slept in the same room, where they could comfort each other when one of them woke from a nightmare in tears. Mary was filled with anger. She didn't want anything around that her mother had given her. She refused to say anything nice about her mother, and if Rose mentioned Linda, Mary frowned. One day Rose overheard the children arguing. "I don't know why she did it," Karen was saying. "Because we were fighting," said Mary. Rose rushed in. "No," she said, "that's not it at all." She explained that their mother's death had nothing to do with them, that their mother had been troubled for reasons of her own. But Mary felt guilty for not saving her mother. "I tried to get her down, Grandma," she'd say, "but I couldn't. I just couldn't." Rose attempted to reassure her: "You're only ten—I couldn't have done it either. You did wonderfully to call Chris." Mary was unconvinced. She had recurring nightmares in which her mother came back to punish her for not saving her life.

One day the children's father, angry that Rose had won temporary custody, called Mary. "What are you and your grandmother trying to do? Do you want me to kill myself, too?" he said. Mary came into the kitchen, where Rose was fixing dinner. "He's going to kill himself," she said. Rose, numb and exhausted, said, "So what?" Mary was matter-of-fact: "Well, then you might as well kill yourself, and I might as well kill myself." Rose answered without thinking, "Not today—I have too much to do."

That afternoon Mary asked Rose if they could visit the grave. When they arrived, Karen laid the roses they had brought on the grave, but Mary, frightened, refused to go near. Nevertheless, Rose was encouraged. "When she asked to go to the grave, that's when I knew she was going to deal with things."

A few weeks after Linda's death the three of them began seeing a therapist, together and separately. Under his gentle questioning Mary opened up. By the second session she was describing every detail of her mother's death to him. She discussed her recurring nightmares and fears that her mother would come back and punish her for not saving her life. The therapist helped Mary and Karen practice what to say to their classmates when they were taunted about their mother hanging herself: "Mummy went to the hospital, went into a coma, and never came out of it." Over the following months he convinced them they were not responsible for their mother's death, and gradually their fears began to subside.

A year after their mother's death, the children's nightmares stopped. Mary and Karen were still afraid to go upstairs to the bathroom alone at night, although they now did so in daylight. Mary's anger eased. She remained reluctant to go to the cemetery, and during a visit on her mother's birthday she kept her distance from the grave. When Mary was very young, her mother had knit her a blue sweater, which Rose kept in the hope chest. One day, Rose took it out and asked Mary if she wanted to wear it. "No," said Mary. "Right now, I wouldn't want to wear it, but maybe someday I will."

# V

# MERRYL:
# THE JIGSAW PUZZLE

───────

IN SEPTEMBER, Merryl began keeping a chart of how she felt. The chart's range was from "suicidal" to "bearable" to "acceptable," and Merryl's graph made precipitous daily zigzags. At the office she was still barely functioning. She couldn't concentrate; she spent all her time thinking about Carl. Gripped by a new worry, a "thought whirl" or a flash of guilt, she would call her mother and talk for an hour. The people in nearby offices heard her weeping but weren't sure what to do. "My supervisor was wonderful, but a lot of people didn't speak to me," she says. "I never felt ostracized, though. They just didn't know what to say." Neither did Merryl. "People asked me how I was, and I didn't know. I couldn't say 'fine,' and I couldn't say 'I want to be dead.' I couldn't say anything. I couldn't smile. For four months I never changed my expression. A friend told me it looked like a bomb had blown up in my face."

Merryl still thought of suicide—or, more accurately, of death. One day in Boston she stepped heedlessly in front of an oncoming trolley car. When she boarded, the conductor shook his head and said, "Next time you do that, the insurance company will pay the fare." Merryl looked at him. "That's exactly what I want," she said. She moved slowly to the back of the car. "I didn't even know what I was doing," remembers Merryl. "But if I'd been hit, I wouldn't have minded." Merryl invented a game: each day, if she could think of one reason to be alive, she would put off dying until the following day. "One morning, I found myself thinking that the autumn leaves were pretty, and I thought, 'I would have missed that if I'd killed myself, so I'll stay alive until tomorrow.'"

Merryl moved into a room over her friend Judith's garage. Judith, an editor at Houghton Mifflin, had lost a close friend to suicide several years earlier and had been one of the first people to call Merryl after Carl's death. She seemed to know just what Merryl needed. Sometimes Merryl would go into her office and talk; other times she'd huddle in a corner and cry quietly while Judith worked. Under Judith's wing Merryl began to go out occasionally, to a lecture, a museum, or a concert. "I felt safe with her," says Merryl. "I could face things. She was like my Seeing Eye dog." Sometimes Merryl sat at home with Judith's husband, an engineer, and listened to him discuss his work. "He could talk for hours about very boring subjects—the concrete used in making bridges, how to build the girders in a skyscraper—and it was just what I needed to hear." By late October the zigzags on Merryl's chart began to settle in the bearable/acceptable range. In November, Merryl laughed for the first time since Carl's death.

Meanwhile, Merryl continued trying to make sense of Carl's suicide. She started jotting down some thoughts about Carl on scraps of paper. Because she was having difficulty separating what had actually happened from what her guilt suggested had happened, she wrote down everything she could remember of those desperate final weeks. Gradually, she recorded many things: incidents she remembered, ideas about Carl's personality, notes from her therapy sessions, raw expressions of wanting to die. Merryl sorted them into three piles: ideas about Carl's character, feelings of guilt, and the details of her day-to-day agony. If she felt strong, she might pick a piece of paper from a pile and pore over it. She dated all her notes. Often she would realize that a question she had written in November she had already asked in October—she had been over that same angle months before, but the wound had reopened. Soon she had hundreds of scraps of paper, which she kept in a black plastic bag she carried everywhere. She and Judith called them "Carl papers." Once, when she accidentally locked them in her car in a friend's driveway, she slept over that night so she could hear if someone tried to break into the vehicle.

Before Carl died it had never occurred to Merryl to read anything on the subject of death. Now her bedside table, once lined with books on maternity, was crowded with books on suicide, bereavement, and widowhood. Even the most basic information fascinated her—that, for instance, four times more men kill themselves than women. She quickly devoured the entries on suicide in her father's four encyclopedias. On weekly trips to the library she and Judith would meet at the checkout desk at closing time, Judith with eight books of poetry, Merryl clutching eight books on death. In bookstores Merryl gravitated toward the psychology and sociology sections. Working in the college division at Houghton Mifflin, she had access to a room filled with shelf after shelf of psychology textbooks. She began to stay late after work, alone in the office, looking up *suicide* in the index of each textbook and reading about depression, self-esteem, and personality theory. She filled another black plastic bag with copies of articles to reread. She learned about Freud and the death instinct, about anomic, egoistic, and altruistic suicide, about the wish to kill, the wish to be killed, and the wish to die, about lethality indexes, ambivalence, and the cry for help.

"I read everything about suicide I could get my hands on," says Merryl. "I was always hoping that the next book would have the answer and was always afraid it would do me in. . . . Only rarely did it help, and some of it hurt." Her mother had told her that hanging was a quick death, but in an encyclopedia she read that suicide by hanging usually takes eight minutes because the body does not fall from a height, as it would in an execution. Merryl couldn't stop shivering for days, thinking of the pain Carl might have felt. In *The Social Reality of Death* she read that a "validating significant other" can mean the difference between life and death for a suicidal person. Merryl was devastated, suddenly certain that she must not have been a "validating significant other." One day in August, she came across *Too Young to Die,* a book on adolescent suicide. She read parts of it in the bookstore and felt she was going to vomit. "It stressed the significance of external events and said that if you had recognized the clues, you could have saved the person," says Merryl. "I was frantic. This book seemed to say that it was really my fault after all, that I could have saved Carl." Merryl ran upstairs to her office and called three friends and her therapist before she began to calm down. "Everything I had put together in two months was coming apart," she says. She was back at square one, reminding herself that she *had* gotten him help, she *had* called a psychiatrist. Merryl gradually began to erect responses so that when a wave of guilt washed over her, she wouldn't be defenseless. One of the things that made her feel worst was the list she had given Carl in Chicago of the twenty-five states she was willing to move to. If she hadn't made those stipulations, she told herself, he'd still be alive—and she would buckle with self-blame. But as she went over and over it, she began to respond more rationally to her self-accusations. She made a mental list of reasons why she should not feel guilty, and when guilt struck, she would recite the list to herself like a mantra:

1. Bad things could have eventually happened to Carl there (like not getting tenure), and he might have gone into despair at that point and killed himself.
2. If we had moved there, I might have been miserable. Then, if he'd gone into despair and killed himself, I would have blamed myself even more for having complained.
3. I had a right to have some influence on where we would live. We had been in Chicago six years solely for his work.
4. Carl agreed to this plan; he could have insisted on his own plan or even moved on his own if it was that important.
5. I did become more flexible when things began going so badly in

Boston and was willing to put his career first completely—but who could know that by that point it would be too late? My perspective is all off now that I know his life was at stake. At the time I made the list I thought we were negotiating with usual and normal stakes and consequences.

Even as Merryl started to cope with feelings of guilt, the sheer ache of missing Carl would flood her: the way his eyes lit up as he laughed; the determined way he walked; his boyish pleasure when he surprised her with a gift. And then there was the loss of the life they had been building together. "What hurt worst is that we were on the verge of so much," says Merryl. "Carl was finally finishing school after eight years of graduate work, and we were thinking of buying a house. Everything was so oriented toward life; there were books all over the house about pregnancy and motherhood. And then every one of my dreams was shattered in a split second, in one phone call. And because we'd been trying to have a child, it felt almost as if there had been two deaths." Guilt over the baby issue gnawed at Merryl. "One of the things I went over and over was, if I had gotten pregnant, would Carl have stayed alive?" Later, her mother-in-law introduced her to a woman whose husband, a graduate student, had killed himself when she was three months pregnant. Her son was now seven. While this helped Merryl realize her pregnancy wouldn't have saved Carl, the overpowering feeling of loss remained—*she* wasn't pregnant, *she* didn't have a child, and now she'd never have Carl's child, maybe never have a child at all. "I was thirty-four and it seemed as if every woman in the world my age was pregnant," she says. "My best friend was pregnant, my two sisters-in-law were pregnant, and a half dozen other friends were pregnant. We had all been on the same track together—college, career, marriage, babies, and here I was a widow and they were all pregnant." For a long time Merryl couldn't bear to think of Carl's nephew, and when she saw babies on the street, she had to look away.

Christmas with Carl had always been special. They had lit candles in the windows, decorated trees with favorite ornaments, and opened the doors on Advent calendars together every December for eight years. This year Merryl spent Christmas with her parents, who had problems of their own. Her father was recovering from a hip replacement, and her mother was suffering pain from advancing cancer. The three of them, wanting to get far away from New England, flew to New Orleans. It was Merryl's first trip since she and Carl had vacationed in Nova Scotia ten months before his death. On the way down, Merryl welcomed each sudden altitude drop or sharp tilt of the plane—"If I were taken away," she thought, "it would solve everything." In the elevator delivering them to their room in an antiseptic, high-rise, downtown hotel, the bellhop said, "It's Christmas Eve; what are you doing here?" Her father answered quietly, "We're here *because* it's Christmas Eve."

The holiday was a nightmare. "We had an abysmal, horrible time," says Merryl. "I told my parents it was a good thing the windows were locked because we were on the fortieth floor and I really felt like leaping." The day after Christmas they went to the zoo. They made a pathetic trio. Merryl's father was in a wheelchair, pushed by Merryl's mother, who wheezed and occasionally cried out in pain. Merryl, hunched over, wrapped in a scarf, wearing glasses (since Carl's death she hadn't worn her contact lenses), looked as if she were in disguise. As they made their way slowly through the zoo, Merryl noticed a young couple strolling toward them, arm in arm, as chipper as a honeymoon couple in an advertisement. The man looked familiar; Merryl realized that she and Carl had known him at the University of Chicago. From the startled look in his eyes Merryl thinks he recognized her. But they passed each other without speaking. On the flight home, seated across from a young man who looked like Carl and was dandling an infant on his knee, Merryl broke into sobs so loud that people craned their necks to see what was wrong.

In January, Merryl moved back into the Brookline apartment. Nothing in it had changed since the day Carl had died. The pencils on his desk were still sharp; his wastebaskets were still filled with notes from his work; his clothes still hung in the closet; his laundry still sat in the hamper; his shoes still sat under his desk; the novel he had been reading still lay on the night table; the calendar in the bedroom was still turned to June.

Over the following months Merryl spent as little time in the apartment as possible. She left the shades drawn except to admit enough light for Carl's plants to survive. She never went shopping, always ate takeout, never used the dishwasher, never vacuumed or dusted. She ignored the growing pile of second-class mail addressed to Carl. She never opened a closet or a dresser drawer; she kept her clothes in piles on the bed she had shared with Carl. She slept on a mattress in Carl's study, where she built a sort of cocoon in the shadow of his desk. Next to her pillow she kept Carl's pajamas and her nightgown from the last night they had slept together. Next to the mattress she arranged an intimate circle of belongings on the floor: her alarm clock, her journals, the Carl papers she was working on, her thirty-third-birthday card from Carl, and a pad of paper on which she kept a tally of the number of days since his death.

In many ways Merryl's own life had stopped in June. For almost a year she didn't watch television, see a movie, or read a "normal" book. "Part of it was that everything seemed so trivial, but a lot of it had to do with the way Carl died," she says. "I couldn't pick up anything that had a story in it without wondering why *these* people didn't commit suicide." She never made phone calls, although she didn't mind getting them. Faced with groups of people, she sought out a room's corners. "I lived a sort of marginal, weird existence. I was living out of shopping bags. If I met someone new and I was asked to explain my life, I would say that I worked at a publishing house and so on, but I really felt like screaming, 'You don't understand! I don't know who's who and what's what, and I don't know who I am.'"

To understand who she was, Merryl felt she had to understand Carl. Until she made some sense of his suicide, she knew she would be unable to move on. Each night after work she took out her Carl papers from the black plastic bag that was by now overflowing and spread the folded yellow pieces of paper on the dining room table, hoping that from all that raw material some answers might emerge. She would stay up late trying to fit together fragments of Carl's life like pieces of a giant jigsaw puzzle. "It would take me two hours to fit one little incident in," she says. She made flow charts with arrows swirling around events in Carl's life, trying to trace the path that had led to his death. Sometimes she went into the study or the bedroom and stood exactly where she had stood seven months earlier, and then she replayed aloud the words they had spoken. "I had this immense need to find out why this person would choose to die when there are so many people in the world who don't," says Merryl. "When a person commits suicide, all his qualities have to be reexamined in light of his death. And that's true only of this kind of death. Someone who dies in an accident is still the same person—you don't go back and analyze their character, wondering who they really were. All the characteristics of the person I'd lived with and loved for eight years—his gentleness, his amazing rapport with children—got thrown into the air. How did they fit in with someone taking his own life so violently? Everyone thought of that gentleness as a good thing, but now I wondered whether it was all just suppressed anger." Sometimes when Merryl passed Carl's portrait on the living room wall, she would stop and gaze at those eyes and wonder who this man really was.

Three times a week Merryl and her therapist talked about Carl. Her therapist helped Merryl realize that the qualities she loved in Carl had not been an illusion. "While there were times Carl should have spoken out, times when he was self-effacing and suffering from a lack of confidence, he had a very gentle, sincere, and responsible way of being," says Merryl. "And if he could have worked through it, if he could have lived, all those good qualities would still be there." Slowly, a picture of Carl began to take shape, of a thoughtful, caring, but troubled man whose high standards had led to great successes—and to great pain when he believed he had fallen short of his ideals.

Merryl's therapist told her about something she called the "all-or-nothing" phenomenon. She explained that certain people, for various developmental reasons, see things as all-or-nothing situations. When they are flooded by negative feelings, any hopeful feelings are often completely forgotten. The person is swept by a black feeling of total hopelessness that may put him at risk for suicide. "As soon as she started talking about that, it clicked," says Merryl. "That's the way Carl was, with his projects, with his job search, and with his dissertation. That perfectionism came even in little things, like baking bread. If it didn't come out exactly right, he was deeply upset." That all-or-nothing quality was also evident in Carl's diary, which Merryl read after his death. In Paris, two nights before he was to fly home from his junior year abroad, Carl had written of the turmoil he felt at the thought of trying to reintegrate himself, with his growing political activism, into the campus he had left as an honors premed student. His life seemed to be changing faster than he could control. As he wandered through the streets of Paris that night, he thought of throwing himself into the Seine. He labeled that journal entry "I want to die."

Although the entry made her inexpressibly sad, it gave Merryl a small measure of understanding, even comfort, to know that Carl's thoughts of death had existed before she'd met him. "I've gone over all this with my therapist, and we feel that something snapped about ten days before he died when he became convinced that there was a fatal flaw in his dissertation," says Merryl. "And that if the dissertation was lost, he was, too. I think that ten days before his death—on some unconscious level—he'd made his decision to kill himself." Gradually, Merryl was able to separate her actions from Carl's. "In the last weeks of his life he was on a separate track. Although I wanted to believe that I could have some control over that, I really don't think I existed for him during that time. In a way that's a relief; understanding that helped ease my feelings of guilt and responsibility. But it's hard to come to terms with the idea that not only are you not responsible but that you probably didn't even matter to the other person at that point."

With the help of her therapist and her friend Judith, Merryl worked out a metaphor that helped put those last weeks into perspective. "It was as if Carl was underwater, and his friends and family and I were on the surface, calling down to him. Occasionally, he would come up and communicate with us. But what was going on for him inside was the part of the water we never see: the undertow, a powerful force churning away down there that we couldn't touch. Suddenly, at the end, that undertow swept him away. It just literally overcame him."

Merryl became increasingly immersed in her exploration; at one point she planned to write an in-depth study of Carl's life. But in early February something nudged her from her obsession and eventually helped her to understand that she had come further in her grieving than she had realized. On the subway one day she bumped into an old acquaintance. The man, also an editor, had always liked Merryl, and after this chance encounter he asked her out. They began seeing each other. At times their dates were eerie when comparisons to Carl flew to her mind: driving together in his car, Merryl would look over and be astonished that the man next to her wasn't Carl; walking the dogs, he would be dragged out the door the way Carl had been; when they kissed, she was surprised not to have to lift her head—Carl had been much taller. Merryl was frightened to be feeling something for someone other than Carl but was pleased to realize that she could feel at all. It was the first time since his death that she had thought for more than sixty minutes about something other than his suicide. Merryl began to take better care of herself: she had her hair cut and curled, she wore her contact lenses again, she ate more, and she went shopping. She had lost so much weight that none of her clothes fit, although she hadn't cared until now. As the relationship grew, all the things that had been ripped from Merryl by Carl's suicide seemed possible once more.

Two months after they met, the man left Merryl for a younger woman. Merryl was devastated, but the obsession of the larger grief had been relieved somewhat by the smaller, newer one. By the time the relationship was over, Merryl no longer kept a running tally of the number of days since Carl's death.

From what she had read, Merryl knew that the first anniversary of Carl's death might be difficult, so she made elaborate preparations. After an impromptu ceremony at the grave with her parents and Carl's family, she drove to Eastham, a small town on Cape Cod, where she spent the night in a hotel. The next morning, exactly one year after Carl's death, she went to the beach with the contents of the suitcase Carl had taken to New York, which had been lying in her parents' basement, unopened, until this week. Now, sitting on the shore among the sunbathers, she spread these things on the sand in front of her: his watch, wallet, and wedding ring. She sang several of her favorite songs. She listened to the waves. She felt she had come a long way since the sight of the sea had meant only one thing: a way for her to die. She felt proud that she had gotten through the year.

In August, fourteen months after Carl's death, Merryl met a new employee at work whom she liked immediately. Ten days after they met, he asked her out. Merryl accepted. On their first date Merryl told him about Carl. "I knew this man was probably going to mean something to me so I wanted it out on the table," she says. "He had to know how much it affected me. I was nervous about telling him, but he was very understanding. We talked a lot about the guilt I felt and the loneliness." Nathan was sympathetic; he had lived a quiet, solitary life in western Massachusetts and knew what it was like to be lonely. Later on during that first date, he asked Merryl what she'd been reading lately. "Other than books about suicide," said Merryl, "nothing." It took a few minutes for the conversation to recover.

Merryl was more cautious this time. "I kept saying to myself, 'I don't want to get involved yet—I'm not ready for this, I'm still too vulnerable.'" But she had grown stronger in therapy, and the more she saw of Nathan, the more she was drawn to him. Like Carl he was sensitive, introspective, and well-spoken. Like Merryl he was fascinated by writing and language. He was a computer buff, a sports nut, and an amateur historian. When he took Merryl to visit *Old Ironsides,* the American frigate from the War of 1812, Nathan was such a knowledgeable, enthusiastic guide that half a dozen tourists abandoned the official tour to follow him. One night Merryl and Nathan went to a showing of

Hitchcock's *Rear Window*. As they kissed and hugged playfully in the dark theater, Merryl had a sudden sense of unreality. "Could I be enjoying life again?" she wondered. "Could this really be me?"

One day in October, about two months after they had met, they spent the day at the beach. At the end of the afternoon Nathan went ahead to get Merryl's car. As Merryl walked toward the car and saw a man's silhouette in the driver's seat, she had a moment of confusion. "I looked through the window, saw that silhouette, and thought, 'It's unbelievable seeing someone else drive the car that Carl and I bought together two years ago.' I had thought no one else would ever sit in that driver's seat. It was eerie. When I got in the car, I shook my head, almost to clear it. Then I looked over, and there was Nathan. I was happy to see him, and I touched his hair gingerly but affectionately." One night, so they wouldn't hear about it secondhand, Merryl called Carl's parents and told them she had met a man she was serious about.

In May, Merryl and Nathan decided to move in together. Merryl spent evenings and weekends in July packing up the Brookline apartment. Everything Carl owned was still untouched. Before she started, Merryl took photographs of the apartment, to record the way it had looked when she and Carl had lived there. And then she began to dismantle the scene of their life together, room by room. She started with the living room, which held the fewest memories. Next, she packed up the dining room, then the kitchen, then the bedroom. The bedroom wasn't too bad: Carl had kept his clothes in a closet in the study. After prolonged internal debate, every item wound up in one of three piles—one to go to the new apartment, one to be given to Goodwill, and one to be thrown away.

She saved the study until last. Almost everything Carl owned was in this room, undisturbed since the day he had died. From her reading she knew all about how bereaved people build shrines to the dead and get "stuck" in grief, but her therapist had agreed it would not be inappropriate for her to keep a box of Carl's clothes. Now Merryl sat on the floor holding up shirts and sweaters she knew so well, trying to decide which to keep, which she would never see again. She saved a green-and-blue-striped Indian bathrobe she had made him for Christmas four years before, one that he'd often studied in; she saved a soft, green velour shirt that reminded her of their Chicago years; she saved a baggy, white mohair sweater she had knitted him during their first year together. When she had stuffed one large carton full and marked it "Carl's clothes," she realized she'd chosen something from each phase of their life together.

It was almost midnight by the time she turned to the old wooden desk where Carl had spent so much of his last eight years. Next to the desk stood the research for his unfinished dissertation—eighteen index card files, enough to catalog a small-town library, crammed with white cards carefully hand-printed with quotations from psychology books, alphabetized and cross-referenced to other cards and to the hundreds of books on Carl's shelves. Merryl sat on a packing crate and stared at the scene of Carl's failure, unable to face it, wishing she hadn't left it to the end. It was midnight, and the movers were due at eight. Then, carefully, as if handling precious, dangerous specimens, she transferred the contents of Carl's desk and files whole into boxes, without stopping to sort through them. The desk drawers took six boxes; the files filled eight. By three in the morning, when Merryl looked up, their home had been broken down to a skyline of stacked boxes. At four o'clock, exhausted, she drove to her new home in Cambridge.

Four hours later the movers arrived, and by that evening eight years of Merryl and Carl's shared life had been scattered to various destinations. A truckload went to Cambridge. Three carloads of clothes and shoes went to Goodwill, so much that it wouldn't fit into the hopper at the shopping mall. The elderly attendant refused to accept the overflow until Merryl, desperate, told him that her husband had recently died. His annoyance disappeared. "He must have been so young," he said sadly, and waved her ahead. Their bed went to Merryl's brother, Carl's desk to her brother's girlfriend. The puppets Carl made for his dissertation research—the elephant, the pilot, the truck two feet long—went into a corner of her father's house at the Cape. Clothes too old for Goodwill, battered suitcases, dead plants, and a seven-foot stack of second-class mail addressed to Carl that had never been thrown out filled thirty green trash bags that lined the sidewalk in front of the Brookline apartment like a lumpy plastic hedge. The Department of Public Works arranged a special pickup because there was so much to haul away. When Merryl drove by the house the next morning, it was gone.

# VI

# A SAFE PLACE

---

"I'M MERRYL MALESKA. My husband committed suicide a year and a half ago."

"I'm Peter Courtney. Our daughter Lisa committed suicide six years ago just before Christmas."

"I'm Liz, Peter's wife."

"I'm Eileen Dowcett. My husband and I lost our son Philip five years ago."

"I'm Rona Marks, and my only daughter committed suicide three months ago."

"I'm Joyce Oldham, and my husband committed suicide thirteen months ago."

"I'm Bailey Barron, and our daughter committed suicide four years ago."

"I'm Stanley Barron."

"I'm Jean Clark. My husband committed suicide three years ago last January."

"I'm Tom Rossi, and my brother Rick committed suicide eight years ago."

On a winter evening nineteen months after Carl's death, Merryl Maleska and ten other people were seated in a semicircle in a small room in a three-story redbrick building in Somerville, Massachusetts. They were members of Safe Place, a support group for survivors of suicide. Group "facilitator" Tom Welch, a young Roman Catholic priest, began the meeting with his customary introduction: "Each of us comes to this circle with a private urgency, even agony and sorrow. Perhaps others we love are carrying their own burdens and aren't always available to comfort us. Let us use this time to create an opportunity for each to share, giving room for silence if that is appropriate, understanding that each has strengths to cope with his or her life, yet all are enriched by compassionate and understanding hearts."

Welch looked around the semicircle at each member of the group. "I wonder if someone might begin by sharing a concern they are presently dealing with."

There was a pause, then Bailey Barron, a middle-aged woman with short blond hair, began, "Fredi committed suicide four years ago . . . today," she said slowly, looking at her hands. "I didn't realize it before we came tonight. It was a Monday, a rainy Monday. . . . It brings back a lot of things. You go through the whole procedure again. Holidays are rough, anniversaries are rough." She shrugged. "Every day is rough."

Welch said gently, "Has anyone else recently experienced an anniversary?"

Peter Courtney, a compact, muscular man in a flannel shirt, nodded. "We're coming very close. Lisa was on a Monday. It was snowing, cold and snowing. I was out on the boat, working, and when I came home, I found out. It's coming right back again now. A couple of weeks."

Joyce Oldham, a prim middle-aged woman in matching blue skirt and jacket, smiled politely. Her earrings trembled. "Just a month ago it was a year for me that my husband killed himself, and I was very depressed." She gave an anxious, apologetic laugh and looked to either side for support. "Does it get any better after the years go by?" She scanned the room nervously.

"Not better," said Bailey softly, staring at the floor. "Different."

---

Merryl Maleska was fortunate in having parents, relatives, friends, and a therapist who were unusually sensitive to her needs. Because the subject of suicide makes many people uncomfortable, survivors often have difficulty finding support. A survivor's need to analyze the suicide may seem unquenchable, and even the most sympathetic friend may eventually find it difficult to listen. But the need to talk may continue long after friends and family have had enough. Some survivors feel that even their closest friends cannot truly understand unless they have themselves lost someone to suicide. It was this need that drew Merryl to Safe Place.

More than one thousand survivors of suicide, ranging in age from twelve to eighty, and coming from as far away as Maine and Vermont, have attended meetings of Safe Place since it started in 1978. Some have lost parents, some husbands, some wives, some children, some grandchildren, some friends. One woman first came to the group a few days after her son had killed himself; another woman first came to the group thirty years after her father had killed himself. Safe Place meets twice a month. People may attend as many or as few meetings as they like. Some come once, find it overwhelmingly painful, and never return; others attend every meeting for years. Most come for a year or so, then gradually stop, perhaps returning for meetings around birthdays, holidays, or the anniversary of the death, when wounds tend to reopen.

When they first hear about Safe Place from a friend or a counselor, survivors are often resistant to the idea, perhaps because of some stiff-upper-lipism, perhaps because they stigmatize others as they themselves have been stigmatized—something *must* be wrong with the people in the group because, after all, someone in their family committed suicide. "When a friend told me about Safe Place, I said no thank you, my husband and I weren't up to it," remembers Arlene Feltz, whose son had hanged himself a few months earlier. "But deep down we felt we didn't belong to this kind of group. I don't know what kind of people we thought they would be—derelicts or something." She laughs. "Somehow I just felt they would look different." When the pain didn't let up, Arlene and her husband decided to try Safe Place. Sitting in a group of twelve people, Arlene, who had always been terrified of speaking in public, was anxious and mute. As the meeting started, there was a pause, and suddenly Arlene was shocked to hear herself talking about her son. "I don't even remember what I said, but that meeting was the biggest uplift since his death."

For many survivors, attending their first Safe Place meeting is like happening upon an oasis. "It was literally my salvation," says a woman who came to the group two months after her husband shot himself. "It was the first time I felt that life might go on." It may be the first time new members have met anyone else who has lost someone to suicide. It may even be the first time they have ever said the word *suicide* out loud. Merely being in the same room with other survivors can be tremendously painful—and tremendously liberating. Tom Rossi, a young priest, came to his first meeting three years after his younger brother's suicide, still dogged by feelings of guilt and low self-esteem. "I looked around at the other people and thought, 'It happened to them, and *they* look like nice, normal people, so maybe I'm not such a horrible person, maybe *I* could be a nice person, too.'"

Merryl Maleska first came to Safe Place three weeks after Carl's death. She hated it. She said nothing, just sat there numb and stone-faced. "I was looking for someone like me, someone young who had lost her husband to suicide but who had come through it," she says. There was one woman close to Merryl's age whose husband, a psychology student, had shot himself, but after two years she still couldn't speak his name without weeping. Merryl left the meeting that night feeling more raw than when she'd arrived. Nevertheless, she continued to attend, even though for many months it seemed only to depress her further. But Merryl had a vague idea it might be good for her someday. And occasionally, lying in her bed or crying at work, she thought of the woman whose husband had shot himself and felt a little less alone. "It helped me to know that this person was going through the same loss, the same torture. In the midst of my pain I would remember her face and think of how she had lost her husband, too. And that communion would somehow help me to make real, tangible, this event that was so unbelievable." After a while Merryl began to speak at meetings. "It was the only place I could talk about nothing but suicide for two hours and not feel guilty for taking up someone's time." Merryl's calendar, which had once been so full, now had only two appointments marked on it each month—meetings of Safe Place.

When Safe Place began in 1978, members of the Samaritans attended the meetings as observers. One night a survivor said that the presence of the Samaritans, whose work is based on the belief that suicide can be prevented, felt like an unspoken accusation. Since that night no one has been allowed in the room who has not lost a family member or close friend to suicide. (The meeting I witnessed was a special one in which Safe Place members had volunteered to be videotaped for educational purposes.) Otherwise, there are few rules. Safe Place has no agenda, no speakers, no required readings, and, although people come looking for them, no answers. There is just a lot of what Welch calls "unloading"—talk, talk, and more talk. But even that is not required; some survivors attend faithfully for a whole season and never say a word. Safe Place meetings are not counseling sessions. There is no advice given. "People can respond to questions and share what works for them," Welch told me, "but they can't suggest that someone else do this, too—it works for me, therefore it works for you." The goal is to create "an atmosphere in which people can safely grieve."

Midway through the meeting Welch turned to Rona, a divorced, middle-aged woman whose daughter had killed herself three months earlier. She was perched on her chair, lips tight, hands folded, as quiet and contained as an owl. She hadn't said a word all night; when someone spoke, she looked not at them but at a point on the floor in their general direction. Welch gently asked whether caring for her remaining children had left her any time for her own grief. Seven words into her answer, Rona began to weep. She could not stop crying but she could not stop talking, and a flood of anxieties gushed out: her children's fears, her son-in-law's drinking, her miserable Thanksgiving. "And I tried to go through my daughter's things, but I couldn't go through them, so my son went through them and he said it's sad but he went through them and I just can't, and every day it's a different pain I have to face, I try to leave it in God's hands as much as I can, and that's helped, and I try to take it one day at a time, and that's helped with my pain, but it also, it . . . just . . . it doesn't . . . I just miss her so much."

As the words and tears poured out, the rest of the group was still. Although it was clear from their faces that they were deeply affected, no one gave her a handkerchief or moved to hug her or even touch her, although Liz Courtney, sitting next to her, unconsciously swung her arm up to rest on the back of Rona's chair. Later, I questioned Welch about their restraint. "If someone starts crying," he explained, "and you immediately pass the Kleenex or run over and hug the person, it stops the feeling. It may make the person feel that tears are inappropriate. Nothing should interrupt whatever someone is feeling. That's why refreshments aren't served until after the meeting. People need to be able to explore their pain without any interference—which is something they don't get to do at home."

Eventually, Rona's sobbing subsided into weeping, her words slowed, and like an accordion that must be squeezed flat before all the notes can escape, she finally stopped. "And I know it's going to be even harder at Christmas, but my son said he would come over and put up the tree because my daughter always did that. And I find as time goes on it's gotten harder instead of easier." There was a long pause, as if the group were giving the spilled pain a chance to settle, and then Merryl said gently, "But three months is like yesterday, really." There were murmurs and nods of assent from the others. Bailey gave a wry smile. "In the beginning I thought that every day would make it better, every step would make it better," she said. "Well, it doesn't, and we all know that. You never go back to the beginning, but it isn't just a steady upward progress." Rona stopped crying. She looked up at the faces of the group, meeting their eyes for the first time.

People feel comfortable at Safe Place talking about things they can't talk about anywhere else: the nightmares and gory details that friends want to be spared but a survivor can't shake, the fear that another family member might complete suicide, the sneaking suspicion they might be going crazy, the sense that they'll never be happy again. "It's amazing how many times I'll unravel an incident and people will say, 'That's how I feel,' or 'That happened to me,'" says a woman whose husband shot himself. A young woman whose lover killed himself a year ago can't tell friends that sometimes, when the pain is overwhelming, she gets in her car, rolls up the windows, and drives back and forth across a bridge, screaming. "You can say anything you want at Safe Place," she says, "and no one will ever laugh at you or think you're a jerk."

One of the most difficult issues for survivors to talk about is their own suicidal thoughts. "They need reassurance that it's okay to have those thoughts," Welch told me. "In the group, people understand those feelings and so it gets said. No one gasps, no one faints." No Safe Place member has ever killed himself, and although a troubled survivor is occasionally referred to counseling, interventions in the group are minimal. More often the group's atmosphere encourages honesty on less dramatic questions. "If friends ask me how I'm feeling and I say I'm feeling bad, they don't know what to say," says the mother of a boy who hanged himself. "So now I just tell them I'm okay. But in group the other night, someone asked me how I was feeling, and I said, 'Terrible.'" She smiles. "It felt good to be able to say that."

At Safe Place comfort comes in peculiar ways. No matter how awful a survivor's situation seems to be, at Safe Place there's always someone whose story sounds even worse. A mother plagued with guilt for not taking her son's suicide threats seriously meets a man who, hoping to shock his wife out of her threats, told her to go ahead and kill herself. A couple whose son shot himself in the heart meets a woman who found her husband shot in the head. A woman angry because her husband left no note meets a woman angry because her husband left a note. A young woman devastated by the suicide of her father meets a woman who lost both her father and her brother to suicide. "Measuring" can also work another way: survivors for whom the wound is unbearably fresh can listen to a survivor whose loss is further in the past and realize that some day their pain may lessen. A woman whose son killed himself four years ago has never told *anybody* it was a suicide. Sitting in silence at Safe Place is the best she can do for now, but listening to survivors who are able to talk about the suicides in their families gives her a seed of hope. And those survivors are comforted to feel that their pain may be of use.

None of which means that a survivor will ever forget. "After five years I feel a lot better," Liz Courtney told the group. Her hands cut quick geometric shapes in front of her as she spoke. "But still, it comes back. The waves keep coming." She looked toward her husband, Peter, who nodded. "Two weeks ago one of our daughters came home from St. Louis for some job interviews," she said, "and she was really excited. Our son had just bought a house, and our other daughter was getting along really well with her beau, and I was so happy that everybody was perking. But then when they left, I just dissolved. I couldn't put my finger on it at first, and then I realized, 'Lisa isn't here to be a part of this.'" Liz's hands folded tightly in her lap as if now that they'd found each other they'd never let go. "I find I can get really upset about something and not have any idea what it's all about until I analyze it. And always it seems to come back to Lisa."

---

Safe Place was born because Liz and Peter Courtney, no matter where they turned, could not find enough room for their grief during the year after their daughter Lisa killed herself on the roof of a five-story building in Newburyport, a small town on the coast north of Boston.

One night, not quite six months after Lisa's death, Liz and Peter were at Peter's brother's house for dinner. Liz had been warned by friends who had been through deaths in their families that she would have six months to "get over" her daughter's death before people would expect her to "shape up her act." But Liz was still reeling with grief, and that night at dinner she began talking yet again about Lisa's suicide. Suddenly her brother-in-law interrupted, "Knock it off. Enough is enough." Liz was mortified but forced a smile. "Wait!" she said. "It's only been five and a half months—I still have two weeks!"

Liz and Peter Courtney laughed when they told me the story. They laughed at their naïveté in thinking they could possibly "shape up their act" in five and a half or even six months. "Five *years* is when we began to feel better," said Liz, a tall, handsome woman who crafts lampshades. Her husband, Peter, a small, rugged-looking lobsterman, nodded. "After five years the salt started to come out of the wound," he said. When I first met them, seven years after their daughter's death, the pain still occasionally struck without warning. For Peter the tears came as suddenly as a summer squall; they rolled down his cheeks until his whole face was wet, and only when he stopped crying did he pull a worn red bandanna from his pocket. Liz dabbed delicately at her tears with a finger before they had a chance to travel far down her face. Recently, she and Peter had been at a friend's house watching *Fanny and Alexander,* the film by Ingmar Bergman. In one scene a woman sees the body of her dead husband for the first time and howls like a jungle animal. "How awful," said one of the Courtneys' friends. "Who could make such a sound?" Liz didn't answer. She had flashed back to a moment seven years before, to the day her daughter died, when she had let out a howl exactly like that.

Lisa Courtney was "born with a crayon in her hand," as her mother said. At an early age she decided she wanted to be an artist; she edited the art quarterly in high school and attended an art school in Philadelphia. A slender girl with long blond hair and milky skin, Lisa was sensitive and shy, though, said Liz, "not painfully so." Liz and Peter were shocked when on Thanksgiving of her junior year at college they got a call from the school counselor at two in the morning telling them Lisa had been found by a night watchman, curled up and whimpering in a public bathroom cubicle. They took off in their station wagon for Philadelphia, terrified. "Lisa was sitting on a bed looking so pathetic," recalled Peter. "I felt so sorry for her. I thought, 'God, if I'd ever known this kid had been this tense . . .'" The doctor, who had given Lisa Thorazine, suggested they take her home for a rest.

Peter and Liz were determined to lick the problem as a family. Each week the three of them went to a husband-and-wife counseling team, and Lisa saw the wife for individual therapy. Over the next few years Lisa gradually seemed to emerge from her shell. She found an apartment, a good job as a jewelry designer, and a few friends. But each fall she went into a funk—a fog, as she called it—that she couldn't shake until Christmas.

The fall when Lisa turned twenty-three, a number of things went wrong: she felt she deserved more pay at her job but was too shy to ask for a raise; her car wasn't working; and worst of all, her boyfriend left her for his old girlfriend. One day Peter got a call. Lisa had stabbed herself, but she was going to be all right. Said Liz, "When we got to the hospital, we asked her what happened, and she said she'd gone out to Plum Island and that she just felt all this fog around her. She thought about stabbing herself out there, but she came back to her apartment and stabbed herself in the kitchen, fell to the floor, and thought, 'Well, this is a dumb thing,' and then she drove herself to the hospital." Peter shook his head. "I remember asking her why she'd done it," he said. "And she said, 'Well, I've never felt real pain, and I *had* to *find out* what *real pain* was *about.*'" Peter pounded the table with his fist at each word. He looked up, puzzled. "And I think that's what shook my boots." Liz spoke quietly: "I think she meant she'd cut herself because she was in such a fog that she needed to feel something sharp."

Lisa came home to live with her parents and went back to work part-time. Each evening the three of them sat by the fire and had "catch-up time," telling each other about their day. "It was a very tense time," remembered Peter, "hoping that Lisa would come out and say, 'This is what was good about the day, and this is what was lousy.' And trying to carry on a smooth conversation with somebody you knew was in a lot of pain." Three times a week they went to their therapists, who taped each session. Afterward, Liz, Peter, and Lisa listened to the tape at home, talking and searching and rehashing, trying to get to the bottom of this, whatever this was. It was an exhausting time for Peter and Liz as they tried to give Lisa enough room but not too much, to be cozy and caring but not suffocating. "It was twenty-four hours a day, it was all for Lisa, trying to help her save her life," said Liz. "And sometimes when I thought that we had done some good work, I felt so elated. I remember walking down the street one day feeling, 'My God, maybe we're really going to get to the root of this problem, maybe we're going to lift Lisa out of this.' "

But Lisa remained brittle and self-conscious. One day in her mother's studio, Lisa looked out the window and saw her old boyfriend and his new girlfriend walking down the street licking ice cream cones. "He never bought ice cream for me," Lisa said in a small voice. Another time she curled up under a table. "I didn't know the word regression then," said Liz. "I didn't see until later it was a step on a long path of making her world smaller and smaller." Lisa worried that she was behaving peculiarly; one day she was mortified that she had driven out of a parking lot the wrong way. "You could always tell she felt a little raw," said Liz. "Her biggest problem was getting up in the morning. She was panicky—afraid to face the day. She'd cry and throw up. I'd hug her and say, 'Come on, let's go,' or 'Don't get up if you don't want to.' " But it got worse. "One morning she said, 'I don't want to live anymore.' I said, 'But, Lisa, just leave it until Friday, until we go back to the therapists.' "

Monday morning it snowed. When Lisa came downstairs, Liz asked her how she felt. "I'm fine," said Lisa. Liz told her daughter that she was going Christmas shopping and her father would be home at noon. "Is there anything you want to talk about now?" she asked. Lisa said no, she was okay, she was going to work.

"But Lisa never went to work," said Liz slowly. "She went to the building where I work. Her ex-boyfriend lives there, too, which is pretty heavy." Liz looked down at the table. "It's an enormous brick shoe factory that was made into artists' studios. And you can go all the way up to the fifth floor where there's a little room with a door that opens out on the roof. People sunbathe out there. Lisa used to go up there at lunchtime with her boyfriend. There's a beautiful view of the ocean. You can see Gloucester." Liz paused. "Afterward, her ex-beau remembered hearing someone up on the roof, walking around this funny little room. He didn't know it was Lisa, he thought it was a kid. She'd gone up to that room where there was a lot of broken glass from kids busting windows over years and years and years, and she did all of this"—Liz made a cutting motion at her wrists—"and this . . . and this"—her hand flashed at her legs, her arms, her neck—"I mean she really wanted *out*." Liz looked away and began to cry. "And then we assumed she just must have rolled off the roof."

In a coma, her skull fractured, her body covered with cuts, Lisa was kept on life-support systems while the family took turns sitting by her bed, talking softly to her, "just to let her know, whether she could hear us or not, that we were there," said Liz. But the doctors told the Courtneys it was hopeless, and they agreed the machines should be turned off. Friday evening they got a call from the hospital. Lisa was dead. "Saturday we saw her without any of the needles or the support systems, and that was a relief," said Liz. "I was glad she was at peace."

After the blur of friends and relatives arriving, the funeral service, friends and relatives departing, there was a sudden lull. Peter and Liz were alone. They talked about Lisa constantly. A sturdy, energetic man, Peter was drained and vulnerable. For weeks he couldn't finish a sentence without crying. About six weeks after the funeral he was painting the ceiling when he felt dizzy and fell off the sawhorse. He was able to telephone Liz, who rushed him to the doctor. Peter's heart had fibrillated; he was weak for weeks afterward.

Peter was angry at his daughter. Four weeks before her suicide, when she had stabbed herself in the stomach, Peter had asked Lisa to let him know if she ever felt like that again. "Don't leave me out of your act," he had said. Now he felt angry that she had broken her promise. Out on his boat he would suddenly cry, "Goddamn it, Lisa, why didn't you come to me?" When he was driving a truckload of lobsters into Boston, a sad tune would come over the radio, and he couldn't stop crying for half an hour. On his boat he would burst into tears, and then, just as quickly, it would be over.

Liz turned inward, wrestling with feelings of guilt. She felt she was a failure as a mother. One moment in particular haunted her, the morning before the suicide when Lisa had come downstairs in silence and Liz had said in frustration, "Please, for once, let me know how you're feeling—don't make me always have to ask."

Lisa had fallen from the tallest building in a small town, and her suicide made headlines in the local newspaper. "There wasn't anybody who didn't know, so there was no hiding, which made it easier in a way," said Liz. "But it also meant we were unable to hide if we wanted to. We knew everyone knew, and they knew we knew they knew." She gave a short, dry laugh. "Our close friends were great. Our medium friends were scared to death of us." Like many survivors, Liz and Peter often found themselves doing the comforting because their would-be comforters were so uncomfortable. Peter remembered one friend who crossed the street every time he saw him coming. "He could get from one side to another faster than a weasel in a chicken coop," said Peter, chuckling, shaking his head. "That went on for a long while, until one day there was a true traffic mess, and he couldn't make it across before I came upon him. I just said, 'Albert, how are you?' I knew he wanted to say something, but he just didn't know what the hell to say. So I said, 'Time's gone on and it's not easy for us, but it's getting better.' I just spilled that out to him, and I could see that just by my talking to him, it released some steam from his boiler."

While friends kept their distance, other survivors, some of whom they hardly knew, seemed to come out of the woodwork. Said Peter, "That spring a fellow fisherman came up to me. 'You've been through a bitch of a winter,' he said. 'My wife tried to kill herself so I know what you're going through, and it's a son of a bitch. The only difference is your kid didn't make it, my wife did.'" Peter tapped his fingers on the table. "It was good to know a guy like that could understand."

Although Peter's need to talk about the suicide gradually diminished, for Liz the ache was continuous. She could still talk to Peter, to their children, and to Peter's brother and his wife. But after a while some of her friends grew weary. "People just didn't want to hear it," said Liz. "I tried to talk about it less, to be more careful about it." She chuckled drily. "To grieve right." But her pain kept spilling over the edges. Years earlier she had been involved in several women's support groups, and now she kept wishing there were a group for this, a group where she could say what she wanted and people would listen whether it had been six months or six years.

Liz decided to look. A sixty-page notebook she kept that fall documents her exhaustive explorations. First she called the Boston Samaritans and talked to its director, Monica Dickens. Dickens was encouraging but knew of no groups for suicide grief; she suggested Liz try the Compassionate Friends, a support group for parents who have lost a child to death. Liz and Peter drove out to a church in Lynnfield one night for a meeting. It was comforting, but none of the other parents had lost a child to suicide. Suicide, Peter and Liz thought, needed a special group of its own. Liz called Massachusetts General Hospital and was referred back to the Samaritans. She called McLean Hospital and was connected to a psychiatrist researching the biochemistry of suicide. She called a specialist in group therapy at Harvard, who seemed surprised by the idea but wished her luck. She called a rabbi who had written books on suicide; he said if a group got started, he would love to write a book about it. She called an Episcopal minister who told her about Erich Lindemann and the importance of grief work. She called another minister, who offered his church to the group if she ever found or founded one. She called a famous grief specialist, who warned her to be careful because groups could be scary and someone might flip out.

After several months Liz had contacted a veritable who's who of bereavement. No one knew of anything in the area for suicide survivors, but they all knew of people who could benefit from such a group. Liz's notebook started filling up with these names—a woman from a farming town whose son had killed himself, a woman from a North Shore village whose son had killed himself. Liz talked to some of these people, and each survivor seemed to lead to another survivor who was looking for help. Then one morning Monica Dickens called and suggested Liz get in touch with Tom Welch, the young priest who had founded Omega, a grief assistance program in Somerville that ran support groups for widows and widowers, and for the terminally ill and their families. Liz called Welch and they arranged to meet. Tom Welch was aware of survivors' needs to talk about suicide, and he was aware of how often those needs went unmet. When he was in the seminary, a fellow priest had killed himself while on a retreat. It was never announced as a suicide. Welch only found out because word spread quickly. During his years at the seminary, two other priests took their lives. Each time there was no discussion or sharing of grief. "The seminary dealt with it very poorly," Welch recalls. "In fact, they didn't deal with it at all."

After meeting with Liz Courtney, Welch did some research of his own and found that although there were a handful of support groups for suicide survivors in the country, the closest was in Detroit, Michigan. "The groups were set up along the Alcoholics Anonymous model," Welch says. "In fact, one of them was called Suicides Anonymous. The *Anonymous* bothered me because it seemed to feed the idea that people need to be anonymous about suicide. It contributes to the conspiracy of silence and to society's inability to acknowledge that suicide is the way some people die. We didn't want to be anonymous about it, but we did want to be safe about it."

On November 9, 1978, almost one year after Lisa Courtney's death, nine people gathered in a small room at the Omega offices in Somerville. After Tom Welch spoke briefly about his ideas for the group, Liz described the research that had led her there. When she finished, there was an awkward pause. Then one man said that before they went any further, he wanted to know who everybody was and what had brought them there. One by one, people in the room introduced themselves. Then, as if a dam had burst, they began to talk about what it felt like to lose someone to suicide. For some of them it had been many years since the death, and talking about it was painful but freeing. At the end of the meeting, one woman stood. "I've said things here tonight that I've never been able to say anywhere else," she said. "This is a safe place."

---

By 2005, Safe Place was one of 270 suicide survivor groups meeting in churches, kitchens, living rooms, and suicide prevention centers across the country. (Now run by the Samaritans, Safe Place has four chapters in New

England, each led by a trained Samaritan volunteer who is also a survivor.) The first group was started in 1971 in San Diego, and others—with names like LOSS, Heartbeat, Seasons, Life Line, Transition, and Life After Suicide— quickly followed. Many groups have informal roots. Two survivors meet, talk over coffee, invite other survivors, and are soon gathering regularly to share their grief as well as advice on such practical matters as how to tell a child, how to manage anniversaries and holidays, or what to do with the dead person's possessions. There are survivor conferences, survivor books, and survivor newsletters such as *Afterwords, Mayday,* and *The Ultimate Rejection,* which print poems, personal stories, and news about survivor research. The Internet has spawned dozens of survivor-themed Web sites, some of which allow survivors to "chat" directly with other survivors around the world. One survivor organization runs separate e-mail support groups for teenagers, adult children, parents, fathers, spouses, adult siblings, grandparents, and support group facilitators. Its Web site also sponsors "Movies to Miss!" in which survivors rate hundreds of films that have suicide-related scenes survivors may find disturbing. (*Best in Show,* a mock documentary about dog shows, in which a few passing jokes about suicide are made, earns one frowny face, indicating "no visuals," while *Titanic,* in which a ship's officer shoots himself, gets five frowny faces—the equivalent of an X rating—signifying "shows the act in detail.")

Because the concept of the "suicide bereaved" as a special population is new, there is disagreement as to what approach best meets survivors' needs. While most of the groups, like Safe Place, are based on sharing personal experience, they range from intense weekly therapy sessions to irregular potluck dinners. One group leader runs "guided fantasies" in which she helps survivors reenact the mourning process—the funeral, burial, and so on—in order to complete issues they may not have had a chance to resolve. Most groups meet once or twice a month and are open-ended, while others hold weekly sessions for two months, with agendas and reading lists. Some groups charge a fee, some pass the hat, most are free. While some prefer members to join as soon after the suicide as possible, others suggest they come when the numbness has begun to wear off. One group won't let survivors join until six months after the death. Some groups are specifically for siblings, others just for mothers. There are a few groups for teenagers only, and at least one for therapists who have lost patients to suicide. Another group sponsors home visits by survivors who hold the same kinship relation to their dead loved one as the survivor to be visited. After being notified of a suicide by the Los Angeles Police Department, the Suicide Prevention Center sends trained survivors to the scene to provide family members with immediate emotional support. And a group in Louisiana brings together survivors with people who have attempted suicide so that survivors may better understand what their loved ones felt, while attempters can see the pain they might cause if they were to complete suicide.

The growth of survivor groups has been so rapid and the variety so wide that in 1984 the American Association of Suicidology, recalling the unsupervised growth of prevention centers in the early seventies, appointed a committee to review survivor groups. The committee found that the main disagreement among groups was over the role of mental health professionals. While about one-third use a therapist or counselor either as coleader or consultant, some are led by survivors with no training. Some professionals worry that these "amateurs" may be in over their head. "A few leaders don't recognize that they'll get involved with people who are severely troubled," says Sam Heilig, the social worker who chaired the AAS committee and for many years led a survivor group at the Los Angeles Suicide Prevention Center. "It's not uncommon for a suicide to trigger a series of underlying problems. In our group we've had people who are mentally ill, psychotic, severely depressed, and suicidal." Heilig is among those who have worried that survivor leaders may overlook people who need professional help. He feels that groups co-led by a therapist and a survivor offer the best of both worlds: the survivor can draw from personal experience, and the professional can answer questions about medication and statistics and act as a "safety net" so a survivor can feel safe falling apart.

Yet some survivors harbor great anger toward the mental health profession, especially if the person they mourn was in therapy. They may feel the "professionals" let them down. A few survivor-leaders insist there should be no professional involvement in groups. They say that they are capable of spotting problems and, when appropriate, of referring the survivor to professional help. "A lot of the literature writes up the pathological cases of survivors, so a few therapists think we're *all* basket cases," says one survivor-leader. "Many therapists look on us as a big pool of potential clients, but many survivors will never be able to go to a therapist." Explains one group leader, "The already stigmatized survivor may see needing therapeutic help as bringing them further stigma by labeling them as sick." At bottom, many survivors feel that no one who is not a survivor himself can understand. An Illinois social worker whose mother killed herself started a group when she realized that many survivors who were already in therapy seemed to need something more. "I feel so safe and warm and understood here," said a woman at her first meeting of the group. "I feel safe and warm at my shrink's office, too, but not always understood."

Whether a group leader is a trained therapist, an untrained survivor running a self-help group, or a counselor-priest like Tom Welch, working with survivors offers a unique perspective on suicide itself. In his years at Safe Place, Welch occasionally got anonymous phone calls from people who were planning to kill themselves and, taking advantage of his reputation as a survivor expert, wanted to know how to make their suicide less painful for their family. What method should they use? Where should they do it? What should they say in their note? Welch listened carefully, suggested some options other than suicide, invited them to call him anytime, but told them their questions were unanswerable. "'There *is* no best way,' I say. I share with them what I learned from the group—that there is really no way to prevent the people who love them from feeling responsible for their death. They could leave them a thousand notes saying they're blameless, but it will never stop affecting them. Their lives will be forever changed."

———————

As the Safe Place meeting continued, the ten survivors became progressively more animated, their voices more sure, their bodies leaning farther into the circle. As I watched the videotape, I got an image of them—Peter, Liz, Merryl, Bailey, and the others—driving to Somerville from homes all over eastern Massachusetts, carrying their pain, coming to this room, and pouring it out as if there were an almost palpable communal pile of shards of grief and guilt and anger on the floor in front of them. Each time their load became a little lighter, although they knew that no matter how much they unloaded, there would always be something left.

"We still have a few more moments," said Tom Welch, "and before we break from the group, I'm wondering if someone has something he'd like to share."

"Earlier, we were talking about the holidays," said Jean, whose husband had shot himself three years ago. "One thing that has been helpful to me is to do something different each year. I haven't had a Christmas in my house or a tree, and that has been helpful. . . . I try to find a totally different scene over the holidays."

"It's a reminder of the happiness you can't participate in," said Welch.

"I don't ever want to have Christmas in my house again," murmured Jean.

"I think one of the things about time is that even though the loss never goes away, other things come up, other things grow," said Tom Rossi. "It's like the pictures now of Mount St. Helens. There's life there, and things fill in some of the spaces that right now are just yawning wounds or huge horrible gaps that it doesn't look like you'd ever get over. So I try not to say that anything's forever—that I'll never celebrate again or that it'll never get any better." He paused. "It'll never be like it was. But new things grow."

"Every Thanksgiving since Fredi's death, we've visited our cousins in North Carolina," Stanley said. "It's always been an escape. But every time we come home, it seems to come right back to that Monday after Thanksgiving when she took her own life." He looked at his wife. "I don't know why, but this Thanksgiving seemed to be the least difficult of all. This year I see things replacing the pain."

Peter nodded. "Lisa's grave is down on Plum Island, not far from where we live," he said. "Every so often I go down there with some flowers I might find on the roadside on the way home from the fishing boat." He looked down at his lap. "For the first three or four years, I couldn't get to the gate without crying. By the time I spoke to the guard and went through the gate I was a basket case." He shook his head. "But last time, I got all the way through the gate before I started crying!" He looked up, shaking his head, and smiled, and everyone in the group began to laugh with him.

After the laughter settled, Welch looked at the faces in the semicircle. "I'd like to make an opportunity for us to chat with one another for a while after we break from this group," he said, "but before that, why don't we spend a few moments in some quiet." And he, Peter, Liz, Merryl, Eileen, Rona, Joyce, Bailey, Stanley, Jean, and Tom joined hands, eyes closed, looking down. After a silence, Welch said, "Just feel all the warmth and support and comfort that's been here in this circle this evening. We can send out our good wishes, our hopes, our concern, our prayers. And remember always to take from this circle what we need for ourselves, to put all of that warmth and support into our own hearts."

# VII

# MERRYL:
# THE BUILDING BLOCKS

SEVENTEEN MONTHS after Carl's death Merryl Maleska spoke at an anniversary service held each year to which all Safe Place members, past and present, are invited. "For each of us in this room life has been torn open with such a shock that our deepest sense of trust in the world has been challenged," said Merryl. ". . . This would all be true of anyone who had lost a loved one in a tragic, sudden, totally unexpected way. For us, though, there are special, unique shadows to the distrust. It is not only the world, after all, that is unpredictable—not only the unforeseeable events of an accident—but the choice, the deliberate, in some sense, actions of our loved one that have so destroyed our sense of the world. Someone we loved terribly has rejected us, has told us we were not enough to stay alive for. Even if we *know* this was not at all his reason for doing what he did, it still *feels* like deep, unutterable abandonment. How can we ever trust another human being with our caring? How can we make ourselves vulnerable again?"

Two years after Carl's death Merryl and Nathan settled into a five-room apartment on the first floor of a three-story frame house on a quiet side street in Cambridge. The furnishings were simple and comfortable; the apartment looked like that of many young professional couples just starting out, building a home. And for Merryl, in many ways, life was just beginning again. Once more she was excited by her work; she had recently been promoted to senior editor at Houghton Mifflin. A social life that had stopped for two years restarted, and her calendar became crowded with entries for movies, birthdays, dinner parties, and concerts. She and Nathan began to invite new friends over for dinner; Merryl began to shop in supermarkets again. "When I walked into Star Market for the first time in two years, I felt like someone from another culture," says Merryl. She gained back the twenty-five pounds she had lost during her first year of grieving. She began to sew again; she made curtains for every room in the house and even knitted gifts for friends' babies. She started wearing jewelry again, resumed writing in her diary, and began, gingerly, to pick up "normal books." *War and Peace* was first, followed ten months later by *Dune.* "Both of them are set in other worlds, so they didn't seem as threatening." And when she and Nathan drove up through Maine to Quebec, it was her first vacation since Carl's death.

As she built a new home, another shared life, Merryl was occasionally swept by waves of fear. "The more I begin trusting someone again, the more afraid I am that I will lose everything again," she told me. "Whenever Nathan is late coming home from a trip, I get worried. If he says he'll call at eight, I'm petrified by nine. I'm just waiting for the worst, for someone to call and say, 'There's been a problem.' We were at the beach not long ago. At the end of the afternoon when we got back to the car, I realized I'd lost an earring. Nathan went back to look for it. It was a long way back to where we'd been sitting, and it was getting dark. He was gone a long time. I got scared that he would disappear into thin air. It was totally irrational; I knew that, and he came back, of course, but I was terrified. When you've had things taken away from you, you are constantly reminded of how fragile life is."

Merryl was forcefully reminded of that when her mother died of cancer a year and a half after Carl's death. Although not unexpected, it was a shock. Merryl's father was overcome with grief, and Merryl made most of the funeral arrangements—with the same home that had handled Carl's death. "The funeral director couldn't believe I was back and that I was functioning," she said. "The last time he'd seen me I was prostrate on the floor." Her mother was buried next to Carl. "It's one of the most important pieces of land in the world to me," she said. "Before Carl died I was afraid of the word *death,* and since then it seems as if I've lived in cemeteries." She chuckled wryly. "Now sometimes I feel more at home there."

For a year and a half Merryl had done little else but think about Carl's life and death. "My relationship with Carl spanned thirteen years—almost my entire adult life up to that point—and his suicide just blew my life open when I was on the verge of so many things," she said. "I thought that Carl's suicide would define my life for a long, long time, but it's no longer primarily how I define myself. It's a major part of my life, but it's no longer the one thing I'm waiting to tell someone. There are lots of pure moments free of Carl—laughing with Nathan or at work. And that's a long way from the night I heard he died when I didn't think I'd be able to live."

In therapy Merryl was still piecing things together about Carl, but gradually she and her therapist focused more on Merryl. For so long her life had seemed bound to Carl's life and his death. "My grief for Carl heightened a lot of the things I need to deal with in myself. I'm trying to come to terms with being a separate person and having a sense of my own self-worth. That's been a big part of separating myself from Carl and going on with life without him. I started feeling I was worth living for, whether or not I had Carl or any other man." Though she kept the black plastic bag of Carl papers in her top desk drawer, she rarely looked at them. After not missing a meeting of Safe Place for more than a year, Merryl began attending only rarely. When she did, she was looked up to as a sort of role model, as someone who had come through. Sometimes she saw someone who had come to Safe Place for the first time, "looking like a waif," and she shivered, remembering her own first meeting.

Merryl still thought of Carl every day. And though she no longer went out of her way to talk about him, she didn't go out of her way not to. "If somebody asks me where I got my car, I can say, 'Oh, Carl and I bought it,'" she said. "I don't unravel anymore. Or if I do start to unravel, I can put myself back together." When Nathan and Merryl were invited to the christening of Nathan's niece, Merryl was terrified she'd be undone by echoes of the christening party for Carl's nephew, the party that never took place. She was cautious but comfortable. She even held the baby. She got back in touch with Carl's brother and sister-in-law, who sent her a snapshot of Carl's nephew. "To me he looks a lot like Carl, which is a little eerie," she said. "But it didn't overwhelm me." One day she came across the pink bathrobe she had worn during her first months of mourning, and she touched the knots her nervous fingers had made of its stray threads. On weekends at her father's house on the Cape, Nathan liked to work in the study, Merryl's former "torture chamber." Merryl sometimes stood in the doorway and watched him. Though the studio couch was folded up, the clock with its insistent red digits still sat on its shelf. "And for a moment that hollow feeling at the pit of my stomach comes back. But then it's just a room again." She paused, then added, "But it'll never be *just* a room."

When Merryl visited New York for the first time since Carl's death, she decided to walk past the hotel where Carl had died, which she had seen so many times in her imagination. As she stood on the sidewalk and looked at the small, ugly, gray building, she was flooded with sadness. Dirty curtains billowed out of open windows. A painted advertisement was peeling on the side of the hotel. "It was no place for a man of Carl's magnitude to die," said Merryl. "But painful as it was, I felt better having seen it. I felt I'd faced down a demon that had been haunting me."

Most of Carl's things that Merryl had saved from the Brookline apartment lay in a corner of the basement. The suitcase Carl had taken to New York. The box marked "Carl's clothes." The portrait Merryl had given him for his thirty-second birthday. The inscribed glass biology prize Carl had won as a sophomore at Tufts, his fraternity "paddle," his master's diploma. Ten eight-foot-tall card files with thousands of neatly lettered file cards. One dozen boxes marked "Carl's files," containing his dissertation. "I will part from these things eventually," said Merryl. "There will come a time in my life when I'm not going to cart around Carl's work, but that time hasn't come yet." Upstairs, in the right-hand drawer of her desk where she kept the Carl papers, Merryl kept an envelope with a lock of Carl's hair she had saved. One day, she opened it and held the brown curl in her hand. "I saw some gray in it, which I'd seen before, but it made me wonder—would his hair have been gray by now? What would he be like? He was only thirty-three—he had so many stages of his life to go through. He was a man who was still unfolding. What would he have been like when he was old?

"Carl will always be a part of me," said Merryl, whose face still lit up when she talked about him. "I'll probably never know anyone else with his intensity and perception. He was so gentle, yet he had a way of cutting through things." She looked away. "I get a tremendous gripping feeling sometimes—at Christmas when I'm writing to his parents or when I'm looking at pictures of him. Suddenly, it will come back—that sense of what a good, rich, deep person he was. I think of the immense waste. It comes over me in an almost nauseating way. The loss of him not just from my world but from the whole world."

# VIII

# A PLACE
# FOR WHAT WE LOSE

---

"WE FIND A PLACE for what we lose," wrote Sigmund Freud to Ludwig Binswanger after the death of his friend's son. "Although we know that after such a loss the acute stage of mourning will subside, we also know that we shall remain inconsolable and will never find a substitute. No matter what may fill the gap, even if it be filled completely, it nevertheless remains something else."

Some say survivors never recover from a suicide. "Life is back to normal, but normal is different now," says a man whose son hanged himself. "Normal will never be the normal it was before a year ago." A man whose teenage daughter killed herself two years ago says it helps him to think of his grief as a physical handicap: "Some people can't see, some people can't walk, and I can't seem to enjoy life," he says matter-of-factly. As Tom Welch told me, "We never really essentially get over anything. We resolve it in such a way that we can go on."

Certainly, the sheer weight of the pain eases with time. In *Madame Bovary,* Flaubert describes a young widower's passage from suicidal depression to something approaching normalcy:

Ah well, slowly but surely, one day chasing another, spring on top of winter, autumn on top of summer, it leaked away, drop by drop, little by little; it left, it went away—it sank down, I should say, because there's always something stays, at the bottom, so to speak . . . a weight there, on

531

the chest! But it's the same for all of us, we mustn't let ourselves go, and want to die just because others are dead.

During this slow healing, signs of recovery may seem minute. One mother visits her son's grave three times a week instead of daily; another dreams of her son once a week instead of every night. "For a year and a half my daughter was the first thing I thought of when I opened my eyes in the morning," says one woman. She smiles faintly. "Now I can make coffee before it hits me." Yet this gradual increase of pain-free moments may be fraught with its own dangers—the pangs of "recovery guilt" many survivors feel for not thinking about the suicide twenty-four hours a day. "It's like if I go on with my life, I must be an awful person," says Tom Rossi. "There's that tug that if things start to go well, then maybe I should punish myself, because what kind of person am I if I can be happy and he's dead?"

Even when the tide of everyday experience takes the edge off the pain, wounds are often reopened. The anniversary of the death may be particularly difficult; merely being asked how many children one has can be devastating. "Sometimes I say, 'I had three but I lost one,'" says a woman whose nineteen-year-old son hanged himself. "Sometimes I say two, but then I feel dishonest, as if I'm denying him." A year after their son killed himself, one couple was desolate when they received his license renewal application in the mail. Another couple, months after their son's suicide, received a Christmas card from his therapist, who had forgotten to remove the boy's name from his computer mailing list. The spring following the suicide of her daughter, a woman burst into tears when she saw purple tulips blooming in her yard; she had forgotten her daughter had planted them. "My hands are just like my mom's," says another woman. "Every time I look at them for the rest of my life I'm going to think of her suicide."

Three years after their daughter's suicide, Liz and Peter Courtney built a one-room addition to their house. As the contractors tore down the walls, Liz grew increasingly anxious. Some days she exploded at them for their seeming inefficiency; at other times she felt helpless, unable to answer their simplest question. She would come downstairs in the middle of the night, pacing off dimensions, fretting about what furniture would go where, calculating how the addition could be made less expensive, wondering whether the project was a mistake. One day Peter was horrified to find her beating her head on the banister. "I can't stand it," she moaned. "I want to give up. I want to die."

In retrospect, Liz, who went back to Lisa's therapists for help, believes she had a nervous breakdown. "I couldn't stand any more destruction," she says. "Lisa had hurt herself so badly, and I felt this house was being hurt, too." At the same time her despair helped her understand how her daughter must have felt. "I never wanted to take my life, but I sure wanted to get out of that pain. And I thought, now I know what feeling awful feels like. Really awful. Really, really awful."

Six months later the addition was completed. "All of a sudden everything lightened," says Liz. "It was the climax; it just came out, and then the worst was over. I look back on it as being Lisa. It was the final hell. And I've felt so much better ever since."

Many grief counselors believe that healing after a suicide can begin only when the survivor realizes that the question why will never be answered. In a survey by Betsy Ross, the founder of an Iowa City support group called Ray of Hope, more than two hundred survivors were asked whether their explanation for the suicide had changed since the death. Over 70 percent said it had not, but they insisted that their relentless questioning was necessary regardless of the results. "I had to search for a reason even though I think I already knew I wouldn't find one," said one survivor. "He had to do it," said another. "I knew that then, and I know that now. I just don't know why. I may never know why, but I couldn't accept that at first and I can now." Observes Tom Welch, "The search for the reason why is part of what people need to do, but finally they understand that no answer is ever enough. Healing and a sense of self-worth come only when one draws away from feeling responsible for the death. When people learn a way to let go, to give permission for what's already happened to them, only then will they be able to move on."

After a suicide, a person's entire life is often seen through his final act, as if it discredits all the good things that came before. "The suicide totally changed the way I viewed our relationship," says a young woman a year after her husband hanged himself. "I really felt we were a model couple, and that's almost embarrassing now. I would like to be able to say to people, 'My husband and I had a great relationship,' but I feel too humiliated to do that." As Tom Rossi told me, "I remember my brother as a happy person—he taught me more about life than anybody. Yet when I tell people about him, about all the good things, I have to have him commit suicide at the end. It's so odd. I have to create him and then destroy him." A more accurate balance is restored only as the survivor works back through the bad memories and the good memories begin to resurface. "It may be a picture or a movie or a piece of music," says the widow of a man who shot himself four years ago, "but now those things remind me of the good times, not the bad." The widow of a man who jumped from an eleven-story building wrote, "I want Dick's death not to be bigger than his life."

Any death shakes our faith in our own world and in the order of the world around us. But suicide in particular forces survivors to question their most basic assumptions, a process in which they may ultimately learn some important things about the person they have lost and about themselves. "I thought I knew my husband," says a middle-aged lawyer. "I was so confident that I understood him and that I understood the world." She shakes her head. "My husband gave me the gift of my beginning to realize how powerless we are, how little we control, and how we have to accept that."

Some survivors speak of positive changes that emerge after a suicide, of families drawn closer together, of becoming more sensitive, loving, attentive, and compassionate. Some speak of the painful lesson of realizing that we can never truly know someone else, that in some way each of us is ultimately alone, and that life is a mystery. Some describe finding inner resources they did not know they had. "The pain I feel is offset by the knowledge that the very worst thing in life has happened to me, and I have survived," says one man. "Maybe we're never quite the same people we were before," says a woman whose son shot himself. "But maybe that's not all bad. Maybe we wouldn't *want* to be that person." In the years since her son's death she has led a survivor group, returned to graduate school, and started to write. "I've become a kinder human being. I listen more closely to people. I try to use the positive approach." Her voice slows with each item on the list. "I'm aware of the good things, but I'd give them up in a minute if I could have him back."

# IX

# MERRYL AND CARL

---

FOUR YEARS AFTER CARL'S DEATH Merryl decided she was ready to sort through the eight cardboard boxes she had packed so hurriedly that final night in her Brookline apartment. And so every weekend for three months she sat in her study, door closed, sifting through the details of her past. Some of it she discarded, some she put aside to send to Carl's parents, and some she placed inside the steamer trunk she had bought to hold the memories she chose to save.

In one box Merryl found evidence of her first year of grieving: dozens of sympathy cards; stubs from bills she had paid; the program from a play she had attended with her friend Judith; a diary she had bought and never written in; comforting letters from her mother. Other boxes held the fragments of the last few months of Merryl's shared life with Carl: dried flowers they had saved from Carl's sister's wedding; ticket stubs from Merryl's business trip to Chicago four weeks before Carl's death; notes for a speech Merryl had given that Carl had attended; a baby picture of Carl grinning and splashing as his mother bathed him in the sink; a baby picture of Merryl that had faced Carl's on her bulletin board; a photograph of Carl's Swedish cousins that his mother had sent him a week before his death; pictures of Merryl and Carl at a family reunion; a card saying "Happy Sailing" that Merryl had been on the verge of mailing to Carl's recently remarried uncle; Merryl's work schedule for the months of June and July; Merryl's clipboard with a long list of things "To Do"; stray notes and clippings for his dissertation that Carl had thrown away in those last weeks; invitations for the christening party for Carl's nephew; tickets for a play they planned to see in July; the novel Merryl was reading at the time of Carl's death.

Then Merryl came across a thin, white folder. She winced, knowing what was inside—Carl's picture from the pigbook. When Carl's mother had learned how much Merryl loved that photograph, she had had an enlargement made. Merryl had kept it in her desk in the Brookline apartment, and as she worked, she occasionally took it out and looked at it. Now, as she held the folder in her hands, she shivered: "I knew I was going to look right into those eyes again." When she opened it, she felt blinded for a moment. There was Carl at age seventeen, looking exactly as he had looked twenty years ago when Merryl had first found his picture and vowed to marry him. "When I looked into those eyes, I remembered Carl in the early way, how I worshiped him. And that shock of attraction and wonder all came back." She gazed into Carl's eyes and thought, "How innocent, how soft, how full of hope, that faraway look, your eyes looking into me. I see in that look all the looks I was to come to know in you; you were a person coming to be. . . . How much did you know then? You cared so much about life, you wanted so much from it—why did it go awry for you? Those eyebrows, so full . . . oh, how you hurt me. And how I loved you."

Then Merryl took a deep breath and looked up. There was a current calendar on her wall. She heard the hum of cars on the street outside and the sound of Nathan puttering in the next room. She was surrounded by the details of her new life. She opened the trunk. "As I picked up the picture, I looked into his eyes again, and it all began to recede. As I looked at him, I thought, 'That was a different life, that was down another path.' And I closed the picture up. 'You suffered a lot, Carl,' I told him. 'But I have to put you away.' "

# ACKNOWLEDGMENTS

IN 1980, JOHN BETHELL, then editor of *Harvard Magazine,* asked me to write an article about suicide. That article, which appeared in 1983 as "The Enigma of Suicide," marked the beginning of my absorption in the subject. I thank John, Kit Reed, Jean Martin, and Gretchen Friesinger for their excellent editorial counsel.

Thanks also to Jim Silberman for seeing the germ of a book in the *Harvard Magazine* piece, and to Ileene Smith and Alane Mason for shepherding the manuscript to publication at Summit Books.

I am grateful to Nan Graham and Susan Moldow at Scribner for granting second life to this book, and to Sarah McGrath and Samantha Martin for smoothing its rebirthing process.

Special thanks to my agent, Amanda Urban, for her wise counsel and infectious enthusiasm throughout.

Among the many people in the field of suicide or suicide prevention who were of help, I am particularly beholden to Patrick Arbore, Karen Dunne-Maxim, Sam Heilig, Derek Humphry, Shirley Karnovsky, Joseph Lowenstein, Terry Maltsberger, Julie Perlman, Charlotte Ross, Ed Shneidman, Tom Welch, and the late Ann Wickett.

For translation, proofreading, typing, hospitality, and help of other varieties, I thank Susan Brenholts, David Breskin, Lisa Colt, Susannah Colt, Naomi Cutner, the late Phil Driscoll, the late Annalee Fadiman, the late Clifton Fadiman, Maureen Fitzpatrick, Campbell Geeslin, June Goldberg, Peter Gradjansky, Eliza Hale, Nina Hale, Douglas Heite, Rob Larsen, Laura Natkins, John Neary, Mark O'Donnell, Linda Pillsbury, Sam Pillsbury, Nancy Skinner, Rod Skinner, John Srygley, Jane Trask Rosen, and Lena Williams.

I cannot thank my parents and my brothers enough for their love and support throughout the years I have worked on this book.

I owe an enormous debt to my cousin and friend Henry Singer, who did the vast majority of the interviewing for part one, and whose sensitivity, emotional generosity, and unflagging energy made him one of the few people I felt I could trust with such a delicate, difficult task. These qualties have been everywhere evident in his subsequent career as a documentary film-maker.

Several months before deciding to write the first edition of this book, I met Anne Fadiman, a writer who was herself in the midst of a long project on suicide, an examination of the right to die. We soon discovered that we had far more in common than our interest in self-destruction; during my work on this book, we married and became parents. Anne's contributions to this book have been varied and immense. She has been a gentle and exacting in-house editor, showing as much care and enthusiasm for the last draft of the second edition as she did for the first draft of the first. In living with me, she also, in a sense, lived with the people who inhabit this book, and not once has she complained about their presence. Without her editorial skill, this book would be less readable; without her love, it would have been unwritable.

I have often been asked, "Isn't it depressing to write a book on suicide?" The question never fails to surprise me, in large part because so many of the people I have met who have had first-hand experience with the subject—who have attempted suicide or have struggled to cope with a suicide in the family, or have worked to prevent the suicide of someone they loved—are so courageous and so admirable. Last and most important, I would like to thank those people whose voices and stories appear in this book,* who gave so generously of themselves, usually in the hope that by sharing their experiences, they might help someone else. I hope that I have not failed them.

*Some of these people, or their families, asked that their real names not be used in this book. This is a list of the pseudonyms I have given them. Part 1: Melinda; Dana Evans; Tammy; Lucy. Part 3: Peter, Barbara, Ruth, Sally, Kathy, and Owen Newell; Bill; Anna; David Kinnell; Ellen Parker; Part 5: Fred and Holly Isham. Part 6: Mary, Karen, Linda, and Rose Vitelli; Chris; Rona Marks.

# NOTES

## PART 1 Adolescent Suicide
## Chapter II The Slot Machine

37  completed suicide: While most people speak of "committing" suicide, prevention groups encourage the use of the less judgmental word "completing" suicide.

38  third leading cause: Each year, about five children between the ages of five and nine kill themselves; for those aged ten to fourteen, the number grows to more than three hundred (a rate of 1.5 per 100,000—one-fifth that of the fifteen-to-nineteen-year-old age group). Suicidal intent is especially difficult to determine in children, however. Each year some twelve thousand children are hospitalized for deliberate self-destructive acts: stabbing, scalding, burning, jumping from high places, running into traffic. Some suicidal children may be motivated by an attempt to escape an intolerable home life, others by self-punishment, others to rejoin a lost loved one—often recently dead—or to gain attention from a neglectful parent. Many have been physically abused by a family member. In a study of 662 preadolescent children treated at the Neuropsychiatric Institute over a five-year period, UCLA psychiatrists found that 5 percent were suicidal or "seriously self-destructive." Many came from families in which the concept of guilt was used to control the child's behavior. Suicide became not only a way of escaping family problems but a form of self-punishment. The child often blamed himself for family problems and came to believe that he deserved to die.

38  Kay Jamison compared: Jamison, *Night Falls Fast,* 22–23.

39  19 percent of high school students: J. A Grunbaum et al., "Youth Risk Behavior Surveillance—United States, 2001," *Morbidity and Mortality Weekly Report, CDC Surveillance Summary* 51 (SS4) (2002): 1–64.

39  No one knows: For a masterful review of recent adolescent suicide research, see Gould et al., "Youth Suicide Risk and Preventive Interventions."

41  more than 90 percent: Y. Conwell et al., "Relationships of Age and Axis I Diagnosis in Victims of Completed Suicide: A Psychological Autopsy Study," *American Journal of Psychiatry* 153 (8) (1996): 1001–8.

42  fifty-six hundred adolescents: Giffin and Felsenthal, *Cry for Help,* 218.

43  not the only answer: After a suicide one often hears family members say, "I don't understand it. He had problems, but he was getting over them. Lately, he seemed so happy." People commonly kill themselves just when they appear to be coming out of a depression. It may be because they have made their decision to kill themselves, and their problems finally seem solved. Ironically, making the decision may help lift the depression—and give them the energy needed to carry out the act. If they have recently been prescribed antidepressant medication, the suicide may be made possible because the medication has taken effect and reduced their depression sufficiently that they are able to act on their self-destructive thoughts.

43  twenty-six depressed patients: Hendin et al., "Desperation and Other Affective States."

43  "This is probably the most primordial": G. Zilboorg, "Some Aspects of Suicide," *Suicide* 5 (3) (1975): 135.

539

43   a "death trend": Moss and Hamilton, "Psychotherapy of the Suicidal Patient."

44   A University of Washington study: T. L. Dorpat et al., "Broken Homes and Attempted and Completed Suicide," *Archives of General Psychiatry* 12 (1965): 213–16.

44   "Loss in all of its manifestations": Styron, *Darkness Visible,* 56.

44   Comparing 505 children: Garfinkel et al., "Suicide Attempts in Children and Adolescents."

44   120 young suicide victims: Gould et al., "Psychosocial Risk Factors."

44   intense mood shifts: Pfeffer's work is described in C. R. Pfeffer, *The Suicidal Child* (New York: Guilford Press, 1986).

45   one of mutual involvement: J. L. Rubenstein et al., "Suicidal Behavior in Adolescents: Stress and Protection in Different Family Contexts," *American Journal of Orthopsychiatry* 68 (1998): 274–84; J. L. Rubenstein et al., "Suicidal Behavior in 'Normal' Adolescents: Risk and Protective Factors," *American Journal of Orthopsychiatry* 59 (1989): 59–71.

45   childhood trauma: For an overview of the link between childhood trauma and suicidal behavior, see "Childhood Trauma" in Goldsmith et al., *Reducing Suicide,* 157–91.

45   at least two disorders: A. B. Silverman et al., "The Long-Term Sequelae of Child and Adolescent Abuse: A Longitudinal Community Study," *Child Abuse and Neglect* 20 (8) (1996): 709–23.

45   9 to 20 percent: Goldsmith et al., *Reducing Suicide,* 183.

45   A review of twenty studies: E. E. Santa Mina and R. M. Gallop, "Childhood Sexual and Physical Abuse and Adult Self-Harm and Suicidal Behaviour: A Literature Review," *Canadian Journal of Psychiatry* 43 (8) (1998): 793–800.

45   study of 159 adolescents: E. Y. Deykin et al., "A Pilot Study of the Effect of Exposure to Child Abuse or Neglect on Adolescent Suicidal Behavior," *American Journal of Psychiatry* 142 (1985): 1299–1303.

46   five times more likely: D. A. Brent et al., "Alcohol, Firearms, and Suicide Among Youth: Temporal Trends in Allegheny County, Pennsylvania, 1960 to 1983," *Journal of the American Medical Association* 257 (24) (1987): 3369–72.

46   drinking within three hours: Powell, "Alcohol Consumption."

47   "A baby repeatedly left": Giffin and Felsenthal, *Cry for Help,* 195.

47   "Nearly every suicidal child": Ibid., 185, 215.

48   had physical fights: M. Peck, "Suicide in Late Adolescence and Young Adulthood," in Hatton and Valente, *Suicide: Assessment and Intervention,* 222.

48   nearly four times more likely: "Suicide Attempts and Physical Fighting Among High School Students—United States, 2001," *Morbidity and Mortality Weekly Report* 53 (22) (2004): 474.

48   psychiatrist David Shaffer found: D. Shaffer and M. Gould, "Study of Completed and Attempted Suicides in Adolescents," *Progress Report: National Institute of Mental Health* (1987).

48   a recent disciplinary crisis: Gould et al., "Psychosocial Risk Factors."

49   fewer than five minutes: T. R. Simon et al., "Characteristics of Impulsive Suicide Attempts and Attempters," *Suicide and Life-Threatening Behavior* 32 (Supplement) (2001): 49–59.

49   "They are like a trivial border incident": Alvarez, *Savage God,* 97.

49   "If youth is the season of hope": G. Eliot, *Middlemarch* (Cambridge: Riverside Press, 1956), 398.

49   permanence of death: In a study of two hundred adolescents, one in five answered yes when asked if they could come back to life following a suicide. Such magical thinking is not limited to young people; some suicidal adults, too, describe death as a temporary state or believe that they will be able to observe the effect of their suicide on family and friends.

50    "I thought death would be": *Newsweek,* August 15, 1983, 74.

50    "I wandered the streets": K. Menninger, *The Vital Balance* (Harmondsworth, England: Penguin, 1977), 267.

52    frequency of moving: Potter et al., "Influence of Geographic Mobility." Each year more than 14 percent of Americans relocate, compared with 8 percent of Britons and 4 percent of Germans.

52    A sixteen-year-old: Giffin and Felsenthal, *Cry for Help,* 125–27.

53    family had recently moved: *San Mateo Times,* February 11, 1983, 10.

54    "Television has brought": J. Anderson, "An Extraordinary People," *New Yorker,* November 12, 1984, 126.

54    more than a thousand studies: Senate Committee on the Judiciary, September 14, 1999, "Children, Violence, and the Media: A Report for Parents and Policy Makers," http://judiciary.senate.gov/mediavio.

54    in video games: In 2005, the American Psychological Association called for a reduction in video game violence. Noting that 73 percent of violent acts in video games go unpunished, APA spokesperson Elizabeth Carll warned that "showing acts of violence without consequences teaches youth that violence is an effective means of resolving conflict." ("APA Calls for Reduction of Violence in Interactive Media Used by Children and Adolescents," www.apa.org/releases/videoviolence05.)

54    six prominent medical groups: Congressional Public Health Summit, July 26, 2000, www.aap.org/advocacy/releases/jstmtevc.htm.

57    therapists attribute the decrease: Columbia University researchers examined teenage suicide rates and use of antidepressants from 1990 to 2000 in 588 regions of the country and found an increase in antidepressant use was associated with a decrease in suicides. (M. Olfson et al., "Relationship Between Antidepressant Medication Treatment and Suicide in Adolescents," *Archives of General Psychiatry* 60 (10) (2003): 978–82.)

## Chapter III Brian

64    settled on a diagnosis: At the time, Brian was thought to be too young for manic depression, which was believed to manifest itself most commonly in the mid- to late twenties. It is now believed that the average age of onset is eighteen.

## Chapter IV Something in the Air

79    "a contagious illness": D. Bushman, "Cluster Suicides," *Reporter Dispatch* (Gannett Westchester Newspapers), December 2, 1984, 1.

79    "sort of like punk rock": Ibid., 16.

80    studied sixty-two patients: B. J. Rounsaville and M. M. Weissman, "A Note on Suicidal Behaviors Among Intimates," *Suicide and Life-Threatening Behavior* 10 (1) (1980): 24–28.

81    columnist Ann Landers: *Reporter Dispatch* (Gannett Westchester Newspapers), April 2, 1985.

83    an article appeared: J. E. Brody, "'Autoerotic Death' of Youths Causes Widening Concern," *New York Times,* March 27, 1984, C1.

83    "The most singular feature": Winslow, *Anatomy of Suicide,* 108.

84    "In the year of Grace": Coleman, *Suicide Clusters,* 17.

84    "Some threw themselves": Fedden, *Suicide,* 150.

84    "Very few of those": Cavan, *Suicide,* 69.

85   "A strange and terrible": Fedden, *Suicide,* 299.

85   "vanity, if not sanity": Alvarez, *Savage God,* 104.

85   "to abandon oneself": A. Wynter, *The Borderlands of Insanity* (London: Henry Renshaw, 1877), 244–45.

85   "The East African societies": Bohannan, *African Homicide and Suicide,* 263.

85   "A child is more open": Friedman, *On Suicide,* 57.

86   "To all this may be added": Mathews, "Civilization and Suicide," 484.

86   "The sensational fashion": Friedman, *On Suicide,* 137.

87   "One 'new Werther'": R. Friedenthal, *Goethe: His Life and Times* (Cleveland and New York: World Publishing Company, 1965), 129–30.

87   "the mischievous influence": Miller, *Guilt, Folly, and Sources of Suicide.*

87   "weakening the moral principles": Winslow, *Anatomy of Suicide,* 87.

87   forty-three Russian roulette deaths: Coleman, *Suicide Clusters,* 126.

88   "When the mind is beginning": Galt, *Treatment of Insanity,* 212.

88   "No fact is better established": Phelps, "Neurotic Books and Newspapers." This paper offers an extensive, if shrill, description of the controversy at the turn of the century.

88   "inducing morbid people": J. A. Motto, "Suicide and Suggestibility: The Role of the Press," *American Journal of Psychiatry* 124 (2) (1967): 157.

89   "literary chamber of horrors": These examples are found in Phelps, "Neurotic Books," 36.

89   found that suicides increase: Phillips, "Influence of Suggestion on Suicide."

89   linking suggestion and suicide: Phillips has also investigated the effect of mass media on aggressive behavior. In a 1979 study of California motor vehicle deaths, he found that front-page suicide stories may provoke an increase in auto fatalities. Three days after a story, fatal car crashes increase by more than 30 percent. The rate of single-car crashes is most affected, suggesting that some of the drivers may have had self-destructive motives. Again, the greater the publicity, the greater the rise in the number of deaths. In addition, he found significant similarities between the dead driver and the person described in the suicide story. Phillips has also linked murder-suicide stories to a rise in U.S. plane crashes. (D. P. Phillips, "Suicide, Motor Vehicle Fatalities, and the Mass Media: Evidence Toward a Theory of Suggestion," *American Journal of Sociology* 84 (5) (1979): 1150–74; D. P. Phillips, "Airplane Accident Fatalities Increase Just After Newspaper Stories About Murder and Suicide," *Science* 201 (1978): 748–50.)

90   numerous other studies: For a review of the literature, see Gould, "Suicide and the Media."

90   yearlong CDC survey: N. D. Brener et al., "Effect of the Incident at Columbine on Students' Violence- and Suicide-Related Behaviors," *American Journal of Preventive Medicine* 22 (3) (2002): 146–50.

90   extends to television news coverage: Examining the effect of thirty-eight nationally televised news or feature stories about suicide from 1973 to 1979, Phillips and a colleague found a significant increase (7 percent) in teenage suicides during the week following the broadcasts. The more networks carrying the story, the bigger the increase. Girls were more susceptible to the influence than boys. They did not find a significant increase in adult suicides following the programs. (D. P. Phillips and L. L. Carstensen, "Clustering of Teenage Suicides After Television News Stories About Suicide," *New England Journal of Medicine* 315 (11) (1986): 685–89.)

90   *fictional* television suicides: In one study, Madelyn Gould and David Shaffer researched the effect of four made-for-TV movies about teenage suicide broadcast in late 1984 and early 1985. Teenage suicide rates in the metropolitan New York area rose in the two

weeks after broadcast for three of the four movies; six more teenagers than would have been expected took their lives. Shaffer suggested that the fourth film, *Silence of the Heart,* did not trigger suicides because it portrayed suicide in a less sensational fashion. In addition, educational materials and training guides were distributed to schools beforehand, suicide prevention hotline numbers were displayed during the broadcast, and a panel discussion on suicide prevention was aired immediately following the movie. (Gould and Shaffer, "Impact of Suicide in Television Movies.") The study was challenged by the television networks, which pointed out that there was no way of knowing whether the teenagers who killed themselves actually saw the movies. Phillips himself contradicted Gould and Shaffer's findings. Looking at the effect of the same movies on teenage suicide in California and Pennsylvania, he found no rise in the rate. (D. P. Phillips and D. J. Paight, "The Impact of Televised Movies About Suicide: A Replicative Study," *New England Journal of Medicine* 317 (13) (1987): 809–11.) Psychologist Alan Berman also questioned the results of the Gould-Shaffer study. Collecting data from 189 medical examiners across the country, representing 20 percent of the U.S. population, he found no increase in youth suicides in the two weeks following three of the TV movies; in some areas there was a decrease. (Berman examined two of the films used in the Gould-Shaffer study, and a third film broadcast after their study had been completed.) He did find evidence that one of the broadcasts may have influenced the choice of methods. (A. Berman, paper presented at a joint meeting of the American Association of Suicidology and the International Association for Suicide Prevention, San Francisco, May 25–30, 1987.)

90  A 1999 English survey: K. S. Hawton et al., "Effects of a Drug Overdose in a Television Drama on Presentations to Hospital for Self Poisoning: Times Series and Questionnaire Study," *British Medical Journal* 318 (1999): 972–77.

90  films from 1917 to 1997: Gould et al., "Media Contagion and Suicide."

91  asks whether cyberspace: K. Becker et al., "Parasuicide Online: Can Suicide Websites Trigger Suicidal Behaviour in Predisposed Adolescents?" *Nordic Journal of Psychiatry* 58 (2) (2004): 111–14.

91  he opposes censorship: From time to time newspapers have been persuaded or pressured into suppressing stories about suicide. In the 1930s, for instance, Mussolini prohibited all reports of suicide in the Italian press; his vision of the modern fascist state did not include the possibility of suicide.

91  fell more than 80 percent: E. Etzersdorfer et al., "Newspaper Reports and Suicide," *New England Journal of Medicine* 327 (1992): 502–3; and E. Etzersdorfer and G. Sonneck, "Preventing Suicide by Influencing Mass-Media Reporting: The Viennese Experience, 1980–1996," *Archives of Suicide Research* 4 (1998): 67–74.

91  issued recommendations: P. W. O'Carroll and L. B. Potter, "Suicide Contagion and the Reporting of Suicide: Recommendations from a National Workshop," *Morbidity and Mortality Weekly Report* 43, RR-6 (1994): 9–18. (See Web site at www.nimh.nih.gov/research/suicidemedia.) In 2001, the CDC and several other groups, including the American Foundation for Suicide Prevention and the American Association of Suicidology, issued media recommendations for reporting on suicide. These can be found in an appendix to Gould et al., "Media Contagion."

91  Annenberg Public Policy Center: K. H. Jamieson, "Can Suicide Coverage Lead to Copycats?" *American Editor,* June 14, 2002. See Web site at www.asne.org.

92  Cobain's death had no effect: D. A. Jobes et al., "The Kurt Cobain Suicide Crisis: Perspectives from Research, Public Health, and the News Media," *Suicide and Life-Threatening Behavior* 26 (1996): 260–71.

## Chapter V Dana

95    125,000 visits: "Suicide and Attempted Suicide," *Morbidity and Mortality Weekly Report* 53 (22) (2004): 471.

95    "Although depression is more common": Jamison, *Night Falls Fast,* 46.

96    "Most people who commit": Stengel, *Suicide and Attempted Sucide,* 87.

96    "The man up there is saying": *Time,* November 25, 1966, 49.

96    "a desperate version": Giffin and Felsenthal, *Cry for Help,* 14.

96    thirteen-year-old Illinois girl: Ibid., 19.

96    Michigan youth hospitalized: A. Wrobleski, *Afterwords,* October 1984, 1. For more on attitudes of hospital staff toward attempters, see T. C. Welu, "Psychological Reactions of Emergency Room Staff to Suicide Attempters," *Omega* 3 (2) (1972): 103–9. Completed suicide also provokes complex reactions in medical personnel. "Something about acute self-destruction is so puzzling to the vibrant mind of a man or woman whose life is devoted to fighting disease that it tends to diminish or even obliterate empathy," writes the surgeon Sherwin Nuland. "Medical bystanders, whether bewildered and frustrated by such an act, or angered by its futility, seem not to be much grieved at the corpse of a suicide." (Nuland, *How We Die,* 151.)

96    chronic psychiatric problems: A. J. Elliott et al., "A Profile of Medically Serious Suicide Attempts," *Journal of Clinical Psychiatry* 57 (1996): 567–71.

97    slashed her wrists lightly: Klagsbrun, *Too Young to Die,* 33–34.

97    lonely sixteen-year-old: Giffin and Felsenthal, *Cry for Help,* 30–31.

## Chapter VI "Use the Enclosed Order Form to Act Immediately. You Could Save a Life"

114    a 1969 article: Cited in C. P. Ross, "Teaching Children the Facts of Life and Death: Suicide Prevention in the Schools," in Peck, Farberow, and Litman, *Youth Suicide,* 153.

116    "Our goal is to help": D. Breskin, "Dear Mom and Dad," 35.

116    "Children with a clearer understanding": G. R. Bernhardt and S. G. Praeger, "Preventing Child Suicide: The Elementary School Death Education Puppet Show" (unpublished paper), 6.

117    "Any school administrator": Quoted in a letter sent by Donna-Marie Buckley, whose son had hanged himself, to President Reagan, June 1984.

118    Shaffer studied the effects: Paper presented at the twenty-first annual meeting of the American Association of Sucidology, Washington, D.C., April 13–17, 1988. See Shaffer et al., "Adolescent Suicide Attempters." See also Shaffer's more general discussion of youth suicide prevention, Shaffer et al., "Preventing Teenage Suicide."

119    115 school-based programs: A. Garland et al., "A National Survey of School-Based, Adolescent Suicide Prevention Programs," *Journal of the American Academy of Child and Adolescent Psychiatry* 28 (1989): 931–34.

119    "By deemphasizing": A. F. Garland and E. Zigler, "Adolescent Suicide Prevention: Current Research and Social Policy Implications," *American Psychologist* 48 (1993): 169–82.

119    A 1994 CDC summary: P. W. O'Carroll et al., "Programs for the Prevention of Suicide Among Adolescents and Young Adults," *Morbidity and Mortality Weekly Report* 43, RR-6 (1994), 1–7.

119    "no justification": Metha et al., "Youth Suicide Prevention."

119    study of twenty-one hundred students: R. H. Aseltine, "An Evaluation of a School Based Suicide Prevention Program," *Adolescent and Family Health* 3 (2003): 81–88. See also

R. H. Aseltine and R. DeMartino, "An Outcome Evaluation of the SOS Suicide Prevention Program," *American Journal of Public Health* 94 (2004): 446–51.

120    significant reductions: J. Kalafat, "School Approaches to Youth Suicide Prevention," *American Behavioral Scientist* 46 (9) (2003): 1211–23.

120    Yellow Ribbon Suicide Prevention Program: See Web site at www.yellowribbon.org.


**PART 2 History**
**Chapter I Primitive Roots: The Rock of the Forefathers**

129    Among the books that describe the history of suicide, from which many of the examples in my discussion are drawn, I owe a special debt to *Biathanatos* by John Donne; *A Full Inquiry into the Subject of Suicide* by Charles Moore; *The Anatomy of Suicide* by Forbes Winslow; *Suicide* by Émile Durkheim; *Suicide* by Henry Romilly Fedden; *To Be or Not To Be* by Louis Dublin and Betty Bunzel; and *The Savage God* by A. Alvarez.

129    "Lo, my name reeks": J. H. Breasted, *Development of Religion and Thought in Ancient Egypt* (New York: Charles Scribner's Sons, 1912), 163–69.

131    "The Baganda were very superstitious": J. Roscoe, *The Baganda: An Account of Their Native Customs and Beliefs* (New York: Barnes & Noble, 1966), 20–21.

132    Primitive fear of the suicide's ghost: Examples of primitive attitudes toward suicide are found in Westermarck, *Origin and Development of the Moral Ideas,* 229–64; Durkheim, *Suicide,* 217–25; Dublin and Bunzel, *To Be or Not To Be,* 137–53.

133    For many years India: For examples of revenge suicide in southern India, see Fedden, *Suicide,* 45–46.

134    "They are a nation lavish": Durkheim, *Suicide,* 218.

134    "They dwell on the red blaze": Dublin and Bunzel, *To Be or Not To Be,* 145.

135    "There is another world": Alvarez, *Savage God,* 53.

135    a king was buried: Herodotus, *The Histories,* trans. A. de Selincourt. (Harmondsworth, England: Penguin, 1988), 294.

135    "keen competition": Ibid., 342.

136    "Should he outrage": A. B. Ellis, *The Tshi-Speaking Peoples of the Gold Coast of West Africa* (The Netherlands: Anthropological Publications, 1970), 287.

136    the village of Deorala: *Los Angeles Times,* October 10, 1987, part I, p. 1.

136    "The government of Madhya Pradesh": "Indian Police Arrest Sons After Woman Commits Suttee," *Sydney Morning Herald,* August 8, 2002, www.smh.com.au/articles/2002/08/07.

137    Yet in Japan: My discussion of suicide in Japan owes much to Iga, *Thorn in the Chrysanthemum*; M. Iga and K. Tatai, "Characteristics of Suicides and Attitudes Toward Suicide in Japan," in Farberow, *Suicide in Different Cultures,* 255–80; J. Seward, *Hara-Kiri: Japanese Ritual Suicide* (Rutland, Vt., and Tokyo: Charles E. Tuttle, 1968).

137    "The Japanese calendar": W. E. Griffis, *The Religions of Japan* (New York: Charles Scribner's Sons, 1895), 112.

138    variety of circumstances: Durkheim noted that "a strange sort of duel is even reported there, in which the effort is not to attack one another but to excel in dexterity in opening one's own stomach." Durkheim, *Suicide,* 222.

138    "The Japanese are an obstinate": Moore, *Full Inquiry,* 140. In 1932, Henry Morton Robinson observed, "If the Samurai code existed in America today, Tammany Hall would be a catacomb of self-slain heroes." (*North American Review* 234 [4] [1932]: 304.)

138    "the very shrine": G. Kennan, "The Death of General Nogi," *Outlook,* October 5, 1912, 258.

139     almost 250 recorded cases: O. D. Russell, "Suicide in Japan," *American Mercury,* July 1930, 341–44.

139     "He mingles with the gods": *Newsweek,* September 24, 1945, 58.

140     "My daughters and myself": *Time,* March 1, 1976, 31. In *The Thorn in the Chrysanthemum,* Mamoru Iga wrote, "The mother who commits suicide without taking her child with her is blamed as an *oni no yō na hito* (demonlike person)" (p. 18). In the United States the opposite is true. In 1985 in Los Angeles, a thirty-two-year-old Japanese immigrant whose husband had been unfaithful walked into the Pacific Ocean carrying her infant daughter and four-year-old son. Although passersby managed to pull her from the surf, her children drowned. Charged with voluntary manslaughter, the woman told police that she had killed her children because she loved them dearly. She was sentenced to eleven years in prison, but after intervention by local Japanese groups, her sentence was reduced to three years' probation. She eventually returned to her husband.

140     the suicide of Yukio Mishima: My description of Mishima's suicide is drawn from newspaper accounts and from Iga and Tatai, "Characteristics of Suicides." For further discussion of Mishima's suicide see Lifton, *Broken Connection,* 262–80.

141     "a sadomasochistic homosexual": *New York Times,* November 9, 1974.

142     "the readiness of the Japanese": Durkheim, *Suicide,* 222.

143     "People didn't know they were suffering": Most of the details in this paragraph are taken from a fascinating article by Kathryn Shulz, "Did Depressants Depress Japan?" (*New York Times Magazine,* August 22, 2004, 39–41.)

143     blend of traditional and contemporary: The historical gulf between primitive and Eastern acceptance of suicide and its condemnation by the West are illustrated in a perhaps apocryphal story told by psychiatrist Joost Meerloo. A sociologist and a psychiatrist who flew to the Orient to attend a conference on alienation and self-destruction were out for a stroll one night when they saw a man hanging from a tree. They rushed to the spot, quickly cut him down, and tried to restore him to consciousness. As they worked feverishly over his prostrate body, a crowd gathered and began to murmur ominously. The air grew thick with tension. Although they had saved the life of the stranger, the sociologist and the psychiatrist were starting to fear for their own lives when a policeman appeared just in time to rescue them from a probable lynching. Relieved at being saved from the mob, these Good Samaritans were shocked when the policeman hauled them off to court, where the judge informed them that they had committed an outrageous offense—they had interfered with the plans of a holy man who wished to join his ancestors. They were ordered to pay a stiff fine, and since the holy man had given away all his earthly possessions in preparation for his suicide, the sociologist and psychiatrist were ordered to assume full responsibility for his material needs for the rest of his life. Meerloo, *Suicide and Mass Suicide,* 93–94.

143     "One single suicide": K. Huus, "Japan's Chilling Internet Suicide Pacts," MSNBC News, www.msnbc.msn.com.

**Chapter II The Classical World: "He Is at Liberty to Die Who Does Not Wish to Live"**

144     "steep down from a high rafter": Homer, *The Odyssey,* trans. R. Fitzgerald (Garden City, N.Y.: Anchor/Doubleday, 1963), 194.

145     "thrusting into their throats": Thucydides, *The History of the Peloponnesian War,* in R. M. Hutchins, ed., *Great Books of the Western World* (Chicago: Encyclopaedia Britannica, 1952), 6: 459.

145     "went quite mad": Herodotus, *Histories,* 414.

145     "to depart from their guard": Dublin and Bunzel, *To Be or Not To Be,* 184.

146    "If one of your own possessions": Plato, *Dialogues of Plato,* trans. B. Jowett, ed. J. D. Kaplan (New York: Washington Square Press/Pocket Books, 1951), 74.

146    "in a spirit of slothful": Plato, *The Laws,* trans. T. J. Saunders (Harmondsworth, England: Penguin, 1975), 391.

146    "To kill oneself to escape": Aristotle, *Ethics,* rev. ed. trans. J. A. K. Thompson (Harmondsworth, England: Penguin, 1976), 130.

146    "The many at one moment": Epicurus, "Letter to Menoeceus," in W. J. Oates, ed., *The Stoic and Epicurean Philosophers* (New York: Random House, 1940), 31.

147    "to weigh carefully": Lecky, *History of European Morals,* 1: 226.

147    "If one day": Fedden, *Suicide,* 81.

147    "as he had advanced": Ibid., 80.

147    "Such a discussion": Moore, *Full Inquiry,* 1: 238.

148    the death of Marcus Porcius Cato: For the story of Cato and his suicide, see Plutarch, *The Lives of the Noble Grecians and Romans,* trans. J. Dryden (New York: Modern Library, 1932), 918–60.

149    "when God himself" and "a noble lesson": Dublin and Bunzel, *To Be or Not To Be,* 186–87.

149    "Jupiter himself": Choron, *Suicide,* 22.

149    "A resolution this": Pliny, *Letters,* trans. W. Melmoth (London: William Heinemann, 1915), 1: 81–82.

149    "Foolish man": Fedden, *Suicide,* 79.

149    "Where had their philosophy gone": For the description of Seneca's death, see Tacitus, *The Annals of Imperial Rome,* trans. M. Grant (London: Penguin, 1989), 376.

151    sheer exhibitionism: The suicide of Peregrinus is described in Fedden, *Suicide,* 66–67. For a more cynical account see *The Works of Lucian of Samosata,* trans. H. W. Fowler and F. G. Fowler (Oxford: Clarendon Press, 1905), 4: 79–95.

151    Frazer reported that in Rome: Fedden, *Suicide,* 84.

151    six suicides in the Old Testament: Quotations from the Bible are from *The Revised Standard Version* (New York: Thomas Nelson & Sons, 1946, 1952).

152    "In the same manner": Sprott, *English Debate,* 147.

153    "the splendid martyrs": Eusebius, *The History of the Church from Christ to Constantine,* trans. G. A. Williamson (New York: New York University Press, 1966), 344.

153    "No City escaped punishment": Donne, *Biathanatos,* 60.

153    "rejoicing and exulting": Eusebius, *History of the Church,* 202.

153    "Amachus, give orders": Fedden, *Suicide,* 121.

153    "Let fire and cross": Eusebius, *History of the Church,* 146.

153    fate of St. Simeon Stylites: For an extensive and graphic description of martyrdom, see Menninger, *Man Against Himself.* Wrote Menninger, "Upon examination, the components of the self-destructive urge in asceticism and martyrdom are apparently identical with those which we found to determine actual suicide—the self-punitive, the aggressive, and the erotic" (p. 125).

153    "Lo! For these thirty years": Ibid., 119.

154    getting out of hand: Aspiring monks who despaired of winning the battle between celibacy and nature often chose suicide by more direct means. The biographer of Pachomius, a young monk who applied asps to himself in an unsuccessful suicide attempt, wrote that in this struggle with the devil "many have destroyed themselves; some, bereft of their senses, have cast themselves from precipices; others laid open their bowels; others killed themselves in divers ways" (Fedden, *Suicide,* 125). Still others, as Gibbon put it, "judged it the most prudent to disarm the tempter" (Ibid., 126). Castration, the church eventually realized, was a partial suicide. A church canon later declared, "He that gelds himselfe cannot be a Clerke, because he is an Homicide of himselfe, and

an enemy to Gods creature." (Quoted in Donne, *Biathanatos,* 133). Perhaps the most revered of all martyrs were the numerous Christian women who preferred death to defilement by heathens. Fifteen-year-old Pelagia, fearing for the loss of her chastity, jumped from a roof to escape a Roman soldier and was canonized for her suicide. "God cannot be offended with this, when we use it but for a remedy," observed St. Ambrose (Ibid., 148).

154   "If it is base": E. Westermarck, *Christianity and Morals* (London: Macmillan, 1939), 253.

154   "monstrous": Quotations are taken from St. Augustine, *City of God,* trans. H. Bettenson (Harmondsworth, England: Penguin, 1984), 26–39.

156   "Let him who hath murdered himself": Dublin and Bunzel, *To Be or Not To Be,* 245.

156   "The madman, or the idiot": Fedden, *Suicide,* 138.

156   "life is a gift": Aquinas's arguments against suicide are found in T. Aquinas, *Summa Theologiae* (New York: McGraw-Hill; London: Eyre & Spottiswoode, 1975), 38: 30–37.

156   the start of the fourteenth century: Dublin and Bunzel pointed out that because of Church prohibitions, civil penalties, and the general stability of institutions and customs in the Middle Ages, individual suicide was practically unheard of during the eight hundred years between Augustine and Aquinas. Yet outside the tight framework of the Church there were sporadic bursts of self-destruction. In the Middle Ages demonic possession was the explanation for most mental disorder, and suicide was considered the ultimate evidence of the devil's work. It has been estimated that in the 250 years prior to the end of the seventeenth century, at least one hundred thousand women were accused of witchcraft, tortured, and burned at the stake. Accused women often sought a less painful and humiliating end by taking their own life. Ironically, their suicides were usually interpreted as proof of their collusion with the devil.

## Chapter III Renaissance and Enlightenment: "It Is His Case, It May Be Thine"

158   "Thou, constrained": G. Pico della Mirandola, "Oration on the Dignity of Man," in E. Cassirer, P. O. Kristeller, and J. H. Randall Jr., eds., *The Renaissance Philosophy of Man* (Chicago: University of Chicago Press, 1948), 225.

159   *"Death is a remedy":* Unless indicated otherwise, quotes in this paragraph are from Montaigne, *The Essays of Montaigne,* trans. J. Florio (New York: Modern Library), 308–20.

159   "All the wisdom": R. Noyes, "Montaigne on Death," *Omega* 1 (4) (1970): 315.

159   "lest men far and wide": D. Erasmus, *The Colloquies of Erasmus,* trans. C. R. Thompson (Chicago and London: University of Chicago Press, 1965), 360.

159   "people who lived next door": D. Erasmus, *The Praise of Folly,* trans. H. H. Hudson (Princeton: Princeton University Press, 1941), 41.

160   "But yf the dysease": T. More, *Utopia.* ed. J. C. Collins (Oxford: Clarendon Press, 1904), 100.

160   "his hand did quake": E. Spenser, *The Faerie Queene,* ed. P. C. Bayley (Oxford: Oxford University Press, 1966), 1: 195–99.

160   M. D. Faber has pointed out: M. D. Faber, "Shakespeare's Suicides: Some Historic, Dramatic and Psychological Reflections," in Shneidman, *Essays in Self-Destruction,* 30–58.

161   "the disease of head-long dying": This and the quotations in the following two paragraphs are from Donne, *Biathanatos,* 62, 50, 47, 17–18.

161   "thirst and inhiation" and "because I had the same desires": C. M. Coffin, ed., *The Complete Poetry and Selected Prose of John Donne* (New York: Modern Library, 1952), 375–76.

162    "I wonder if *Biathanatos*": Alvarez, *Savage God,* 155–56.

162    "because it is upon": Coffin, *Complete Poetry,* 387.

162    "hevy, thoghtful, and wrawe": G. Chaucer, *The Canterbury Tales,* ed. W. Skeat (New York: Modern Library, 1929), 581.

162    "If there be a hell": For Burton quotations, see Burton, *Anatomy of Melancholy,* 281–88.

163    "There be two sorts": Faber, "Shakespeare's Suicides," 31–32.

163    preached three sermons: A description of Neser's work can be found in G. Rosen, "History," in Perlin, *Handbook for the Study of Suicide,* 18.

163    an English country clergyman: Quotations in this paragraph are from Hunter and Macalpine, *Three Hundred Years of Psychiatry, 1535–1860,* 113–15, and Fedden, *Suicide,* 185.

164    "as cruelly as possible": Fedden, *Suicide,* 142.

164    "brought through the town": Dublin and Bunzel, *To Be or Not To Be,* 207.

164    "harled through the town": Westermarck, *Christianity and Morals,* 255.

164    "until he be persuaded": H. Silving, "Suicide and Law," in Shneidman and Farberow, *Clues to Suicide,* 83.

165    "The body is drawn": Moore, *Full Inquiry,* 1: 304.

165    "the worst kind of murder": Kushner, *Self-Destruction in the Promised Land,* 15.

165    "felloniously and willfully": The case of Abraham Harris can be found in Noble, "Glance at Suicide."

165    "Wheresoever you finde": Donne, *Biathanatos,* 93.

166    "is now growne so common": Sprott, *English Debate on Suicide,* 32.

166    "Cato was not so much" and "What Cato did": Fedden, *Suicide,* 240–41.

166    three hundred suicides: MacDonald, *Mystical Bedlam,* 278.

166    "These actions, considered": Winslow, *Anatomy of Suicide,* 319–20.

167    "To be *happy* or not to be": Gruman, "Historical Introduction to Ideas," 99.

167    "When I am overcome": For quotations in this paragraph, see Montesquieu, *Persian Letters,* trans. C. J. Betts (Harmondsworth, England: Penguin, 1987), letter 76, pp. 152–54.

167    "Every man has a right": For Rousseau's discussion of suicide, see letters 21 and 22 in *Julie ou la Nouvelle Héloïse* (Paris: Garnier-Flammarion, 1967), 278–91.

168    "his goods are given": Fedden, *Suicide,* 224.

169    "Each one has his reasons": Ibid., 204.

169    "We kill ourselves": Ibid., 237.

169    "It is a decision": Ibid., 205.

169    "If suicide be criminal": For Hume quotations, see Hume, "On Suicide," in *Essays Moral, Political and Literary,* 585–96.

171    "The carcass," "sons of perdition," and "contribute somewhat": Sprott, *English Debate on Suicide,* 122.

171    "It might not only": Moore, *Full Inquiry,* 1: 339.

171    "Many of those": These and other quotes in this paragraph are found in Hey, *Three Dissertations,* 179–80, 208.

171    "Freedom, then": Gruman, "An Historical Introduction," 97.

172    "The rule of morality": I. Kant, *Lectures on Ethics,* trans. L. Infield (Gloucester, Mass.: Peter Smith, 1978), 152.

172    "The causes of misery": De Staël quotations are drawn from M. de Staël, *The Influence of Literature Upon Society* (Hartford: S. Andrus & Son, 1844), 99–112.

173    "The excuse of not being": Moore, *Full Inquiry,* 1: 324.

173    "A penniless poor dog": Ibid., 1: 323–24.

173    the result of its reputation: For material in these two paragraphs, see Bartel, "Suicide in Eighteenth-Century England."

173     "We do not find": Montesquieu, *The Spirit of Laws,* rev. ed. trans. T. Nugent (New York: Colonial Press, 1899) 1: 231 (bk. 14, chap. 12).

173     a letter to a friend: A. A. Lipscomb, ed., *The Writings of Thomas Jefferson* (Washington, D.C.: Thomas Jefferson Memorial Association, 1904), 11: 64. In a letter dated February 8, 1805, Jefferson observed, "I prefer much the climate of the United States to that of Europe. I think it is a more cheerful one. It is our cloudless sky which has eradicated from our constitutions all disposition to hang ourselves, which we might otherwise have inherited from our English ancestors."

174     "No urgent motive": Moore, *Full Inquiry,* 1: 343.

174     "in order to avoid": Winslow, *Anatomy of Suicide,* 79.

174     "With the greatest pleasure": Ibid., 133.

174     "There are little domestic news": W. S. Lewis, ed., *Horace Walpole's Correspondence* (New Haven: Yale University Press, 1941), 35: 236.

175     "By this conviction": Winslow, *Anatomy of Suicide,* 86.

176     "practised it as one": Alvarez, *Savage God,* 204. My description of the Romantics owes much to Alvarez's chapter "The Romantic Agony," 194–205.

176     "We swung between madness": Ibid., 204.

## Chapter IV Science: Moral Medicine and Vital Statistics

177     "hypertrophy of the poetic organ": Choron, *Death and Western Thought,* 159.

178     "Whatever may be the cause": R. Hunter and I. Macalpine. eds., *A Treatise on Madness and Remarks on Dr. Battie's Treatise on Madness* (London: Dawsons, 1962), 36–37.

178     "Few, perhaps, are aware": Winslow, *Anatomy of Suicide,* 136–37. Of course, it is likely that many young suicides were caused not by masturbation but by guilt over the act.

178     "Suicide presents" and "the treatment of suicide": Choron, *Suicide,* 63.

179     "A lady, shortly after": For this and the following two quotations see Winslow, *Anatomy of Suicide,* 174–75, 203.

179     "A pint every hour": Galt, *Treatment of Insanity,* 212.

179     "Once in a while": M. Fuller, "Suicide Past and Present: A Note on Jean-Pierre Falret," *Life-Threatening Behavior* 3 (1) (1973): 62.

179     holding the patient under: Bucknill and Tuke, *Manual of Psychological Medicine,* 465. Referring to this treatment, Bucknill and Tuke quote Pinel approvingly: "One must blush at this medical delirium, worse, perhaps, than that of the madman whose reason it was to restore."

180     "travelling, agreeable society": Winslow, *Anatomy of Suicide,* 166.

180     "I should as soon": Bucknill and Tuke, *Manual of Psychological Medicine,* 473.

180     "How many females": Galt, *Treatment of Insanity,* 341.

181     "As no rational being": Winslow, *Anatomy of Suicide,* 222. In the debate over whether suicides were insane, many nineteenth-century writers complained that suicides in their day lacked the heroism and cool rationality of the ancient Greeks and Romans. One physician asserted that 10 percent of classical suicides were insane and 90 percent were rational, while 10 percent of nineteenth-century suicides were rational and 90 percent were insane.

181     "I am far from from supposing": T. Chevalier, *Remarks on Suicide* (London: 1824), 4.

181     "Two cases have occurred": Mathews, "Civilization and Suicide," 474.

181     "We know, as a fact": This and the following quotes in this paragraph are from Strahan, *Suicide and Insanity,* 188, 30, 75, 78.

181   "All the superstitious fear": Fedden, *Suicide,* 260.

182   "Agnis Miller wieff": Shneidman, *Deaths of Man,* 115–16.

182   "I dare ensure": Quote and information in this paragraph may be found in J. Graunt, *Natural and Political Observations made upon the Bills of Mortality* (Baltimore: Johns Hopkins University Press, 1939), 31–36.

183   "The evil frequently appears": Masaryk, *Suicide,* 48.

183   "On this area": Morselli, *Suicide,* 37.

184   "extremes of heat and cold": Strahan, *Suicide and Insanity,* 154.

184   "Suicide and madness": Morselli, *Suicide,* 72.

184   "Nationality has a noticeable effect": Masaryk, *Suicide,* 121.

184   "A very low suicide frequency": Ibid., 42.

184   "The frequency of suicide": Morselli, *Suicide,* 102.

184   "From whence this fact proceeds": Ibid., 76.

185   a German priest calculated: S. Gargas, "Suicide in the Netherlands," *American Journal of Sociology* 37 (5) (1932): 698.

185   "The certainty of the figures": Morselli, *Suicide,* 16. At the time it was believed that suicide was virtually unknown in "primitive" societies except in cases of "economic" suicide. Then in 1984, Alfred Vierkandt, a German sociologist, reported mass suicides among tribes in New Zealand and in Madagascar, and since then studies have found suicide in primitive societies throughout the world.

187   an entire society may experience anomie: Prior to the fall of the Berlin Wall in 1989, West Berlin had one of the highest suicide rates in the world, more than twice that of West Germany as a whole. Alienated not only geographically but spiritually, culturally, and politically, it was the embodiment of anomie.

187   "Lack of power": Durkheim, *Suicide,* 254.

187   "suicide varies inversely": Ibid., 209.

187   "are very often combined": Ibid., 287.

187   "social facts must be studied": Ibid., 37–38.

188   "When we learn": Friedman, *On Suicide,* 110.

188   "Thus the unconscious": Ibid., 119.

188   "the decisive factor": Ibid., 71, 76.

188   "No one kills himself": Ibid., 87.

188   "Let us suspend": Ibid., 141.

188   Robert Litman has pointed out: Much of my discussion of Freud is drawn from Litman, "Sigmund Freud on Suicide."

188   "I have long since resolved": E. Jones, *The Life and Work of Sigmund Freud* (New York: Basic Books, 1953), 1: 132.

189   "In the two opposed situations": S. Freud, *Mourning and Melancholia* (1917), in J. Strachey, ed., *Standard Edition of the Complete Psychological Works* (London: Hogarth Press, 1953–65), 14: 252.

189   "A patient over whom": S. Freud, *The Psychopathology of Everyday Life* (1901), in Strachey, ed., *Works,* 6: 3.

189   "We find that impulses": S. Freud, *Totem and Taboo* (1913), in Strachey, ed., *Works,* 13: 154.

189   a kind of inverted murder: Freud might also have agreed with the English comedy troupe Monty Python, who observed that "a murder is nothing but an extroverted suicide."

189   "After long hesitancies": S. Freud, *An Outline of Psycho-Analysis* (1940), in Strachey, ed., *Works,* 23: 148.

190   "We find that": S. Freud, *The Ego and the Id* (1923), in Strachey, ed., *Works,* 19: 53.

## Chapter V Faith, Hopelessness, and 5HIAA

193　the NYSPI researchers: The work of NYSPI on serotonin can be found in J. J. Mann et al., "Evidence for the 5-HT Hypothesis of Suicide: A Review of Post-Mortem Studies," *British Journal of Psychiatry* (Supplement) (8) (1989): 7–14; Underwood et al., "Morphometry of the Dorsal Raphe Nucleus"; Mann et al., "Serotonin Transporter Gene Promoter"; Arango et al., "Genetics of the Serotonergic System"; Underwood et al., "Serotonergic and Noradrenergic Neurobiology"; Arango et al., "Serotonin 1A Receptors"; and Boldrini et al., "More Tryptophan Hydroxylase." For a concise overview of the field, see J. J. Mann and V. Arango, "The Neurobiology of Suicidal Behavior," in Jacobs, *Harvard Medical School Guide,* 98–114. See also J. J. Mann and V. Arango, "Neurobiology of Suicide and Attempted Suicide," in Wasserman, *Suicide,* 29–34. And V. Arango and M. Underwood, "Serotonin Chemistry in the Brain of Suicide Victims," in R. W. Maris, M. M. Silverman, and S. S. Canetto, *Review of Suicidology, 1997* (New York: Guilford Press), 237–50. A few of the details in my description of NYSPI's work have been taken from media accounts, in particular Ezzell, "Why?" For an extensive and extraordinarily lucid discussion of chemical and biological factors in suicide, I recommend K. R. Jamison's *Night Falls Fast,* 163–212.

193　"the emotional seat belt": J. Mann, *Psychiatric News,* April 7, 2000, www.psych.org/pnews/00–04–07/serotonin.html.

194　"sadness, anxiety, moral dejection": Solomon, *Noonday Demon,* 286.

194　"surgery of the soul": *New York Times,* June 7, 1937, in Whitaker, *Mad in America,* 116.

194　Robert Whitaker cites: Ibid., 73–138.

195　suicide and serotonin: Much of my description of Åsberg's work is drawn from Pines, "Suicide Signals." See also Åsberg et al., "5-HIAA in the Cerebrospinal Fluid." And Åsberg, "Neurotransmitters and Suicidal Behavior." For an interview with Åsberg, see the American Foundation for Suicide Prevention Web site at www.afsp.org/about-us/asberg.htm.

196　"the more lethal": Ezzell, "Why?" For the study, see Oquendo et al., "Positron Emission Tomography."

196　Mice with low serotonin: The information on serotonin and animal studies can be found in Jamison, *Night Falls Fast,* 185–89, and Solomon, *Noonday Demon,* 254.

197　four to six times higher: *Psychiatric News,* www.psych.org/pnews/98–01–19/suicide.html.

197　massive Danish study: P. Qin et al., "Suicide Risk in Relation to Family History of Completed Suicide and Psychiatric Disorders: A Nested Case-Control Study Based on Longitudinal Registers," *Lancet* 360 (9340) (2002): 1126–30.

198　2002 study by psychiatrist David Brent: D. A. Brent et al., "Familial Pathways to Early-Onset Suicide Attempts: A High-Risk Study," *Archives of General Psychiatry* 59 (2002): 801–7.

198　1985 study of the Old Order Amish: J. A. Egeland and J. N. Sussex, "Suicide and Family Loading for Affective Disorders," *Journal of the American Medical Association* 254 (7) (1985): 915–18.

198　"racing one's horse" and "excessive use of the public telephone": Jamison, *Night Falls Fast,* 170.

198　psychiatrist Alex Roy found: Roy et al., "Suicide in Twins."

199　Looking at attempted suicide: Roy et al., "Attempted Suicide."

199　adoptions in Copenhagen: R. Schulsinger et al., "A Family Study of Suicide," in M.

Schou and E. Stromgren, eds., *Origins, Prevention and Treatment of Affective Disorder* (New York: Academic Press, 1979), 277–87.

199    "Reducing suicide": *New York Times,* October 8, 1985, C8.

200    "what is being measured:" Shneidman, *Comprehending Suicide,* 72, 73.

200    "French runs in families": "High-Suicide Families Eyed by Genetic Scientists," *Boston Globe,* www.healthyplace.com/communities/depression/related/suicide.

201    "Taking all evidence": V. Arango and M. Underwood, "Serotonin Chemistry in the Brain of Suicide Victims," in Maris et al., *Review of Suicidology, 1997,* 238.

201    1895 address: Quotations in this paragraph are from "Is Life Worth Living?" in James, *Essays on Faith and Morals,* 1–31.

202    "Have we a right": Zilboorg, "Considerations on Suicide," 15.

202    "The contemporary physician": Szasz, *Theology of Medicine,* 68.

202    "Perhaps the greatest contribution": Hastings, *Encyclopaedia of Religion and Ethics,* 12: 24.

203    product of psychological disturbance: A few pundits, however, felt that increasing attention to psychological factors created too much sympathy toward suicide. "It is high time for the pulpit and religious press to emphasize strongly the wickedness of suicide," wrote Bishop Oldham in 1932. ". . . The warranted revolt from the barbarous practice of former centuries, whereby those who took their own lives were buried at a crossroads at midnight, and a stake driven through their bodies, has resulted in a weak sentimentality, and we have ceased to express and, perhaps, to feel the horror we ought." *Literary Digest,* July 16, 1932, 20.

203    In England: For a discussion of twentieth-century English suicide law, see Williams, *Sanctity of Life,* 278–83.

203    "unless there is some outstanding feature": Ibid., 279.

203    "Intentionally causing": Larue, *Euthanasia and Religion,* 37.

204    "There is but one": A. Camus, *The Myth of Sisyphus and Other Essays,* trans. J. O'Brien (New York: Vintage Books, 1955), 3.

204    examined fluctuations: Henry and Short, *Suicide and Homicide.*

204    Jack Gibbs and Walter Martin refined: Gibbs and Martin, *Status Integration and Suicide.*

204    Departing from Durkheim: Douglas, *Social Meanings of Suicide.*

204    "A wealthy man": Menninger, *Man Against Himself,* 19.

205    "To say that the death instinct": Zilboorg, "Considerations on Suicide," 17.

205    a mathematical formula: M. L. Farber, *Theory of Suicide* (New York: Funk & Wagnalls, 1968), 75.

**PART 3 The Range of Self-Destructive Behavior**
**Chapter I Winner and Loser**

209    "one calm summer night": E. A. Robinson, "Richard Cory," in F. O. Matthiessen, ed., *The Oxford Book of American Verse* (New York: Oxford University Press, 1950), 469–70.

**Chapter II Under the Shadow**

221    "No one ever lacks": Pavese, *Burning Brand,* 99.

222    reported rarity of suicides: Several death-camp survivors have pointed out that there were ways of killing oneself other than active suicide; one had only to approach the

barbed-wire fences to be shot by guards, or to relax one's struggle for survival to succumb. "We all had to fight constantly against the wish to go passively into death," a survivor told psychiatrist Joost Meerloo. "There is always a moment when a man surrenders, with his soul, with his will, and with his dreams. If that happened in the camps he was lost. Suicide was not even needed." Meerloo, *Suicide and Mass Suicide,* 130.

222   "The day was dense": P. Levi, *The Drowned and the Saved* (New York: Summit, 1988), 76.

222   "It is impossible": D. J. Enright, ed., *The Oxford Book of Death* (Oxford: Oxford University Press, 1983), 106.

222   "There is no refuge": J. Bartlett, *Familiar Quotations* (Boston: Little, Brown, 1980), 450.

223   Manes pulled a knife: Suicide was not an unfamiliar option for Manes; his father, despondent after his wife's death, killed himself, reportedly by stabbing, when Manes was a young man. Three years after Donald Manes's death, his twin brother, who had been in treatment for depression, attempted suicide, also by stabbing himself in the chest.

223   he shot himself: Kammerer's story is told in A. Koestler, *The Case of the Midwife Toad* (New York: Random House, 1972).

223   David Kelly, a fifty-nine-year-old: The circumstances leading to Kelly's suicide are detailed in J. Cassidy, "The David Kelly Affair," *New Yorker,* December 8, 2003, www.newyorker.com/fact/content.

223   "I have only myself": *Time,* November 17, 1980, 94.

224   "Dearest, I feel certain": L. Woolf, *The Journey Not the Arrival Matters: An Autobiography of the Years 1939 to 1969* (New York: Harcourt Brace Jovanovich, 1969), 93–94.

224   "Paradoxical and tragic": L. S. Kubie, "Multiple Determinants of Suicide," in Shneidman, *Essays in Self-Destruction,* 458.

225   "To whom concerned": P. Friedman, "Suicide Among Police: A Study of Ninety-three Suicides Among New York City Policemen, 1934–1940," in Shneidman, *Essays in Self-Destruction,* 438.

225   a few general types: Many of the details in my discussion of murder followed by suicide have been taken from the excellent overview of the subject provided in M. K. Nock and P. M. Marzuk, "Murder-Suicide: Phenomenology and Clinical Implications," in Jacobs, *Harvard Medical School Guide,* 188–209.

225   eighty-eight women who had murdered a child: Hendin, *Suicide in America,* 100–101.

225   "Although such events": Nock and Marzuk, "Murder-Suicide," 199.

225   "One central theme": Ibid.

226   "Good creatures": A. E. Housman, *Complete Poems* (New York: Henry Holt, 1959), 185.

226   "If I commit suicide": Alvarez, *Savage God,* 125.

226   "Suicide always seeks": Lifton's discussion of suicide is found in Lifton, *Broken Connection,* 239–61.

227   "The impulse to death" and "for some, organic death": Hillman, *Suicide and the Soul,* 63, 83.

227   "The suicidal attempt": Kubie, "Multiple Determinants of Suicide," 455.

228   "Is it conceivable": Quotations in this paragraph are found in Pavese, *Burning Brand,* 89, 48, 365, 366.

229   "being imprisoned": Styron, *Darkness Visible,* 50.

229   "as if I were being stuffed": Plath quotations are from Plath, *Bell Jar,* 105, 152, 193.

229   "an experience of harassment": E. Ringel, "The Presuicidal Syndrome," *Suicide and Life-Threatening Behavior* 6 (3) (1976): 131.

229   "Everything was like": Shneidman, *Voices of Death,* 15–16.
230   "The logic of suicide": Alvarez, *Savage God,* 116.
230   "some standard domestic squabble": The description of Alvarez's attempt and the quotes in this paragraph are from *Savage God,* 257–72.


## Chapter III The Manner of Dying

233   "Take a look at them": J. M. Cain, *Double Idemnity* (New York: Vintage Books, 1978), 67.
233   was considered "unseemly": Jamison, *Night Falls Fast,* 136.
234   "What a low-minded wretch": Moore, *Full Inquiry,* 1: 357.
234   "Hanging is a type of death": Fedden, *Suicide,* 231.
234   "Not only have they": Alvarez, *Savage God,* 131–32.
234   "Since many Norwegians": Hendin, *Suicide in America,* 144.
235   "Sexual experience": Ibid., 145.
235   a rash of ninety-three suicides: P. Friedman, "Suicide Among Police," in Shneidman, *Essays in Self-Destruction,* 414–49.
235   people have completed suicide by: About half of this list is taken from a similar list compiled by George Kennan in an article for *McClure's* and quoted in Menninger, *Man Against Himself,* 55. The other, more recent, examples are drawn from a variety of books and news clippings.
236   Yet on closer inspection: The nineteenth-century Parisienne who applied one hundred leeches to her body may well have been attempting to cure rather than kill herself, in an era when leeches were a common remedy for suicidal depression.
236   "That the various methods": S. Freud, "The Psychogenesis of a Case of Homosexuality in a Woman" (1920), in Strachey, *Works,* 18: 162.
236   "The choice of the manner": Ellis and Allen, *Traitor Within,* 125–26.
237   "jumping out": Meerloo, *Suicide and Mass Suicide,* 74.
237   stab or shoot themselves: Hendin, *Suicide in America,* 147–48.
237   "Some suicides use their control": Ibid., 149.
237   "the multiplicity of methods": Ibid.
238   "Suicides have a special language": A. Sexton, *The Complete Poems* (Boston: Houghton Mifflin, 1981), 142–43.
238   go to great lengths: And they will go to great lengths to insist on suicide. Wrote Pavese: "There is nothing ridiculous or absurd about a man who is thinking of killing himself being afraid of falling under a car or catching a fatal disease. Quite apart from the question of the degree of suffering involved, the fact remains that to want to kill oneself is to want one's death to be significant, a *supreme* choice, a deed that cannot be misunderstood. So it is natural that no would-be suicide can endure the thought of anything so meaningless as being run over or dying of pneumonia. So beware of draughts and street corners." (Pavese, *Burning Brand,* 87.) Pity, then, poor Heliogabalus, a Roman emperor renowned for his eccentricity. Told by Syrian priests that he'd take his own life, he obtained a golden sword, a rope of imperial purple and gold, and a priceless ring filled with poison. And in case he decided on jumping, he ordered a pavement of jewels to be laid beneath one of his towers to receive his body. Unfortunately, before he had a chance to take advantage of his elaborate preparations, he was murdered by his guards.
238   "A man who has attempted": Winslow, *Anatomy of Suicide,* 210.
238   six people who survived leaps: D. H. Rosen, "Suicide Survivors: Psychotherapeutic Implications of Egocide," *Suicide and Life-Threatening Behavior* 6 (4) (1976): 209–15.
239   Thomas Lynch describes: T. Lynch, *The Undertaking: Life Studies from the Dismal*

*Trade* (New York: Penguin, 1998), 153. I first read of the story in Jamison, *Night Falls Fast,* 134–35.

239    In one early project: For a brief summary of research on suicide notes, see C. J. Frederick, "Suicide Notes: A Survey and Evaluation," *Bulletin of Suicidology,* March 1969, 17–26.

239    psychiatrist Calvin Frederick: C. J. Frederick, "An Investigation of Handwriting of Suicide Persons Through Suicide Notes," *Journal of Abnormal Psychology* 73 (3) (1968): 263–67.

240    "Suicide notes often seem like parodies": Shneidman, *Voices of Death,* 58. Collections of suicide notes can be found in Shneidman, *Voices of Death,* 41–76; Shneidman and Farberow, *Clues to Suicide,* 197–215; Ellis and Allen, *Traitor Within,* 170–85; H. Wolf, "Suicide Notes," *American Mercury,* November 1931, 264–72; and M. Etkind, . . . *Or Not to Be: A Collection of Suicide Notes* (New York: Riverhead Books, 1997).

240    "Whether the writers": Stengel, *Suicide and Attempted Suicide,* 44.

240    "'You are not to blame'": Hendin, *Suicide in America,* 155.

## Chapter IV The Numbers Game

245    A six-year study: Paper presented at a joint meeting of the American Association of Suicidology and the International Association for Suicide Prevention, San Francisco, May 25–30, 1987.

245    studying suicide in Scandinavia: Material in this and the following two paragraphs is from Hendin, *Suicide and Scandinavia.*

247    at least twenty: D. Baum, "The Price of Valor," *New Yorker,* July 12 and 19, 2004, 49.

247    sociologist M. Harvey Brenner: *New York Times,* April 6, 1982, C1.

248    "The suicide rate seems to mirror": Kushner, *Self-Destruction in the Promised Land,* 150–51.

248    "the struggle for existence": "Suicide in Cities," *American Journal of Sociology* 10 (4) (1905): 562.

249    Minneapolis suicides: C. F. Schmid, "Suicide in Minneapolis, Minnesota: 1928–32," *American Journal of Sociology* 39 (1) (1933): 30–48.

249    district-by-district survey: P. Sainsbury, *Suicide in London: An Ecological Study* (London: Chapman and Hall, 1955).

249    studies by psychiatrist Alex Pokorny: A. D. Pokorny, "Suicide and Weather," *Archives of Environmental Health* 13 (1966): 255–56; and Pokorny et al., "Suicide, Suicide Attempts."

250    "A suicidal depression": Alvarez, *Savage God,* 79.

250    "It was a spring day": Kaysen, *Girl, Interrupted,* 52.

250    "If a person works": Ellis and Allen, *Traitor Within,* 21.

250    Steven Stack points out: Stack, "Occupation and Suicide."

251    "Dentists suffer": The Straight Dope, www.straightdope.com.

251    one in three psychiatrists: C. L. Rich and F. N. Pitts Jr., "Suicide by Psychiatrists: A Study of Medical Specialists Among 18,730 Consecutive Physician Deaths During a Five-Year Period, 1967–72," *Journal of Clinical Psychiatry* 41 (8) (1980): 261–63.

251    "a vocational hazard": Beam, *Gracefully Insane,* 217.

251    "It draws workaholics": *Time,* February 16, 1981.

252    "You can't kill yourself by jumping": R. H. Seiden, "We're Driving Young Blacks to Suicide," *Psychology Today,* August 1970, 24.

253    "Many of these subjects" and "It does not seem surprising": Hendin, *Black Suicide,* 139, 145.

253    "To be a Negro": Seiden, "We're Driving Young Blacks," 28.

253    "They believe they have": *Time,* September 16, 1985, 33.

254    "You ache with the need": Ibid.

254    analyzed 437 shootings: Hutson et al., "Suicide by Cop."

254    "The problem with such speculations": A. F. Poussaint, "Black Suicide" (paper presented at "The Enigma of Suicide," a conference sponsored by the Samaritans in Boston, March 24, 1984), 11–12.

255    posttraumatic slavery syndrome: Poussaint and Alexander, *Lay My Burden Down,* 15. This book offers a comprehensive overview of African-American suicide, and my discussion owes much to it.

255    "There is a type of suicide": Durkheim, *Suicide,* 276.

255    "Their expectations of life": Poussaint, "Black Suicide," 12.

255    "Black Poets should live": Poussaint and Alexander, *Lay My Burden Down,* 110.

256    a study of marital status and suicide: S. Stack, "The Effect of Marital Integration in African American Suicide," *Suicide and Life-Threatening Behavior* 26 (4) (1996): 405–14.

256    Charles Prudhomme predicted: C. Prudhomme, "The Problem of Suicide in the American Negro," *Psychoanalytic Review* 25 (1938): 187–204, 372–91.

256    Harlem's suicide rate: K. B. Clark, *Dark Ghetto: Dilemmas of Social Power* (New York: Harper and Row, 1965).

256    A 1998 study traced the rise: J. Neeleman et al., "Suicide Acceptability in African and White Americans: The Role of Religion," *Journal of Nervous and Mental Disease* 186 (1) (1998): 16.

257    "Perhaps these unifying": Seiden, "Why Are Suicides," 5. Also see R. H. Seiden, "Mellowing with Age: Factors Influencing the Nonwhite Suicide Rate," *International Journal of Aging and Human Development* 13 (4) (1981): 265–84. And Seiden, "Current Development in Minority Group Suicidology."

257    a study by Alton Kirk: A. R. Kirk, "Socio-Psychological Factors in Attempted Suicide Among Urban Black Males" (Ph.D. diss., Michigan State University, 1976).

257    "try to become more assimilated": A. R. Kirk, "Psycho-Social Modes of Adaptation and Suicide Among Blacks" (unpublished paper, Michigan State University), 10.

257    Part is historical: The medical community's patronizing attitudes toward African-Americans date back at least as far as 1851, when one prominent Southern physician identified a type of insanity peculiar to slaves: "drapetomania"—the desire to run away. The cure? Light beatings and hard labor. (These attitudes have persisted. In a 1988 experiment, 290 psychiatrists reviewed case studies in which the patients were alternately described as white male, white female, black male, and black female; their diagnoses diverged in two directions: more severe for black males, less severe for white males.) (See Whitaker, *Mad in America,* 173.) Minorities in general may avoid seeking help from the mental health care system, which is hardly surprising given that, in a system predominately run by and geared toward whites, they have less access. And, according to recent government-sponsored reports, "When they utilize care, minorities are more likely than whites to be misdiagnosed or to receive inferior quality of care." (Goldsmith, *Reducing Suicide,* 355.)

257    considered depression: National Mental Health Association, "Depression and African-Americans Fact Sheet" (Alexandria, Va.: National Mental Health Association, 2000).

257    "The internal strength": Poussaint and Alexander, *Lay My Burden Down,* 26.

258    Things have changed: After her twenty-year-old son killed himself in 1990, Donna Holland Barnes sought out support groups to help her cope with her grief. She was surprised not to see any other African-Americans. In 1998, Holland, a professor of sociology, cofounded the National Organization for People of Color Against Suicide (NOPCAS),

a nonprofit organization devoted to suicide prevention and awareness in the African-American community.

258    "Blacks view suicide": Kirk, "Psycho-Social Modes," 11.

258    One of the few large-scale studies: J. C. Smith et al., "Comparison of Suicides Among Anglos and Hispanics in Five Southwestern States," *Suicide and Life-Threatening Behavior* 15 (1) (1985): 14–26.

259    nearly twice as likely: "Youth Risk Behavior Surveillance—United States, 2000," *Morbidity and Mortality Weekly Report, CDC Surveillance Summary* 49 (SS05) (2000): 1–96.

259    "After they were confined": L. H. Dizmang, "Suicide Among the Cheyenne Indians," *Bulletin of Suicidology,* July 1967, 9.

260    new ways to vent aggression: The Native American death rate from cirrhosis of the liver is far higher than for any other race, especially among the young. The rates of homicide and violent accidents are also high, although there is evidence that they have decreased somewhat over the past few decades.

260    the causes were numerous: "Suicide Among Aboriginal People," Royal Commission Report, February 23, 1995, prepared by Nancy Miller Chenier, Political and Social Affairs Division, Canadian Parliament.

261    "Inuit culture is rooted": "Tragedy of Inuit Suicides Must End: New Measures Needed on World Suicide Prevention Day," press release issued September 7, 2004, by Stephen Hendrie, director of communications, Inuit Tapiriit Kanatami.

261    "Prior to the development": Rofes, *"I Thought People,"* 25. My discussion of gay and lesbian suicide owes much to this pioneering work.

261    "Homosexuality used to be": Ibid., 11.

262    "The homosexual act in itself": Meerloo, *Suicide and Mass Suicide,* 72. Among the eminent psychiatrists who believed homosexuality to be inherently suicidal were Karl Menninger and Gregory Zilboorg. Zilboorg, in fact, suggested that male suicide was invariably connected to homosexuality. Pointing out that far more men than women kill themselves, Zilboorg suggested that "man's suicide has more to do with the inner struggles created by passivity and feminine strivings, i.e., by homosexuality. This would perhaps explain why more men shoot themselves than women, shooting having obviously something to do (symbolically) with passive homosexual wishes." Zilboorg, "Considerations on Suicide," 25.

262    "Have lesbians and gay men": Rofes, *"I Thought People,"* 14.

262    survey of 3,648 men: Cochran and Mays, "Lifetime Prevalence of Suicide Symptoms."

262    1986 study concluded: C. L. Rich et al., "San Diego Study I: Young vs. Old Subjects," *Archives of General Psychiatry,* 43 (6) (1986): 577–82.

262    A study of male twins: Herrel et al., "Sexual Orientation and Suicidality."

262    A 1978 Kinsey report, for instance: A. P. Bell, and M. S. Weinberg, *Homosexualities: A Study of Diversity Among Men and Women* (New York: Simon and Schuster, 1978).

262    A gay suicidologist likened this: www.virtualcity.com/youthsuicide/sltb.

263    One frequently cited paper: D. Shaffer et al., "Sexual Orientation in Adolescents Who Commit Suicide," *Suicide and Life-Threatening Behavior* 25 (Supplement 4) (1995): 64–71.

263    "Less than two months ago": J. Nelson, "Documentation Regarding Some Relationships Between Adolescent Suicide and Homosexuality" (unpublished paper, March 1987).

263    one of the first systematic studies: *New York Times,* March 4, 1988. See P. Marzuk et al., "Increased Risk of Suicide in Persons with AIDS," *Journal of the American Medical Association* 259 (1988): 1333–37.

264    has been linked to increased anxiety: "You and AIDS: The HIV/AIDS Portal for Asia Pacific," www.youandaids.org.

264 "exchange formulas for suicide": R. Shilts, "Talking AIDS to Death," in J. Kaplan, ed., *The Best American Essays 1990* (New York: Ticknor & Fields, 1990), 243.

264 survey of 113 men: S. C. Kalichman et al., "Depression and Thoughts of Suicide Among Middle-Aged and Older Persons Living with HIV-AIDS," *Psychiatric Services* 51 (7) (2000): 903–7.

264 survey of 3,365 students: Garofolo et al., "Sexual Orientation and Risk."

264 survey of nearly forty thousand: Remafedi et al., "Relationship Between Suicide Risk."

264 "All of the problems": This and other Gibson quotes are from P. Gibson, "Gay Male and Lesbian Youth Suicide" (paper presented at a joint meeting of the American Association of Suicidology and the International Association for Suicide Prevention, San Francisco, May 25–30, 1987). For a critique of this paper, see P. LaBarbera, "The Gay Youth Suicide Myth," www.leaderu.com/jhs/labarbera.

265 study by the Los Angeles Suicide Prevention Center: S. Schneider et al., "Suicidal Behavior in Adolescent and Young Adult Gay Men" (paper presented at a joint meeting of the American Association of Suicidology and the International Association for Suicide Prevention, San Francisco, May 25–30, 1987).

266 "He wanted to be normal": The material on Jim Wheeler was taken from several Web sites, including www.jimwheeler.org.

## Chapter V Backing into the Grave

267 survey of the etymology: Daube, "Linguistics of Suicide." For much of the material in these first three paragraphs I am indebted to this fascinating paper.

268 Alvarez cites an earlier usage: Alvarez, *Savage God,* 48.

268 "One barbarous word": Fedden, *Suicide,* 29.

269 "*eating* to gluttony": Ibid., 184.

269 "the daredevil": Durkheim, *Suicide,* 45–46.

269 "I have now learnt" and "When a member of my family": S. Freud, *The Psychopathology of Everyday Life* (1901), in Strachey, *Works,* 6: 178–82.

270 "in the end each man": Menninger, *Man Against Himself,* vii.

270 two armies at war: Meerloo, *Suicide and Mass Suicide,* 92.

270 "The development of symptoms": K. Menninger, "Expression and Punishment," in Shneidman, *On the Nature of Suicide,* 71.

271 self-mutilation: In *Man Against Himself,* Menninger offers an extensive analysis of self-mutilation. For a brief but comprehensive summary of the syndrome, see M. A. Simpson, "Self-Mutilation and Suicide," in Shneidman, *Suicidology,* 281–315. See also A. R. Favazza, "Self-Mutilation," in Jacobs, *Harvard Medical School Guide,* 125–45.

272 about 3 percent: G. E. Murphy et al., "The Lifetime Risk of Suicide in Alcoholism," *Archives of General Psychiatry* 47 (1990): 383–92.

272 115 times that: G. E. Murphy, *Suicide in Alcoholism* (New York: Oxford University Press, 1992). As cited in Goldsmith et al., *Reducing Suicide,* 84.

272 "a form of self-destruction": Menninger, *Man Against Himself,* 161.

272 147 suicidal male alcoholics: Hendin, *Suicide in America,* 127.

272 one-third of alcoholic suicides: Murphy et al., "Suicide and Alcoholism."

273 "I didn't think I was worth anything": Giffin and Felsenthal, *Cry for Help,* 53.

273 review of more than thirty studies: A. Gardner and C. Rich, "Eating Disorders and Suicide," in R. Yufit, ed., *Proceedings of the 21st Annual Meeting of the American Association of Suicidology* (Denver: American Association of Suicidology, 1999), 171–72.

274 Melvin Selzer has demonstrated: Selzer and Payne, "Automobile Accidents."

274 In a subsequent study: *New York Times,* April 1, 1968, 35.

274 "lifelong war against boredom": Greene describes playing Russian roulette and making several adolescent suicide attempts in G. Greene, *A Sort of Life* (New York: Touchstone, 1971), 73–88, 128–33.

274 "They use risk-taking behavior": The quote and a description of the study are taken from *Washington Post,* June 9, 1987, Health Section, 5.

275 "I would describe myself": M. Begley, "Risky Business," *Backpacker,* May 1986, 38. Yukio Mishima compared athletes who sought such extreme experience to kamikaze pilots. But most rock climbers, skydivers, and so on are not, of course, suicidal. "Generally speaking, all dangerous activities (for example, auto racing, mountain climbing, acrobatics, etc.) *could* reflect suicidal tendencies," writes Jean Baechler. "There is no question of considering all race-car drivers as suicidal but simply of having available a form of suicidal behavior that is revealed in taking risks." Baechler, *Suicides,* 19. Some, however, may be attracted to such risky endeavors partially because of their self-destructive possibilities. The British climber Menlove Edwards was famous for his risky expeditions and bold routes. The feats that in public won him medals had a pathetic parallel in his private life. A homosexual who never found lasting love, he was tormented by depression. When depressed, he liked to row far out into the open sea in a battered boat, then ride huge waves to shore, scrambling to safety as they crashed on the rocks. At age thirty-four he suffered a breakdown and made three suicide attempts. He lived the last fourteen years of his life as a recluse, cared for by his sister, although he continued to climb. In 1958 he completed suicide by swallowing potassium cyanide.

275 "Life is impoverished": Alvarez, *Savage God,* 253.

275 "Many soldiers have the fantasy": Meerloo, *Suicide and Mass Suicide,* 75.

275 In his 1950s study of murder: M. E. Wolfgang, "Suicide by Means of Victim-Precipitated Homicide," in H. L. P. Resnik, ed., *Suicidal Behaviors* (Boston: Little, Brown, 1968), 90–104.

275 a forty-three-year-old German man: M. Landler, "German Court Convicts Internet Cannibal of Manslaughter," *New York Times,* January 31, 2004.

276 A twenty-two-year-old babysitter: Quite the opposite of people who use murder as a means of suicide are those political prisoners who are murdered and are called "suicides." During the 1930s when the National Socialists imprisoned and killed many of their opponents and insisted they were suicides, the French revived the caustic phrase *être suicidé*—"to be suicided." In the 1980s and early 1990s, this occurred among anti-apartheid prisoners in South Africa who were said to have killed themselves while in detention.

276 creativity: On the other hand, some artists make art of self-destruction, an aesthetic of asceticism. Like a contemporary St. Simeon Stylites, one New York performance artist spent five days and nights in a two-by-three-foot locker without food. Another sat on a shelf in an art gallery for twenty-two days. Then there was the man who lived in a cage for a year.

276 "Most people are no longer alive": Meerloo, *Suicide and Mass Suicide,* 19.

277 "backing into the grave": Pretzel, "Philosophical and Ethical Considerations," 32.

277 examples of self-destruction: Steincrohn, *How to Stop Killing Yourself.*

277 "One must be careful": Baechler, *Suicides,* 18.

277 "There is a little murder": K. Menninger, *Sparks,* ed. L. Freeman (New York: Thomas Y. Crowell Company, 1973), 142.

277 "A thousand people": J. Carroll, *The Winter Name of God* (Kansas City: Sheed and Ward, 1975), 87–88.

**PART 4 Prevention**
**Chapter II Suicidology**

291 until 1906: There were a few exceptions. During the Enlightenment, when there was great interest in using scientific advances to extend the human life span, societies were formed in which physicians, clergy, and laymen essentially acted as eighteenth-century paramedics. The members of one such group, London's Royal Humane Society, founded in 1774, were trained to restore life "to the drowned, those suspended by the cord, or otherwise suffocated: likewise in cases of intense cold; the aweful and tremendous stroke of lightning; and other premature, accidental or sudden deaths." Members were paid four guineas for each successful revival; unsuccessful attempts earned two. While preventing suicide was not its primary goal, the society came in contact with many attempted suicides. "By the Annual Reports of this society it appears, that since its first institution not fewer than five hundred cases of suicide have fallen under its cognizance," observed the Reverend G. Gregory in 1797, "in about three hundred and fifty of which its interposition has been providential enough to restore the despairing culprit to himself, to his friends, and to society; and to rescue the soul of the sinner from the overwhelming pressure of despondency, and, perhaps from the danger of everlasting condemnation."

Although the society considered suicide a "horrid crime," its members were among the first to realize that suicidal people can and should be helped. They also recognized a characteristic of suicidal people that would be crucial to subsequent prevention efforts: ambivalence. After describing the rescue and rehabilitation of a homeless woman who attempted suicide in 1778, one member wrote, "This happy issue must give pleasure to every reflecting mind. It proves that there is no life so miserable but it may be worthy of our endeavours to save it; and it is an additional argument, to the many others Our Society has afforded, against a prevailing sentiment, that all attempts to save a suicide are in vain; for, they will repeat the act. A sentiment this, neither founded in the knowledge of human nature, nor justified by experience." In 1797, a year in which, according to society records, eleven would-be suicides were saved and "all of them were reconciled to life," the RHS held an anniversary celebration. The evening's highlight was "the Procession of the Persons restored to Life by the efforts of the Humane Society, and its Medical Assistants." Odes "To Sympathy" and "To Science" were recited, which seems appropriate considering that the society's good works were inspired as much by the spirit of scientific inquiry as by sympathy for the suicidal. (Material on the Royal Humane Society from G. Gregory, *A Sermon on Suicide* (London: J. Nichols, 1797).)

In the nineteenth century, there were a few organized prevention efforts. Like the Royal Humane Society, the Lemberg Volunteer Rescue Society (with a branch office in Budapest) was an emergency paramedical service whose cases included suicides and suicide attempts. According to a 1906 German newspaper article the society had attended to 720 suicides and suicide attempts since its founding in 1893. Fedden reports that toward the end of the century an association was formed in Foochow, China, to keep four boats patrolling the Foochow Bridge to save would-be suicides from drowning.

295 "Prior to the 1950s": Frederick, "Current Trends," 172.

296 broke the key: E. S. Shneidman and N. L. Farberow, "Some Comparisons Between Genuine and Simulated Suicide Notes," *Journal of General Psychology* 56 (1957): 251–56.

300 "Both of those have given way": A. B. Tulipan and S. Feldman, eds., *Psychiatric Clinics in Transition* (New York: Brunner-Mazel, 1969), 128.

304 "The goal of the NIMH Center": E. S. Shneidman, "The NIMH Center for Studies of Suicide Prevention," *Bulletin of Suicidology,* July 1967, 2.

304     coined by Shneidman: Shneidman subsequently learned that the word *suicidologie* had been used in 1929 by Dutch professor W. A. Bonger.

304     "massive public education": E. S. Shneidman, "A Comprehensive NIMH Suicide Prevention Program" (1966) (a thirty-six-page memorandum to Stanley Yolles, then director of NIMH), 14.

304     "The 'early signs' of suicide": Ibid., 2.

305     "Just as there are fire stations": Ibid., 7.

305     The suicide prevention movement: Psychiatrist Erwin Ringel, who in 1947 founded Vienna's Lebensmuedenfuersorge (Society for the Care of People Who Are Tired of Life), frequently expressed his belief in the efficacy of such centers by maintaining that "if Romeo had had a crisis intervention clinic handy, neither he nor Juliet would have died." (*Washington Post,* January 21, 1973, C5.)

305     "How to Set Up a Suicide Prevention Center": N. Allen, "How to Set Up a Suicide Prevention Center," *California's Health,* January 1970.

305     wide variations: Much of the information on prevention centers in these paragraphs is drawn from Fisher, *Suicide Prevention and/or Crisis Services.*

306     Shneidman even pointed out: Shneidman, "Comprehensive NIMH Suicide Prevention Program," 29.

306     "One of the problems": D. Lester, "Spiritualism and Suicide," *Omega* 12 (1) (1981): 45–49.

306     A 1972 summary: D. Lester, *Why People Kill Themselves* (Springfield, Ill.: Charles C. Thomas, 1972).

306     psychologist Richard McGee: R. K. McGee et al., "A Survey of Telephone Answering Services in Suicide Prevention and Crisis Intervention Agencies," *Life-Threatening Behavior* 2 (1) (1972): 42–47.

307     CSSP-sponsored task force: H. L. P. Resnik and B. C. Hathorne, eds., *Suicide Prevention in the 70's* (Washington, D.C.: U.S. Government Printing Office, 1973), 3.

307     When a 1968 study: C. Bagley, "The Evaluation of a Suicide Prevention Scheme by an Ecological Method," *Social Science and Medicine* 2 (1968): 1–14; and R. Fox, "The Recent Decline of Suicide in Britain: The Role of the Samaritan Suicide Prevention Movement," in Shneidman, *Sucidology,* 499–524.

307     more carefully controlled study: C. Jennings et al., "Have the Samaritans Lowered the Suicide Rate? A Controlled Study," *Psychological Medicine* 8 (1978): 413–22.

307     compared eight cities: D. Lester, "Effect of Suicide Prevention Centers on Suicide Rates in the United States," *Health Services Reports* 89 (1974): 37–39.

307     institute's top priority: At the same time, the federal government was at the height of its commitment to community mental health centers. Emphasis shifted from research to direct services. The government's goal was to reach more people for less money. With the move toward crisis intervention and youth problems, suicide research received decreasing support, and the suicide prevention center per se was swallowed up in the extraordinary growth of hotlines of all varieties. By 1974 there were almost seven hundred hotlines in the United States; St. Louis alone was alleged to have ninety-three. There were hotline newsletters and hotline conventions. National magazines and TV melodramas offered histrionic accounts of tearful calls and heroic rescues. "At this very moment, thousands of hotlines are ringing," began a book describing the hotline phenomenon. "People are calling for help about problems that deal with pregnancy, illegal drugs, boy-girl problems, family hassles, alcohol abuse, suicide, loneliness, child abuse, runaways, rape, and more." The book, which included instructions on how to start a hotline, described the LASPC as "the grandfather of all hotlines." Its progeny now included Rap Shop, Some Body Loves You Baby, Awakening Peace, Fort Help, Mother, Need, The Way Out, Listening Post, Pulse, Inc., Oz, Yell Inc., Sunshine Line, and Tele-

Mom (M. O. Hyde, *Hotline!* [New York: McGraw-Hill, 1976]). In a 1972 issue of Romaine Edwards's *Hotline Newsletter,* the author, who claimed to have founded fifteen hotlines, captured the hotline fever: "The word got around quickly: You didn't need a battalion of degreed headshrinkers to start helping local folk with their big and little problems. . . . All you needed were a couple of phone numbers, a few friends, and a little publicity, and presto!"

308    study of ten centers: Hendin, *Suicide in America,* 183.

308    half of the four thousand calls: Lester and Lester, *Suicide,* 162.

308    psychiatrist Jerome Motto: J. A. Motto, "Evaluation of a Suicide Prevention Center by Sampling the Population at Risk," *Suicide and Life-Threatening Behavior* 2 (1) (1971): 18–22.

308    eighteen-month follow-up: R. E. Litman and C. I. Wold, "Beyond Crisis Intervention," in Shneidman, *Suicidology,* 525–46.

310    "The committee finds": Goldsmith et al., *Reducing Suicide,* 9.

310    University of Alabama study: H. L. Miller et al., "An Analysis of the Effects of Suicide Prevention Facilities on Suicide Rates in the United States," *American Journal of Public Health* 74 (4) (1984): 340–43.


## Chapter III Treatment

313    "People say": Giffin and Felsenthal, *Cry for Help,* 41.

314    A twenty-year follow-up study: Brown et al., "Risk Factors for Suicide."

314    Reasons for Living scale: M. M. Linehan et al., paper presented at the Fourteenth Annual Meeting of the American Association of Suicidology, Albuquerque, N.M., 1981.

314    Risk-Rescue Rating: A. D. Weisman and J. W. Worden, "Risk-Rescue Rating in Suicide Assessment," *Archives of General Psychiatry* 26 (1972): 553–60.

314    like the weather: Simon, "Suicide Prevention Contract."

315    SAD PERSONS scale: W. M. Patterson et al., "Evaluation of Suicidal Patients: The SAD PERSONS Scale," *Psychosomatics* 24 (4) (1983): 343–49.

315    "Patient Monitoring of Suicidal Risk": R. C. Drye et al., "No-Suicide Decisions: Patient Monitoring of Suicidal Risk," *American Journal of Psychiatry* 130 (2) (1973): 171–74.

315    whether they actually work: A recent study of seventy-six people who completed suicide either as hospital inpatients or immediately after discharge found that more than three-quarters denied suicidal thoughts or intent as their last communication to mental health professionals. "Many clinicians use a patient's denial of suicide to relieve their anxiety," warned psychiatrist Jan Fawcett, a coauthor of the study. "But this denial is not to be relied upon." K. A. Busch et al., "Clinical Correlates of Inpatient Suicide," *Journal of Clinical Psychiatry* 64 (1) (2003): 14–19. See also E. Bender, "Suicide Expert Calls for More Aggressive Screening," *Psychiatric News* 38 (11) (2003): 28.

315    survey at Harvard Medical School: M. C. Miller et al., "Talisman or Taboo? The Controversy of the Suicide Prevention Contract," *Harvard Review of Psychiatry* 6 (1998): 78–87. For an overview of the subject, see M. C. Miller, "Suicide-Prevention Contracts: Advantages, Disadvantages, and an Alternative Approach," in Jacobs, *Harvard Medical School Guide,* 463–81.

315    "the use of such clinical contracts": M. Goin, "The 'Suicide-Prevention Contract': A Dangerous Myth," *Psychiatric News* 38 (14) (2003), pn.psychiatryonline.org.

315    "The contract against self-harm": Simon, "Suicide Prevention Contract."

316    proved unsuccessful: Pokorny, "Prediction of Suicide."

316     computer was shown to be more accurate: J. H. Greist et al., "A Computer Interview for Suicide-Risk Prediction," *American Journal of Psychiatry* 130 (12) (1973): 1327–32.

316     brought to emergency rooms: A. Spirito et al., "Attempted Suicide in Adolescence: A Review and Critique of the Literature," *Clinical Psychology Review* 9 (3) (1989): 335–63.

316     getting the person: It has been estimated that only 12 percent of those who attempt suicide receive medical attention. Indeed, it is said that over 90 percent of people who complete suicide have a diagnosable mental disorder. Yet two-thirds of all people with diagnosable mental disorders do not receive treatment. (Of those who do receive treatment, only half see mental health professionals. And only about half of those who receive treatment—be it from a mental health professional or a physician—are diagnosed and treated appropriately.) There are a number of reasons for this. Suicidal people face stigma on two fronts, the diminishing but still considerable stigma of mental illness, and the stigma of suicide. Many face financial obstacles: 16 percent of Americans have no medical insurance (for minorities, the figure is even higher), and even those who are insured are unlikely to receive adequate coverage; carriers commonly have greater restrictions for coverage of mental illness than for other health conditions. Many of those who end up taking medications stop prematurely. Some are discouraged by unpleasant side effects, which usually start before the therapeutic benefit is felt. Others give up because they begin to feel better and want to see if they can do without the medications. (Patients must often try several different drugs or combinations of drugs at different dosage levels before one works. After each new medication is introduced, several weeks or more must pass before patient and clinician can determine whether it is effective.) Compliance rates for patients on antidepressants run about 65–80 percent; for lithium, about 60 percent; for anticonvulsants, about 55 percent. (The FDA stresses the importance of close monitoring, especially during the first few months of treatment—patients are most likely to become suicidal within the first nine days of starting antidepressant medication—or whenever dosages are altered or medications changed.) See "Barriers to Effective Treatment and Intervention," in Goldsmith et al., *Reducing Suicide,* 331–73.

317     "The immediate goal" and "I did several things": Shneidman, *Definition of Suicide,* 229.

318     "Suicidal behaviors": J. A. Motto, "Recognition, Evaluation, and Management of Persons at Risk for Suicide," *Personnel and Guidance Journal* 26 (1978): 537–43.

318     "Suicide proneness": D. H. Buie and J. T. Maltsberger, "The Psychology and Assessment of Suicide" (unpublished paper), 18.

318     "In our age the triumph": D. Merkin, "Psychoanalysis: Is It Science or Is It Toast?" *New York Times Book Review,* September 5, 2004, 9.

319     "immobile" and "waxlike": Whitaker, *Mad in America,* 154.

319     Prozac Nation: E. Wurtzel, *Prozac Nation* (Boston: Houghton Mifflin, 1995).

319     thirteen times more likely: R. J. Baldessarini et al., "Treating the Suicidal Patient with Bipolar Disorder: Reducing Suicide Risk with Lithium," *Annals of the New York Academy of Sciences* 932 (2001): 24–38.

319     a German study: K. Thies-Flechtner et al., "Effect of Prophylactic Treatment on Suicide Risk in Patients with Major Affective Disorders. Data from a Randomized Prospective Trial," *Pharmacopsychiatry* 29 (3) (1996): 103–7.

320     suicidal acts rose sixteenfold: Baldessarini et al., "Effects of Lithium."

320     only 8–17 percent: Goldsmith et al., *Reducing Suicide,* 237.

320     6–14 percent: Ibid., 237.

321     Those concerns resurfaced: Much of my discussion of the SSRI controversy is taken from articles in the *New York Times* in 2004.

322     only 20 percent: Mahler, "Antidepressant Dilemma," 61.

322     "It is probably the case": A. Solomon. "A Bitter Pill," *New York Times,* March 29, 2004.

322    439 depressed teenagers: J. March, "Fluoxetine, Cognitive-Behavioral Therapy, and Their Combination for Adolescents with Depression: Treatment for Adolescents with Depression Study (TADS) Randomized Controlled Trial," *Journal of the American Medical Association* 292 (7) (2004): 807–20.

323    "Medicine alone is not sufficient": Goldsmith et al., *Reducing Suicide,* 258.

323    modus operandi: Electroconvulsive therapy, for instance, is said by some clinicians to be the most effective treatment for severe suicidal depression, because when it works, it works so quickly. (As to *why* it works, doctors are still at a loss to explain.) Overused and abused in the days when it was known as shock treatment, ECT may now, in a kinder, gentler incarnation, be underutilized because of its lingering stigma. (ECT has not been subject to clinical studies, and there is no conclusive evidence that ECT has a long-term effect on suicide rate and suicidal behavior.)

324    "psychodynamic formulation": Buie and Maltsberger, *Practical Formulation of Suicide Risk.* See also J. T. Maltsberger, "The Psychodynamic Understanding of Suicide," in Jacobs, *Harvard Medical School Guide,* 72–82.

326    no better than radiologists: A. L. Berman, "Notes on Turning 18 (and 75): A Critical Look at Our Adolescence" (paper presented at the Eighteenth Annual Meeting of the American Association of Suicidology, Toronto, Canada, April 18–21, 1985).

326    A 1983 survey: Study by A. L. Berman, ibid.

326    "relatively superficial in nature": Ellis et al., "Patient Suicide."

326    "Residents are trained": See Light, *Becoming Psychiatrists*; Light, "Psychiatrists and Suicide"; Light, "Professional Problems"; and Light, "Treating Suicide."

327    "During the course": Stone, "Suicide Precipitated by Psychotherapy."

327    a series of papers: A. A. Stone and H. M. Shein, "Psychotherapy of the Hospitalized Suicidal Patient," *American Journal of Psychotherapy* 22 (1) (1968): 15–25; H. M. Shein and A. A. Stone, "Psychotherapy Designed to Detect and Treat Suicidal Potential," *American Journal of Psychiatry* 125 (9) (1969): 141–45; and Shein and Stone, "Monitoring and Treatment." The story of Shein's suicide is told in Beam, *Gracefully Insane,* 222–32. Sociologist Rose Coser's nuanced examination of the rash of suicides about which Shein and Stone wrote can be found in Coser, *Training in Ambiguity.*

327    "Some patients almost ready": J. T. Maltsberger, and D. H. Buie Jr., "Common Errors in the Management of Suicidal Patients" (unpublished paper, 1980), 14.

328    Impressed with the jocular: Stone, "Suicide Precipitated by Psychotherapy," 5.

328    In one of the few papers: Maltsberger and Buie, "Countertransference Hate."

328    William Wheat isolated: Hendin, *Suicide in America,* 169. In 2001, the authors of a study in which data were collected from twenty-six therapists who had had a patient complete suicide came to a similar conclusion. "The 26 suicide cases we studied suggest that therapists working with suicidal patients frequently fail to recognize the severity of the emotional crises they experience," they wrote. "Our data indicate that only a small percentage of persons who are intent on killing themselves while in treatment give the therapist little or no indication of their crisis." Hendin et al., "Recognizing and Responding."

329    more than two hundred therapists: Litman, "When Patients Commit Suicide."

330    describe a man: N. L. Farberow et al., "Suicide Among Schizophrenic Mental Hospital Patients," in Farberow and Shneidman, *Cry for Help,* 90.

331    ascendancy of HMOs: In 1999, 72 percent of Americans with health insurance were covered by managed care, which promotes treatment of mental health in primary care, limits access to mental health specialists, and has severely reduced coverage of inpatient and outpatient care (between 1988 and 1998, managed care plans cut their spending on psychiatric treatment by 55 percent). Although the influence of managed care on suicide itself is largely unexamined, a 1999 study of 1,204 outpatients with depression in seven different HMOs, which found that only 48–60 percent received some sort of men-

tal health care, concluded that patients with suicidal ideation were at particular risk for receiving inappropriate treatment. (K. B. Wells et al., "Quality of Care for Primary Care Patients with Depression in Managed Care," *Archives of Family Medicine* 8 [6] [1999]: 529–36.) People who complete suicide have substantially more difficulty *getting* health care at all. A study of 22,957 deceased people of all ages found that, compared with people who died of illnesses or injuries, those who complete suicide are three times more likely to have difficulty accessing health care (and twice as likely to refuse needed care)—because of trouble paying bills, difficulty being admitted to a treatment facility, problems finding a doctor, and so on. (C. L. Miller and B. Druss, "Datapoints: Suicide and Access to Care," *Psychiatric Services* 52 [12] [2001]: 1566.)

331 perhaps least prepared: There is evidence that physician training might impact the suicide rate. In the 1980s, on the Swedish island of Gotland, where most treatment is provided by GPs, suicide prevention experts trained island physicians about recognition and treatment of depressed and suicidal people. Despite physician fears that they'd trigger suicides if they asked their patients about suicide, the island's suicide rate was lower by 60 percent (almost entirely due to a decrease in suicide by females; the male rate was essentially unchanged), a decrease exceeding that of Sweden as a whole over that same time. Although the rate eventually rose back to pretraining levels, coinciding with the departure of about half the island's physicians, the results were nevertheless promising. (W. Rutz et al., "Long-Term Effects of an Educational Program for General Practitioners Given by the Swedish Committee for the Prevention and Treatment of Depression," *Acta Psychiatrica Scandinavica* 85 [1992]: 83–88; Z. Rihmer et al., "Depression and Suicide on Gotland: An Intensive Study of All Suicides Before and After a Depression-Training Programme for General Practitioners," *Journal of Affective Disorders* 35 (1995): 147–52.)

331 "leaves them in the role": From a speech to the APA's annual Institute on Psychiatric Services, October, 1997, as reported in *Psychiatric News,* www.psych.org/pnews/97–12–05/primary.

331 widespread lack of knowledge: J. W. J. Williams et al., "Primary Care Physicians' Approach to Depressive Disorders: Effects of Physician Speciality and Practice Structure," *Archives of Family Medicine* 8 (1) (1999): 58–67.

331 more than half of patients with depression: E. S. Higgins, "A Review of Unrecognized Mental Illness in Primary Care: Prevalence, Natural History, and Efforts to Change the Course," *Archives of Family Medicine* 3 (10) (1994): 908–17.

331 72 percent had prescribed SSRIs: Voelker, "SSRI Use Common," 1882.

331 Philadelphia medical schools: Light, *Becoming Psychiatrists,* 30.

332 91 percent of physicians: Giffin and Felsenthal, *Cry for Help,* 28.

332 believe the old canard: K. Michel, "Suicide Prevention and Primary Care," in K. Hawton and K. van Heeringen, eds., *International Handbook of Suicide and Attempted Suicide* (Chichester, UK: John Wiley and Sons, 2000), 661–74.

332 primary care physicians: Williams et al., "Primary Care Physicians' Approach."

333 "hundreds of ways": Reynolds and Farberow, *Suicide.*

333 a study of hospitalized patients: Jamison, *Night Falls Fast,* 152.

333 suicides at Metropolitan State Hospital: A. R. Beisser and J. E. Blanchette, "A Study of Suicides in a Mental Hospital," *Diseases of the Nervous System* 22 (1961): 365–69.

333 a study attributing a decline: L. F. Woolley and A. H. Eichert, "Notes on the Problem of Suicide and Escape," *American Journal of Psychiatry* 98 (1941): 110–18.

333 "rather hesitantly": Styron's account of his hospitalization can be found in *Darkness Visible,* 67–75.

334 "begin planning for discharge": American Psychiatric Association, "Psychiatric Hospitalization," www.psych.org/public_info/hospital.

334   "extremely difficult": Okin, "Future of State Hospitals," 579.

335   "Often caught in the dilemma": Jamison, *Night Falls Fast,* 153.

336   A study by San Francisco psychiatrist: Motto and Bostrom, "Randomized Controlled Trial."

337   "one of the ways that the Lord": The story of the lawsuit is told in M. A. Weitz, *Clergy Malpractice in America: Nally v. Grace Community Church of the Valley* (Lawrence: University Press of Kansas, 2001).

338   "Suicide can best be understood": Shneidman, *Definition of Suicide,* 226.

338   appeared on the television news show: Giffin and Felsenthal, *Cry for Help,* 162–63.


## Chapter IV Social Studies

340   One August day: For historical material on the Golden Gate Bridge, see A. Brown, *Golden Gate: Biography of a Bridge* (Garden City, N.Y.: Doubleday, 1965).

341   "almost any place in Japan": O. D. Russell, "Suicide in Japan," *American Mercury,* July 1930, 342.

341   On January 7, 1933: The description of the suicides at Mihara-Yama is drawn from newspaper and magazine accounts of the time, and from Ellis and Allen, *Traitor Within,* 94–99.

342   A study of 116 people: Y. Takahashi, "Aokigahara-Jukai: Suicide and Amnesia in Mt. Fuji's Black Forest" (paper presented at a joint meeting of the American Association of Suicidology and the International Association for Suicide Prevention, San Francisco, May 25–30, 1987). In today's industrialized Japan, several Tokyo skyscrapers have taken their places as suicide landmarks. The Takashimadaira public housing complex, sixty-four apartment buildings on the edge of Tokyo, opened in April 1972. Within eight years, more than seventy people leaped from its rooftops—some journeying from as many as 120 miles away—earning it the nickname Mecca for Suicide.

342   "At one time there seemed": W. Sweetser, *Mental Hygiene: or, an Examination of the Intellect and Passions* (New York: George P. Putnam, 1850), 292.

344   the names of 515 people: Seiden, "Where Are They Now?"

344   David Rosen interviewed: D. H. Rosen, "Suicide Survivors: Psychotherapeutic Implications of Egocide," *Suicide and Life-Threatening Behavior* 6 (4) (1976): 209–15.

344   second study by Seiden: Seiden and Spence, "Tale of Two Bridges."

345   moot political issue: In 1977, the bridge's fortieth anniversary year, pro-barrier activists held a Memorial Day rally on the bridge to commemorate the more than six hundred bridge suicides. Ironically, one of the speakers was the Reverend Jim Jones, who arrived with three busloads of his People's Temple followers. "It is entirely fitting that on Memorial Day we are here on account of the hundreds of people who are not casualties of war, but casualties of society," he said. "For, in the final analysis, we have to bear collective responsibility for those individuals who could not find a place to go with their burdens, who came to that place of total helplessness, total despondency, where they took their own lives here on this beautiful bridge, this Golden Gate Bridge, a symbol of human ingenuity, technological genius but social failure." Eighteen months later he would lead 912 of his followers into mass suicide in the jungles of Guyana. The text of Jones's speech is reprinted in R. H. Seiden, "Reverend Jones on Suicide," *Suicide and Life-Threatening Behavior* 9 (2) (1979): 116–19.

345   "grandeur": A. Blum, "Suicide Watch," *New York Times,* March 20, 2005.

347   "Much could be gained": Friedman, *On Suicide,* 52–53. The opposite prevention strategy was proposed in the seventeenth century by Richard Capel. He suggested that instead of avoiding bridges that might tempt one to jump, one should march firmly

across with a constant heart, and the urge would be conquered. "A false meanes is for a man to yeeld to much to feares, so as to thinke to avoid tentation, by declining, and not by resisting, as some dare not carry a knife about them, or when their knife is out, cast it from them, this is to yeeld too much to Satan: neither doth it helpe the matter, but rather keepe the tentation in. . . . The way to drive away our tentation is to keepe our knives about us . . . to fight it out against Satan, by setting the Word and Christ against him." Sprott, *English Debate,* 46.

347   a landmark 1983 study: J. H. Boyd, "The Increasing Rate of Suicide by Firearms," *New England Journal of Medicine* 308 (15) (1983): 872–74.

347   the strictness of state gun-control laws: D. Lester and M. E. Murrell, "The Influence of Gun Control Laws on Suicidal Behavior," *American Journal of Psychiatry* 137 (1) (1980): 121–22.

348   "Where there are more guns": A. Marcus, "Study: Handgun Ownership Raises Risk of Suicide," Health on the Net News, www.hon.ch/News. See Hemenway and Miller, "Association of Rates." See also Miller and Hemenway, "Relationship Between Firearms and Suicide."

348   eighty-two consecutive suicides: Seiden, "Suicide Prevention," 271.

348   King County, Washington, firearms study: A. L. Kellerman and D. T. Reay, "Protection or Peril? An Analysis of Firearm-Related Deaths in the Home," *New England Journal of Medicine* 314 (24) (1986): 1557–60.

348   "If some persons": Seiden, "Suicide Prevention," 271.

348   "get the guns out of the house": Apparently, few people heed such advice. In a study of depressed adolescents who entered psychotherapy, only 27 percent of parents who, at intake, reported having guns in their home removed them after being urged to do so by the therapist. (D. A. Brent et al., "Compliance with Recommendations to Remove Firearms in Families Participating in a Clinical Trial for Adolescent Depression," *Journal of the American Academy of Child and Adolescent Psychiatry* 39 [10] [2000]: 1220–26.)

348   study of 238,000 people: Wintemute et al., "Mortality Among Recent Purchasers."

349   "It is unlikely": R. W. Hudgens, "Preventing Suicide," *New England Journal of Medicine* 308 (15) (1983): 897–98.

349   "The NRA is not for gearing": A. Parachini, "Gun Deaths: Suicides Versus Murders," *Los Angeles Times,* April 19, 1983, pt. V, p. 5.

349   twenty-year-old manager: This and subsequent examples are taken from newspaper and magazine accounts.

350   As a term project: L. Moss, "Help Wanted: A Limited Study of Responses to One Person's Cry for Help," *Life-Threatening Behavior* 1 (1) (1971): 55–66.


## Chapter V Life or Liberty

352   "Suicide is a fundamental": T. Szasz, *The Second Sin* (Garden City, N.Y.: Anchor/Doubleday, 1973), 67.

352   "If the psychiatrist is to prevent": T. Szasz, in a speech given at the conference "Suicide: What Is the Clinician's Responsibility?" Boston, February 1, 1985.

352   "In fact, I firmly believe": T. Szasz, in a debate with Edwin Shneidman in 1972 at the University of California, Berkeley. Taped by Audio-Digest Foundation, Suite 700, 1930 Wilshire Blvd., Los Angeles, CA 90057.

353   a lawsuit filed by the widow: The lawsuit against Szasz is described in Jamison, *Night Falls Fast,* 254.

353   Abraham Lincoln: Psychiatrist Ronald Fieve has written that if Lincoln had been his

patient today, he would insist on immediate "hospitalization, observation for suicidal intent, anti-depression drugs, and later, lithium as the treatment of choice." Lincoln survived his depression without such help; gun control seems to have been the form of suicide prevention he could most have benefited from.

353    "The 'right' to suicide": Murphy, "Suicide and the Right to Die."

353    survived six-story jumps: Hendin, *Suicide in America,* 210.

353    "The right to kill oneself": Ibid., 225.

353    "Suicide is not a 'right'": Shneidman, "Aphorisms of Suicide," 322.

354    "Although such cases": S. E. Wallace, "The Survivor's Rights," in Wallace and Eser, *Suicide and Euthanasia,* 67.

354    "Suicidal persons are succumbing": M. Boldt, "The Right to Suicide," *Suicide Information and Education Centre Current Awareness Bulletin* 1 (2) (1985): 1.

354    "the act [of suicide] clearly represents an illness": Szasz, *Theology of Medicine,* 68.

354    "If a sociologist predicted": A. Brandt, *Reality Police: The Experience of Insanity in America* (New York: William Morrow, 1975), 146.

355    "If a middle-aged lady": Debate between Szasz and Shneidman in 1972, University of California, Berkeley.

355    "If everyone who evinces": Friedman, *On Suicide,* 84–85. The difficulty of drawing the line between sickness and health was described by Melville: "Who in the rainbow can draw the line where the violet tint ends and the orange tint begins? Distinctly we see the difference of the colors, but where exactly does the one first blendingly enter into the other? So with sanity and insanity. In pronounced cases there is no question about them. But in some supposed cases, in various degrees supposedly less pronounced, to draw the exact line of demarcation few will undertake, though for a fee becoming considerate some professional experts will. There is nothing namable but that some men will, or undertake to, do it for pay." (H. Melville, *Billy Budd, Sailor and Other Stories* [New York: Bantam, 1981], 52–53.)

355    "The argument connecting": Green and Irish, *Death Education,* 120.

356    A Harvard University study: Hendin, *Suicide in America,* 189–90.

356    "Suicide is pre-judged": Quotes in this paragraph can be found in Hillman, *Suicide and the Soul,* 36, 37, 87, 93, 92.

356    review of Hillman's book: R. E. Litman, "Concern for Suicide: Before and After," in Shneidman, Farberow, and Litman, *Psychology of Suicide,* 637–40.

356    "In regarding the desire": Szasz, *Theology of Medicine,* 81.

357    "Some of the things": Green and Irish, *Death Education,* 120.

357    "If the person says": Ibid., 121.

## PART 5 The Right to Die

In updating this part, I relied heavily on two indispensable essay collections, *The Case Against Assisted Suicide,* edited by Kathleen Foley and Herbert Hendin, and *Physician-Assisted Dying,* edited by Timothy E. Quill and Margaret P. Battin, as well as on Marilyn Webb's exploration of end-of-life issues, *The Good Death.*

## Chapter I A Fate Worse Than Death

364    "Among the Karens": Westermarck, *Origin and Development of the Moral Ideas,* 231.

365    "Thus was he blessed": Suetonius, *The Lives of the Twelve Caesars,* ed. J. Gavorse (New York: Modern Library, 1931), 115.

365 "if any man labour": Fedden, *Suicide,* 72.

365 "Just as a landlord": Lecky, *History of European Morals,* 1: 232–33.

365 "I will not relinquish": Ibid., 232.

365 "do away with the sufferings": Humphry and Wickett, *Right to Die,* 4.

366 "the most excusable cause": Moore, *Full Inquiry,* 270.

366 "I esteem it the office": F. Bacon, *Selected Writings,* ed. H. G. Dick (New York: Modern Library, 1955), 277. For pointing the way to this quote and to numerous other tidbits of helpful information, and for helping me clarify my thinking on right-to-die issues, I am indebted to Anne Fadiman and to her essay "The Liberation of Lolly and Gronky."

366 "We have very great pity": Mannes, *Last Rights,* 64.

366 "should not torment his patient": Hendin, *Death as a Fact of Life,* 82–83.

366 "in cases of incurable": Russell, *Freedom to Die,* 57–58.

366 "practices of savages": Ibid., 62.

366 "Vast numbers of human beings": R. G. Twycross, "Voluntary Euthanasia," in Wallace and Eser, *Suicide and Euthanasia,* 88.

367 "Some are proposing": Y. Kamisar, "Euthanasia Legislation: Some Non-Religious Objections," in Downing, *Euthanasia,* 115.

367 only the beginning: "Of the five identifiable steps by which the Nazis carried out the principle of 'life unworthy of life,' coercive sterilization was the first," writes Lifton. "There followed the killing of 'impaired' children in hospitals; and then the killing of 'impaired' adults, mostly collected from mental hospitals, in centers especially equipped with carbon monoxide gas. This project was extended (in the same killing centers) to 'impaired' inmates of concentration and extermination camps and, finally, to mass killings, mostly of Jews, in the extermination camps themselves." (R. J. Lifton, *The Nazi Doctors: Medical Killing and the Psychology of Genocide* [New York: Basic Books, 1986].) Lifton's book offers a comprehensive description of the Nazi "euthanasia" program.

368 "For every illness": *New York Times,* January 18, 1985, B1.

368 "The classical deathbed scene" and "Where can we draw the line": J. Fletcher, "The Patient's Right to Die," in Downing, *Euthanasia,* 65–66.

368 "I do not remember": M. Angell, "The Quality of Mercy," in Quill and Battin, *Physician-Assisted Dying,* 16

368 dedication to life: It has been suggested that what one skeptical doctor calls "their crusade to slay the dragon of death" may be a function of doctors' neuroses as much as of their concern for patients; on psychological tests, doctors score high on death anxiety.

368 "The dignity starts with": Clark, *Whose Life Is It Anyway?,* 143.

369 "We are discovering": Hendin, *Death as a Fact of Life,* 79.

369 terminally ill seventy-eight-year-old: This story is told in Barnard, *Good Life,* 88.

369 growing acceptance of passive euthanasia: In active and passive euthanasia, the patient has requested to die; in "mercy killing," the "killer" takes matters into his or her own hands because the patient is no longer able to express his or her wishes, as in the case of a coma victim or someone suffering from Alzheimer's disease.

369 "Thou shalt not kill": H. Gardner, ed., *The New Oxford Book of English Verse* (New York and Oxford: Oxford University Press, 1972), 682.

370 "Basic to our considerations" and "It is morally justifiable": Wanzer et al., "Physician's Responsibility," 955, 958.

370 According to a study reported: *USA Today,* January 4, 1985, 1.

370 "When inevitable death is imminent": "The Vatican's Declaration on Euthanasia, 1980," in Larue, *Euthanasia and Religion,* 42.

371 Doctors have been sued: In 1981, at the request of the patient's family, two California doctors disconnected the respirator of a comatose patient named Clarence Herbert. (In

the past he had told his wife he did not want to become "another Karen Ann Quinlan.") When he did not die, they disconnected his feeding tube as well. When Herbert died six days later, the Los Angeles district attorney charged the doctors with murder. Although the case was eventually dismissed, it was the first time doctors had ever been charged for removing life-support equipment, and it sent shock waves through the medical community. But doctors can also be sued for *not* following a request to cease life-sustaining measures. William Bartling was a seventy-year-old retired dental-supply salesman suffering from emphysema, arteriosclerosis, chronic respiratory failure, an abdominal aneurysm, and a malignant lung tumor. In 1984, kept alive by a respirator, feeding and drainage tubes, and a device that vacuumed his throat every two hours, he requested to be disconnected from life-support systems and allowed to die. His doctors refused—and, for a time, tied his hands down so he could not pull out the tubes himself. After the state superior court ruled in favor of the doctors, a California appellate court overturned the decision, ruling that the hospital had violated Bartling's right to "self-determination as to his own medical treatment." Bartling, however, died twenty-three hours before the appellate court could hear his plea and two months before the courts affirmed his right to die.

371 estimates that 70 percent: Webb, *Good Death,* 189. Ironically, in the last decade, physicians working with dying patients have noticed that in an increasing number of cases, it is the family members and not the doctors who are insisting on keeping suffering loved ones alive at any cost.

372 66 percent of physicians: Humphry and Clement, *Freedom to Die,* 188.

372 nine thousand terminally ill patients: W. A. Knaus et al., "A Controlled Trial to Improve Care for Seriously Ill Hospitalized Patients," *Journal of the American Medical Association* 274 (1995): 1591–98.

372 the case of Terri Schiavo: My account is drawn largely from articles in the *New York Times* published during March and April 2005, as well as from D. Eisenberg, "Lessons of the Schiavo Battle," *Time,* April 4, 2005, 23–30.

374 "I have learned from my life": Barnard, *Good Life,* 15. Barnard would later stir controversy in the right-to-die movement by insisting that the decision of when to perform euthanasia was best made by the doctor—not by the the patient or the patient's family.

375 "Can doctors who remove": P. Singer, *Rethinking Life and Death* (New York: St. Martin's Press, 1994), 221.

375 "the morphine drip is undeniably euthanasia": T. A. Preston, "Killing Pain, Ending Life," *New York Times,* November 1, 1994, A27.

375 "What, morally, is the difference": Fletcher, "Patient's Right to Die," 68.

375 described her mother's death: Rollin, *Last Wish.*

375 In one recent case: The story of Huntington Williams and John Welles is from W. Yardley, "For Role in Suicide, a Friend to the End is Now Facing Jail," *New York Times,* March 4, 2005, A1, and W. Yardley, "Probation for Connecticut Man, 74, Who Aided Suicide," *New York Times,* April 8, 2005, A24.

376 have come to public attention: In a particularly poignant example, in 1985, John Kraai, a seventy-six-year-old general practitioner in a small town near Rochester, New York, injected a lethal dose of insulin into his patient and friend of more than forty years, an eighty-one-year-old nursing-home resident suffering from Alzheimer's disease and gangrene of the feet. Shortly after he was charged with second-degree murder, Kraai killed himself by lethal injection.

376 Michigan pathologist: My account of Dr. Kevorkian's activities is taken largely from Michael Betzold's *Appointment with Doctor Death* and Jack Kevorkian's *Prescription: Medicide,* as well as from numerous newspaper accounts, and from my interviews with

Geoffrey Fieger and Janet Good. See also J. Lessenberry, "Death Becomes Him," *Vanity Fair*, July 1994. Information about Kevorkian in prison is from T. Ward, "Dr. K: I Expect to Die in Prison," *Daily Oakland Press*, April 11, 2004.

380   the man she called "the doctor": Kevorkian called Janet Good his "associate" and to show his appreciation gave her a signed print of one of his paintings, *The Gourmet (War)*. In it, a Roman centurion stands behind a decapitated man who, his neck dripping with blood, holds a plate on which his severed head reposes, an apple in its mouth. Good was proud of the gift but kept it behind her computer desk, and showed it only to a few friends. "I don't think any sane person would hang that on the wall," she told me.

383   Gallup poll in 1947: E. D. Stutsman, "Political Strategy and Legal Change," in Quill and Battin, *Physician-Assisted Dying*, 247.

383   1995 study: Doukas et al., "Attitudes and Behaviors on Physician-Assisted Death: A Study of Michigan Oncologists," *Journal of Clinical Oncologists* 13 (5) (1995): 1055–61.

383   1996 study of physicians: A. L. Back et al., "Physician-Assisted Suicide and Euthanasia in Washington State: Patient Requests and Physician Responses," *Journal of the American Medical Association* 275 (1996): 919–25.

384   1997 *New England Journal of Medicine* report: L. R. Slome et al., "Physician-Assisted Suicide and Patients with Human Immunodeficiency Virus Disease," *New England Journal of Medicine* 336 (6) (1997): 417–21.

384   the same journal reported: D. E. Meier et al., "A National Survey of Physician-Assisted Suicide and Euthanasia in the United States," *New England Journal of Medicine* 338 (17) (1998): 1193–1201.

384   1996 survey of 852: D. A. Asch, "The Role of Critical Care Nurses in Euthanasia and Assisted Suicide," *New England Journal of Medicine* 334 (1996): 1374–79.

384   "I feared the effects": T. Quill, "Death and Dignity: A Case of Individualized Decision Making," *New England Journal of Medicine* 324 (10) (1991): 691–94. For a discussion of "nonabandonment," see T. E. Quill and C. K. Cassel, "Nonabandonment," in Quill and Battin, *Physician-Assisted Dying*, 24–38.

384   seemed quite civilized: Comparing Quill and Kevorkian, bioethicist Arthur Caplan wrote, "I am convinced that what Kevorkian did in helping Janet Adkins die is completely immoral. Yet I do not believe that Quill acted unethically. . . .

"Kevorkian did not know Adkins prior to attaching her to his homemade suicide device; Quill had known Diane as a patient and as a friend for many years before her death. Kevorkian scoured the country looking for someone upon whom he could use his machine. Quill did all that he could to get his patient to choose life, not death.

"Kevorkian helped to her death a woman who was questionably competent, was in no pain and who was not terminally ill; Quill wrote a prescription for sleeping pills for a terminally ill, competent woman who was in a great deal of pain. Kevorkian personally hitched Janet Adkins to a machine that he himself had built, promoted and fervently hoped someone would use; Quill fervently hoped he could help manage Diane's suffering so that she never would choose to end her life." (Betzold, *Appointment with Doctor Death*, 146.)

385   Ballot initiatives: After the bills including provisions for both physician-assisted suicide and voluntary euthanasia had been defeated in California and Washington, Oregon dropped voluntary euthanasia from its proposed bill to maximize the chances of its passage.

386   "For many people": D. Colburn, "Fewer Turn to Assisted Suicide," *Oregonian*, March 11, 2005. The *Oregonian* has provided the most detailed coverage of the Death with Dignity Act.

386 "I don't know if I'd ever take it": D. Colburn, "Assisted Suicide Advocate Dies at 79," *Oregonian,* October 28, 2003.

386 deaths have been gentle: The stories of Oregonians who have used the Death with Dignity Act are taken mostly from Lee, *Compassion in Dying.* An exception is the story of the fifty-four-year-old former health care worker, which was taken from J. Estrin, "In Oregon, Choosing Death Over Suffering," *New York Times,* June 1, 2004, F4. The story of Peggy Sutherland is taken both from Lee, *Compassion in Dying,* and from a lovely piece by Todd Schwartz, "A Death of Her Choosing," *Oberlin Alumni Magazine,* Summer 2003, www.oberlin.edu/alummag/summer2003.

388 not always foolproof: In some 18 percent of physician-assisted suicides in the Netherlands, patients lived more than three hours after taking the lethal dose; doctors usually intervened with a lethal injection—a practice that would, of course, be illegal in Oregon.

389 "To confine legalized": Humphry and Clement, *Freedom to Die,* 336.

389 one country: In 2002, Belgium became the second country to legalize physician-assisted suicide and voluntary euthanasia. In 1996–97, voluntary euthanasia was legal for nine months in Australia's Northern Territory, a rural area where little palliative care is available; four people were given lethal doses of medications before the territorial law was overturned by Australia's national parliament. In Switzerland, assisted suicide (but not euthanasia) has long been permitted, by doctors and laypeople alike, if done for "altruistic purposes." There is evidence that more than a few people have traveled to Switzerland for the express purpose of receiving assisted suicide.

## Chapter II "Your Good End in Life Is Our Concern!"

392 "There is only one prospect worse": A. Koestler, in *Exit: A Guide to Self-Deliverance,* preface, 3.

395 the formation of the Hemlock Society: Hemlock is one of forty-six right-to-die societies in twenty-three countries from Australia to Israel to Zimbabwe. Although most societies share a common goal—to guarantee people the right to choice in their own death—the groups disagree on the lengths to which they will go. The groups range from those that favor only passive euthanasia to those that wish to legalize assisted suicide and voluntary euthanasia.

399 by writing *Final Exit*: Quotes from this and the following two paragraphs are from Humphry, *Final Exit.*

400 deaths by plastic bag: P. M. Marzuk et al., "Increase in Suicide by Asphyxiation in New York City After the Publication of *Final Exit,*" *New England Journal of Medicine* 329 (20) (1993): 1508–10; and P. M. Marzuk et al., "Increase in Fatal Suicidal Poisonings and Suffocations in the Year *Final Exit* Was Published: A National Study," *American Journal of Psychiatry* 151 (1994): 1813–14.

400 "This misuse I regret": D. Humphry, *Final Exit,* 3rd ed. (New York: Dell, 2002), xv.

401 no one had ever written: A few books and pamphlets have tackled the subject in a darkly comic mode, most notably *21 Delightful Ways of Committing Suicide,* written and illustrated by Jean Bruller and published in the United States in 1930.

401 "It is the sovereign right": *Guide to Self-Deliverance,* 31.

402 "I feel no remorse": *Boston Globe,* September 20, 1982.

404 a fatal overdose: The story of Wickett's death is told in *Deadly Compassion* by Rita Marker, an antieuthanasia activist who had debated Humphry over the years. Surprisingly, after Humphry left her, a distressed Wickett turned to Marker, and they became friends. According to Marker, Wickett came to believe that legalizing physician-assisted

suicide or voluntary euthanasia would be a mistake, because it might coerce vulnerable, elderly people to seek a premature death. Wickett believed her mother had not, in fact, wanted to die, but had felt subtle pressure from her father to go along with him. Marker, *Deadly Compassion,* 213.

406   "Compassion is not an advocacy": Michaele Houston in Coombs Lee, *Compassion in Dying,* 50. For my description of Compassion in Dying's work I have relied heavily on this book, and on B. C. Lee, "A Model That Integrates Assisted Dying with Excellent End-of-Life Care," in Quill and Battin, *Physician-Assisted Dying,* 190–201.

407   launched Caring Friends: The description of the Caring Friends program comes from several Web sites, including www.endoflifechoices.org; from R. Marker, "Patience and Plastic Bags," *Human Life Review,* Spring 2003; and from a speech by Dr. Richard MacDonald, "The Caring Friends Program—Five Years of Peaceful Dying," delivered at a picnic in Milwaukee, as reported in an End-of-Life Choices chapter newsletter, vol. 14, no. 3, http://communities.madison.com/endoflifechoiceswis.

408   "This isn't rocket science:" Marker, "Patience and Plastic Bags." The description of the Exit Bag is also taken from this article.

408   "the helium makes the voice": "Helium," *Hemlock Timelines* 83 (Spring 2000): 12.

408   "I'm sort of a midwife": Marker, "Patience and Plastic Bags."

410   "If you can't get your sulfuric acid": *Age,* May 31, 2003, www.theage.com.au/ articles/2003/05/31.

412   "Then—the highlight of the weekend": "Network Trains 15 Exit Guides in St. Louis!" Final Exit Network Newsletter, vol. 1., no. 1, www.finalexitnetwork.org/newsletter.

412   "We have 33 cases": "We Are 'Transparent,'" Final Exit Network Newsletter, vol. 1, no. 2, www.finalexitnetwork.org/newsletter.


## Chapter III "The Limits Are Obscure . . . and Every Errour Deadly"

415   "whether it was logical": Mannes, *Last Rights,* 62–63.

415   "It seems unimaginable": Fletcher, *Morals and Medicine,* 193.

415   "Their argument turns": Battin, *Ethical Issues in Suicide,* 179.

415   interferes with God's will: In 1847, when ether was first used in the delivery room, many people protested that labor pains were divinely ordained and to use anesthetics went against God's will.

415   "If it is for God alone": J. Rachels, *The End of Life: Euthanasia and Morality* (Oxford: Oxford University Press, 1986), 163.

415   "Human life consists": Mannes, *Last Rights,* 141.

416   "When life is more terrible": Choron, *Suicide,* 78.

416   "The final stage": Maguire, *Death by Choice,* 151.

416   "Even if this is true": Seneca, "Letter to Lucilius, No. 70," in *The Stoic Philosophy of Seneca,* trans. M. Hadas (Gloucester, Mass.: Peter Smith, 1965), 203.

416   forty-four-year-old Maryland woman: *People,* October 13, 1986, 43–44.

417   "People say they want": T. Schwartz, "A Death of Her Choosing," *Oberlin Alumni Magazine,* Summer 2003, www.oberlin.edu/alumnimag/summer2003.

417   In 1919, German psychiatrist: A year later, Hoche coauthored *The Permission to Destroy Life Unworthy of Life.*

417   Richard Brandt compared: R. Brandt, "The Rationality of Suicide," in Battin and Mayo, *Suicide,* 117–32.

418   described six cases: Jackson and Youngner, "Patient Autonomy."

418   "How free or informed": L. R. Kass, "'I Will Give No Deadly Drug': Why Doctors Must Not Kill," in Foley and Hendin, *Case Against Assisted Suicide,* 24.

418    uncompleted suicide pacts: M. Rosenbaum, "Crime and Punishment: The Suicide Pact," *Archives of General Psychiatry* 40 (1983): 979–82. See also Fishbain et al., "A Controlled Study."

418    emotionally coerced: If Koestler is to be blamed, however, the blame must be not for his wife's death but for her life. "A good man would have weaned her," wrote Barbara Grizzuti Harrison. ". . . I think it's fair to say he killed her." But to call Koestler a murderer seems as patronizing and demeaning to Cynthia as her husband may have been, denying her any volition of her own. "For a man in grave and failing health, self-deliverance was the final right," wrote Hemlock Society cofounder Ann Wickett. "For Cynthia, it was the final act of devotion. That too was her right. One regrets, however, less the nature of her death, than the nature of her life. She deserved more."

419    "She was his appendix": A. Wickett, "Why Cynthia Koestler Joined Arthur," *Hemlock Quarterly,* January 1985, 4–5.

419    "It is hardly an exaggeration": Ibid.

419    "Some writers opposed": M. P. Battin, "Suicide: A Fundamental Human Right?" in Battin and Mayo, *Suicide,* 279.

419    "Activists draw": A. Solomon, *Noonday Demon,* 268.

419    suicide prevention experts are sympathetic: Some may describe it as something other than suicide. "We need not argue the issue of whether it is rational for an individual with a painful terminal illness to refuse extraordinary life-saving measures or to arrange more actively to end his life," writes Herbert Hendin (*Suicide in America,* 214–15). ". . . The person facing imminent death who is in intractable pain and arranges to end his life may be a suicide in the dictionary definition of the term, but not in the psychological sense." Many others in the field object to the right-to-die movement, while reserving the right to an assisted death for themselves. "I believe in suicide prevention, but I have Alzheimer's in my family, and I'm fearful of death without dignity," a leader in suicide prevention told me. "If you're incompetent, they keep you from killing yourself. Well, the point at which I want out is when I lose competence. I have made a suicide pact with two of my sisters." Edwin Shneidman participated in the initial Hemlock think tank and delivered the keynote address at Hemlock's 1985 national conference. "I like Derek Humphry and I approve of what he does," he told the audience. "But I'm not a card-carrying Hemlock member, and I maintain some substantial differences with the goals of the organization." A friend of Shneidman's interprets: "Ed doesn't believe in rational suicide—except for himself."

420    "From an intellectual standpoint": Seiden, "Self-Deliverance or Self-Destruction?"

420    "Physician-assisted suicide is mistakenly understood": D. Callahan, "Reason, Self-determination, and Physician-Assisted Suicide," in Foley and Hendin, *Case Against Assisted Suicide,* 60.

420    "the limits are obscure": Donne, *Biathanatos,* 216.

421    oft-quoted 1949 essay: L. Alexander, "Medical Science Under Dictatorship," *New England Journal of Medicine* 241 (2) (1949): 39–47.

421    "I think there is no way": Quoted on "Rational Suicide?" produced by Barry Lando for *60 Minutes,* CBS-TV, October 12, 1980.

422    "Once any group": Humphry and Wickett, *Right to Die,* 164.

422    "Miss Voluntary Euthanasia": Y. Kamisar, "Euthanasia Legislation: Some Non-Religious Objections," in Downing, *Euthanasia,* 115.

422    "I have seen the true wish": Wallace and Eser, *Suicide and Euthanasia,* 102.

422    "Where is the sense": Humphry and Wickett, *Right to Die,* 313.

422    government-sponsored study: The studies were summarized in P. J. van der Maas et al., "Euthanasia, Physician-Assisted Suicide, and Other Medical Practices Involving the End of Life in the Netherlands, 1990–1995," *New England Journal of Medicine* 335 (1996): 1699–1705.

422    a slippery crevasse: Criticism of the Dutch program can be found in Hendin, *Seduced by Death*; H. Hendin, "The Dutch Experience," in Foley and Hendin, *Case Against Assisted Suicide,* 97–121; Jochemsen and Keown, "Voluntary Euthanasia Under Control?"; J. Keown, "Some Reflections on Euthanasia in the Netherlands," in J. C. Willke et al., *Assisted Suicide and Euthanasia, Past and Present* (Cincinnati: Hayes Publishing Company, 1998). See also H. Hendin, "Suicide, Assisted Suicide, and Euthanasia," in Jacobs, *Harvard Medical School Guide,* 540–60.

424    "Virtually every guideline": H. Hendin, "Summary for Congressional Subcommittee on the Constitution. Suicide, Assisted Suicide and Euthanasia: Lessons From the Dutch Experience," http://www.house.gov/judiciary/2169.htm.

424    "The man, afraid of being left": Hendin, "Dutch Experience," 109.

426    "Given legal sanction": Ibid., 117.

426    "It may be more than ironic": Hendin, "Summary for Congressional Subcommittee."

427    "I am concerned": B. Steinbock, "The Case for Physician Assisted Suicide: Not (Yet) Proven," *Journal of Medical Ethics* 31 (2005): 235–41.

427    a woman in her mideighties: The case of the first patient is described in E. Hoover and G. H. Hill, "Two Die Using Oregon Suicide Law," *Oregonian,* March 26, 1998, A1. Criticism of the case can be found in, among others, K. Foley and H. Hendin, "The Oregon Experiment," in Foley and Hendin, *Case Against Assisted Suicide,* 144–74. Also in Steinbock, "Case for Physician Assisted Suicide." Compassion in Dying's senior medical adviser offers a spirited rebuttal in P. Goodwin, "The Distortion of Cases in Oregon," in Quill and Battin, *Physician-Assisted Dying,* 184–89.

428    "If I get rebuffed": W. Claiborne, "An Oregon Statute Is Blunting Death's Sting," *Washington Post,* April 29, 1998, A1, as quoted in Foley and Hendin, "Oregon Experiment," 148.

429    "Under these conditions": Ibid., 146.

429    "The fears that we had": M. Vitez, "Oregon Is the Laboratory in Assisted-Suicide Debate," *Philadelphia Inquirer,* March 13, 2005.

429    25 percent of cancer patients: Webb, *Good Death,* 114.

430    only 6 percent felt confident: L. Ganzini et al., "Attitudes of Oregon Psychiatrists toward Physician-Assisted Suicide," *American Journal of Psychiatry* 157 (2000): 595–600.

430    an eighty-five-year-old widow: E. H. Barnett, "Is Mom Capable of Choosing to Die?" *Oregonian,* October 16, 1999. See also Lee, *Compassion in Dying,* 72–83.

431    no Kevorkianesque abuses: Which is no guarantee that they will never happen. Surgeon and author Sherwin Nuland, while generally supportive of physician-assisted suicide in some form, would like to see the Oregon Death with Dignity requirements strengthened to include repeated requests made to a physician with whom the patient has had a long-standing relationship; mandatory consultation with a physician whose specialty is in the area of the patient's disease; evidence that all therapeutic options have been exhausted; mandatory consultation with a palliative-care expert—"not just the local anesthesiologist but a true palliative care expert"; mandatory evaluation by a psychiatrist experienced with end-of-life care; mandatory pastoral consultation of some sort; and mandatory notification of next of kin ("I'm not talking about veto power but about a frank discussion with people important in your life. When one takes one's own life, it has a profound and permanent influence on the lives of other people, and they should be involved"). Nuland's final recommendation? That a council of wise, civic-minded individuals should be convened to discuss the case and grant final consent. "I believe that by permitting physician-assisted suicide, a society is commenting on its values," he says. "And therefore, I believe it's the responsibility of society to validate these decisions."

431    "They have one way only": Herodotus, *The Histories* (London: Penguin, 1972), 128.

431    The Tschuktschi of northern Siberia: Some of this list is drawn from Humphry and Wickett, *Right to Die,* 2.

431    The perhaps apocryphal story: Maguire, *Death by Choice,* 86.

431    "Like leaves which fall": *Time,* April 9, 1984, 68.

432    "The time is not far off": Lamm, "Long Time Dying," 21.

432    "our technological sophistication": J. Hardwig, "Is There a Duty to Die?" *Hastings Center Report* 27 (2) (1997): 39–42.

433    "the postponement of an individual's death": *New York Times,* September 5, 1984.

433    "creatively and honorably accepting": Callahan quotes are from *Time,* November 2, 1987, 76.

433    "Any sophisticated doctor": *Los Angeles Times,* May 25, 1984, pt. 5, p. 27.

434    "The report entirely ignored": N. G. Hamilton, "Oregon's Culture of Silence," in Foley and Hendin, *Case Against Assisted Suicide,* 180.

434    "One must look at": Humphry and Clement, *Freedom to Die,* 313.

434    "Today, the needs of the individual": Portwood, *Common-Sense Suicide,* 46–47.

434    "Assisted suicide and euthanasia": New York State Task Force on Life and the Law, "When Death Is Sought: Assisted Suicide and Euthanasia in the Medical Context" (Albany, N.Y.: May, 1994), 43.

435    "When asked to describe" and "The primary issue": D. Coleman, "Not Dead Yet," in Foley and Hendin, *Case Against Assisted Suicide,* 220, 225. (Not Dead Yet was particularly incensed when Dr. Kevorkian's assistant Janet Good remarked, "People can endure pain. But once children have to wipe their butts, that's the end. When that dignity is gone, no one wants to live.") Historian Paul Longmore has observed, "If a nonhandicapped person expressed a desire to commit suicide, that person would immediately get crisis intervention therapy. Let a disabled person express such despair, and he or she is assumed to be 'rational.' " (Marker, *Deadly Compassion,* 301.)

435    "We argue" and "conclude in support": A. I. Batavia, "Disability and Physician-Assisted Dying," in Quill and Battin, *Physician-Assisted Dying,* 63, 70.

436    "creatures born defective": Humphry and Wickett, *Right to Die,* 14. The notion that the "incurably mentally ill" should be euthanized cropped up throughout the first several decades of the twentieth century, in part as an outgrowth of the eugenics movement, which held that many mentally and physically disabled people should be sterilized (see Whitaker, *Mad in America,* 65–66). Decrying the money spent to warehouse "gangsters and lunatics," Nobel Prize–winning physician Alexis Carrel, in 1935, suggested they be "humanely and economically disposed of in small euthanasic institutions supplied with proper gases." (Ibid., 66.) The discussion was silenced by the advent of World War II and the eventual knowledge of the horrors of the Third Reich.

436    "Sentimental prejudice": Humphry and Wickett, *Right to Die,* 14–15.

436    "If a chronically sick man": E. Slater, "Choosing the Time to Die," in Battin and Mayo, *Suicide,* 202.

436    "a slobbering wreck": Marker, *Deadly Compassion,* 97.

436    her sixteen-year-old cat: K. L. Lyle, *Newsweek,* March 2, 1992, as described in E. Newman, "Ethical Issues in Terminal Health Care, Part Three: Local Perspectives on the Right-to-Die Debate," www.cp.duluth.mn.us.

436    "there can be no possibility": M. R. Barrington, "Apologia for Suicide," in Downing, *Euthanasia,* 159.

436    "These type of statistics": Humphry, *Good Euthanasia Guide 2005,* 27.

437    "including the depressed": *National Review* Online, www.nationalreview.com/interrogatory.

437    "It is realistic": Seiden, "Self-Deliverance or Self-Destruction?" 10.

437    "At best, the living old": Butler, *Why Survive?,* xi.

437 "Many elders suffer": J. Levin and A. Arluke, "Our Elderly's Fate?" *New York Times,* September 29, 1983, 27.

437 the suicide rate of elderly Americans: For an excellent overview of elderly suicide, see Conwell, "Suicide in Later Life."

438 50 percent of elderly suicides: Barraclough, "Suicide in the Elderly."

438 "In general, where the 'geriatric case'": Wrobleski, *Afterwords,* January 1985, 2.

439 "Since the elderly depressed": *Los Angeles Times,* November 13, 1984.

439 elderly nursing home patients: *New York Times,* July 16, 1982.

440 "The discovery and cure": Humphry and Clement, *Freedom to Die,* 58.

440 1,177 physicians: Foley and Hendin, *Case Against Assisted Suicide,* 298.

440 40 to 80 percent: Humphry and Clement, *Freedom to Die,* 55.

440 9,000 terminally ill patients: W. A. Knaus et al., "A Controlled Trial to Improve Care for Seriously Ill Hospitalized Patients," *Journal of the American Medical Association* 274 (1995): 1591–98.

440 897 physicians: J. H. Von Roenn et al., "Physician Attitudes and Practice in Cancer Pain Management: A Survey from the Eastern Cooperative Oncology Group," *Annals of Internal Medicine* 119 (1993): 121–26.

440 90 patients: Webb, *Good Death,* 120–22.

441 survey of oncologists: E. J. Emanuel, "Report of the ASCO Membership Survey on End of Life Care," *Proceedings of the American Society of Clinical Oncology* 17 (Alexandria, Va.: 1998). Cited in K. Foley and H. Hendin, "Changing the Culture," in Foley and Hendin, *Case Against Assisted Suicide,* 315.

441 "Physicians who unwisely prolong": Ibid.

441 the less physicians know: R. K. Portenoy et al., "Determinants of the Willingness to Endorse Assisted Suicide: A Survey of Physicians, Nurses, and Social Workers," *Psychosomatics* 38 (1997): 277–87.

441 "You don't have to kill": Quoted on "Rational Suicide?" *60 Minutes.*

441 change their mind: Z. Zylicz, "Palliative Care and Euthanasia in the Netherlands: Observations of a Dutch Physician," in Foley and Hendin, *Case Against Assisted Suicide,* 122–43.

441 "If all the care": C. Saunders, "Dying They Live: St. Christopher's Hospice," in H. Feifel *New Meanings of Death* (New York: McGraw-Hill, 1977), 159.

442 "are no more mutually exclusive": M. Angell, "The Quality of Mercy," in Quill and Battin, *Physician-Assisted Dying,* 23.

442 "not only compatible" and "the highest rate": T. E. Quill and M. P. Battin, "Excellent Palliative Care as the Standard, Physician-Assisted Dying as a Last Resort," in Quill and Battin, *Physician-Assisted Dying,* 329.

442 "Where we proponents": M. P. Battin and T. E. Quill, "False Dichotomy versus Genuine Choice: The Argument over Physician-Assisted Dying," in Quill and Battin, *Physician-Assisted Dying,* 2.

442 "Often people ask": N. Speijer, "The Attitude of Dutch Society Toward the Phenomenon of Suicide," in Farberow, *Suicide in Different Cultures,* 164.

443 "When an older woman leaves": Portwood, *Common-Sense Suicide,* 17–18.

443 for the Holy Stone: R. Gillon, "Suicide and Voluntary Euthanasia: Historical Perspective," in Downing, *Euthanasia,* 182

444 "What we want": G. B. Rolfe, "The Right to Die," *North American Review* 157 (6) (1893): 758.

445 "In a rational state": Ibid.

445 "Robert Lowell once remarked": Alvarez, *Savage God,* 130.

445 "People are going to help": *USA Today,* May 15, 1985, 8A.

445   "I believe that the classical": *New York Times,* April 25, 1983, B8.

445   "I myself believe": M. P. Battin, "Manipulated Suicide," in Battin and Mayo, *Suicide,* 179.

## PART 6 Survivors
## Chapter I Merryl and Carl

455   "There are always two parties": A. Toynbee, *Man's Concern with Death* (New York: McGraw-Hill, 1969), 267, 271.

## Chapter II The Mark of Cain

466   French engraving: Reproduced in J. B. C. I. Delisle de Sales, *De la Philosophie de la Nature* (London: 1789).

467   "decapitated": This list is taken partially from a similar list in Cain, *Survivors of Suicide,* 29.

467   In 1289, it is recorded: Fedden, *Suicide,* 138.

468   "What punishment": J. W. Ehrlich, ed., *Ehrlich's Blackstone* (Westport, Conn.: Greenwood Press, 1973), 838.

468   the case of Lancelot Johnson: MacDonald, *Mystical Bedlam,* 137–38.

468   The jury's verdict: The colonies were more lenient. In 1700, for instance, in his charter to Pennsylvania, William Penn recommended "that if any person, through temptation or melancholy, shall destroy himself, his estate, real and personal, shall, notwithstanding, descend to his wife, children, or relations, as if he had died a natural death." (S. Yorke, "Is Suicide a Sin?" *North American Review,* February 1890, 277.)

468   Marc-Antoine Calas: Fedden, *Suicide,* 231–32.

469   "He plants a dagger": Gregory, *Sermon on Suicide,* 12–13.

469   "Stay then, guilty man!": Miller, *Guilt, Folly, and Sources of Suicide,* 24–25.

469   "The *Sorrow* which arises": Hey, *Three Dissertations,* 202–3.

470   "With reference to suicide": Winslow, *Anatomy of Suicide,* 152.

470   at the Annual Meeting: J. M. S. Wood and A. R. Urquhart, "A Family Tree Illustrative of Insanity and Suicide," in Cain, *Survivors of Suicide,* 40–43.

470   George P. Mudge constructed: G. P. Mudge, "The Mendelian Collection of Human Pedigrees: Inheritance of Suicidal Mania," in Cain, *Survivors of Suicide,* 44–51.

470   "Many are induced": Winslow, *Anatomy of Suicide,* 96–97.

471   "The suicide by his last act": Strahan, *Suicide and Insanity,* 90.

471   "in the hope": Ibid., vi.

471   "But the worst of all": J. Joyce, *Ulysses* (New York: Random House, 1961), 96.

471   "Nothing lowered": Fedden, *Suicide,* 248.

472   "he placed the mark": E. Lindemann and I. M. Greer, "A Study of Grief: Emotional Responses to Suicide," in Cain, *Survivors of Suicide,* 67.

473   "I believe that the person": E. S. Shneidman, "Foreword," in Cain, *Survivors of Suicide,* x.

473   A 1967 study: Bergson, "Suicide's Other Victims," 104.

473   "Given the present stage": H. L. P. Resnik, "Psychological Resynthesis: A Clinical Approach to the Survivors of a Death by Suicide," in Cain, *Survivors of Suicide,* 177.

473   A bibliography of publications: J. L. McIntosh, "Survivors of Suicide: A Comprehensive Bibliography," *Omega* 16 (4) (1986): 355–70. Also J. L. McIntosh, "Survivors of Suicide: A Comprehensive Bibliography Update, 1986–1995," *Omega* 33 (2) (1996): 147–75.

473 A 2003 conference: "AFSP Releases Report on Survivors of Suicide Research Workshop," www.afsp.org/survivor/sosworkshop903.

473 "Historically, one of the most": McIntosh, "Suicide Survivors," 339.

474 "To the tragic legion": Styron, *Darkness Visible,* 33.

475 One study compared: L. G. Calhoun et al., "Reactions to the Parents of the Child Suicide: A Study of Social Impressions," *Journal of Consulting and Clinical Psychology* 48 (1980): 535–36.

475 "Even in the numbness": Wechsler, *In a Darkness,* 13.

## Chapter III Merryl: The Torture Chamber

483 Carl had left no suicide note: In 1989, nearly seven years after his death, Merryl learned that Carl had left a suicide note. Believing it would do Merryl more harm than good, her parents and in-laws had withheld it from her. Merryl wrote to Carl's parents, who sent her a photocopy. In the four-line note, which began, "She will get over it." Carl weighed the "misery" of staying alive against the "control" and "freedom" he would gain by killing himself. "I wish the note had not been kept from me for so long," says Merryl. "Although reading the note gave me great pain—at seeing Carl's handwriting, at feeling more acutely his torturous state—the overall feeling was one of relief at having the fuller knowledge and at knowing that I was in Carl's thoughts at the end."

## Chapter IV The O'er-Fraught Heart

487 "Although mourning involves": S. Freud, *Mourning and Melancholia* (1917), in Strachey, *Works,* 14: 243–44.

487 "Mourning has a quite specific": S. Freud, *Totem and Taboo* (1913), in Strachey, *Works,* 13: 65.

487 A study by the National Academy of Sciences: Osterweis, Solomon, and Green, *Bereavement.*

488 "There's a tendency": Worden, *Grief Counseling,* 32.

489 "Sooner or later": Ibid., 14.

489 10 to 15 percent: Ibid., 1.

489 "The first response": K. Lorenz, *On Aggression,* trans. M. K. Wilson (New York: Harvest/Harcourt Brace Jovanovich, 1966), 208.

490 "psychic numbing": R. J. Lifton, *Death in Life* (New York: Random House, 1967), 86–87.

491 Sheila Weller described: Weller, "Whose Death Was It, Anyway?"

492 "Guilt is a way:" E. Dunne and K. Dunne-Maxim, F. Walsh, and M. McGoldrick, *Living Beyond Loss: Death in the Family* (New York: W. W. Norton, 2004), 276.

492 "There is an especially": E. Lindemann and I. M. Greer, "A Study of Grief: Emotional Responses to Suicide," in Cain, *Survivors of Suicide,* 66.

492 one in ten: S. Wallace, *After Suicide* (New York: Wiley, 1973).

492 "Some feel guilty": A. Pangrazzi, "Suicide: How Christians Can Respond Today," *Catholic Update,* July 1984, 3.

494 In his poem "The Portrait": S. Kunitz, *The Poems of Stanley Kunitz, 1928–1978* (Boston and Toronto: Atlantic Monthly Press/Little, Brown, 1979), 86.

495 "I spit upon": J. Berryman, *The Dream Songs* (New York: Farrar, Straus and Giroux, 1969), 406.

495 fatally stabbed herself: Giffin and Felsenthal, *Cry for Help,* 173.

496   "I see now": Alvarez, *Savage God,* 258.

496   serve a preventive role: The thought of a suicide's effect on survivors has long been a
restraint on—and occasionally a spur to—potential suicides. Suffering from a bout of
chronic catarrh, Seneca, who championed the idea of suicide as man's ever-available freedom, wrote, "Reduced to a state of complete emaciation, I had arrived at a point were
the catarrhal discharges were virtually carrying me away with them altogether. On many
an occasion I felt an urge to cut my life short there and then, and was only held back by
the thought of my father, who had been the kindest of fathers to me and was then in his
old age. Having in mind not how bravely I was capable of dying but how far from bravely
he was capable of bearing the loss, I commanded myself to live." (Battin, *Ethical
Issues,* 78.) On the other hand, many suicidal people are beyond the ability to consider
the effect their death might have on friends and family. "Decisions about suicide are not
fleeting thoughts that can be willed away in deference to the best interests of others,"
writes Kay Jamison, who attempted suicide as a young woman. "Suicide wells up from
cumulative anguish or is hastened by impulse; however much it may be set in or set off
by the outer world, the suicidal mind tends not to mull on the well-being and future of
others. If it does, it conceives for them a brighter future due to the fact that their lives are
rid of an ill, depressed, violent, or psychotic presence." *Night Falls Fast,* 292.

497   "For children": Osterweis, Solomon, and Green, *Bereavement,* 125.

497   Children are even more apt: Many parents mistakenly believe that a child is too young
to grieve. "They think, 'She's only three—she won't feel it,'" says Sandra Fox. Until
recently, in fact, it was believed that because they cannot comprehend the permanence
of death until about age nine, children are unable to mourn. Today, experts say that children begin to sense separation and loss at six months and may be able to grieve by age
three. Children of any age express their grief differently from adults, through physical
symptoms such as restlessness, colds, and upset stomachs, or through misbehavior, academic problems, and delinquency.

498   forty-five children: A. C. Cain and I. Fast, "Children's Disturbed Reactions to Parent
Suicide: Distortions of Guilt, Communication, and Identification," in Cain, *Survivors of
Suicide,* 93–111.

498   seventeen patients: T. L. Dorpat, "Psychological Effects of Parental Suicide on Surviving Children," in Cain, *Survivors of Suicide,* 121–42.


## Chapter VI A Safe Place

523   One survivor organization runs: See Web site at www.1000deaths.com.

524   "I feel so safe": S. Slepicka, "The Role of Support Groups in the Healing Process of Suicide Survivors" (unpublished paper).


## Chapter VIII A Place for What We Lose

531   "We find a place": Worden, *Grief Counseling,* 17.

531   "Ah well, slowly but surely": D. J. Enright, *The Oxford Book of Death* (Oxford: Oxford
University Press, 1983), 113–14.

533   "I want Dick's death not to be bigger": Kenyon, "Survivor's Notes."

# SELECTED BIBLIOGRAPHY

The literature on suicide is massive. These are the books and papers I found most useful or thought-provoking in the preparation of this work.

## Books

Ackerman, D. *A Slender Thread.* New York: Random House, 1997.

Alcohol, Drug Abuse, and Mental Health Administration. *Report of the Secretary's Task Force on Youth Suicide.* 4 vols. Washington, D.C.: U.S. Government Printing Office, 1989.

Alvarez, A. *The Savage God.* New York: Bantam Books, 1973.

Baechler, J. *Suicides.* Trans. B. Cooper. New York: Basic Books, 1979.

Barnard, C. *Good Life/Good Death.* Englewood Cliffs, N.J.: Prentice-Hall, 1980.

Battin, M. P. *Ethical Issues in Suicide.* Englewood Cliffs, N.J.: Prentice-Hall, 1982.

Battin, M. P., and D. J. Mayo, eds. *Suicide: The Philosophical Issues.* New York: St. Martin's Press, 1980.

Beam, A. *Gracefully Insane.* New York: Public Affairs, 2001.

Betzold, M. *Appointment with Doctor Death.* Troy, Mich.: Momentum Books, 1993.

Bohannan, P., ed. *African Homicide and Suicide.* New York: Atheneum, 1967.

Bolton, I., with C. Mitchell. *My Son . . . My Son . . .* Atlanta: Bolton Press, 1983.

Bruller, J. *21 Delightful Ways of Committing Suicide.* New York: Covici, Friede, 1930.

Bucknill, J. C., and D. H. Tuke. *A Manual of Psychological Medicine.* London: John Churchill, 1858.

Buie, D. H., and J. T. Maltsberger. *Practical Formulation of Suicide Risk.* Cambridge: Firefly Press, 1983.

Burton, R. *The Anatomy of Melancholy.* New York: Empire State Book Co., 1924.

Butler, R. N. *Why Survive? Being Old in America.* New York: Harper Colophon Books, 1975.

Cain, A. C., ed. *Survivors of Suicide.* Springfield, Ill.: Charles C. Thomas, 1972.

Callahan, D. *Setting Limits.* New York: Simon and Schuster, 1987.

Cavan, R. S. *Suicide.* New York: Russell & Russell, 1965.

Choron, J. *Death and Western Thought.* New York: Collier/Macmillan, 1973.

———. *Suicide.* New York: Charles Scribner's Sons, 1972.

Clark, B. *Whose Life Is It Anyway?* New York: Avon, 1980.

Coleman, L. *Suicide Clusters.* Boston and London: Faber and Faber, 1987.

Coser, R. L. *Training in Ambiguity.* New York: Free Press/Macmillan, 1979.

Donne, J. *Biathanatos.* New York: Arno Press, 1977.

Douglas, J. D. *The Social Meanings of Suicide.* Princeton: Princeton University Press, 1973.

Downing, A. B., ed. *Euthanasia and the Right to Death.* Los Angeles: Nash Publishing Company, 1970.

Dublin, L. I. *Suicide: A Sociological and Statistical Study.* New York: Ronald Press, 1963.

Dublin, L. I., and B. Bunzel. *To Be or Not To Be.* New York: Harrison Smith and Robert Haas, 1933.

Dunne, E. J., J. L. McIntosh, and K. Dunne-Maxim, eds. *Suicide and Its Aftermath.* New York: W. W. Norton, 1987.

Durkheim, E. *Suicide.* Trans. J. A. Spaulding, and G. Simpson. New York: Free Press, 1966.

Ellis, E. R., and G. N. Allen. *Traitor Within: Our Suicide Problem.* Garden City, N.Y.: Doubleday, 1961.

Evans, G., and N. L. Farberow. *The Encyclopedia of Suicide.* New York: Facts on File, 1988.

Exit. *A Guide to Self-Deliverance.* London: Executive Committee of Exit, 1981.

Faber, M. D. *Suicide and Greek Tragedy.* New York: Sphinx Press, 1970.

Farberow, N. L., ed. *The Many Faces of Suicide.* New York: McGraw-Hill, 1980.

———. *Suicide in Different Cultures.* Baltimore: University Park Press, 1975.

———. *Taboo Topics.* New York: Atherton Press, 1963.

Farberow, N. L., and E. S. Shneidman, eds. *The Cry for Help.* New York: McGraw-Hill, 1965.

Fedden, H. R. *Suicide: A Social and Historical Study.* New York: Arno Press, 1980.

Fisher, S. A. *Suicide Prevention and/or Crisis Services: A National Survey.* Canton, Ohio: Case Western Reserve University, 1972.

Fletcher, J. *Morals and Medicine.* Princeton: Princeton University Press, 1954.

Foley, K., and H. Hendin, eds. *The Case Against Assisted Suicide.* Baltimore: Johns Hopkins Paperbacks, 2004.

Friedman, P., ed. *On Suicide.* New York: International Universities Press, 1967.

Galt, J. M. *The Treatment of Insanity.* New York: Harper and Brothers, 1846.

Gates, B. T. *Victorian Suicide.* Princeton: Princeton University Press, 1988.

Gibbs, J. P., and W. T. Martin. *Status Integration and Suicide: A Sociological Study.* Eugene: University of Oregon Press, 1964.

Giffin, M., and C. Felsenthal. *A Cry for Help.* Garden City, N.Y.: Doubleday, 1983.

Goethe, J. W. *The Sorrows of Young Werther.* Trans. E. Mayer and L. Bogan. New York: Vintage Books, 1973.

Goldsmith, S. K., T. C. Pellmar, A. M. Kleinman, and W. E. Bunney, eds. *Reducing Suicide: A National Imperative.* Washington, D.C.: National Academies Press, 2002.

Green, B. R., and D. P. Irish eds. *Death Education: Preparation for Living.* Cambridge, Mass.: Schenkman, 1971.

Gregory, G. *A Sermon on Suicide.* London: J. Nichols, 1797.

Grollman, E. A. *Suicide: Prevention, Intervention, Postvention.* Boston: Beacon Press, 1971.

Guillon, C., and Y. LeBonniec. *Suicide, Mode d'Emploi: Histoire, Technique, Actualité.* Paris: Éditions Alain Moreau, 1982.

Hankoff, L. D., ed. *Suicide: Theory and Clinical Aspects.* Littleton, Mass.: PSG Publishing Company, 1979.

Hastings, J., ed. *Encyclopaedia of Religion and Ethics.* New York: Charles Scribner's Sons, 1922.

Hatton, C. L., and S. M. Valente, eds. *Suicide: Assessment and Intervention.* Norwalk, Conn.: Appleton-Century-Crofts, 1984.

Hayes, L., and B. Kajdan. *And Darkness Closes In . . . A National Study of Jail Suicides.* Washington, D.C.: National Center on Institutions and Alternatives, 1981.

Hendin, D. *Death as a Fact of Life.* New York: W. W. Norton, 1984.

Hendin, H. *Black Suicide.* New York: Basic Books, 1969.

———. *Seduced by Death: Doctors, Patients, and the Dutch Cure.* New York: Norton, 1997.

———. *Suicide and Scandinavia.* Garden City, N.Y.: Doubleday/Anchor Books, 1965.

———. *Suicide in America.* New York: W. W. Norton, 1982.

Henry, A. F., and J. F. Short Jr. *Suicide and Homicide.* New York: Free Press, 1965.

Hewett, J. H. *After Suicide.* Philadelphia: Westminster Press, 1980.

Hey, R. *Three Dissertations; On the Pernicious Effects of Gaming, On Duelling, and on Suicide.* Cambridge: J. Smith, 1812.

Hillman, J. *Suicide and the Soul*. Dallas: Spring Publications, 1985.

Hoffman, F. *Suicide Problems*. Newark: Prudential Press, 1928.

Hume, D. *Essays Moral, Political and Literary*. London: Oxford University Press, 1963.

Humphry, D. *Final Exit*. Eugene, Oreg.: Hemlock Society, 1991.

———. *The Good Euthanasia Guide 2005*. Junction City, Oreg.: Norris Lane Press/ERGO, 2005.

———. *Let Me Die Before I Wake*. Los Angeles: Hemlock, 1982.

Humphry, D., and M. Clement. *Freedom to Die: People, Politics and the Right-to-Die Movement*. New York: St. Martin's Press, 1998.

Humphry, D., and A. Wickett. *The Right to Die: Understanding Euthanasia*. New York: Harper & Row, 1986.

Hunter, R., and I. Macalpine. *Three Hundred Years of Psychiatry, 1535–1860*. London: Oxford University Press, 1963.

Iga, M. *The Thorn in the Chrysanthemum: Suicide and Economic Success in Modern Japan*. Berkeley: University of California Press, 1986.

Jackson, S. W. *Melancholia and Depression*. New Haven: Yale University Press, 1986.

Jacobs, D. G., ed. *The Harvard Medical School Guide to Suicide Assessment and Intervention*. San Francisco: Jossey-Bass, 1999.

James, W. *Essays on Faith and Morals*. New York: Longmans, Green, 1947.

Jamison, K. R. *Night Falls Fast: Understanding Suicide*. New York: Vintage Books, 2000.

Kastenbaum, R., and R. Aisenberg. *The Psychology of Death*. New York: Springer Publishing Company, 1976.

Kaysen, Susanna. *Girl, Interrupted*. New York: Vintage Books, 1994.

Kevorkian, J. *Prescription: Medicide*. Buffalo, N.Y.: Prometheus Books, 1991.

Klagsbrun, F. *Too Young to Die: Youth and Suicide*. New York: Pocket Books, 1981.

Knauth, P. *A Season in Hell*. New York: Pocket Books, 1977.

Kobler, A., and E. Stotler. *The End of Hope*. New York: Free Press of Glencoe, 1964.

Kübler-Ross, E. *On Death and Dying*. New York: Macmillan, 1969.

Kushner, H. I. *Self-Destruction in the Promised Land*. New Brunswick, N.J.: Rutgers University Press, 1989.

Larue, G. A. *Euthanasia and Religion*. Los Angeles: Hemlock Society, 1985.

Lecky, W. E. H. *History of European Morals from Augustus to Charlemagne*. London: Longmans, Green, 1869.

Lee, B. C. *Compassion in Dying: Stories of Dignity and Choice*. Troutdale, Oreg.: New Sage Press, 2003.

Lester, D. *Making Sense of Suicide*. Philadelphia: Charles Press, 1997.

Lester, G., and D. Lester. *Suicide: The Gamble with Death*. Englewood Cliffs, N.J.: Prentice-Hall, 1971.

Lieberman, L. *Leaving You: The Cultural Meaning of Suicide*. Chicago: Ivan R. Dee, 2003.

Lifton, R. J. *The Broken Connection*. New York: Simon and Schuster, 1980.

Light, D. *Becoming Psychiatrists: The Professional Transformation of Self*. New York: W. W. Norton, 1980.

Lukas, C., and H. M. Seiden. *Silent Grief: Living in the Wake of Suicide*. New York: Charles Scribner's Sons, 1987.

MacDonald, M. *Mystical Bedlam*. Cambridge: Cambridge University Press, 1981.

Mack, J. E., and H. Hickler. *Vivienne: The Life and Suicide of an Adolescent Girl*. Boston: Little, Brown, 1981.

Maguire, D. C. *Death by Choice*. New York: Schocken Books, 1975.

Maltsberger, J. T., and M. J. Goldblatt. *Essential Papers on Suicide*. New York: NYU Press, 1996.

Mannes, M. *Last Rights*. New York: William Morrow, 1974.

Marker, Rita. *Deadly Compassion*. New York: William Morrow, 1993.

Masaryk, T. G. *Suicide and the Meaning of Civilization*. Trans. W. B. Weist and R. G. Batson. Chicago: University of Chicago Press, 1970.

Meerloo, J. A. M. *Suicide and Mass Suicide*. New York: E. P. Dutton & Co., 1968.

Menninger, K. A. *Man Against Himself*. New York: Harvest/Harcourt, Brace & World, 1938.

Miller, A. *Death of a Salesman*. New York: Bantam Books, 1951.

Miller, S. *The Guilt, Folly, and Sources of Suicide*. New York: T and J Swords, 1805.

Moore, C. *A Full Inquiry on the Subject of Suicide*. London: 1790.

Morselli, H. *Suicide: An Essay on Comparative Moral Statistics*. New York: Arno Press, 1975.

New York State Task Force on Life and the Law. *When Death Is Sought: Assisted Suicide and Euthanasia in the Medical Context*. Albany, N.Y.: 1994.

Norman, M. *'Night, Mother*. New York: Dramatists Play Service, 1983.

Nuland, S. B. *How We Die*. New York: Vintage Books, 1995.

Osterweis, M., F. Solomon, and M. Green, eds. *Bereavement: Reactions, Consequences, and Care*. Washington, D.C.: National Academy Press, 1984.

Pavese, C. *The Burning Brand: Diaries, 1935–1950*. Trans. A. E. Murch. New York: Walker & Company, 1961.

Peck, M. L., N. L. Farberow, and R. E. Litman, eds. *Youth Suicide*. New York: Springer Publishing Company, 1985.

Perlin, S., ed. *A Handbook for the Study of Suicide*. New York: Oxford University Press, 1975.

Plath, S. *The Bell Jar*. New York: Bantam Books, 1972.

Portwood, D. *Common-Sense Suicide*. New York: Dodd, Mead, 1978.

Poussaint, A. F., and A. Alexander. *Lay My Burden Down: Understanding Suicide and the Mental Health Crisis among African-Americans*. Boston: Beacon Press, 2000.

Quill, T. E., and M. P. Battin, eds. *Physician-Assisted Dying*. Baltimore: Johns Hopkins University Press, 2004.

Reynolds, D. K., and N. L. Farberow. *Suicide: Inside and Out*. Berkeley: University of California Press, 1976.

Roberts, A. R., ed. *Self-Destructive Behavior*. Springfield, Ill.: Charles C. Thomas, 1975.

Robitscher, J. *The Powers of Psychiatry*. Boston: Houghton Mifflin, 1980.

Rofes, E. E. *"I Thought People Like That Killed Themselves": Lesbians, Gay Men and Suicide*. San Francisco: Grey Fox Press, 1983.

Rollin, B. *Last Wish*. New York: Linden Press/Simon and Schuster, 1985.

Roman, J. *Exit House*. New York: Seaview Books, 1980.

Rosenfeld, L., and M. Prupas. *Left Alive: After a Suicide Death in the Family*. Springfield, Ill.: Charles C. Thomas, 1984.

Russell, O. R. *Freedom to Die: Moral and Legal Aspects of Euthanasia*. New York: Human Sciences Press, 1977.

Shneidman, E., ed. *Death and the College Student*. New York: Behavioral Publications, 1972.

———, ed. *Definition of Suicide*. New York: John Wiley & Sons, 1985.

———, ed. *Voices of Death*. New York: Harper & Row, 1980.

Shneidman, E. S. *Autopsy of a Suicidal Mind*. New York: Oxford University Press, 2004.

———. *Comprehending Suicide: Landmarks in 20th-Century Suicidology*. Washington, D.C.: American Psychological Association, 2001.

———. *Deaths of Man*. Harmondsworth, England: Penguin, 1974.

———, ed. *Essays in Self-Destruction*. New York: Jason Aronson, 1967.

———, ed. *On the Nature of Suicide*. San Francisco: Jossey-Bass, 1973.

———, ed. *Suicide Thoughts and Reflections, 1960–1980*. New York: Behavioral Sciences Press, 1981.

———, ed. *Suicidology: Contemporary Developments*. New York: Grune and Stratton, 1976.

Shneidman, E. S., and N. L. Farberow, eds. *Clues to Suicide.* New York: McGraw-Hill, 1957.

Shneidman, E. S., N. L. Farberow, and R. E. Litman, eds. *The Psychology of Suicide.* New York: Science House, 1970.

Smolin, A., and J. Guinan. *Healing After the Suicide of a Loved One.* New York: Fireside, 1993.

Solomon, A. *The Noonday Demon: An Atlas of Depression.* New York: Scribner, 2001.

Sprott, S. E. *The English Debate on Suicide from Donne to Hume.* La Salle, Ill.: Open Court, 1961.

Steincrohn, P. J. *How to Stop Killing Yourself.* New York: Ace Books, 1950.

Stengel, E. *Suicide and Attempted Suicide.* New York: Jason Aronson, 1974.

Stern, D. *The Suicide Academy.* New York: Arbor House, 1985.

Stimming, M., and M. Stimming, eds. *Before Their Time: Adult Children's Experiences of Parental Suicide.* Philadelphia: Temple University Press, 1999.

Strahan, S. A. K. *Suicide and Insanity.* London: Swan Sonnenschein, 1893.

Styron, W. *Darkness Visible.* New York: Vintage, 1992.

Szasz, T. *The Manufacture of Madness.* New York: Harper Colophon Books, 1977.

———. *The Theology of Medicine.* Baton Rouge: Louisiana State University Press, 1977.

Wallace, S., and A. Eser, eds. *Suicide and Euthanasia.* Knoxville: University of Tennessee Press, 1981.

Wasserman, D. *Suicide: An Unnecessary Death.* London: Martin Dunitz, 2001.

Webb, M. *The Good Death: The New American Search to Reshape the End of Life.* New York: Bantam, 1999.

Wechsler, J. A. *In a Darkness.* New York: W. W. Norton, 1972.

Weisman, A. D. *On Dying and Denying.* New York: Behavioral Publications, 1972.

Westermarck, E. *The Origin and Development of the Moral Ideas.* London: Macmillan, 1912.

Whitaker, R. *Mad in America.* Cambridge: Perseus, 2003.

Williams, G. *The Sanctity of Life and the Criminal Law.* New York: Alfred A. Knopf, 1957.

Winslow, F. *The Anatomy of Suicide.* London: Henry Renshaw, 1840.

Worden, J. W. *Grief Counseling and Grief Therapy.* New York: Springer Publishing Company, 1982.

**Papers and Articles**

Anonymous. "Ex-Suicide." *Harper's Monthly* 165 (1932): 426–35.

Applebome, P. "Between Two Worlds." *Texas Monthly,* January 1985, 104.

Arango, V., et al. "Genetics of the Serotonergic System in Suicidal Behavior." *Journal of Psychiatric Research* 37 (2003): 375–86.

———. "Serotonin 1A Receptors, Serotonin Transporter Binding and Serotonin Transporter mRNA Expression in the Brainstem of Depressed Suicide Victims." *Neuropsychopharmacology* 25 (6) (2001): 893–903.

Åsberg, M. "Neurotransmitters and Suicidal Behavior: The Evidence from Cerebrospinal Fluid Studies." *Annals of the New York Academy of Sciences* 836 (1997): 158–81.

Åsberg, M., L. Tråskman, and P. Thorén. "5-HIAA in the Cerebrospinal Fluid." *Archives of General Psychiatry* 33 (1976): 1193–97.

Asimos, C. T. "Dynamic Problem-Solving in a Group for Suicidal Persons." *International Journal of Group Psychotherapy* 29 (1) (1979): 109–14.

Atlas, J. "The Survivor's Suicide." *Vanity Fair,* January 1988, 78.

Baker, W. E. "Diary of a Suicide." *The Glebe* 1 (2) (1913).

Bakwin, H. "Suicide in Children and Adolescents." *Journal of Pediatrics* 50 (6) (1957): 749–69.

Baldessarini, R. J., et al. "Effects of Lithium Treatment and Its Discontinuation on Suicidal

Behavior in Bipolar Manic-Depressive Disorders." *Journal of Clinical Psychiatry* 60 (Supplement 2) (1999): 77–84.

Barraclough, B. M. "Suicide in the Elderly: Recent Developments in Psychogeriatrics." *British Journal of Psychiatry* (Special Supplement 6) (1971): 87–97.

Bartel, R. "Suicide in Eighteenth-Century England: The Myth of a Reputation." *Huntington Library Quarterly,* February 1960, 145–58.

Basescu, S. "The Threat of Suicide in Psychotherapy." *American Journal of Psychotherapy* 19 (1965): 99–105.

Battin, M. P. "Age Rationing and the Just Distribution of Health Care: Is There a Duty to Die?" *Ethics* 97 (1987): 317–40.

———. "The Least Worst Death." *Hastings Center Report* 13 (2) (1983): 13–16.

Beck, A. T., M. Kovacs, and A. Weissman. "Assessment of Suicidal Intention: The Scale for Suicide Ideation." *Journal of Consulting and Clinical Psychology* 47 (2) (1979): 343–52.

Bergson, L. "Suicide's Other Victims." *New York Times Magazine,* November 14, 1982, 100–108.

Berman, A. L., and R. Cohen-Sandler. "Childhood and Adolescent Suicide Research: A Critique." *Crisis* 3: 3–15.

Bernikow, L. "Sickness Unto Death: Young Women and Suicide." *Mademoiselle,* April 1983, 150.

Billings, J. H., et al. "Observations on Long-Term Group Therapy with Suicidal and Depressed Persons." *Life-Threatening Behavior* 4 (3) (1974): 160–70.

Blair, G. "The Heart of the Matter." *Manhattan, Inc.,* October 1984, 72–79.

Blum, D. "A Loss of Balance." *New York,* January 13, 1986, 32–37.

Boldrini, M., et al. "More Tryptophan Hydroxylase in the Brainstem Dorsal Raphe Nucleus in Depressed Suicides." *Brain Research* (2005) (forthcoming).

Bongar, B., and M. Harmatz. "Clinical Psychology Graduate Education in the Study of Suicide: Resources and Importance." *Suicide and Life-Threatening Behavior* 21 (3) (1991): 231–44.

Bradley, K. A., and T. A. Raffin. "Life and Death Decisions: Ethical Decision Making When Resources Are Limited." Unpublished paper.

Breed, W. "Five Components of a Basic Suicide Syndrome." *Life-Threatening Behavior* 2 (1) (1972): 3–18.

Breskin, D. "Dear Mom and Dad." *Rolling Stone,* November 8, 1984, 26.

Brown, G. K., et al. "Risk Factors for Suicide in Psychiatric Outpatients: A 20-Year Prospective Study." *Journal of Consulting and Clinical Psychology* 68 (3) (2000): 371–77.

Brown, G. L., et al. "Aggression, Suicide, and Serotonin: Relationships to CSF Amine Metabolites." *American Journal of Psychiatry* 139 (6) (1982): 741–46.

Cantor, P. "The Adolescent Attempter: Sex, Sibling Position, and Family Constellation." *Life-Threatening Behavior* 2 (4) (1972): 252–61.

Cantor, P. C. "Personality Characteristics Found Among Youthful Female Suicide Attempters." *Journal of Abnormal Psychology* 85 (3) (1976): 324–29.

Cassity, J. H. "Are You the Suicide Type?" *American Mercury,* October 1939, 172–77.

Centers for Disease Control. "Youth Suicide Prevention Programs: A Resource Guide." Atlanta: Centers for Disease Control, 1992.

Cochran, S. D., and V. M. Mays. "Lifetime Prevalence of Suicide Symptoms and Affective Disorders Among Men Reporting Same-Sex Sexual Partners: Results from NHANES III." *American Journal of Public Health* 90 (4) (2000): 573–78.

Comstock, B. S. "Suicide in the 1970's: A Second Look." *Suicide and Life-Threatening Behavior* 9 (1) (1979): 3–13.

Conwell, Y. "Suicide in Later Life: A Review and Recommendations for Prevention." *Suicide and Life-Threatening Behavior* 31 (Supplement) (2001): 32–47.

Conwell, Y., et al. "Risk Factors for Suicide in Later Life." *Biological Psychiatry* 52 (2002): 193–204.

Crocker, L. G. "The Discussion of Suicide in the Eighteenth Century." *Journal of the History of Ideas* 13 (1952): 47–72.

Danto, B. L. "New Frontiers in the Relationship Between Suicidology and Law Enforcement." *Suicide and Life-Threatening Behavior* 9 (4) (1979): 195–204.

———. "Practical Aspects of the Training of Psychiatrists in Suicide Prevention." *Omega* 7 (1) (1976): 69–73.

Daube, D. "The Linguistics of Suicide." *Suicide and Life-Threatening Behavior* 7 (3) (1977): 132–82.

Eisenberg, L. "Adolescent Suicide: On Taking Arms Against a Sea of Troubles." *Pediatrics* 66 (1980): 315–20.

Ellis, T. E., and T. O. Dickey. "Procedures Surrounding the Suicide of a Trainee's Patient: A National Survey of Psychology Internships and Psychiatry Residency Programs." *Professional Psychology: Research and Practice* 29 (5) (1998): 492–97.

Ellis, T. E., et al. "Patient Suicide in Psychiatry Residency Programs: A National Survey of Training and Postvention Practices." *Academic Psychiatry* 22 (1998): 181–89.

Emery, P. E. "Adolescent Depression and Suicide." *Adolescence* 18 (70) (1983): 245–58.

Engelhardt, H. T., Jr., and M. Malloy. "Suicide and Assisting Suicide: A Critique of Legal Sanctions." *Southwestern Law Journal* 36 (4) (1982): 1003–37.

Ezzell, C. "Why? The Neuroscience of Suicide." *Scientific American,* February 2003. www.sciam.com.

Faber, M. D. "Seneca, Self-Destruction, and the Creative Act." *Omega* 9 (2) (1978): 149–65.

———. "Shakespeare's Suicides: Some Historic, Dramatic and Psychological Reflections." In E. S. Shneidman, ed. *Essays in Self-Destruction,* 30–58. New York: Jason Aronson, 1967.

Fadiman, A. "The Liberation of Lolly and Gronky." *Life,* December 1986, 71–94.

Farberow, N. L. "Ten Years of Suicide Prevention—Past and Future." *Bulletin of Suicidology* 6 (Spring 1970): 6–11.

Farberow, N. L., D. R. MacKinnon, and F. L. Nelson. "Suicide: Who's Counting?" *Public Health Reports* 92 (3) (1977): 223–32.

Fishbain, D. A., et al. "A Controlled Study of Suicide Pacts." *Journal of Clinical Psychiatry* 45 (1984): 154–57.

Frederick, C. J. "Current Trends in Suicidal Behavior in the United States." *American Journal of Psychotherapy* 32 (1978): 172–200.

———. "The Present Suicide Taboo in the United States." *Mental Hygiene* 55 (2) (1971): 178–83.

Frederick, C. J., and H. L. P. Resnik. "Interventions with Suicidal Patients." *Journal of Contemporary Psychotherapy* 2 (2) (1970): 103–9.

Freeman, W. "Psychiatrists Who Kill Themselves: A Study in Suicide." *American Journal of Psychiatry* 124 (6) (1967): 154–55.

Friend, T. "Jumpers." *New Yorker,* October 13, 2003, 48–59.

Garfinkel, B. D., A. Froese, and J. Hood. "Suicide Attempts in Children and Adolescents." *American Journal of Psychiatry* 139 (10) (1982): 1257–61.

Garofolo, R., et al. "Sexual Orientation and Risk of Suicide Attempts among a Representative Sample of Youth." *Archives of Pediatrics and Adolescent Medicine* 153 (1999): 487–93.

Gibson, P. "Gay Male and Lesbian Youth Suicide." Paper presented at a joint meeting of the American Association of Suicidology and the International Association for Suicide Prevention, San Francisco, May 25–30, 1987.

Gould, M., et al. "Media Contagion and Suicide Among the Young." *American Behavioral Scientist* 46 (9) (2003): 1269–84.

————. "Youth Suicide Risk and Preventive Interventions: A Review of the Past 10 Years." *Journal of the American Academy of Child and Adolescent Psychiatry* 42 (4) (2003): 386–405.

Gould, M. S. "Suicide and the Media." In H. Hendin and J. J. Mann. "The Clinical Science of Suicide Prevention." *Annals of the New York Academy of Sciences* 932 (2001): 200–224.

Gould, M. S., and D. Shaffer. "The Impact of Suicide in Television Movies: Evidence of Imitation." *New England Journal of Medicine* 315 (11) (1986): 690–94.

Gould, M. S., et al. "Psychosocial Risk Factors of Child and Adolescent Completed Suicide." *Archives of General Psychiatry* 53 (1996): 1155–62.

Groenewoud, J. H., et al. "Physician-Assisted Death in Psychiatric Practice in the Netherlands." *New England Journal of Medicine* 336 (25) (1997): 1795–1801.

Gruman, G. J. "An Historical Introduction to Ideas about Voluntary Euthanasia." *Omega* 4 (2) (1973): 87–138.

Gurland, B. J., and P. S. Cross. "Suicide Among the Elderly." From M. K. Aronson, R. Bennett, and B. J. Gurland, eds. *The Acting-Out Elderly,* 55–65. New York: Haworth Press, 1983.

Hackel, J., and C. T. Asimos. "Resistances Encountered in Starting a Group Therapy Program for Suicide Attempters in Varied Administrative Settings." *Suicide and Life-Threatening Behavior* 10 (2) (1980): 100–105.

Hansen, L. C., and C. A. McAleer. "Terminal Cancer and Suicide: The Health Care Professional's Dilemma." *Omega* 14 (3) (1983): 241–48.

Haughton, A. "Suicide Prevention Programs in the United States—an Overview." *Bulletin of Suicidology,* July 1968, 25–29.

Havens, L. L. "The Anatomy of a Suicide." *New England Journal of Medicine* 272 (8) (1965): 401–6.

Heilig, S. M., et al. "The Role of Nonprofessional Volunteers in a Suicide Prevention Center." *Community Mental Health Journal* 4 (4) (1968): 287–95.

Hemenway, D., and M. Miller. "Association of Rates of Household Handgun Ownership, Lifetime Major Depression, and Serious Suicidal Thoughts with Rates of Suicide Across U.S. Census Regions," *Injury Prevention* 8 (2002): 313–16.

Hendin, H., et al. "Desperation and Other Affective States in Suicidal Patients." *Suicide and Life-Threatening Behavior* 34 (4) (2004): 386–94.

————. "Recognizing and Responding to a Suicide Crisis." *Suicide and Life-Threatening Behavior* 31 (2) (2001): 115–28.

Herrel, R., et al. "Sexual Orientation and Suicidality: A Co-Twin Control Study in Adult Men." *Archives of General Psychiatry* 56 (1999): 867–74.

Holinger, P. C., and D. Offer. "Prediction of Adolescent Suicide: A Population Model." *American Journal of Psychiatry* 139 (3) (1982): 302–7.

Holmes, J. H. "Is Suicide Justifiable?" *John Day Pamphlets* 42 (1934).

Hutson, H. R., et al. "Suicide by Cop." *Annals of Emergency Medicine* 32 (6) (1998): 665–69.

Jackson, D. L., and S. Youngner. "Patient Autonomy and 'Death with Dignity': Some Clinical Caveats." *New England Journal of Medicine* 301 (8) (1979): 404–8.

Jochemsen, H., and J. Keown. "Voluntary Euthanasia Under Control? The Latest Empirical Evidence on Euthanasia in the Netherlands." *Journal of Medical Ethics* 25 (1) (1999): 16–21.

Kalafat, J. "School Approaches to Youth Suicide Prevention." *American Behavioral Scientist* 46 (9) (2003): 1211–23.

Kastenbaum, R. "On the Future of Death: Some Images and Options." *Omega* 3 (4) (1972): 319–30.

Kelly, W. A. "Suicide and Psychiatric Education." *American Journal of Psychiatry* 130 (4) (1973): 463–68.

Kenyon, K. "A Survivor's Notes." *Newsweek,* April 30, 1979, 17.

King, R. A., et al. "Psychosocial and Risk Behavior Correlates of Youth Suicide Attempts and Suicidal Ideation." *Journal of the American Academy of Child and Adolescent Psychiatry* 40 (7) (2001): 837–46.

Kirk, A. R. "Psycho-Social Modes of Adaptation and Suicide Among Blacks." Unpublished paper, Michigan State University.

Klein, J. "A Mystery of Three Suicides." *Rolling Stone,* February 10, 1977, 34–39.

Klugman, D. J., R. E. Litman, and C. I. Wold. "Suicide: Answering the Cry for Help." *Social Work* 10 (4) (1965): 43–50.

Kobler, J. "Suicides Can Be Prevented." *Saturday Evening Post,* March 27, 1948, 20.

Kovacs, M., A. T. Beck, and A. Weissman. "Hopelessness: An Indicator of Suicidal Risk." *Suicide* 5 (2) (1975): 98–103.

Lamm, R. D. "Long Time Dying." *New Republic,* August 27, 1984, 20–23.

LeBlanc, A. N. "You Wanna Die with Me?" *New England Monthly,* December 1986, 76.

Light, D. "Professional Problems in Treating Suicidal Persons." *Omega* 7 (1) (1976): 59–67.

———. "Psychiatrists and Suicide." Unpublished paper.

———. "Treating Suicide: The Illusions of a Professional Movement." *International Social Science Journal* 25 (4) (1973): 475–88.

Litman, R. E. "Sigmund Freud on Suicide." In E. S. Shneidman, ed., *Essays in Self-Destruction,* 324–44. New York: Science House, 1967.

———. "Suicide Prevention Center Patients: A Follow-up Study." *Bulletin of Suicidology* 6 (Spring 1970): 12–17.

———. "When Patients Commit Suicide." *American Journal of Psychotherapy* 14 (1965): 570–76.

Mahler, J. "The Antidepressant Dilemma." *New York Times Magazine,* November 21, 2004, 58.

Malcolm, A. H. "Many See Mercy in Ending Empty Lives." *New York Times,* September 23, 1984, 1.

———. "Some Elderly Choose Suicide Over Lonely, Dependent Life." *New York Times,* September 24, 1984, 1.

———. "To Suffer a Prolonged Illness or Elect to Die: A Case Study." *New York Times,* December 16, 1984, 1.

Maltsberger, J. T., "The Descent into Suicide." *International Journal of Psycho-Analysis* 85 (2004): 653–68.

Maltsberger, J. T., and D. H. Buie. "Countertransference Hate in the Treatment of Suicidal Patients." *Archives of General Psychiatry* 30 (1974): 625–33.

———. "The Devices of Suicide: Revenge, Riddance, and Rebirth." *International Review of Psycho-Analysis* 7 (1980): 61–72.

Mann, J. J. "A Current Perspective of Suicide and Attempted Suicide." *Annals of Internal Medicine* 136 (4) (2002): 302–11.

Mann, J. J., et al. "A Serotonin Transporter Gene Promoter Polymorphism (5-HTTLPR) and Prefrontal Cortical Binding in Major Depression and Suicide." *Archives of General Psychiatry* 57 (2000): 729–38.

Maris, R. "Rational Suicide: An Impoverished Self-Transformation." *Suicide and Life-Threatening Behavior* 12 (1) (1982): 4–16.

Marzuk, P. M., et al. "HIV Seroprevalence Among Suicide Victims in New York City, 1991–1993." *American Journal of Psychiatry* 154 (1997): 1720–25.

Mathews, W. "Civilization and Suicide." *North American Review,* April 1891, 470–84.

McIntosh, J. L. "Epidemiology of Suicide in the Elderly." In D. Lester and M. Tallmer, eds. *Suicide and the Older Adult,* 15–35. New York: The Guilford Press, 1992.

———. "Suicide Among Native Americans: Further Tribal Data and Considerations." *Omega* 14 (3) (1983): 215–29.

———. "Suicide Among the Elderly: Levels and Trends." *American Journal of Orthopsychiatry* 55 (2) (1985): 288–93.

———. "Suicide Prevention in the Elderly (Age 65–99)." *Suicide and Life-Threatening Behavior* 25 (1) (1995): 180–92.

———. "Suicide Survivors: The Aftermath of Suicide and Suicidal Behavior." From C. D. Bryant, *Handbook of Death and Dying.* Vol. 1, *The Presence of Death,* 339–350. Thousand Oaks, Calif.: Sage Publishing, 2003.

McIntosh, J. L., and J. F. Santos. "Changing Patterns in Methods of Suicide by Race and Sex." *Suicide and Life-Threatening Behavior* 12 (4) (1982): 221–33.

McIntosh, J. L., R. W. Hubbard, and J. F. Santos. "Suicide Facts and Myths." Paper presented at the sixteenth annual meeting of the American Association of Suicidology, Dallas, Texas, April 21–24, 1983.

Menninger, K. "Psychoanalytic Aspects of Suicide." *International Journal of Psychoanalysis* 14 (1933): 376–90.

Metha, A., et al. "Youth Suicide Prevention: A Survey and Analysis of Policies and Efforts in the 50 States." *Suicide and Life-Threatening Behavior* 28 (1998): 150–64.

Miller, H. L., et al. "Suicide Prevention Services in America." *Alabama Journal of Medical Science* 16 (1) (1979): 26–31.

Miller, M., and D. Hemenway. "The Relationship Between Firearms and Suicide: A Review of the Literature." *Aggression and Violent Behavior* 4 (1999): 59–75.

Mintz, R. S. "Basic Considerations in the Psychotherapy of the Depressed Suicidal Patient." *American Journal of Psychotherapy* 25 (1971): 56–73.

———. "Some Practical Procedures in the Management of Suicidal Persons." *American Journal of Orthopsychiatry* 36 (1966): 896–903.

Moss, L. M., and D. M. Hamilton. "The Psychotherapy of the Suicidal Patient." *American Journal of Psychiatry* 112 (1956): 814–19.

Motto, J. A. "New Approaches to Crisis Intervention." *Suicide and Life-Threatening Behavior* 9 (3) (1979): 173–84.

———. "Newspaper Influence on Suicide: A Controlled Study." *Archives of General Psychiatry* 23 (1970): 143–48.

———. "The Psychopathology of Suicide: A Clinical Model Approach." *American Journal of Psychiatry* 136 (4B) (1979): 516–20.

———. "Rational Suicide and Medical Ethics." In M. D. Basson, ed. *Rights and Responsibilities in Modern Medicine* 2, 201–9. New York: Alan R. Liss, 1981.

Motto, J. A., and A. G. Bostrom. "A Randomized Controlled Trial of Postcrisis Suicide Prevention." *Psychiatric Services* 52 (6) (2001): 828–33.

Murphy, G. E. "Suicide and the Right to Die." *American Journal of Psychiatry* 130 (4) (1973): 472–73.

Murphy, G. E., et al. "Suicide and Alcoholism." *Archives of General Psychiatry* 36 (1) (1979): 65–69.

Nisbet, P. A. "Protective Factors for Suicidal Black Families." *Suicide and Life-Threatening Behavior* 26 (4) (1996): 325–41.

Noble, J. "A Glance at Suicide as Dealt With in the Colony and in the Province of the Massachusetts Bay." *Proceedings of the Massachusetts Historical Society* 16 (1902): 521–32.

Nuland, S. B. "The Principle of Hope." *New Republic,* May 27, 2002, 25–30.

———. "The Right to Live." *New Republic,* November 2, 1998, 29–35.

Okin, R. L. "The Future of State Hospitals: Should There Be One?" *American Journal of Psychiatry* 140 (5) (1983): 577–81.

Oquendo, M. A., et al. "Adequacy of Antidepressant Treatment After Discharge and the Occurrence of Suicidal Acts in Major Depression: A Prospective Study." *American Journal of Psychiatry* 159 (2002): 1746–51.

———. "Inadequacy of Antidepressant Treatment for Patients with Major Depression Who Are at Risk for Suicidal Behavior." *American Journal of Psychiatry* 156 (1999): 190–94.

———. "Positron Emission Tomography of Regional Brain Metabolic Responses to a Serotonergic Challenge and Lethality of Suicide Attempts in Major Depression." *Archives of General Psychiatry* 60 (2003): 14–22.

Peck, M. L. "Suicide Motivations in Adolescents." *Adolescence* 3 (9) (1968): 109–18.

———. "Youth Suicide." *Death Education* 6 (1982): 29–47.

Peck, M. L., and R. E. Litman. "Current Trends in Youthful Suicide." In J. Bush, ed. *Suicide and Blacks: A Monograph for Continuing Education in Suicide Prevention,* 13–27. Los Angeles: Fanon Research and Development Center, 1975.

Pepitone-Arreola-Rockwell, F. "Death Anxiety: Comparison of Psychiatrists, Psychologists, Suicidologists, and Funeral Directors." *Psychological Reports* 49 (1981): 979–82.

Phelps, E. B. "Neurotic Books and Newspapers as Factors in the Mortality of Suicide and Crime." *Bulletin of the American Academy of Medicine* 12 (5) (1911): 264–306.

Phillips, D. P. "The Influence of Suggestion on Suicide: Substantive and Theoretical Implications of the Werther Effect." *American Sociological Review* 39 (1974): 340–54.

Phillips, D. P., and L. L. Carstensen. "Clustering of Teenage Suicides After Television News Stories About Suicide." *New England Journal of Medicine* 315 (11) (1986): 685–89.

Pines, M. "Suicide Signals." *Science* 83 (October 1983), 55–58.

Pokorny, A. D. "A Follow-up Study of 618 Suicidal Patients." *American Journal of Psychiatry* 122 (1966): 1109–16.

———. "Prediction of Suicide in Psychiatric Patients." *Archives of General Psychiatry* 40 (1983): 249–57.

Pokorny, A. D., F. Davis, and W. Harberson. "Suicide, Suicide Attempts, and Weather." *American Journal of Psychiatry* 120 (1963): 377–81.

Potter, L. B., et al. "The Influence of Geographic Mobility on Nearly Lethal Suicide Attempts." *Suicide and Life-Threatening Behavior* 32 (Supplement) (2001): 42–48.

Powell, K. E. "Alcohol Consumption and Nearly Lethal Suicide Attempts." *Suicide and Life-Threatening Behavior* 32 (Supplement) (2001): 30–41.

Pretzel, P. W. "Philosophical and Ethical Considerations of Suicide Prevention." *Bulletin of Suicidology,* July 1968, 30–38.

Raffin, T. A. "The Right to Live, the Right to Die." *Stanford Magazine,* Spring 1983, 25–31.

Remafedi, G., et al. "The Relationship Between Suicide Risk and Sexual Orientation: Results of a Population-Based Study." *American Journal of Public Health* 88 (1) (1998): 57–60.

Ringel, E. "The Presuicidal Syndrome." *Suicide and Life-Threatening Behavior* 6 (3) (1976): 131–49.

Robbins, D., and R. C. Conroy. "A Cluster of Adolescent Suicide Attempts: Is Suicide Contagious?" *Journal of Adolescent Health Care* 3 (1983): 253–55.

Robinson, H. M. "The Case of Suicide." *North American Review* 234 (4) (1932): 303–8.

Rollin, B., "Whose Life Is It, Anyway?" *O,* February 2003.

Ross, C. P. "Mobilizing Schools for Suicide Prevention." *Suicide and Life-Threatening Behavior* 10 (4) (1980): 239–43.

Ross, C. P., and J. A. Motto. "Group Counseling for Suicidal Adolescents." In H. S. Sudak, A. B. Ford, and N. B. Rushforth, eds. *Suicide in the Young.* Boston: John Wright-PSG Inc., 1984.

Roy, A., et al. "Attempted Suicide among Living Co-Twins of Twin Suicide Victims." *American Journal of Psychiatry* 152 (7) (1995): 1075–76.

———. "Suicide in Twins." *Archives of General Psychiatry* 48 (1) (1991): 29–32.

Rubey, C. T., and J. L. McIntosh. "Suicide Survivors Groups: Results of a Survey." *Suicide and Life-Threatening Behavior* 26 (4) (1996): 351–58.

Ruggieri, C. "Narrative of the Crucifixion of Matthew Lovat, Executed by His Own Hands, at Venice, in the Month of July, 1805." *Pamphleteer* (London) 3 (6) (1814).

Santa Mina, E. E., and R. M. Gallop. "Childhood Sexual and Physical Abuse and Adult Self-Harm and Suicide Behavior: A Literature Review." *Canadian Journal of Psychiatry* 43 (1998): 793–800.

Saunders, J. M., and S. M. Valente. "Suicide Risk Among Gay Men and Lesbians: A Review." *Death Studies* 11 (1987): 1–23.

Sayre, J. "The Man on the Ledge." *New Yorker,* April 16, 1949, 34.

Scheinin, A.-G. "The Burden of Suicide." *Newsweek,* February 7, 1983, 13.

Schuyler, D. "Counseling Suicide Survivors: Issues and Answers." *Omega* 4 (4) (1973): 313–21.

Schwartz, A. J. "Inaccuracy and Uncertainty in Estimates of College Student Suicide Rates." *College Health* 28 (1980): 201–4.

Schwartz, D. A., D. E. Flinn, and P. F. Slawson. "Suicide in the Psychiatric Hospital." *American Journal of Psychiatry* 132 (2) (1975): 150–53.

Seiden, R. H. "Current Developments in Minority Group Suicidology." *JBHP* 1 (4) (1974): 29–50.

———. "Self-Deliverance or Self-Destruction?" Paper presented at the sixteenth annual meeting of the American Association of Suicidology, Dallas, Texas, 1983.

———. "A Study of Student Suicide." *Journal of Abnormal Psychology* 71 (6) (1966): 389–99.

———. "Suicide and Public Health: A Brief Appraisal." *Life-Threatening Behavior* 2 (2) (1972): 99–103.

———. "Suicide Capital? A Study of the San Francisco Suicide Rate." *Bulletin of Suicidology,* December 1967, 1–10.

———. "Suicide: Preventable Death." *Public Affairs Report* (Bulletin of the Institute of Governmental Studies, University of California, Berkeley) 15 (4) (1974): 1–5.

———. "Suicide Prevention: A Public Health/Public Policy Approach." *Omega* 8 (3) (1977): 267–76.

———. "Where Are They Now? A Follow-up Study of Suicide Attempters from the Golden Gate Bridge." *Suicide and Life-Threatening Behavior* 8 (4) (1978): 203–16.

———. "Why Are Suicides of Young Blacks Increasing?" *HSMHA Health Reports* 87 (1) (1972): 3–8.

Seiden, R. H., and M. C. Spence. "A Tale of Two Bridges: Comparative Suicide Incidence on the Golden Gate and San Francisco–Oakland Bay Bridges." *Crisis* 3 (1) (1982): 32–40.

Seiden, R. H., and R. K. Tauber. "Pseudocides vs. Suicides." *Proceedings, Fifth International Conference for Suicide Prevention* (1970): 219–22.

Seligman, M. E. P. "Giving Up on Life." *Psychology Today,* May 1974, 80–85.

Seligson, M. "Are You Suicidal?" *Harper's Bazaar,* August 1972.

Selkin, J. "The Legacy of Émile Durkheim." Paper presented at the fifteenth annual meeting of the American Association of Suicidology, New York City, April 15–18, 1982.

Selzer, M. L., and C. E. Payne. "Automobile Accidents, Suicide and Unconscious Motivation." *American Journal of Psychiatry* 119 (1962): 237–40.

Shaffer, D. "Suicide in Childhood and Early Adolescence." *Journal of Child Psychology and Psychiatry* 15 (1974): 275–91.

Shaffer, D., and P. Fisher. "The Epidemiology of Suicide in Children and Young Adolescents." *Journal of the American Academy of Child Psychiatry* 20 (1981): 545–65.

Shaffer, D., et al. "Adolescent Suicide Attempters: Response to Suicide-Prevention Programs." *Journal of the American Medical Association* 264 (24) (1990): 3151–55.

———. "Preventing Teenage Suicide: A Critical Review." *Journal of the American Academy of Child and Adolescent Psychiatry* 27 (6) (1988): 675–87.

———. "Psychiatric Diagnosis in Child and Adolescent Suicide." *Archives of General Psychiatry* 53 (1996): 339–48.

Shein, H. M. "Suicide Care: Obstacles in the Education of Psychiatric Residents." *Omega* 7 (1) (1976): 75–81.

Shein, H. M., and A. A. Stone. "Monitoring and Treatment of Suicidal Potential Within the Context of Psychotherapy." *Comprehensive Psychiatry* 10 (1) (1969): 59–70.

Shneidman, E. S. "Aphorisms of Suicide and Some Implications for Psychotherapy." *American Journal of Psychotherapy* 38 (3) (1984): 319–28.

———. "The Suicidal Logic of Cesare Pavese." *Journal of the American Academy of Psychoanalysis* 10 (4) (1982): 547–63.

Siegel, K. "Society, Suicide, and Social Policy." *Journal of Psychiatric Treatment and Evaluation* 4 (1982): 473–82.

Simon, R. I. "The Suicide Prevention Contract: Clinical, Legal, and Risk Management Issues." *Journal of the American Academy of Psychiatry Law* 27 (3) (1999): 445–50.

Singular, S. "Local Hero." *Denver Post Magazine,* September 9, 1984, 11.

Stack, S. "Occupation and Suicide." *Social Science Quarterly* 82 (2) (2001): 384–96.

Stack, S., and A. Haas. "The Effect of Unemployment Duration on National Suicide Rates: A Time Series Analysis, 1948–1982." *Sociological Focus* 17 (1) (1984): 17–29.

Stannard, D. E. "Death and Dying in Puritan New England." *American Historical Review* 78 (5) (1973): 1305–30.

Stearns, A. W. "Suicide in Massachusetts." *Mental Hygiene* 5 (4) (1921): 752–77.

Stone, A. A. "Suicide Precipitated by Psychotherapy: A Clinical Contribution." Paper presented at the ninth national scientific meeting of the Association for the Advancement of Psychotherapy, May 10, 1970.

———. "A Syndrome of Serious Suicidal Intent." *Archives of General Psychiatry* 3 (1960): 331–39.

Terman, L. M. "Recent Literature on Juvenile Suicides." *Journal of Abnormal Psychology* 9 (1914): 61–66.

Tishler, C. L., P. C. McKenry, and K. C. Morgan. "Adolescent Suicide Attempts: Some Significant Factors." *Suicide and Life-Threatening Behavior* 11 (2) (1981): 86–92.

Toolan, J. M. "Suicide in Children and Adolescents." *American Journal of Psychotherapy* 29 (3) (1975): 339–44.

———. "Therapy of Depressed and Suicidal Children." *American Journal of Psychotherapy* 32 (2) (1978): 243–51.

Tucker, S. J., and P. C. Cantor. "Personality and Status Profiles of Peer Counselors and Suicide Attempters." *Journal of Counseling Psychology* 22 (5) (1975): 423–30.

Underwood, M. D., et al. "Morphometry of the Dorsal Raphe Nucleus Serotonergic Neurons in Suicide Victims." *Biological Psychiatry* 46 (1999): 473–83.

———. "Serotonergic and Noradrenergic Neurobiology of Alcoholic Suicide." *Alcoholism: Clinical and Experimental Research* (Supplement) 28 (5) (2004): 57S-69S.

U.S. Public Health Service. "Report of the Surgeon General's Conference on Children's Mental Health: A National Action Agenda." Washington, D.C.: Department of Health and Human Services, 2000.

———. "The Surgeon General's Call to Action to Prevent Suicide." Washington, D.C., Department of Health and Human Services, 1999.

van der Maas, P. J. "Evaluation of the Notification Procedure for Physician-Assisted Death in the Netherlands." *New England Journal of Medicine* 335 (22) (1996): 1706–12.

Van Praag, H. M. "Depression, Suicide, and the Metabolism of Serotonin in the Brain." *Journal of Affective Disorders* 4 (1982): 275–90.

Wanzer, S. H., et al. "The Physician's Responsibility Toward Hopelessly Ill Patients." *New England Journal of Medicine* 310 (1984): 955–59.

Weaver, P., Jr. "A Legal Suicide, 1996." *Overland Monthly* 28 (1896): 680–90.

Weis, S., and R. H. Seiden. "Rescuers and the Rescued: A Study of Suicide Prevention Center

Volunteers and Clients by Means of a Death Questionnaire." *Life-Threatening Behavior* 4 (2) (1974): 118–30.

Weisman, A. D. "Is Suicide a Disease?" *Life-Threatening Behavior* 1 (4) (1971): 219–31.

Weller, S. "Whose Death Was It, Anyway? Reflections on the Suicide of a Friend." *Village Voice,* December 9–15, 1981, 25–27.

Winegarten, R. "On the Love of Suicide." *Commentary,* August 1972, 29–34.

Winn, M. "The Loss of Childhood." *New York Times Magazine,* May 8, 1983.

Wintemute, G. J., et al. "Mortality Among Recent Purchasers of Handguns." *New England Journal of Medicine* 341 (21) (1999): 1583–89.

Wold, C. I. "Characteristics of 26,000 Suicide Prevention Center Patients." *Bulletin of Suicidology* 6 (Spring 1970): 24–28.

Wold, C. I., and R. E. Litman. "Suicide After Contact with a Suicide Prevention Center." *Archives of General Psychiatry* 28 (1973): 735–39.

Wolf, H. "Suicide Notes." *American Mercury,* November 1931, 264–72.

Wrobleski, A. "Rational Suicide: A Contradiction in Terms." An address given at the First Unitarian Society, Minneapolis, Minnesota, February 27, 1983.

Wyden, P. "Suicide." *Saturday Evening Post,* August 19, 1961, 18.

Zilboorg, G. "Considerations on Suicide, with Particular Reference to That of the Young." *American Journal of Orthopsychiatry* 7 (1937): 15–31.

———. "Some Aspects of Suicide." *Suicide* 5 (3) (1975): 131–39.

# RESOURCES

The following organizations will be of help to those who wish to learn more about suicide.

American Association of Suicidology
5221 Wisconsin Avenue, N.W.
Washington, DC 20015
(202) 237-2280
www.suicidology.org

American Foundation for Suicide Prevention
120 Wall Street, 22nd floor
New York, NY 10005
(888) 333-2377
www.afsp.org

Centers for Disease Control and Prevention
1600 Clifton Road
Atlanta, GA 30333
(800) 311-3435
www.cdc.gov

National Institute of Mental Health
6001 Executive Boulevard
Bethesda, MD 20892
(866) 615-6464
www.nimh.nih.gov

Suicide Prevention Action Network
1025 Vermont Avenue, N.W., Suite 1066
Washington, DC 20005
(202) 449-3600
www.spanusa.org

For those who need immediate help: National Hopeline 1-800-SUICIDE; National Suicide Prevention Lifeline 1-800-273-TALK.

# INDEX

AA (Alcoholics Anonymous), 62, 73–74,
103, 109, 121, 324, 522
AAS (American Association of Suicidology), 116, 118, 201, 258, 304, 309,
310, 350–51, 417, 524
Abimelech (biblical figure), 151
abortion, 144, 317
Abram, Morris, 368
accidents, 269–70, 273–74
*accidie,* 162
active listening, 287
Addison, Joseph, 166
Adkins, Janet, 376, 378, 379, 382, 384, 385,
399, 572*n*
Adler, Alfred, 188
Admiraal, Pieter, 390–91
"Admonitions of a Sage," 129–31
adolescent depression, 41–43, 321, 322, 331
adolescent suicide, 15–126
of African Americans, 252–53
antidepressant medication and, 3, 57,
319, 321–22
attempts vs. completion of, 38–39,
95–97, 438
case histories, 15–37, 59–79, 93–94,
97–110, 121–26, 518–20
causality of, 39–58
childhood trauma and, 45, 60, 61,
252–53
clusters of, 2, 11, 39, 78–83, 85–86, 87,
92, 114–15, 116, 259
cultural influences on, 53–55, 86–92,
139, 542*n*–43*n*
depression as factor in, 41–43, 322
home location of, 95
as impulsive act, 48–49
in Japan, 139
of males vs. females, 38, 39, 97, 260,
264
mother-infant bonding issues linked
with, 46–47

of Native Americans, 259, 260
parental loss and, 43–44
parents' divorces after, 125
peer reactions to, 31–34, 36, 37, 81,
123–24, 126
prevention programs on, 2, 32, 37, 79,
111–20, 259, 260–61
psychiatric hospitalization and, 63–65,
71–72, 103–4, 105–10
rates of, 2, 3, 11, 37–39, 51, 56–57, 197,
252, 314, 539*n*
serotonin dysfunction in, 47–48
sexual-identity concerns and, 48, 66,
101–2, 264–66
substance abuse and, 46, 48, 62, 73–74,
93, 99–100, 101, 103–5, 106
triggering events of, 48–49
Viennese psychoanalytic panel on, 86,
188
adrenaline junkies, 275
advance directives, 371–72
adversity, responses to, 222, 256
AEA (autoerotic asphyxiation), 83
Aedesius, 152
African Americans, 234–35, 251–58, 263,
557*n*–58*n*
*African Homicide and Suicide* (Bohannan),
85
African tribal cultures, 131–32, 133, 135,
364
*Age of Reason, The* (Paine), 87
aggression, psychoanalytic theories of, 188,
189–90
aggressive behavior:
antidepressants in reduction of, 320
mass media violence coverage vs., 542*n*
serotonin function vs., 196
suicide as, 224–26, 239
suppression of, 245
in young male suicides, 47–48
Ahithophel (biblical figure), 152